DIGEST

OF

DECISIONS RELATING TO INDIAN AFFAIRS.

Compiled under supervision of Hon. W. A. JONES, Commissioner of Indian Affairs,

BY

KENNETH S. MURCHISON.

IN TWO VOLUMES.
VOL. I.
JUDICIAL.

PUBLISHED BY AUTHORITY OF CONGRESS.

WASHINGTON:
GOVERNMENT PRINTING OFFICE.
1901.

KRAUS REPRINT CO.
Millwood, New York
1973

Library of Congress Cataloging in Publication Data

United States. Bureau of Indian Affairs.
   Digest of decisions relating to Indian affairs.

   Reprint of the ed. issued as no. 538, in series:
56th Congress, 2d Session, House document.
   No more published.
   1. Indians of North America — Legal status, laws,
etc. — Digests. I. Murchison, Kenneth S., comp. II.
United States. Courts. III. Title. IV. Series: United
States. 56th Congress, 2d session, 1900-1901. House.
Document no. 538.
KF8204.1901   342'.701'02648   73-16017
ISBN 0-527-92015-0

AUTHORITY OF CONGRESS.

To pay the expense of the preparation of a digest, under the direction of the Commissioner of Indian Affairs, of the decisions of the courts and the Interior Department, and the opinions of the Attorney-General relating to Indian Affairs, three thousand dollars. (Act June 10, 1896, 29 Stat. L., 341.)

For completion of the digest, now being prepared under the direction of the Secretary of the Interior, of the decisions of the courts and the Interior Department, and of the opinions of the Attorney-General relating to Indian Affairs, under authority of the Indian Appropriation Act approved June tenth, eighteen hundred and ninety-six, two thousand dollars: *Provided,* That the Secretary of the Interior may authorize said work to be performed by a clerk of the Indian Office out of office hours and pay a proper compensation to such clerk therefor. And the accounting officers of the Treasury are hereby authorized and directed to settle the accounts of Kenneth S. Murchison, allowing him credit for such sums as he has disbursed under the appropriation heretofore made or may hereafter disburse under this appropriation for this purpose to himself or to Millard F. Holland, under authority of the Secretary of the Interior, for services heretofore, or that may be hereafter, rendered by them in connection with the preparation of said digest. (Act June 7, 1897, 30 Stat. L., 87.)

For printing and binding in two volumes not exceeding two thousand copies of the digest of decisions relating to Indian Affairs, authorized by Indian appropriation Acts of June tenth, eighteen hundred and ninety-six, and June seventh, eighteen hundred and ninety-seven, five thousand dollars, or so much thereof as may be necessary: *Provided,* That the Secretary of the Interior is authorized to donate thirty copies to Kenneth S. Murchison, the compiler of said digest, for complimentary distribution by him. (Act May 31, 1900, 31 Stat. L., 24.)

KRAUS REPRINT CO.
A U.S. Division of Kraus-Thomson Organization Limited

Printed in Germany

PREFACE.

When the compilation of this digest was entered upon, it was with a view to gathering together in compact form a complete line of decisions by the courts, Federal, State, and Territorial, and by the Executive Departments on the many and varied questions arising relative to Indian affairs, the rights of Indians as individuals, as tribes under treaties and acts of Congress, and the relation of the individual and the tribe to the General Government and the State within which they reside and where their reservations are located.

The necessity for such a compilation has been for a long time felt in the Indian Department, as can be readily understood in view of the peculiar position occupied by the Indians, who are generally not citizens, but are yet under the supervision and control of the General Government as wards, and whose very status has been the prolific cause of litigation growing out of their intercourse with the white citizens of the United States, who have gradually encroached on their reservations and so surrounded them as to make it impossible for them to avoid daily contact.

This work is a pioneer in the field occupied by it, and many difficulties had to be encountered and overcome in order to make it the helper to the departments of the Government and the legal profession which it was hoped it would become. The primary object of this digest was to furnish to the Executive Departments, in such a form as would be the greatest help in dealing with Indian affairs, not only what the law is as laid down by the courts on questions that have been drawn directly into litigation, but also what probably would be held to be the intent and effect of the law on questions not directly decided, as indicated by the *dicta* of learned jurists used in opinions delivered by them.

As in all works of this character covering a field of decisions not heretofore closely digested, this digest will doubtless be found to be imperfect in some respects, but every effort was made to have it as nearly correct and as complete as possible, and it is hoped that the Executive Departments of the Government and the legal profession will find it of much value and great usefulness as a helper in the solving of the many problems presented in dealing with the Indian question.

K. S. M.

3

ARTICLE I.—JURISDICTION AND GOVERNMENT OF INDIANS AND INDIAN COUNTRY.

CHAPTER I.—WHAT IS INDIAN COUNTRY?

SECTION 1. The Indians and their country are considered by foreign nations, as well as ourselves, as being so completely under the sovereignty and dominion of the United States that any attempt to acquire their lands, or to form a political connection with them, would be considered by all as an invasion of our territory and an act of hostility. *Cherokee Nation v. Georgia, 5 Pet., 1.*

SEC. 2. The power to define originally the "Indian country" within which the unlicensed introduction and sale of liquors were prohibited, necessarily includes that of enlarging the prohibited boundaries whenever, in the opinion of Congress, the interests of Indian intercourse and trade will be best subserved.
United States v. 43 Gals. Whiskey, 93 U. S., 188.

SEC. 3. The presumption is that the Congress of the United States and the judges who administered the laws must have found in the definition of the Indian country, in the act of 1834 (4 Stat. L., 729), such an adaptability to the altered circumstances of what was then Indian country as to enable them to ascertain what it was at any time since then, and that, therefore, no new definition was necessary to be furnished. *Bates v. Clark, 95 U. S. 204.*

SEC. 4. All the country described by the act of 1834 (4 Stat. L., 729) as Indian country remains Indian country so long as the Indians retain their original title to the soil, and ceases to be Indian country whenever they lose that title in the absence of any different provision by treaty or by act of Congress.
Bates v. Clark, 95 U. S., 204. Ex parte Crow Dog, 109 U. S., 556.

5

SEC. 5. Section 1 of the act of June 30, 1834 (4 Stat. L., 729), was not reenacted in the Revised Statutes, although other parts of the act were, and it was therefore repealed; but it may be referred to for the purpose of determining what was meant by the term "Indian country" when found in sections of the Revised Statutes which are reenactments of other sections of that act. The repeal of section 1 does not of itself change the meaning of the term it defines when found elsewhere in the original connection, and the reenacted sections are to be given the same meaning they had in the original statute unless a contrary intention is plainly manifested.

Ex parte Crow Dog, 109 U. S., 556.   United States v. Le Bris, 121 U. S., 278.   In re Jackson, 40 Fed. Rep., 372. Pelcher v. United States, 3 McCrary, 510.

SEC. 6. The definition of Indian country now applies to all the country within the limits of the United States to which the Indian title has not been extinguished, even when not within a reservation expressly set apart for the exclusive occupancy of Indians, although much of it has been acquired since the passage of the act of 1834, and notwithstanding the former definition in that act has been dropped from the statutes, excluding however any territory embraced within the exterior geographical limits of a State not excepted from its jurisdiction by treaty or by statute at the time of its admission into the Union; but saving even in respect to territory not thus excepted, but actually in the exclusive occupancy of Indians, the authority of Congress over it under the constitutional power to regulate commerce with the Indian tribes, and under any treaty made in pursuance of it.

Ex parte Crow Dog, 109 U. S., 556.   United States v. Barnhart, 22 Fed. Rep., 285.   Kie v. United States, 27 Fed. Rep., 351.   In re Jackson, 40 Fed. Rep., 372.

SEC. 7. The reservation of the Red Lake and Pembina Indians in Polk County, Minn., is Indian country within the meaning of section 2139, Revised Statutes.   United States v. Le Bris, 121 U. S., 278.

SEC. 8. The treaties of 1853 (10 Stat. L., 1013), 1865 (14 Stat. L., 717), and 1867 (15 Stat. L., 581) show that as late as 1867 the "Public Land Strip" (No Man's Land), in the mode of its use, had some connection with Indians west of the Mississippi, and especially with some of those now occupying permanent reservations in the Indian Territory. That strip has not been occupied by Indians since 1867, but it was not open to settlement, and could have been used for any of the purposes that the Government had in view for Indians.

Cook v. United States, 138 U. S., 157.

SEC. 9. In an official communication from the Commissioner of the General Land Office to the Secretary of the Interior, under date of January 29, 1886, embodied in a report made on February 11, 1886, by the Judiciary Committee of the House of Representatives upon a proposed bill extending the laws of the United States over certain unorganized territory south of Kansas, it was stated that "it appears that the Cherokees claimed the Public Land Strip, now so called, as the outlet above mentioned, and the official maps down to 1869 or later designated said strip as a part of the Indian Territory." *Ibid.*

SEC. 10. The White Mountain Indian Reservation was a legally constituted Indian reservation. True, when the Territory of Arizona was organized, on February 24, 1863, there was no such reservation, and it was created in the first instance by order of the President in 1871. Whatever doubts there might have been, if any, as to the validity of such Executive order are put at rest by the act of Congress of February 8, 1887 (24 Stat. L., 388), relating to the allotment of lands in severalty to Indians. *In re Wilson, 140 U. S., 575.*

SEC. 11. The necessary effect of the legislative recognition in the first clause of section 1 of the act of February 8, 1887 (24 Stat. L., 388), of Executive order reservations was to confirm the Executive order and establish beyond challenge the Indian title in the White Mountain Indian Reservation. *Ibid.*

SEC. 12. The treaty of 1854 (10 Stat. L., 1109) with the Chippewa Indians did not operate to defeat the prior right of occupancy which the Indians had to the particular section 16 in question, but by including it in the new reservations, made as a condition of the cession of large tracts of land in Wisconsin, continued it in force. The State, therefore, had no such control over that section or right to it as would prevent its being set apart by the United States, with the consent of the Indians, as a part of their permanent reservation. *United States v. Thomas, 151 U. S., 577.*

SEC. 13. By authority of their original right of occupancy, which has continuously existed in the Chippewa Indians, as well as by the fact that the section 16 in question is included within the tract set aside as a portion of the permanent reservation in consideration of the cession of lands, the title never vested in the State, except as subordinate to the right of occupation of the Indians. *Ibid.*

SEC. 14. By virtue of the treaty of 1842 (7 Stat. L., 591), in the absence of any proof that the Chippewa Indians have surrendered their right of occupancy, the right still remains with them, and the title and right which the State may claim ultimately to the sixteenth section of every township for the use of schools is subordinate to this right of occupancy of the Indians, which has never been released to any of their lands except as it may be inferred from the provisions of the treaty of 1854. *Ibid.*

SEC. 15. The provision in the treaty of February 24, 1869 (15 Stat. L., 673), with the Bannock Indians, whose reservation was within the limits of what is now the State of Wyoming, that they shall have the right to hunt upon the unoccupied lands of the United States so long as game may be found thereon, etc., does not give them the right to exercise this privilege within the limits of that State in violation of its laws.

Ward v. Race Horse, 163 U. S., 504.

SEC. 16. An Indian reservation established in Nevada March 3, 1874, by a mere Executive order for "the use" of certain Indians, and afterwards recognized as such by Congress, was "Indian country" within the meaning of sections 2133, 2139, and 2148 of the Revised Statutes.

United States v. Bridleman, 7 Fed. Rep., 894. Also 7 Saw., 243.

SEC. 17. The treaty of June 9, 1855 (12 Stat. L., 445), establishing the Umatilla Reservation was not modified or repealed by the act of Congress admitting Oregon into the Union, and all laws for the punishment of crimes committed in the Indian country are applicable thereto and may be enforced in the United States courts.   *Ibid.*

SEC. 18. Colored persons who were never held as slaves in the Indian country, but who may have been slaves elsewhere, are like other citizens of the United States, and have no more rights in the Indian country than other citizens of the United States.

United States v. Payne, 8 Fed. Rep., 883.

SEC. 19. Section 1 of the act of June 30, 1834 (4 Stat. L., 729), defining the "Indian country" as "all that part of the United States west of the Mississippi, and not within the States of Missouri and Louisiana or the Territory of Arkansas, and also that part of the United States east of the Mississippi River and not within any State, to which the Indian title has not been extinguished," was repealed by section 5596, Revised Statutes, and consequently the description of the "Indian country" found in the said section 1 of the act of 1834 is no longer a part of the law of the land. The question as to what is the Indian country, since the repeal of that section, not decided. (See sec. 6, ante.)   *43 Gals. Cognac Brandy, 11 Fed. Rep., 47.*

SEC. 20. The carrying of spirituous liquors into a territory purchased by the United States, after March 30, 1802, although frequented and inhabited exclusively by Indians, is not an offense within the meaning of the acts of Congress so as to subject it to forfeiture. (See sec. 6, ante.)   *Ibid.*

SEC. 21. The fact that a tract of country has sometimes been referred to in treaties and official reports as the "Red Lake Reservation" is not sufficient to authorize the court, in a *quasi* criminal case, to declare it to be such.   *43 Gals. Cognac Brandy, 14 Fed. Rep., 539. Same, 4 McCrary, 616.*

SEC. 22. A particular portion of the public domain on which an Indian tribe has been suffered long to remain, while other portions have been opened to settlement, or set apart particularly for Indian occupancy, does not constitute such tract an Indian reservation.

Ibid.

SEC. 23. "Indian country" as used in the Revised Statutes now includes only that portion of the public domain which is set apart as a reservation, or as reservations, for the use and occupancy of the Indians, and not the whole vast extent of the national domain to which the Indian title has not been extinguished.   (See sec. 6, ante.)

United States v. Martin, 14 Fed. Rep., 817.   Same, 8 Saw., 473.
Pelcher v. United States, 3 McCrary, 510.

SEC. 24. Since the repeal of section one of the Indian intercourse act (4 Stat. L., 729) by section 5596 of the Revised Statutes, the only Indian country in the United States within the purview of that phrase as used in chapter 4, Title XXVIII of the Revised Statutes, is the tract of country set apart by the United States for the exclusive use and occupancy of particular Indian tribes, and known as Indian reservations; and the Umatilla Reservation in Oregon is such Indian country.

Ibid.   Same, 8 Saw., 473.

SEC. 25. The Cherokee Nation is neither a State nor Territory; it is an autonomy; but it does not come within the meaning of either State or Territory, but is part of what is called "Indian country."

Ex parte Morgan, 20 Fed. Rep., 298.   Cherokee Nation v. So. Kan.
Ry. Co., 33 Fed. Rep., 900.

SEC. 26. The Umatilla Reservation is a place within the geographical limits and general jurisdiction of the State of Oregon, but is also a tract of country to which the Indian title is not extinguished, and which has been permanently set apart by treaty as a reservation for the sole and exclusive use of the Indians thereon and is therefore "Indian country" within the meaning of that phrase as used in the Revised Statutes.

United States v. Barnhart, 22 Fed. Rep., 285.   Same, 10 Saw., 491.

SEC. 27. Although a reservation was never expressly excepted from the jurisdiction of the State by either treaty or statute, it is nevertheless territory to which the Indian title was never extinguished, and "actually in the exclusive occupancy of Indians" in pursuance of a treaty of the United States.   This brings it within the definition or description of "Indian country" in Ex parte Crow Dog.   (See sec. 6, ante.)

Ibid.

SEC. 28. Prior to the act of Congress of January 6, 1886, the Cherokee outlet was in the jurisdiction of the United States court for the western district of Arkansas.   That act did not put it in the jurisdiction of the United States court of Kansas, as then and now it is Indian country, set apart for, and occupied by, the Cherokees.

United States v. Rogers, 23 Fed. Rep., 658.

SEC. 29. Alaska was not described or included in the act of 1834, the same being at the time foreign territory, and for the further reason that, if it had been, Congress has since made special provision concerning the intercourse therein between the aborigines and others.

Kie v. United States, 27 Fed. Rep., 351.

SEC. 30. Alaska was purchased from Russia in 1867.   Article III of the treaty of purchase (15 Stat. L., 539) provides that such of "the inhabitants of the ceded territory" as "prefer to remain" therein, with the exception of the uncivilized native tribes, shall be admitted to all the rights, advantages, and immunities of citizens of the United States, and shall be maintained and protected in the free enjoyment of their liberty, property, and religion.   The uncivilized tribes will be subject to such laws and regulations as the United States may from time to time adopt in regard to the aboriginal tribes of that country.   *Ibid.*

SEC. 31. Alaska is not "Indian country" in the sense in which that phrase is used in the intercourse act of 1834 and the Revised Statutes.

Ibid.   8 Saw., 579.

SEC. 32. Alaska is held to be "Indian country" only in so far as the liquor traffic is concerned.   *United States v. Nelson, 29 Fed. Rep., 202.*

SEC. 33. The act of March 3, 1873 (17 Stat. L., 530), extending to Alaska two sections of the act of June 30, 1834 (4 Stat. L., 729), known as the "Indian intercourse laws," and relating principally to the interdiction of the liquor traffic among the Indians, is to be construed to make said Territory "Indian country" only to the extent of the prohibited commerce, and did not put the Alaska Indians on a general footing with Indians in other parts of the United States.

In re Sah-Quah, 31 Fed. Rep., 327.

SEC. 34. Section 3 of the act of Congress approved April 3, 1864 (13 Stat. L., 40) provides "that the several Indian reservations in California which shall not be retained for Indian reservations under the provisions of the preceding section of this act" shall be surveyed and sold.   The Klamath reservation was not selected or retained under the provisions of said act, and it therefore ceased to be "Indian country."

*United States v. Forty-eight Pounds of Tea, 38 Fed. Rep., 400.
Same, 13 Saw., 298.*

SEC. 35. The Klamath Indian reservation was not, at the time of suit, "Indian country" within the meaning of section 2133 of the Revised Statutes, prescribing the penalty for unauthorized trading in the Indian country.   *Ibid.*

SEC. 36. The act of 1889 (25 Stat. L., 783) established a United States court with jurisdiction extending over the Indian Territory, bounded so as to include "No Man's Land."   Section 17 attached to the eastern district of Texas all of the Indian Territory not otherwise assigned, which included this land, if it was a part of the Indian Territory. *Held:* That the jurisdiction of the United States court for the eastern district of Texas over this tract of land was sufficiently clear to warrant a removal to the State of Texas of one indicted by that court for a crime committed in "No Man's Land" and arrested in another State.   *In re Jackson, 40 Fed. Rep., 372.*

SEC. 37. The expression "Indian country" and "Indian territory" are used interchangeably in the statutes.   We speak of the "Indian territory;" but politically this is a mistake.   There is no organization. It is more properly a territory referring simply to geographical extension and not to any political organization.   At the time the act of 1834 was passed "No Man's Land" was not a part of the United States, and did not come within the "Indian country" as defined.

Ibid.

Sec. 38. The villages within the Allegany Reservation which were located under the act of Congress of February 19, 1875 (18 Stat. L., 330), are not "Indian country" within the meaning of section 2139 of the Revised Statutes, prohibiting the introduction of spirituous liquors into the Indian country.   Benson v. United States, 44 Fed. Rep., 178.

Sec. 39. Inasmuch as the Indian reservations in the State of New York were not Indian country in 1834, and as no lands are now included within that country which were not within it then, sections 2133, 2134, and 2139 of the Revised Statutes have no application to these reservations.   Some of the lands in the reservations of this State are now occupied by Indians who still maintain their tribal relations.   Ibid.

Sec. 40. Since 1834 the Indian reservations in New York have not been embraced in the Indian country of the laws of Congress.   The term "Indian country" originated in the acts of Congress passed in or prior to 1834 to regulate trade and intercourse with the Indian tribes, which contained the identical provisions which are now embodied in sections 2133, 2134, and 2139 of the Revised Statutes.   Ibid.

Sec. 41. Irrespective of the act of 1875 (18 Stat. L., 330), the villages of the Allegany Reservation can not be considered Indian country within the meaning of section 2139 of the Revised Statutes, as the act of June 30, 1834, which contained the provision now embodied in that section, in describing what lands should be deemed "Indian country" for the purposes of the act, included only lands outside the territorial limits of any State then existing, and by providing that "the general laws of the United States as to the punishment of crimes committed in any place within the sole and exclusive jurisdiction of the United States * * * shall extend to the Indian country," showed that by such country was meant territory "within the sole and exclusive jurisdiction of the United States."   Ibid.

Sec. 42. A plea that the whisky when seized was in the claimant's possession, and that he was then on his way from a town named to another town not named, neither of said towns being within the Indian country, is bad, since it does not show that the whisky was in transit when seized or that the unnamed town was off the Indian reservation.

United States v. 29 Gals. Whisky, 45 Fed. Rep., 847.

Sec. 43. In a libel to forfeit whisky alleged to have been introduced into the Indian country, a plea that claimant did not unlawfully introduce said whisky into any Indian country, and that he did not introduce it intending to sell or dispose of it to any Indian, is bad, since the first allegation is a conclusion of law, and the second is irrelevant. *Ibid.*

SEC. 44. The title to the sixteenth sections of the surveyed lands vested in the State when it became a member of the Union under the act of 1846 (9 Stat. L., 58), and the title to the sixteenth sections of the unsurveyed public domain in the State vested in it when those sections were subsequently located and defined by surveys. The sixteenth sections within the exterior boundaries of the Lac Courte d'Oreilles Reservation, as it was agreed upon and established in 1859, had belonged to the State since 1855, and the Government had no more right to take them for Indian reservations than it had to take the lands of individuals for the same purpose. (See sec. 13, ante.)

United States v. Thomas, 47 Fed. Rep., 488.

SEC. 45. The State's right of dominion over these sections, including the right to sell, became complete when they were located by the survey in 1855. The Government's right to occupy or otherwise control them then ceased, and it follows that the Indians thereafter acquired no right of occupancy from the Government. (See sec. 12, ante.) *Ibid.*

SEC. 46. If the title or general legislative or governmental jurisdiction is not a necessary element in the question, the only inquiry is whether the murder was committed within the limits of an Indian reservation, set apart and recognized by the Government and actually occupied by the Indians for reservation purposes, and that it was is evident from the testimony and undisputed facts. (Dissenting opinion of Bunn, J., in.) *Ibid.*

SEC. 47. Section 16 is within the outside limits of the reservation; it is a part of the land actually selected for the Indians by the commissioners pursuant to their treaty; it was platted and set apart by the Government for the use of the Indians, and though in 1865 the State of Wisconsin assumed to sell it, and the purchaser went on and stripped it of its timber, it has been vacant and unoccupied always, except as used and occupied by the Indians prior to the treaty of 1854 (10 Stat. L., 1109) under their own possessory right. It is, therefore, thought to be within the true meaning of the act of 1885 (23 Stat. L., 385), so far as the question of jurisdiction is concerned. (Dissenting opinion of Bunn, J., in.) *Ibid.*

SEC. 48. It can not be questioned that the Indian reservation found within the borders of Charles Mix County forms part of what is known as "Indian country," and that the same was, so far as was necessary for the protection of the Indians, within the exclusive jurisdiction of the United States up to the time of the admission of South Dakota as a State of the Union.

United States v. Ewing, 47 Fed. Rep., 809.

Sec. 49. The act of February 22, 1889 (25 Stat. L., 676), providing for the organization of the States of North Dakota and South Dakota, declared that "the people of said States do agree and declare that they forever disclaim all right and title * * * to all lands lying within said limits owned or held by any Indian or Indian tribes," and that the same "shall be and remain under the absolute jurisdiction and control of the Congress of the United States."

United States v. Ewing, 47 Fed. Rep., 809.

Sec. 50. The simple criterion is that, as to all lands thus described, it was Indian country whenever the Indian title had not been extinguished, and it continued to be Indian country so long as the Indians had title to it, and no longer. As soon as they parted with their title, it ceased to be Indian country without any further act of Congress, unless by the treaty by which the Indians parted with their title, or by some act of Congress, a different rule was made applicable in the case.

United States v. Partello, 48 Fed. Rep., 670.

Sec. 51. Prior to the admission of Montana as a State, the Crow Reservation situated therein was part of the "Indian country," within the meaning of section 2145 of the Revised Statutes, extending the general criminal laws of the United States over the Indian country.

Ibid.

Sec. 52. The act of July 1, 1892 (27 Stat. L., 62), opening a part of the Colville Indian Reservation, in the State of Washington, annulled from that date the Executive order creating the reservation and restored the lands to the public domain, subject only to the rights of the Indians to make selections for allotments in severalty; but the mineral lands contained therein are not subject to such selection, it being the intent of the law to award to each Indian agricultural land for his home. Collins v. Bubb, 73 Fed. Rep., 735.

Sec. 53. For the purpose of giving the Indians the full benefit of the right to select from the whole tract, settlements upon and entries of agricultural lands on the Colville Reservation must be postponed, under the act of July 1, 1892 (27 Stat. L., 62), until six months after the President's proclamation opening the lands to settlement and entry; but prospectors and miners are not required to wait for the proclamation to open the tract to exploration for minerals. Ibid.

Sec. 54. That part of the Indian reservation described and provided for in the treaty made with the Chippewa Indians February 22, 1855 (10 Stat. L., 1166), which was granted to the chief Hole in the Day, under the exception and stipulation contained in the subsequent treaty of May 7, 1864 (13 Stat. L., 693), continued to retain its character as an Indian reservation notwithstanding such grant.

Note to Karrahor v. Adams, 1 Dill., 344. United States v. Shanks,
15 Minn., 369.

Sec. 55. The owner of land may replevy timber cut by a wrongdoer; and accordingly it has been held that the United States may maintain replevin for timber cut on the public lands, and even for timber cut and sold by Indians on land reserved for them, as the fee is in the Government, and only a right of occupancy in the Indians.

Note to Bly v. United States, 4 Dill., 469.

SEC. 56. All Indian reservations held under treaty stipulations with the Government must be deemed and taken to be a part of the *Indian country* within the meaning of our laws on that subject.

United States v. Crook, 5 Dill., 453.

SEC. 57. The Indian country, within the meaning of the act declaring it a crime to introduce spirituous liquors therein, is only that portion of the United States which has been declared to be such by act of Congress; and although Alaska is owned or inhabited by Indians in whole or in part, it is not, therefore, necessarily a part of the "Indian country."

United States v. Seveloff, 2 Sawyer, 311.

SEC. 58. In an "opinion" by Attorney-General Cushing (7 Opin., 295) it was held that Oregon was a part of "Indian country" because at the date of such opinion, 1855, it was "a part of the United States west of the Mississippi."

Ibid.

SEC. 59. In an opinion rendered in 1855 (7 Opin., 295) Attorney-General Cushing held that "the Indian country" in the acts of Congress is not limited by any specific boundaries, but includes generally all "such portions of the acquired territory of the United States as are in the actual occupation of the Indian tribes," while the Indian title thereto is unextinguished.

Ibid.

SEC. 60. The act of 1834 defines the Indian country absolutely by metes and bounds, and no subsequent purchase of lands within these limits would of itself operate to take them out of the category of Indian country or except them from the laws regulating trade and commerce with Indians who might be found thereon; nor can the act of 1834 be held to have extended itself over Alaska upon its cession by Russia.

Ibid.

SEC. 61. Section 23 of the act of 1834 (4 Stat. L., 729), which authorizes the President to employ the military force of the United States to make arrests in the Indian country, was in force in Alaska so far as the introduction and disposition of spirituous liquors therein is concerned from and after the extension of said sections 20 and 21 of said act over said Territory.

In re John A. Carr, 3 Sawyer, 316.

SEC. 62. Section 5 of the act of June 5, 1850 (9 Stat. L., 437), making Oregon Indian country, so far as the disposition of liquor to the Indians is concerned, is not repealed by section 5596, Revised Statutes.

United States v. Winslow, 3 Sawyer, 337.

SEC. 63. Alaska is not "Indian country" in the technical sense of that phrase only so far as the introduction and disposition of spirituous liquors is concerned, and, subject to this restraint, it is open to occupation and trade generally.

Waters v. Campbell, 4 Sawyer, 12

SEC. 64. The laws of the United States extending the laws regulating intercourse with the Indian tribes over the tribes in Utah, Nevada at the time of their passage being a part of Utah, do not make Nevada Indian country. *United States v. Leathers, 6 Sawyer, 17.*

SEC. 65. The tract of country called the Pyramid Lake Indian Reservation was set apart by competent authority (Executive order) for the use of Pah Utes and other Indians residing thereon, and it is "Indian country" within the meaning of sections 2133 and 2139, Revised Statutes. *Ibid.*

SEC. 66. Reservations established by Executive order are established by competent authority, and are therefore "Indian country." *Ibid.*

SEC. 67. The provisions of law applicable to Indian tribes may be enforced without first being obliged to declare the Territories in which those tribes live Indian country. The laws are extended over the *tribes* and not over any specified territory. *Ibid.*

SEC. 68. The very extensive powers given to the President by sections 462 to 465 in the management of Indian affairs might well be held to include the power to establish a reservation if there were no other acts in relation to the matter. *Ibid.*

SEC. 69. Acts of Congress from 1790 to 1856 referring to "Indian country" and "Indian territory" discussed. *Ibid.*

SEC. 70. Alaska was not "the Indian country" within the purview of section 21 of the act of March 27, 1854 (10 Stat. L., 270; sec. 2142, Rev. Stat.), defining the crime of an assault by a white person within such country with a deadly weapon, with intent to kill. *United States v. Williams, 6 Sawyer, 244.*

SEC. 71. As section 1 of the act of 1834 defining the then limits of the "Indian country," was repealed by title 74 of the Revised Statutes (Dec. 1, 1873) there is now no "Indian country," unless the several reservations set apart for the exclusive use of the Indians are considered to be such. *United States v. Bridleman, 7 Sawyer, 243.*

SEC. 72. There is no express definition in the Revised Statutes, as there ought to be, of what constitutes Indian country. Section 1 of the intercourse act of June 30, 1834 (4 Stat. L., 729), defining the boundaries of the then Indian country, has been repealed by section 5596 of the Revised Statutes. *United States v. Martin, 8 Saw., 473.*

SEC. 73. An Indian reservation is a part of the public domain set apart by proper authority for the use and occupation of a tribe of Indians. It may be set apart by treaty, act of Congress, or Executive order. *Ibid.*

SEC. 74. The Umatilla Reservation is a place within the geographical limits and general jurisdiction of the State of Oregon, but is also a tract of country to which the Indian title is not extinguished, and which has been permanently set apart by treaty as a reservation for the exclusive use of the Indians thereon, and is therefore "Indian country" within the meaning of that phrase as used in the Revised Statutes.   *United States v. Barnhart, 10 Saw., 491.*

SEC. 75. The Secretary of the Interior was dealing with the lands of the Klamath Reservation as directed by the third section of the act of 1864 (13 Stat. L., 40), and *some* steps had been taken to carry out the provisions of that section. That said lands continued to constitute a reservation in the sense that they were not open to entry under the general land laws is undoubtedly true; but they constitute an abandoned reservation, to be disposed of as specifically provided for in said section 3.
United States v. 48 pounds Rising Star Tea, 13 Saw., 298.

SEC. 76. The Ute Reservation in Colorado was not at the time of the passage of the act of June 3, 1834 (4 Stat. L., 729) a part of the United States, but was subsequently acquired from Mexico. It was originally embraced within the territorial limits of Utah (9 Stat. L., 453).
United States v. Berry, 2 McCrary, 58.

SEC. 77. Section 7 of the act of February 27, 1851 (9 Stat. L., 587) extended all the laws then in force regulating trade and intercourse with the Indian tribes over the Indian tribes in the Territories of New Mexico and Utah, including what is now the Ute Reservation in Colorado; but whether the effect of this was to make New Mexico and Utah Indian country is a question.   *Ibid.*

SEC. 78. An Indian reservation is a part of the public domain set apart by proper authority for the use and occupation of a tribe or tribes of Indians. It may be set apart by an act of Congress, by treaty, or by Executive order; but it is not thought that it can be established by custom or prescription. The fact that a particular tribe or band of Indians has for a long time occupied a particular tract of country does not constitute such tract an Indian reservation.
Forty-three Cases Cognac Brandy, 4 McCrary, 616.

SEC. 79. Originally all of the public domain was occupied by Indians, and the reservation policy was adopted with a view of locating them in certain districts and opening the remainder of the public land for white settlement.   *Ibid.*

SEC. 80. In the officers of The Interior Department are vested the judgment and discretion of determining, when applications for public lands are presented, whether the lands applied for are public lands open for settlement, or whether they are Indian lands, or whether, for any other reason, they are not open to settlement; and the determination of this question will not be interfered with by the courts, by injunction, in behalf of a homestead applicant, prior to the time the question has gone beyond the control of the Interior Department by the disposal of the lands, and their becoming the subject of private instead of Governmental ownership.

Wilbourne v. Baldwin et al., 47 Pacific Reporter, 1045.

SEC. 81. The territory in which Deadwood is situated was, under the treaty with the Sioux Indians, proclaimed February 24, 1869, a part of an Indian reservation, until February 28, 1877, and during such time no rights whatever therein could be acquired by any settler.   Where, prior to February 28, 1877, one undertook to lease to another certain lots in Deadwood, then part of an Indian reservation, the contract for such leasing was illegal and absolutely void, and courts would not lend their aid to enforce any pretended right resting on such contract.

Uhlig v. Garrison. 2 N. W. Rep:, 253.   Same, 2 Dak., 71.   French v. Lancaster, 2 Dak., 276.   Caledonia Mining Co. v. Noonan, 3 Dak. (Smith), 201.

SEC. 82. The *locus in quo* was Indian country, to which the Indian title was not relinquished until by force of the agreement of February 28, 1877.   *Uhlig v. Garrison, 2 Dak. (Smith), 71.   Same, 2 N. W. Rep., 253.*

SEC. 83. The Indian country includes such portions of the public domain as are exclusively reserved for the use and occupation of the several bands and tribes of Indians, and which are not included within the jurisdiction of any State or Territory.

United States v. Knowlton, 13 N. W. Rep., 573.   Same, 3 Dak., 59.

SEC. 84. Lands ceded to the United States by its Indian occupants cease from that time to be a part of the Indian country, within the meaning of the intercourse act of 1834 (4 Stat. L., 729) and its amendment (13 Stat. L., 29).

Clark v. Bates, 46 N. W. Rep., 510.   Same, 1 Dak. (Bennett), 42.

SEC. 85. The preemption law of 1841 (5 Stat. L., 456) provides that no "Indian reservations to which the title has been extinguished by the United States at any time during the operation of this act   *   *   * shall be liable to entry under and by virtue of the provisions of this act."   June 16, 1820, the Chippewas ceded certain lands at Sault Ste. Marie to the United States, certain rights being reserved and guaranteed to them as follows: "The United States will secure to the Indians a perpetual right of fishing at the falls of St. Mary, and also a place of encampment upon the tract hereby ceded," etc. (7 Stat. L., 206). March 28, 1836, the Ottawas and Chippewas ceded to the United States certain lands including said lands, the treaty providing that "it is understood that the reservation for a place of fishing and encampment, made under the treaty of St. Mary's of the 16th of June, 1820, remains unaffected by this treaty" (7 Stat. L., 497).   In 1845 the United States surveyed and set apart to the Indians a tract as an Indian reservation under the treaty of 1820.   The Chippewas on

August 2, 1855, relinquished to the United States the right of fishing and encampment secured to them by said treaty. *Held*, that the said tract surveyed and set apart to the Indians was not subject to preemption under said act of 1841 in 1859, though in act of Congress of August 26, 1852, granting the right of way to the State of Michigan for the canal at Sault Ste. Marie, this land is termed and treated as a military reservation.   *Spaulding v. Chandler, 47 N. W. Rep., 593.*

SEC. 86. In 1818 the Hot Springs, Arkansas, were in the Indian country, to which, of course, no public surveys extended.
Gaines v. Hale 26 Ark., 168.

SEC. 87. The purpose and effect of the non-intercourse act of 1834 was to declare and proclaim what was then Indian country; country in which the manners, customs, and laws of the Indian tribes prevailed, and in which the United States should protect them in all their natural and guaranteed rights, and not to declare or maintain that to be Indian country which was not in fact in the occupation and under the control of the Indians.
Clark v. Bates, 1 Dakota (Bennett), 42.   Same, 46 N. W. Rep., 510.

SEC. 88. The policy of all branches of the Government from the earliest times has been to protect all citizens in the occupation of the ceded Indian country, and to secure cessions as fast as demanded by the increase of our population, and when territory has once been solemnly ceded by the Indians it has never afterwards been considered or treated as Indian country for any purpose.   *Ibid.*

SEC. 89. The nonintercourse act of 1834, wherein it fixed and determined the limits of the Indian country, was modified and changed by the treaty with the Dakota nation of Indians, made in 1868, as it had been by various other preceding treaties.   *Ibid.*

SEC. 90. Cessions by treaty, duly proclaimed by the President, have always been considered and treated by the people of the United States as an invitation from the Executive Department to all people to come upon and possess the ceded country.   *Ibid.*

SEC. 91. The authority of the President to withdraw from sale a portion of the public domain and set it apart for the use of the several tribes of Sioux Indians as an addition to their existing treaty reservation can not be questioned.   *United States v. Knowlton, 3 Dakota, 59.*

SEC. 92. The provisions of the twenty-fifth section of the act of Congress of 1834, regulating trade and intercourse with the Indians, is as applicable to the Indian tribes in the Territory of Idaho as any portion of the act; hence the Territory is Indian country, but only so far as the rights of the persons and property of the Indian tribes are concerned, and, therefore, to that extent within the sole and exclusive jurisdiction of the United States.

Prickett v. United States, 1 Prickett (Idaho), 523.

SEC. 93. Indian land possesses no intrinsic quality distinguishing it from *domesticated* land and enabling it to repel the jurisdiction of civilized people. An Indian tribe or other political community or nation can not, on becoming extinct or on abandoning its territory, leave behind it adhering to the land a thing called *jurisdiction* capable of excluding other jurisdictions from the vacant territory. Much less could this be effected by an *imaginary* tribe having no existence *in* fact.

Tilford v. Barney, 1 Greene (Iowa), 575.

SEC. 94. Oregon was not a part of the Indian county as defined by the act of Congress of June 30, 1834, and consequently the provisions of that act did not originally extend to Oregon. The act of June 5, 1850, by extending the act of June 30, 1834, to Oregon, so far as its provisions may be applicable, conferred upon the judiciary of the Territory the power to determine how far and in what respects said act is applicable to the same. So much of the act of Congress of June 30, 1834, as prohibits the selling, exchanging, giving, bartering, or disposing of any spirituous liquors or wines to an Indian is applicable to Oregon, and, therefore, the law of the Territory.

United States v. Tom, 1 Oregon (Wilson), 27.

SEC. 95. Evidence that there are settlements of white men in a certain section of Montana is not admissible to prove that it is not a part of the Indian country. All the country within the limits of Montana Territory is regarded as Indian country under the laws of the United States regulating trade and intercourse with Indian tribes. The fourth article of the treaty of 1855 between the United States and the Blackfoot tribe of Indians (11 Stat. L., 657) makes that portion of Montana in which Camp Cook is situated the home of the Blackfeet nation, and it is Indian country in the fullest acceptation of the term.

United States v. 196 Buffalo Robes, 1 Mon., 489.

SEC. 96. Throughout the year 1857 the premises now comprising lot 7, section 22, in township 111 north, of range 32 west, according to the plat of the survey by the Government of the United States in Minnesota, were embraced in an Indian reservation, and were not subject to preemption or private sale. Scrip issued under the act of Congress entitled "An act to authorize the President of the United States to cause to be surveyed the tract of land in the Territory of Minnesota belonging to the half-breeds or mixed bloods of the Dakota or Sioux nation of Indians, and for other purposes," approved July 17, 1854, could not be located upon said premises during said year, and a location thereof upon the same during said year and a patent issued upon such location are void.

Sharon v. Wooldrich, 18 Minn., 354.

SEC. 97. In contemplation of the Indian intercourse act of June 30, 1834, and the amendment of March 3, 1847, Washington Territory is Indian country. The latter act does not repeal the former, but the second section adds the penalty of imprisonment.

Fowler v. The United States, 1 Allen (Wash.), 3.

CHAPTER II.—POWERS OF CONGRESS.

SEC. 98. In the grant of judicial powers the term "foreign states" stands naked without any qualification accompanying it as to Indian tribes; and it is, therefore, to be taken in its largest sense, and with reference to the great principle of constitutional policy in view, which was the preservation of the peace and the maintenance of the faith and justice of the Union.

Opinion of Chancellor Kent as counsel in Cherokee Nation v. Georgia, "Peters Cherokee Case," 225.

SEC. 99. The abstract right of every section of the human race to a reasonable portion of the soil, by which to acquire the means of subsistence, can not be controverted, and it is equally clear that the range of nations or tribes who exist in the hunter state may be restricted within reasonable limits. They shall not be permitted to roam, in the pursuit of game, over an extensive and rich country while in other parts human beings are crowded so close together as to render the means of subsistence precarious. The law of nature, which is paramount to all other laws, gives the right to every nation to the enjoyment of a reasonable extent of country, so as to derive the means of subsistence from the soil. (McLean's concurrent opinion.)

Worcester v. Georgia, 6 Pet., 515—483.

SEC. 100. The Indian tribes residing within the territorial limits of the United States are subject to their authority, and where country occupied by them is not within the limits of any one of the States, Congress may by law punish any offense committed there, no matter whether the offender be a white man or an Indian.

United States v. Rogers, 4 How., 567.

SEC. 101. The act of Congress passed in 1851 (9 Stat. L., 595), creating the western judicial district of Arkansas, with criminal jurisdiction over the crimes committed against the laws of the United States within the Indian country by others than Indians, did not take away the power and jurisdiction of the circuit court of the United States for the eastern district to try an indictment for murder pending in that court at the time.

United States v. Dawson, 15 How., 467.

SEC. 102. The policy of the act of February 13, 1862 (12 Stat. L., 339), is the protection of those Indians who are, by treaty or otherwise, under the pupilage of the Government from the debasing influence of the use of spirits, and it is not easy to perceive why that policy should not require their protection from this, to them, destructive poison, when they are outside a reservation as well as within it. The evil effects are the same in both cases.

United States v. Holliday, 3 Wall., 407.

SEC. 103. The constitutional power of Congress extends to the regulation of commerce with the Indian tribes and with the individual members of such tribes, although the traffic and the Indian with whom it is carried on are wholly within the territorial limits of a State.

Ibid.

SEC. 104. Neither the constitution of a State nor any act of its legislature can withdraw the Indians from the influence of an act of Congress which that body has the constitutional right to pass concerning them, notwithstanding any rights that may be conferred by the State on such Indians as electors or citizens.

Ibid.

SEC. 105. Commerce or traffic or intercourse carried on with an Indian tribe, or with a member of an Indian tribe, is subject to be regulated by Congress, although within the limits of a State.

Ibid.

SEC. 106. There can be no question of State sovereignty in the case, as Kansas accepted her admission into the family of States on condition that the Indian rights should remain unimpaired and the General Government at liberty to make any regulation respecting them, their lands, property, or other rights, which it would have been competent to make if Kansas had not been admitted into the Union.

The Kansas Indians, 5 Wall., 737.

SEC. 107. If the Shawnees are under the control of Congress, of necessity there can be no divided authority. It may be that they can not exist much longer as a distinct people in the presence of the civilization of Kansas; but until they are clothed with the rights and bound to all the duties of "citizens" they enjoy the privilege of total immunity from State taxation.

Ibid.

SEC. 108. Congress has no constitutional power to settle the rights under treaties except in cases purely political. The construction of them is the peculiar province of the judiciary when a case shall arise between individuals.

Wilson v. Wall, 6 Wall., 83.

SEC. 109. Congress has the power to impose a restriction on the right of alienation of their lands by Indian reservees as a safeguard against the improvidence of the Indians.

Ibid.

SEC. 110. The power to define originally the "Indian country," within which the unlicensed introduction and sale of liquors were prohibited, necessarily includes that of enlarging the prohibited boundaries whenever, in the opinion of Congress, the interests of Indian intercourse and trade will be best subserved.

United States v. 43 Gals. Whisky, 93 U. S., 188.

SEC. 111. Congress, under its constitutional power to regulate commerce with the Indian tribes, may not only prohibit the unlicensed introduction and sale of spirituous liquors in the "Indian country," but extend such prohibition to territory in proximity to that occupied by the Indians.   *Ibid.*

SEC. 112. Of necessity the limitations in the articles of confederation on the power of the United States to regulate the trade and manage all affairs with the Indians rendered the power of no practical value; but the Congress now has the exclusive and absolute power to regulate commerce with the Indian tribes, which is a power as broad and as free from restrictions as that to regulate commerce with foreign nations.   *Ibid.*

SEC. 113. Congress has power to exclude spirituous liquors from existing Indian country and from that ceded to the United States.
                    Ibid.

SEC. 114. The power of Congress to regulate commerce with the Indian tribes is in no wise affected by the magnitude of the traffic or the extent of the intercourse. As long as these Indians remain a distinct people, with an existing tribal organization, recognized by the political departments of the Government, Congress has the power to say with whom and on what terms they shall deal, and what articles shall be contraband.   *Ibid.*

SEC. 115. Congress, from whom the power of a Territory to exercise jurisdiction emanates, has undoubted authority to exclude therefrom any part of the soil of the United States, or of that whereto the Indians have the possessory title, when, by our solemn treaties with them, a stipulation to that effect is made.
                    Langford v. Monteith, 102 U. S., 145.

SEC. 116. If land reserved for the exclusive occupancy of Indians lies outside the exterior boundaries of any organized Territorial government, it would require an act of Congress to attach it to a judicial district; the latest instance of which is the act of January 6, 1883 (22 Stat. L., 400), by which a part of the Indian Territory was attached to the district of Kansas and a part to the northern district of Texas.
                    Ex parte Crow Dog, 109 U. S., 556.

SEC. 117. The Sioux Indians, notwithstanding the pledge contained in their agreement that the United States would secure them in self-government, were to be subject to the laws of the United States, not in the sense of citizens, but as they had always been, as wards subject to a guardian; not as individuals, constituted members of the political community of the United States, with a voice in the selection of representatives, and the framing of the laws, but as a dependent community who were in a state of pupilage; advancing from the condition of a savage tribe to that of a people who, through the discipline of labor and by education, it was hoped might become a self-supporting and a self-governing society.   *Ibid.*

SEC. 118. The Indian tribes, being within the territorial limits of the United States, were not, strictly speaking, foreign states; but they were alien nations, distinct political communities with whom the United States might and habitually did deal as they thought fit, either through treaties made by the President and Senate or through acts of the Congress in the ordinary forms of legislation.

Elk v. Wilkins, 112 U. S., 94.

SEC. 119. The power of the General Government over these remnants of a race once powerful, now weak and diminished in numbers, is necessary to their protection as well as to the safety of those among whom they dwell. It must exist in that Government, because it never has existed anywhere else, because the theater of its exercise is within the geographical limits of the United States, because it has never been denied, and because it alone can enforce its laws on all the tribes.

United States v. Kagama, 118 U. S., 375.

SEC. 120. Because of the local ill feeling the people of the States where Indians are found are often their deadliest enemies, and from their weakness and helplessness, so largely due to the course of dealing of the Federal Government with them and the treaties in which it has been promised, there arises the duty of protection, and with it the power.   *Ibid.*

SEC. 121. While it can not be seen in either of the clauses of the Constitution and of its amendments referring to Indians any delegation of power to enact a code of criminal law for the punishment of the worst crimes known to civilized life when committed by Indians, there is a suggestion in the manner in which the Indian tribes are introduced in the clause (relating to commerce with them), not as states, nor as nations, nor as possessing the full attributes of sovereignty, but as separate people, with the power of regulating their own internal and social relations, and thus far not brought under the laws of the Union or of the State within whose limits they reside, which may have a bearing on the subject.   *Ibid.*

SEC. 122. The expression "excluding Indians not taxed," used in the Constitution declaring the basis on which representation in the lower House of Congress and direct taxation should be apportioned, and in the fourteenth amendment, do not shed much light on the power of Congress over the Indians in their existence as tribes, distinct from the ordinary citizens of a State or Territory, and the mention of Indians in the Constitution which has received most attention is that found in the clause which gives Congress "power to regulate commerce * * * with the Indian tribes."   *Ibid.*

SEC. 123. The first clause of the ninth section of the act of March 3, 1885 (23 Stat. L., 385), is new in legislation by Congress, which has heretofore only undertaken to punish an Indian who sustains the usual relation to his tribe, and who commits the offense in the Indian country or on an Indian reservation, in exceptional cases, as where the offense was against the person or property of a white man or was some violation of the trade and intercourse regulations imposed by Congress on the Indian tribes; and the second clause is a still further advance, as asserting exclusive jurisdiction over Indians within the limits of a State of the Union.   *Ibid.*

SEC. 124. While the Government of the United States has recognized in the Indian tribes heretofore a state of semiindependence and pupilage, it has the right and authority, instead of controlling them by treaties, to govern them by acts of Congress, because they are within the geographical limits of the United States, and are necessarily subject to the laws which Congress may enact for their protection and for the protection of the people with whom they come in contact.   *Ibid.*

SEC. 125. The question is no longer an open one as to whether a railroad is a public highway, established primarily for the convenience of the people and to subserve public ends, and therefore subject to governmental control and regulation, and it is because it is a public highway and subject to such control that the corporation by which it is constructed, and by which it is to be maintained, may be permitted under legislative sanction to appropriate private property for the purposes of a right of way upon making just compensation to the owner in the mode prescribed by law.

Cherokee Nation v. So. Kan. Rwy. Co., 135 U. S., 641.

SEC. 126. The provision of section 3 of the act of 1884 (23 Stat. L., 73) relating to the ascertainment of the compensation justly payable to the Cherokee Nation by the railway company is sufficiently reasonable, certain, and adequate to secure the just compensation to which the nation is entitled, and by it the requirements of the Constitution that the owner of lands taken for public purposes is entitled to reasonable, certain, and adequate provision for obtaining compensation before his occupancy is disturbed have been fully met.   *Ibid.*

SEC. 127. It was competent for Congress to give the enumerated courts jurisdiction over not only controversies immediately relating to or growing out of the construction of the road, but over all controversies between the nations and tribes, or the inhabitants thereof through whose territory the railroad might be constructed, and the company.   *So. Kan. Rwy. Co. v. Briscoe, 144 U. S., 133.*

SEC. 128. Unquestionably a treaty may be modified or abrogated by an act of Congress, but the power to make and unmake is essentially political and not judicial, and the presumption is wholly inadmissible that Congress sought, in referring the claim of these Indians to the courts for adjudication, to submit the good faith of its own action or the action of the Government to judicial decision by authorizing the stipulations in the Cherokee treaty of 1846 (9 Stat. L., 871) to be overthrown upon an inquiry of the character suggested, and the act of February 25, 1887 (24 Stat. L., 694), giving the courts jurisdiction of this case does not in the least degree justify any such inference.

United States v. Old Settlers, 148 U. S., 427. United States v. Tobacco Factory, 1 Dill., 264. United States v. Reese, 5 Dill., 405. Webster v. Reid, 1 Morris (Iowa), 467. Ryan v. Knorr, 19 Hun. (N. Y.), 540.

SEC. 129. The Indians of the country are considered as wards of the nation, and whenever the United States set apart any land of their own as an Indian reservation, whether within a State or Territory, they have full authority to pass such laws and authorize such measures as may be necessary to give to these people full protection in their persons and property, and to punish all offenses committed against them or by them within such reservations.

United States v. Thomas, 151 U. S., 577.

SEC. 130. Whatever the reason for the omission to make mention of the Indian reserve, the power existed in Congress to invade the sanctity of the reservation and disregard the guaranty contained in the Chippewa treaty of 1820 (7 Stat. L., 206), even against the consent of the Indians, parties to that treaty, and as the requirements of the grant to Michigan of the right to locate a canal at the Falls at St. Mary's River necessarily demanded the possession of the portion of the reserve through which the canal was to pass, the effect of the act was to extinguish so much of the Indian title in the reservation as was embraced in the grant to the State for canal purposes.

Spalding v. Chandler, 160 U. S., 394.

SEC. 131. The provision in the treaty of February 24, 1869, with the Bannock Indians, whose reservation was within the limits of what is now the State of Wyoming, that "they shall have the right to hunt upon the unoccupied lands of the United States so long as game may be found thereon," etc., does not give them the right to exercise this privilege within the limits of that State in violation of its laws.

Ward v. Race Horse, 163 U. S., 504.

SEC. 132. The existence of the right in Congress to regulate the manner in which the local powers of the Cherokee Nation shall be exercised does not render such local powers Federal powers arising from and created by the Constitution of the United States, and as the powers of local self-government enjoyed by the Cherokee Nation existed prior to the Constitution, they are not operated upon by the fifth amendment of the Constitution. *Talton v. Mayes, 163 U. S., 376.*

SEC. 133. By treaties and statutes of the United States the right of the Cherokee Nation to exist as an autonomous body, subject always to the paramount authority of the United States, has been recognized (5th art., treaty of 1835, 7 Stat. L., 478; 13th art., treaty of 1866, 14

Stat. L., 799; secs. 30 and 31, act May 2, 1890, 26 Stat. L., 81).   And from this fact there has consequently been conceded to exist in that nation power to make laws defining offenses and providing for the trial and punishment of those who violate them when the offenses are committed by one member of the tribe against another one of its members within the territory of the nation.   *Ibid.*

SEC. 134. The treaty between the United States and the several bands of Utes proclaimed March 2, 1868 (15 Stat. L., 619), is not repealed by the Colorado enabling act approved March 3, 1875 (18 Stat. L., 474), and the Ute reservation still remains within the sole and exclusive jurisdiction of the United States.   *United States v. Berry, 4 Fed. Rep., 779.*

SEC. 135. The Indian intercourse act of June 30, 1834 (4 Stat. L., 729), was extended over Oregon by the act of June 5, 1850 (9 Stat. L., 437), and was not modified or repealed by the admission of the State into the Union.   *United States v. Bridleman, 7 Fed. Rep., 894.*

SEC. 136. The treaty-making power can reserve a part of the public domain for a specific lawful purpose, because this is but the exercise of a less higher power than that which conveys title.
*United States v. Payne, 8 Fed. Rep., 883.   United States v. Reese,
5 Dill., 405.   Parker v. Winsor, 5 Kans., 362.*

SEC. 137. Congress may exercise its power to regulate commerce with the Indian tribes to the same extent as with foreign nations.
Note to Forty-three Galls. Cognac Brandy, 11 Fed. Rep., 51.

SEC. 138. When the Indian territory is within the limits of a State, Congress is limited to the regulation of commercial intercourse with such tribes as exist as a distinct community, governed by their own laws and resting for their protection on the faith of treaties and the laws of the Union, and the State can not withdraw them from the operation of the laws of the Congress.   *Ibid.*

SEC. 139. "The Government of the United States had, in the earliest and purest days of the Republic, watched with great anxiety over the property of the Indians intrusted to their care. It must have been immaterial from what source the property proceeded, and whether it was owned by tribes or families or individuals. *If it was Indian property in land*, it had a right to protection from us as against our own people."   *Wau-pe-mau-qua v. Aldrich, 28 Fed. Rep., 489.*

SEC. 140. The treaty of March 30, 1867 (15 Stat. L., 539), by which the Territory of Alaska was ceded to the United States, made the uncivilized tribes therein subject to such laws and regulations as the United States might adopt in regard to them.
In re Sah-Quah, 31 Fed. Rep., 327.

SEC. 141. The right of eminent domain does not grow out of the tenure by which lands are held. When a government asserts the right, it admits title in the one against whom the right is asserted. The right of eminent domain exists independent of the consideration whether the lands would escheat to the Government in case of failure of heirs.

Cherokee Nation v. So. Kan. Ry. Co., 33 Fed. Rep., 900.

SEC. 142. By sovereignty, in its largest sense, is meant supreme, absolute, uncontrollable power, the *jus summi imperii*, the absolute right to govern. Sovereignty in government is that public authority which directs or orders that which is to be done by each member of society in relation to the end of the association or organization. Government is not sovereignty, but is the machinery or expedient for expressing the will of the sovereign power. *Ibid.*

SEC. 143. Eminent domain pertains alone to sovereignty. It belongs to no other power. It is one of the attributes of sovereignty. *Ibid.*

SEC. 144. Eminent domain is the rightful authority which exists in every sovereignty which controls and regulates those rights of a public nature which pertain to its citizens in common, and to appropriate and control individual property without the consent of the owners, upon the payment of just compensation to the owners, for the public benefit, as the public safety, necessity, or convenience may demand.

Ibid.

SEC. 145. By the treaty of 1855 (12 Stat. L., 948) the Umatilla Indians engaged to submit to any rule that might be prescribed by the United States for their government. This obviously includes the power to organize and maintain an Indian court and police, and to specify the acts or conduct of which it shall have jurisdiction. This treaty is an "act" or "law" relating to Indian affairs; and by section 465 of the Revised Statutes the power to prescribe a rule for carrying the same into effect is given the President, who has exercised it in this case through the proper instrumentality, the Secretary of the Interior. *United States v. Clapox, 35 Fed. Rep., 575.*

SEC. 146. Indians are frequent suitors in the courts of the various States, and while the Supreme Court of the United States reversed the supreme court of Kansas in the case of the Kansas Indians, the right of the Indian to sue in the courts of the State was not questioned.

Felix v. Patrick, 36 Fed. Rep., 457.

SEC. 147. There is nothing in the act of Congress authorizing the defendant to build its road permitting it to lease it. The laws of Kansas granting the extraordinary power to defendant to lease its road can not operate beyond the sovereignty of Kansas. Before defendant could lease its road in the Indian country it must have the consent of the other party to the contract—the United States.

Briscoe v. So. Kan. Ry. Co., 40 Fed. Rep., 273

SEC. 148. The nations of Indians through whose lands the 120 miles of the Southern Kansas Railway runs have many rights that may be affected or destroyed by the tortious acts of the defendant, and Congress did not intend that these Indians should be left without a remedy for an injury to personal property caused by the negligent and tortious acts of the defendant.   *Ibid.*

SEC. 149. It is a fundamental principle that the laws of a State can have no binding force *proprio vigore*, outside of the territorial limits of the State enacting them. The charter of this road, or the laws of Kansas under which it exists, does not give it the right to exercise its powers beyond the State of Kansas. Its powers under its Kansas charter can not be exercised in the Indian country unless permitted to be so exercised by the act of Congress, and they can be exercised only to the extent permitted.   *Ibid.*

SEC. 150. The case at bar is within the jurisdiction of the United States courts, not on the ground of exclusive jurisdiction because of the Government's owning the land, or having general or exclusive jurisdiction over the territory embraced within an Indian reservation, but because of the subject-matter, which is the management, control, and government of the Indians under the charge of the United States, and is necessarily one of national cognizance.

> *Dissenting opinion of Bunn, J., in United States v. Thomas, 47 Fed. Rep., 488.*

SEC. 151. The question is not one of power in the National Government, for, as has been shown, Congress may provide for the punishment of this crime (murder) wherever committed in the United States. Its jurisdiction is coextensive with the subject-matter—the intercourse between the white man and the tribal Indians—and is not limited to place or other circumstances.   *Ibid.*

SEC. 152. The act of February 22, 1889 (25 Stat. L., 676), providing for the organization of the States of North Dakota and South Dakota, declared that "the people of said States do agree and declare that they forever disclaim all right and title * * * to all lands lying within said limits, owned or held by any Indian or Indian tribes," and that the same "shall be and remain under the absolute jurisdiction and control of the Congress of the United States."

> *United States v. Ewing, 47 Fed. Rep 809.*

SEC. 153. In view of the fact that the United States has always assumed control over the Indians, as the wards of the nation, to the exclusion of the States, the relinquishment by the State of jurisdiction over the Indians' reservation was for a "Federal purpose."

> *United States v. Partello, 48 Fed. Rep., 670.*

SEC. 154. As an incident of the right of the United States to govern Indians by its own laws, would be the right to hold lands upon which to locate them. It was urged that while the United States could have jurisdiction over such lands as far as the Indians are concerned, it would have no right over white men found within an Indian reservation, such as the Crow Reservation. The statute and the ordinance the court have been considering in this case say the jurisdiction and control is absolute, not a divided jurisdiction or control; and this seems proper.   *Ibid.*

SEC. 155. Where a controversy between citizens of the Creek Nation is an action in the United States court for the Indian Territory, the rule of decision, in the absence of evidence as to what the Creek law is, is the law of the forum, which is to be found in Mansfield's Digest of the Laws of Arkansas, put in force in the Indian Territory by the act of Congress May 2, 1890 (26 Stat. L., 84).

Davison v. Gibson, 56 Fed. Rep., 443.

SEC. 156. Citing the case of Johnson *v.* McIntosh (8 Wheat., 585), the court quotes: "It has never been doubted that either the United States or the several States had a clear title to all the lands within the boundary lines described in the treaty with Great Britain of 1783 (8 Stat. L., 80) subject only to the Indian right of occupancy, and that the exclusive power to extinguish that right was vested in the Government, which might constitutionally exercise it."

Caldwell v. Robinson, 59 Fed. Rep., 653.

SEC. 157. The act of 1887 (24 Stat. L., 388), which confers citizenship on Indian allottees clearly does not emancipate the Indians from all control of the Government or abolish the reservations. Section 3 of the act of 1891 (26 Stat. L., 794), amendatory of that of 1887, provides for leasing lands under certain contingencies and under the regulations of the Secretary of Interior, and the proviso of the section contemplates agents in charge of the reservations. The patents to the Puyallup Indian allottees have clear words of prohibition against alienation, and even if they had omitted them the treaties and laws imposed them. The power of the Government to impose the restraints is not questioned, and its purpose is certainly not ambiguous.

Eells v. Ross, 64 Fed. Rep., 417.

SEC. 158. By the act of July 27, 1868 (15 Stat. L., 228), Congress authorized and directed the Secretary of the Interior and Commissioner of Indian Affairs to take the same supervisory charge of the Eastern Band of Cherokees as of other tribes, and there is a necessary implication of power that if, in the exercise of such supervisory charge, it becomes necessary to resort to a court of equity for remedy and relief, a suit may be properly instituted by such supervisory department in the name of the United States to obtain adequate redress.   *United States v. Boyd, 68 Fed. Rep., 577.*

SEC. 159. The supreme court of North Carolina, in Rollins *v.* Cherokees (67 N. C., 229), fully recognized the power and right of the United States to supervise and control the affairs, lands, and contracts of the North Carolina Cherokees. The court refers with approbation to the acts of Congress regulating contracts with Indians, and

expresses the opinion that such laws apply to contracts with the North
Carolina Cherokee Indians.   *Ibid.*

SEC. 160. Neither the constitution of a State nor any act of its
legislature, however formal or solemn, whatever rights it may confer
on these Indians or withhold from them, can withdraw them from the
influence of an act of Congress which that body has the constitutional
right to pass concerning them. Any other doctrine would make the
legislature of the State the supreme law of the land instead of the
Constitution of the United States and the laws and treaties made in
pursuance thereof.   *Ibid.*

SEC. 161. In the exercise of its exclusive power of legislation for
the Indian Territory, Congress, by the act of May 2, 1890 (26 Stat.
L., 81), for the purpose of remedying the defects in the act of 1889
(25 Stat. L., 783), enacted a complete code of substantive laws for the
Territory, to be administered by the court it had previously created.
This code of laws was taken from the revised statutes of the State of
Arkansas, and it embraced the body of the statute law of that State.
Man'f'g Co. v. Needles, 69 Fed. Rep., 68.

SEC. 162. Under the act of May 2, 1890 (26 Stat. L., 81), adopting
for the Indian Territory certain statutes of Arkansas, including chapter
60 of the statutes of that State relating to executions, and providing
a penalty for the failure of an officer to whom an execution is delivered
to execute or return the writ, is an act of Congress within the Territory, of the same force and effect as if adopted by Congress, without
any reference to the Arkansas statutes, and is to be enforced by the
United States courts as such.   *Ibid.*

SEC. 163. If the United States, by a treaty duly made with an Indian
tribe, has assumed a given duty or obligation to the Indians, the power
exists to properly perform this duty within the boundaries of a State
as well as within a Territory. The power to enforce its laws, and the
treaties made by it, in pursuance of the provisions of the Constitution,
is paramount and supreme, and rests upon every foot of soil within
the national boundaries.   *United States v. Flournoy, etc., Co., 69 Fed. Rep., 886.*

SEC. 164. If the executive branch of the Government deems it
necessary for the proper performance of its treaty stipulations with
the Indians to forbid the occupancy of allotted tracts by white men,
it has the right to do so, particularly in view of the fact that, in all
the legislation touching the same, Congress has uniformly prohibited
the alienation of the lands, and has expressly declared that all contracts
between the Indians and persons not native members of the tribe shall
be wholly null and void.   *Ibid.*

SEC. 165. The relation of an unnaturalized Indian segregated from
his tribe and residing in a State, in respect to both Federal and State
authority and jurisdiction, is peculiar, and often gives rise to difficult

and perplexing questions. But no such questions are presented by this record; and, inasmuch as there is no provision in the act of March 3, 1887 (24 Stat. L., 552), or the amendatory act of August 13, 1888 (25 Stat. L., 438), or in any act of Congress conferring jurisdiction on the circuit courts of the United States in civil controversies or suits by or against Indians, it follows necessarily that the petition for removal must be denied. *Paul v. Chilsoquie, 70 Fed. Rep., 401.*

SEC. 166. While the paramount title to all lands in Alaska is in the United States, Congress and the General Government have recognized for a great many years the right of the American citizens to go onto public lands, occupy, possess, use, and improve the same, with the view of ultimately obtaining title thereto from the General Government, whenever the same shall be opened to purchase, and in this district this right is expressly recognized by Congress in the first proviso of section 8 of the act of May 17, 1884 (23 Stat. L., 24), providing a civil government for Alaska. When Congress enacted this law, it undoubtedly had in view the condition of affairs in this country, and, to protect the settlers upon the public lands here, incorporated into said act the proviso above mentioned, which is in the following language: "That the Indians or other persons in said district shall not be disturbed in the possession of any lands actually in their use or occupation or now claimed by them, but the terms under which such persons may acquire title to such lands is reserved for future legislation by Congress." *Carroll v. Price, 81 Fed. Rep., 137.*

SEC. 167. Section 2124 of the Revised Statutes was not intended to limit the United States to an action of debt to collect the penalties provided, but prescribed the procedure in cases where the penalty was sought to be collected by an informer.
United States v. Stocking, 87 Fed. Rep., 857.

SEC. 168. It was not the purpose of Congress, by the act of February 16, 1889 (25 Stat. L., 673), empowering the President, in his discretion, from year to year, to authorize the Indians on a reservation to cut and sell or dispose of the dead timber thereon, to permit a few to monopolize the privilege; nor can it be supposed that such has heretofore been the purpose of the President in granting such authority; and where a contract made by an Indian to cut and deliver to a purchaser a certain quantity of timber, "more or less" or "about," to be taken from the dead timber on a reservation is approved by the President, the quantity stated limits the amount which can be sold, or to which the purchaser can obtain title thereunder, allowance being made only for small and accidental variation.
United States v. Logging and Improvement Co., 89 Fed. Rep., 907.

SEC. 169. The act of March 2, 1895 (28 Stat. L., 906), prohibiting any Indian agent or other employee of the Government from using compulsory means, such as withholding rations or the like, to induce the parents or next of kin of any Indian child to consent to the removal of such child beyond the limits of the reservation, is applicable to the Sac and Fox tribe of Indians in Iowa and is paramount to any regulation of the Department. Under such statute the agent of the tribe and the superintendent of the school established therefor not only have no power to compel children to attend the school which is situated outside the reservation, but the consent of the parents or next of kin of such children is required to authorize their removal thereto.

In re. Lelah puc ka chee, 98 Fed. Rep., 429.

SEC. 170. The fact that an Indian girl, a minor, while in attendance at a Government school which is outside the reservation of the tribe of which she is a member, contracts a marriage in accordance with the custom of her tribe, with another member, does not entitle her husband to a writ of habeas corpus to remove her from the school, nor can she be detained there against her own will; but in such case her marriage releases her from parental authority, and she has the right to remain or not, at her own election. So long as she remains unmarried her attendance during her minority is subject entirely to the will of her parents or those who stand to her in the parental relation.   Ibid.

SEC. 171. The act of August 14, 1848 (9 Stat. L., 323), organizing the Territory of Oregon, provided by section 1 "That nothing in this act contained shall be construed to impair the rights of persons or property now pertaining to the Indians in said Territory, so long as such rights shall remain unextinguished by treaty between the United States and such Indians, or to affect the authority of the Government of the United States to make any regulations by treaty, law, or otherwise respecting such Indians, their lands, property, or other rights which it would be competent for the Government to make if this act had never passed."   Johnson v. United States, 2 C. Cl., 155.

SEC. 172. The purchase of supplies to subsist Indians in California in 1851 was a purchase under authority of law, within the meaning of the act of June 30, 1834 (4 Stat. L., 729), although the treaty pursuant to which the supplies were purchased had not then been ratified and was subsequently rejected by the Senate.

Belt v. United States, 15 C. Cl., 92.

SEC. 173. When the Commissioner of Indian Affairs, being informed of the course which a subagent intends to pursue, approved it, his approval was a ratification of the agent's acts, rendering them valid.

Ibid.

SEC. 174. The action of the Commissioner of Indian Affairs must be presumed to be the action of the President.   Ibid.

SEC. 175. When a statute requires a subordinate officer to obey the instructions of the Secretary of the Interior and to carry into effect such regulations as the President may prescribe, and his acts receive subsequently the approval of the Commissioner of Indian Affairs, the law is substantially complied with. *Ibid.*

SEC. 176. The statutory authority of Indian agents in 1851 to purchase necessary supplies for Indians with the approval of the President examined and stated. *Ibid.*

SEC. 177. The restrictions upon purchases for the public service established by the act of May 1, 1820 (3 Stat. L., 568), did not extend to the business of Indian affairs, nor were there any such restrictions applicable to purchases for Indians in 1851.

Ibid.

SEC. 178. The court refrains from expressing an opinion as to whether interest should be allowed on the sum of $240,164.58, which should be credited to the Chickasaw Nation, as the question must necessarily be taken to the legislative department of the Government, which alone has the power to grant relief, which will consider the equities of the case and which will decide whether it is one wherein the doctrine should be waived that as the sovereign does no wrong and is ever ready and willing to pay its just debts, the Government pays no interest. *Chickasaw Nation v. United States, 22 C. Cls., 222.*

SEC. 179. Section 2052, Revised Statutes, authorized the President to appoint 42 Indian agents at specified salaries, but every subsequent appropriation act has disregarded those provisions, both as to number and salary. *Belknap v. United States, 24 C. Cls., 433.*

SEC. 180. The authority of the King to regulate and control purchases from the Indians within these colonies was not questioned on the argument and can not be denied. Any purchases made by Stedman in violation of such regulations must be void, and he could acquire no right whatever thereby, not even the Indian right of occupancy, and he must have been an intruder by any entry made under such purchase. *Jackson, ex. dem. Sparkman v. Porter, 1 Paine, 457.*

SEC. 181. The peculiar relation which a tribe of Indians residing within the limits of a State bears to the Federal and State governments renders every exercise of jurisdiction over their persons and property, by the Federal Government a matter of great delicacy and importance. *United States v. Cisna, 1 McLean, 254.*

SEC. 182. The validity of the numerous treaties and laws made with and for the Indians has not been questioned, it is believed, so far as they act upon the Indian tribes and our own citizens beyond the boundaries of any State. But serious questions have arisen, and are likely to again arise, between the Federal and State authorities respecting the jurisdiction of the former over territory of Indians situated within a State sovereignty. *Ibid.*

SEC. 183. No express provision has been made in treaties or by act of Congress at what period or under what circumstances the power of the Federal Government to regulate commerce with the Wyandotte or any other tribe of Indians living within a State shall be terminated.

Ibid.

SEC. 184. If it be conceded that under the power of peace and war, to make treaties and to regulate commerce with the Indian tribes, Congress could, in the absence of reserved right to do so, withdraw Indians living within the limits of a State entirely from State jurisdiction and the reach of its criminal laws and process for offenses against its citizens committed off a reservation, it would seem most improbable that such a power would ever be exercised. In point of fact Congress has not undertaken to exercise it, and therefore this court, which can take cognizance only of offenses created by some act of Congress, has no jurisdiction of the crime charged in the indictment.

United States v. Yellow Sun, 1 Dill., 271.

SEC. 185. The power of the Government may be employed to effect the removal of trespassers from a reservation; but where the removal is effected it is the duty of the troops to convey the persons so removed, by the most convenient and safe route, to the civil authorities of the judicial district in which the offense may be committed, to be proceeded against in due course of law.

United States v. Crook, 5 Dill., 453.

SEC. 186. The case of the Cherokee Tobacco (11 Wall., 616) presented a clear and necessary repugnance between an act of Congress and a preexisting Indian treaty, and therefore one in which the latter repealed the former, it being held that the internal-revenue laws, made to apply *anywhere within the exterior boundaries of the United States*, did not apply to the Cherokees because of a provision to the contrary in a former treaty. *United States v. Berry, 2 McCrary, 58.*

SEC. 187. If the treaty of 1868 (15 Stat. L., 619) with the Utes was one of the laws of the United States which, by the terms of the act of June 26, 1876 (19 Stat. L., 61), was to remain in force in the State of Colorado after its admission, it follows that the Ute Reservation remains within the exclusive jurisdiction of the United States by virtue of said treaty. *Ibid.*

SEC. 188. Many of the provisions of the Ute treaty of 1868 (15 Stat. L., 619) necessarily require for their enforcement that the reservation shall remain under the sole and exclusive jurisdiction of the United States; and to hold that this jurisdiction is superseded by that of the State would be to render nugatory nearly every provision of the treaty.

Ibid.

SEC. 189. The policy of keeping the Indian reservations within the exclusive jurisdiction of the National Government until such time as the rights of the Indians therein are extinguished has been uniformly pursued with respect to all the Indian reservations in the country, and it is expressed so plainly in the treaty of 1868 with the Utes that it is impossible to suppose that it was the intention of Congress by the organization of the State of Colorado to annihilate the treaty and to deprive the Indians of their right to protection under it.   *Ibid.*

SEC. 190. The act of March 3, 1875 (18 Stat. L., 474), admitting Colorado into the Union did not take from the United States jurisdiction over the Ute Reservation.   *Ibid.*

SEC. 191.   An express statute conferring special rights and privileges is never held to be repealed by implication unless the intent to effect such repeal is clear.   *Ibid.*

SEC. 192. By virtue of the treaty-making power the United States had, prior to the organization and admission of the State of Colorado, brought the Ute Reservation within their sole and exclusive jurisdiction, and no doubt is entertained that the Federal courts had, prior to the admission of Colorado, complete jurisdiction to try and determine all cases of murder committed within the limits of that reservation.

Ibid.

SEC. 193. Congress has the constitutional power to pass laws punishing Indians for crimes and offenses committed against the United States.   *United States v. Cha-to-kah-na-pe-sha et al., 1 Hemp., 27.*

SEC. 194. Congress had power to authorize the President to regulate or prohibit the introduction of distilled spirits into the district of Alaska, under penalties, as prescribed by act of July 27, 1864 (15 Stat. L., 241).   *The Louisa Simpson, 2 Saw., 57.*

SEC. 195. The power of Congress to regulate the intercourse between the inhabitants of the United States and the Indian tribes therein is not limited by State lines or governments, but may be exercised and enforced wherever the subject-Indian tribes exist.

United States v. Bridleman, 7 Saw., 243.

SEC. 196. The power to regulate commerce with Indian tribes includes not only traffic in commodities, but intercourse with such tribes, the personal conduct of the white and other races to and with such tribes and the members thereof, and *vice versa.*   *Ibid.*

SEC. 197. Intercourse with Indians is a subject of Federal jurisdiction, the same as the naturalization of aliens, etc., and therefore Congress may pass laws regulating or even prohibiting it and providing for the punishment of acts or conduct growing out of it resulting in injury to either the Indian or the other party, or calculated to interrupt or destroy its peaceful or beneficial character.   *Ibid.*

SEC. 198. The power given to the President and to the Secretary of the Interior to require a bond from an Indian agent with "conditions" will not be construed to authorize them to exact or impose conditions not relative to the duties and obligations of the office.

United States v. Barnhart, 9 Saw., 159.

SEC. 199. The power of Congress over a territory of the United States extends to all rightful subjects and methods of legislation not denied to it by the Constitution, and consistent with the spirit of the same and the purpose for which such territory may have been acquired.

Nelson v. United States, 12 Saw., 285.

SEC. 200. Congress has power to prohibit the importation, manufacture, and sale of intoxicating liquors in the district of Alaska, and to make the violation of such prohibition punishable by fine and imprisonment.　　　　　　　　　　　　　　　　　　　　　*Ibid.*

SEC. 201. The treaty between the United States and the Blackfeet Indians provides that the Indians shall send their young children to school and that the agent shall see that this stipulation is carried into effect. But no penalty is provided for its violation, and the United States is given no authority over the children and can not reclaim them by a writ of *habeas corpus* from a person who has taken them from the agency, possibly with the parents' consent.

United States ex rel. Young v. Imoda, 1 Pac. Rep., 721.

SEC. 202. Under the treaty of the United States with the Yakima Nation or tribe of Indians, entered into June 9, 1855, conferring on them the right of taking fish at all usual and accustomed places, in common with the citizens of Washington Territory, etc., the privilege is reserved to them to enjoy all the fisheries they had theretofore done, and where a person, under an act of Congress passed subsequently to the treaty, obtained a patent for homestead land abutting upon the "Tum Water Fishery," and erected and maintained a fence thereon which obstructed the approaches to the fishery and prevented the enjoyment by the Indians of the right which had been so reserved to them, equity will interfere by injunction and cause the removal of the obstruction.　　　*United States v. Taylor, 13 Pac. Rep., 333.　Same, 1 Wash. (Struve), 88.*

SEC. 203. Under the second section of the act of August 4, 1886 (24 Stat. L., 219) lands patented by the United States to a deceased allottee of the Kickapoo Indian tribe in Kansas descend to the heirs of said allottee in accordance with the rule of succession provided by the laws of the State of Kansas.　　　*Edde v. Pash-pah-o et al., 48 Pac. Rep., 884.*

SEC. 204. The common law did not prevail in the Indian Territory prior to the passage of the act of May 2, 1890 (26 Stat. L., 94).

Johnson v. State, 60 Ark., 308.

SEC. 205. Congress lacks the Constitutional power to enact laws invalidating contracts entered into within the limits of a State, whether with an Indian or a resident of a sister State or subject of a foreign Government, this being one of the reserved rights retained by the States.　　　　　　　　　　　　*Hicks v. Ewhartonah, 21 Ark., 106.*

Sec. 206. When the Indians occupy a territory of limited extent, surrounded by a white population which necessarily have daily intercourse with them, and it becomes impossible to enforce the United States laws, the Federal jurisdiction must cease. *Ibid.*

Sec. 207. Congress has the exclusive right of preemption to all Indian lands lying within the territories of the United States.

Thompson v. Doaksum, 68 Cal., 593.

Sec. 208. The legislature and the executive departments of the State of Kansas have recognized the power of the Federal Government, by treaty, to exempt Indian lands from taxation, notably so by the act approved by the governor February 10, 1864.

Parker v. Winsor, 5 Kans., 362.

Sec. 209. The Bluejacket case was taken to the Supreme Court of the United States (5 Wall., 759), and that court went further than the supreme court of Kansas did, not only holding that the Government, by treaty, had the power to exempt such lands from taxation, but that it had actually done so; holding that the words "levy and sale," as there used, had a broader significance than that given to them by the supreme court of Kansas; holding that these words mean, respectively, a "levy of taxes" and a "sale for taxes," as well as a levy of an execution and a sale on execution, thereby overruling the decision of the supreme court of Kansas in this respect. *Ibid.*

Sec. 210. In the Bluejacket case (3 Kans., 368) the court commented upon various treaties exempting lands from taxation, levy, sale, or forfeiture. Elaborate argument was made to prove that the words "levy, sale, and forfeiture," as used in the Miami treaty, do not mean, respectively, "a levy of taxes," "sale for taxes," or "a forfeiture for taxes;" but nowhere does it seem to have occurred to the court that the Government had no power to make such a treaty, or to exempt such lands from taxation. *Ibid.*

Sec. 211. The supreme court of Kansas, in the case of Miami County v. Wan-zop-pe-che (3 Kans., 364), seem to have recognized the power of the United States to exempt Indian lands from taxation. *Ibid.*

Sec. 212. The power of the President and the Senate of the United States by a treaty with the Indians, without the consent of the House of Representatives, to dispose of the public domain held or occupied by Indian tribes, giving said public domain to a few railroad companies, questioned. *Ibid.*

Sec. 213. In a conflict between the law of the State and a treaty of the United States in regard to Indian lands in the State the former must give way. Neither the title nor possession of the Indian owner, secured by treaty, can be disturbed by State legislation, and the occupying claimant act has no application in this case.

Maynes v. Veale, 20 Kans., 374.

SEC. 214. In 1862 Congress had the exclusive right and dominion over the Delaware Reservation in Kansas, and had full power to permit the construction of a railroad over such reservation either with or without compensation to be paid by the company.

Ginter v. K. P. Ry. Co., 23 Kans., 642.

SEC. 215. Under the act of Congress of July 1, 1862 (12 Stat. L., 489), the company had the authority in 1863, without paying compensation to the Delaware allottees, to enter upon the reservation for the purpose of locating its line of road and of constructing and operating its road over and across said land.

Ibid.

SEC. 216. As to the power of the United States to regulate the mode of conveyance of lands belonging to the United States, or to Indians, or to both, free from and independent of State statutes, see 61 U. S., 588; 38 U. S., 436; 20 Kans., 374.

McGannon v. Straightlegs, 32 Kans., 524.

SEC. 217. The right of the United States to dispose of lands to which it holds the fee has ever been recognized by the courts of highest resort in this country, and this rule is true with regard to lands in which the Indians have the right of possession, as well as to the public lands belonging to the Government.

Roberts v. M. K. & T. Ry. Co., 43 Kans., 102.

SEC. 218. Congress having full control over the lands in Kansas known as the "Osage trust and diminished reserve lands," may make them subject to State taxation upon such conditions as are deemed proper, not in conflict with the provisions of the constitution and laws of the State.

Logan v. Commissioner, 51 Kans., 747.

SEC. 219. The power given to Congress to regulate commerce with the Indian tribes does not include navigation with the Penobscot or any other tribe of Indians. It is confined to that sort of trade of which navigation constitutes no part.

Moor v. Veazie, 32 Maine, 343.

SEC. 220. "The Indian tribes" referred to in the constitution were those tribes which were in a condition to determine for themselves with whom they would have commerce, or in a condition to have Congress determine it for them, and not those tribes or remnants of tribes yet denominated tribes which had before that time and have ever since continued to be under the control and guardianship of a State, and were without the power to carry on commerce, except by permission and under the control of State laws.

Ibid.

SEC. 221. The fact that a parcel of land embraced within the Indian reserve at Sault Ste. Marie was at one time within the so-called "military reservation," or at least surrounded by it, did not alter its character, or take away or destroy the right of the Indians to its use for the purposes for which it was set apart and reserved; nor could Congress, by naming the land as a "military reservation" in the act of Congress of August 26, 1852, granting the right of way to the State of Michigan for the canal at Sault Ste. Marie, or by any other legislation, directly or indirectly, destroy the reservation after it had been set apart to and used by the Indians under the treaty of 1820, the voluntary cession of the land to the United States by the Indians themselves being necessary to deprive it of its character as an Indian reservation. *   *Spalding v. Chandler, 84 Mich. (Fuller), 140.*

SEC. 222. It would not have been in the power of the Indians, or of the Government by treaty stipulation, without the express assent of the State, to vest the Indian with the absolute property in the land and at the same time say it shall not be subject to execution for debts lawfully contracted. That would be trenching too far on State sovereignty.   *Saffarans v. Terry, 20 Miss., 690.*

SEC. 223. The United States had the power to deal with the lands occupied by the Indian tribes according to its pleasure. It could respect their title and pretensions as it saw fit; but, as the several treaties and acts of Congress show, the Government never regarded the absolute title to the soil as residing in the United States until ceded by the Indians, nor did they undertake to dispose of them until the acquisition of the Indian title.   *Minter v. Shirley, 45 Miss., 376.*

SEC. 224. The character of the Indian Territory was discussed in United States v. Rogers (4 How., 567), and it was adjudged that the Territory was within the territorial limits of the United States, and that the Indians residing therein were subject to their authority, and Congress may by law punish offenses committed there whether the offender be a white man or an Indian.

Tush ho yo tabby v. Barr, 45 Miss., 189.

SEC. 225. The United States did not intend to yield or divide its authority over the Indians in their domestic affairs; the Territorial legislature had no right to exercise it, and the presumption is that it did not intend to do so.   *State v. McKenny, 18 Nev., 182.*

SEC. 226. In report No. 367, Forty-third Congress, first session, the Committee on Indian Affairs of the House of Representatives, to whom was referred the bill conferring jurisdiction upon the United States courts, and for the punishment of crimes committed by and against Indians, reported "* * * that it is doubtful whether Congress has the power to confer exclusive jurisdiction upon the courts of the United States over Indian reservations within the several States without their consent. This difficulty does not exist in the Territories, where the authority is ample and undisputed. * * *"   *Ibid.*

SEC. 227. By the act admitting Nevada as a Territory, in March, 1861 (12 Stats., 209) it was declared "that nothing in this act contained shall be construed to impair the rights of person or property now pertaining to the Indians in said Territory so long as such rights shall remain unextinguished by treaty between the United States and such Indians;   *   *   *   or to affect the authority of the Government of the United States to make any regulations respecting such Indians, their lands, property, or other rights, by treaty, law, or otherwise, which it would have been competent for the Government to make if this act had not been passed."   *Ibid.*

SEC. 228. The rights of person and property referred to in the organic act of Nevada could not have been treaty rights only, as the first treaty with the Shoshones in the Territory was concluded in 1863 (18 Stat. L., 685); nor could it have been intended to guard the Indians against lawlessness on the part of the Territory.   *Ibid.*

SEC. 229. Mr. Wharton, in his Conflict of Laws (sec. 252), says: "He (the person adopted by a tribe) may be indicted, it is true, in State or Territorial courts for crimes committed by him on persons not of his tribe, but for offenses against members of his tribe he is only justiciable before the tribal authorities. So far as concerns his domestic relations, he is governed not by Territorial but by tribal law.   *   *   * In short, while he retains his subjection to the Territorial government (State or Federal) in all that relates to transactions outside of the tribe, his allegiance is to the tribe, and he is governed exclusively by tribal law."   *Ibid.*

SEC. 230. The act of Congress of February 19, 1875, authorizing the Seneca Nation of New York Indians to lease lands within their reservations and confirming existing leases was intended to give validity to all existing leases given by Indians to white persons, for the period of at least five years from the passage of said act, and to render them binding upon the parties thereto and upon the Seneca Nation. Even if this act of 1875 was in conflict with the provisions of the prior treaties entered into between the United States and the Indians, yet the act superseded the prior treaties, and the consequences arising from such conflict are beyond the sphere of judicial cognizance. When an Indian, prior to the passage of said act, leased the same land to two different persons, the one who received the first lease had the better title.   *Ryan v. Knorr, 19 Hun. (N. Y.), 540.*

SEC. 231. The treaty of 1785 (7 Stat. L., 18) with the Cherokees uses the language of "allotting to the Cherokees lands for their hunting grounds." These, with all the treaties, make the Indians acknowledge the protection of the United States, which is very different from the rights of complete sovereignty.   *Glasgow v. Smith, 1 Overton (Tenn.), 111.*

SEC. 232. The Cherokee treaty of 1791 (7 Stat. L., 739) abridged the rights of citizens and extended those of the Indians; consequently a great quantity of land sold by North Carolina to her citizens was thrown by this treaty within the Indian boundary. While this was severe it was obligatory, having been made by the United States under the authority of the Constitution.   *Ibid.*

Sec. 233. In 1789 the soil and sovereignty of what is now the State of Tennessee was transferred by North Carolina to the United States, and in the same year the treaty-making power and the right to regulate intercourse with the Indians was vested in the United States.

Cornet v. Winton, 2 Yerger (Tenn.), 143.

Sec. 234. The Cherokee Nation did not cease to exist east of the Mississippi and within the limits of Tennessee upon the ratification of the treaty of 1835 (7 Stat. L., 478) for their removal west of the river, but remained a nation, subject to the laws of the United States, during the two years allowed for removal; and it was, therefore, a good defense to an action of trespass for destroying liquor within the limits of the nation that the liquor had been brought into the nation contrary to the laws of the United States, and that the defendant had destroyed it under the order of the military commander assigned to command the public forces in that nation.

Morrow v. Blevens, 4 Humph. (Tenn.), 223.

Sec. 235. The power of Congress to enact the laws of 1802 (2 Stat. L., 139), 1832 (4 Stat. L., 596), and 1834 (4 Stat. L., 729) can not be successfully questioned.

Ibid.

CHAPTER III.—OF OFFENSES.

Sec. 236. The Indian tribes residing within the territorial limits of the United States are subject to their authority; and where country occupied by them is not within the limits of any one of the States, Congress may by law punish any offense committed there, no matter whether the offender be a white man or an Indian.

United States v. Rogers, 4 How., 567.

Sec. 237. A white man adopted into an Indian tribe is not an Indian within the exception of the act of 1834, as to crimes by one Indian against another.

Ibid.

Sec. 238. The act of 1834, section 25, repeated in section 2146 of the Revised Statutes, expressly excepts from the operation of the enactments extending the laws of the United States to the Indian country, crimes committed by one Indian against the person or property of another Indian.

Ibid. Ex parte Crow Dog, 109 U. S., 556. United States v. Kagama, 118 U. S., 375.

Sec. 239. A white man, an adopted member of an Indian tribe, indicted for the murder within the Indian country of another white man, likewise an adopted member of the same tribe, is within the jurisdiction of the proper United States courts, and if he is found guilty on the indictment he is liable to the punishment provided by the act of June 30, 1834 (4 Stat. L., 729), and is not within the exception in relation to Indians.

United States v. Rogers, 4 How., 567.

SEC. 240. A white man by adoption may become entitled to certain privileges in an Indian tribe and make himself amenable to their laws and usages. Yet he is not an Indian; and the exception contained in the proviso to section 25 of the act of June 30, 1834, that the provisions of that section "shall not extend to crimes committed by one Indian against the person or property of another Indian," is confined to those who by the usages and customs of the Indians are regarded as belonging to their race.   *Ibid.*

SEC. 241. It is the duty of the courts to expound and execute the law as they find it. It is too firmly and clearly established to admit of dispute that the Indian tribes residing within the territorial limits of the United States are subject to their authority, and where the country occupied by them is not within the limits of one of the States, Congress may, by law, punish any offense committed there, no matter whether the offender be a white man or an Indian.

Ibid. Cherokee Tobacco Tax, 11 Wall., 616.

SEC. 242. The act of Congress passed in 1851 (9 Stat. L., 594) creating the western judicial district of Arkansas, with criminal jurisdiction over crimes committed against the laws of the United States within the Indian country by others than Indians, did not take away the power and jurisdiction of the circuit court of the United States for the eastern district to try an indictment for murder pending in that court at the time.   *United States v. Dawson, 15 How., 467.*

SEC. 243. The offense of selling spirituous liquors to an Indian, declared by the act of February 12, 1862 (12 Stat. L., 139), to be cognizable in the district courts was, by virtue of the judiciary act of 1789 (1 Stat. L., 73), also cognizable in the circuit courts of the United States.

United States v. Holliday, 3 Wall., 407. United States v. Mayrand, C. L. E. 18, 699.

SEC. 244. Parties are liable for the offense if they sold liquors to Indians under the charge of a superintendent or agent, wherever they may be, although living on land which they own and voting at county and town elections.   *Ibid.*

SEC. 245. The circuit court of the United States for the district of Colorado has no jurisdiction of an indictment against a white man for the murder of another white man within the Ute Reservation in the State of Colorado. The act admitting Colorado as a State makes no exception of jurisdiction over the reservation.

United States v. McBratney, 104 U. S., 621. Draper v. United States, 164 U. S., 240.

SEC. 246. The case of the *Cherokee Tobacco Tax* (11 Wall., 616), can not be treated as authority against the conclusion the court have reached in this case, for the decision only disposed of that case, as three of the judges of the court did not sit in it and two dissented from the judgment pronounced by the other four.

United States v. 43 Gals. of Whisky, 108 U. S., 491.

SEC. 247. A Territorial district court has two distinct jurisdictions. As a Territorial court it administers the local law; as invested by act of Congress with jurisdiction to administer the laws of the United States, it has all the authority of circuit and district courts, and in the former character it may try a prisoner for murder committed in the Territory proper under the local law, which (in Dakota) requires the jury to determine whether the punishment shall be death or imprisonment for life, and, in the other character, try another prisoner for murder committed within an Indian reservation under the laws of the United States, which imposes the death penalty on conviction,

Ex parte Crow Dog, 109 U. S., 556.

SEC. 248. The exception contained in section 2146 of the Revised Statutes is not repealed by the operation and legal effect of the treaty with the Sioux Indians of April 29, 1868 (15 Stat. L., 635), and an act of Congress approved February 28, 1877 (19 Stat. L., 254), to ratify an agreement with the Sioux Indians, etc. *Ibid.*

SEC. 249. The district court of a Territory, within the geographical boundaries of whose district an Indian reservation lies, may exercise jurisdiction under the United States laws over offenses made punishable by them, committed within the limits of the reservation, but such jurisdiction does not extend to an indictment for murder of one Indian by another. *Ibid.*

SEC. 250. The general laws of the United States for the punishment of offenses may be constitutionally extended to embrace Indians in the Indian country by the mere force of a treaty, without the aid of any legislation by Congress. *Ibid.*

SEC. 251. The laws of the United States, to which the Sioux were declared by the agreement of 1877 (19 Stat. L., 256) to be subject, were the laws then existing, and which applied to them as Indians, and, of course, they included the statute excepting from the operation of the general laws of the United States crimes committed within the Indian country by one Indian upon the person or property of another Indian. Declaring them subject to the laws made them so, if it effected any change in their situation, only in respect to laws in force and existing, and did not effect any change in the laws themselves. The phrase can not have a more extended meaning than the acknowledgment of their allegiance as Indians to the laws of the United States, made, or to be made, in the exercise of legislative authority over them as such.

Ibid.

SEC. 252. The ninth section of the Indian appropriation act of March 3, 1885 (23 Stat. L., 385), is separable into two distinct definitions of the conditions under which Indians may be punished for the same crimes as defined by the common law. The first of these is where the offense is committed within the limits of a Territorial government, whether on or off an Indian reservation. The second is where the offense is committed by one Indian against the person or property of another Indian within the limits of a State of the Union but on an Indian reservation. The first clause subjects the offender within the limits of a Territory to the laws of that Territory and to its courts for trial; while the second, which applies solely to offenses by Indians committed within the limits of a State and on a reservation, subjects him to the laws of the United States passed for the government of places under the exclusive jurisdiction of those laws and to trial by the courts of the United States.   *United States v. Kagama, 118 U. S., 375.*

Sec. 253. Section 9 of the Indian appropriation act of March 3, 1885 (23 Stat. L., 385), is valid and constitutional in both its branches, viz: That which gives jurisdiction to the courts of the Territories of the crimes named committed by Indians within the Territories, and that which gives jurisdiction in like cases to the courts of the United States for the same crimes committed on an Indian reservation within a State of the Union.   *Ibid.*

Sec. 254. The crimes mentioned in the Indian appropriation act of March 3, 1885 (23 Stat. L., 385), section 9, are murder, manslaughter, rape, assault with intent to kill, arson, burglary, and larceny.   *Ibid.*

Sec. 255. While there can not be seen in either of the clauses of the Constitution, and of its amendments referring to Indians, any delegation of power to enact a code of criminal law for the punishment of the worst crimes known to civilized life, when committed by Indians, there is a suggestion in the manner in which the Indian tribes are introduced into the clause (relating to commerce with them), not as States, nor nations, nor as possessed of the attributes of sovereignty, but as a separate people, with the power of regulating their internal and social relations, and thus far not brought under the laws of the Union or of the State within whose limits they reside which may have a bearing on the subject.   *Ibid.*

Sec. 256. The first clause of the ninth section of the act of March 3, 1885 (23 Stat. L., 385), is new in legislation by Congress, which has heretofore only undertaken to punish an Indian who sustains the usual relation to his tribe, and who commits the offense in the Indian country, or on an Indian reservation, in exceptional cases; as where the offense was against the person or property of a white man, or was some violation of the trade and intercourse regulations imposed by Congress on the Indian tribes; and the second clause is a still further advance, as asserting exclusive jurisdiction over Indians within the limits of a State of the Union.   *Ibid.*

SEC. 257. It is of consequence that in the new departure which Congress has made in the ninth section of the act of 1885 (23 Stat. L., 385), of subjecting the Indians, in a limited class of cases, to the same laws which govern the whites within the Territories where they both reside, the Indian shall at least have all the advantages which may accrue from that change, which transfers him as to the punishment of these crimes from the jurisdiction of his own tribe to the jurisdiction of the government of the Territory in which he lives.

Gon-shay-ee, Petitioner, 130 U. S., 343.

SEC. 258. The ninth section of the act of 1885 (23 Stat. L., 385) is very clearly a continuation of the policy upon which Congress entered several years previously, of attempting, so far as possible and consistent with justice and existing obligations, to reduce the Indians to individual subjection to the laws of the country and dispense with their tribal relations. *Ibid.*

SEC. 259. That part of section 9 of the act of 1885 (23 Stat. L., 385) which relates to crimes committed by Indians within a Territory, and to the trial and punishment of the offenders therefor, was enacted to transfer to the Territorial courts established by the General Government (as all courts of general jurisdiction are in the Territories) jurisdiction to try the crimes described in it under the Territorial laws when sitting as and exercising the functions of such Territorial court. *Ibid.*

SEC. 260. The phrase "within the exclusive jurisdiction of the United States," as used in the ninth section of the act of 1885 (23 Stat. L., 385), is well understood as applying to the crimes which are committed within the premises, grounds, forts, arsenals, navy-yards, and other places within the boundaries of a State, or even within a Territory, over which the United States Government has by cession, by agreement, or by reservation exclusive jurisdiction. *Ibid.*

SEC. 261. Prior to the act of 1885 (23 Stat. L., 385), so far as Indians could be punished for offenses of the kind charged in this case in any court, either Federal or Territorial, the jurisdiction would belong to the one sitting under the first branch and exercising the judicial functions appropriate thereto. *Ibid.*

SEC. 262. In the case of Captain Jack, petitioner, the fact that the crime charged was committed outside a reservation, and that the Indian was sentenced to imprisonment in Ohio, does not take the case out of the rule laid down in Gon-shay-ee, and the prisoner must be released, the only difference being that the writ in this case must be directed to the keeper of the penitentiary at Columbus, Ohio, instead of the United States marshal for Arizona. *Captain Jack, Petitioner, 130 U. S., 353.*

SEC. 263. The words "punishable by imprisonment at hard labor" in the act of March 1, 1889 (25 Stat. L., 783), to establish a United

States court in the Indian Territory, embrace offenses which although not imperatively required by statute to be so punished may, in the discretion of the court, be punished by imprisonment in a penitentiary. To hold otherwise would impute to Congress a purpose to invest the court with jurisdiction of offenses it could not punish for want of authority to impanel a grand jury to return presentment or indictments against the offenders.   *In re Mills, 135 U. S., 263.*

SEC. 264. Upon a careful scrutiny of the act of 1889 (25 Stat. L., 783), giving full effect to all its clauses, according to the reasonable meaning of the words used, yet interpreting it in the light of the previous history of the Public Land Strip (No Man's Land), and of the information communicated to Congress by public officers, the court has no doubt that Congress intended to bring that strip within the jurisdiction of the court established for the Indian Territory and to attach it for limited judicial purposes to the eastern district of Texas.   *Cook v. United States, 138 U. S., 157.*

SEC. 265. Before the act of 1885 (23 Stat. L., 385) the jurisdiction of the United States courts was not sole and exclusive over all offenses committed within the limits of an Indian reservation. The words "sole and exclusive" in section 2145 do not apply to the jurisdiction extended over the Indian country, but are only used in the description of the laws which are extended to it.   *In re Wilson, 140 U. S., 575.*

SEC. 266. Section 2145 of the Revised Statutes extends to the Indian country the general laws of the United States for the punishment of crimes committed in any place within the sole and exclusive jurisdiction of the United States, except as to crimes the punishment of which is otherwise expressly provided for; but this is limited by the section following it so as not to extend to crimes committed by one Indian against the person and property of another Indian, nor to any Indian committing any offense in the Indian country, who has been punished by the local law of the tribe, as to any case where by treaty stipulations, the exclusive jurisdiction of such offenses is or may be secured to the Indian tribes respectively. "The White Mountain Apache Indian Reservation is a part of the Indian country within the meaning of these sections."   *Ibid.*

SEC. 267. The jurisdiction of the United States over Indian reservations and the power of Congress to provide for the punishment of all offenses committed therein, by whomsoever committed, are not open questions, and this power being a general one, Congress may provide for the punishment of one class of offenses in one court and another class in a different court. There is no necessity for and no constitutional provision compelling full and exclusive jurisdiction in one tribunal, and the policy of Congress for a long time has been to give only a limited jurisdiction to the United States courts.   *Ibid.*

SEC. 268. Prior to 1885 the district court of a Territory (sitting as a district court of the United States) had jurisdiction over the crime of murder committed by any person other than an Indian upon an Indian reservation within its Territorial limits, and such jurisdiction has not been taken away by the legislation of that year. *Ibid.*

SEC. 269. The effect of the act of 1885 (23 Stat. L., 385) was not the transfer to Territorial courts a part of the sole and exclusive jurisdiction of United States courts, but only a part of the limited jurisdiction then exercised by such courts, together with jurisdiction over offenses not theretofore vested therein. There has been no transfer of part of a sole and exclusive jurisdiction, carrying by implication, even in the absence of express language, a transfer of all jurisdiction, but only a transfer of a part of an already limited jurisdiction, and neither by language nor implication transferring that theretofore vested and not in terms transferred. *Ibid.*

SEC. 270. The general object of treaties and statutes cited affecting the courts of the Cherokee Nation is to vest in those courts jurisdiction of all controversies between Indians, or where a member of the nation is the only party to the proceedings, and to reserve to the courts of the United States jurisdiction of all actions to which its own citizens are parties on either side. *In re Mayfield, 141 U. S., 107.*

SEC. 271. While the crime of adultery is punishable simply in the penitentiary for a term not exceeding three years, such imprisonment may, under chapter 9, title 70, of the Revised Statutes, be executed in a penitentiary, where hard labor is exacted of all convicts, and it follows that it is, in effect, imprisonment at hard labor and therefore not within the jurisdiction of the courts established by the act of March 1, 1889 (25 Stat. L., 783), for the Indian Territory. *Ibid.*

SEC. 272. The object of the proviso to article 13 of the Cherokee treaty of 1866 (14 Stat. L., 799) seems to be not so much the establishment of a new jurisdiction dependent upon the happening of a certain event as a recognition of a jurisdiction already existing. *Ibid.*

SEC. 273. The act of March 3, 1887 (24 Stat. L., 635) "to amend an act entitled 'An act to amend section fifty-three hundred and fifty-two of the Revised Statutes of the United States, in reference to bigamy, and for other purposes,' approved March twenty-second, eighteen hundred and eighty-two," is applicable to cases of offenses prohibited therein committed within the territory of the Cherokee Nation, by virtue of section 2145 of the Revised Statutes, but its operation within that nation is limited by section 2146 of the Revised Statutes, excepting "crimes committed by one Indian against the person or property of another Indian," etc., from the operation of the general criminal laws of the United States extended over the Indian country by the preceding section. *Ibid.*

SEC. 274. As the Southern Kansas Railway Company acquired all its rights in the matter of the construction and operation of its road within the Indian Territory under and by virtue of a law of the United States enacted by Congress in the exercise of its powers over the Territories, controversies arising by reason of the exercise of its rights therein were necessarily controversies arising under the laws of the United States.   *So. Kan. Rwy. Co. v. Briscoe, 144 U. S., 133.*

SEC. 275. The addition of the words "so far as may be necessary to carry out the provisions of this act" to the eighth section of the act of July 4, 1884 (23 Stat. L., 73), was not intended as a limitation of the jurisdiction of the courts of the northern district of Texas and western district of Arkansas to controversies growing out of the construction of the road merely, since the section in terms applies to "all controversies."   *Ibid.*

SEC. 276. It was competent for Congress to give the enumerated courts jurisdiction over not only controversies immediately relating to or growing out of the construction of the road, but over all controversies between the nations and tribes or the inhabitants thereof, through whose territory the railroad might be constructed, and the company.   *Ibid.*

SEC. 277. The Indians of the country are considered as wards of the nation, and whenever the United States sets apart any land of their own as an Indian reservation, whether within a State or Territory, they have full authority to pass such laws and authorize such measures as may be necessary to give to these people full protection in their persons and property, and to punish all offenses committed against them, or by them within such reservation.
United States v. Thomas, 151 U. S., 577.

SEC. 278. It is a general doctrine that there can be no certificate of a division of opinion between the judges of the circuit court on a motion for a new trial, but where a motion of the kind or of a similar kind may present for consideration a question going directly to the merits, and a decision of which may determine the point in controversy, the court will consider the question submitted on a certificate of division of opinion between the judges of the court below.   *Ibid.*

SEC. 279. In the trial of a Cherokee Indian for the crime of murder charged to have been committed within the Cherokee Nation, the Government is bound to establish as a fact that the murdered man was a white man and not an Indian, and if it failed to introduce any evidence upon that point, defendant was entitled to an instruction to that effect, and if no other reasonable inference could have been drawn from the evidence than that the man on whom the murder is alleged to have been committed was an Indian, defendant was entitled, as matter of law, to an acquittal.   *Smith v. United States, 151 U. S., 50.*

SEC. 280. Horse stealing on November 12, 1890, in the Indian country, within the boundaries of Oklahoma Territory, as defined by the act of May 2, 1890 (26 Stat. L., 81), was not a crime against the United States and punishable under the act of February 15, 1888 (25 Stat. L., 33), denouncing horse stealing in the Indian Territory.

United States v. Pridgeon, 153 U. S., 48.

SEC. 281. The act of Congress of February 15, 1888 (25 Stat. L., 33), which provided in its first section for the punishment of the crime of horse stealing in the Indian Territory, was superseded by the act of May 2, 1890 (26 Stat. L., 81), with respect to so much of the Indian Territory as was included within the boundaries and made part of the Oklahoma Territory. *Ibid.*

SEC. 282. It admits of no question that under the various provisions of the act of May 2, 1890 (26 Stat. L., 81), the district court for the first judicial district within and for Logan County, Okla., and for the Indian country attached thereto for judicial purposes, sitting as a district court of the United States, had jurisdiction of offenses committed against the laws of the United States in the Cherokee Outlet, which by the statute and the action of the supreme court of Oklahoma was attached to Logan County, Okla., for judicial purposes. *Ibid.*

SEC. 283. It is clear, in respect to the Cherokee Outlet attached to Logan County for judicial purposes, that at the passage of the act of May 2, 1890 (26 Stat. L., 81), it was, and continued to be, Indian country, coming within the provisions of the act of February 15, 1888 (25 Stat. L., 33), and that the offense of horse stealing committed therein on November 4 and 12, 1890, was an offense against the United States. *Ibid.*

SEC. 284. The act of March 1, 1889 (25 Stat. L., 783), establishing a United States court for the Indian Territory, and extending the jurisdiction of the United States courts over the Indian Territory, which was divided and annexed for judicial purposes to the district of Kansas and the eastern district of Texas, has no application to that portion of the Cherokee Outlet referred to in the ninth section of the act of May 2, 1890 (26 Stat. L., 81), attached to Logan County, Okla., for judicial purposes. *Ibid.*

SEC. 285. There is nothing on the face of the indictment to show affirmatively that the district court for the first judicial district within and for Logan County, Okla., and for the Indian country attached thereto for judicial purposes, sitting with the powers of a district court of the United States, did not have jurisdiction of the offense of horse stealing, so as to render its sentence void on collateral attack as by *habeas corpus.* *Ibid.*

SEC. 286. Under the rule laid down in *Ex parte* Karstendick (93 U. S., 396) and *In re.* Mills (135 U. S., 263), while the act of February

15, 1888 (25 Stat. L., 33), denouncing horse stealing in the Indian Territory, does not specifically authorize the imposition of "hard labor" as a part of the sentence of imprisonment, still it was competent for the court to sentence the party convicted to imprisonment in a penitentiary where "hard labor" is a part of the usual discipline; so that the provision for "hard labor" in the sentence is nothing more nor less than a sentence to simple imprisonment in the Ohio penitentiary, subject to its rules, regulations, and discipline, and if the sentence had been imposed in this form it could not justify the release of the prisoner on *habeas corpus*.   *Ibid.*

SEC. 287. The first clause of section 2146 of the Revised Statutes is taken from the twenty-fifth section of the act of June 30, 1834 (4 Stat. L., 729, 733), and it was held in United States *v.* Rogers (4 How., 567), that the adoption into an Indian tribe did not bring the party thus adopted within the scope of such exception, the court saying: "Whatever obligations the prisoner may have taken upon himself by becoming a Cherokee by adoption his responsibility to the laws of the United States remains unchanged and undiminished. He was still a white man of the white race, and therefore not within the exception of the act of Congress." The term "Indian" in section 2146 is one descriptive of race, and therefore the defendant, described as a white man and not an Indian, is shown to be outside the first two clauses of the section.   *Westmoreland v. United States, 155 U. S., 545.*

SEC. 288. While it may be conceded that the expression in an indictment for murder charged to have been committed in the Indian Territory, that the defendant and the deceased were not "citizens of the Indian Territory," is not apt to describe the citizenship in an Indian tribe, yet it is not an unreasonable construction to hold that it refers to all citizenship which could possibly be acquired in the Indian Territory, including therein citizenship in an Indian tribe domiciled within such limits.   *Ibid.*

SEC. 289. The fact that a man murdered in the Indian Territory was a white man had no bearing on the question of the *corpus delicti*, or of the fact that the defendant, a Cherokee Indian, murdered him, and bore only on the jurisdiction of the court.

Isaacs v. United States, 159 U. S., 487.

SEC. 290. An indictment for murder in the eastern district of Texas which alleges that the accused and the deceased were not Indians or citizens of the Indian Territory is sufficient, without the further allegation that they were not citizens of any Indian tribe or nation.

Wheeler v. United States, 159 U. S., 523.

SEC. 291. The decision of the question as to the competency of a child as a witness rests primarily with the trial judge, who sees the proposed witness, notices his manner, his apparent possession or lack of intelligence, and who may resort to any examination which will tend to disclose his capacity and intelligence as well as his understanding of the obligations of an oath. As many of these matters can not be photographed into the record, the decision of the trial judge will not be disturbed on review, unless from that which is preserved it is clearly erroneous. *Ibid.*

SEC. 292. A boy 5 years old is not, as a matter of law, absolutely disqualified as a witness; there is no precise age which determines the question of competency, which depends on the capacity and intelligence of the child, his appreciation of the difference between truth and falsehood, as well as of his duty to tell the former. *Ibid.*

SEC. 293. Alberty, a negro born in slavery, who became a citizen of the Cherokee Nation under the ninth article of the treaty of 1866 (14 Stat. L., 799), is alleged to have committed murder on the person of one Phil. Duncan, the illegitimate child of a Choctaw Indian by a negro slave in the Cherokee Nation. *Held*, that for purposes of jurisdiction Alberty must be treated as a member of the Cherokee Nation, but not an Indian, and Duncan as a colored citizen of the United States, and that for the purposes of this case the court below had jurisdiction. *Alberty v. United States, 162 U. S., 499.*

SEC. 294. Duncan was the illegitimate child of a Choctaw Indian, by a colored woman who was not his wife, but a slave in the Cherokee Nation. As his mother was a negro slave, under the rule *partus sequiter ventrem*, he must be treated as a negro by birth and not as a Choctaw Indian; and there is an additional reason for this in the fact that he was an illegitimate child and took the status of the mother.

Ibid.

SEC. 295. It will be observed that while the thirtieth and thirty-first sections of the act of May 2, 1890 (26 Stat. L., 81), follow the Cherokee treaty of 1866 (14 Stat. L., 799), so far as recognizing the jurisdiction of the Cherokee Nation as to all cases in the country in which members of the nation, by nativity or adoption, are the sole and only parties, it omits that portion of the thirteenth article of the treaty wherein is reserved to the judicial tribunals of the nation exclusive jurisdiction "where the cause of action shall arise in the Cherokee Nation," and to that extent apparently supersedes the treaty. *Ibid.*

SEC. 296. The proposition which harmonizes best with the intention of Congress in the enactments concerning jurisdiction of crimes within the Cherokee Nation is that which treats the victim whose person or property has been invaded as a party, under which construction the word "parties" as used in the act of May 2, 1890 (26 Stat. L., 81), and the Cherokee treaty of 1866 (146 Stat. L., 799) would really mean parties to the crime and not simply to the prosecution of the crime, in which case the Federal court would have jurisdiction in all cases in which the victim is a white man or other than an Indian.   *Ibid.*

SEC. 297. The crime of murder committed by one Cherokee Indian upon the person of another within the jurisdiction of the Cherokee Nation is not an offense against the United States, but an offense against the local laws of the Cherokee Nation, and the statutes of the United States which provide for an indictment by a grand jury and the number of persons who shall constitute such a body have no application.   *Talton v. Mayes, 163 U. S., 376.*

SEC. 298. The fifth amendment to the Constitution of the United States does not apply to local legislation of the Cherokee Nation so as to require all prosecutions for offenses committed against the laws of that nation to be initiated by a grand jury in accordance with the provisions of that amendment.   *Ibid.*

SEC. 299. As under the present condition of the laws pertaining to the Choctaw tribe negroes who have been adopted into the tribe are within the jurisdiction of its judicial tribunals, it follows that the averment in the indictment that the murdered man was a negro and not an Indian was the averment of a jurisdictional fact which it was necessary for the prosecution to sustain by competent evidence. Such averment implied that there were negroes who were and those who were not Indians in a jurisdictional sense.   *Lucas v. United States, 163 U. S., 612.*

SEC. 300. On the trial of a Choctaw Indian for the murder of a negro in the Choctaw Nation, in the Indian country, the status of the deceased is a question of fact to be determined by the evidence, and the burden of proof is on the Government to sustain the jurisdiction of the court by evidence.   *Ibid.*

SEC. 301. The fact that a person murdered in the Choctaw Nation was a negro does not raise the presumption that he was a citizen of the United States and not a member of the Choctaw tribe, and therefore not an Indian in a jurisdictional sense; and it was error in the court below in instructing the jury that they had a right to find that the deceased was not a member of the Choctaw Nation from the mere fact that he was a negro.   *Ibid.*

SEC. 302. When the enabling act admitting a State into the Union contains no exclusion of jurisdiction as to crimes committed on an Indian reservation by others than Indians, or against Indians, the State courts are vested with jurisdiction to try and punish such crimes.   *Draper v. United States, 164 U. S., 240.*

SEC. 303. The act of 1834 (4 Stat. L., 729) conferred upon the national courts jurisdiction of offenses against the laws of the United States committed on Indian reservations in Kansas, but the act admitting the State into the Union so far modified that act as to deprive the circuit court of jurisdiction in that particular case, which was an indictment of murder committed by one white man upon another upon a reservation set apart for the Kansas tribe of Indians.

United States v. Bridleman, 7 Fed. Rep., 894.

SEC. 304. The power of Congress to regulate commerce with Indian tribes is coextensive with the subject, and applies to individuals constituting the tribes, although off a reservation and within the limits of a State, and therefore the act of 1864 (13 Stat. L., 29) for the punishment of a person who disposes of spirituous liquor to an Indian under the charge of an agent is constitutional, although the disposition took place within the limits of a State to an Indian not upon or belonging to a reservation. *Ibid.*

SEC. 305. The circuit court, having concurrent jurisdiction with the district court over crimes, has jurisdiction over the offense of selling liquor to Indians, although jurisdiction may be vested by statutes in the district court. *Note to Forty Gallons Cognac Brandy, 11 Fed. Rep., 51.*

SEC. 306. Where the country occupied by Indians is not within the territorial limits of a State, Congress may provide for the punishment of offenses there, no matter by whom committed. *Ibid.*

SEC. 307. The power to regulate intercourse between the tribes and individual Indians includes the power to prohibit the traffic in spirituous liquors. *Ibid.*

SEC. 308. In McBratney's case the defendant, a white man, was convicted in the United States circuit court for Colorado of the murder of a white man on the Southern Ute Reservation. Upon a motion in arrest of judgment the opinion of the circuit justice and district judge differed upon the question of whether the circuit court had jurisdiction, and the same was certified to the Supreme Court, who answered it in the negative. *United States v. Martin, 14 Fed. Rep., 817.*

SEC. 309. In the exercise of its constitutional power to regulate intercourse with the Indian tribes Congress may define and punish crimes committed by white men upon the person or property of an Indian, and *vice versa*, within as well as without the limits of a State. *Ibid.*

SEC. 310. Congress having provided for the punishment of murder committed in the Indian country (secs. 2145, 5339, Rev. Stats.) the United States circuit court for the district of Oregon has jurisdiction of the crime of murder committed on the Umatilla Reservation by an Indian upon a white man, and therefore it is a violation of section 5389 of the Revised Statutes for anyone to resist or obstruct the execution of an order made by a circuit court commissioner engaged in the examination of an Indian charged with murder. *Ibid.*

SEC. 311. The policy of the act (4 Stat. L., 729) is the protection of those Indians who are, by treaty or otherwise, under the pupilage of the

Government from the debasing influence of the use of spirits, and it is not easy to perceive why that policy should not require their preservation from this, to them, destructive poison, where they are outside of a reservation as well as within it.   The evil effects are the same in both cases.   *United States v. Earl, 17 Fed. Rep., 75.*

SEC. 312. Section 2148 of the Revised Statutes, section 2 of the act of August 18, 1856 (11 Stat. L., 80), is in legal effect a prohibition against any person who has been removed from the Indian country returning thereto, and the penalty therein provided for its violation may be enforced by indictment or information.

United States v. Howard, 17 Fed. Rep., 639.

SEC. 313. Section 2124 of the Revised Statutes ought to be construed as only applicable to penalties imposed by the act of June 30, 1834 (4 Stat. L., 729), of which it is a part; but if considered applicable at all to section 2148, as being included in Title XXVIII of the Revised Statutes, the remedy therein provided for the enforcement of the penalty for returning to an Indian reservation is not exclusive of the common law remedy by indictment or information, but only cumulative.   *Ibid.*

SEC. 314. Section 2148 of the Revised Statutes, being in legal effect a prohibition against the defendant's returning to the Siletz Reservation, as he did, the penalty for which he is thereby made liable for so doing may be enforced against him by indiction or information.   *Ibid.*

SEC. 315. The Cherokee Nation being neither State nor Territory, the Constitution of the United States and the laws of Congress did not authorize the governor of the State of Arkansas to honor the demand of the chief of the Cherokee Nation for the extradition of Morgan.   *Ex parte Morgan, 20 Fed. Rep., 298.*

SEC. 316. B. and A. were indicted in the United States court for the crime of manslaughter, committed in killing Indian William on the Umatilla Reservation, and pleaded to the indictment a former acquittal, from which plea it appeared that they had been indicted and tried in the State court for the murder of said Indian, and acquitted, to which plea there was a demurrer. *Held,* that the crime for which the defendants were acquitted in the State court was not the same as that charged in the indictment in the United States court, and therefore the plea was bad.   *United States v. Barnhart, 22 Fed. Rep., 285.*

SEC. 317. The United States court of the district of Oregon has jurisdiction over all crimes committed on the Umatilla Reservation by a white man on the person or property of an Indian, and *vice versa,* so far as the same has been defined by an act of Congress.   *Ibid.*

SEC. 318. The proper proceeding in case of return after removal from the Indian country is by action under section 2124 Revised Statutes to recover the penalty prescribed for such offenses.

United States v. Payne, 22 Fed. Rep., 426.

SEC. 319. The plaintiff in error, being convicted of manslaughter under the law of Oregon, instead of under the act of 1875 (18 Stat. L., 473), whereby his imprisonment was authorized for twenty days in excess of the punishment allowed by said act. *Held*, that the judgment was erroneous, and the same was reversed, with the direction to have the plaintiff in error sentenced according to law.

Kie v. United States, 27 Fed. Rep., 251.

SEC. 320. The district court of Alaska has jurisdiction, under sections 5339 and 5341 of the Revised Statutes, to try and punish any inhabitant of the district for the crime of murder committed by killing of any human being therein; but the law of Oregon defining the crime of murder or manslaughter and prescribing the punishment therefor is not in force in Alaska.

Ibid.

SEC. 321. The prohibition against the jurisdiction of the courts of the United States to try an Indian for an offense committed on another Indian applies only when the offense is committed in the Indian country. When an Indian commits a crime outside the Indian country (although the crime may be against another Indian) he is, like any other person, amenable to the criminal laws of the place where the crime is committed.

In re Wolf, 27 Fed. Rep., 606.

SEC. 322. When an Indian is outside of the Indian country, he is entitled to the full measure of protection afforded by the laws of the nation; and if he commits a crime outside of the Indian country, whether upon one of his own race or another, he is amenable to the law of the place where the crime is committed.

Ibid.

SEC. 323. The "Cherokee Outlet" is within that portion of the Indian Territory placed within the jurisdiction of the United States district court of Kansas by the act of January 6, 1883 (22 Stat. L., 400), and jurisdiction of a murder committed there is in that court, and not in the district court for the western district of Arkansas.

United States v. Soule, 30 Fed. Rep., 918.

SEC. 324. The Alaska Indians, while not citizens of the United States within the full meaning of the term, are dependent subjects, amenable to the penal laws of the United States, and subject to the jurisdiction of its courts. The act of Congress of March 3, 1885 (23 Stat. L., 385), making all Indians amenable to the criminal laws of the United States for the offenses therein designated, is to be regarded as aiding this construction of the law, and the act of March 3, 1871 (16 Stat. L., 566), prohibiting future recognition of tribal independence among the Indians, is to be construed in the same connection.

In re Sah Quah, 31 Fed. Rep., 327.

SEC. 325. Where an Indian prisoner escapes from the reservation, taking with him an Indian girl 11 years old and forcibly has sexual intercourse with her, he is not guilty of abduction under the laws of

Alabama for taking a girl under 14 years of age from the person having legal charge of her, for purposes of prostitution, marriage, or concubinage.   *United States v. Zes Claya, 35 Fed. Rep., 493*

SEC. 326. The place or manner of the prisoner's commitment is immaterial. She might have been committed to the custody of the police officer or any house or enclosure provided for that purpose. Nor need the process have been in writing. From this Indian court and police in this, their first effort in the administration of justice, written process and proceedings could not have been expected.
    United States v. Clapox, 35 Fed. Rep., 575. Same, 13 Saw., 349.

SEC. 327. A crime is said to be committed against a State or sovereign when the act which constitutes it is a violation of a penal law of such State or sovereign. In this case the United States, by virtue of its power and authority in the premises, has established a rule which is, in effect, a law prohibiting the commission of adultery by an Indian on the Umatilla Reservation, and providing for the arrest and punishment of any Indian guilty of a violation of the same. Minnie was committed for a violation of this law, and was, therefore, committed for a crime against the lawmaker—the United States.   *Ibid.*

SEC. 328. The term "misdemeanor," as used in No. 9 of the rules promulgated by the Secretary of the Interior December 2, 1882, for the government of the Indians on the Umatilla and other reservations, includes "adultery."   *Ibid. Same, 13 Sawyer, 349.*

SEC. 329. An Indian woman, arrested by the Indian police on the Umatilla Reservation on a charge of adultery committed thereon, was committed to the Indian jail for trial before the "court of Indian offenses," and, while so committed, was rescued and set at liberty by the defendants. *Held,* that they thereby committed the crime of rescue, as defined by section 5401 of the Revised Statutes, for forcibly setting a person at liberty who was committed for a crime against the United States.   *Ibid.*

SEC. 330. The President is authorized by the treaty of June 9, 1855 (12 Stat. L., 948), and the Revised Statutes (secs. 441, 463, and 465) to make rules for the government of the Indians on the Umatilla Reservation, including the establishment of an Indian court and police, and the definition of "Indian offenses" and the measure of punishment therefor.   *Ibid.*

SEC. 331. The act with which these defendants are charged (rescue) is in flagrant opposition to the authority of the United States on this reservation and directly subversive of the laudable effort to accustom and educate these Indians in the habits and knowledge of self-government. It is, therefore, appropriate and needful that the power and name of the Government of the United States should be invoked to restrain and punish them under section 5411, Revised Statutes.   *Ibid.*

SEC. 332. The act of Congress of March 3, 1885 (23 Stat. L., 385), provides that "immediately upon and after the passage of this act all Indians committing against the person or property of another Indian or other person any of the following crimes, viz, murder, manslaughter," etc., shall be subject to the same laws and tried in the same courts as all other persons. *Held*, that on the indictment of an Indian for the killing of another Indian, in obedience to tribal resolutions, it was no defense that defendants had no notice of the statute.

United States v. Whaley, 37 Fed. Rep., 145. Same, 13 Saw., 548.

SEC. 333. The grand jury impaneled by the United States court at Muskogee, Ind. T., was impaneled without authority of law. An indictment found by it would be simply a nullity.

Ex parte Wilson, 40 Fed. Rep., 66.

SEC. 334. The United States court at Muskogee, Ind. T., has no power to impanel a grand jury. as no such power is given by the act creating it, and section 808 of the Revised Statutes has reference only to United States circuit or district courts, and the court at Muskogee is neither. The power to impanel a grand jury is not an inherent power of a court of the United States, but is derived from the statutes.

Ibid.

SEC. 335. The United States court for the Indian Territory, created by the act of March 1, 1889 (25 Stat. L., 783), has no jurisdiction of an assault with intent to kill, but has of an aggravated assault.

Ex parte Brown, 40 Fed. Rep., 81.

SEC. 336. The United States court at Muskogee, Ind. T., can not carve out of an assault with intent to kill an aggravated assault and try the latter, because it does not have jurisdiction of the greater crime. *Ibid.*

SEC. 337. To bring a defendant within the provisions of the act of March 3, 1885 (23 Stat. L., 385), providing for the punishment of Indians committing certain offenses, it must be shown that his father was an Indian, as the child follows the condition of the father.

United States v. Ward, 42 Fed. Rep., 320. Same, 14 Saw., 472.

SEC. 338. The son of a negro father by an Indian mother is not an Indian within the meaning of the act of March 3, 1885 (23 Stat. L., 385), providing for the punishment of Indians committing certain offenses, as the child follows the condition of the father. *Ibid.*

SEC. 339. The Federal Government has the right and authority, instead of controlling the Indian tribes by treaties, to govern them by acts of Congress, and the Indians being necessarily subject to the laws which Congress may enact for their protection and for the protection of the people with whom they may come in contact, the States have no such power over them as long as they maintain their tribal relations.

Benson v. United States, 44 Fed. Rep., 178.

SEC. 340. It is unnecessary to consider the question of the power of Congress over the Indian reservations in the State of New York, even to the exclusion of any State jurisdiction over the lands of the Indians or over criminal offenses committed within their territory, so long as the reservations are occupied by Indians in tribal organization.   *Ibid.*

SEC. 341. Transporting ardent spirits as an article of commerce through the Indian country, between places outside the same, is not in violation of section 2139 of the Revised Statutes, which provides that "no ardent spirits shall be introduced, under any pretense, into the Indian country."   *United States v. 29 Gals. Whisky, 45 Fed. Rep., 847.*

SEC. 342. If the title, or the general legislative or governmental jurisdiction is not a necessary element in the question, the only inquiry is whether the murder was committed within the limits of an Indian reservation, set apart and recognized by the Government, and actually occupied by the Indians for reservation purposes; and that it was is evident from the testimony and undisputed facts.   *Dissenting opinion of Bunn, J., in United States v. Thomas, 47 Fed. Rep., 488.*

SEC. 343. The subject-matter of the act of 1885 (23 Stat. L., 385) is the government of the Indians, who are the wards, and under the charge and tutelage of the nation; and it is the subject-matter, and not the title to the land whereon the crime is committed, which gives the Federal courts jurisdiction.   *Ibid.*

SEC. 344. The argument that the reservation of absolute jurisdiction and control over the Indian lands contained in the omnibus act (25 Stat. L., 676) is to be confined to the mere matter of the ownership of the title and control of the right of taxation is a limited construction that is not admissible. The reservation was meant to be broad as the duty which the United States assumed in regard to these lands, which was to secure to the Indians the peaceful possession thereof as their homes, and to protect their persons and property.   *United States v. Ewing, 47 Fed. Rep., 809.*

SEC. 345. Under the terms of the act of March 2, 1861 (12 Stat. L., 239) there was reserved to the United States jurisdiction over the Indian reservations in Dakota, with full power and authority to make provision for the proper protection of the personal and property rights of the Indians against all wrongs committed by white men within the boundaries of the reservations.   *Ibid.*

SEC. 346. An indictment for a larceny committed in the county of Charles Mix, in the district aforesaid, and at a place in said county within the Great Sioux Indian Reservation and within the Indian country, sufficiently alleges the venue, although the name "Great

Sioux Reservation" is more properly applicable to another Sioux reservation in the State. *Ibid.*

SEC. 347. The United States court has jurisdiction of an indictment against a white man for stealing the horses of an Indian on the Yankton Reservation, under the act of April 30, 1790 (section 5356, Revised Statutes), which provides for the punishment of larceny committed "within any of the places under the sole and exclusive jurisdiction of the United States." *Ibid.*

SEC. 348. The act of February 22, 1889 (25 Stats., 676), admitting Montana and other Territories, provides in section 4 that "the people inhabiting said proposed States do agree and declare that they forever disclaim" all right to the lands therein held by Indian tribes, and that until the Indian title is extinguished the same shall remain subject to the disposition and "under the absolute jurisdiction and control" of Congress, and this provision was incorporated into the constitution of Montana. *Held*, that, in view of the fact that the United States, by the treaty of 1868 (15 Stat. L., 649), with the Crow Indians, agreed that no persons except certain employees of the Government should ever be permitted to "pass over, settle upon, or reside in" the reservation thereby set apart to them in Montana, the jurisdiction reserved to the United States was intended to apply to persons as well as to the lands themselves; and hence, under section 2145 of the Revised Statutes, which extends the general criminal laws of the United States to "the Indian country," the Federal courts have jurisdiction to punish a rape committed by a white man against a white woman. *United States v. Partello, 48 Fed. Rep., 670.*

SEC. 349. The word "jurisdiction" as used in section 4 of the act of February 22, 1889 (25 Stat. L., 676), admitting Montana, when applied to Congress, means the power of governing such lands; the power or right of exercising authority over them; to legislate for them. *Ibid.*

SEC. 350. Section 5345 of the Revised Statutes provides for the punishment of rape committed in any of the places mentioned in section 5339, among others, "any fort * * * or district of country under the exclusive jurisdiction of the United States." Section 2145 declares that "except as to crimes the punishment of which is expressly provided for in this title, the general laws of the United States as to the punishment of crimes committed within the sole and exclusive jurisdiction of the United States * * * shall extend to the Indian country." *Held*, that, as the punishment of rape is not specified in the title mentioned, a rape committed in the Indian country is punishable under section 5345. *Ibid.*

SEC. 351. An information lodged with the United States commissioner charged the accused with "introducing 10 gallons of beer into the Indian country, the same then and there being a spirituous liquor, in violation of section 2139, Revised Statutes." *Held*, that introducing spirituous liquor into an Indian country was an offense under section 2139; that the commissioner had jurisdiction over such offenses and the power to determine if beer was a spirituous liquor; and that his decision on that question could not be reviewed on a writ of *habeas corpus*.   *In re Boyd, 49 Fed. Rep., 48.*

SEC. 352. It is competent for a private person to make a conveyance of real property, and to withhold from the donee, for a season, the power to sell or otherwise dispose of it. And we can conceive of no sufficient reason why the United States, in the exercise of its sovereign power, should be denied the right to impose similar conditions, especially when it is dealing with a dependent race like the Indians.
                                Beck v. Flournoy & Co., 65 Fed. Rep., 30.

SEC. 353. The civilized nations in the Indian Territory are probably better guarded against suits than the States themselves, for the States may consent to be sued, but the United States has never given its permission that these Indian nations might be sued generally, even with their consent.   *Thebo v. Choctaw Tribe, 66 Fed. Rep., 372.*

SEC. 354. The constitutional competency of Congress to pass acts authorizing suits to be brought against the Choctaw Nation has never been questioned, but no court has presumed to take jurisdiction of a cause against any of the Five Civilized Nations in the Indian Territory in the absence of any act of Congress expressly conferring the jurisdiction in a particular case.   *Ibid.*

SEC. 355. It has been the settled policy of the United States not to authorize suits to be brought against the Choctaw Nation except in a few cases where the subject-matter of the controversy was particularly specified, and was of such a nature that the public interests, as well as the interests of the nation, seem to require the exercise of the jurisdiction.   *Ibid.*

SEC. 356. *Habeas corpus* will not lie to release an Indian, convicted and imprisoned under the law of 1885 (23 Stat. L., 385), for assault with intent to kill, on the ground that he is entitled to be tried under the laws of the State of his residence by virtue of the act of February 8, 1887 (24 Stat. L., 388), declaring Indians born within the United States, to whom land has been allotted, to be citizens of the United States, such facts being matter of defense, and reviewable by writ of error.   *In re Blackbird, 66 Fed. Rep., 541.*

SEC. 357. The act of May 2, 1890 (26 Stat. L., 81), which put in force in Indian Territory among other laws the statute of frauds making void conveyances to defraud creditors, has no retrospective effect, and before the passage of said act it was competent for an insolvent debtor to give away his property and deprive his creditors, who had obtained liens, of the opportunity to collect their claims for such property.   *McClellan v. Pyeatt, 66 Fed. Rep., 843.*

SEC. 358. One M., a citizen of the Cherokee Nation, mortgaged certain cattle to the plaintiffs; subsequently he used a part of the cattle so mortgaged to purchase the improvements on certain lands, which he then conveyed to his wife. *Held*, that M. was a trustee of the cattle for plaintiffs, and they had the right to follow the proceeds of the trust property in the hands of M.'s wife; and that, under the act of March 1, 1889 (25 Stat. L., 783), creating the United States court in the Indian Territory, that court had power to enforce such right. *Ibid.*

SEC. 359. If a Cherokee court has acquired jurisdiction of a case where a citizen of that country is charged with larceny, the fact that such citizen is naturalized under the act of May 2, 1890 (26 Stat. L., 81), does not, after jurisdiction has once attached, divest the court of jurisdiction. *Ex parte Kyle, 67 Fed. Rep., 306.*

SEC. 360. Having assumed the duty of securing the use and occupancy of these lands to the Indians, and being charged with the duty of enforcing the provisions of the act of Congress (24 Stat. L., 388) forbidding all alienation of lands until the expiration of the period of twenty-five years after the allotment thereof, the Government of the United States, through the executive branch thereof, has the right to invoke the aid of the courts to compel parties wrongfully in possession of land held in trust by the United States for the Indians to yield possession thereof and to restrain such parties from endeavoring to obtain or retain possession of these lands in violation of law.

United States v. Live Stock and Real Estate Co., 69 Fed. Rep., 886.

SEC. 361. The United States holds the lands of the tribe of Omaha and Winnebago charged with the trust created by the treaties with said Indians, and it is its duty to do whatever is necessary to protect the Indians in proper use and occupancy thereof. *Ibid.*

SEC. 362. The power and right of the United States to do whatever is necessary for the fulfillment of its treaty duties, trusts, and obligations toward the Indians rests upon every foot of soil and upon every individual within the boundaries of the reservations, and this power and right is paramount and supreme. *Ibid.*

SEC. 363. The Government has the power to invoke the aid of the courts to remove from the lands of the Indians under its supervision and control persons who have intruded thereon under unauthorized leases from the Indians, and to restrain such persons from procuring other such leases from the Indians. *Ibid.*

SEC. 364. A member of the Indian police is not an officer of the United States within the meaning of the first clause of section 5398, Revised Statutes, imposing a penalty for resisting any officer of the United States in serving a writ or process, but such police are included among the other persons who may be authorized to serve writs or process, within the last clause of that section.

United States v. Mullin, 71 Fed. Rep., 682.

Sec. 365. Prior to March 3, 1871, the United States always exercised its power and jurisdiction over the Indian tribes by means of treaties, but on that day a radical change was made in the preexisting policy by the enactment of a law (16 Stats., 566) which, while continuing every obligation of any treaty, theretofore lawfully made and ratified with any tribe, declared that thereafter "no Indian Nation or tribe within the Territory of the United States shall be acknowledged or recognized as an independent nation, tribe, or power with whom the United States may contract by treaty."

Trascott v. Hurlbut Land and Cattle Co., 73 Fed. Rep., 60.

Sec. 366. The failure of an Indian agent through clerical errors to include in his accounts property which, in fact, remains at the agency, and which is not lost to the Government, does not entitle the United States to recover the value thereof in a suit on his bond; and he may show these facts in his defense. The technical failure to account would authorize the recovery of no more than nominal damages.

73 Fed. Rep., 801.

Sec. 367. The offense of assault with intent to commit rape, committed by an Indian upon an Indian woman, both residing upon an Indian reservation, is not cognizable as a crime by any statute of the United States, and the United States courts have no jurisdiction of such offenses.

United States v. King, 81 Fed. Rep., 625.

Sec. 368. When a statute creating a forfeiture does not prescribe the mode of collecting it, either debt, information, or indictment will lie, and indictment will lie to recover the penalty provided by section 2148 of the Revised Statutes for the return to the Indian country of a person removed therefrom by the Superintendent of Indian Affairs or Indian agent.

United States v. Stocking, 87 Fed. Rep., 857.

Sec. 369. The act of August 18, 1856 (11 Stat. L., 80, sec. 2), prescribing a penalty of $1,000 for the return of a person removed from the Indian country is not an amendment, but is a supplement to section 10 of the act of June 30, 1834 (4 Stat. L., 730), authorizing and directing the removal of intruders in the Indian country, and therefore the provisions of section 27 of the said act of 1834, providing for collection of penalties under said act in an action of debt, does not apply to the act of 1856.

Ibid.

Sec. 370. The act of June 30, 1834 (4 Stat. L., 733), section 27, provided for the collection of all penalties accruing under "this act" by an action of debt, etc. The act of August 18, 1856 (11 Stat. L., 80), section 2, provided a penalty for an infraction of the act of 1834. Upon revision the act of 1856 was printed under the same title with the act of 1834, as section 2148 of the Revised Statutes. The section providing for the collection of penalties (sec. 2124, R. S.) was changed to provide for the collection of penalties under "this title" instead of under "this act." By section 5600 of the revision it is provided that no presumption of a legislative construction shall be drawn by reason of the title under which any particular section is placed by the revision. *Held*, that section 2124 does not limit the right of the United States to an action of debt to recover the penalty prescribed in section 2148.

Ibid.

SEC. 371. A stock of liquors is not introduced into the Indian country by being transported across a reservation to a place where it may be lawfully sold, and is not subject to seizure while in transit, or after it reaches its destination.

United States v. 4 Bottles Sour Mash Whisky, 90 Fed. Rep., 720.

SEC. 372. An offense committed upon an Indian reservation within a State is not cognizable in a Federal court under act of Congress, March 3, 1885 (23 Stat. L., 385), unless the offender is an Indian.

United States v. Hadley, 99 Fed. Rep., 437.

SEC. 373. Half-breed Indians, who are citizens by birth, can not be brought to trial in the Federal courts under a statute which limits the jurisdiction of offenses committed by Indians.

Ibid.

SEC. 374. Amnesty, by the very nature of peace, is necessarily included in it. A special provision of amnesty for "all past offenses" must be held to include all prior offenses without regard to time, and not merely those committed during a recent war.

Garrison v. U. S. et al., 30 C. Cls., 272.

SEC. 375. "A general amnesty of all past offenses committed by any member of the Creek Nation against the laws of the United States is hereby declared," being clear and comprehensible language in a treaty, the preamble can not be consulted to ascertain its meaning.

Ibid.

SEC. 376. An indictment was found against two Indians for killing a white man named Davis, on a public road passing through the Cherokee lands, ceded by treaty with the Cherokee Nation to the United States. A plea to the jurisdiction being filed, the court decided against the jurisdiction on the ground that there was no law of the United States which "makes the facts as charged and laid in said indictment a crime, affixes a punishment, and declares the court which shall have jurisdiction of it."

United States v. Bailey, 1 McLean, 234.

SEC. 377. If in a community or neighborhood composed principally of whites, a citizen of the Indian race, not within the exception of the fourteenth amendment, should propose to lease and cultivate a farm, and a combination should be formed to expel him and prevent him from accomplishing his purpose on account of his race or color, it can not be doubted that this would be a case within the power of Congress to remedy and redress. But if that person should be injured in his person or property by any wrongdoer for the mere felonious purpose of malice, revenge, or gain, without any design to interfere with his rights of citizenship or equality before the laws, it would be an ordinary crime punishable by the State laws only.

United States v. Crukshank, 1 Woods, 308.

SEC. 378. From the provisions of section 1 of the act of 1817 (3 Stats., 385), no doubt can be entertained that it was the intention of Congress to punish all offenses specified, and especially the crime of murder committed in the Indian country, though within the limits of a State; and the jurisdiction of the court must be sustained, unless the said act shall be found to be repugnant to the Constitution of the United States.   *United States v. Bailey, 1 McLean, 234.*

SEC. 379. The crime of murder charged against a white man for killing another white man within the Cherokee country, in the State of Tennessee, can not be punished in the courts of the United States.

Ibid.

SEC. 380. Congress can not punish for an offense within the Indian territory, in a State, which has no relation to the Indians, and which can not affect their commerce.   *Ibid.*

SEC. 381. The State of New York for many years has punished its citizens for crimes committed in the Indian territory within its limits; and the State of Georgia, before its laws were extended over the Cherokee country, within the State, punished its own citizens for offenses committed within that territory; and it does not appear that the right of either State to do this has been questioned.

Ibid.

SEC. 382. There is nothing in the treaties with the Cherokees which gives to the court jurisdiction of the offense charged in the indictment.

Ibid.

SEC. 383. The act of Congress, 1817, asserts a general jurisdiction for the punishment of offenses over the Indian territory, though it be within the limits of a State. To the exercise of this jurisdiction within a territorial government there can be no objection, but the case is wholly different, as it regards Indian territory within the limits of a State. In such case the power of Congress is limited to the regulation of a commercial intercourse with such tribes of Indians as exist, as a distinct community, governed by their own laws, and resting for their protection on the faith of treaties and laws of the Union. Beyond this the power of the Federal Government in any of its departments can not be extended.   *Ibid.*

SEC. 384. A murder committed by one white person on another within the Indian territory, and within a State, is in no respect an act connected with the commerce of the Cherokee Indians, or interferes with their property or safety.   *Ibid.*

SEC. 385. The Cherokee country can in no sense be considered a territory of the United States over which the Federal Government may exercise exclusive jurisdiction, nor has there been any cession of jurisdiction by the State of Tennessee, or any prohibition to its exercise of jurisdiction over this territory, constitutionally, except such as the rights recognized and guaranteed to the Indians by treaties and the laws regulating commerce with them may impose.   *Ibid.*

SEC. 386. That Congress has power to inflict punishment on all who violate the laws which regulate a commercial intercourse with the Indians is admitted, but because this is a legitimate exercise of power, it does not follow that the jurisdiction may be extended without limit.   *Ibid.*

SEC. 387. The question of jurisdiction which is raised by the demurrer is whether the law under which this indictment has been found (1802) can be carried into effect within the Wyandott Reserve. And whether this is properly a judicial question may admit of some controversy.   *United States v. Cisna, 1 McLean, 254.*

SEC. 388. The act of June 30, 1834 (4 Stat. L., 729), confers upon the Federal courts jurisdiction of offenses against the laws of the United States committed on Indian reservations in Kansas, unless subsequent legislation has withdrawn the locality from that jurisdiction.
        United States v. Ward, 1 Woolw., 17.   Same, 1 Banks & McCahon, 601.

SEC. 389. Jurisdiction is claimed here to punish this homicide, because it was committed on an Indian reservation.   That circumstance alone is not sufficient to give the United States court jurisdiction. There is no act of Congress giving Federal courts jurisdiction of every murder committed on any Indian reservation.   These courts have jurisdiction only when such reservation is within the sole and exclusive jurisdiction of the United States.
        United States v. Ward, 1 Woolw., 17.   Same, 1 Banks & McCahon, 601.

SEC. 390. Ever since the organization of this court it has sat here administering and enforcing the laws of the United States over the Indian country, trying and punishing Indians, in some cases capitally. They are prohibited from trafficking in certain articles.   Until recently they could not sell their cattle without permission of the United States agent (13 Stat. L., 563).   They can not alienate their lands, neither can they permit citizens of the United States to settle within their country without the consent of the United States.   By permission of the United States they have jurisdiction of offenses committed by one Indian on the person or property of another Indian. But this power is granted them from considerations of policy only, and no one doubts that Congress might invest this court with that jurisdiction.   They are without a single attribute that marks them as a sovereign and independent people.
        United States v. Tobacco Factory, 1 Dill., 264.

H. Doc. 538——5

SEC. 391. In the United States *v.* Bailey (1 McLean, 235) a case is referred to in the Tennessee district where, in 1816, two Indians were indicted in the United States circuit court for the murder of a white man *on a reservation* in the Cherokee country, within the limits of the State; and this decision in the Tennessee case was the cause of the passage of the act of 1817 (3 Stat. L., 383), which was subsequently repealed by the act of June 30, 1834 (4 Stat. L., 728), whereby Congress provided for the punishment in the national courts of offenses committed by Indians or others upon lands within the State limits.

United States v. Yellow Sun, 1 Dill., 271.

SEC. 392. In view of the peculiar relations which the General Government sustains to the Indian tribes, the court does not fully assent to the opinion which Mr. Justice McLean seems to have held in Bailey's case (1 McLean, 235), that Congress had no power to pass the act of 1817 (3 Stat. L., 383)—that is, that Congress could not, if it saw fit, make punishable in the national courts offenses committed by or against Indians *upon reservations in State limits.*   *Ibid.*

SEC. 393. If it be conceded that, under the power of peace and war to make treaties and to regulate commerce with the Indian tribes, Congress could, in the absence of reserved right to do so, withdraw Indians living within the limits of a State entirely from State jurisdiction and the reach of its criminal laws and process for offenses against its citizens committed off a reservation, it would seem most improbable that such a power would ever be exercised. In point of fact Congress has not undertaken to exercise it, and, therefore, this court, which can take cognizance only of offenses created by some act of Congress, has no jurisdiction of the crime charged in the indictment.   *Ibid.*

SEC. 394. There are two statutes relating to murder cognizable by the United States courts—the statute of 1790 and that of 1825. They declare that if a person commits murder within certain places he shall be punished. The case at bar falls within none of the provisions of either of these statutes. They do not undertake to punish murder generally, but only when committed at a place within the exclusive jurisdiction of the United States.   *Ibid.*

SEC. 395. It is settled that there are no common-law offenses cognizable by the courts of the United States; that before these courts can take cognizance of an offense it must be declared such by an act of Congress; and that it is not competent for Congress to enact a criminal code punishing offenses generally, but those only which relate to the General Government, or which are committed in places over which Congress has exclusive jurisdiction.   *Ibid.*

SEC. 396. The court, in a capital case against Indians, committed off their reservation, though neither party asked it, and both demanded a judgment on a verdict of guilty, arrested the judgment on its own motion for want of jurisdiction over the offense charged. *Ibid.*

SEC. 397. A major-general in command of an army may lawfully issue an order to arrest a person therein who has induced friendly Indians to steal cattle from him, with a view to turning such cattle over to the Government under contracts to supply the army with beef; and the fraudulent possessor of such cattle can not recover for them against the officer who, for such reasons, ordered their seizure.

Holmes v. Sheridan, 1 Dill., 351.

SEC. 398. The act of 1833 (4 Stat. L., 634) provides that the Federal judges shall have the power to grant writs of *habeas corpus* in all cases of a prisoner in jail or confinement where he shall be committed or confined on or by any authority or law for any act done or omitted to be done in pursuance of a law of the United States or any order, process, or decree of any judge or court thereof.

Ex parte Forbes, 1 Dill., 363.

SEC. 399. The judiciary act of 1789 gave the general power to issue the writ of habeas corpus, but, in a proviso, declared "that it in no case shall extend to prisoners in jail, unless they are in custody under, or by color of, the authority of the United States; or are committed for trial before some court of the same; or are necessary to be brought into court to testify." *Ibid.*

SEC. 400. By the laws of the United States, the Supreme, circuit, and district courts have power to grant the writs of habeas corpus within their respective jurisdictions. *Ex parte Kenyon, 5 Dill., 385.*

SEC. 401. The Indian Territory is within the jurisdiction of the western district of Arkansas. A writ of *habeas corpus* issued by the United States court of that district will run in that Territory. *Ibid.*

SEC. 402. If a person is held in custody in violation of the Constitution, laws, or treaties of the United States—it matters not by whom he is held—the courts of the United States, within their respective territorial jurisdictions, have power to issue the writ of habeas corpus to inquire into the cause of his imprisonment. *Ibid.*

SEC. 403. If the petitioner were tried, convicted, and sentenced by a court of the Cherokee Nation without its having jurisdiction, then he is held in violation of the Constitution, laws, and treaties of the United States; but how far this court will examine into the case to ascertain if such person is held contrary to such Constitution, laws, and treaties is a question. *Ibid.*

SEC. 404. If there were any crime committed at any time, it was committed not only beyond the place over which the Cherokee court had jurisdiction, but, at the time it was committed, by one over whose person such court did not have jurisdiction; because, to give that court jurisdiction of the person of an offender, such offender must be an Indian, and the one against whom the offense is committed must also be an Indian. *Ibid.*

SEC. 405. The jurisdiction over the person, the place, and the act committed must all concur to give any court of limited jurisdiction the right to try. If either one of these elements of jurisdiction is wanting, the right to try and convict does not exist. *Ibid.*

SEC. 406. In order to give this court jurisdiction of the crime of murder, of which the defendant stands charged, it must appear that the crime was committed in the Indian country, and that the person who committed it is not one of the persons known as an Indian, or, if he is an Indian, that the person upon whom the crime was committed was not an Indian. *Ex parte Reynolds, 5 Dill., 394.*

SEC. 407. If the person charged and the person upon whom the murder was committed are both Indians, under section 2146 of the Revised Statutes this court has no jurisdiction, because, by the terms of said section, the general laws of the United States defining crimes and providing for their punishment do not extend to "offenses committed by one Indian upon the person or property of another Indian," but the same are left by the laws of the United States to be dealt with by the Indian authorities. *Ibid.*

SEC. 408. In time of peace, no authority, civil or military, exists for transporting Indians from one section of the country to another without the consent of the Indians, nor to confine them to any particular reservation against their will, and where officers of the Government attempt to do this, and arrest and hold Indians who are at peace with the Government for the purpose of removing them to and confining them on a reservation in the Indian Territory, they will be released on habeas corpus. *United States v. Crook, 5 Dill., 453.*

SEC. 409. By reference to sections 751, 752, and 753, Revised Statutes, it will be seen that when a *person* is in custody or deprived of his liberty under color of authority of the United States, or in violation of the Constitution or laws or treaties of the United States, the Federal judges have jurisdiction, and the writ of *habeas corpus* can properly issue. *Ibid.*

SEC. 410. The power of the Government may be employed to effect the removal of trespassers from a reservation, but where the removal is effected it is the duty of the troops to convey the persons so removed, by the most convenient and safe route, to the civil authorities of the judicial district in which the offense may be committed, to be proceeded against in due course of law. *Ibid.*

SEC. 411. The punishment of the crime of murder is nowhere expressly provided for in the Revised Statutes under the title "Indians," and it follows that where that crime is committed in the Indian country, it is within the exclusive jurisdiction of the United States. *United States v. Berry, 2 McCrary, 58.*

SEC. 412. The Ute Reservation, though within the State of Colorado, having been set aside as such by treaty, and the exclusive jurisdiction to punish crime therein being by the terms of the treaty vested in the United States, and this treaty not being in terms repealed by act of Congress, the treaty remains in force as the law; and the United States district court has jurisdiction to try and punish offenses for crimes committed within the reservation. *Ibid.*

SEC. 413. Congress has passed a law expressly giving this court jurisdiction of offenses committed by Indians, such as the one charged against the prisoners, and as there is no doubt of its constitutionality, the court is bound to carry its provisions into effect. *United States v. Cha-to-kah-na-pe-sha, 1 Hemp., 27.*

SEC. 414. The Osage Nation were in amity with the United States and had no intention of going to war by the murder of which the prisoners are found guilty. *United States v. Cha-to-kah-na-pe-sha, 1 Hemp., 27.*

SEC. 415. The indictment of the defendant for the homicide of a citizen of the United States in the country occupied by the Osage Nation of Indians was bad, but the prisoner was remanded to custody on proof before the court of the commission of the homicide. *United States v. Town-maker, 1 Hemp., 299.*

SEC. 416. Congress specifically defined the boundaries of the State of Arkansas, and by giving the district court thereof such powers only as were conferred on the district court of Kentucky by the judiciary act of 1789 necessarily excluded jurisdiction beyond the boundaries of the State of Arkansas; and therefore a crime committed in the Indian country west of Arkansas is not triable in this court. *United States v. Ta-wan-ga-ea, 1 Hemp., 304.*

SEC. 417. The prisoner was indicted for murder at a term of the superior court of the late Territory of Arkansas. That court was competent to try him for the crime, as a law of the United States had conferred upon it jurisdiction of capital crimes committed in that part of the Indian country west of Arkansas. *Ibid.*

SEC. 418. All the laws giving to the circuit and district courts of the United States jurisdiction of crimes committed in the Indian country have been passed since 1789. *Ibid.*

SEC. 419. Robbery, when committed in the Indian country, is indictable and punishable only as larceny. *Note to United States v. Terrel, 1 Hemp., 411.*

SEC. 420. If robbery committed in "a place within the sole and exclusive jurisdiction of the United States" be punishable with death, then, if committed in the Indian country, it is also punishable with death, and not otherwise.   *Ibid.*

SEC. 421. There is no law of Congress punishing the crime of robbery committed on land, and judgment on an indictment therefor will be arrested.   *United States v. Terrel, 1 Hemp., 411.*

SEC. 422. Acts of Congress of March 30, 1802 (2 Stat. L., 139), and of June 30, 1834 (4 Stat L., 729), to regulate intercourse with the Indian tribes and preserve peace on the frontiers; the act of March 3, 1825 (4 Stat. L., 115), relating to crimes against the United States; the act of June 15, 1836, admitting Arkansas into the Union, and the act of March 3, 1837 (5 Stat. L., 176), amendatory of the judicial system of the United States, commented on and explained.

United States v. Alberty, 1 Hemp., 444.

SEC. 423. The circuit court of this district, in the absence of any statute attaching the Indian country west of Arkansas thereto, has no jurisdiction over such Indian country and can not punish an offense committed therein.   *Ibid.*

SEC. 424. Until the act of June 17, 1844 (4 Stat. L., 733), was passed by Congress the courts of the United States had no jurisdiction to hear, try, and punish offenses committed in the Indian country west of Arkansas.   *United States v. Starr, 1 Hemp., 469.*

SEC. 425. The act of June 17, 1844 (4 Stat. L., 733), conferring jurisdiction on United States courts to try and punish offenses committed in the Indian country west of Arkansas, was prospective and did not operate on the past.   *Ibid.*

SEC. 426. By the act of June 30, 1834 (4 Stat. L., 729), so much of the laws of the United States as provided for the punishment of crimes committed in any place within the sole and exclusive jurisdiction of the United States are declared to be in force in the Indian country west of Arkansas, but not to extend to crimes committed by one Indian against the person or property of another Indian. And for the sole purpose of giving jurisdiction to the Territorial court that part of the Indian country was annexed to the Territory of Arkansas (4 Stat. L., 723; 4 Story, Laws U. S., 2399; 9 Laws U. S., 128).   *Ibid.*

SEC. 427. The plea of former trial and acquittal for this offense under the Cherokee laws in the Cherokee country is insufficient upon the ground that the Cherokee court had no jurisdiction of the case.

United States v. Ragsdale, 1 Hemp., 479.

SEC. 428. The United States circuit court for Arkansas has no jurisdiction to punish offenses under the intercourse law of 1834, committed by one Indian against the person or property of another Indian.

United States v. Sanders, 1 Hemp., 483.

SEC. 429. The prisoner did not rest his defense on his innocence, but on the want of jurisdiction in this court to punish him at all. He is charged in the indictment to be a Cherokee Indian, and the deceased to have been a white boy and not an Indian, thus presenting a case, as far as the indictment is concerned, within the jurisdiction of the court.
Ibid.

SEC. 430. The second article of the treaty of August 6, 1846, with the Cherokees (9 Stat. L., 871) had not the effect to pardon an offense previously committed by an Indian in the Cherokee country west of Arkansas against a white man who had been adopted by that tribe and become a part of it. *United States v. Ragsdale, 1 Hemp., 497.*

SEC. 431. The killing of a white man in the Cherokee country west of Arkansas prior to its annexation to the district of Arkansas by the act of June 17, 1844, is not a case in the jurisdiction of the circuit court of the United States to try. *United States v. Ivy, 1 Hemp., 562.*

SEC. 432. Persons indicted in 1845 in the circuit court of the United States for the district of Arkansas for a felony committed in the Indian country west of Arkansas, and which territory was transferred to the western district of Arkansas by the act of March 3, 1851 (9 Stat. L., 594), are subject to trial in the court where the indictment was found, and the court in the western district has no jurisdiction. That act did not deprive the court where an indictment was pending of the right to try and determine the same.
United States v. Dawson et al., 1 Hemp., 643.

SEC. 433. No person arrested by the military authority in the Indian country for the introduction or disposition of spirituous liquors therein contrary to law can be lawfully detained by such authorities more than five days after such arrest before removing him for delivery to the civil authorities for trial. *In re Carr, 3 Sawyer, 316.*

SEC. 434. In an indictment under section 2139, Revised Statutes, for disposing of spirituous liquors to an Indian, it is necessary to allege that the defendant is not an "Indian in the Indian country."
United States v. Winslow, 3 Sawyer, 337.

SEC. 435. The exception in section 2139, Revised Statutes, "an Indian in the Indian country," does not apply to the offense, but only to the person who may commit it. *Ibid.*

SEC. 436. After a State has been admitted into the Union, the fact that within its boundaries land, the fee of which is in the United States, is set apart as an Indian reservation is not enough of itself to give a United States court jurisdiction to try a person for a murder committed within the limits of such reservation.
Ex parte Sloan, 4 Sawyer, 330.

SEC. 437. There is no question as to the extent of the power of Congress to regulate commerce with the Indian tribes. The courts of the

United States have no criminal jurisdiction except such as is given to them by some law of the United States, and Congress has not yet attempted to create the crime of murder under the power given it to regulate commerce with the Indian tribes.   *Ibid.·*

SEC. 438. A person arrésted by military force for violation of sections 20 or 21 of the act of June 30, 1834 (4 Stat. L., 729,) is not a military prisoner subject to the Articles of War, but a citizen charged with a non-military crime, and must be removed for trial by the civil authorities within five days from his arrest or discharged; and his detention thereafter under any circumstances is unlawful.   *Waters v. Campbell, 5 Saw., 17.*

SEC. 439. A person under arrest for violation of sections 20 or 21 of the act of June 30, 1834 (4 Stat. L., 729), may be confined in a military prison, but he can not be lawfully required to labor or perform any duty other than taking care of his person.   *Waters v. Campbell, 5 Saw., 17.*

SEC. 440. The treaty of June 9, 1855 (12 Stat. L., 445), establishing the Umatilla Reservation for the exclusive use of certain Indian tribes was not modified or repealed by the act admitting Oregon into the Union, and from the date of such treaty, and by reason thereof, such reservation was and is "Indian country," and all laws for the punishment of crimes committed in such country are applicable thereto, and may be enforced in the United States courts for the district of Oregon.
United States v. Bridleman, 7 Saw., 243.

SEC. 441. It is immaterial that the State has power to, and does, punish for larceny committed within its limits. So it has the power to regulate and control the disposition of spirituous liquors; but in neither case does this power exclude or supersede the paramount authority of the National Government where the larceny or disposition touches upon or affects a subject within its jurisdiction and power.
Ibid.

SEC. 442. In the exercise of its constitutional power to regulate intercourse with the Indian tribes Congress may define and punish crimes committed by white men upon the person or property of an Indian, and *vice versa*, within as well as without the limits of a State.
United States v. Martin, 8 Saw., 473.

SEC. 443. Congress having provided for the punishment of murder committed in the Indian country (secs. 2145, 5339, Rev. Stat.), the United States circuit court for the district of Oregon has jurisdiction of the crime of murder committed on the Umatilla Reservation by an Indian upon a white man; and therefore it is a violation of section 5398, Revised Statutes, for anyone to resist or obstruct the execution of an order made by a circuit court commissioner engaged in the examination of an Indian charged before him with the commission of murder under such circumstances.   *Ibid.*

SEC. 444. Section 2148, Revised Statutes, is in legal effect a prohibition against any person who has been removed from the Indian country returning thereto, and the penalty therein provided for its violation may be enforced by indictment or information.

United States v. Howard, 9 Saw., 155.

Sec. 445. Section 2124 of the Revised Statutes ought to be construed as only applicable to the penalties imposed by the act of June 30, 1834 (4 Stat. L., 729), of which it is a part; but if considered applicable at all to section 2148, as being included in Title XXVIII, Revised Statutes, the remedy therein provided for the enforcement of the penalty for returning to an Indian reservation is not exclusive of the common-law remedy by indictment or information, but only cumulative.

Ibid.

Sec. 446. The party committing the act prohibited by section 2148, Revised Statutes, might have been prosecuted therefor criminally. There was no other mode of proceeding provided in the act.   *Ibid.*

Sec. 447. The United States courts of the district of Oregon have jurisdiction over all crimes committed on the Umatilla Reservation by a white man on the person or property of an Indian, and *vice versa*, so far as the same have been defined by an act of Congress.

United States v. Barnhart, 10 Saw., 491.

Sec. 448. The prisoners were indicted in the United States court for the crime of manslaughter committed on the Umatilla Reservation and pleaded to the indictment a former acquittal, from which plea it appeared that they had been indicted and tried in the State court for the murder and acquitted. *Held,* that the crime of which the defendants were acquitted in the State court was not the same as that charged in the indictment in the United States court, and therefore the plea was bad.   *Ibid.*

Sec. 449. Courts of different sovereignties can not have concurrent jurisdiction of the same offense unless it is one arising under some law common to them all—as the law of nations.   *Ibid.*

Sec. 450. It is impossible that the United States can maintain its paramount authority over the subjects committed by the Constitution to their jurisdiction and at the same time allow a trial in a State court on a criminal charge growing out of an act that Congress has defined to be a crime, to be a bar to a prosecution therefor, in its own courts and according to its own law.   *Ibid.*

Sec. 451. The district court of Alaska has jurisdiction, under sections 5339 and 5341 of the Revised Statutes, to try and punish any inhabitant of the district for the crime of murder or manslaughter committed by the killing of any human being therein, but the law of Oregon, defining the crime of murder or manslaughter and prescribing the punishment therefor, is not in force in Alaska.

Kie v. United States, 11 Saw., 579.

Sec. 452. Alaska has been since 1867 "a district of country under the exclusive jurisdiction of the United States." Therefore, the statutory provisions concerning the commission and punishment of murder and manslaughter are in force therein and necessarily exclude the operation or application there of any law of Oregon on these subjects.

Ibid.

Sec. 453. In 1879 Kat ko wat, and in 1882 Ki ta tah, both aborigines of Alaska, were tried and convicted in this court, under the statute, for murder committed in Alaska, and were punished with death. *Ibid.*

Sec. 454. It is not necessary in an indictment for the violation of section 14 of the act of May 17, 1884 (23 Stat. L., 24), by the sale of intoxicating liquor in the district of Alaska, to allege that such sale was not made for mechanical, medicinal, or scientific purposes; but the same may be shown, if at all, as a defense. *Nelson v. United States, 12 Saw., 285.*

Sec. 455. By section 7 of the act of 1884 (23 Stat. L., 24) jurisdiction is given this court of writs of error to the district court of Alaska in the criminal cases mentioned in the act of 1879 (20 Stat. L., 354). But the provision in section 1 of the latter act concerning the tender and allowance of a bill of exceptions in a district court of the United States is not made applicable to proceedings in the district court of Alaska. *Ibid.*

Sec. 456. In an indictment for the violation of section 14 of the act of May 17, 1884 (23 Stat. L., 24), the name of the purchaser, if known, ought to be alleged, as a convenient means of identifying the transaction; but the omission to do so is not a sufficient cause for the reversal of the judgment on error. *Ibid.*

Sec. 457. No "appeal" lies to this court from the judgment of the district court of Alaska. It can only review the judgments of said court in criminal cases on a writ of error, which must be allowed by the circuit judge or justice, who may order a stay of proceedings thereon and take a bond that the same will be prosecuted to effect, and the defendant will abide the judgment of the court thereon.

Ibid.

Sec. 458. By section 1955 of the Revised Statutes, the President was given power to "restrict and regulate, or to prohibit the importation and use * * * of distilled spirits into the Territory of Alaska. * * * And any person violating such regulations shall be fined not more than five hundred dollars, or imprisoned not more than six months." *Ibid.*

Sec. 459. In United States *v.* Stephens (8 Saw., 119), it was held that as the law then (1882) was, the introduction of spirituous liquors and wine into Alaska was "absolutely prohibited, subject to the power of the War Department to permit the same for the use of the Army, and the power of the President to permit the introduction of distilled spirits, but not wine, for any purpose." *Ibid.*

SEC. 460. Nebraska was organized into a Territory by the act May 30, 1854 (10 Stat. L., 277), and by sections 4 and 37 of that act the rights of Indians therein are preserved unimpaired, and the authority of the United States to make regulations respecting them, their property, and other rights, retained. The Pawnee tribe then, as now, resided within the limits of the Territory thus created.

United States v. Sa coo da cot, 1 Abbott, 377.

SEC. 461. There are two statutes relating to murder cognizable by the United States courts—the statute of 1790 and that of 1825. *Ibid.*

SEC. 462. The opinion which Mr. Justice McLean seems to have entertained in Bailey's case (1 McLean, 234), that Congress had no power to make punishable in the national courts offenses committed by or against Indians upon reservations within a State, criticised.

Ibid.

SEC. 463. The criminal laws of this State (Wisconsin) extend over the Oneida Reservation, and crimes committed within such reservation, whether by Indians of that tribe or others, are triable in the State courts and punishable under such laws.

State of Wis. v. Doxtater, jr., 2 N. W. Rep., 439; 36 Conover (Wis.), 278.

SEC. 464. The opinion of the court in the case of State *v.* Doxtater disposes of the exceptions of the defendant in this case adversely to her. In that opinion it is expressly held that the criminal laws of the State extend to all parts of the State, including the Oneida Reservation, within the boundaries of which the offense charged against the defendant was committed, and as the evidence shows she was not an Indian and did not belong to the tribe of Oneida Indians, there can be no pretense that she was not subject to the criminal laws of the State on any grounds personal to herself, as was claimed in the case of Doxtater. *State v. Harris, 2 N. W. Rep., 543; same, 36 Conover (Wis.), 278.*

SEC. 465. An indictment for murder in the Indian country was entitled in the caption as follows: "The United States of America, Territory of Dakota, second judicial district, ss: In the district court in and for the second judicial district and Territory of Dakota, having and exercising the jurisdiction of a United States circuit and district court; United States *v.* Silas Frank Beebe." *Held*, not to show that it was presented to a court not having jurisdiction. A court will take judicial notice of Indian reservations and all leading public proclamations affecting matters relating to its jurisdiction. An indictment charged that a crime was committed at a place near the Crow Creek Indian Agency, in the Indian country, in a place and district of country under the exclusive jurisdiction of the United States, in the said second judicial district and Territory of Dakota, and within the jurisdiction of this court, sufficiently states the place of the commission of the offense.   *Beebe v. United States, 11 N. W. Rep., 505.*

SEC. 466. The courts of this State (Nevada) have no authority to prosecute and punish one Indian for a crime committed against another on the reservation to which they belong so long as they maintain their tribal relations.   *Ex parte Cross, 30 N. W. Rep., 428.*

SEC. 467. The sale of liquor to an Indian is a misdemeanor, and not a felony, under Revised Statutes United States, section 2139, providing that one who sells spirituous liquor to an Indian shall be punishable by imprisonment for not more than two years and by fine not exceeding $300.

On an indictment charging in one count a sale of intoxicating liquor to an Indian and in another a gift, a general verdict of guilty is sufficient, though based on proof of a single transaction.

Brugier v. United States, 46 N. W. Rep., 502.

SEC. 468. Under the laws of the United States authorizing the condemnation of any boat introducing intoxicating liquor into the Indian country on a seizure made by the Superintendent of Indian Affairs, an Indian agent or subagent, or the commanding officer of a military post, there is no jurisdiction unless the libel shows a seizure by one of the officers mentioned, and an amended libel is fatally defective which shows only a seizure by the marshal under a writ based on the original libel.   *United States v. The Cara, 46 N. W. Rep., 503.*

SEC. 469. A sale of spirituous liquors to an Indian under the charge of an Indian superintendent or agent, though not made within the Indian country, is an offense under sec. 2139, of the Revised Statutes of the United States, providing that "every person, except an Indian,[1] in the Indian country, who sells spirituous liquor to any Indian under the charge of any Indian superintendent or agent, shall be punishable."

United States v. Burdick, 46 Northwestern Rep., 571.

SEC. 470. Unless otherwise provided by treaty with an Indian tribe, or by the act admitting the State into the Union, the criminal laws of the State, except so far as restricted by the authority of Congress to regulate commerce with the Indian tribes, extend to all crimes committed on an Indian reservation by persons other than tribal Indians.

State v. Campbell, 55 N. W. Rep., 553.

SEC. 471. Mr. Wharton in his Conflict of Laws, under the head of "Adoption in a North American Indian Tribe" (sec. 252), says: "He (the person adopted) may be indicted, it is true, in State or Territorial courts, for crimes committed by him on persons not of his tribe; but for offenses against members of his tribe, he is only justifiable before

---

[1] The exception of Indians in the Indian country from the liability to the penalties of the law has been repealed by the act of July 23, 1892 (27 Stats., 260).

the tribal authorities. So far as concerns his domestic relations, he is governed not by Territorial, but tribal law. * * * In short, while he retains his subjection to the Territorial government (State or Federal as the case may be) in all that relates to transactions outside of the tribe, so far as concerns transactions within the tribe his allegiance is to the tribe, and he is governed exclusively by tribal laws." *State v. McKenney, 2 Pacific Reporter, 178.*

SEC. 472. An Indian agent in carrying out the provisions of the law to prevent the introduction of spirituous liquors into the reservations is justified in seizing the property of a third party which is being used by the person making such introduction of liquors as a means to his purpose.

The answer of an Indian agent in an action brought against him for the seizure of plaintiff's property is defective if it shows that such property, when seized, was being used to violate the law as to the introduction of liquors into the reservations, and yet does not show that the offender so using it was a "white man," or an "Indian."

Webb, sr., v. Nickerson, 4 Pacific Reporter, 1126.

SEC. 473. When both the defendant, in a prosecution under an indictment for murder, and the deceased are full-blood Indians, but it does not appear that defendant is a member of any tribe of Indians having its chief or tribal laws, nor that his ancestral tribe had treated with the Government, but it does appear that he had lived among the whites several years, the State courts of California have jurisdiction to punish him for the crime. *People v. Ketchem, 15 Pa. Rep., 353.*

SEC. 474. An Indian who has severed his tribal relations may be prosecuted in the courts of the State, whether the crime was committed within or without the reservation, and an Indian who retains his tribal relations may be prosecuted in the courts of a State for a crime committed at a place without the limits of a reservation. An information filed in the superior court of a county containing within its limits an Indian reservation, against a person described in the information as an Indian, need not aver that such person does not sustain tribal relations or that the offense was not committed within such reservation.

State v. Williams, 43 Pa. Rep., 15.

SEC. 475. Under the penal code, section 397 (as amended in 1893), providing that "every person who sells or furnishes * * * intoxicating liquors to any Indian is guilty of a felony," an information charging that defendant did "willfully and unlawfully sell and furnish intoxicating liquor * * * to two Indians," etc., is sufficient without naming the Indians. *People v. Faust, 45 Pacific Reporter, 261.*

SEC. 476. Under act of Congress of March 3, 1885 (23 Stat. L., 385) giving Territorial and Federal courts jurisdiction to punish Indians for murder and other crimes committed by one Indian against another, whether on or off a reservation, an Indian, tribal or otherwise, is amenable to State jurisdiction for the murder of another Indian outside of the reservation within the State.   *Pablo v. People, 46 Pa. Rep., 636.*

SEC. 477. It is sufficient, in an indictment for murder, to charge that the deceased was a "Wyandot Indian whose name is to the jurors unknown," without averring that the deceased was a human being.

Reed v. The State, 16 Ark., 499.

SEC. 478. Where an indictment for murder describes the deceased as a Wyandot Indian, the description is material, and the race of the accused must be proved as alleged.   *Ibid.*

SEC. 479. The court judicially knows that a "Wyandot Indian" is a human being, and especially when it is alleged that he was in the peace of the State and was murdered.   *Ibid.*

SEC. 480. Where an indictment for murder describes the deceased as a Wyandot Indian, such description may be proved by reputation; and although it would not be sufficient if the witness stated that "he did not know except from what he had heard" that the deceased was a Wyandot Indian, yet the jury would be warranted in finding the fact where a witness stated "that he had heard from those with the Indian who was killed that he was a Wyandot Indian," when it was in proof that there was a band of Indians encamped together, of whom the deceased was one.   *Ibid.*

SEC. 481. When a thief takes property stolen in Arkansas into the Indian Territory, with continuing intent to appropriate it to his own use, the Federal court at Fort Smith and the State court of the county in which the property is stolen, have concurrent jurisdiction to try him for the larceny, and the court first obtaining possession of the case will not be interfered with by the other. But if the Federal court, or the judge at chambers, after making the arrest releases him before trial to the State officers, the State court may proceed to trial and conviction.   *Elmore v. State, 45 Ark., 243.*

SEC. 482. There is no law of the Cherokee Nation making it an offense for one to shoot another's mule trespassing on his premises.

Carter v. Goode, 50 Ark., 155.

SEC. 483. The act of April 22, 1850, conferring on justices of the peace the power to punish Indians convicted of larceny by whipping, is by necessary implication repealed by act of 1856, which prescribes the punishment for both grand and petit larceny. The act of April 20, 1863, concerning courts of justice of this State, confers upon the county courts jurisdiction to try and determine indictments for grand larceny, and in effect it takes from justices of the peace the jurisdiction of grand larceny attempted to be conferred upon them by the act of April 22, 1850.   *The People v. Juan Antonio, 27 Cal., 404.*

SEC. 484. The fact that the deceased and the defendant were both Indians does not deprive the superior court of jurisdiction over the defendant charged with murder committed within its jurisdiction.

People v. Turner, 85 Cal., 432.

SEC. 485. A forged order for the delivery of intoxicating liquor to bearer is, upon its face, capable of being used to defraud those who may act upon it as genuine, and is within the statute against forgery; and the fact that the defendants accused of the forgery are Indians, and that the furnishing of intoxicating liquor to Indians is positively prohibited by law and made a felony, does not prevent the order from being the subject of forgery; and the fact that it was presented and passed by the defendants is a false factor as to its being a subject of forgery, and the defendants may be properly convicted of forgery.

People v. James, 110 Cal., 157.

SEC. 486. The Territory of Colorado is not a place or district of country under the sole and exclusive jurisdiction of the United States within the meaning of section 3 of the act of Congress of 1790 (1 Stat. L., 113), and an indictment based upon said section, in which it is alleged that the murder was committed "at the said county of Gilpin," without further description of the place, or without any averment as to the jurisdiction of the United States, is not sufficient.

Franklin v. United States, 1 Colo., 35.

SEC. 487. The selling or giving spirituous liquors to an Indian under the charge of an Indian agent by the statutes of the United States is a misdemeanor, not a felony. An indictment describing a thing by its general term is supported by proof of a species which is clearly comprehended within such description. If the indictment charges that the defendant sold, to wit, one pint of whisky, it is sustained if it be proved that he sold or gave to the Indian spirituous liquors.

Brugner v. United States, 1 Dakota (Bennett), 5.

SEC. 488. On a trial for homicide (Fleury, a half-breed Indian, in his house on Fort Buford Reservation) a witness for the prosecution, being the only person present at the shooting, on cross-examination for the purpose of affecting his credulity, was asked certain questions tending to show that she had married one A at the age of 13 years and had never been divorced from him; that thereafter she had lived with one B for several years as his wife, until he, becoming jealous, shot and dangerously wounded her, and then shot and killed himself; that subsequently she had lived with deceased as his wife, for a time, and then married him; such cross-examination being excluded by the trial court. *Held,* to be error.

United States v. Wood, 4 Dakota (Smith), 455.

SEC. 489. A district court has jurisdiction over Indian reservations in any organized county of this Territory, and its process may run and be served there if there be no treaty to the contrary with the Indians thereof.

Hyde v. Harkness, 1 Prichett (Idaho), 536.

SEC. 490. Where one member of the "United Tribes" (Kaskaskia, Piankashaw, and Wea) killed another member in the State of Kansas, outside of an Indian reservation, the offender can not claim more than a foreigner whose nation has treaty relations with us that there are no general exemptions of foreigners from the duty of observing our laws, while here; and law binds and protects alike all persons, native or foreign, found within our territory (Bishop, Crim. Law, secs. 584, 593), to which rule Indians are subject.   *Hunt v. The State, 4 Kans., 60.*

SEC. 491. There is no law, or regulation of the President, that makes it a punishable offense for an Indian to leave his reservation to go to Washington, at his own expense, against the order of the Commissioner of Indian Affairs.
Wiley v. Keokuk, 6 Kans., 94.   Wiley v. Man-a-to-wah, 6 Kans., 111.

SEC. 492. While keeping the peace and disobeying no law, human or divine, an Indian can not be the subject of arrest or imprisonment by anyone, except at the peril of the offender. His rights are regulated by law, and when he appeals to the law for redress it is not in the power of any tribunal to say "you are an Indian, and your rights rest in the arbitrary decrees of executive officers and not in the law."   *Ibid.*

SEC. 493. By article 7 of the Cherokee treaty of 1866 (14 Stat. L., 799) it is provided that the United States district court nearest to the Cherokee Nation shall have exclusive original jurisdiction of all civil and criminal cases.   *Holderman v. Pond, 45 Kans., 411.*

SEC. 494. An action for the conversion of certain corn grown and standing upon land in the Indian Territory, leased in violation of law and the treaty of 1866 with the Cherokees (14 Stat. L., 799), brought by a citizen of Kansas against a person residing in said Territory, but personally served with summons, can not be maintained in Kansas.
Ibid.

SEC. 495. The primary right of the plaintiff below to recover rested upon a tort committed where the remedy was confined to the nearest United States district court, which had exclusive original jurisdiction.
Ibid.

SEC. 496. The tort charged and the remedy must be determined by the law of the Territory where the wrong was committed. The rule is well settled that if there is no right to recover for alleged injuries in the State or Territory where they are said to have been committed, there can be none in any other State; and if the State in which the alleged injuries are committed has declared the consequences and defined the liabilities therefor, that law must govern.   *Ibid.*

SEC. 497. In an indictment, under the act of 1830, prohibiting any persons other than Indians from making settlements within their territory it is necessary to aver that the defendant is not an Indian.
The State v. Craft, 1 Miss. (Walker), 409.

SEC. 498. By statutes of Mississippi (1858, p. 180) the crime of rape was extended to Indian women.   *George v. State, 37 Miss., 316.*

SEC. 499. The character of the Indian Territory was discussed in the case of United States *v.* Rogers (4 How., 567), and it was adjudged that the Territory is within the territorial limits of the United States, and that the Indian tribes residing therein were subject to their authority and Congress may by law punish offenses committed there, whether the offender be a white man or an Indian.
                Tush-ho-yo-tubby v. Barr, 45 Miss., 189.

SEC. 500. Upon the trial of the appellant under an indictment charging him with selling, unlawfully, spirituous liquor to an Indian in the Indian country, the affidavit of the district attorney, in support of his motion for a continuance, set forth that he could not proceed to a trial without the testimony of absent witnesses who would testify that they saw the appellant so sell said liquor. The appellant, in open court, then offered to admit that the witnesses, if present, would testify to the facts stated in the affidavit, and the motion was denied. *Held*, that the affidavit was admissible as evidence against the appellant upon the trial.   *United States v. Sacramento, 2 Mon., 239.*

SEC. 501. The Federal courts have no jurisdiction of the crime of larceny alleged to have been committed on an Indian reservation in the State of Nebraska.   *Painter v. Ives, 4 Nebraska, 122.*

SEC. 502. The courts of this State have jurisdiction and authority to try and punish persons for crimes committed on Indian reservations within the State.   *Marion v. The State, 20 Nebraska, 233.*

SEC. 503. The courts of this State have no authority to prosecute or punish one Indian for a crime committed against another on the reservation to which they each belong so long as they maintain their tribal relations.   *Ex parte Jesse Cross, 20 Nebr., 417.*

SEC. 504. The State courts may be given jurisdiction by the legislature over crimes committed by an Indian against the person and property of another Indian by extending the criminal laws over them.
                State v. McKenny, 18 Nev., 182.

SEC. 505. There is no statute (State) extending the criminal laws over the Indian tribes, or the individuals thereof. The statute under which the indictment is found is the general act concerning crimes and punishments.   *Ibid.*

SEC. 506. The territory had a right to subject tribal Indians, like other persons, to punishment for crimes against its own citizens. (What. Conf. Laws, 252.)   *Ibid.*

SEC. 507. The State of Tennessee was admitted into the Union in 1796 "on an equal footing with the original States in all respects whatsoever." In 1833 the legislature extended the civil jurisdiction of several counties to include the territory within the occupancy of the

Cherokee Indians. The statute also gave the courts jurisdiction of three crimes committed within the Indian country—murder, rape, and larceny—but allowed to the Indians their usages and customs in all other respects. *Ibid.*

SEC. 508. The courts of this State have no jurisdiction to try an Indian belonging to a tribe which is recognized and treated with as such by the Government of the United States, having its chief and tribal laws for killing another Indian belonging to the same tribe.

Ibid.

SEC. 509. As both Indians were under the authority and subjection of such tribal laws, the authorities of the tribe alone have the right to take cognizance of the crime. It was not the intention of the legislature that the Territorial or State laws defining crimes and providing for their punishment should apply to crimes committed by Indians against each other living in their tribal relations. The courts of this State could only obtain jurisdiction of such offenses by an act of the legislature or self-acting clause of the constitution. *Ibid.*

SEC. 510. The murder by an uncivilized Mescalero Apache Indian of a white man, within an Indian reservation and the Territory of New Mexico, is an offense within the jurisdiction of the Territorial court, sitting as a district or circuit court of the United States, and not within the jurisdiction of such court sitting as a court of the Territory. *United States v. Monte, 3 N. Mex. (Johnson), 126. Same (Gild.), 173.*

SEC. 511. In an action brought to recover for an assault and battery, both of the parties being members of the Seneca Nation of Indians, the jury estimated the damages of the plaintiff at the sum of $325. An exception was taken by the defendant to the denial of a motion made by him for a nonsuit upon the ground that the plaintiff has brought the action by attorney other than the "Attorney of the Seneca Nation of Indians," in violation of section 2 of chapter 150, laws of 1845. *Held,* That the motion was properly denied, as, by section 14 of chapter 365, of 1847, any Indian of said nation who had any demand or right of action which exceeded the amount which might be awarded by the peacemakers was authorized to maintain and prosecute actions in the courts of this State, in the same manner and with the like effect as between white citizens.

Jemmison v. Kennedy, 55 Hun. (N. Y.), 47.

SEC. 512. A number of Indians had been taken at a dance house and a fight had occurred there to which the prisoner and the deceased were parties; at the breaking up of the dance the prisoner and another, who was also charged with the murder, were walking together toward their homes, when the deceased came up, and another fight ensued between the prisoner and his companion on one side and the deceased upon the other, in the course of which the killing occurred. *Held,*

I. That these facts constituted no evidence of a combination between the persons charged to commit the homicide.

II. That it was error to instruct the jury that if there were previous malice on the part of the prisoner toward the deceased, then, even in case the prisoner fought in self-defense, he was guilty of murder; and as the court to which the prisoner appealed could not tell how much the latter may have been prejudiced by the charge, even where the verdict was for manslaughter only, a new trial should be granted.

State v. Ta cha na tah, 3 Phillips (64 N. C.), 614.

SEC. 513. The Cherokee Indians who reside in North Carolina are subject to its laws. Cohabitation between an Indian man and woman, according to the ancient customs of their tribe, which leave the parties free to dissolve the connection at pleasure, is not marriage, and therefore the parties to such relation may be compelled to testify against each other. *Ibid.*

SEC. 514. Section 2139, Revised Statutes, is applicable to all Indians who are in any degree under the control or charge of an Indian agent. The fact that an Indian received allotted lands in Kansas in the year of 1866 and took the oath of allegiance to the United States, and became an elector of the State of Kansas, and is above the age of 21 years, is not sufficient to take him out of the inhibition contained in that section, provided he has not been released by the Government from the charge, supervision, and control of an Indian agent. Neither does the fact that an Indian may be living upon allotted land and not drawing any annuity from the Government authorize the sale to such Indian of intoxicating liquors, provided such Indian is still under the supervision or control of an Indian agent.

Renfrow v. United States, 3 Okla. (Dale), 161.

SEC. 515. One who sells liquors to Indians may be punished for the same act under the law of the Territory and the law of the United States. *Territory of Oregon v. Coleman, 1 Oreg. (Wilson), 192.*

SEC. 516. W., jr., without authority, introduced upon an Indian reservation a quantity of spirituous liquors. N., the Indian agent in charge of said reservation, arrested him and seized the wagon and team which were conveying said liquors. His father, claiming to be the owner of the team and harness, brought an action against the agent for a wrongful taking and detention. *Held,* that under section 2140, Revised Statutes, the agent had the right, if W., jr., belonged to either of the classes of persons named in said section, to so seize said team, harness, and wagon. In justifying the seizure under the acts aforesaid it was necessary to allege that W., jr., was either a "white person" or an "Indian." Under the code, matter which constitutes only a partial defense may be set up by way of answer, but in such case it should be pleaded as a partial defense. By surrendering the team and

harness to W., sr., the agent did not waive his right to justify the original taking aforesaid.   *Webb v. Nickerson, 11 Oregon (Odeneal), 382.*

Sec. 517. A person committing larceny in a foreign country and con-
verting the stolen property to his own use in this State, either personally or by innocent agents, is guilty of larceny in this State.
                                         Oregon v. Barnett, 15 Oregon (Holmes), 77.

Sec. 518. The South Carolina law of 1740, providing for the trial of
offenses committed by negro and mulatto slaves by a court composed
of a magistrate and two freeholders, did not apply to free Indians.
                          Gray v. Magistrates and Freeholders, 3 McCord (S. C.), 175.

Sec. 519. Free Indians in South Carolina have invariably been tried
by a judge and jury, and not under the act of 1740, by justices and
freeholders.   *State v. Belmont, 4 Strob. (S. C.), 445.*

Sec. 520. If under tribal laws an Indian be put to death in the Indian
Territory by another, under circumstances which by the laws of the
State would make such homicide a murder, the slayer is not punishable by the law of the State, though the fact were perpetrated within
its limits, for he has acted agreeably to the law of his nation.
                                         Holland v. Pack, 1 Peck (Tenn.), 119.

Sec. 521. By the Indian nations, war, when lawfully declared, is conducted according to the forms and usages which they themselves have
established, and when made captives they are treated as prisoners of
war and not as offenders against the laws of this State or of the United
States.   *Ibid.*

Sec. 522. When a man put up at an inn in the Cherokee Nation, and
his horse was missing in the morning, if he sues in the courts of this
State he must show what his rights and the defendants' responsibilities
are by the law of the Cherokees.   *Ibid.*

Sec. 523. If war be declared by the Cherokee Nation and one of
them kill one of the people against whom war is declared, he is not
subject to punishment as a criminal therefor, because he is acting under
the authority and laws of his nation.   *Ibid.*

Sec. 524. An Indian by carrying on war against us can not be
treated as a traitor or rebel, and he is only then subject to our law
when he comes within the limits of the State and beyond the territories of his own nation.   *Ibid.*

Sec. 525. The act of 1833 (Tennessee) extending the criminal laws
of the State so as to give jurisdiction to the courts of the State over
certain crimes committed within the Indian Territory by any Cherokee
Indian residing therein is constitutional.
                                         State v. Foreman, 8 Yer. (Tenn.), 256.

Sec. 526. It was admitted that the property belonged to the appellant at the time it was stolen, and that he demanded it of the appellee
soon after its recapture from the Indians, but the restoration was

refused upon the alleged ground that the taking and possession by the Indians for more than twenty-four hours divested the right and ownership of the appellant, and that the recapture vested the property in the recaptors, of whom appellee was one. *Held*, that if recaptors of property from the grasp of the Indian robber were entitled to the full benefit of *postliminium*, with its rigid and unqualified rule of limitation against the rights of the original owner, it would be indirectly holding out inducements to the commission of the offenses against which the laws should provide a penalty. The depraved and discontented of all classes and nations would thus have a premium held out to them to encourage Indian robberies. We can not regard this case in any other way than as a robbery coming strictly within the rules of the municipal law, and which entitles the owner of stolen property, upon the establishment of his title according to the mode there pointed out, to be restored to his original rights.

Dass v. Craddock, 1 Dallam (Texas), 592.

SEC. 527. The criminal laws of the State extend to all parts of the State, including the Oneida Reservation.

State v. Harris, 36 Conover (Wis.), 298.

CHAPTER IV.—REGULATIONS AS TO TRADE AND OTHER MATTERS.

SEC. 528. Proof that spirituous liquors were carried into the Indian country by an Indian trader and were there found among his goods is *prima facie* proof of the violation of the act of March 30, 1802 (2 Stat. L., 139), and throws the burden of proof upon him.

Sundry Goods v. United States, 2 Pet., 358.

SEC. 529. Where an Indian trader carries spirituous liquors into an Indian country in violation of act of 1802 (2 Stat. L., 139), all his goods there are forfeited, and not merely those among which the liquors are found. *Ibid.*

SEC. 530. Under the act of Congress of 1802 (2 Stat. L., 139), a seizure of *ardent spirits* belonging to an Indian trader can not be made in a territory purchased by the United States of the Indians, although inhabited exclusively by the Indians. *Ibid.*

SEC. 531. The Cherokee Nation can maintain a suit in the Supreme Court of the United States against the State of Georgia, founded on a violation of their rights under the operation of the act of that State, and the process of injunction may issue to stay the execution of the statute.   *Cherokee Nation v. Georgia, 1 Appendix, "Cherokee Cases," 225.*

Sec. 532. If one of the United States violates the treaties of the Nation made with the Indian tribes or the security afforded to them under the intercourse act of 1802 (2 Stat. L., 139) by attacking their national privileges and rights of property, there must be a civil remedy within the contemplation of law, or the Government would be lamentably imperfect in its organization and competence. It would be destitute of ordinary means of self-preservation.   *Ibid.*

SEC. 533. The Constitution evidently intended to reach and cover all controversies between two or more States, or between one of them and a foreign state, by the interposition and reasoning powers of the courts of justice; and controversies between the States and Indian tribes are within the reason and policy of the provision.   *Ibid.*

SEC. 534. The judicial power extends originally to controversies "between a State and foreign state, citizens or subjects." In those cases in which a "State shall be a party," the Supreme Court had, and still has, original jurisdiction. But by the amendment to the Constitution, the judicial power does not extend to any suit in law or equity commenced or prosecuted against one of the United States by citizens of another State, "or by citizens or subjects of any foreign state," leaving thereby the judicial power as it originally stood in respect to "controversies between a State and foreign states."   *Ibid.*

SEC. 535. If the Supreme Court has original jurisdiction in the case it follows, of course, that they may grant an injunction on a bill filed by the Cherokee Nation, and stating their right and title. The process would go to restrain the officers of Georgia, under the law of that State, from executing any process within the Indian Territory incompatible with their rights and privileges as heretofore enjoyed and recognized by the laws and treaties of the United States.   *Ibid.*

SEC. 536. In 1776 Congress admonished the Indians that "their safety as nations depended on their preserving peace and friendship with the white people of this land;" they declare that they will take all the care in their power that no interruption or disturbance be given to their security and settlement, and that none of the white people should be suffered by force or fraud to deprive them of any of their land, or settle them without a fair purchase and their free consent. Congress particularly guaranteed to the Delawares all their Territorial rights in the most ample manner as bounded by former treaties.   *Ibid.*

SEC. 537. In 1776 Congress undertook to regulate trade with the Indians and prevent any "unjust advantage of their distress and intemperance," and to declare that no traders should go into the Indian territories without license, etc.   *Ibid.*

SEC. 538. The Articles of Confederation gave to Congress what indeed they had before asserted, the full and exclusive right and power of determining on war and peace, and entering into treaties and alliances; and the exclusive power of "regulating the trade and managing all affairs with the Indians not members of any of the States, provided that the legislative right of any State within its own limits be not infringed or violated."   *Ibid.*

SEC. 539. In 1788 Congress, by proclamation, declared its determination to protect the Cherokees in their rights under the treaty of November 28, 1785 (7 Stat. L., 18), and to employ force, if necessary, to drive off intruders upon their lands and hunting grounds. *Ibid.*

SEC. 540. Georgia had been a member of the Union from July, 1775, and was equally bound with the other States of the Confederacy to all the acts, resolutions, and treaties of the Federal head. There had been a question raised by the States of North Carolina and Georgia respecting the construction of the sixth article of the Confederation, giving to Congress the right "to regulate trade and manage affairs with the Indians." The article had been differently construed by Congress and these two States, and the latter had actually pursued measures in conformity to their own construction, for North Carolina had undertaken to assign land to the Cherokees, and Georgia had proceeded to treat with the Creeks concerning their lands. *Ibid.*

SEC. 541. The Constitution put an end to the difficulty arising from the words in the Articles of Confederation "By Indians not citizens of any State," by dropping the obnoxious proviso and vesting in the Government the exclusive power to declare war, to make treaties, and to regulate commerce with the Indian tribes. *Ibid.*

SEC. 542. In pursuance of the general powers conferred by the Constitution, Congress, as early as July, 1790, passed a law (1 Stat. L., 137) to regulate trade and intercourse with the Indian tribes, and to declare void all sales of lands by any tribe or nation of Indians within the United States to any person *or State* except under the like authority. *Ibid.*

SEC. 543. For laws of the State of Georgia respecting the Cherokee Indians and their lands in that State, see "Peters Cherokee case." Appendix IV, section 281–286.

SEC. 544. The power of regulating the whole intercourse between the United States and the Cherokee Nation is, by our Constitution and laws, vested in the Government of the United States.

Worcester v. Georgia, 6 Peters 515.

SEC. 545. The Federal Government has the exclusive regulation of the intercourse with the Indians, and so long as this power shall be exercised it can not be obstructed by a State. But if a contingency shall occur which shall render the Indians who reside in a State incapable of self-government, either by moral degradation or reduction of their numbers, it would undoubtedly be in the power of a State government to extend to them the *ægis* of its laws, and under such circumstances the agency of the General Government, of necessity, must cease. *Ibid.*

SEC. 546. On August 7, 1786, an ordinance for the regulation of the Indian affairs was adopted which repealed the former system. *Ibid.*

SEC. 547. The Cherokee Nation is a distinct community, occupying its own territory, with boundaries accurately described, in which the law of Georgia can have no force, and which the citizens of Georgia have no right to enter but with the assent of the Cherokees themselves, or in conformity with the treaties and the acts of Congress; the whole intercourse between the United States and this nation is, by our Constitution and laws, vested in the Government of the United States.

Ibid.

SEC. 548. Congress has passed acts to regulate trade and intercourse with the Indians which treat them as nations, respect their rights, and manifest a firm purpose to afford the protection which treaties stipulate; all these acts, and especially that of 1802 (2 Stat. L., 139), manifestly consider the several Indian tribes as distinct political communities, having territorial boundaries in which their authority is exclusive, and having a right to all the lands within those boundaries, which is not only acknowledged, but guaranteed by the United States.   *Ibid.*

SEC. 549. The Indian intercourse laws act upon our own citizens, and not upon the Indians, the same as laws restrictive of trade passed under the constitutional power to regulate commerce with foreign nations act upon our own citizens in foreign commercial intercourse.

Ibid.

SEC. 550. The relations between the Indians and the Government of Spain were considered as matters of deepest political concern, in no wise connected with its fiscal operations. The commerce with the Indians was intrusted exclusively to the governors of the Spanish provinces. It was a part of his oath, as prescribed by the law of the Indies, "that you shall take care of the welfare, increase, and protection of the Indians."   *Mitchel v. United States, 9 Peters, 711.*

SEC. 551. The act of the War Department in requiring that the fractional section on which trading houses for conveniently carrying on trade with the Indians to be reserved was in legal contemplation the act of the President. The President speaks and acts through the heads of the several departments in relation to subjects appertaining to their several duties.   *Wilcox v. McConnel, 13 Peters, 496.*

SEC. 552. The money appropriated to the payment of the Cherokee Indians upon their removal and cession of their lands was properly public money, and within the provisions of the statutes as to commissions upon its disbursement.   *Minis v. United States, 15 Peters, 423; 10—791.*

SEC. 553. Indian trade within the province of Louisiana while that province belonged to Spain was regulated by ordinance from the King, and one Todd had obtained, prior to 1796, the privilege to carry on the Indian trade within said province and to exclude others from doing so without his consent.   *Chonteau v. Molony, 16 Howard, 203.*

SEC. 554. The policy of the act of February 12, 1862 (12 Stat. L., 139), is the protection of those Indians, who are, by treaties or otherwise, under the pupilage of the Government, from the debasing influence of the use of spirits, and it is not easy to perceive why that policy should not require their preservation from this, to them, destructive poison, when they are outside a reservation as well as within it. The evil effect is the same in both cases.

United States v. Holliday, 3 Wallace, 407.

SEC. 555. The constitutional power of Congress extends to the regulation of commerce with the Indian tribes and with the individual members of such tribes, although the traffic and the Indians with whom it is carried on are wholly within the territorial limits of a State.

Ibid.

SEC. 556. Where an Indian to whom liquor was sold had a piece of land on which he lived, and voted in county and town elections as he was authorized to do by the laws of the State, still, if he lived with his tribe and received his annuity, he was a member of his tribe and under the charge of an Indian agent. *Ibid.*

SEC. 557. By the act of February 12, 1862 (12 Stat. L., 338), Congress intended to make it penal to sell spirituous liquors to an Indian under charge of an Indian agent, although it was sold outside of any Indian reservation and within the limits of a State. The said act is constitutional, and is based on the power of Congress to regulate commerce with the Indian tribes. *Ibid.*

SEC. 558. Commerce is undoubtedly traffic; but it is something more, it is intercourse. The law of February 12, 1862 (12 Stat. L., 338), amending section 20 of the act of June 30, 1834 (4 Stat. L., 729), professes to regulate traffic and intercourse with the Indian tribes. It manifestly does both; it relates to buying and selling and exchanging commodities, which is the essence of all commerce, and it regulates the intercourse between the citizens of the United States and those tribes, which is another branch of commerce, and a very important one. *Ibid.*

SEC. 559. Commerce with Indian tribes means commerce (which includes traffic and intercourse) between citizens of the United States and the individuals composing those tribes, and the act of February 12, 1862 (12 Stat. L., 338), amending the intercourse act of June 30, 1834 (4 Stat. L., 729), describes this precise kind of traffic or commerce, and therefore comes within the terms of the constitutional provision giving Congress the power to "regulate commerce with the Indian tribes." *Ibid.*

SEC. 560. The facts show distinctly "that the Secretary of the Interior and Commissioner of Indian Affairs deem that it is necessary, in order to carry into effect the provisions of said treaty, that the tribal organization should be preserved." In reference to all matters of this kind, it is the rule of this court to follow the action of the executive and other political departments of the Government, whose more especial duty it is to determine such affairs. If by them those Indians are recognized as a tribe, this court must do the same. If they are a tribe, then, by the Constitution, they are placed for certain purposes within the control of the laws of Congress. This control extends to the subject of regulating the liquor traffic with them, and this power residing in Congress that body is necessarily supreme in its exercise.   *Ibid.*

SEC. 561. The act of July 20, 1868 (15 Stat. L., 125), imposing taxes on distilled spirits, tobacco, etc., applies to the country of the Cherokee Nation and is valid, notwithstanding the treaty with that Nation.   *Boudinot v. United States, 11 Wallace, 616.*

SEC. 562. Congress, under its constitutional power to regulate commerce with the Indian tribes, may not only prohibit the unlicensed introduction and sale of spirituous liquors in the "Indian country," but extend such prohibition to territory in proximity to that occupied by the Indians.   *United States v. 43 Gallons Whisky, 93 U. S., 188.*

SEC. 563. Of necessity, the limitation in the Articles of Confederation on the power of the United States to regulate the trade and manage all affairs with the Indians rendered the power of no practical value; but Congress now 'has the exclusive and absolute power to regulate the commerce with the Indian tribes, which is a power as broad and as free from restrictions as that to regulate commerce with a foreign nation.   *Ibid.*

SEC. 564. The power of Congress to regulate commerce with the Indian tribes is in no wise affected by the magnitude of the traffic or the extent of the intercourse; as long as these Indians remain a distinct people, with an existing tribal organization, recognized by the political department of the Government, Congress has the power to say with whom and on what terms they shall deal and what articles shall be contraband.   *Ibid.*

SEC. 565. Traffic with Indians is so profitable that white men are constantly encroaching on Indian territory to engage in it. The difficulty of preventing this intrusion and procuring convictions for offenses committed on the confines of civilization are the obstacles in the way of carrying into effect the intercourse laws.   *Ibid.*

SEC. 566. It is competent for the United States, in the exercise of the treaty-making power, to stipulate in a treaty with an Indian tribe that within the territory thereby ceded the laws of the United States, then or thereafter enacted, prohibiting the introduction and sale of spirituous liquors in the Indian country shall be in full force and effect until otherwise directed by Congress or the President of the United States; and such stipulation operates *proprio vigore*, and is binding upon the courts, although the ceded territory is situated within an organized county of a State.   *Ibid.*

SEC. 567. It has been decided by this court (2 Pets., 314) "that a treaty is to be regarded in courts of justice as equivalent to an act of the legislature whenever it operates of itself without the aid of any legislative provision." No legislation is required to put the seventh article of the Chippewa treaty of 1863 (13 Stat. L., 667) in force, and it must become a rule of action if the contracting parties had power to incorporate it in the treaty. *Ibid.*

SEC. 568. The principle that Federal jurisdiction must be everywhere the same under the same circumstances, has not been departed from in the seventh article of the Chippewa treaty of 1863 (13 Stat. L., 667). The prohibition contained therein rests on grounds which, so far from making a distinction between the States, apply to them all alike. The fact that the ceded territory lies within the limits of Minnesota is a mere incident, for the act of Congress incorporated into the treaty applies alike to all Indian tribes occupying a particular country, whether within or without State lines. *Ibid.*

SEC. 569. The tribes for whom the act of 1834 (4 Stat. L., 729) was made were those semidependent tribes whom our Government has always recognized as exempt from our laws whether within the limits of an organized State or Territory, and, in regard to their domestic government, left to their own rules and traditions, in whom we have recognized the capacity to make treaties, and with whom the Governments, State and national, deal, with few exceptions only, in their national or tribal character, and not as individuals.

United States v. Joseph, 94 U. S., 614.

SEC. 570. The court being informed who they are by the description of them in the petition, as "pueblo Indians of the pueblo of Taos," is not bound, by the use of the additional word "tribe," to disregard that knowledge and assume that they are tribal Indians within the meaning of the statute regulating the intercourse of the white man with this latter class of Indians. *Ibid.*

SEC. 571. It is clear that the eleventh section of the act of June 30, 1834 (4 Stat. L., 729), could have no application to the Seneca or Oneida Indians of New York. *Ibid.*

SEC. 572. Military officers can no more protect themselves than civilians for wrongs committed in time of peace under orders emanating from a source which is itself without authority in the premises. Hence a military officer seizing liquors supposed to be in the Indian country, when they are not, is liable to an action as a trespasser.

Bate v. Clark, 95 U. S., 204.

SEC. 573. If the place where the whisky was seized had been Indian country and it had turned out that the plaintiff below had a license or did not intend to sell or introduce the goods, the fact that the defendants acted on reasonable grounds would have exempted them from liability; but the plaintiffs violated no law in having the whisky for sale at the place where it was seized, and the plea that the defendants had good reason to believe that it was Indian country, and that they acted in good faith, while it might excuse them from punitory damages is no defense to the action.   *Ibid.*

Sec. 574. There may be no good reason for any longer restricting the liability of the United States under sections 2154 and 2155 to acts of whites, but until Congress sees fit to change the statute in this particular the courts are not at liberty to disregard the law as it is left to stand.   *United States v. Perriman, 100 U. S., 235.*

Sec. 575. The United States, under sections 2154 and 2155 of the Revised Statutes, is not liable to pay the value of property stolen by a negro from a friendly Indian within the Indian country. Those sections relate only to crimes committed by white persons.   *Ibid.*

Sec. 576. The establishment of a collection district embracing Indian country did not authorize—nor was it intended to authorize— business which was otherwise specifically forbidden.
                            United States v. 43 Gals. Whiskey, 108 U. S., 491.

Sec. 577. The unauthorized introduction of liquors into territory ceded in the Chippewa treaty of October 2, 1863 (13 Stat. L., 667), constitutes the offense, although if they were not sold or given away no injurious consequences would follow; but once allow them to be indiscriminately or generally introduced, and the law would be evaded without the possibility of detection. The introduction is therefore forbidden, unless permitted by order of the War Department or of some officer of that Department authorized by it.   *Ibid.*

Sec. 578. The evils resulting from the use of spirituous liquors are so many and so appalling that the Government has, from an early period of our history, labored to prevent their introduction among the Indians, and in order more effectually to secure this result, laws prescribing severe penalties have been enacted and authority vested in the Indian agents to arrest traffickers in the prohibited article, and to seize and confiscate their property found with it. It would require very clear expressions in any general legislation to authorize the inference that Congress purposed to depart from its long-established policy in regard to a matter of so vital importance to the peace and to the material and moral well-being of these wards of the nation.   *Ibid.*

Sec. 579. The Second Auditor of the Treasury is charged by law with the duty of receiving and examining all accounts relating to Indian affairs and transmitting them to the Second Comptroller for his decision thereon.   *United States v. Brindle, 110 U. S., 688.*

Sec. 580. It would be a strained construction of the constitutional clause to hold that a system of criminal laws for Indians living peaceably on their reservations, which left out the entire code of trade and intercourse laws justly enacted under that provision, and establish punishments for certain common-law crimes of the higher degrees, without any reference to their relation to any kind of commerce, was authorized by the grant of power to regulate commerce with the Indian tribes. *United States v. Kagama, 118 U. S., 375.*

SEC. 581. The railroad authorized by the act of 1884 (23 Stat. L., 73) to be constructed and maintained will have, if constructed and operated, direct relation to commerce with the Indian tribes, as well as with commerce among the States, especially with the States immediately north and south of the Indian Territory, and while it is true that the company authorized to construct and maintain it is a corporation created by the laws of a State, it is none the less a fit instrumentality to accomplish the public objects contemplated by the act, and therefore it was in the power of Congress to adopt it as a means conducive to that end. *Cherokee Nation v. So. Kan. Ry. Co., 135 U. S., 641.*

SEC. 582. Such enactments as sections 2103, 2104, and 2105 of the Revised Statutes, intended to protect the Indians from improvident and unconscionable contracts, by no means create a legal obligation on the part of the United States to see that the Indians perform their part of such contracts. *In re Sanborn, 148 U. S., 222.*

SEC. 583. Lager beer is not " spirituous liquors" nor " wine" within the meaning of those terms as used in section 2139 of the Revised Statutes. *Sarlls v. United States, 152 U. S., 570. In re McDonough, 49 Fed. Rep., 360.*

SEC. 584. So far as popular usage goes, according to the leading authorities, " lager beer," as a malt liquor made by fermentation, is not included in the term " spirituous liquor," the result of distillation. *Ibid.*

SEC. 585. The act of Congress providing for the punishment of persons charged with selling liquor to Indians under charge of an Indian agent, duly appointed by the Government of the United States, has force and validity in this case. *United States v. Mayrand, 154 U. S., 552.*

SEC. 586. The disposition of spirituous liquors to an Indian, under the charge of an agent, who has abandoned his nomadic habits and tribal relations and adopted the habits of civilized life, violates section 2139 of the Revised Statutes. *United States v. Osborn, 2 Fed. Rep., 58.*

SEC. 587. An Indian occupying land in severalty, and voting at elections in the State of Michigan, can not be sold liquor without violation of the law. *Ibid.*

SEC. 588. The power of Congress to regulate the intercourse between the inhabitants of the United States and the Indian tribes therein is not limited by State lines or governments, but may be exercised and enforced wherever the subject—Indian tribes—exists. *United States v. Bridleman, 7 Fed. Rep., 894. United States v. Martin, 14 Fed. Rep., 817.*

SEC. 589. The power to regulate commerce with Indian tribes includes not only traffic in commodities, but intercourse with such tribes and the members thereof, and *vice versa*.   *Ibid.*

SEC. 590. The power of Congress to regulate commerce with the Indian tribes does not cease on their being included within the limits of a State, but the Federal jurisdiction must cease, or is lost, where the Indians occupy a very limited territory and are practically absorbed by the surrounding white population.   *Ibid.*

SEC. 591. The power of Congress to regulate commerce with the Indian tribes is coextensive with the subject, and applies to individuals constituting the tribes, although off a reservation and within the limits of a State, and therefore the act of 1864 (13 Stat. L., 29) for the punishment of a person who disposes of spirituous liquor to an Indian, under the charge of an agent, is constitutional, although the disposition took place within the limits of a State to an Indian not upon or belonging to a reservation.   *Ibid.*

SEC. 592. A search for and seizure of liquors under the provisions of section 2140 of the Revised Statutes, which provides for the enforcement of a penalty and forfeiture for introducing spirituous liquors and wines into the Indian country, in a case where the liquors found were not claimed to have been seized within the limits of an Indian reservation, was held unauthorized.   *43 Galls. Cognac Brandy, 11 Fed. Rep., 47.*

SEC. 593. The carrying of spirituous liquors into a territory purchased by the United States after March 30, 1802, although frequented and inhabited exclusively by Indians, is not an offense within the meaning of the acts of Congress so as to subject it to forfeiture.   (Note.)   *Ibid.*

SEC. 594. If Indians occupy territory of very limited extent, surrounded by a white population which necessarily have daily intercourse with them and it becomes impracticable to enforce the law, the Federal jurisdiction must cease.   (Note.)   *Ibid.*

SEC. 595. Congress may exercise its power to regulate commerce with the Indian tribes to the same extent as with foreign nations. (Note.)   *Ibid.*

SEC. 596. The circuit court having concurrent jurisdiction with the district court over crimes, has jurisdiction over the offense of selling liquor to Indians although jurisdiction may be vested by statute in the district court.   (Note.)   *Ibid.*

SEC. 597. By the act of March 3, 1873 (17 Stat. L., 530), the introduction of spirituous liquors and wine into Alaska is absolutely prohibited, except for Army uses; and *semble*, that section 2 of the Alaska act of June 27, 1868 (15 Stat. L., 250) (sec. 1954, Rev. Stat.), which gave the President "power to restrict and regulate or to prohibit the importation and use of distilled spirits" into Alaska, is still so far in force, notwithstanding the passage of said act of March 3, 1873 (17 Stat. L., 530), as to authorize him to permit the introduction of said spirits, but no more, as a regulation of the subject.

United States v. Stephens, 12 Fed. Rep., 52.

SEC. 598. The policy of the act (12 Stat. L., 338) is the protection of those Indians who are, by treaty or otherwise, under the pupilage of the Government, from the debasing influence of the use of spirits; and it is not easy to perceive why that policy should not require their preservation from this, to them, destructive poison, where they are outside of a reservation as well as within it. The evil effects are the same in both cases. *United States v. Earl, 17 Fed. Rep., 75.*

SEC. 599. The Government of the United States is charged with the duty of regulating intercourse between the Indian tribes and other inhabitants of the country, and to this end may inaugurate and pursue that policy in regard to such intercourse as may be for the best interest of all concerned. *Ibid.*

SEC. 600. It is the duty of Congress to regulate the intercourse with the Indians, and to that end may provide for the punishing the giving of spirituous liquor to them on or off a reservation within or without a State. *Ibid.*

SEC. 601. The United States has jurisdiction over intercourse with tribal Indians, and Congress may prohibit and provide for the punishment of acts relating to or affecting such intercourse anywhere in the United States. *United States v. Barnhart, 22 Fed. Rep., 285.*

SEC. 602. Act of March 3, 1873 (17 Stat. L., 530), extending to Alaska two sections of the act of June 30, 1834 (4 Stat. L., 729), known as the "Indian Intercourse Laws" and relating principally to the introduction of the liquor traffic among the Indians, is to be construed to make said territory "Indian country" only to the extent of the prohibited commerce, and did not put the Alaska Indians on general footing with Indians in other parts of United States.

In re Sah-Quah, 31 Fed. Rep., 327.

SEC. 603. By the treaty of 1855 (12 Stat. L., 948) the Umatilla Indians engaged to submit to any rule that might be prescribed by the United States for their government. This obviously includes the power to organize and maintain an Indian court and police and to specify the acts or conduct of which it shall have jurisdiction. This treaty is an "act" or "law" relating to Indian affairs; and by section 456 of the Revised Statutes the power to prescribe a rule for carrying the same into effect is given the President, who has exercised it in this case through the proper instrumentality, the Secretary of Interior.

United States v. Clapox, 35 Fed. Rep., 575.

SEC. 604. The Klamath Indian Reservation was not at the time of suit "Indian country" within the meaning of the Revised Statutes, section 2133, which prescribes the penalty for unauthorized trading in the Indian country.   *United States v. Rising Star Tea, etc., 38 Fed. Rep., 400.*

SEC. 605. In 1832 the Supreme Court, in Worcester *v.* State (6 Pets., 515), declared that the whole intercourse between the United States and an Indian nation was by our Constitution and laws vested in the Government of the United States, and that within the territory occupied by such Indians in the State of Georgia the laws of Georgia have no force unless with the assent of the Indians themselves, so in conformity with treaties and acts of Congress.   *Benson v. United States, 44 Fed. Rep., 178.*

SEC. 606. The purpose of the statute (section 2139, Revised Statutes) was undoubtedly to prevent the placing of whisky or spirituous liquors in such a place as would make them accessible to the Indians. It was not the purpose of that statute to interfere in any manner with the commerce in spirituous liquors between sections of the country not Indian.   The construction of that statute which would allow the seizure of liquors without reference to the purposes in regard to which it came there, would prevent the transportation of such liquors from the East to the Pacific coast on the line of the Northern Pacific Railroad.   *United States v. Whisky, etc., 45 Fed. Rep., 847.*

SEC. 607. The proper construction of section 2139, Revised Statutes, as to the terms, "No ardent spirits shall be introduced, under any pretense, into the Indian country," is as follows: Whenever such liquors are taken into an Indian country as their place of destination or use, then they have been introduced into such country. In other words, when such liquors reach an Indian country as the end of their journey, they have, within the meaning of the statute, been introduced into such country.   It is not necessary to show that they were brought there for the purpose of sale to the Indians or to anyone.   The transportation of such liquors through an Indian country, between places outside the same, as an article of commerce is not, within the meaning of that statute, introducing them into said country.   *Ibid.*

SEC. 608. Transporting ardent spirits as an article of commerce through an Indian country, between places outside of same, is not in violation of section 2139, Revised Statutes, which provides that "no ardent spirits shall be introduced, under any pretense, into the Indian country."   *Ibid.*

SEC. 609. The question is not one of power in the National Government, for, as has been shown, Congress may provide for the punishment of the crime (murder) wherever committed in the United States. Its jurisdiction is coextensive with the subject-matter, the intercourse between the white man and the tribal Indians is not limited to place or other circumstances.   *United States v. Thomas, 47 Fed. Rep., 488.*

SEC. 610. By the terms of the sections 2103 and 2104, Revised Statutes, no money belonging to Indians arising from the sale or lease of their lands, or claims growing out of or in reference to their annuities, etc., under laws or treaties of the United States, shall be paid to any agent or attorney by any officer of the United States, unless certain conditions are complied with.   Section 2105, Revised Statutes, prescribes the punishment for the violation of certain provisions of the preceding sections.   *Unitea States v. Crawford, 47 Fed. Rep., 561.*

SEC. 611. By the act of March 1, 1889 (25 Stat. L., 757), Congress intended to change the rule as prescribed by section 2103, Revised Statutes, and by said act it provided when a contract with an Indian or with an Indian tribe for the payment of money to an agent or attorney was a valid contract, and when money might be legally paid by an officer of the Government to an agent or attorney of an individual Indian or Indian tribe without violation of the law.   But the said act of 1889 (25 Stat. L., 757) was only intended to apply to the particular case embraced in the act of Congress, and said act used appropriate language to change the law as prescribed by section 2103, Revised Statutes, as far as the case in the act was concerned.   *Ibid.*

SEC. 612. If the money was paid by the officers of the Government, without the direction of the Creek National Council, it would be a payment of the money not in violation of the section, 2103 Revised Statutes, but of the act of March 1, 1889 (25 Stat. L., 757), and it would be a case where the Government should sue the party who wrongfully received the money for money had and received, but such suit could not be based on a cause of action arising under section 2103.
                                                                         Ibid.

SEC. 613. The compliance with the conditions of section 2103, Revised Statutes, requiring the approval of contracts by the Secretary of Interior and Commissioner of Indian Affairs, was unquestionably required up to March 1, 1889, when Congress passed an act (25 Stat. L., 757) authorizing the payment of a certain sum of money belonging to the Creek Nation, by the Secretary of the Treasury, to an agent or attorney, without the approval of the contract by the Secretary of Interior or Commissioner of Indian Affairs.   *Ibid.*

SEC. 614. In view of the general law as it stood at the time of the adoption by Congress of section 2103, Revised Statutes, the reasonable and just construction of the words "any court of the United States" at the time of their enactment was any circuit or district court where defendant might be found; but since the laws of 1789 (1 Stat. L., 73) and 1875 (18 Stat. L., 112), in regard to where suits may be brought, have been repealed by the laws of 1887 (24 Stat. L., 552) and 1888 (25 Stat. L., 434), the true and reasonable construction of the words "any court of the United States" seems to be any court of any district of which the party sued is an inhabitant, and that this must be so until Congress, by express legislation, authorizes the service of summons outside the district, and as this has not been done, the defendant is not in court and can not be brought in unless he becomes an inhabitant of the district, or voluntarily appears.   *Ibid.*

SEC. 615. All contracts or agreements made in violation of any of the conditions prescribed by the sections 2103 and 2104, Revised Statutes, are null and void, and it is because of the failure to comply with the provisions thereof requiring the approval of certain officers of the Government that this suit is brought.   *Ibid.*

SEC. 616. It would seem from the decision in United States *v.* McBratney (104 U. S., 621) that although a portion of a State was not excepted from the jurisdiction thereof by treaties or statutes, yet if occupied by Indians Congress might have jurisdiction over the same under its constitutional power to regulate commerce with the Indian tribes, and under any treaty made in pursuance of it. Under the last power it would appear that the offense charged in some way interfered with commerce with the Indian tribes. But the right to legislate for Indian country was not so limited.   *United States v. Partello, 48 Fed. Rep., 670.*

SEC. 617. An information lodged with the United States commissioner charged the accused with "introducing ten gallons of beer into the Indian country, the same being then and there spirituous liquor, in violation of section 2139." *Held,* That introducing spirituous liquors into an Indian country was an offense under section 2139; that the commissioner had jurisdiction over such offenses and the power to determine if beer is a spirituous liquor; and that his decision on that question could not be reviewed on writ of *habeas corpus.*
        In re Boyd, 49 Fed. Rep., 48.

SEC. 618. The act of July 4, 1884 (23 Stat. L., 94), declaring that section 2139 shall not be a bar to the prosecution of any officer, soldier, or employee of the Government who shall furnish "liquors, wines, beer, or any intoxicating beverage whatever to any Indian," is not a legislative construction of such section.
        In re McDonough, 49 Fed. Rep., 360.

SEC. 619. There are two cases which define "spirituous liquors" so as to include beer. They are Levin *v.* Ladne (3 Denis, 43), State *v.* Giersch (98 North Carolina, 720). In the first of these cases the court gives the definition of "beer" as defined by Webster.   *Ibid.*

SEC. 620. It was obviously the purpose of section 2139, Revised Statutes, to keep out of the Indian country liquors which cause intoxication in that country and destroy the people. It was to suppress it, to prohibit it from being taken in there. Then we are to interpret or construe the statute by that rule of interpretation or construction which would enable us to effectuate the purpose of those who passed that law.   *United States v. Ellis, 51 Fed. Rep., 808.*

SEC. 621. Under the provisions of section 14 of the organic act of Alaska (act May 17, 1884, 23 Stat. L., 24) and of section 1955,

Revised Statutes, an indictment charging the defendant with selling liquor to two Indian women states a punishable offense, and it is immaterial under the law whether the sale is to Indians or white persons, the allegation as to Indian women being mere surplusage.

United States v. Warwick, 51 Fed. Rep., 280.

SEC. 622. No particular question was made on the construction of section 14 of the organic act of Alaska (23 Stat. L., 24), but as it covers the whole ground the most reasonable conclusion is that it supersedes or repeals all former laws on the subject of intoxicating liquors in Alaska.   *Ibid.*

SEC. 623. According to the true sense of the words "spirituous liquor" as used in section 2139, Revised Statutes, lager beer is comprehended by its terms, and it is spirituous liquor, and its introduction into Indian country was intended to be prohibited by the statutes, and the words "spirituous liquor" are comprehensive enough to embrace lager beer.   *Ibid.*

SEC. 624. Section 2139, Revised Statutes, is a section of law that is to be construed in the light of contemporaneous history, in the light of things then and now. The manifest purpose of said statute was to prevent intoxication. If that be true, we have the key which opens the way to the correct interpretation of the law. Wherever we find that which produces intoxication, if that subject comes within the definition of spirituous liquors, we have that which has been pro hibited and which has been said by the statute shall not be introduced. The words "ardent" and "spirituous" are used indiscriminately as having the same meaning, and include lager beer.   *Ibid.*

SEC. 625. It is not a crime, under section 2139, Revised Statutes, to dispose of spirituous liquor to British Columbia Indians, or Indians upon whom the rights of citizenship have been conferred by the laws of the United States; and the said statute is not applicable to any case of selling or disposing of liquor to an Indian not at the time subject to the general authority given by law to the officers of Indian affairs.   *United States v. Hurshman, 53 Fed. Rep., 543.*

SEC. 626. Section 3 of the act of 1887 (24 Stat. L., 388) provides for leasing lands under the regulations of the Secretary of the Interior, and the proviso of the section contemplates agents in charge of the reservations. Besides, the practice of the Department is and has been to maintain them, and this practice is respectable evidence of a correct interpretation of the statute by the officers who may have suggested the policy and written the provisions of the statute.

Eells v. Ross, 64 Fed. Rep., 417.

SEC. 627. The act of 1887 (24 Stat. L., 388), which confers citizenship, clearly does not emancipate the Indians from all control or abolish the reservation.   *Ibid.*

Sec. 628. From its relations to the title, and from the terms of the treaty with the Puyallup Indians (10 Stat. L., 1132), the Government had the power to make such conditions relative to alienation as it might deem expedient, and they were not destroyed by making the Indians citizens. Such effect can not be deduced from the act of 1887 (24 Stat. L., 388), for if Congress could do so, Congress did explicitly clog the title with a condition of nonalienation for twenty-five years and absolutely nullified all contracts made touching the same before the expiration of such time.   *Ibid.*

Sec. 629. That the abolition of the reservations and of the guardianship of the Indians is the ultimate hope of the policy contemplated by the general allotment act (24 Stat. L., 388) there can be no doubt, but it will not be soonest realized by attributing fanciful qualities to the Indians, or supposing that their natures can be changed by legislative enactment.   *Ibid.*

Sec. 630. Some of the restraints of a reservation may be inconsistent with the rights of citizens. The advantages of a reservation are not; and if, to secure the latter to the Indians, others not Indians are excluded it is not clear what right they have to complain.   *Ibid.*

Sec. 631. On June 5, 1850 (9 Stat. L., 437), Congress, recognizing the fact that the law of 1834 (4 Stat. L., 729) was not in force in Oregon Territory, enacted " that the law regulating trade and intercourse with the Indian tribes east of the Rocky Mountains, or such provisions of the same as may be applicable, be extended over the Indian tribes in the Territory of Oregon."   *Robinson v. Caldwell, 67 Fed. Rep., 391.*

Sec. 632. For the purpose of securing the North Carolina Cherokees against the evil consequences of injudicious contracts with more intelligent and designing white men, a State statute was enacted requiring all contracts, equal to $10 or more, with Cherokee Indians to be in writing, signed in the presence of two witnesses who shall subscribe the same (1 Code N. C., sec. 1553). This law of the State imposed upon them a restriction which was not imposed upon other citizens, except as to transactions coming within the statute of frauds and a few other cases.   *United States v. Boyd, 68 Fed. Rep., 577.*

Sec. 633. The occupancy of the lands of the Winnebagoes by the defendants results in antagonizing the authority and control of the Government over the Indians, and is clearly detrimental to their best interests, and materially interferes with the rules and regulations of the Department charged with the duty of carrying out the treaty stipulations under which the land forming the reservation was set apart for the benefit and occupancy of the Indians.

United States v. Flournoy, &c., Co., 69 Fed. Rep., 886.

Sec. 634. The Constitution expressly delegates to the United States exclusive jurisdiction to regulate intercourse with Indians, and the power thus delegated may be exercised by the Government either by legislative enactment or under the treaty-making power conferred upon it by the Constitution.   *In re Race Horse, 70 Fed. Rep., 598.*

SEC. 635. By the express terms of the treaty of March 8, 1865 (14 Stat. L., 671), and by the provisions of sections 2114, 2118, 2119, and 2149 of the Revised Statutes, the Executive Department is charged with the duty of removing all intruders from the Winnebago Reservation and protecting the Indians in the use and occupancy of the reservation, and by the rules and regulations of the Interior Department, as well as by the express provisions of section 2119 of the Revised Statutes, the Indian agent is the officer charged with the performance of this duty, and an order issued by him, within the scope of his powers, is a legal writ.   *United States v. Mullin, 71 Fed. Rep., 682.*

SEC. 636. Notwithstanding the fact that portions of the Winnebago Reservation have been allotted, or if it were true that the entire reservation had been allotted in severalty, the United States is yet bound to protect the Indians, whether citizens or wards of the nation, in the use and occupancy of the reservation lands which have never been opened to occupancy by the whites.   *Ibid.*

SEC. 637. The Federal Government, by the terms of the treaty of March 8, 1865 (14 Stat. L., 671), with the Winnebago Indians, is charged with the duty of protecting the Indians in the use and occupancy of the reservation lands, whether allotted in severalty or not, and the Executive Department, acting through the Indian agents on the reservation, has full power to do whatever may be necessary for the proper performance of this duty.   *Ibid.*

SEC. 638. The Government is not relieved from its duty of guardianship and protection of the members of an Indian tribe, assumed by treaty with such tribe, in consequence of the Indians becoming citizens of the United States.   *Ibid.*

SEC. 639. A written order of an Indian agent, acting in pursuance of instructions from the Interior Department, for the purpose of fulfilling the duty of the Government to protect the Indians, is a legal writ or process, within the meaning of section 5398 of the Revised Statutes, imposing a penalty for resisting the service of such writ or process.   *Ibid.*

SEC. 640. An Indian woman, arrested by the Indian police on the Umatilla Reservation on a charge of adultery committed thereon, was committed to the Indian jail for trial before the court of Indian offenses, "and, while so committed, was rescued and set at liberty by the defendants." *Held*, that they thereby committed the crime of rescue as defined by section 5401 of the Revised Statutes, for forcibly setting at liberty a person who was committed for a crime against the laws of the United States.   *United States v. Clapox, 35 Fed. Rep., 575.*

SEC. 641. The President is authorized by the treaty of June 9, 1855 (12 Stat. L., 948), and sections 441, 463, and 475 of the Revised Statutes to make rules for the government of the Indians on the Umatilla Reservation, including the establishment of an Indian court and police, and the definition of "Indian offenses" and the measure of punishment therefor. *Ibid.*

SEC. 642. The act with which these defendants are charged (rescue) is in flagrant opposition to the authority of the United States on this reservation, and directly subversive of a laudable effort to accustom and educate these Indians in the habit and knowledge of self-government. It is therefore appropriate and needful that the power and name of the Government of the United States should be invoked to restrain and punish them under section 5411 of the Revised Statutes. *Ibid.*

SEC. 643. If the contention of the defendant as to jurisdiction be true, the nation or tribe, or the inhabitants thereof, were left by Congress without any remedy for torts committed by the railroad company; for as there is no remedy for torts, such as was sued for in this case, at the place where the same was committed, there could be no remedy anywhere, as an action for tort not founded upon a breach of contract must be actionable or punishable by the law of the place in which it was done. *Briscoe v. So. Kan. Ry. Co., 40 Fed. Rep., 273.*

SEC. 644. Every right the defendant has in the Indian country is derived from the act of Congress, and this is sufficient to raise a Federal question. *Ibid.*

SEC. 645. Prior to the act of July 4, 1884 (23 Stat. L., 73), the plaintiff could have had no remedy in the Indian country for the injury caused by the tort of defendant; therefore he had no remedy elsewhere. *Ibid.*

SEC. 646. To give this court jurisdiction, the right to claim it must grow out of the subject-matter. When it appears that some title, right, privilege, or immunity on which the recovery depends will be defeated by one construction of a law of the United States, or sustained by the opposite construction, the case will be one arising under a law of the United States, and the Federal courts have jurisdiction regardless of the citizenship of the parties. *Ibid.*

SEC. 647. The act of Congress approved June 1, 1886 (24 Stat. L., 73), authorized the Kansas and Arkansas Valley Railway Company to construct and operate a railroad through the Indian Territory, and to take and use a certain strip of land for that purpose.
Payne v. Railway Co., 46 Fed. Rep., 546.

SEC. 648. The act of February 18, 1888 (25 Stat. L., 35), conferring upon the circuit courts for the western district of Arkansas and the northern district of Texas concurrent jurisdiction of all suits between the Choctaw Coal and Railway Company and the inhabitants of the

Indian nations or tribes through which that railway should run, is not repealed by the act of March 1, 1889 (25 Stat. L., 783), establishing a court in the Indian Territory, nor by the act of May 2, 1890 (26 Stat. L., 81), enlarging the jurisdiction of that court.

Gowen v. Harley, 56 Fed. Rep., 973.

SEC. 649. Under the act of February 18, 1888 (25 Stat. L., 35), evidence that plaintiff lived with his wife in his house in the Territory of the Choctaw Nation when the cause of action arose, and for a year thereafter, is sufficient proof of inhabitancy to give the circuit court for the western district of Arkansas jurisdiction of a suit wherein the Choctaw Coal and Railway Company is defendant, whether plaintiff dwelt there rightfully or wrongfully.   *Ibid.*

SEC. 650. Under the act of May 2, 1890 (26 Stat. L., 94), putting in force in the Indian Territory the statutes of Arkansas and Mansfield's Digest, Arkansas, sections 1053–1061, providing that every poor person not being able to sue may be permitted to bring his action without liability for costs or fees, the privilege of suing *in forma pauperis* under order of court is granted to every poor person in the United States, and not merely to poor persons residing in the Indian Territory,   *Railway Co. v Farr, 56 Fed. Rep., 994.*

SEC. 651. Equitable liens on personalty by contract of the parties being enforceable only in equity, jurisdiction of a case arising in the Choctaw Nation upon suit by nonresidents to enforce such lien against an administrator is in the United States court for the Indian Territory and not in the probate court of the Choctaw Nation.

Riddle v. Hudgins, 58 Fed. Rep., 490.

SEC. 652. In the suit by the owners and mortgagees of the cattle to declare void a judgment of a court of the Creek Nation imposing a fine on the owners for bringing the cattle into the nation contrary to its laws, and making it a lien of the cattle in accordance with such law it will, on demurrer to the answer, be held that the Creek court had jurisdiction to render the judgment, the answer alleging that such court had jurisdiction of the owners of the cattle.   *Cornells v. Shanon, 63 Fed. Rep., 305.*

SEC. 653. The judgments of the courts of the Creek Nation are entitled to the same respect and the same faith and credit as the judgment of the Territorial courts of the United States, and white men residing in the Indian Territory who appear and submit themselves to the jurisdiction of the courts of the nation are bound by their judgments.

Ibid.

SEC. 654. An act of the council of the Creek Nation entitled "An act establishing quarantine regulation against foreign cattle and to prevent smuggling cattle into the Creek Nation," approved October 29, 1891, makes it unlawful for any citizen of the nation "to introduce or invite into the Creek Nation cattle of any kind at any time," except between

January 1 and March 31 of each year, and declares that any citizen
violating this provision of the act "shall be fined a sum that will be
the equivalent of $3 per head for each and every head of cattle" unlaw-
fully introduced. The act makes it a lien on the cattle unlawfully
introduced.   *Ibid.*

SEC. 655. The United States court in the Indian Territory has no
jurisdiction of an action against the Choctaw Nation or the chief executive officer thereof when sued in their capacity as such for an alleged
debt or liability of the nation, and when the judgment will operate
against the nation. Jurisdiction is not conferred by the acts of March
1, 1889 (25 Stat. L., 783), or May 2, 1890 (26 Stat. L., 93).

Thebo v. Choctaw Indians, 66 Fed. Rep., 372.

SEC. 656. The act of March 1, 1889 (25 Stat. L., 783), provides for
the appointment of certain judicial officers and a court for the Indian
Territory and adopted a code of procedure, but did not adopt any
substantive laws for the court to enforce, or by which the rights and
obligations of the citizens in the Territory subject to the jurisdiction
of the court should be regarded and determined.

Manufacturing Co. v. Needles, 69 Fed. Rep., 68.

SEC. 657. Equity has jurisdiction by a bill brought by the United
States, as trustee for the Indians to whom lands have been allotted in
severalty, pursuant to treaties or acts of Congress providing that the
United States will hold the land so allotted in trust for the benefit of
the allottees, against persons who have illegally secured leases of such
lands and taken possession thereof, such bill seeking to oust such
intruders and to restrain them from inducing the Indian to make further leases and from the interfering with the Indian agent in the performance of his duties, since the remedy by action of ejectment, even
if such action could be maintained, would be inadequate.

United States v. Flournoy &c. Co., 69 Fed. Rep., 886.

SEC. 658. The United States has the right, as guardian and trustee
of a tribe of Indians, to bring a suit to protect their rights secured by
treaty.   *United States v. Winans, 73 Fed. Rep., 72.*

SEC. 659. The fact that a purchaser had paid for a large quantity
of timber delivered by and received from Indians, under a contract
approved by the President, in excess of the quantity stated in the contract, does not give him title thereto, and is no defense to a suit for
its recovery by the Government.

United States v. Logging and Improvement Co., 89 Fed. Rep., 907.

SEC. 660. An agent of the Government charged with the duty of
superintending the cutting and removal of timber from an Indian
reservation under contracts with the Indians can not, by his acquiescence in the delivery of quantities in excess of those called for by the

contracts, bind the Government, the provisions of the contract being obligatory upon him as well as the parties thereto. *Ibid.*

SEC. 661. The act of February 16, 1889 (25 Stat. L., 673), empowering the President to authorize the cutting and removal by Indians from their reservations of "dead timber, standing or fallen," includes in such designation not only standing trees that are entirely dead, but also those which are so vitally injured that a prudent landowner would cause them to be forthwith cut to preserve their value. It does not include living and uninjured trees merely because they stand among trees a large portion of which are dead. *Ibid.*

SEC. 662. An agent of the United States charged with the duty of superintending the cutting and removal of dead timber from an Indian reservation under certain contracts, to the end that no green or growing timber should be cut, is vested with a discretion to determine whether injured trees are so badly hurt that they ought to be classified as dead timber within the statute; and the Government is bound by his decision, if made in good faith, while exercising proper care and diligence in the performance of his duties. But the parties to such contracts can not found rights upon his dereliction of duty, nor obtain a title to living and uninjured trees the cutting of which was prohibited by law because he assented to the cutting or was cognizant thereof. *Ibid.*

SEC. 663. The superintendent of logging on an Indian reservation could not legalize a trespass committed by the cutting of live trees in violation of the statute by agreeing, after they were cut and thus become "dead timber," that they might pass under the contract; and such agreement can not estop the Government from recovering the value of such trees. *United States v. Logging, &c., Co., 89 Fed. Rep., 907.*

SEC. 664. Under the regulations established by the President for the cutting of dead timber on Indian reservations, pursuant to the act of February 16, 1889, 10 per cent of the proceeds of such timber when sold is required to be paid into the poor fund of the tribe. *Held,* that such a payment made directly into such fund by a purchaser, under the terms of his contract, was not a payment to the United States for which such purchaser was entitled to credit on a recovery by the Government against him for a wrongful conversion of a part of the timber received and paid for under such contract. *Ibid.*

SEC. 665. It is not unlawful for an Indian having a contract, approved by the President, to cut and deliver a certain quantity of dead timber from a reservation, to employ other Indians to cut and deliver timber thereunder in his name. *Ibid.*

SEC. 666. The Government is always at liberty to change its policy, and can not be held pecuniarily liable for so doing, nor can the prerogatives of legislative discretion be made subservient to the rights of an individual. Therefore, although the Government for many years recognized assignments by the Indian tribes to their agents, and although the claimants act upon the faith of that policy and hold a power coupled with an interest, of which the Government has notice, still a treaty may be made which provides for the payment of all appropriations directly to the Indians, and declares that the fund shall not be assignable. *Kendall v. United States, 1 C. Cls., 261.*

SEC. 667. When an Indian tribe employs agents to prosecute a claim against Government for a percentage of what may be obtained and it is afterwards provided by treaty that the funds shall be paid to the Indians per capita, an action will not lie against the Government in favor of the agent, even though the Indians, after the treaty, direct the Secretary of War to pay the agent out of any moneys coming to them under the treaty or otherwise. *Ibid.*

SEC. 668. The United States had the right to make the treaty that was made without consulting plaintiffs or incurring any liability to them. The act of Congress which appropriated the money only followed the treaty in securing its payment to the individual Indians, without deduction for agents, and both the act and treaty are inconsistent with the payment of any part of the sum thus appropriated to plaintiffs. *Ibid.*

SEC. 669. The act of August 14, 1848 (9 Stat. L., 323), organizing the Territory of Oregon, provided by section 1, "That nothing in this act contained shall be construed to impair the rights of person or property now pertaining to the Indians in said Territory so long as such rights shall remain unextinguished by treaty between the United States and such Indians, or to affect the authority of the Government of the United States to make any regulations by treaty, law, or otherwise respecting such Indians, their lands, property, or other rights, which it would be competent for the Government to make if this act had never passed." *Johnson v. United States, 2 C. Cls. R., 155.*

SEC. 670. From the earliest history of the Government it has been the habit of the United States to remove the Indians from the encroaching white settlements to reservations provided for them to avoid collisions and bloodshed, and to there subsist them and provide for them until they are able to supply themselves in their new homes or are removed to new hunting grounds. *Fremont v. United States, 2 C. Cls., 461.*

SEC. 671. In January, 1851, the commissioners sent by the Government, charged with the duty of making and preserving peace with the Indians in California, proceeded into the Indian country, accompanied by a force of United States troops, and made treaties and compacts whereby the Indians consented to relinquish their lands and remove onto limited tracts, called reserves, on condition of being fed in their new location until they could feed themselves.   *Ibid.*

SEC. 672. In 1851 the Indians in California removed to the reserves under the superintendence of the commissioners and the military force, and a military force was stationed to compel them to stay there.   The treaties and the removal of the Indians were all within the scope of the authority of the commissioners, and when done was fully approved by the Department.   *Ibid.*

SEC. 673. The powers and duties of the Commissioner of Indian Affairs are conferred and prescribed by the act of July 9, 1832 (4 Stat. L., 564), which provides that "The President shall appoint, by and with the advice and consent of the Senate, a Commissioner of Indian Affairs, who shall, under the direction of the Secretary of War, and agreeably to such regulations as the President may from time to time prescribe, have the direction and management of all Indian affairs and of all matters arising out of Indian relations."   *Ibid.*

SEC. 674. August 30, 1852 (10 Stat. L., 56), Congress made an appropriation "for the preservation of peace with the Indians who have been dispossessed of their lands in California until permanent arrangements be made for their future settlement."   And by the act of March 3, 1853, the President was authorized to make military reservations from the public lands in the State of California and remove the Indians thereto.   *Ibid.*

SEC. 675. Under the act of September 28, 1850 (9 Stat. L., 519), Redick McKee, George W. Barbour, and Oliver M. Wozencraft were appointed Indian agents for the State of California, but after the passage of the act of September 30, 1850 (9 Stat. L., 558), the functions of these Indian agents were suspended and they became commissioners for the State of California under the provisions of the last-named act, their duties being to hold treaties with the various Indian tribes in that State.   *Ibid.*

SEC. 676. The contract made by the Kendalls with the Western Cherokees was in all respects a legal and valid contract in law—it would have been sustained and enforced by any court having jurisdiction over the subject-matter—and was one which every just government should sanction and approve.   *Kendall v. United States, 2 C. Cls., 592.*

SEC. 677. In May, 1869, a commissary of subsistence had no authority to contract for the subsistence of Indians under the appropriation act, April 10, 1869 (16 Stat. L., 40), until the determination of the Government to place the Indians within the care of the commissary department, and instructions issued in pursuance thereof.

                                   Ryan v. United States, 8 C. Cls., 265.

SEC. 678. Where a commissary of subsistence is without statutory authority to contract for the support of Indians a contract entered into by him for beef cattle "in such numbers and at such times as may be required," founded on proposals for supplying beef "to the troops and others at Camp Supply," can not be construed to include cattle subsequently needed for Indians at the same camp; and no action will lie for a breach if the commissary subsequently, under authority, enter into a contract with a third party for supplying the Indians. The first contract will be construed to have been limited in purpose to the subsistence of troops and ordinary camp followers.

Ibid.

SEC. 679. Where a contract provides that the contractor "shall have all the hides of beef cattle slaughtered for Indians at Fort Sill" which the superintendent of Indian affairs at that place shall decide are not required for the comfort of the Indians, the number of hides to be about 4,000, "and the superintendent, after the contractor has made ready to receive the hides, turns over the cattle on the hoof to the Indians by whom they were slaughtered, there is no breach of the contract, for the decision of the superintendent is to the effect that all the hides are required for the comfort of the Indians, and the contract is made subject to that decision.

Labenstein v. United States, 9 C. Cls., 135.

SEC. 680. It has been the declared policy of the Government from an early day to prohibit any settlement of lands belonging to the Indians. *Hale v. United States, 11 C. Cls., 238.*

SEC. 681. This court is without jurisdiction to enforce an obligation assumed by the Government for the Indians by treaty. (Sec. 1066, Rev. Stat.) *Langford v. United States, 12 C. Cls., 338.*

SEC. 682. By the act of March 3, 1849 (9 Stat. L., 395), establishing the Interior Department, the supervisory and appellate powers previously exercised by the Secretary of War in relation to all the acts of the Commissioners of Indian Affairs were transferred to the Secretary of the Interior, and Indian affairs were placed under the newly created department. *Belt v. United States, 15 C. Cls., 92.*

SEC. 683. The history of the policy pursued by the Government in regard to the California Indians examined and stated. *Ibid.*

SEC. 684. Where the Quartermaster's Department enters into a contract the subject-matter of which is the transportation of "*such military, Indian, and Government stores*" as may be turned over to the contractor for transportation "by the officers or agents of the Quartermaster's Department," the contractor is not bound to transport and has no right to the transportation of Indian stores which are not in the custody of the Quartermaster's Department.

Hazlett v. United States, 16 C. Cls., 450.

SEC. 685. The Indian Bureau is charged by law, under the Secretary of the Interior, with the duty of contracting for the purchase and transportation of Indian supplies of all kinds under the several annual appropriations therefor, and the court will take notice that its ordinary and regular course of action is, and has been, to make annually contracts for those purposes in pursuance of the law. *Ibid.*

SEC. 686. The Commissioner of Indian Affairs can not buy supplies with money appropriated for expenditures of one fiscal year and transport them to agencies with money appropriated for the expenditures of another fiscal year.

Wilder v. United States, 16 C. Cls., 528.

SEC. 687. There is no statute requiring an Indian transportation supply contract to be approved by the Board of Indian Commissioners or by the Secretary of the Interior. If such approval be required by regulation or otherwise it will relate back whenever given to the date of the contract. *Power v. United States, 18 C. Cls., 263.*

SEC. 688. Section 2107 of the Revised Statutes, which forbids the payment of more than 50 per cent of the amount due for transportation of Indian supplies until the accounts, etc., have been submitted to the Board of Indian Commissioners, does not apply to a claim for damages which that board has no jurisdiction to settle. *Ibid.*

SEC. 689. Section 10 of the Cherokee treaty of July 19, 1866 (14 Stat. L., 799), provides that " every Cherokee and freed person within the Cherokee Nation shall have the right to sell any products of his farm, including his or her live stock, or any merchandise, or manufactured products, and to ship and drive the same to market without restraint, paying any taxes thereon which are now or may be levied by the United States on the quantity sold outside the Indian Territory."

Boudinot v. United States, 18 C. Cls., 716.

SEC. 690. The only authority in 1880 for the appointment of an Indian agent at the Quapaw Agency by that name is found in the appropriation acts which fix the salary at $1,200.

Dyer v. United States, 20 C. Cls., 166.

SEC. 691. The Interior Department has not considered it the duty of the Commissioner of Indian Affairs or of the Department to interfere with the affairs of the Cherokee Nation, except in the case especially provided for by treaty with that nation.

Eastern Band Cherokee v. United States et al., 20 C. Cls., 499.

SEC. 692. The Cherokee Nation has a right to stand upon the contracts of its treaties in relation to the funds now in question, and no acts of Congress and no proceedings of the political departments of the Government in connection therewith can take away its vested rights guaranteed by such treaties. *Ibid.*

SEC. 693. Where the Quartermaster's Department enters into a contract the subject-matter of which is the transportation of " such military, Indian, and Government stores" as may be turned over to the contractor for transportation " by the officers or agent of the Quartermaster's Department," the contractor is not bound to transport and has no right to the transportation of Indian stores which are not in the custody of the Quartermaster's Department.   Judgment of court below affirmed.   (115 U. S., 291.)

Choctaw Nation v. United States, 21 C. Cls., 493.

SEC. 694. The agents of the Government were warranted in chartering steamers to transport the Chickasaws under the treaty of 1834 (7 Stats. L., 450), and the contractor in making preparations to transport 4,000; but he was not entitled to demurrage, which would be refunded to the Chickasaws.   *Chickasaw Nation v. United States, 22 C. Cls., 222.*

SEC. 695. Certain assignments made by Chickasaws, designated in the treaties as " incompetents," were void, and payments made thereon, contrary to the terms of the treaties, should not be credited to the United States.   *Ibid.*

SEC. 696. The cost of conductors of emigration under the Chickasaw treaty, 1834 (7 Stat. L., 450), was to be borne by the United States.

Ibid.

SEC. 697. The court refrains from expressing an opinion as to whether interest should be allowed on the sum of $240,164.58, which should be credited to the Chickasaw Nation, as the question must necessarily be taken to the legislative department of the Government, which alone has power to grant relief, which will consider the equities of the case, and which will decide whether it is one wherein the doctrine should be waived that, as the sovereign does no wrong and is ever ready and willing to pay its just debts, the Government pays no interest.   *Ibid.*

SEC. 798. The rules applicable to controversies between the Government and the Indian tribes are not so strict as those governing differences between guardian and ward; but doubts are to be resolved in favor of the Indians, who are not to be prejudiced by technical construction, and words of doubtful import are to be taken most strongly against the United States.   *Ibid.*

SEC. 699. Where the Government acted as trustee without remuneration in surveying and selling Chickasaw lands and in holding and applying the proceeds, it is entitled to reimbursement for clerks, stationery, and incidental governmental expenses.   *Ibid.*

SEC. 700. Where by treaty the Government was bound to feed Indians and furnished damaged food, equity and justice require that, like a delinquent trustee, it should reimburse the costs to which the Indians were put in procuring legislative redress. *Ibid.*

SEC. 701. Certain payments made to orphans in the manner provided by treaty can not be charged to the United States because of errors or frauds on the part of chiefs and head men who were properly the representatives of orphan Chickasaws. *Ibid.*

SEC. 702. When there has been a wrongful payment made to an incompetent, and where the payment had been made to a person having no right to receive it, and no person is entitled to receive money by virtue of an assignment from an individual confessedly incompetent to manage his own affairs, then if the incompetent has in fact been defrauded, as he evidently was to some extent in the case at bar, then and to that extent the United States should account to the Chickasaw Nation. *Ibid.*

SEC. 703. The treaty of 1852 (10 Stat. L., 974) applies to this case, and while no doubt is entertained that individual orphans were badly treated, it is not found that the Government is responsible therefor to the tribe whose members and selected officials and responsible representatives were parties to whatever wrong was done. *Ibid.*

SEC. 704. Where an agreement is to do six distinct things, upon a specific consideration for each, it is severable, and in the case of such a contract with Indians the Interior Department may approve one provision and reject the others. *Rollins & Presbrey v. United States, 23 C. Cls., 106.*

SEC. 705. Where a contract purports to be by the authority vested in the chief of the band which has never been questioned, and the Indians had the benefit of the services of the other party, the power to make the contract will be deemed established without positive proof. *Ibid.*

SEC. 706. The regulations for Indian Affairs, 189, 193, prescribed by the President under the Revised Statutes, section 465, can not be construed to lengthen a term of office limited by the Constitution and by section 1769 of the Revised Statutes, nor to give the salary of the office to the incumbent holding over contrary to sections 1762, 1769. *Romero v. U. S., 24 C. Cls., 331.*

SEC. 707. The course of Indian legislation since 1874 shows a settled legislative purpose to regulate the Indian agency service according to the exigencies of each year, without reference to the general provisions of the Revised Statutes. *Belknap v. United States, 24 C. Cls., 433.*

SEC. 708. The decision of the court below is affirmed on the same grounds, except as to two items, the Supreme Court concurring substantially in the conclusions reached by the Court of Claims. *Western Cherokee Indians v. United States, 27 C. Cls., 1.*

SEC. 709. Congress has always legislated with regard to the rights of Indians on the theory that they are so dependent and helpless that the nation has the right to assume unlimited control over them.

Jaeger v. United States et al., 27 C. Cls., 278.

SEC. 710. The jurisdictional act does not authorize the court to treat perpetual annuities as ended and allow a recovery for the valuation of the same.   *Pottawatomie Indians v. United States, 27 C. Cls., 403.*

SEC. 711. A statutory obligation to furnish supplies to Indians must be treated as a legal obligation resting upon the Government, though not one known to the common law.

Baker v. United States, 28 C. Cls., 370.

SEC. 712. When cattle intended for the subsistence of the Indians were seized by them while in the contractor's possession, and the agent treated the seizure as an issue to them, and gave a voucher, which was approved by the Secretary of the Interior and charged by him to the appropriation for the support of Indians at that agency, the Government acquired a benefit from the transaction, and a contract must be implied, under the rule in Solomon's case (19 Wall., 17).   *Ibid.*

SEC. 713. Where cattle intended for the subsistence of Indians are seized by them while still in the hands of the contractor, the Government has an election either to regard the cattle as not having been delivered and furnish the Indians with others, or to treat the seizure as a quasi delivery for the benefit of the Indians, and charge them with the issue.   *Ibid.*

SEC. 714. The treaty with the Shawnees, 1825 (7 Stat. L., 284), and that of 1831 (7 Stat. L., 355), require the United States to "Support and keep a blacksmith for the term of five years, or as long as the President may deem it advisable." The President having kept a blacksmith there more than five years his action bound the United States, and the claimants can not be charged with the cost of it.

Blackfeather v. United States, 28 C. Cls., 447.

SEC. 715. The treaty of 1831 (7 Stat. L., 355) provides for an advance of $13,000, "to be reimbursed from the sales of the lands herein ceded." This was simply a loan and must be charged against the Shawnees, though the United States ultimately received a benefit from the improvements made with the fund.   *Ibid.*

SEC. 716. The treaty of 1831 (7 Stat. L., 355) requires the United States to sell the Ohio lands of the Shawnees "at public sale to the highest bidder," and requires the sales to be made "in the manner of selling the public land." This brought the sales within the restriction of the land laws, then making $2 the minimum price per acre.   *Ibid.*

SEC. 717. The treaty of 1831 (7 Stat. L., 355) provides for the retention of a fund in the hands of the Government to bear the expenses of the Shawnees in Michigan "should they ever wish to follow." The money being still held for this contingency, the claimants are not entitled to be credited with it.   *Ibid.*

SEC. 718. The act of April 1, 1880 (21 Stat. L., 70), which provides for the deposit of Indian trust funds in the Treasury and directs the payment of interest thereon, does not create a right to interest where none is assured by treaty.   *Ibid.*

SEC. 719. Where a balance now found by the court should have been paid by the United States into an interest-bearing treaty fund (treaty 1831, article 7) interest may be recovered.   *Ibid.*

SEC. 720. Under the treaty 1854 (10 Stat. L., 1053), "the portions of orphan children shall be appropriated by the President in the manner deemed best by him for their interest." This makes the United States responsible for the money of orphans misapplied or lost. But the Shawnees as a tribe have no claim to the money which belongs and is decreed to be paid to the individual orphan children or their representative.   *Ibid.*

SEC. 721. Article 8 of the treaty of 1854 (10 Stat. L., 1053) places upon the President a different responsibility in regard to the "incompetents" than in regard to the "orphans;" as to the former he must consult the Shawnee council; as to the latter he has absolute power and single responsibility.   *Ibid.*

SEC. 722. The decision of the court below is reversed as to article 7 of the treaty of 1831 (7 Stat., 355) in regard to the amount allowed, on the ground that the attention of the court below had not been called to the act of April 24, 1820, fixing the statutory price of the public lands at $1.25 per acre instead of $2 per acre, the amount allowed by the court as fixed by prior statutes. It is also reversed as to an allowance of $10,506.39, on the ground that the record was defective in not showing how much of the orphan fund was embezzled by the Indian superintendent. Upon all other points the decision was affirmed.
                                                       Ibid.

SEC. 723. It has been the policy of the United States to protect the Indian tribes by legislation from the misapplication of their funds. (Rev. Stat., 2097, 2098.)   *Leighton v. United States, 29 C. Cls., 288.*

SEC. 724. The Indians being within the jurisdiction and control of the United States as "domestic dependent nations," it is their duty to submit to the constituted authorities; but if, instead of submitting, they resort to arms as a band, tribes, or nation, to maintain or contest their rights, a want of amity in fact arises, and by reason of their recognized tribal relations by the political departments and the favorable rules of interpretation to which they are entitled, their rights as belligerents will be respected by the courts on construing the remedial act of 1891.   *Ibid.*

SEC. 725. The treaty of Buffalo Creek (7 Stat. L., 550) provided that if the Indians do not remove to "their new homes within five years, or such other time as the President may from time to time appoint," they "shall forfeit all interest in the lands." Under this the duty of removal was on the Government, and a forfeiture could be based only upon a refusal by the Indians to emigrate.

New York Indians v. United States, 30 C. Cls., 413.

SEC. 726. Legislative action is not necessarily a precedent for judicial. Where Congress awards damages to an Indian tribe and refers the claims of others to this court for investigation and adjudication, it must be deemed that Congress was convinced that the one tribe had been injured, but was not convinced that the others had been.

Ibid.

SEC. 727. The act of January 28, 1893 (27 Stat. L., 426), conferring jurisdiction on this court to hear and enter judgment "as if it had original jurisdiction of said case" contains no admission of a right. It is a grant of jurisdiction with a waiver of the statute of limitations.

Ibid.

SEC. 728. The Buffalo Creek treaty (7 Stat. L., 550) has expired, leaving no rights or duties behind it, so far as this litigation is involved. Both parties allowed it to lapse. The Indians can not maintain a suit under it for either the lands in Kansas or the lands in Wisconsin.

Ibid.

SEC. 729. Under the act of October 1, 1890 (26 Stat. L., 636), the court is without jurisdiction to award the complainants more than their proportional part of the communal fund which is the subject of these suits.   *Journeycake v. Cher. Nation et al., 31 C. Cls., 140.*

SEC. 730. Where both parties have classed the "adopted citizens" of the Cherokee Nation as a part of the body of citizens who make up the whole number of the nation, a court of equity will not be justified in awarding a portion of the communal fund which may be theirs to the complainants before the court, though the defendants consent thereto.

Ibid.

SEC. 731. Where a decree was entered by consent of the defendant's attorneys for a larger amount than the court had decided the complainants were entitled to recover, it will be set aside on the court's own motion.   *Ibid.*

SEC. 732. The treaty with the Cherokee Nation, July 19, 1866 (14 Stat. L., 799), provides that the freedmen of the nation who "are now residents therein, or who may return within six months, and their descendants" shall be entitled to dwell and occupy land in the Cherokee country. This was intended for the protection of the Cherokee

Nation. That is to say, freedmen and the descendants of freedmen who did not return within six months are excluded from the benefits of the treaty and of the decree.   *Ibid.*

SEC. 733. The period of six months within which the freedmen were to acquire certain rights in the Cherokee Nation under the treaty of 1866 (14 Stat. L., 799), extended from the date of the promulgation of the treaty, August 11, 1866, and did not expire until February 11, 1867.   *Ibid.*

SEC. 734. The act of March 2, 1895 (28 Stat. L., 910) prescribes the manner in which payments per capita shall be made, and that the matter of payment is exclusively within the jurisdiction of the Secretary of the Interior.   *Ibid.*

SEC. 735. The word "commerce," as used in the Constitution, is not necessarily limited to the purposes of trade; but may well be construed to embrace every species of intercourse which the Federal Government may think proper to establish with the Indian nations.

United States v. Bailey, 1 McLean, 234.

SEC. 736. That the word "commerce" does refer to trade would seem to be clear from its being used in the same sentence in reference to foreign nations; but it is admitted that the "power to regulate commerce with the Indian tribes" confers on Congress the right of selecting such means as may be necessary to attain the object of the power. But these means must have a direct relation to the object.

Ibid.

SEC. 737. Congress has power to regulate commerce among the several States, and if the same power, given in the same words, in relation to the Indians, may be exercised as contended, Congress could legislate on crimes for the States generally.   *Ibid.*

SEC. 738. If the State of Tennessee has no jurisdiction or had failed to exercise it, it does not follow that the Federal Government has a general and unlimited jurisdiction over the territory, for its powers are delegated and can not be assumed to supply any defect of power on the part of the State.   *Ibid.*

SEC. 739. It is clear that the State of Tennessee either by failing to exercise jurisdiction or by positive enactment, short of a cession of jurisdiction for purposes specified in the Constitution, can neither enlarge nor diminish the powers of Congress on the subject.   *Ibid.*

SEC. 740. All intercourse with a foreign nation may be prohibited, or it may be admitted under a license or permit. Our agents abroad are protected, and we punish depredations committed by our own citizens on the persons or property of a foreign people with whom we are at peace. Thus far it would seem the power may be exercised by

Congress, both as it relates to foreign nations and to our Indian tribes.   *Ibid.*

SEC. 741. All the provisions of the act of 1802 (2 Stat. L., 139) come clearly within the scope of the power to regulate commerce with the Indian tribes; and substantially the same power has been exercised in regulating commerce with foreign nations.   *Ibid.*

SEC. 742. Under the intercourse law of 1802 Congress has the right to select the means, which have a direct relation to the object, in the regulation of commerce with the Indians; but Congress can not under this investure of power exercise a general jurisdiction over an Indian territory within the limits of a State.   *Ibid.*

SEC. 743. That Congress has power to inflict punishment on all who violate the laws which regulate a commercial intercourse with the Indians is admitted; but because this is a legitimate exercise of power it does not follow that the jurisdiction may be extended without limit.
Ibid.

SEC. 744. No express provision has been made in treaties or by act of Congress at what period or under what circumstances the power of the Federal Government to regulate commerce with the Wyandot or any other tribe of Indians living within a State shall be terminated.
United States v. Cisna, 1 McLean, 254.

SEC. 745. Under the power to regulate commerce with the Indian tribes, Congress has power to prohibit all intercouse with them except under a license.   *Ibid.*

SEC. 746. The Federal relations should be withdrawn from the Indians within a State by the concurrent acts of the Federal and State governments.   But if no such acts take place, and the Indians occupy a territory of very limited extent, surrounded by a white population, which necessarily have daily intercourse with the Indians, and it becomes impracticable to enforce the law, the Federal jurisdiction must cease.   *Ibid.*

SEC. 747. The power of Congress to regulate commerce with the Indian tribes does not necessarily cease on their being included within the limits of a State.   *Ibid.*

SEC. 748. The laws regulating intercourse with the Indian tribes were intended to operate on communities somewhat remote from white population.   The exception in the act of 1802 refers to Indian tribes at that time surrounded by white settlements, as the remnant of tribes in Connecticut, Massachusetts, and other States.   *Ibid.*

SEC. 749. Congress can not effectually regulate commerce with the Indian tribes, without adopting such provisions by law as shall preserve those tribes from an indiscriminate commercial intercourse with our own citizens; such is their inferiority in the business of commerce while in an uncivilized state that their interest would be sacrificed if left to an unrestricted intercourse. *Ibid.*

SEC. 750. No one can read the laws for the regulation of our intercourse with the Indian tribes without perceiving that they were designated to operate on and protect communities of Indians remotely situated from our own population. *Ibid.*

SEC. 751. The power to regulate commerce with foreign nations and with Indian tribes is given to Congress by the Constitution. And under this and the treaty-making power numerous treaties have been made and laws enacted to regulate commercial intercourse with the numerous Indian tribes which live within the Federal limits. *Ibid.*

SEC. 752. By the proclamation of Congress, at Princeton, September 12, 1783, "all persons were prohibited from making settlements on lands inhabited or claimed by Indians, without the limits or jurisdiction of any particular State, and from purchasing or receiving any gift or cession of such lands or claims, without the express authority and direction of the United States in Congress assembled."

Doe. ex. dem. Chinn v. Darnell, 4 McLean, 440.

SEC. 753. So much of article 10 of the treaty of July 19, 1866, with the Cherokee (14 Stat. L., 799) as is repugnant to the provisions of the act of Congress July 20, 1868, imposing taxes on manufactured tobacco, is thereby abrogated. *United States v. Tobacco Factory, 1 Dill., 264.*

SEC. 754. The internal-revenue laws imposing taxes on manufactured tobacco are in force in the Indian country. Section 107 of the internal-revenue act of July 20, 1868, which was thus construed, declares that the internal-revenue laws shall be held and construed to extend to the articles therein mentioned, produced anywhere within the exterior boundaries of the United States, whether the same shall be within a collection district or not. Not only is the Cherokee Nation within the letter of said section 107, but it is also within the reason and policy of the internal-revenue laws relative to the manufacture of tobacco.

Ibid.

SEC. 755. Nebraska was organized as a Territory by the act of May 30, 1854, and by that act the rights of Indians therein are preserved unimpaired, and the authority of the United States to make regulations respecting them, their property, and other rights, by treaty, law, or otherwise, retained. The Pawnee tribe then, as now, resided within the limits of the Territory thus created.

United States v. Yellow Sun, 1 Dill., 271.

SEC. 756. At the time of the passage of the act of June 30, 1834 (4 Stat. L., 728), it applied to the locality where the offense in question was committed, but it ceased to be operative within the limits of Nebraska at the moment when the latter was admitted into the Union as a State upon equal footing with the original States.   *Ibid.*

SEC. 757. Under the act of March 15, 1864 (13 Stat. L., 29), prohibiting the sale of liquor to any Indian under the charge of an Indian agent, actual control or immediate supervision by such agent over the individual Indian to whom the liquor is sold is not essential if the tribe to which the Indian belongs is under the charge of such agent and the Indian himself still maintains his tribal relations.

United States v. Flynn, 1 Dill., 451.

SEC. 758. Legislation prohibiting the sale of liquor to Indians has been held by the Supreme Court of the United States to be constitutional, and authorized by the power of Congress to regulate commerce with the Indian tribes.   *Ibid.*

SEC. 759. Notwithstanding the broad language of the first article of the treaty of 1855 (10 Stat. L., 1159), as to the dissolution of the tribal relation of the Wyandotte Indians, and as to their becoming citizens of the United States and subject to its laws and the laws of the Territory of Kansas, it is evident from a view of the whole treaty that their property rights were regulated by it, and that the Wyandotte council, which was a tribunal with executive and judicial functions, was still to continue in force, at least for a time.   *Gray v. Coffman, 2 Dill., 393.*

SEC. 760. The Commissioner of Indian Affairs has ample authority for removing from an Indian reservation all persons found thereon without authority of law or whose presence may be detrimental to the peace and welfare of the Indians.   *United States v. Crook, 5 Dill., 453.*

SEC. 761. Section 7 of the act of February 27, 1851 (9 Stat. L., 587), extended all the laws then in force regulating trade and intercourse with the Indian tribes over the tribes in the Territories of New Mexico and Utah, including what is now the Ute Reservation in Colorado; but whether the effect of this was to make New Mexico and Utah Indian country is a question.   *United States v. Berry, 2 McCrary, 58.*

SEC. 762. By article 7 of the treaty of March 2, 1868, with the Utes (15 Stat. L., 619), it is stipulated "That the United States may pass such laws on the subject of alienation and descent of property, and on all subjects connected with the government of the Indians on said reservation and the internal police thereof, as may be thought proper."

Ibid.

SEC. 763. The policy of keeping the Indian reservations within the exclusive jurisdiction of the National Government until such time as the rights of the Indians therein are extinguished has been uniformly pursued with respect to all the Indian reservations in the country, and it is expressed so plainly in the treaty of 1868 with the Utes that it is impossible to suppose that it was the intention of Congress, by the organization of the State of Colorado, to annihilate the treaty and to deprive the Indians of their right to protection under it.   *Ibid.*

SEC. 764. A search for and seizure of liquors under the provisions of section 2140, Revised Statutes, which provides for the enforcement of a penalty and forfeiture for introducing spirituous liquors and wines into the Indian country, in a case where the liquors found were not claimed to have been seized within the limits of an Indian reservation, was held unauthorized.   *Pelcher et al. v. United States, 3 McCrary, 510.*

SEC. 765. Acts of Congress of March 30, 1802, and of June 30, 1834 (4 Stat. L., 729), to regulate intercourse with the Indian tribes and preserve peace on the frontiers; the act of March 3, 1825, relating to crimes against the United States; the act of June 15, 1836, admitting Arkansas into the Union, and the act of March 3, 1837, amendatory of the judicial system of the United States, commented on and explained.   *United States v. Alberty; 1 Hemp., 444.*

SEC. 766. The circuit and district courts of the United States can take cognizance of civil and criminal matters only so far as the power to do so is conferred upon them by statutes of the United States.   *Ibid.*

SEC. 767. Distilled spirits are imported into the district of Alaska when brought from an American port outside of said district into the waters within the headlands of Point Hope and Cape Prince of Wales and there unladen or disposed of, or with the intent to so unlade or dispose of them.   *The Louisa Simpson, 2 Sawyer, 57.*

SEC. 768. Section 20 of the act of 1834, as amended by the act of March 15, 1864 (13 Stat. L., 29), making the disposing of spirituous liquors to Indians a crime, is in this respect a general act, and *prima facie* applies wherever the subject-matter exists—an Indian under the charge of an agent appointed by the United States; but Alaska being acquired by the United States after the enactment of such amendment, it is doubtful whether it was extended over that territory *propria vigore* upon its acquisition; and the act of July 27, 1868 (15 Stat. L., 240), having provided for the subject of the introduction and use of distilled spirits in Alaska, by implication Congress thereby excluded such amendment therefrom.   *United States v. Seveloff, 2 Sawyer, 311.*

SEC. 769. In 1853 the supreme court of the Territory of Oregon, in United States *v.* Tom, 1 Or., 27, held that the act of 1834 was not in force to the westward of the Rocky Mountains until specifically extended over the Territory of Oregon by the act of June 5, 1850. (9 Stat. L., 437.)   *Ibid.*

SEC. 770. The act of July 27, 1868 (15 Stat. L., 240), extending the laws "relating to customs, commerce, and navigation" over Alaska, construed not to extend the Indian intercourse act of 1834 (4 Stat. L., 729) over that country, although the latter is a regulation of commerce "with the Indian tribes." *Ibid.*

SEC. 771. The act of June 30, 1834 (4 Stat. L., 729), defining the limits of the "Indian country" and regulating the trade and intercourse with the Indian tribes therein, is a local act, and was therefore not extended *propria vigore* over the territory of Alaska upon its cession to the United States. *Ibid.*

SEC. 772. Under article 1, section 8, of the Constitution, Congress exercises the power to regulate trade and intercourse with the Indian tribes as well without as within the Indian country. *Ibid.*

SEC. 773. In Am. Fur. Co. *v.* United States (2 Pet., 358) it was held, in an action to forfeit an Indian trader's goods for taking whisky into "the Indian country" for the purpose of disposing of it, that a country purchased from the Indians subsequent to the act of March 30, 1802 (2 Stat. L., 139), and therefore no longer within the specified limits of "the Indian country," as defined by section 1 of said act, was not such country within the meaning of the trade and intercourse act, although it was then frequented and inhabited exclusively by Indians. *Ibid.*

SEC. 774. The word *person*, in section 20 of the act of 1834 (4 Stat. L., 729), as amended by the act March 15, 1864 (13 Stat. L., 29), includes an Indian, and under such section an Indian may be punished for disposing of spirituous liquors to another Indian.
United States v. Shaw-mux, 2 Sawyer, 364.

SEC. 775. In United States *v.* Tom, (1 Or., 26) the defendant was an Indian, and was indicted and convicted under the section for selling liquor to Indians. The case was considered at length, but this precise question does not appear to have been raised. But the fact could not have escaped the attention of the counsel and the court, and the inference is that it was not deemed material. *Ibid.*

SEC. 776. Congress has power to regulate intercourse *between* Indian tribes and the members thereof, and may, therefore, prohibit the traffic in spirituous liquors between such tribes or members, within as well as without the limits of a State. *Ibid.*

SEC. 777. The clause in section 6 of the act of February 17, 1873 (17 Stat. L., 463), providing for the abolishing of Indian superintendencies after June 30, did not of itself abolish any such superintendency, but only took effect when and as the President designated and appointed.
United States v. Wirt, 3 Sawyer, 161

SEC. 778. The provisions of the general appropriation act of March 3, 1873 (17 Stat. L., 530), extending sections 20 and 21 of the Indian intercourse act of June 30, 1834, over Alaska, being local in its character, was not repealed by the repealing clause of section 1954, Rev. Stats.   *Waters v. Campbell, 4 Sawyer, 121.*

SEC. 779. There is no law of the United States requiring persons to be licensed to trade in Alaska, even with the Indians.   *Ibid.*

SEC. 780. Where a statute prescribes the penalty and conditions of a bond, one given in a greater penalty, or upon substantially other or different conditions, is so far illegal and void.
                                    United States v. Humason, 5 Sawyer, 537.

SEC. 781. In the absence of any statute upon the subject, a bond voluntarily given the United States to secure the payment of a debt or the performance of official duty is valid.   *Ibid.*

SEC. 782. An Indian agent appointed for Oregon, under section 4 of the act of June 5, 1850 (9 Stat. L., 137), was required to give bond in the penal sum of $2,000, as provided in section 4 of the act of June 30, 1834 (4 Stat. L., 729); and he was also a person "charged or trusted" with the disbursement or application of money or property on account of the Indian Department within the purview of section 8 of said act of 1834, and therefore might be' required by the President to give a bond in a larger sum than $2,000 for the performance of his official duties.   *Ibid.*

SEC. 783. The law presumes that official duty has been duly performed, and, therefore, where the Indian Department took a bond from an Indian agent in Oregon in a larger amount than $2,000, the presumption of the law is that the increase in the penalty was required by the Executive, and the bond is valid until the contrary appears.
                                                              Ibid.

SEC. 784. Section 8 of the act of 1834 (4 Stat. L., 729) is prospective, and applies, wherever, by any subsequent legislation or Executive regulation, an Indian agent is required to disburse money or property on account of the Indian Department.   *Ibid.*

SEC. 785. Section 1 of the act June 27, 1846 (9 Stat. L., 20), provides that "no superintendent, Indian agent, or other disbursing officer in such service shall have advanced to him on Indian or public account any money to be disbursed in future" until he has settled his accounts for the preceding year and the balances in his hand are ready to be paid over.   *Ibid.*

SEC. 786. Section 1 of the act of March 3, 1857 (11 Stat. L., 169), authorizes the President to direct the payment of money to Indians by the superintendent in the presence of witnesses.   *Ibid.*

SEC. 787. Ignorance of the lines of the reservation will not excuse a man for being within them and carrying on a trade with the Indians that is prohibited by law.   *United States v. Leathers, 6 Sawyer, 17.*

SEC. 788. The military force may be used to remove persons from reservations under sections 2147 and 2149. These sections show that whether it is proper to permit a trader to remain in the Indian country, or whether any person is detrimental to the welfare of the Indians, are questions left in the one case to the agent and in the other to the commissioner and Secretary of the Interior.

United States v. Sturgeon, 6 Sawyer, 29.

SEC. 789. A reservation having been set apart by competent authority for the use of the Indians, anything which deprives them of that use is unlawful and contrary to law.   *Ibid.*

SEC. 790. The Indian intercourse act of June 30, 1834 (4 Stat. L., 729), was extended over Oregon, so far as the same was applicable thereto, by the act of June 5, 1850 (9 Stat. L., 437). *Held* that the provision of said act of 1834 providing for the punishment of a white man for stealing the property of an Indian, and *vice versa* was applicable to Oregon, and thereafter in force there, and that the same was not modified or repealed by the admission of the State into the Union, February 14, 1859.   *United States v. Bridleman, 7 Saw., 243.*

SEC. 791. Intercourse with Indians is a subject of Federal jurisdiction, the same as the naturalization of aliens, etc., and therefore Congress may pass laws regulating or even forbidding it, and providing for the punishment of acts or conduct growing out of it, resulting in injury to either the Indian or the other party, or calculated to interrupt or destroy its peaceful or beneficial character.   *Ibid.*

SEC. 792. The power to regulate commerce with Indian tribes includes not only traffic in commodities, but intercourse with such tribes—the personal conduct of the white and other races to and with such tribes and the members thereof, and *vice versa.*   *Ibid.*

SEC. 793. The power of Congress to regulate the intercourse between the inhabitants of the United States and the Indian tribes therein is not limited by State lines or governments, but may be exercised and enforced wherever the subject—Indian tribes—exists.   *Ibid.*

SEC. 794. The publication of an advertisement for supplies was authorized by the Secretary of the Interior within the meaning of section 3828, Revised Statutes, and the payment therefor was a lawful expenditure of the public money intrusted to the superintendent, and ought to be allowed in his accounts.

United States v. Odeneal, 7 Saw., 451.

SEC. 795. It is the duty of Congress to regulate the intercourse with the Indians, and to that end may provide for punishing the giv-

ing of spirituous liquors to them on or off a reservation, within or
without a State.   *United States v. Earl, 9 Saw., 79.*

Sec. 796. The United States claims and has rightfully exercised the
power to place Indians upon reservations and appoint agents to take
charge of them there, as its wards, without any treaty to that effect,
but simply upon its own volition manifested by an act of Congress or
other proper department of the Government.   . *Ibid.*

Sec. 797. Lumber made at the sawmill on the Grand Ronde Reservation is the "property" of the Indians thereon, and not that of the
United States, within the purview of section 3618, Revised Statutes,
and the agent, subject to the instructions of the Commissioner of
Indian Affairs, may dispose of any portion of the same and apply the
proceeds to the mill or otherwise for the support of the Indians, without reference to section 3617, Revised Statutes, requiring money
received for the use of the United States to be deposited to its credit.
                  United States v. Sinnott, 11 Saw., 398.   Same in Fed. Rep.

Sec. 798. The Sevalaff case (2 Saw., 311) was decided in December,
1872, and on March 3, 1873, Congress apparently gave its sanction
to the theory of that case (17 Stat. L., 530) by amending section 1 of
the Alaska act of 1868 (15 Stat. L., 240) so as to extend over the
country sections 20 and 21 of the intercourse act of 1834 prohibiting
the introduction and disposition of spirituous liquors therein.
                                    Kie v. United States, 11 Saw., 579.

Sec. 799. The unorganized Alaska act of July 27, 1868 (15 Stat. L.,
240), is also continued in force except as modified by the act of 1884
(sec. 14) and "the importation, manufacture, and sale of intoxicating
liquors in said district, except for medicinal, mechanical, and scientific
purposes," is thereby prohibited under the penalties prescribed in
section 4 of the act of 1868 (sec. 1955, Rev. Stat.) "for the importation of distilled spirits."   *Ibid.*

Sec. 800. Even supposing that the population of Alaska was not
Indian, but white, Congress would have the same right to forbid the
manufacture and sale of intoxicating liquors therein. During its
minority the Territory, in this, as well as in other respects, is very
properly in Congressional leading strings.

                              Nelson v. United States, 12 Saw., 285.

Sec. 801. By act of April 8, 1864 (13 Stat. L., 39), the President
was authorized to set apart not exceeding four tracts of land in California for Indian reservations, and in his discretion to include therein
existing reservations. The lands in existing reservations not thus
retained were to be sold as therein provided. Four reservations were
accordingly set apart, among which the present existing Klamath Reservation was not included; but possession of the latter, which contained

about 40 square miles, was retained by the United States, and some steps were taken toward its disposition. *Held*, that the Klamath Reservation was not Indian country within the meaning of section 2133 of the Revised Statutes prescribing the penalty for unlicensed trading in the Indian country.

United States v. Rising Star Tea, 13 Saw., 208.   Same, 14 Saw., 19.

SEC. 802. "Courts of Indian offenses" are not the constitutional courts provided for in section 1, article 3, of the Constitution, but merely educational and disciplinary instrumentalities by which the Government is endeavoring to improve and elevate the condition of these dependent tribes.

United States v. Clapox, 13 Saw., 349.   Same in Fed. Rep.

SEC. 803. The President is authorized by treaty of June 9, 1855 (12 Stat. L., 948), and the Revised Statutes (secs. 441, 463, 465), to make rules for the government of the Indians on the Umatilla Reservation, including the establishment of an Indian court and police, and the definition of "Indian offenses," and the measure of punishment therefor.

Ibid.

SEC. 804. The court in a capital case against Indians, though neither party asked it and both demanded judgment, arrested judgment, on its own motion, for want of jurisdiction over the offense charged in the indictment; but instead of at once ordering the discharge of the Indians, the court turned them over to the State authorities.

United States v. Sa-coo-da-cot, 1 Abbott, 377.

SEC. 805. The intercourse act of 1802 (2 Stat. L., 137), by which Congress defined the "Indian country" and provided for the punishment by the United States courts of Indians who left the Indian country and committed offenses in any State or Territory, was repealed, so far as it relates to the Indian tribes west of the Mississippi, by the act of June 30, 1834 (4 Stat. L., 729).

Ibid.

SEC. 806. Expenditures made by an Indian agent for the benefit of the Indians, and on a tract of land reserved and held by themselves, are not to be charged to the United States.

United States v. Duval, 1 Gilpin, 356.

SEC. 807. Trading with Indians without a license on lands west of the Mississippi River to which the Indian title has been extinguished is not prohibited by the act of Congress of June 30, 1834 (4 Stat. L., 729), regulating trade with the Indians "in the Indian country," section 1 of that act providing that "all that part of the United States west of the Mississippi and not within the States of Missouri and Louisiana or the Territory of Arkansas, and also that part of the United States east of the Missouri River and not within any State to which the Indian title has not been extinguished shall, for the purpose of this act, be taken to be Indian country."

United States v. Certain Property, 25 Pacific Reporter, 517.

SEC. 808. The claimant's goods were seized for a violation of the act of 1834.   He had a store on land open to settlement near the line of a reservation, and traded at his store without a license with Indians from the reservation and others.   *Held*, that there was no error in refusing a certificate of probable cause under 1 U. S. Stat. L., p. 696, sec. 89, providing that, if it should appear that there was reasonable cause for the seizure, the court should cause a proper certificate or entry thereof to be made.   *Ibid.*

SEC. 809. The intercourse act of March 30, 1802 (2 Stat. L., p. 145, sec. 19), provided that the act should not be construed to prevent trade or intercourse with Indians living on lands surrounded by settlements of citizens of the United States.   The act of 1834, section 29, provided that the repeal of the act of 1802 should not affect it so far as it related to tribes east of the Mississippi River.   The organic act of New Mexico provided that the laws of the United States not locally inapplicable should have the same force and effect in the Territory as elsewhere in the United States, and this provision was by organic act of Arizona, section 2, made applicable to that Territory.   *Held*, that section 19 of the act of 1802 was extended to the Territory of Arizona by its organic act.   *Ibid.*

SEC. 810. A contract by which G and K, who were the holders of a license to trade with the Indians at Fort Peck Indian Agency, agreed to pay K and S the one-half of the net profits of such trade for the consideration of the said K and S purchasing all goods and supplies necessary and proper for said trade at their own account and credit, and immediately resell and invoice such goods to said G and S at said agency at cost price, cost for transportation and insurance added, and one of the said K and S take entire charge, management, and control of said business, devoting his entire time and attention thereto, and residing at Fort Peck, is *held* to be illegal, for the reason that it contemplates the violation of the statute (Rev. Stat., U. S., secs. 2129, 2130, 2133, p. 372) as well as the public policy of the Government of the United States.   *Goul et al. v. Kendall et al., 19 Northwestern Reporter, 483.*

SEC. 811. Section 2129 (Rev. Stat.) provides as follows: "No person shall be permitted to trade with any Indians in the Indian country without a license therefor from the superintendent of Indian affairs, or Indian agent or subagent, which license shall be issued for a term of not exceeding two years for the tribes east of the Mississippi, and not exceeding three years for tribes west of that river."

Section 2133 (Rev. Stat.) provides that "any person, other than an Indian, who shall attempt to reside in the Indian country as a trader, or to introduce goods, or to trade therein, without such license, shall forfeit all merchandise offered for sale to the Indians or found in his possession, and shall, moreover, be liable to a penalty of five hundred dollars."

Held, That "it will be thus seen that a license to reside in the Indian country as a trader, and to trade with the Indians, is a personal privilege of a high official character, so that if C. L. Bristol was the holder of such a license he possessed no right to sell it, either in whole or in part, and a pretended or simulated sale thereof would convey no right or franchise whatever to the purchaser. Also, that no court of law or equity will lend its assistance in any way toward carrying out an illegal contract, therefore such contract can not be enforced by one party against another, either directly, by asking the court to carry it into effect, or indirectly, by claiming damages or compensation for a breach of it.   *Hobbie v. Zaepffel, 23 N. W. Rep., 514.*

SEC. 812. In Lobenstien *v.* United States, 91 U. S., 324, the contract was that L. should have all the hides of beef cattle slaughtered for Indians at Fort Sill "which the superintendent of Indian affairs at that place shall decide are not required for the comfort of the Indians, the number of hides to be about 4,000, more or less." The court held that by the express terms of the contract L. was only entitled to such hides as the superintendent of Indian affairs decided were not required for the comfort of the Indians, and having decided that there were none such, that the comfort of the Indians required that the cattle be issued to them on foot, and that they have the hides, L. was bound by the decision of the superintendent, who, by the contract, was constituted the final arbiter in the matter; that he had agreed in advance that his right to hides should depend upon the superintendent's decision as to what was required for the comfort of the Indians; and that the number "about 4,000, more or less," was an estimated, not a guaranteed number, and still subject to the general condition that the superintendent might decide whether or not there were any hides not required for the comfort of the Indians.

Glecher v. Slavens, 59 N. W. Rep., 328.

SEC. 813. The Indians upon our Western frontier, since their removal from their former homes east of the Mississippi, have been, to some extent, under the parental guardianship and protection of the Government of the United States; have been receiving annuities under treaty stipulations, and being of an inferior race and easily imposed upon, Congress deemed it expedient to pass the clause in section 3 of the act of March 3, 1847 (9 Stat. L., 203) to guard them against impositions.   *Clark v. Crosland, 17 Ark., 43.*

SEC. 814. A contract made by an Indian in the Indian country, to pay money at a future day, can not be enforced in the courts of Arkansas, because prohibited by an act of Congress.   *Ibid.*

SEC. 815. The latter clause of the third section of the act of Congress

March 3, 1847 (9 Stat. L., 203), amendatory of acts in relation to the Department of Indian Affairs, and to trade and intercourse with the Indians, is too broad and comprehensive in its terms to be restricted to contracts for spirituous liquors. *Ibid.*

SEC. 816. An executory contract entered into, in this State, between an Indian and a white man, may be enforced—Congress possessing no constitutional power to invalidate contracts entered into within the limits of a sovereign State, whether with Indians or others.

Hicks v. Ewhartonah, 21 Ark., 106.

SEC. 817. Congress lacks the constitutional power to enact laws invalidating contracts entered into within the limits of a sovereign State, whether with an Indian or a resident of a sister State or subject of a foreign Government, this being one of the reserved rights retained by the State. *Ibid.*

SEC. 818. The case of Clark *v.* Crosland (17 Ark., 43) furnishes no precedent in this. There the writing obligatory was executed by the Indian in the Indian country, where the *lex loci* applied, as it does in this case, and must as a settled rule in all cases of a similar character.

Ibid.

SEC. 819. Congress has not undertaken to say that an executory contract made by an Indian within the limits of one of the States of the Union shall be void and shall not be enforced in our courts; and if Congress were so to enact, the court would be slow to concede the constitutional validity of the act. *Taylor v. Drew, 21 Ark., 485.*

SEC. 820. When an Indian goes into one of the States and makes a contract there its validity must depend, as a general rule, upon the laws of that State; and so an executory contract made by an Indian within the State will be enforced. *Ibid.*

SEC. 821. Congress, exercising a parental guardianship over the Indian people, has enacted laws for their protection from imposition within their own country; but when an Indian goes into any one of the States, and makes a contract there, its validity must depend, as a general rule, upon the laws of that State. *Ibid.*

SEC. 822. That Congress has the constitutional power "to regulate commerce with foreign nations, and among the several States, and with the Indian tribes," is beyond question. But the clause of the intercourse act declaring that executory contracts made by an Indian for the payment of money or goods shall be null and void was no exercise of the power to "*regulate* commerce," within the meaning of the Constitution. *Ibid.*

SEC. 823. The acts of Congress to protect Indians from the payment of money on executory contracts (acts of March 3, 1847, and June 30, 1834) do not relieve white men from the discharge of their obligations to Indians. *Rogers v. Duval, 23 Ark., 77.*

SEC. 824. A white man licensed to trade in the Indian country who sells out his business and abandons his post has no right to remain in such country, and he may, together with his property, be ousted therefrom.   *Echols v. Tate, 53 Ark., 12.*

SEC. 825. The President of the United States is charged with the duty of putting unauthorized persons out of the Indian country, and when he determines that the exigency has arisen requiring his action, there is no power to review the correctness of his conclusion.   *Ibid.*

SEC. 826. All persons improperly within the Indian country shall be removed. (Sec. 2147, U. S. Rev. Stat.; United States v. Payne, 8 Fed. Rep., 883.)   *Ibid.*

SEC. 827. The United States Indian agents are to manage and superintend all the affairs of the agency, including the intercourse of the whites with the Indians, and execute such regulations as may be prescribed by the President, the Secretary of the Interior, and the Commissioner of Indian Affairs, or the superintendent. (U. S. Rev. Stat., 2058.)   *Ibid.*

SEC. 828. The Indians by treaty are guaranteed that white men, except those designated in sections 2128–2129, Rev. Stat., shall not come into their country. Any man who attempts to settle there or to mark the boundaries of a habitation shall be fined $1,000. (Sec. 2118, Rev. Stat.) The President shall remove them. (Id.)   *Ibid.*

SEC. 829. A contract for the sale of cattle by a citizen of Arkansas to a Choctaw Indian, whereby the cattle were to be delivered at the vendee's place of residence in the Choctaw Nation, the title to remain in the vendor until paid for, does not contravene a law of the Choctaw Nation which prohibits a noncitizen from owning, controlling, or holding stock in that country, and prohibits a citizen from evading or assisting any noncitizen to evade the law by a sham sale without consideration, of stock to be held by such citizen for the use and benefit of such noncitizen within the limits of such nation.
                                              Morris v. Cohen, 55 Ark., 401.

SEC. 830. Section 2117, Revised Statutes, which imposes a penalty on any person "who drives any horses, mules, or cattle to range or feed on any land belonging to any Indian or Indian tribe, without the consent of said tribe," is not violated by driving cattle into the Indian country for delivery to one of its citizens under his contract to purchase them.   *Ibid.*

SEC. 831. Under section 31 of the act of Congress, May 2, 1890 (26 Stat. L., 94, 95), a licensed trader in the Indian Territory is entitled to claim his exemptions, as provided by Mansfield's Digest, chapter 60.   *King v. Hargadine-McKittrick Dry Goods Company, 60 Ark., 1.*

SEC. 832. In the absence of proof of the laws and customs of the

Indian Nation at the time of the marriage of defendant and Paralee Sivils, and such as were applicable to them, the defendant should not have been convicted.   *Johnson v. State, 60 Ark., 308.*

SEC. 833. A marriage between first cousins in the Indian Territory since May 2, 1890, is void, as on that day an act of Congress (26 Stat. L., 94) extended the Arkansas laws on the subject of marriage over the Indian Territory.   *Ibid.*

SEC. 834. The policy of all branches of the Government from the earliest times has been to protect all citizens in the occupation of ceded Indian lands and to secure cessions as fast as demanded by the increase of our population; and when territory has once been solemnly ceded by the Indians it has never afterwards been considered or treated as Indian country for any purpose.

Clark v. Bates, 1 Dak. (Bennett), 42.   Same, 46 N. W. Rept., 510.

SEC. 835. The act of Congress organizing the Territory of Oregon reserved to the Government of the United States the right to make rules and regulations respecting the person and property of the Indians which it would have been competent for the Government to make had the act never been passed.

Pickett v. United States, 1 Prichett (Idaho), 522.

SEC. 836. It was by virtue of the act of Congress of June 5, 1850, and not the act of June 30, 1834, that the law regulating trade and intercourse with the Indian tribes east of the Rocky Mountains, or such provisions of the same as were applicable, were extended over the Indian tribes of Oregon.   *Ibid.*

SEC. 837. This Territory having been originally a portion of Oregon, and Congress, in organizing it, having reserved the right to make such regulations respecting the persons and property of the Indians as in the Oregon Territory, the act of 1850 and the provisions of the act of 1834, so far as applicable, remain in force in this Territory.   *Ibid.*

SEC. 838. By the first section of the act of Congress of June 30, 1834 (4 Stat. L., 729), it is provided that all that part of the United States west of the Mississippi and not within the States of Missouri and Louisiana or the Territory of Arkansas, for the purposes of this act, shall be taken and deemed to be Indian country. The Supreme Court of the United States in giving an interpretation of this section says: "The Indian Territory is admitted to compose a part of the United States." (Cherokee Nation *v.* Georgia, 5 Peters, 171.) "The treaties and laws of the United States contemplate the Indian Territory as completely separated from that of the States, and provide that all intercourse with them shall be carried on exclusively by the Government of the Union." (Worcester *v.* Georgia, 6 Peters, 547.) They are not foreign but dependent domestic nations. They occupy a territory to which we assert a title independent of will, which must take effect in point of possession when their right of possession ceases.

Ibid.

SEC. 839. The provisions of the twenty-fifth section of the act of Congress of 1834, regulating trade and intercourse with the Indians, is as applicable to the Indian tribes in this Territory as any portion of the act, hence the Territory of Idaho is Indian country, but only so far as the rights of the persons and property of the Indian tribes are concerned, and therefore to that extent within the sole and exclusive jurisdiction of the United States.

At the time of the passage of the act of 1834 none of the country which was subsequently organized into the Territory of Oregon was embraced by the provisions of this act within the Indian country, it being at that time jointly occupied by the United States and Great Britain. By the act of Congress organizing the Territory of Oregon (9 Stat. L., 323) it is provided among other things: That nothing in said act shall be construed to impair the rights of person or property of the Indians in said Territory so long as the same shall remain unextinguished by treaty between the United States and such Indians, or to affect the authority of the Government of the United States to make any regulation respecting such Indians, their lands, etc. *Ibid.*

SEC. 840. The prohibitory principle, with respect to liquor traffic, was adopted partially in regard to certain classes, as Indians; contingently all over the State by the township vote, and in certain localities directly. *Harris v. Doe ex dem. Spencer, 3 Indiana, 494.*

SEC. 841. An indictment for selling spirituous liquor to an Indian can not be objected to merely because the name of the Indian is not inserted, if the indictment state that the name is unknown to the jurors. *State v. Jackson, 4 Blackf. (Ind.), 49.*

SEC. 842. Assumpsit brought by an administrator on a written contract, by which the defendant sold to the intestate one-half of a claim on some Indians, with a guarantee, etc.; each of the parties was to assist in the collection of the claim at the next Indian treaty, and a certain void obligation, held by the intestate on the defendant, was to be given up. On the trial under the general issue the contract was proved, but there was no evidence that the intestate had assisted in the collection of said claim or that said void obligation had been given up. *Held*, that the plaintiff could not recover.

Ewing v. Coombs, 8 Blackf. (Ind.), 357.

SEC. 843. A contract to prosecute a claim against the Government on account of the Potawatomi Indians, and pay all expenses, and to receive as compensation therefor a certain portion of the amount recovered if successful and nothing if not successful, is champertous and void. *Coquillard's Admr. v. Bearss et al., 21 Ind., 479.*

SEC. 844. It could not have been intended by Congress, in the enactment of sections 2103 to 2106, Revised Statutes, to prevent an Indian from directing the application of his moneys to the payment of his debts, except such as were contracted upon the consideration expressed in the statute.   *Godfroy v. Scott, 70 Ind., 259.*

SEC. 845. In an attachment suit against a nonresident, wherein garnishment was resorted to, the court found specially that the defendant was a Miami Indian entitled to an annuity from the United States; that the defendant had verbally directed the Indian agent to pay the annuity to the garnishee, in part satisfaction of a debt due from the defendant to the garnishee; that payment had accordingly been made, and that, subsequent to the giving of such order, but prior to such payment, the writ of garnishment had been issued. *Held*, as a conclusion of law, that, as the special finding does not show the nature of the consideration of the debt of the defendant to the garnishee, it will not be presumed that such debt was for any of the things mentioned in section 2103 of the Revised Statutes of the United States, and therefore such order was valid.   *Ibid.*

SEC. 846. The third article of the ordinance of 1787, which has been judicially declared to be in force in Indiana, is as follows: "The utmost good faith shall always be observed toward the Indians; their lands and property shall never be taken from them without their consent, and in their property, rights, and liberty they shall never be invaded or disturbed, unless in just and lawful wars authorized by Congress; but laws founded in justice and humanity shall, from time to time, be made for preventing wrongs being done them, and for preserving peace and friendship with them.
    Board of Com'rs of Allen Co. v. Simons, 129 Ind., 193.

SEC. 847. By the act of June 10, 1816, the Territorial legislature of Indiana made a solemn compact with the United States, by the terms of which certain portions of the ordinance of 1787, among which was the one relating to Indians, were kept in force. This clause is a provision in favor of the Indian tribes residing on Indiana territory, and as such is to be liberally construed in their favor.   *Ibid.*

SEC. 848. In the month of April, 1816, Congress passed an act which provided that the people of the Indiana Territory might form a constitution and be admitted into the Union, provided that the same, when formed, should be republican, and not repugnant to the ordinance of July 13, 1787, which was declared to be irrevocable between the original States and the people and the States of the territory northwest of the Ohio River, etc.   *Ibid.*

SEC. 849. The "nonintercourse act" of June 30, 1834 (4 Stat. L., 729), does not prohibit all contracts between white men and Indians.
    Jones v. Eisler, 3 Kans., 134.

SEC. 850. An answer to a petition on a promissory note, setting forth that the defendant is an " Ottawa Indian," lives with that tribe on the "Ottawa Reserve" in Kansas, where the note was executed, does not contain sufficient allegations to bring the case within the prohibitions of that act of Congress. *Held*, that the sustaining of a demurrer to such answer was not error, and that an Ottawa Indian may be sued.   *Ibid.*

SEC. 851. The allegations do not bring the case within the provisions of the act of June 30, 1834. If it were admitted that the place where the note was made was without the limits of the then Territory of Kansas, and was the "Indian country" as defined by the act referred to, and that the maker was an Indian belonging to the tribe occupying that locality, it would not follow that his contract with a white man would be void; a contract made out of the Territory is not for that reason void.   *Ibid.*

SEC. 852. A contract between a white man and an Indian made in the "Indian country" would be void if prohibited by the act of Congress. But the act does not prohibit all contracts made between white men and Indians. When made under certain circumstances they are prohibited.   *Ibid.*

SEC. 853. An Indian may build a house in the "Indian country," and may, with the consent of the Government, employ mechanics to do the work, and when the work has been performed that assent will be presumed.   *Ibid.*

SEC. 854. The clerk of the council of the Wyandotte tribe is not a public officer competent to authenticate copies of public records.
Cooper v. Armstrong, 4 Kans., 30.

SEC. 855. It is settled in the Bluejacket case (5 Wallace, 756) that " Kansas accepted her admission into the family of States on condition that the Indian rights should remain unimpaired and the General Government at liberty to make any regulation respecting them, their lands, property, or other rights which it would have been competent to make if Kansas had not been admitted into the Union."

Parker v. Winsor, 5 Kans., 362.

SEC. 856. Under the Kansas Territorial organic act, and the act of admission, no right that the Indians had before the admission, or before the Territory was organized, can be impaired " so long as such rights shall remain unextinguished by treaty between the United States and such Indians."   *Ibid.*

SEC. 857. The Miamis of Kansas employed Sims to prosecute certain matters pending before the departments and in Congress. To assist Sims, McBratney was employed. The exact terms of the contract and the exact nature of the services rendered are not shown. If all that was contemplated was the preparing of briefs, the making of oral arguments before the departments or a committee of Congress, the contract was valid and the services legitimate; but if the employment of plaintiff was as a lobbyist, the contract was against public policy and void.

McBratney v. Chandler, 22 Kans., 35.

SEC. 858. It is not the presumption that a party is a wrongdoer in going into or being within any State or Territory of the United States. It is known that the Indian Territory is set apart for the occupation of Indians, because the court takes judicial notice of the laws and treaties of the United States, and in those treaties express reservation is made of the right to license the building and running of a railroad through that Territory. (Creek treaty of 1866, 14 Stat. L., 787; Choctaw and Chickasaw treaty, 14 Stat. L., 771.)

Speer v. M., K. & T. Ry. Co., 23 Kans., 571.

SEC. 859. Carter had a license to trade with the Potawatomi Indians in Kansas. Being of limited means and credit he formed a partnership with plaintiff's son under an arrangement that plaintiff would sell goods from his store at Topeka to the firm, and the firm would dispose of the goods under the license and in the name of Carter on the reservation. Carter obtained a permit from the Government for plaintiff's son to live upon the reservation, and the latter took charge of the store operated in Carter's name. *Held*, that the sale of goods at Topeka by the plaintiff to Carter or the firm was not in violation of sections 2128, 2129, or 2133 United States Revised Statutes, or contrary to public policy.

Dunn v. Carter, 30 Kans., 294.

SEC. 860. A mortgagee from an entryman of a tract of Osage trust and diminished reserve lands, after final receipt is given, and before the issuance of the patent, takes his mortgage subject to the supervisory power of the Commissioner of the General Land Office of the United States.

Freese v. Scanten, 53 Kans., 347.

SEC. 861. The Commissioner of the General Land Office, before the issuance of the patent, has full authority, upon a valid contest, to pass and decide upon the qualification of an applicant to enter and purchase a tract of the Osage trust land.

Ibid.

SEC. 862. All that is required of an applicant to make an entry and purchase of the Osage trust and diminished reservation lands is, that he shall have all the qualifications of a preemptor; that he shall be an actual settler on the land at the date of the entry, and that he shall make full payment therefor.

Ibid.

SEC. 863. By the statute of 1824, ch. 271, a sale to a foreigner of trees, timber, or grass standing or growing on the Passamaquoddy Indian Township, whether made by the agent or by a citizen of Maine who had purchased of the agent is void, and transfers no title to such foreigner.

Boies v. Blake, 13 Maine, 381.

SEC. 864. Where the Indian agent gave to Dudley a written license to cut all the grass on Passamaquoddy Township, with a provision in the license that it was understood that Dudley was to permit Boies to cut a certain specified portion thereof for a compensation; and B. offered to D. such reasonable compensation, who refused to receive it, and afterwards transferred his right and license to a foreigner; B. cut the grass, made it into hay, and stacked it, it was held that B. had such interest in the hay as would enable him to maintain trespass against a foreigner acting under such trespass.   *Ibid.*

SEC. 865. The agent of the Passamaquoddy Indians had authority to dispose of the hay in question. The instrument in writing between him and John Dudley is evidence that when the plaintiff went in and cut the hay, he had the license and consent of the agent.   *Ibid.*

SEC. 866. Though there were difficulties attending plaintiff's title to the hay cut on the Passamaquoddy land, he had cut it and had it in actual possession. He might, therefore, maintain trespass against a wrongdoer for taking it away.   *Ibid.*

SEC. 867. If the contract of sale of logs taken from the Passamaquoddy Reservation be illegal, as contravening the statute 1824, chapter 271, but a full consideration is paid and the logs are delivered, the seller can neither reclaim the logs, nor recover their value by an action therefor.   *Marks v. Hapgood, 24 Maine, 407.*

SEC. 868. "The Indian tribes" referred to in the Constitution were those tribes which were in a condition to determine for themselves with whom they would have commerce, or in a condition to have Congress determine it for them; and not those small tribes or remnants of tribes yet denominated tribes which had before that time, and have ever since, continued to be under the control and guardianship of a State, and were without power to carry on commerce, except by permission and under the control of State laws.   *Moor v. Veazie, 32 Maine, 343.*

SEC. 869. The power given to Congress to regulate *commerce* with the Indian tribes does not include *navigation* with the Penobscot or any other tribe of Indians. It is confined to that sort of trade of which navigation constitutes no part.   *Ibid.*

SEC. 870. The admission that commerce includes navigation is not intended to include commerce with the Indian tribes. The language must have been used with reference to such commerce with them as was known to have existed. The treaties made with them before the Union, and the ordinance made by Congress under the confederation, recognize and provide for trade or traffic with them; but no national, conventional, or constitutional law or ordinance is known to have recognized or authorized navigation to be carried on with any Indian tribe.   *Ibid.*

SEC. 871. So early as the year 1633 the general court of Massachusetts ordered "that no person whatsoever shall henceforth buy any land of any Indian without license first had and obtained. In 1650 the French, Dutch, and other foreigners were forbidden to trade with them. In 1657 the Commonwealth declared its right to all the fur trade with them. It had before that time forbidden the sale to them of guns, gunpowder, and other munitions of war. In 1693 an act was passed "for the better rule and government of the Indians in their several places and plantations." *Ibid.*

SEC. 872. The first section of the act of 1693 (Massachusetts) provided for the appointment of persons "to have the inspection and more particular care of the Indians in their respective plantations," and these persons were authorized to determine "pleas betwixt party and party" and to punish criminal offenses. Such a course of legislative control was continued until Maine was separated from Massachusetts, although contracts called "treaties" were made with them by the colony for the relinquishment of their title to lands. By the act of separation Maine assumed the performance of all obligations made by Massachusetts to the Indians within her jurisdiction, and in 1812 passed an act for the regulation of the Penobscot and Passamaquoddy tribes of Indians. *Ibid.*

SEC. 873. The early laws relating to the Penobscots and Passamaquoddies may be ascertained by reference to the ancient charters and statutes of Massachusetts under the title "Indians." Neither the Congress under the confederation nor the Government of the United States appears to have at any time exercised any control over them, or to have made any contract or treaty with the Indians within the jurisdiction of Maine or Massachusetts. Vide American State Papers; title, Indian affairs. *Ibid.*

SEC. 874. Col. John Allan was appointed by Congress in 1777 "agent for Indian affairs in the eastern department," and held that office till 1784. He was instructed to visit "the tribes of Indians, inhabitants of St. John and Nova Scotia," and by threats, persuasions, and arguments of various kinds to convince them that it would be better for their interests not to take part against the United States in the war then raging. He made his headquarters at Machias and assumed a general supervision over the various tribes of Indians from the St. John to the Penobscot. *State v. Newell, 84 Maine, 465.*

SEC. 875. Many of Col. John Allan's letters have been preserved by the Indians and by them submitted to the court. They are full of kindly assurances of protection, including hunting, but it can not be claimed that they amount to a treaty between two political communities. *Ibid.*

SEC. 876. The decision of the United States land officers upon the location of scrip issued pursuant to the act of Congress of July 17, 1854, entitled "An act to authorize the President of the United States to cause to be surveyed the tract of land in the Territory of Minnesota belonging to the half-breeds or mixed bloods of the Dakotah or Sioux nation of Indians, and for other purposes," is final and conclusive.   *Monette v. Cratt, 7 Minn. (Gilfillan), 176.*

SEC. 877. An assignment by defendant to plaintiff of a portion of certain claims held and owned by the defendant on and before the 8th of December, 1860, and then existing in favor of the defendant, for goods, wares, and merchandise sold and delivered by the defendant to certain Indians of the Sioux or Dakotah tribe, which were still to be examined, allowed, and affirmed by the United States under the provisions of the treaty between the United States and Sisseton and Wahpaton bands of the Dakotah or Sioux tribe of Indians, concluded in Washington June 19, 1858, ratified by the Senate March 9, 1859, is void under the act of Congress entitled "An act to prevent frauds upon the Treasury of the United States," approved February 26, 1853.

Becker v. Sweetzer, 15 Minn., 427.

SEC. 878. The seventh article of the Chickasaw treaty, 1816 (7 Stat. L., 150), provides that any person whomsoever, of the white people, who shall bring goods and *sell* them contrary to this article, shall forfeit the whole of his or her goods, etc.

Mingo & Allen v. Goodman, 2 Miss., 552.

SEC. 879. The defendant justified under the treaty for seizing certain goods and merchandise, and set out the seventh article thus: that any person or persons whatsoever, of the white people, who *shall bring goods to sell* and offer to sell them in said nation, etc.; the variance was fatal.   *Ibid.*

SEC. 880. To constitute the offense under the treaty it is not only necessary that the goods should be brought and offered for sale, but there must be an actual sale.   *Ibid.*

SEC. 881. The purchase is regulated by treaty, prior to which the Indians were entitled to be protected in their possession; but the fee simple in the soil, and the right of preemption belongs to the Government. The Indians can sell neither to States nor individuals; and this principle is now extended to all their commerce and intercourse, which are wholly under the control of the Federal Government.

Tush-ho-yo-tubby v. Barr, 45 Miss., 189.

SEC. 882. The fact that both parties to a suit in chancery in a State court claim the land in controversy, under a treaty to which the United States is a party, has in itself nothing to exclude the jurisdiction of the State court.   *Land v. Land, 1 S. & M. Chancery (Miss.), 158.*

SEC. 883. Citizens of the United States, and those who have declared their intention to become such, have the right to carry spirituous liquors through the Indian country for the purpose of lawfully selling the same in other places.   *United States v. Carr, 2 Montana, 234.*

Sec. 884. A sale of whisky in Montana outside of an Indian reservation to an Indian belonging to a tribe living upon a reservation in charge of an Indian agent is not commerce "with the Indian tribes" within the meaning of the Constitution of the United States, Article I, section 8, subdivision 3.   *Territory v. Guyott, 9 Montana, 46.*

Sec. 885. The United States did not intend to yield or divide its authority over the Indians in their domestic affairs; the Territorial legislature had no right to exercise it, and the presumption is that it did not intend to do so.   *State v. McKenney, 18 Nev., 182.*

Sec. 886. By the act of admitting Nevada as a Territory in March, 1861, it was declared "that nothing in this act contained shall be construed to impair the rights of person or property now pertaining to the Indian in said Territory so long as such rights shall remain unextinguished by treaty between the United States and such Indians; * * * or to affect the authority of the Government of the United States to make any regulations respecting such Indians, their lands, property, or other rights, by treaty, law, or otherwise, which it would have been competent for the Government to make if this act had never been passed."   *Ibid.*

Sec. 887. The rights of person and property referred to in the organic act (1861) could not have been treaty rights only, as the first treaty with the Shoshones in the Territory was concluded in 1863 (18 Stat. L., 685), nor could it have been intended to guard Indians against lawlessness on the part of the Territory.   *Ibid.*

Sec. 888. In Boyer *v.* Dively (58 Mo., 529) it was held that although within the State lines, yet, so long as their tribal customs are adhered to and the Federal Government manages their affairs by agents, the Indians are not regarded as subject to State laws, so far at least as marriage, inheritance, etc., are concerned. No State legislation was attempted to the contrary, and it is useless to inquire if it had been whether it would have been valid.   *Ibid.*

Sec. 889. All persons employed in Indian affairs were prohibited from having any interest or concern in any trade with the Indians except for or on account of the United States. (Secs. 1840 and 2070, Rev. Stats.)   *Ibid.*

Sec. 890. Statutes for the regulation of trade and intercourse with the Indian tribes which impose fines and forfeitures are to be construed strictly as penal laws.   *United States v. Lucero, 1 N. M. (Gild), 422.*

Sec. 891. All contracts for the purchase or sale or occupation of land made with any of the tribes of Indians within this State, without the previous consent of the State, are by the constitution and laws of the State illegal and absolutely void.

The St. Regis Indians v. Dunn, 19 John. (N. Y.), 126.

SEC. 892. Under the statute (2 R. L., 153, sec. 2) declaring that no person shall sue or maintain an action upon a contract made with any Indian belonging to certain tribes (By the act of 1790, against any Indian residing upon any lands reserved to the Oneida, Onondaga, and Cayuga Indians. By the act of 1801 this inability to be sued was extended to the Stockbridge and Brotherhood Indians, and in 1807 to the Senecas) within this State (including the Onondagas), a judgment upon contract rendered against an Onondaga Indian, without appearance on his part, is void.

An Indian may appear and plead his exemption from suit upon his contracts, but he is not obliged to do so. The courts have no authority to render judgment against him.

Hastings v. Farmer et al., 4 Comstock (N. Y. App.), 293.

SEC. 893. The legislature can not empower Indian nations to make, or others to take from them, grants or leases of lands within Indian reservations. It is only pursuant to Federal authority that lands belonging to an Indian reservation can be granted or demised or acquired by conveyance or lease from an Indian nation.

Chapter 316 of the laws of 1836 of New York, authorizing railroad companies to contract with Indian nations for the right to construct railroads over Indian lands, is not within the legislative power of the State so as to give a railroad company, by virtue of a lease made in accordance with its provisions by the Seneca Nation, without the intervention of Federal authority, prior to the act of Congress of February 19, 1875, of lands in the village of Salamanca, in the Allegany Indian Reservation, a right to the possession of such lands superior to that of an individual in possession under a prior lease, which, although originally invalid and giving no right as against the Seneca Nation, had been ratified and validated under the said act of Congress by a renewal thereof by the Seneca Nation.

Buffalo, etc., R. R. Co. v. Larery, 75 Hun (N. Y.), 396.

SEC. 894. Section 2139, Revised Statutes, is applicable to all Indians who are in any degree under the control or charge of an Indian agent. The fact that an Indian received allotted lands in Kansas in the year 1866 and took the oath of allegiance to the United States and became an elector of the State of Kansas, and is above the age of 21 years, is not sufficient to take him out of the inhibition contained in section 2139, provided he has not been released by the Government from the charge, supervision, and control of an Indian agent. Neither does the fact that an Indian may be living upon allotted lands and not drawing any annuity from the Government authorize the sale to such Indian of intoxicating liquors, provided such Indian is still under the supervision or control of an Indian agent.

Renfrow v. United States, 3 Okla. (Dale), 161.

SEC. 895. The act in relation to contracts with Cherokee Indians

(Rev. Code, ch. 50, sec. 16) applies as well to contracts made by one Indian with another as to those made by an Indian with a white man.

Lovingood v. Smith, 7 Jones (N. C. Law), 601.

SEC. 896. The Constitution of the United States gave the power to the General Government to regulate intercourse with the Indians and to make treaties. The Constitution was a dead letter until the treaties and the laws of the United States pointed out the principles of this intercourse. By treaty there are certain lands within which the citizens are not to hunt, survey, or even go without permission. But neither the Constitution nor the laws of the United States take from the sovereign rights of the State further than is compatible with these regulations.

Glasgow v. Smith, 1 Overton (Tenn.), 111.

SEC. 897. The penalty imposed by the act of Congress, 1802 (2 Stat. L., 139), is only incurred when a person, without permit, goes into the Indian country and trades with the Indians. But the possession and enjoyment of the tract where the traffic in question was carried on are secured to the United States as a military post, and of course the penalty is no more incurred than if the trading had been in this place.

Luty v. Purdy, 2 Overton (Tenn.), 543.

SEC. 898. It is no justification for the seizure and imprisonment of a citizen that the defendant was commandant of a military post and had authorized the plaintiff, upon his application, to sell goods to the soldiers, but prohibited him from selling liquors to soldiers or Indians, and that plaintiff had violated that order, for which he was imprisoned.

Ibid.

SEC. 899. A number of Choctaws having reported themselves to the agent to be registered for reservations, which for some cause the agent neglected or refused to do, they made contracts with attorneys to secure to them their reservations of land, the consideration being a grant by the Indians of a portion of the lands secured to them.

Maney v. Porter, 3 Humph. (Tenn.), 347.

SEC. 900. In contemplation of the Indian intercourse act of June 30, 1834 (4 Stat. L., 729), and the amendment of March 3, 1847, Washington Territory is Indian country. The latter act does not repeal the former, but the second section adds the penalty of imprisonment.

Fowler v. United States, 1 Allen (Wash.), 3.

SEC. 901. The act of Congress organizing the Territories of Kansas and Nebraska, by implication, repeals the act of June 30, 1834, regulating intercourse with Indians so far as it prohibits settlement by foreigners and manufactures by or commerce among persons not belonging to Indian tribes and not on the land of such tribes.

McCracken v. Todd, 1 Banks & McCahon, 146.

SEC. 902. From the date of the cession of the Delaware "trust lands" and of the "outlet," July 17, 1854, these lands and their occupants (not Indian) became subject to the laws of Kansas as other lands in the State and their occupants, except as the treaty contained provisions of special and local application to them. The only provisions in the treaty (10 Stat. L., 1048) ceding these lands of such special application are article 2, by which the Government agrees, for preemptors, to offer the "trust lands" at public auction, and the provisions in article 16, extending, so far as applicable, to the lands ceded in the treaty the act of March 3, 1807, which prohibits any person from making settlement on any land secured to the United States by any treaty made with a foreign nation or by a cession by any State, which lands shall not have been previously disposed of by the United States, and which prohibits the surveying without authority of law of any of such lands.	*McCracken v. Todd, 1 Banks & McCahon, 146.*

SEC. 903. An averment in an indictment as follows: "That Louis Laurent did * * * unlawfully and knowingly sell, exchange, give, barter, and dispose of to one Cheek wah, then and there being an Indian of the Pottawatomie tribe and nation and not a citizen of the United States nor of the State of Kansas, certain spirituous liquors and wines, to wit: One pint of whisky, one pint of brandy, and one pint of wine, the same not having been directed by any physician for medical purposes or otherwise," charges an offense in the language required by law and contains all the negative averments required by the statute. Sufficient appears to describe the crime and the person charged and to enable the court to pronounce judgment on a conviction.	*Laurent v. State, 1 Banks & McCahon, 296.*

SEC. 904. It is probable that the intention of Governor Micheltorena was not merely to restore the houses, orchards, etc., to the Fathers, but, by placing all the lands of the Missions under their administration and subjecting the Indians to tutelage, to collect and protect that dispersed and oppressed people.	*Larkin v. United States, 1 Hoffman's Land Cases, 313.*

CHAPTER V.—STATE AND TERRITORIAL CONTROL.

SEC. 905. The royal proclamation in 1763 establishing a reservation in the Province of Georgia for the use of the Indians suspended for a time the settlement of the country reserved and the power of the royal governor within it, but did not amount to an alteration of the boundaries of the Georgian colony.	*Fletcher v. Peck, 6 Cranch, 142.*

SEC. 906. Under the Constitution no State can enter into any treaty, and it is not believed that since its adoption any State, under its own authority, has held a treaty with the Indians.

Worcester v. Georgia, 6 Peters, 575.

SEC. 907. Various acts of the legislature of Georgia furnish conclusive evidence that her former opinion as to the rights of the Indians to lands they occupied concurred with those entertained by the other States and the Government of the United States; that their territory was separate from that of any State within whose chartered limits they might reside by a boundary line established by treaties; that within their boundary they possessed rights with which no State could interfere, and that the whole power of regulating intercourse with them was vested in the United States. *Ibid.*

SEC. 908. The Georgia act of 1830 making it a misdemeanor for any person to reside within the Cherokee Nation without a license from the State is unconstitutional and void. *Ibid.*

SEC. 909. The Federal Government has the exclusive regulation of intercourse with the Indians, and so long as this power shall be exercised it can not be obstructed by a State. But if a contingency shall occur which shall render the Indians who reside in a State incapable of self-government, either by moral degradation or reduction of their numbers, it would undoubtedly be in the power of a State government to extend to them the ægis of its laws, and under such circumstances the agency of the General Government of necessity must cease. *Ibid.*

SEC. 910. The Cherokee Nation is a distinct community, occupying its own territory, with boundaries accurately described, in which the laws of Georgia can have no force, and which the citizens of Georgia have no right to enter but with the assent of the Cherokees themselves, or in conformity with the treaties and acts of Congress. The whole intercourse between the United States and this nation is, by our Constitution and laws, vested in the Government of the United States. *Ibid.*

SEC. 911. The chartered limits of the individual States have never been construed by the United States, in any period of its history, to confer jurisdiction over territories contained within those limits; and claimed, defined, and occupied, not by wandering savages, as in New South Wales, but by tribes of Indians acting regularly in a national capacity. *Cherokees v. Georgia, Appendix 1, "Peters Cherokee Case," sec. 225.*

SEC. 912. The compact with the United States was ratified by the legislature of Georgia, June 16, 1802; and it would appear to follow that the State of Georgia is *estopped* by her solemn and deliberate act, done in the face of the Union, from questioning the rights and liberties of the Cherokees, as now by them declared and asserted. *Ibid.*

SEC. 913. The bill filed on behalf of the Cherokees seeks to restrain a State from the forcible exercise of legislative power over a neighboring people asserting their independence, their right to which the State denies. On several of the matters alleged in the bill, for example on the laws making it criminal to exercise the usual powers of self-government in their own country by the Cherokee Nation, the court can not interpose, at least in the form in which those matters are presented.

That part of the bill which respects the land occupied by the Indians may be more doubtful.   The mere question of right might perhaps be decided by this court in a proper case, with proper parties; but the court is asked to do more than to decide on the title.   The bill requires us to control the legislature of Georgia, and restrain the exercise of its physical force.   The propriety of such an interposition by the court may well be questioned.   It savors too much of the exercise of the political power to be within the proper province of the judicial department.   *Ibid.*

SEC. 914.   The act of the legislature of Georgia (19th December, 1829,) is repugnant to the treaties made between the United States and the Cherokees (7 Stat. L, 311) and the act of Congress of 1802 (2 Stat. L., 139) regulating intercourse with the Indian tribes, and to the Constitution of the United States authorizing that act and those treaties; and the conclusion appears to follow that it is an unconstitutional act, and one which the courts of the United States would not sustain.   *Ibid.*

SEC. 915.   The act of the legislature of the State of New York in 1822, asserting exclusive criminal jurisdiction over the Senecas and other tribes of Indians within the limits of the State, even as to crimes and offenses committed by Indians against each other *upon their own territory*, is to be cited as an anomalous case, which can not be easily reconciled to sound principles, or to the authority of the act of Congress of 1802 (2 Stat. L., 139), or to the treaties made with the Six Nations.   *Ibid.*

SEC. 916.   Notwithstanding the peculiar relation which the Seneca Nation of Indians hold to the Government of the United States, the State of New York had the power of a sovereign over their person and property, so far as it was necessary to preserve the peace of the commonwealth and protect those feeble and helpless bands from imposition and intrusion.   The power of the State to make police regulations to preserve the peace of the community is absolute, and has never been surrendered.   *New York v. Dibble, 21 How., 366.*

SEC. 917.   Proceedings under the statute of the State of New York providing for the summary removal of persons other than Indians from the Indian lands within that State did not deprive persons thus removed of property or any rights secured to them by any treaty or act of Congress.   *Ibid.*

SEC. 918.   The New York statute which authorizes the summary removal of persons other than Indians who settle or reside upon lands belonging to or occupied by Indians is not contrary to the Constitution of the United States, or any treaty, or any act of Congress.   Unless such persons have the right of entry into these lands by the treaty of May 20, 1842 (7 Stat. L., 586) between the United States and the Seneca

Indians, they can not allege that such summary removal, by authority of the statute of New York, is in conflict with the treaty.   *Ibid.*

SEC. 919. No State can, by either its constitution or other legislation, withdraw the Indians within its limits from the operation of the laws of Congress regulating trade with them, notwithstanding rights it may confer on such Indians as electors or citizens.

United States v. Holliday, 3 Howard, 407.

SEC. 920. There can be no question of State sovereignty in the case, as Kansas accepted her admission into the family of States on condition that the Indian rights should remain unimpaired and the General Government at liberty to make any regulation respecting them, their lands, property or other rights, which it would have been competent to make if Kansas had not been admitted into the Union.

The Kansas Indians, 5 Wallace, 737.

SEC. 921. If the Shawnees are under the control of Congress, of necessity there can be no divided authority. It may be that they can not exist much longer as a distinct people in the presence of the civilization of Kansas, "but until they are clothed with the rights and bound to all the duties of citizens," they enjoy the privilege of total immunity from taxation.   *Ibid.*

SEC. 922. Indians with separate estates have the same rights in the tribe of Shawnee Indians as those whose estates are held in common.

Blue Jacket v. Johnson Co., 5 Wallace, 737.

SEC. 923. By conferring rights and privileges on the Indians the State of Kansas can not affect their situation, which can only be changed by treaty stipulation or voluntary abandonment of their tribal organization.   *The Kansas Indians, 5 Wallace, 737.*

SEC. 924. If the tribal organization of Indian bands is recognized by the political department of the National Government as existing— that is to say, if the National Government makes treaties with, and has its Indian agent among them, paying annuities and dealing otherwise with the "head men" in its behalf—the fact that the primitive habits and customs of the tribe when in a savage state have been largely broken into by their intercourse with the whites in the midst of whom, by the advance of civilization, they have come to find themselves, does not authorize a State government to regard the tribal organization as gone and the Indians as citizens of the State where they are, and subject to its laws.   *Ibid.*

SEC. 925. The situation of the Weas and their property in the State of Kansas is the same as that of the Shawnees, and the fact that they have applied to the courts of the State, sometimes voluntarily, and, in certain specified cases, by the Secretary of the Interior, does not necessarily imply that they have submitted themselves to all the laws of the State; and until the tribe is disbanded the Indians can not look to Kansas for protection, nor can the general laws of the State taxing real estate within its limits reach their property.   *Ibid.*

SEC. 926. The situation of the Miamis in Kansas is the same as that of the Shawnee and Wea tribes. It is sufficient to state that they are a nation of people, recognized as such by the General Government in making of treaties with them, and the relation always maintained toward them, and can not, therefore, be taxed by the authorities of Kansas.   *Ibid.*

SEC. 927. The land belonging to the tribe of Shawnee, Wea, and Miami Indians, residing in Kansas, are not taxable by the State.

> *The Kansas Indians, 5 Wall., 737.   Yellow Beaver v. Miami Co., Ibid., 757.   Won zop e ah v. Miami Co., Ibid., 759.*

SEC. 928. The exercise by the State of New York of authority over the Indian lands in that State, as in the assessment and levy of taxes on them, is an unwarrantable interference, inconsistent with the original title of the Indians and offensive to their tribal relations.

> *The New York Indians, 5 Wall., 761.*

SEC. 929. At the adjustment of the dispute between New York and Massachusetts in respect to the lands occupied by the Indians in New York, those two States dealt exclusively with the preemption right after the Indian right was extinguished and with the government and jurisdiction over the territory. They possessed no power to deal with the Indian rights or title, and, therefore, the stipulation "that the lands so granted, and the occupants thereof, shall, during said period (fifteen years), be subject to town and county charges or taxes only" can in no way affect the Indian occupants.   *Ibid.*

SEC. 930. The right of the Indians in their lands does not depend upon the act of 1841, or any other statutes of the State of New York, but upon treaties, which are the supreme law of the land; and it is to these treaties that we must look to ascertain the nature of these rights and the extent of them.   *Ibid.*

SEC. 931. Where Indians, under arrangements approved by the United States, agree to sell their lands to private citizens and to give possession of them at the expiration of a term of years named, a taxation of the land before the efflux of the term is premature, even though a sale for the nonpayment of taxes might not take place until after the time when, if they fulfilled their agreements, the Indians would have left the land, and even though such would be subject to the proviso that the right of the Indians to occupy the land should not in any manner be affected thereby.   *Ibid.*

SEC. 932. Where Indians being in possession of lands, their ancient and native homes, the enjoyment of which "without disturbance by the United States" has been secured to them by treaty with the Federal Government, with the assurance that "the lands shall remain theirs until they choose to sell them," the State in which the lands lie has no power to tax them, either for ordinary town and county purposes or for the special purpose of surveying them and opening roads through them. *Ibid.*

SEC. 933. A statute of a State authorizing a sale of Indian lands for taxes so laid is void, even though the statute provides that no sale for the purpose of collecting the tax shall in any manner affect the right of the Indians to occupy the land. *Ibid.*

SEC. 934. The taxes assessed by the laws of the State of New York upon the three Indian reservations (Buffalo Creek, Allegany, and Cattaraugus) are illegal and void, as in conflict with the tribal rights of the Seneca Nation as guaranteed to it by treaties with the United States. *Ibid.*

SEC. 935. The seventh article of the Chippewa treaty of 1863 (13 Stat. L., 667) is based exclusively on the Federal authority over the *subject-matter*, and there is no disturbance of the principle of State equality. *United States v. 43 Gals. Whisky, 93 U. S., 188; 23—846.*

SEC. 936. The territory reserved for the Shoshone Indians in the Territory of Idaho by the treaty of July 3, 1868 (15 Stat. L., 674), was as much beyond the jurisdiction, legislative or judicial, of the government of Idaho as if it had been set apart with the limits of another country or of a foreign State. Its lines marked the bounds of that government, and the process of one of its courts, consequently, served beyond those lines, could not impose upon the defendant any obligation of obedience, and its disregard could not entail upon him any penalties. The service was an unlawful act of the sheriff.
Harkness v. Hyde, 98 U. S., 476.

SEC. 937. Congress, from whom the power of a territory to exercise jurisdiction emanates, has undoubted authority to exclude it from any part of the soil of the United States, or of that whereto the Indians have the possessory title, when by our solemn treaties with them a stipulation to that effect is made. *Longford v. Montieth, 102 U. S., 145.*

SEC. 938. The court in Harkness v. Hyde (98 U. S., 476), relying upon an imperfect extract found in the brief of counsel, inadvertently inferred that the treaty with the Shoshones, like that with the Shawnees, contains a clause excluding the land of the tribe from the Territorial or State jurisdiction. In this it seems that the court was laboring under a mistake. *Ibid.*

SEC. 939. Where no clause excluding the lands of the tribe from the State or Territorial jurisdiction, or language equivalent to it is found in a treaty with Indians within the exterior limits of Idaho, the lands held by them are a part of the Territory and subject to its jurisdiction, so that process may run there, however the Indians themselves may be exempt from that jurisdiction; and as there is no such treaty with the Nez Perce tribe, on whose reservation the premises in dispute are situated, and as this is a suit between white men, citizens of the United States, the justice of peace had jurisdiction of the parties if the subject-matter was one of which he could take cognizance.

Ibid.

SEC. 940. Where an act of Congress admitting a State into the Union, or organizing a Territorial government, provides, in accordance with a treaty stipulation, that the lands in the possession of an Indian tribe shall not be a part of such State or Territory, the new government has no jurisdiction over them.   *Ibid.*

SEC. 941. By accepting the provisions of Article X of the Sac and Fox treaty of 1859 (15 Stat. L., 467) and the benefit arising out of that article and article 17 of the treaty of 1867 (15 Stat. L., 495) a half-breed Indian woman of the confederated Sac and Fox tribes of the Mississippi who was married to a white man had renounced all claim to share in the proceeds of lands in the reservation sold by the United States under said treaty of 1859, and her subsequent relation to her tribe as a member of it, if she chose to keep it up, can not affect the jurisdiction of the State over her property for governmental purposes. She might have followed her tribe; she can now do it; but as the tribe has left the State of Kansas while she remains, and has taken a title carrying with it absolute ownership, with a right of free disposition at her will, she and her property has come under the control of the State, and are subject to its laws, entitled to its protection, and bound to bear a portion of its burdens.

Pennock v. Commissioners, 103 United States, 44.

SEC. 942. The circumstances being different in that case, the opinion of the court in the case of the Kansas Indians is not in conflict with the views expressed in this case. The tribal organizations of the Kansas Indians continuing in the State, and the United States treating with them as distinct political communities, the legislature of Kansas could not interfere with their lands or lands of individual members of the tribes, and subject them to taxation.   *Ibid.*

SEC. 943. Whenever, upon admission of a State into the Union, Congress has intended to except out of it an Indian reservation, or the sole and exclusive jurisdiction over that reservation, it has done so by express words.   *United States v. McBratney, 104 United States, 621.*

SEC. 944. The State of Colorado, by its admission into the Union by Congress upon an equal footing with the original States in all respects whatever, without such exception as has been made in the treaty with the Ute Indians and in the act establishing a Territorial government, has acquired criminal jurisdiction over its own citizens and other white persons throughout the whole of the territory within its limits, including the Ute Reservation, and that reservation is no longer within the sole and exclusive jurisdiction of the United States.

Ibid.

SEC. 945. A Territorial district court has two distinct jurisdictions. As a Territorial court it administers the local laws; as invested by act of Congress with jurisdiction to administer the laws of the United States it has all the authority of circuit and district courts, and in the former character it may try a prisoner for murder committed in the Territory proper under the local law, which (in Dakota) requires the jury to determine whether the punishment shall be death or imprisonment for life, and in the other character try another for murder committed in the Indian reservation under the law of the United States which imposes on conviction the death penalty.

Ex parte Crow Dog, 109 United States, 556.

SEC. 946. If the plaintiff lawfully constructed and now operates a railroad through the Fort Hall Reservation, it is not perceived that any just rights of the Indians under treaty can be impaired by taxing the road and property used in operating it, and by the force of the cession made in the agreement of July 18, 1881 (22 Stat. L., 148), and the act of Congress of July 3, 1882 (22 Stat. L., 148), the road and property thereupon became subject to the laws of Idaho relating to railroads, including those under which the tax is imposed, as if the Indian reservation did not exist.

Railroad Co. v. Fisher, 116 United States, 28.

SEC. 947. Process of the courts of Idaho may run into an Indian reservation like Fort Hall Reservation, where the subject-matter or controversy is otherwise within their cognizance. To uphold the jurisdiction of the United States in all cases and to the fullest extent would undoubtedly interfere with the enforcement of the treaty stipulations, and might thus defeat provisions designed for the security of the Indians; but it is not necessary to insist upon such general jurisdiction for the Indians to enjoy the full benefit of the stipulations for their protection.

Ibid.

SEC. 948. By force of the cession of the land upon which the road and other property of the Utah and Northern Railroad Company are situated, it was, so far as necessary for railroad purposes, withdrawn from the Indian reservation. The taxation of such property by the Territory of Idaho does not impair the treaty rights of the Indians.

Ibid.

SEC. 949. The Fort Hall Indian Reservation is subject to the general jurisdiction of the Territory of Idaho as to all matters not interfering with the rights secured to the Indians by treaty.

Ibid.

SEC. 950. The act of March 1, 1863 (12 Stat. L., 808), creating the Territory of Idaho, excludes from the jurisdiction of that Territory only such Indian lands as by treaty with the Indian tribes were not, without their consent, to be included in the limits of any State or Territory. There is no such treaty provision relating to the Fort Hall Reservation, and the provision on that head has therefore no application. It was held to the contrary in Harkness v. Hyde (98 Stat. L., 476) upon the mistaken belief that such a treaty existed. *Ibid.*

Sec. 951. The ninth section of the act of March 3, 1885 (23 Stat. L., 385), does not interfere with the process of the State courts of California within the Hoopa Valley Reservation, nor with the operation of the State laws upon white people found there.

United States v. Kagama, 118 United States, 375.

Sec. 952. The States have no control, power, or government over the Indians as long as they maintain their tribal relations. They owe no allegiance to a State within which their reservation may be established, and the States give them no protection. *Ibid.*

Sec. 953. The Indian appropriation act of March 3, 1885, section 9 (23 Stat. L., 385), is valid and constitutional in both its branches, viz, that which gives jurisdiction to the courts of the Territory of the crimes named committed by the Indians within the Territories, and that which gives jurisdiction in the like cases to the courts of the United States for the same crimes committed on an Indian reservation within a State of the Union. *Ibid.*

Sec. 954. The ninth section of the Indian appropriation act of March 3, 1885 (23 Stat. L., 385), is separable into two distinct definitions of the condition under which Indians may be punished for the same crimes as defined by the common law. The first of these is where the offense is committed within the limits of a Territorial government, whether on or off an Indian reservation. The second is where the offense is committed by one Indian against the person or property of another Indian, within the limits of a State of the Union, but on an Indian reservation. The first clause subjects the offender within the limits of a Territory to the laws of that Territory and to its courts for trial, while the second, which applies solely to offenses by Indians committed within the limits of a State and on a reservation, subjects him to the laws of the United States passed for the government of places under the exclusive jurisdiction of those laws and to trial by the courts of the United States. *Ibid.*

Sec. 955. That part of section 9 of the act of 1885 (23 Stat. L., 385) which relates to crimes committed by Indians within a Territory, and to trial and punishment of the offenders therefor, was enacted to transfer to the Territorial courts established by the General Government, as all courts of general jurisdiction are, in the Territories, jurisdiction to try the crimes described in it under the Territorial laws, when sitting as and exercising the functions of such Territorial court.

Gon-shay-ee, Petitioner; 130 U. S., 343.

SEC. 956. Prior to the act of 1885 (23 Stat. L., 385), so far as Indians could be punished for offenses charged in this case in any court, either Federal or Territorial, the jurisdiction would belong to the one sitting under the first branch and exercising the judicial functions appropriate thereto.   *Ibid.*

SEC. 957. Indians within a Territory are subjected by the act of 1885 (23 Stat. L., 385) to the laws of the Territory and not to the laws of the United States as respects their trial and punishment for the offenses named in the ninth section of that act; and the definition of those offenses must be governed by the laws of the Territory, so far as they furnish any definition of them.   *Ibid.*

SEC. 958. The effect of the act of 1885 (23 Stat. L., 385) was not to transfer to Territorial courts a part of the sole and exclusive jurisdiction of the United States courts, but only part of a limited jurisdiction then exercised by such courts, together with jurisdiction over offenses not theretofore vested therein.   There has been no transfer of part of a sole and exclusive jurisdiction, carrying by implication, even in the absence of express language, transfer of all jurisdiction, but only a transfer of a part of an already limited jurisdiction, and neither by language nor implication transferring that theretofore vested and not in terms transferred.   *In re Wilson, 140 U. S., 575.*

SEC. 959. The treaty of 1854 (10 Stat. L., 1109) did not operate to defeat the prior right of occupancy which the Indians had to the particular section 16 in question, but, by including it in the new reservations, made as a condition of the cession of large tracts of land in Wisconsin, continued it in force.   *United States v. Thomas, 151 U. S., 577.*

SEC. 960. As it appears that the decision of the court of appeals (126 N. Y., 122) was rendered, in addition to other grounds, upon a distinct and independent ground not involving any Federal question, and sufficient in itself to maintain the judgment, the writ of error falls within the well-settled rule on that subject and can not be maintained.
                              Seneca Nation v. Christy, 162 U. S., 283.

SEC. 961. The Seneca Nation availed itself of the act of the State of New York passed May 8, 1845 (N. Y. Rev. Stat., 7th ed., 295), in bringing this action, which was subject to the provision as held by the court of appeals (126 N. Y., 122), that it could only be brought and maintained "in the same manner and within the same time as if brought by citizens of this State in relation to their private individual property and rights," and under the circumstances the fact that the plaintiff was an Indian tribe can not make Federal questions of the correct construction of the act and the bar of the the statute of limitations.
                                                                Ibid.

SEC. 962. The proper construction of the act of the legislature of the State of New York passed May 8, 1845 (N. Y. Rev. Stats., 7th ed., 295), enabling the Indians within that State to prosecute and maintain in all courts of law and equity in that State any action, suit, or proceeding necessary or proper to protect their rights and interests in and to their reservations, and the time within which an action might be brought and maintained thereunder, it was the province of the State courts to determine.   *Ibid.*

SEC. 963. The scrip certificates issued to the Chippewas of mixed blood were intended to be located only by the half-breeds to whom they were issued, and patents were to be issued only to the persons named in those certificates, and, consequently, the right to alienate the lands was not given until after the issue of the patents.
                                    Fee v. Brown, 162 U. S., 602.

SEC. 964. The Ottawa tribe of Indians, including the bands of Blanchard's Fork and Roche de Boeuf, proposed to continue its organization and relations to the United States and the Government accepted the proposition; the State of Kansas has never objected, even if it had any right to object, and it does not lie in the power of any individual to assert any supposed political right of the State or challenge the action of the nation and the Indians in this behalf. The treaty of 1867 (15 Stat. L., 513) was valid and determined the status of the Indians politically and in respect to this treaty.
                                Wiggan v. Conolly, 163 U. S., 56.

SEC. 965. The fifth amendment to the Constitution of the United States does not apply to local legislation of the Cherokee Nation so as to require all prosecutions for offenses committed against the laws of that nation to be initiated by a grand jury in accordance with the provisions of that amendment.   *Talton v. Mayes, 163 U. S., 376.*

SEC. 966. The question whether a statute of the Cherokee Nation which was not repugnant to the Constitution of the United States or in conflict with any treaty or law of the United States had been repealed by another statute of that nation, and the determination of what was the existing law of the Cherokee Nation as to the constitution of the grand jury, is solely a matter within the jurisdiction of the courts of that nation, and the decision of such a question in itself necessarily involves no infraction of the Constitution of the United States.   *Ibid.*

SEC. 967. The statute of the Creek Nation prohibiting noncitizen licensed traders from cutting and putting up hay from the common pasturage of the nation implies that citizens of the nation might cut hay without hindrance from such pasturage, as the prohibition is limited to noncitizen traders.   *Eddy v. Lafayette, 163 U. S., 456.*

SEC. 968. The provision in the enabling act of Montana that the " Indian lands shall remain under the absolute jurisdiction and control of the Congress of the United States" does not affect the application of the general rule laid down in United States *v.* McBratney (104 U. S., 621) to the State of Montana.   *Draper v. United States, 164 U. S., 240.*

SEC. 969. When the enabling act admitting a State into the Union contains no exclusion of jurisdiction as to crimes committed on an Indian reservation by others than Indians or against Indians, the State courts are vested with jurisdiction to try and punish such crimes.

Ibid.

SEC. 970. The act of the legislature of the Territory of Oklahoma of March 5, 1895, which provided that "when any cattle are kept or grazed or any other personal property is situated in any * * * reservation of this Territory, such property shall be subject to taxation in the organized county to which said * * * reservation is attached for judicial purposes," was a legitimate exercise of the Territory's power of taxation, and, when enforced in the taxation of cattle belonging to persons not resident in the Territory grazing upon Indian reservations therein, does not violate the Constitution of the United States.   *Thomas v. Gay, 169 U. S., 264.*

SEC. 971. In a case of appropriation for dower, on the part of the widow, in lands held by her husband during coverture, the law of the State on limitations applies.   *Pka-o-wah-ash-kum v. Sorin, 8 Fed. Rep., 740.*

SEC. 972. When the Indian territory is within the limits of a State, Congress is limited to the regulation of commercial intercourse with such tribes as exist as a distinct community, governed by their own laws, and resting for their protection on the faith of laws and treaties of the Union, and the State can not withdraw them from the operation of the laws of Congress.   *Note to Brandy etc., 11 Fed. Rep., 51.*

SEC. 973. If Indians occupy territory of very limited extent, surrounded by white population which necessarily have daily intercourse with them, and it become impracticable to enforce the law, the Federal jurisdiction must cease.   *Ibid.*

SEC. 974. In the case of the State *v.* Doxtater (47 Wis., 278) it was decided that the State had jurisdiction of the crime of adultery committed on the Oneida Reservation by an Indian man on a white woman; but that does not touch upon the question of whether the United States has the jurisdiction of the crime of murder committed on the Umatilla Reservation by an Indian upon a white man.

United States v. Martin, 14 Fed. Rep., 817.

SEC. 975. It may be conceded that the admission of Oregon into the Union upon an equality with the other States, without any special reservation of jurisdiction over the place then known and occupied as the Umatilla Indian Reservation, extended the jurisdiction of the State thereover as to all subjects constitutionally within its power of legislation; but the subject of the intercourse between the Indians and other people in Oregon still remain a matter within the jurisdiction of the United States just as much as when the country was a Territory.   *Ibid.*

SEC. 976. The courts of the Cherokee Nation have jurisdiction and can try only for the crime of murder when the person murdered is an Indian and the one charged with the crime is also an Indian.

Ex parte Morgan, 20 Fed. Rep., 298.

SEC. 977. In all cases not provided for by the laws of the United States the law of the State will apply and govern, and the treaty and local law must be construed together so that both shall stand as far as they can be reconciled, the law of the treaty prevailing in case of unavoidable conflict.   *Love v. Pamplin, 21 Fed. Rep., 755.*

SEC. 978. As the subject of intercourse between the white man and the Indian is committed by the Constitution to the Government of the United States, and as Congress has provided for the punishment of a white man for the felonious killing of an Indian upon a reservation, and *vice versa*, it is not admitted that the State has any authority over such killing, or power to punish or absolve the person committing the same.   *United States v. Barnhart, 22 Fed. Rep., 285.*

SEC. 979. It may be that the State can punish acts growing out of the intercourse between the whites and Indians until Congress vests the jurisdiction thereof exclusively in the national courts, but be this as it may, the plea of former acquittal in a State court is not good.   *Ibid.*

SEC. 980. When an Indian is outside of the Indian country he is entitled to the full measure of protection afforded by the laws of the nation, and if he commits a crime outside of the Indian country he is amenable to the law of the place where the crime is committed.

In re Wolf, 27 Fed. Rep., 606.

SEC. 981. It has always been competent for the State of Indiana to send its officers with process, civil and criminal, into the reservations and lands of the Miamis within its borders, whether held by the tribe or by individuals, and, possibly, to exercise police powers over the Indians themselves to some extent. This much, it would seem, is within the scope of the last clause of the third article of the ordinance of 1787, but quite different, and by no means necessarily implied, would be the right to levy taxes or to impose other pecuniary burdens, which might work a forfeiture or affect substantially the Indian right of exclusive and free enjoyment.

Wan pe man qua v. Aldrich, 28 Fed. Rep., 489.

SEC. 982. Without some clause or language to the contrary, in a treaty with Indians with respect to a reservation within the exterior boundaries of a Territory, the lands held by them are a part of the Territory (Idaho) and subject to its jurisdiction, *so that process may run* there, however the Indians themselves may be exempt from that jurisdiction.   *Ibid.*

SEC. 983. Under the Nebraska bill of rights (section 13), providing that all courts shall be open to every person for any injury done him in his lands, goods, person, or reputation, shall have a remedy, and, under section 2126, Revised Statutes of the United States, relating to actions between an Indian and a white man about a right of property, an Indian may come into the courts and legislate his title to land, and, where he is not shown to be uneducated or unfamiliar with the laws, the statute of limitations will run against him.   *Felix v. Patrick, 36 Fed. Rep., 457.*

SEC. 984. It is argued because the Indians seek the courts of Kansas for the preservation of rights and redress of wrongs, sometimes voluntarily, and in certain specified cases by direction of the Secretary of the Interior, that they submit themselves to all the laws of the State.   *Ibid.*

SEC. 985. It is a fundamental principle that the laws of a State can have no binding force *proprio vigore* outside of the territorial limits of the State enacting them. The character of this road, or the laws of Kansas under which it exists, does not give it the right to exercise its powers beyond the State of Kansas. Its powers under its Kansas charter can not be exercised in the Indian country unless permitted to be exercised by the act of Congress, and they can be exercised only to the extent permitted.   *Briscoe v. Kansas Railroad Co., 40 Fed. Rep., 273.*

SEC. 986. The Federal Government has the right and authority, instead of controlling the Indian tribes by treaties, to govern them by acts of Congress, and the Indians being necessarily subject to the laws which Congress may enact for their protection and for the protection of the people with whom they may come in contact, the States have no power over them as long as they maintain their tribal relations.   *Benson v. United States, 44 Fed. Rep., 178.*

SEC. 987. The State of New York always exercised its sovereign powers within the reservations in its borders, and since 1858, when the case of New York *v.* Dibble (21 Howard, 366) was decided by the Supreme Court, its right to do so, so far as necessary to protect the persons and property of the Indians in said State and to preserve the public peace, has never been questioned.   *Ibid.*

SEC. 988. The act of March 2, 1861 (12 Stat. L., 239), creating the Territory of Dakota, provides that nothing therein contained shall be construed to "impair the right of person or property pertaining to the Indians in said Territory," and that all the Indian lands therein shall be excepted out of its boundaries and jurisdiction "until the Indian title is extinguished by treaty with the United States."

United States v. Ewing, 47 Fed. Rep., 809.

SEC. 989. The people of Montana had full power, under the Constitution, to relinquish to the United States all jurisdiction over the Indian reservations located in that State.

United States v. Partello, 48 Fed. Rep., 670.

SEC. 990. In the case of United States *v.* Ward (1 Woolw., 17), Justice Miller, while holding that the act admitting Kansas into the Union repealed the jurisdiction of the United States over any portion of the State which had before that time been classed as Indian country within its borders, which was not excepted from the limits of the State by any treaty with the Indians and some provision in the admission act, says: "And the converse of this proposition is inferable; that is, that Congress intended to and did concede to the new State, and it acquired and holds irrevocable, except as it sees fit to surrender the same, full right and authority to legislate to enforce her laws and to exercise plenary jurisdiction over all parts of her territory as were not covered by such treaties."   *Ibid.*

SEC. 991. It would be an anomaly in government if it should be conceded that the United States has full right to govern the Indians, and yet has no right to any lands upon which to place them with that object. Considering what was said of the relation of the Indians to the State in United States *v.* Kagama (118 U. S., 375), with such a view we would behold a Government without a country.   *Ibid.*

SEC. 992. In the case of United States *v.* Ward (1 Woolw., 17), Mr. Justice Miller, after speaking of the treaty with the Shawnee Indians, which excluded their reservation from the State of Kansas, and, after declaring to some extent the effect of the act admitting Kansas into the Union, said further: "Or rather, to express the matter more exactly, all territory which was not covered by such treaties was included within the State, its jurisdiction, and within its territory, and thus irrevocably and exclusively."   *Ibid.*

SEC. 993. In view of the fact that the United States has always assumed control over the Indians, as the wards of the nation, to the exclusion of the States, the relinquishment by the State of jurisdiction over the Indian reservations was for a Federal purpose.   *Ibid.*

SEC. 994. While it is not held that when an Indian commits a crime off the reservation he can not be punished by the laws of the State where the offense was committed, the State can not regulate in any manner the social relations of the members of an organized tribe among themselves.   *United States v. Barnaby, 51 Fed. Rep., 20.*

SEC. 995. The indictment in the case of Nelson *v.* United States (30 Fed. Rep., 112) did not contain the name of the vendee of the liquor, but it was held that the name can only be required for the more convenient identification of the transaction.   It was not a necessary ingredient of the offense, particularly where the prohibition to sell is general irrespective of parties.

United States v. Warwick, 51 Fed. Rep., 280.

SEC. 996. The registry of Kansas does not apply to a chattel mortgage executed in Kansas by a resident of the Indian Territory upon property situated in the Territory.

Pyeatt v. Powell, 51 Fed. Rep., 551.

SEC. 997. The grantees of certain lots on the Puyallup Reservation under the treaty of December 26, 1854 (10 Stat. L., 1132), were, by the act of February 8, 1887 (24 Stat. L., 388), made citizens of the United States, with all the rights, privileges, and immunities of other citizens; and subsequently the Territory was admitted as a State. This deprived the Government of the power to coerce such Indians into making or annulling contracts or to molest persons who were on the granted premises by the license of the grantees, and transferred to the State government the power to preserve peace and good order, regulate the making of private contracts, and the use and descent of private property, and, therefore, no power remained in the United States to interfere with a person who was building a railroad across the granted lands with the consent and approval of the grantees, and an injunction *pendente lite* would be granted to restrain an army officer from attempting such interference.   *Ross v. Eells, 56 Fed. Rep., 855.*

SEC. 998. For the purpose of securing the North Carolina Cherokees against the evil consequences of injudicious contracts with more intelligent and designing white men, a State statute was enacted requiring all contracts equal to ten dollars or more with Cherokee Indians to be in writing, signed in the presence of two witnesses, who shall subscribe the same (1 Code N. C., sec. 1553). This law of the State imposed upon them a restriction which was not imposed upon other citizens, except as to transactions coming within the statute of frauds, and a few other cases.   *United States v. Boyd, 68 Fed. Rep., 577.*

SEC. 999. Neither the constitution of a State nor any act of its legislature, however formal or solemn, whatever rights it may confer on these Indians, or withhold from them, can withdraw them from the influence of an act of Congress, which that body has the constitutional right to pass concerning them. Any other doctrine would make the legislature of that State the supreme law of the land instead of the Constitution of the United States and the laws and treaties made in pursuance thereof.   *Ibid.*

SEC. 1000. Race Horse, a Bannock Indian, killed some elk in Wyoming, outside of the reservation, during the prohibited season, for which he was arrested by the State. *Held*, that the federal court had jurisdiction, under section 753, Revised Statutes, to issue a writ of habeas corpus to determine whether or not Race Horse was restrained of his liberty in violation of the treaty of July 3, 1868 (15 Stat. L., 673), with the Bannocks. *In re Race Horse, 70 Fed. Rep., 598.*

SEC. 1001. The effect of the admission of Wyoming as a State, upon an equal footing with the original States, as well as in respect of the exercise of the police power as otherwise, did not abrogate the provisions of the treaty in reference to the rights of the Indians in the lands within the State. *Ibid.*

SEC. 1002. In the case of Lawton *v.* Steele, 152 United States, 133, 14 Supreme Court, 499, Mr. Justice Brown says:

The preservation of game and fish, however, has always been treated as within the proper domain of the police power, and laws limiting the season within which birds and wild animals may be killed or exposed for sale, and prescribing the time and manner in which fish may be caught, have been repeatedly upheld by the courts. *Ibid.*

SEC. 1003. It is undoubtedly true that upon its admission into the Union, Wyoming became vested with all the powers of a sovereign State, and, among the powers thus conferred, was the police power, under which the State may unquestionably pass laws which are essential to public health, safety, and morals. The limitations upon this power are (1) that the interests of the public generally, as distinguished from those of a particular class, require such interference; and (2) that the means are reasonably necessary for the accomplishment of the purpose, and not unduly oppressive to individuals. Under this power the State has unquestionable right to pass laws placing restrictions upon the time and manner of taking wild game and fish. *Ibid.*

SEC. 1004. It seems perfectly clear that if the United States had the right, by virtue of the treaty-making power conferred upon it by the Constitution, to take away from a sovereign State, after its admission into the Union, the power to levy taxes upon the lands of Indians within the State, it would certainly have that power prior to the admission of the State into the Union, and that the treaty provisions would be in full force after admission, unless the act of Congress admitting the State was so inconsistent with the provisions of the treaty that it furnished an exclusive rule, so that the court could not, by fair construction, give effect to both. The same rule applies to an exercise of the police power of the State. *Ibid.*

SEC. 1005. In the absence of Congressional legislation, or a treaty with the Indians, they would doubtless be subject to the provisions of the State law, but no such question arises in this case. We are here dealing with a question which has been the subject of treaty stipulation between the National Government and the tribe of Bannock Indians. *Ibid.*

SEC. 1006. The United States has never yet been released from the treaty stipulations and obligations by which it assumed to preserve the lands of the Omaha and Winnebago Indians for their use and benefit.
United States v. Flournoy, etc., Co., 71 Fed. Rep., 576.

SEC. 1007. In Langford *v.* Monteith (102 U. S., 145, 147) it was held that, where, by treaty, the reservation was not excluded from the limits of the Territory, civil process in a suit between white men in a court of the Territory may run into the reservation, notwithstanding the Indians themselves are exempt from that jurisdiction.

Truscott v. Hurlbut, etc., Co., 73 Fed. Rep., 60.

SEC. 1008. There is no good reason why the authority of the State may not also include the taxation of all personal property found within its limits, although upon an Indian reservation, provided that the Indians are in no way interested in it. *Ibid.*

SEC. 1009. So far as concerns the government and protection of the Crow Indians, and for all purposes relating to the treaty and agreements between that tribe and the United States, the reservation in question is within the sole and exclusive jurisdiction of the United States; but it is not to be regarded as without the jurisdiction of Montana for all purposes. *Ibid.*

SEC. 1010. By section 41 of the code of Montana, it was declared that all legal process of the State, whether civil or criminal, may be served upon persons and property found within any of the military reservations or on any Indian reservation in all cases where the United States has not exclusive jurisdiction. *Ibid.*

SEC. 1011. The constitution of Montana, in compliance with the conditions of the enabling act (25 Stat. L., 676), contains, section 4, a disclaimer of right to any public lands owned or held by Indian tribes, and provides that, until the Indian title is extinguished, such lands shall remain under the absolute jurisdiction and control of Congress. *Held*, that the provision does not prevent the State or its counties from taxing cattle of a corporation grazing upon an Indian reservation under a contract with the Indians which is sanctioned by the United States. *Ibid.*

SEC. 1012. The act of May 26, 1864 (13 Stat. L., 85), organizing the Territory of Montana, provides that no lands included therein which, by treaty with any Indian tribe, were not, without its consent, to be included in any Territory or State. *Held* that as there was no treaty existing at the passage of the act with any Indian tribe containing such a provision in respect to the lands constituting the present Crow Reservation, that reservation was included in the boundaries and jurisdiction of the Territory and State of Montana. *Ibid.*

SEC. 1013. An act of the council of the Creek Nation entitled "An act establishing quarantine regulations against foreign cattle and to prevent smuggling cattle into the Creek Nation," approved October 29, 1891, makes it unlawful for any citizen of the nation "to introduce or invite into the Creek Nation cattle of any kind at any time," except between January 1 and March 31 of each year, and declares that any citizen violating this provision of the act "shall be fined a sum that will be equivalent of $3 per head for each and every head of cattle" unlawfully introduced. The act makes it a lien on the cattle unlawfully introduced.   *Cornells v. Shannon, 63 Fed. Rep., 305.*

SEC. 1014. In a suit by the owners and mortgagees of cattle to declare void a judgment of a court of the Creek Nation imposing a fine on the owners for bringing the cattle into the nation contrary to its law, and making it a lien on the cattle in accordance with such law, it will, on demurrer to the answer, be held that the Creek court had jurisdiction to render the judgment, the answer alleging that such court had jurisdiction of the owners of the cattle.   *Ibid.*

SEC. 1015. The judgments of the courts of the Creek Nation are entitled to the same respect and to the same faith and credit as the judgments of the Territorial courts of the United States, and white men residing in the Indian Territory who appear and submit themselves to the jurisdiction of the courts of the nation are bound by their judgment.   *Ibid.*

SEC. 1016. A legislative enactment declaring that certain lands which should be purchased for the Indians should not thereafter be taxed, constituted a contract which could not be rescinded by a subsequent legislative act, such repealing act being void under that clause of the Constitution of the United States which prohibits a State from passing any law impairing the obligation of contracts.
                     New Jersey v. Wilson, 7 Cranch, 164.

SEC. 1017. Kentucky legislated for her entire territory, subject to the restrictions imposed by the treaty of Hopewell with the Chickasaws, which was recognized by the State as the paramount law until its restrictions were removed by a treaty of cession, then the act of 1809 and all the other laws of the State had effect west of the Tennessee River and operated alike in all parts of the State.
                     Porterfield v. Clark, 2 How., 76.

SEC. 1018. The act of May 26, 1864, organizing the Territory of Montana, provides that no lands shall be included therein which, by treaty with any Indian tribe, were not, without its consent, to be included in any Territory or State. *Held* that as there was no treaty existing at the passage of the act with any Indian tribe containing such a provision in respect to the lands constituting the present Crow Reservation, that reservation was included in the boundaries and jurisdiction of the Territory and State of Montana.
                     Truscot v. Hurlbut, etc., Co., 73 Fed., 60.

SEC. 1019. The provision in the treaty of 1867 with the Pottawatomie Indians, giving the probate court authority to appoint administrators and settle the estates of deceased allottees, gave such court no authority to appoint administrators of an Indian unless he had been an allottee under the treaty and was dead.
                     Laughton v. Nadeau et al., 75 Fed., 789.

SEC. 1020. Article 5 of the treaty of January 22, 1855, with the several Indian tribes of Washington Territory (12 Stat. L., 928), which provides that "the right of taking fish at usual and accustomed grounds and stations is further secured to said Indians in common with all citizens of the Territory, and of erecting temporary houses for the purpose of curing," was not intended to secure to the Indians exclusive rights at any particular places, but only such rights as might be enjoyed by all citizens in common, and valid State laws effective to abridge the fishing rights of citizens are equally effective as against the Indians.   *United States v. Alaska Packing Assn., 79 Fed., 152.*

SEC. 1021. The National Government, as original proprietor, has the power to dispose of public lands, even within an Indian reservation, without the consent of the Indians, and even if the Indian treaty of January 22, 1855 (12 Stat. L., 928), be regarded as making a reservation of fishing grounds and lands adjacent necessary for the use of the Indians, Congress still had the power to make disposition of the same grounds, notwithstanding the treaty.

In the control of fisheries within a State the State government is supreme.   *Ibid.*

SEC. 1022. In view of the cession by the legislature of Iowa to the United States of jurisdiction over the reservation in Tama County occupied by a portion of the Sac and Fox tribe of Indians, and the acceptance of such cession by Congress in the general Indian appropriation act of June 10, 1896 (26 Stat. L., 331), a district court of the State of Iowa has no jurisdiction to appoint a guardian for the person of a minor of such tribe residing on the reservation.

In re Lelah-Puc-ka-chee, 98 Fed. Rep., 429.

SEC. 1023. It appears that Mr. Ewart was under contract in writing with the proper authorities of the Eastern Band of Cherokee Indians to effect a sale of timber for them.   The timber was sold.   The sale has been affirmed in court in proceedings to which the United States and the Eastern Band of Cherokee Indians were parties.   *Held* that the United States courts protect attorneys in their fees, and therefore in a suit by the United States to enjoin a sale of timber effected by an attorney for a band of Indians, the timber having been sold, and the sale affirmed by the court, it is proper to permit the attorney to intervene for the allowance of his claim for services in effecting the sale to be paid out of the proceeds.

United States v. Boyd et al., 79 Fed. Rep., 858.

SEC. 1024. While the paramount title to all lands in Alaska is in the United States Congress, and the General Government have recognized for a great many years the right of the American citizen to go onto public lands, occupy, possess, use, and improve the same with the view of ultimately obtaining title thereto from the General Government, whenever the same shall be opened to purchase, and in this district this right is expressly recognized by Congress in the first proviso of section 8 of the act of May 17, 1884, providing a civil government for Alaska. (23 Stat. L., 24; Sup. Rev. Stat., 2d ed., p. 433.) When Congress enacted this law it undoubtedly had in view the condition of affairs in this country, and, to protect settlers upon the public lands here, incorporated into said act the proviso above mentioned, which is in the following language:

"That the Indians or other persons in said district shall not be disturbed in the possession of any lands actually in their use or occupation or now claimed by them, but the terms under which such persons may acquire title to such lands is (are) reserved for future legislation by Congress."   *Carroll v. Price, 81 Fed. Rep., 137.*

SEC. 1025. Montours Island was within the original charter boundaries of Virginia; so that as far as royal jurisdiction and Indian surrender are involved, the sovereignty and property of that State was complete.   *Sims, lessee, v. Irvin, 3 Dallas, 425.*

SEC. 1026. The State of Pennsylvania raised and maintained troops for the defense of her western frontier from hostile incursions by Indians from March, 1791, until the spring of 1796.

Commonwealth v. Tench Coxe 4 Dallas, 170.

SEC. 1027. If in a community or neighborhood composed principally of whites, a citizen of the Indian race, not within the exception of the fourteenth amendment, should propose to lease and cultivate a farm, and a combination should be formed to expel him and prevent him from accomplishing his purpose on account of his race or color, it can not be doubted that this would be a case within the power of Congress to remedy and redress. But if that person should be injured in his person or property by any wrongdoer for the mere felonious purpose of malice, revenge, or gain, without any design to interfere with his rights of citizenship or equality before the laws, it would be an ordinary crime punishable by the State laws only.

United States v. Cruikshank, 1 Woods, 308.

SEC. 1028. It is not necessary in determining the question of jurisdiction in this case to decide whether any or what jurisdiction may be exercised by the State of Tennessee over the Cherokee country within her limits.   *United States v. Bailey, 1 McLean, 234.*

SEC. 1029. The Wyandott reserve is situated in Crawford County, Ohio, which for some years has been regularly organized as a county; and at the last session of the legislature of Ohio a law was passed which declared "that all white inhabitants now or hereafter resident in said Wyandott Reservation shall be, and they are hereby, made subject to the laws of Ohio for the purpose of taxation, and for all civil, criminal, or military purposes, as other white citizens are now or hereafter may be in the different townships in the said county of Crawford, any law or custom to the contrary notwithstanding."

United States v. Cisna, 1 McLean, 254.

SEC. 1030. If the State of Tennessee has no jurisdiction or has failed to exercise it, it does not follow that the Federal Government has a general and unlimited jurisdiction over the territory, for its powers are delegated, and can not be assumed to supply any defect of power on the part of the State.   *United States v. Bailey, 1 McLean, 234.*

SEC. 1031. It is clear that the State of Tennessee, either by failing to exercise jurisdiction or by positive enactment short of accession of jurisdiction, for purposes specified in the Constitution, can neither enlarge nor diminish the powers of Congress on the subject.   *Ibid.*

SEC. 1032. The validity of the numerous treaties and laws made with and for the Indians has not been questioned, it is believed, so far as they act upon the Indian tribes and our own citizens beyond the boundaries of any State; but serious questions have arisen, and are likely to again arise, between the Federal and State authorities respecting the jurisdiction of the former over the territory of Indians situated within a State sovereignty.   *United States v. Cisna, 1 McLean, 254.*

SEC. 1033. The Indian territory within a State can not be considered as a foreign jurisdiction. Under certain circumstances it has been decided that a State can not extend its laws over the Indian territory within it, and especially when those laws are incompatible with constitutional regulations by the Federal Government. But the jurisdiction is not foreign. If the State have the fee of the Indian lands it may dispose of that fee subject to the Indian right of occupancy.   *Ibid.*

SEC. 1034. The State of New York has not only punished its own citizens for offenses committed within an Indian reserve in that State, but has extended its jurisdiction in criminal cases over the Indians.
Ibid.

SEC. 1035. The supreme court of Ohio has not decided whether offenses under the State laws, if committed within the Wyandott reserve by a white person, may be punished, but a lower court has decided that no punishment can be inflicted in such case.   *Ibid.*

SEC. 1036. Except by compact, or the voluntary legislative action of the State, Indian lands within its limits can not be withdrawn from its ordinary action.   *Lowry v. Weaver, 4 McLean, 82.*

SEC. 1037. The grantee of the Government in this case was capable of making contracts, and was legally responsible under them; and although by the restrictions of the grant he could not alien there would seem to be no inconsistency in saying that the State law may substitute an agency through which the land may be reached by creditors.   *Ibid.*

SEC. 1038. The act admitting Kansas into the Union withdraws all its territory from the Federal jurisdiction except territory of Indians having treaties with the United States, which provide that without their consent such territory shall not be subjected to State jurisdiction.

United States v. Ward, 1 Woolw., 17.   Same, 1 Banks & McCahon, 601.

SEC. 1039. Indian territory in Kansas not protected by treaty is brought within and subjected to State jurisdiction.   *Ibid.*

SEC. 1040. The last treatv made with the Kansas tribe of Indians in 1859 (12 Stats., 1111) does not contain a guarantee that their lands shall never be included within the State, and it follows that the State of Kansas has jurisdiction to try the defendant for the crime of murder.

Ibid.

SEC. 1041. By a proviso annexed to the clause admitting Kansas as a State, all territory was excepted out of and was not included within the State which belonged to a tribe having a treaty excepting their lands from State jurisdiction.   *Ibid.*

SEC. 1042. There were at the time of the admission of the State of Kansas tribes of Indians within the boundaries of the new State with which the United States had treaties, and in these treaties the Government stipulated that their lands should never be brought within the bounds nor subjected to the jurisdiction of the new State. Among such tribes may be mentioned the Shawnees.   *Ibid.*

SEC. 1043. The United States, when it admitted Kansas into the Union, although retaining the title to the land which it then owned within the State, parted with the jurisdiction over it, except the lands of Indian tribes having treaties with the United States, which exempt them from State jurisdiction, and the right to tax lands of the United States and of the Indians.   *Ibid.*

SEC. 1044. It will appear from the numerous citations in this case that New York, Ohio, and 'other States have at times passed acts declaring that their civil and criminal jurisdiction extended to Indians and to Indian reservations, and that such legislation has been considered valid when not in conflict with some treaty or constitutional act of Congress.   *United States v. Yellow Sun, 1 Dill., 271.*

SEC. 1045. Indians, though belonging to a tribe which maintains the tribal organization, but occupying a reservation within the limits of a State, where there are no statute or treaty provisions granting or retaining jurisdiction in favor of the United States over offenses committed by them, are amenable to State laws for murder or other offenses committed off the reservation and within the limits of the State.   *Ibid.*

SEC. 1046. In the case of the Kansas Indians (5 Wall., 737) the United States Supreme Court, in speaking of the Shawnees, says: "As long as the United States recognizes their tribal character they are under the protection of treaties and the laws of Congress and their property is withdrawn from the operation of State laws." There can be no question of the applicability of this language to the suit in Wyandotte County. The Secretary of the Interior has never approved the deeds under which petitioners claim and the deeds are entirely void until approved by that officer. Until they are so approved the lands of the Shawnees are as wholly beyond the jurisdiction of the State courts as if it were situated beyond its geographical limits.

Ex parte Forbes, 1 Dill., 363.

SEC. 1047. It will be conceded, for the purposes of this case, that the Senate amendment to article 8 of the treaty of 1867 with the Pottawatomies (15 Stat. L., 536) gave the probate court authority to appoint administrators and settle the estates of deceased allottees of the tribe. But it gave the probate court no authority to appoint administrators of an Indian unless he had been an allottee under the treaty and was dead.

United States v. Payne, 4 Dill., 387.

SEC. 1048. The grant of administration on the estate of a member of the Pottawatomie tribe of Indians by a probate court in Kansas by virtue of the treaty of 1867 (15 Stat. L., 536) when such member is in fact alive, is void as respects the administrator, and money paid to him by the United States in that capacity may be recovered back.

Ibid.

SEC. 1049. Without the assent of the General Government the probate courts of a State have no jurisdiction to administer upon the property or credits of Indians who were members of a tribe which maintains toward the United States its tribal relations.

Ibid.

SEC. 1050. If the tribal organization of Indian bands is recognized by the political departments of the Government as existing, the fact that the primitive habits and customs of the tribe, when in a savage state, have been largely broken into by their intercourse with the whites, in the midst of whom, in the advance of civilization they have come to find themselves, does not authorize the State government to regard the tribal organization as gone and the Indians as citizens of the State where they are and subject to its laws.

Ex parte Reynolds, 5 Dill., 394.

SEC. 1051. If the jurisdiction claimed by the State be conceded, then it follows that the State may not only enforce such criminal laws as now exist on its statute books as against all persons on the reservation, but it may exact other laws, if it so wills, in direct conflict with the rights guaranteed to the Indians by treaty, as well as destructive of the policy of Congress with respect to that people.

United States v. Berry, 2 McCrary, 58.

SEC. 1052. The answer to the claim that the State may have jurisdiction within the limits of the reservation for the purpose of enforcing its criminal laws is that one of the obligations imposed upon the United States by the plain terms of the treaty is to enforce their own criminal laws against all classes of offenders within the limits of the reservation.

Ibid.

SEC. 1053. It is manifest that if the enabling act repeals the treaty for one purpose it repeals it for all purposes. If the State has jurisdiction over any part of the Territory and people of the reservation for the purpose of enforcing its criminal laws, it has jurisdiction over the whole of the Territory and over all the people, whether whites or Indians.

Ibid.

SEC. 1054. In the attempt of the State of Georgia in 1829 to extend its legislation over the reservation of the Cherokee Nation in that State the Supreme Court of the United States held, in Worcester v. Georgia (6 Pet., 515), that the State legislation was void because in conflict with a treaty with the Cherokee Indians, which was held to be the supreme law of the land.

Ibid.

SEC. 1055. The jurisdiction of the district court for Oregon over offenses committed in Alaska is conferred by section 7 of the act of July 27, 1868 (15 Stat. L., 240), and by such section confined to violations of that act and the laws "relating to customs, commerce, and navigation," and therefore it has no jurisdiction over the crime of distilling spirits therein without paying a tax therefor.

United States v. Seveloff, 2 Sawyer, 311.

SEC. 1056. By its admission and the act of May 5, 1866 (14 Stat. L., 43), Nevada acquired the same right over the land now embraced in the Moapa Reservation as over any other portion of its territory, and that an Executive order made long afterwards could not, proprio vigore, take away the power of the State to legislate for this territory and confer it exclusively on the United States is a plain proposition.

Ex parte Sloan, 4 Sawyer, 330.

SEC. 1057. Section 3 of the act of 1884 provides for a district court for the district of Alaska "with the civil and criminal jurisdiction" of a district court of the United States; and section 7 declares that "the general laws of the State of Oregon," then in force, shall "be the law in said district so far as the same may be applicable and not in conflict with the provisions "of that act or the laws of the United States."

Kie v. United States, 11 Saw., 579.

SEC. 1058. No law of Oregon is to have effect in Alaska if it is in conflict with a law of the United States.   There is such a conflict within the meaning of the statute, not only when these laws contain different provisions on the same subject, but when they contain similar or identical ones.   *Ibid.*

SEC. 1059. Indians, though belonging to a tribe which maintains the tribal organization, but occupying a reservation *within* the State, if there is no valid statute of Congress or treaty to the contrary, are amenable to State laws for murder or other offenses against such laws committed by them off the reservation and within the limits of the State.   But whether United States courts have jurisdiction, under such circumstances, of offenses committed by the Indians *upon* reservations, is a question.   *United States v. Sa-coo-da-cot, 1 Abbott, 377.*

SEC. 1060. There is no exception in the State constitution of Nebraska, or in the acts of Congress, of the Pawnee Reservation or the Pawnee Indians, from the Territorial or civil jurisdiction of the State.
                                                                          Ibid.

SEC. 1061. The relations which Indians, residing within State limits, sustain to the State and the United States, and their respective laws, discussed.   *Ibid.*

SEC. 1062. It seems impossible to hold that this court has jurisdiction in this case without necessarily implying that the courts of the State have not; and if they have not, then we decide that the State of Nebraska has not the power to make her ordinary criminal statutes coextensive with the State limits, and enforce them against all persons living or found therein.   Such a power we are not prepared to deny to the State in the absence of some conflicting treaty stipulation or valid act of Congress.   *Ibid.*

SEC. 1063. New York, Ohio, and other States have passed acts declaring that the civil and criminal jurisdiction of these States extended to Indians and to Indian reservations, and that such legislation has been considered valid when not in conflict with some treaty or constitutional act of Congress.   *Ibid.*

SEC. 1064. As to State authority over Indians, see Goodell *v.* Jackson, 21 Johns, 693, and constitutional provisions and act of April 12, 1822 (2 Rev. Stat., 881); Murray *v.* Wooden, 17 Wend., 531; Swan's Ohio Stat., 304; Rev. Stat., Mass., 148; Clay *v.* State, 4 Kans., 49; People *v.* Antonio, 27 Cal., 484; Hicks v. Euhartonah, 21 Ark., 106; Id., 485; Peters Case, 2 Johns, Cas., 344.   *Ibid.*

SEC. 1065. None of the lands embraced within the boundaries of Idaho Territory are excepted out of said Territory by the provisions of section 1 of the organic act, except such as by the provisions of preexisting treaties with Indian tribes were not, without the consent of such Indian tribes, to be included within the limits of any State or Territory.   At the time of the passage of the organic act of Idaho Territory no treaty existed between the United States and any Indian tribes providing that the lands embraced within the Fort Hall Indian Reservation should not, without the consent of the Indians, be included within any State or Territory; such lands, therefore, became part of Idaho Territory upon the passage of said organic act, March 3, 1863 (12 Stat., 808), and have not since been withdrawn from or excepted out of said Territory.   *Utah & N. Ry. Co. v. Fisher, 3 Pa. Rep., 3.*

SEC. 1066. In the case of McCracken *v.* Todd (1 Kans., 148), taken by writ of error to the supreme court of Kansas, one of the questions presented was whether certain judicial proceedings, which took place on the lands belonging to the Delaware Indians when Kansas Territory was organized, were not transacted without the Territory, and therefore null and void.   That court, after reciting the proviso, said: "This ground of objection calls for no comment by the court further than a statement that nowhere in any treaty with the Delaware Indians is there a provision that the lands of that tribe shall not, without their consent, be included within the territorial limits of any State or Territory.   All the lands of that tribe within the boundaries specifically described in the law referred to were therefore included within the limits of the Territory."   *Ibid.*

SEC. 1067. In the case of Langford *v.* Monteith (102 U. S., 145) the court held, "the act of Congress of March 3, 1863 (12 Stat. L., 808), to provide a temporary government for the Territory of Idaho contains a clause precisely similar to that admitting Kansas into the Union. This court in Harkness *v.* Hyde relying upon an imperfect extract found in the brief of counsel inadvertently inferred that the treaty with the Shoshones, like that with the Shawnees, contains a clause excluding the lands of the tribe from Territorial or State jurisdiction. In this it seems we were laboring under a mistake.   Where no such clause or language equivalent to it is found in a treaty with Indians within the exterior limits of Idaho, the lands held by them are a part of the Territory and subject to its jurisdiction, so that process may run there, however the Indians themselves may be exempt from that jurisdiction.   *Ibid.*

SEC. 1068. A post trader on an Indian reservation is an agent of the Federal Government, in performing the obligations of its treaty with the Indians, and therefore the Territorial government can not tax the stock in trade of such post trader.   *Fremont County v. Moore, 19 Pacific Reporter, 438.*

SEC. 1069. An action for the conversion of certain corn and cornstalks, grown and standing upon land in Indian Territory, leased in violation of law and the treaty between the United States and the Cherokee Nation (August 11, 1866; 14 U. S. Stat. L., 800), brought by a citizen of this State against a person residing in such Territory, but personally served with summons, can not be maintained in this State.   *Holderman v. Pond, 25 Pacific Reporter, 872.*

SEC. 1070. When the country of Oklahoma was originally set apart for the Indians, the previous laws made for the government of the whites and in force then were withdrawn, and the subsequent settlement of the country by whites after the purchase of the lands from the Indians did not revive those laws.

Even if the act of Congress of June 4, 1812 (sec. 14), providing that, if the public exigencies make it necessary for the common preservation to demand particular services of any person full compensation shall be made, were in force in Oklahoma at the time the country was opened to the whites, a person can not recover under this section for services performed as recorder of the provisional government of Oklahoma City, since there was no law requiring records to be kept, no authority for anyone to employ him for such duties, and no public necessities for his services.   *Blackburn v. Oklahoma City, 33 Pa. Rep., 708.*

SEC. 1071. Under act of Congress of March 3, 1885 (23 Stat. L., 385), giving Territorial and Federal courts jurisdiction to punish Indians for murder and other crimes committed by one Indian against another, whether on or off a reservation, an Indian, tribal or otherwise, is amenable to State jurisdiction for the murder of another Indian outside of the reservation within the State.
Pablo v. People, 46 Pacific Reporter, 636.

SEC. 1072. Entry on Indian lands by an officer to levy an execution issued by a State court on property of one not an Indian, but residing on the Indian land by consent of the tribe, is not interdicted by the provision of the enabling act of Montana that all Indian lands in the State "shall remain under the absolute jurisdiction and control of the Congress of the United States."   *Stiff v. McLaughlin, 48 Pacific Reporter, 232.*

SEC. 1073. Under the second section of the act of August 4, 1886 (24 Stat. L.), lands patented by the United States to a deceased allottee of the Kickapoo Indians in Kansas descend to the heirs of said allottee in accordance with the rule of succession provided by the laws of the State of Kansas.   *Edde v. Pash-pah-o et al., 48 Pacific Rep., 884.*

SEC. 1074. Defendant in error presented the question and made the contention that "the evidence shows that the alleged crime for which defendant was convicted was committed, if at all, upon a tract of land set apart for the sole and exclusive use of the Otoe and Missouri tribes of Indians under the laws of Congress and treaties between the said Indian tribes and the United States, and the district court of Gage County had no jurisdiction over the said offense." *Held*, that "This territory, known as the Otoe Reservation, being within the boundaries of this State (Nebraska), is subject to its laws, and the courts of this State have jurisdiction and authority to try and punish parties for crimes committed on the Indian reservations within this State."

Marion v. State, 20 Northwestern Reporter, 290, 291.

SEC. 1075. The State (Wisconsin) may include an Indian reservation, or any part of it, within the boundaries of a town.

Schriber v. Town of Langlade, 29 Northwestern Reporter, 547.

SEC. 1076. The courts of this State (Nebraska) have no authority to prosecute and punish one Indian for a crime committed against another on the reservation to which they each belong so long as they maintain their tribal relations.   *Ex parte Cross, 30 Northwestern Reporter, 428.*

SEC. 1077. Certain lands having been ceded to the United States by the Indian occupants, a stock of goods therein containing intoxicating liquor was seized by officers of the United States Army for violation of the nonintercourse act. They notified the United States attorney, who filed a libel, and the marshal took the goods under a writ issued thereon, but afterwards returned them to the owners. *Held*, in trespass *de bonis asportatis* against the officers and the marshal, that the measure of damages was the difference in the value of the goods at the time of the seizure and when they were returned to the owners.

Clark v. Bates, 46 N. W. Rep., 510.

SEC. 1078. The act of Congress of June 15, 1836, providing for the admission of Michigan into the Union, required the State legislature to provide by an irrevocable ordinance that said State should "never interfere with the primary disposition of the soil by the United States, or with any regulation Congress may find necessary for securing the title in such soil to the *bona fide* purchasers thereof, and that no tax should be imposed on land the property of the United States." July 25, 1836, the Michigan legislature passed the ordinance required. By the treaty of October 18, 1864 (14 Stat. L., 657), the Saginaw, Swan Creek, and Black River Chippewa Indians were divided into those "competent" to prudently manage their own affairs and those "not so competent," and it was provided that patents for land allotted to the latter class should contain a clause forbidding the alienation. *Held*, that lands patented to Indians designated "not so competent" could not be taxed by the State.   *Auditor v. Williams, 53 N. W. Rep., 1097.*

SEC. 1079. Unless otherwise provided by treaty with an Indian tribe or by the act admitting the State into the Union, the criminal laws of the State, except so far as restricted by the authority of Congress "to regulate commerce with the Indian tribes," extend to all crimes committed on an Indian reservation by persons other than tribal Indians.   *State v. Campbell et al., 55 N. W. Rep., 553.*

SEC. 1080. Indians while preserving their tribal relations and residing on a reservation set apart for them by the United States are the wards of the General Government, and as such the subject of Federal authority, and the power to legislate for them is exclusively in the Congress, and for acts committed within the limits of the reservation they are not answerable to the criminal laws of the State.   *Ibid.*

SEC. 1081. Compiled laws of Dakota, section 425, provide that the civil and criminal jurisdiction of justices of the peace in a judicial subdivision containing one or more unorganized counties shall extend over all such unorganized counties, and that the expenses of all criminal prosecutions arising in such unorganized counties shall be audited and paid out of the State treasury when the same is certified and allowed in the manner prescribed therein. *Held*, that such statute applies to unorganized counties which were a part of the Great Sioux Indian Reservation at the time the statute was enacted.

Morgan v. State, 68 N. W. Rep., 538.

SEC. 1082. General Statutes, 1894, section 2002, forbids the sale of intoxicating liquors to any Indian without regard to the question whether he has or has not severed his tribal relations, adopted the habits of civilization, and become a citizen of the United States by complying with the provisions of the United States "land and severalty act" of February 8, 1887 (24 Stat. L., 388). As thus construed the statute is a valid exercise of the police power of the State, and is not in conflict with either section 33 of article 4 of the constitution of the State, or section 1 of the 14th amendment of the Federal Constitution.

State v. Wise, 72 N. W. Rep., 843.

SEC. 1083. By treaty of 1831, recognized by the legislature (Laws 1849, c. 355), the disposition of the annuities between the Indians at Sandusky and those in New York was determined. The question is therefore with the legislature and not with the Commissioners of the Land Office. The petitions seek to establish a debt against the State. The commissioners can not declare one. The Commissioners can not rescind a *treaty* already made, nor interfere with an arrangement which the State has perfected. No power to annul or vary the existing treaty was delegated to the Commissioners. Until the State otherwise directs it must stand. (Note.—This case contains full account of treaties, etc., with the Cayuga Indians by the State of New York.)

That portion of the Cayuga Indians residing in Canada v. State, 1 North Eastern Reporter, 764–770.

SEC. 1084. Simeon (Indian), claimant for 500 by 200 varas, in Los Angeles County, Cal., granted June 1, 1846, by Pio Pico, to Simeon. Confirmed by the commission December 13, 1853, by the district court February 18, 1856, and appeal dismissed February 24, 1857.

1 Hoffman's Land Cases, Appendix, p. 62.

SEC. 1085. A State has the constitutional right to extend its civil and criminal jurisdiction over any tract of Indian country within her limits, where the Indian title is not extinguished.

An offense committed in the Indian territory to which title has not been extinguished, but over which territory the jurisdiction of the State court has been extended, is properly cognizable in the courts of the State, and the conviction of one for felony on such lands is legal.

All the rights of sovereignty exercised by the British Government before the Revolution is vested in the States, not collectively, but severally, within their respective limits. This sovereignty remains with the States to the full extent exercised by the British Crown, if not abridged by concessions made to the Federal Government.

Stewart v. Potter, 1 Ala., 327.

SEC. 1086. A plea alleging *that the defendants were served with process out of the county of Blount,* in the Cherokee Nation, held bad without the further averment *that the defendants were not residents of the county of Blount,* as by act of 1818 process was authorized to be served on Indian lands upon any one *resident* of the county from which issued.

Callison et al. vs. Lemons, 2 Por. (Ala.), 145.

SEC. 1087. In several of the States regulations have been passed forbidding the enforcement of contracts entered into with Indians, showing the repeated exercise of power by the States to enact such laws.

Hicks v. Ewhartonah, 21 Ark., 106.

SEC. 1088. In New York (Murray *v.* Wooden, 17 Wendell, 351) it is held that a deed from an Indian, executed in accordance with the laws of that State, *is valid,* notwithstanding the inhibition of Congress that no grant of lands by an Indian shall be valid unless made by treaty or convention entered into in pursuance of the Constitution of the United States.

Ibid.

SEC. 1089. In New York, where the State law forbids the bringing of any suit against an Indian, upon penalty of treble costs, it is held that the disability must be pleaded.

Ibid.

SEC. 1090. When the Indians occupy a territory of limited extent, surrounded by a white population, which necessarily have daily intercourse with the Indians, and it becomes impracticable to enforce the United States laws, the Federal jurisdiction must cease.

Ibid.

SEC. 1091. A white man living in the Indian nation, and owning property there, having undertaken to dispose of it by will, his right to make a will and the mode of making it, if its validity be contested, would be determined by the laws and usages of the Indian nation; but his executor having taken possession of his property and acted under the will, and having appeared in the chancery court of this State and submitted to be treated as executor or trustee under the will, without objecting to the jurisdiction of the court, the court will proceed to settle the rights of the parties under the will.

Atkins v. Guice, Admr., 21 Ark., 164.

SEC. 1092. The usual presumption that the common law prevails in another State does not apply to the Creek Nation of Indians, but the usages and customs that constitute their laws must be proven.
Du Val v. Marshall, 30 Ark., 230.

SEC. 1093. When a thief takes property stolen in Arkansas into the Indian Territory, with continuing intent to appropriate it to his own use, the Federal court at Fort Smith and the State court of the county in which the property is stolen have concurrent jurisdiction to try him for the larceny, and the court first obtaining possession of the case will not be interfered with by the other. But if the Federal court, or the judge at chambers, after making the arrest, releases him before trial to the State officers, the State court may proceed to trial and conviction.
Elmore v. The State, 45 Ark., 243.

SEC. 1094. Dunwell mortgaged certain personal property, then being on the Nez Perce Indian Reservation, and Nixon and the Aukeys, with full knowledge of plaintiff's mortgage, and with intent to cheat and defraud him out of the same, disposed of said property.
"The fact that the property is not within the jurisdiction of the court constitutes no bar in a court of equity, for a court of equity acts upon the person."
Gamble v. Dunwell, 1 Cummings (Idaho), 268.

SEC. 1095. The act of Congress organizing the Territory of Oregon reserved to the United States the right to make any regulations respecting the person and property of the Indians which it would have been competent for the Government to make had the act never been passed.
Picket v. United States, 1 Prickett (Idaho), 523.

SEC. 1096. Though act of March 3, 1863, section 1 (organic act of Idaho, 12 Stat. L., 808) provides that there shall not be included in Idaho any territory which, by treaty with any Indian tribes, is not, without the consent of the tribe, to be included within the Territorial limits or jurisdiction of any Territory, yet insomuch as the tract of land known as the "Fort Hall Indian Reservation" was included within the Territory by the act supra, and as there is no Indian treaty which would exclude such tract, it is within the jurisdiction of the Territory, and consequently the property of a railroad within this tract is subject to taxation for Territorial purposes.
Utah & N. Ry. Co. v. Fisher, 2 Idaho, 54.

SEC. 1097. The statute of 1834 (Indiana), which expressly requires the taxing of certain lands reserved to individual Miamis, instead of being unconstitutional is only declaratory of the previously existing law relating to the revenue.
Frederickson v. Fowler et al., 5 Blackf. (Ind.), 409.

SEC. 1098. The provision in the act of 1816 (Indiana), exempting certain lands from taxes for five years from the time of sale, does not apply to lands reserved to individuals by an Indian treaty.
Ibid.

SEC. 1099. The act of the Indiana legislature, February 11, 1848, repealing the act for the relief of the Miami Indians of February 3, 1841, and the act relative to suits against the Miami Indians of February 11, 1843, did not repeal the third section of chapter 28, Revised Statutes, 1843.   *Doe ex dem. Lafontaine v. Avaline, 8 Ind., 6.*

SEC. 1100. The laws of the State of Indiana relative to Indians are in *pari materia*, and must be construed together, whether repealed or not.   *Ibid.*

SEC. 1101. Laws of the State of Indiana relating to Indians and their lands considered and distinguished.
          Doe ex dem. Lafontaine v. Avaline, 8 Ind., 6.

SEC. 1102. A marriage between a male and female of the Miami tribe of Indians, formed according to the customs of the tribe, while the parties to it were residents of Indiana, can not be recognized as a valid marriage under the laws of Indiana.   *Roche v. Washington, 19 Ind., 53.*

SEC. 1103. After the act of Congress of 1834, the half-breed tract was to the fullest extent individual property, and as such, by the organic act, placed under the municipal regulations of the Territory of Iowa.   *Webster v. Reid, 1 Morris (Iowa), 467.*

SEC. 1104. Lands not under Indian government, but held by individual Indians as tenants in common, are subject to the jurisdiction of the State or Territory in which they lie. The half-breed tract, after Congress released the reversion to the half-breeds, became subject to the jurisdiction of Iowa, and the partition made in 1841 by the Territorial court is valid, and is conclusive evidence against all persons of legal title in those to whom the shares were allotted.
          Telford v. Barney, 1 Greene (Iowa), 575.

SEC. 1105. It is the right and duty of the judicial power in the State to declare all acts of the legislature made in violation of the Constitution to be void.

An act of the legislature of the Territory of Wisconsin entitled "An act for the partition of the half-breed land, and for other purposes," approved January 16, 1838, and an act supplementary thereto, approved January 16, 1838, and also an act passed by the Iowa legislature, approved January 25, 1839, to repeal both of said acts, are repugnant to the ordnance of 1787, and also to the organic law of Wisconsin and Iowa, and are therefore void. So also are judgments rendered by virtue of said laws.   *Reed v. Wright, 2 Greene (Iowa), 15.*

SEC. 1106. Since the act of Congress of 1834 the half-breed lands in Lee County have been subject to the laws and courts of Iowa to the same extent as other lands owned by individuals.
          Wright v. Marsh, Lee, and Delavan, 2 Greene (Iowa), 94.

SEC. 1107. The Wyandotte treaty of January 31, 1855 (10 Stat. L., 1159), provided for the sale to the highest bidder of the Wyandotte

Ferry, and for a conveyance thereof by patent from the United States to the purchaser, which was done, to plaintiff in error. At the time, the Wyandottes were running a ferry from the land so conveyed across the river to a landing on land now owned by defendant but then owned by the United States. *Held*, That the Wyandottes had no right of ferriage good against a franchise granted by the legislature.

Walker v. Armstrong, 2 Kans., 198.

SEC. 1108. The Wyandottes had no right of ferriage good against a franchise granted by the legislature, and Walker could get by his purchase from them no greater rights than they had to sell.   *Ibid*

SEC. 1109. An exclusive ferry right prohibits competitors from landing t'eir boats in tle highway or upon their own soil within the limits covered by the franchise, as fully as elsewhere.   *Ibid.*

SEC. 1110. The Federal Constitution, laws of the United States, and all treaties made under their authority are the supreme law controlling organic acts and State laws in this as in Federal courts, despite any notions of State sovereignty.

Charles Blue Jacket v. Comsrs. of Johnson Co., 3 Kans., 299.

SEC. 1111. Under the constitution and laws of the State of Kansas all the property therein not specifically exempted is subject to taxation. The lands of the United tribes of Shawnees held in severalty are included unless controlled by exemptions in a paramount law.   *Ibid.*

SEC. 1112. Under the Kansas Territorial organic act and the act of admission no rights that Indians had before the admission or before the Territory was organized can be impaired "so long as such rights shall remain unextinguished by treaty between the United States and such Indians."   *Parker v. Winsor, 5 Kans., 362.*

SEC. 1113. The clause of article 9 of the Ottawa treaty of 1831 (7 Stat. L., 361), whereby the United States guarantee that the lands reserved to the Ottawas shall never be within the bounds of any State or Territory, is abrogated by the provisions of the Ottawa treaty of July 16, 1862 (12 Stat. L., 1237).   *McCullagh v. Allen, 10 Kans., 150.*

SEC. 1114. The Ottawa treaty of 1862 (12 Stat. L., 1237) stipulates that at the expiration of five years the members of the tribe shall become citizens of the United States and their tribal relations be dissolved. Meanwhile their lands are to be disposed of by special allotments and sale in various ways. Some of the stipulations of the treaty are inconsistent with the idea that the reservation is without the limits of the State while others seem to clearly recognize the laws of Kansas as in force from that time forward.   .   *Ibid.*

SEC. 1115. If the Ottawa Reservation did not by virtue of the treaty of 1862 become a part of the State of Kansas, it is not now a part of it. The making of the tribe citizens after five years did not necessarily in terms make the reserve a part of the State, though it must be admitted as one of many stipulations in the treaty abrogating the excluding clause of the treaty of 1831.   *Ibid.*

SEC. 1116. If the land in question was a part of the lands belonging to the Cherokee Nation by the treaty of 1835 (7 Stat. L., 478), there can be no doubt that the court below had no jurisdiction, for the fifth article of that treaty expressly stipulates that the lands reserved by that treaty to the Cherokees "shall in no future time, without their consent, be included within the territorial limits of jurisdiction of any State or Territory."   *Ephraim v. Garlick, 10 Kans., 280.*

SEC. 1117. John Rubideaux, a Miami Indian chief, bought a piece of land in Miami County, Kans., from Jack Vallie, and in consideration therefor gave Vallie a promissory note. After maturity of the note Vallie sued Rubideaux thereon in the district court of Miama County; *Held*, that said court had jurisdiction to hear and determine the case.
                                        Rubideaux v. Vallie, 12 Kans., 28.

SEC. 1118. There is no law of the United States, or of the State of Kansas, that authorizes Indians to purchase lands in Kansas and then to refuse to pay for the same. Neither is there any law that prohibits the courts of Kansas from taking jurisdiction of the persons and property of Indians found within the territorial boundaries of Kansas, except while such Indians or property are actually situated on a reserve excluded from the jurisdiction of the State.   *Ibid.*

SEC. 1119. Neither the title nor possession of the Indian owner, secured by treaty, can be disturbed by State legislation; and if Mrs. Goodell were plaintiff in the action, seeking to recover possession, it is probable she would be entitled to both land and improvements. But this property protection, guaranteed to the Indians, is a personal privilege and does not run with the land. Mrs. Goodell has parted with the title, and the protection which the Federal law threw around the land has ceased.   *Krause v. Means, 12 Kans., 335.*

SEC. 1120. In a conflict between the law of the State and a treaty of the United States in regard to Indian lands in the State the former must give way. Neither the title nor possession of the Indian owner, secured by treaty, can be disturbed by State legislation; and the occupying claimant act has no application in this case.
                                        Maynes v. Veale, 20 Kans., 374.

SEC. 1121. The State courts have jurisdiction over lands ceded by the Kansas Indians to the United States, in trust, under the treaty of 1860 (12, Stat. L., 1129).   *Webster v. Cooke, 23 Kans., 637.*

SEC. 1122. It appearing that the tribal organization of the Shawnees was still recognized by the political department of the United States Government, under the decision of the Supreme Court of the

United States in the case of the Kansas Indians (5 Wall., 737), the descent of the lands allotted under the treaty of May 10, 1854 (10 Stat. L., 1053), is governed not by the Kansas law, but by the Shawnee law   *Brown v. Steele, 25 Kans., 672.*

SEC. 1123. The cases of Parker *v.* Winsor, 5 Kans., 362, and Douglas Co. *v.* R. R. Co., 5 Kans., 615, are cited to show that the lands in controversy are not taxable until after final payment. In those cases the facts were that the General Government, as the owner of certain Indian reservations, had contracted to sell them under a contract, which provided that if full payment was not made there should be a total and absolute forfeiture. And the court held that neither the legal nor equitable title had passed away from the Government, and that therefore the lands, as property of the Government, were not subject to taxation.   *Comss. of Dickinson Co. v. Baldwin, 29 Kans, 540.*

SEC. 1124. As to the power of the United States to regulate the mode of conveyance of lands belonging to the United States, or to the Indians, or to both, free from and independent of State statutes, see Irvine *v.* Marshall, 61 U. S., 558; Bagnell *v.* Broderick, 38 U. S., 436; Maynes *v.* Veale, 20 Kans., 374.   *McGannon v. Straightlege, 32 Kans., 524.*

SEC. 1125. So early as the year 1633 the general court of Massachusetts ordered "that no person whatsoever shall henceforth buy any land of any Indian without license first had and obtained." In 1650 the French, Dutch, and other foreigners were forbidden to trade with them. In 1657 that Commonwealth declared its right to all the fur trade with them. It had before that time forbidden the sale to them of guns, gunpowder, and other munitions of war. In 1693 an act was passed "for the better rule and government of the Indians in their several places and plantations."   *Moore v. Veazie, 32 Maine, 343.*

SEC. 1126. The Penobscots own all the island in the Penobscot River above Oldtown Falls, some of which they occupy. Said tribe of Indians always have been, and now are, under the jurisdiction and guardianship of the State.   *Ibid.*

SEC. 1127. That the Penobscot Indians were, when the Constitution of the United States was adopted, under the complete control of State laws and without the power to conduct commerce or trade, except by permission of the State, will appear by reference to State enactments.
Ibid.

SEC. 1128. The Penobscot tribe of Indians always have been, and now are, under the jurisdiction and control of this State. This tribe can not, therefore, be one of those referred to in the Constitution of the United States.   *Ibid.*

SEC. 1129. The wandering and improvident habits of the remnants of the Indian tribes in the State of Maine led the legislature at an early day to make them the wards of the State, and especially to take control and regulate the tenure of their lands. Numerous acts looking to this end were passed in different years, which are now gathered together in chapter 9 of the Revised Statutes.

John v. Sabattis, 69 Maine, 473.

SEC. 1130. Chapter 158 of the laws of 1835 (Maine) was designed to promote an interest in agricultural pursuits among the Indians. But it relates to lands other than those which are the subject of this suit. The assignment of the house and garden lots on Indian Oldtown Island was regulated by chapter 396 of the laws of 1839, and the provisions of sections 15–18 of chapter 9, Revised Statutes, have no connection with those of sections 22 and 23 in the same chapter.   *Ibid.*

SEC. 1131. The lots assigned under chapter 158, laws of 1835 (Maine), according to section 4 of that chapter, could not be sold by the Indians to whom they were assigned to any person in or out of the tribe with or without the permission of the agent, and the same construction must be given to section 18, chapter 9, Revised Statutes, so far as the sale of lots there ordered to be assigned for agricultural purposes is concerned.   *Ibid.*

SEC. 1132. The Indians of Maine are as completely subject to the State as any other inhabitants can be. They can not now invoke treaties made centuries ago with Indians whose political organization was in full vigor.   *State v. Newell, 84 Me., 465.*

SEC. 1133. While the Indians of Maine have a partial organization for tenure of property and local affairs, they have now no separate political organization, and are subject as individuals to all the laws of the State.   *Ibid.*

SEC. 1134. Whatever the status of the Indian tribes in the West may be, all the Indians of whatever tribe remaining in Massachusetts and Maine have always been regarded by those States and by the United States as bound by the laws of the State in which they lived. Their position is like that of those Cherokees who remained in North Carolina.   *Ibid.*

SEC. 1135. Land patented to a "not-so-competent Indian," under a treaty prohibiting its alienation by the patentee without the consent of the Government, which provision is incorporated in the patent, is not subject to taxation.   *Attorney-General v. Williams, 94 Mich. (Fuller), 180.*

SEC. 1136. The State has no authority to levy taxes upon property within the Indian reservations.

Foster v. Commissioners, 7 Minn. (Gilfillan), 84 (7 Minn. R., 140).

SEC. 1137. Unless otherwise provided by treaty with an Indian tribe or by the act admitting the State into the Union, the criminal laws of the State, except so far as restricted by the authority of Congress "to regulate commerce with the Indian tribes," extend to all crimes committed on an Indian reservation by persons other than tribal

Indians.   But Indians while preserving their tribal relations and residing on a reservation set apart for them by the United States are the wards of the General Government, and as such the subject of Federal authority, and the power to legislate for them is exclusively in Congress.   And for acts committed within the limits of the reservation they are not subject to the criminal law of the State.

State v. Campbell, 53 Minn., 354.

SEC. 1138. White persons living in the Indian country within the limits of Montana are subject to the laws of this Territory. The clause in the treaty of 1855 which gives the Indians of the Blackfoot Nation the exclusive control over a certain region was adopted to prevent the United States from interfering with the customs and tribal relations of the nation. In the proviso of the first section of the organic act the United States has expressly reserved the right to make regulations respecting the Indians within this Territory.

United States v. Buffalo Robes, 1 Mon., 489.

SEC. 1139. Under the legislative power of Territories, extended by section 1851, Revised Statutes of the United States, there is no limitation upon the authority of a Territory to pass laws for the regulation and restriction of "the sale of articles deemed injurious to the health or morals of the community."   Territory v. Guyott, 9 Montana, 46.

SEC. 1140. In the year 1829 the limits or jurisdiction of Monroe County, Miss., was extended over that portion of the Chickasaw Territory in which defendant and his wife resided, and the property in controversy remained in the possession of the latter down to the time of the levy.   Fisher v. Allen, 3 Miss., 611.

SEC. 1141. The right of sovereignty was never enforced by the State of Mississippi against the individuals composing the different tribes of Indians within her limits until 1830, when the legislature abolished the tribal character of the Choctaws and Chickasaws and conferred upon them the rights of citizenship.   Ibid.

SEC. 1142. By the act of the legislature of 1830, abolishing the tribal customs of the Chickasaw Indians, and extending the laws of the State over their territory, it is enacted that all marriages and matrimonial connections entered into by virtue of any custom or usage of the Indians, and by them deemed valid, shall be held as valid and obligatory as if the same had been solemnized by the laws of the State.   Ibid.

SEC. 1143. By the customs of the Chickasaws the husband acquired no right to the property of the wife which she possessed at the time of marriage. No community of interest was produced by the marriage contract with respect either to the original property of the parties or to the acquests and gains during its continuance.   Ibid.

H. Doc. 538——12

SEC. 1144. It would not have been in the power of the Indians or of the Government by treaty stipulation, without the express assent of the State, to vest the Indian with the absolute property in the land and at the same time say it shall not be subject to execution for debts lawfully contracted. That would be trenching too far on State sovereignty.   *Saffarans v. Terry, 20 Miss., 690.*

SEC. 1145. All the territory embraced within the boundaries of the State of Nebraska was withdrawn from the jurisdiction of the Federal courts by the act admitting the State into the Union.
                                                     Painter v. Ives, 4 Nebraska, 122.

SEC. 1146. The act of the Territorial legislature of March 17, 1855, entitled "An act defining the boundaries of counties therein named, and for other purposes," in so far as it defines the boundaries of Blackbird County, is inoperative and void, as being in violation of the act of Congress approved May 30, 1854, entitled "An act to organize the Territory of Nebraska," and which reserved from within the boundaries of the Territory the Indian reservation of which said Blackbird County was a part.   *State v. Thayer, 22 Nebraska, 413.*

SEC. 1147. For the several laws of New Jersey and decisions of its courts relating to Indian lands in that State, see
                                          State, Given, pros., v. Wright, 41 N. J., 478.

SEC. 1148. The private property of the Seneca Indians is not within the jurisdiction of our laws respecting administration, and letters of administration granted by a surrogate upon the estate of a deceased Indian are void.

The distribution of the property of a deceased Indian among his relatives according to the custom of the nation passes a good title, which the courts of this State will not disturb.   *2 N. Y. (Barbour), 639.*

SEC. 1149. The laws of Nevada exempt "uncivilized American Indians" from poll and road taxes.   *Hassett v. Walls, 9 Nev., 387.*

SEC. 1150. In Boyer *v.* Dively, 58 Mo., 529, it was held that although located within the State lines, yet, so long as their tribal customs are adhered to, and the Federal Government manages their affairs by agents, the Indians are not regarded as subject to State laws, so far, at least, as marriage, inheritance, etc., are concerned. No State legislation was attempted to the contrary, and it is useless to inquire, if it had been, whether it would have been valid.
                                              State v. McKenney, 18 Nev., 182.

SEC. 1151. In Langford *v.* Monteith, 102 U. S., 147, after referring to the organic act, the court said: "The court, in Harkness *v.* Hyde, 98 U. S., 476, relying upon an imperfect brief of counsel, inadvertently inferred that the treaty with the Shoshones, like that with the Shawnees, contains a clause excluding the lands of the tribe from Territorial or State jurisdiction. In this the court labored under a mistake. Where no such clause or language equivalent is found in a treaty with Indians within the exterior limits of Idaho, the lands held by them are a part of the Territory and subject to its jurisdiction, so that process may run there, however the Indians themselves may be exempt from that jurisdiction."　*Ibid.*

SEC. 1152. Mr. Otis, in his book on the Indian question, published in 1878, concludes that we should sweep away the tribal organizations and subject the Indian to territorial law. But he admits that the codes of civilized States will not answer for the purpose. Commenting on his conclusions, Mr. Wharton, in a note at section 253, says: "Waiving the question out of our right to destroy, under the Constitution, tribal sovereignty, it will be a task exceedingly difficult to frame a code to which Indians can be properly subjected."　*Ibid.*

SEC. 1153. It admits of serious doubt at least whether it would be good policy even now to subject Indians, as to their own matters, to our laws; but it would be less open to objection, now than it would have been in 1861. To have done so then would have been "cruel and absurd." (Whart. Conf. Laws, sec. 9.)　*Ibid.*

SEC. 1154. In report No. 367, Forty-third Congress, first session, the Committee on Indian Affairs, to whom was referred the bill conferring jurisdiction upon the United States courts, and for the punishment of crimes committed by and against Indians, reported "That it is doubtful whether Congress has the power to confer exclusive jurisdiction upon the courts of the United States over Indian reservations within the several States without their consent. This difficulty does not exist in the Territories, where the authority is ample and undisputed."　*Ibid.*

SEC. 1155. Mr. Wharton, in his Conflict of Laws (sec. 252), says: "He (the person adopted by a tribe) may be indicted, it is true, in State or Territorial courts for crimes committed by him on persons not of his tribe; but for offenses against members of his tribe he is only justiciable before the tribal authorities. So far as concerns his domestic relations, he is governed not by Territorial but by tribal law. * * * In short, while he retains his subjection to the Territorial government (State or Federal) in all that relates to transactions outside of the tribe, his allegiance is to the tribe, and he is governed exclusively by tribal law."　*Ibid.*

SEC. 1156. The courts of the State have no jurisdiction to try an Indian belonging to a tribe which is recognized and treated with as such by the Government of the United States, having its chief and tribal laws, for killing another Indian belonging to the same tribe.　*Ibid.*

SEC. 1157. The State courts may be given jurisdiction by the legislature over crimes committed by one Indian against the person or property of another Indian by extending the criminal laws over them.   *Ibid.*

SEC. 1158. There is no statute (State) extending the criminal laws over the Indian tribes or the individuals thereof. The statute under which the indictment is found is the general act concerning crimes and punishments.   *Ibid.*

SEC. 1159. In Lovingood *v.* Smith, 7 Jones (N. C. Law), 601, it was *held* that on examination of the treaty of New Echotah, Ga., on the 29th of December, 1835, between the United States and the Cherokee Indians, we find that by Article XII it is provided that individuals and families who were averse to moving west of the Mississippi River might remain and become citizens of the States where they resided. Our civil laws have been extended over these Indians, at least ever since 1838 (Rev. Code, chapter 50, section 16), and this statute applies as well where the contract is between two Indians as where one of the parties is white. *   *The State v. La-cha-na-tah., 64 N. C., 614.*

SEC. 1160. The treaty of Holston between the United States and the Cherokee Indians did not have the effect to repeal or modify the entry laws of this State.   *Brown v. Brown, 103 N. C., 213.*

SEC. 1161. It appears from the petition that the town-site of Chandler was set apart by the Secretary of the Interior as a county seat and was a part of the lands purchased from the Sac and Fox Indians. *Held,* that section 17 of the act of Congress approved March 3, 1891 (26 Stat. L., 1026), modifies section 2387, United States Revised Statutes, repudiates the act of Oklahoma legislature, approved December 2, 1890, and adopts the statutes of Kansas determining the jurisdiction of probate judges in town-site matters, and presenting the regulations for executing such trust. The only laws in Oklahoma regulating the duties of probate judges in the town-site matters are the laws of the United States and the State of Kansas.   *Brown v. Parker, 2 Okl. (Dale), 258.*

SEC. 1162. From 1777 to 1816 State laws alone were of force in the territory of the Cherokee Nation in South Carolina, and when, in 1816, the State wished to acquire complete sovereignty over this territory, she, under the auspices of the United States Government, entered into negotiations with them which resulted in the treaty of March 22, 1816 (7 Stat. L., 138).   *Thomas v. Daniel, 2 McC. (S. C.), 354.*

SEC. 1163. South Carolina never attempted to exercise civil or criminal jurisdiction over the tribes of Indians living within her limits and maintaining a separate existence. It was when individuals wandered off from their tribes or their tribes had become extinct that they became amenable to the State laws.

Miller v. Dawson & Brown, 1 Dudley (S. C.), 174.

SEC. 1164. The act of the legislature of North Carolina, 1783, chapter 2, without consulting the Cherokee Indians, reserved such part of their lands to them as the legislature thought proper. The balance, extending as far as the Mississippi, was authorized to be sold for the benefit of the Indians and was sold.   *Glasgow v. Smith, 1 Overton (Tenn.), 111.*

SEC. 1165. The Constitution of the United States gave the power to the General Government to regulate intercourse with the Indians and to make treaties. The Constitution was a dead letter until the treaties and the laws of the United States pointed out the principles of this intercourse. By treaty certain lands within the limits of the State are secured to the Indians within which the citizens are not to hunt, survey, or even go there without permission. But neither the Constitution nor the laws of the United States take from the sovereign rights of the State further than is compatible with these regulations.   *Ibid.*

SEC. 1166. A judgment will bind land within the Indian limits as well as without, provided the district or county in which the judgment was rendered extended there.   *Ibid.*

SEC. 1167. The rights of the aborigines as a sovereign people are not recognized, neither in the charter of Charles II nor the constitution of North Carolina. The first does not seem to recognize them at all, and the second in very different language from that which is usual when mentioning a people sovereign in fact.   *Ibid.*

SEC. 1168. The rights of these people are best understood by referring to the acts of North Carolina when possessing jurisdiction over the country now the State of Tennessee, the Constitution of the United States, and the laws made in pursuance of it.   *Ibid.*

SEC. 1169. The Indian laws must govern the transactions which happen within their own borders, and the legal claims which are founded upon them, in whatever court of other nations the satisfaction for an injury sustained may be demanded. This action is not founded upon their law, but upon the law of Tennessee, and there is no evidence produced to show what the Cherokee law is. The verdict of the court below is reversed.   *Holland v. Pack, 1 Peck (Tenn.), 119.*

SEC. 1170. At the time the execution was issued the land lay within the Indian boundary and the Indian title thereto was not then extinguished.   *Pound v. Pullen, 3 Yer., 338.*

SEC. 1171. The North Carolina act of 1783 provides "that the Cherokee Indians shall have and enjoy all that tract of land bounded as follows: * * * And that the lands included within the aforesaid bounds shall be and are hereby reserved unto the said Cherokee Indians and their nation forever." The sixth and seventh sections provide that said reserved lands shall not be granted to others or the possession of the Indians obtruded upon.   *Blair v. Pathkiller, 2 Yer., 407.*

SEC. 1172. The theory of legislating for the Cherokees which is supposed to have been assumed by North Carolina was visionary. The treaty under consideration admits the Indians not to be citizens, and the eighth article provides the mode of their naturalization. *Ibid.*

SEC. 1173. North Carolina had no right to legislate for the Cherokees without first incorporating them into the body politic. They were not represented, nor was the grant made by the act of 1783 accepted by them. *Ibid.*

SEC. 1174. North Carolina had the ultimate title, er.cumbered with the Indian right of occupancy, but that she had the right to exercise legislative power over the nation is negatived by her own acts. Hence the act of 1783 is in its character not even conventional in respect to the Cherokees who were not parties thereto. *Ibid.*

SEC. 1175. North Carolina, by her legislative acts, had the right to grant lands within the Indian boundary to her citizens, and while such grants were binding between the State and her grantees, they did not affect the Indian title. *Ibid.*

SEC. 1176. The act of 1801 (Tennessee) provides that nothing therein contained shall be so construed as to authorize any person to violate the law of the United States, so far as it relates to such parts of certain counties lying within the Indian boundary; or to authorize the sheriffs to levy executions or sell any real property lying within the Indian boundary, until the same is extinguished. *Pound v. Pullen, 3 Yer., 338.*

SEC. 1177. Before the passage of the act of 1833, chapter 16 (Tennessee), the State did not claim jurisdiction to tax persons within the Cherokee boundary, nor did the State have such jurisdiction. That act partially extended it, but on the subject of taxation excepts "any native Cherokee residing within the limits of said tract of country at the passage of this act." This exception does not include those to whom the rights of citizenship have been extended.

The State v. Ross, 7 Yer. (Tenn.), 74.

SEC. 1178. A Cherokee native, keeping a store within the limits of the Cherokee Nation, to whom the rights of citizenship were not extended, was, by the express terms of the act of 1833, chapter 16, exempt from taxation. *The State v. Ross, 7 Yer., 74.*

SEC. 1179. The act of 1833, chapter 16 (Tennessee), extending the criminal laws of the State so as to give jurisdiction to the courts of the State over certain crimes committed within the Indian Territory by any Cherokee Indian residing therein, is constitutional.

State v. Foreman, 8 Yer. (Tenn.), 256.

SEC. 1180. The State of Tennessee exercises the power of perfecting titles to land within her borders by virtue of the compact made with North Carolina in 1804. This compact was confirmed by Congress in 1806, but the power given by it was restricted to land north and east of what has been called "the Congressional reservation line," and to which the Indian title shall have been extinguished.

Gillespie v. Cunningham, 2 Humph. (Tenn.), 19.

SEC. 1181. The State courts recognize as valid all marriages made in the Cherokee Nation entered into in accordance with the forms and usage of that nation.   *Morgan v. McGhee, 5 Humph (Tenn.), 12.*

SEC. 1182. It has been settled that grants from North Carolina of lands reserved to the Cherokees under their treaties were void under the laws of that State, though, in the absence of laws expressly declaring such entries and grants void, it might be a question whether the State could not have granted the fee subject to the right of the Indians.

Calloway v. Hopkins, 11 Heiskell (Tenn.), 349.

SEC. 1183. To tax a Cherokee Indian, resident within the limits of the State, without at the same time extending to him the rights of citizenship, would be to practice the same despotic power against which our ancestors rebelled.   *Pope v. Phifer, 3 Heiskell (Tenn.), 682.*

SEC. 1184. The right of those Indian nations residing within the limits of a State to regulate their own civil polity has never been questioned unless the State authority has by some affirmative act claimed a jurisdiction incompatible with such right. Their laws and customs regulating property, contracts, and the relations between husband and wife have been respected when drawn into controversy in the courts of the State and of the United States.

Statutes of one State can not be judicially known to the courts of another State, and they must be proven as other foreign laws. The courts can only judicially know the acts of Congress and public treaties.   *Jones v. Laney et al., 2 Webb & Duval (Texas), 342.*

SEC. 1185. Under the laws of the Territory of Michigan, an order of the county court, and a license issued under such order, empowering the administrator to sell the real estate of the intestate (who was of Indian descent) for the payment of debts, is conclusive upon the subject, and the presumption of law is that the court had all the necessary evidence before it to authorize such order and license; and the heirs at law of the intestate can not, in a collateral suit, contest the validity of the order and license, for the purpose of setting aside a sale and conveyance made by the administrator under such order and license, on the ground of mere error, or that the court exercised its jurisdiction irregularly or improvidently. The presumption is that every necessary step was taken to give the court jurisdiction.

Jackson v. Astor et al., 1 Pinney (Wisc.), 138.

SEC. 1186. The criminal laws of this State apply to the Indians on their reservations within the State; and the circuit court for Brown County has jurisdiction of all violations of such laws committed, whether by Indians or others, in the Oneida Reservation, which is included within the boundaries of that county, as fixed by law.

The State v. Doxtater, 36 Wisc., 278. Same, 2 N. W. Rep., 439.

Sec. 1187. The jurisdiction of a State, when not restricted by existing treaties with Indian tribes, or by the act admitting such State into the Union, and, except so far as it is restricted by authority of Congress under the Federal Constitution to regulate commerce with the Indian tribes, extends to all members of such tribes within the territorial limits of the State.   *The State v. Doxtater, 36 Wisc, 278.*

Sec. 1188. The criminal laws of this State extend to all parts of the State, including the Oneida Reservation. (State *v.* Doxtater, ante, p. 278.)   *State v. Harris, 36 Wisc, 298.*

, Sec. 1189. The opinion of the court in the case of State *v.* Doxtater disposes of the exceptions of the defendant in this case adversely to her. In that opinion it is expressly held that the criminal laws of the State extend to all parts of the State, including the Oneida Reservation, within the boundaries of which the offense charged against the defendant was committed; and, as the evidence shows she was not an Indian and did not belong to the tribe of Oneida Indians, there can be no pretense that she was not subject to the criminal laws of the State, on any grounds personal to herself, as was claimed in the case of Doxtater.   · *State v. Harris, 2 Northwestern Reporter, 543.   Same, 36 Wisc., 278.*

Sec. 1190. Revised Statutes of the United States, section 1839, provides that " nothing in this title (the Territories) shall be construed to impair the rights of person or property pertaining to the Indians in any Territory so long as such rights remain unextinguished by treaty,   *   *   *   or to include any territory which, by treaty with any Indian tribe, is not, without the consent of such tribe, to be embraced within the territorial limits or jurisdiction of any State or Territory, but all such territory shall be excepted out of the boundaries and constitute no part of any Territory now or hereafter organized." The treaty of July 3, 1868, with the Shoshones, pursuant to which their reservation was established, contains no reservation or exception whereby it should be excluded and excepted out of the Territory within which it is situated. *Held,* that the reservation was included within the Territory and that cattle thereon, belonging to a white person in no wise connected with the Indians, were subject to taxation in the county within which the reservation lay.

        Torry v. Baldwin, 3 Wyoming, 430.

Sec. 1191. From the date of the cession of the Delaware " trust lands " and of the " outlet," July 17, 1854, these lands and their occupants (not Indians) became subject to the laws of Kansas as other lands in the State and their occupants, except as the treaty contained provisions of special and local application to them. The only provisions in the treaty (10 Stat. L., 1048) ceding these lands, of such special application, are, article 2, by which the Government agrees, for preemptors, to offer the " trust lands " at public auction, and the provision in article 16, extending, *so far as applicable*, to the lands ceded in the treaty the act of March 3, 1807, which prohibits any person making settlement on any land secured to the United States by any treaty made with a foreign nation, or by a cession by any State, which lands shall not have been previously disposed of by the United States, and which prohibits the surveying without authority of law of any such lands. *McCracken v. Todd, 1 Banks & McCahon, 146.*

SEC. 1192. The process of all the courts of the Territory could have been legally executed anywhere within the limits defined by the Territorial laws, whether on the Indian or military tracts, except only on those Indian reservations excluded by express treaty stipulations from the limits or jurisdiction of the Territory; and the State has like power within the limits defined by the State laws, except only on those Indian reservations in like manner excluded from the limits of the State by treaty provisions in force at the date of the admission of Kansas into the Union. *Ibid.*

SEC. 1193. A tract of land included within the 200,000 acres reserved to the Shawanees by the treaty of 1854 (10 Stat. L., 1053) and thereafter patented to one of the tribes, and by such patentee conveyed by an approved deed, is, notwithstanding the proviso to the first section of the act of admission, within the territorial limits of the State of Kansas, and wholly subject to its laws. *State of Kansas v. O'Laughlin, 29 Kans., 20.*

CHAPTER VI.—OF CIVIL ACTIONS, DEPREDATION, AND OTHER CLAIMS.

SEC. 1194. A legislative enactment declaring that certain lands which should be purchased for the Indians should not thereafter be taxed constituted a contract, which could not be rescinded by a subsequent legislative act, such repealing act being void under that clause of the Constitution of the United States which prohibits a State from passing any law impairing the obligations of contracts.

New Jersey v. Wilson, 7 Cranch, 164.

SEC. 1195. The Supreme Court has appellate jurisdiction under the twenty-fifth section of the judiciary act (1 Stat. L., 85) in case of a decision in the highest court of law or equity in Georgia, under the said act, in favor of its validity or against the Constitution, treaties, and laws of the United States.

Cherokee Nation v. Georgia, Appendix 1, " Pets., Cherokee Case."

SEC. 1196. The new inhibition to sue a State imposed by the Constitution only applies to the citizens or subjects of foreign states, and does not extend to the foreign state itself. *Ibid.*

SEC. 1197. At the commencement of the war of the Revolution it was to be expected, on account of Great Britain's policy toward the

Indian nations, recognizing their title to the lands they occupied and had not ceded and their right of self-government, that as her allies they would add the force of their arms to hers.   The early journals of Congress therefore exhibit a most anxious desire to conciliate the Indians.   Far from advancing a claim to their lands or asserting any right of dominion over them, Congress resolved "that the securing and preserving the friendship of the Indians appears to be a subject of the utmost moment to these colonies."

Worcester v. Georgia, 6 Peters, 515.

SEC. 1198. The moneys appropriated in and stipulated by treaty to be paid to the Cherokees on their removal and cession of their lands were properly public moneys, and the disbursement thereof was on account of the United States and for their use and benefit, in fulfillment of the obligations of the treaty.   *Minis v. United States, 15 Peters, 423.*

SEC. 1199. The thirteenth section of the act of June 30, 1834, chapter 162, Revised Statutes, is designed to exclude military officers, who might be called upon to perform duties in connection with the general Indian agent by direction of the President, from any other compensation than their traveling expenses, as well as those officers who might be directed by the President to perform the duties of general Indian agents.   *Ibid.*

SEC. 1200. Kentucky legislated for her entire territory, subject to the restrictions imposed by the treaty of Hopewell with the Chickasaws, which was recognized by the State as the paramount law until its restrictions were removed by a treaty of cession, when the act of 1809 (2 Stat. L., 516) and all the other laws of the State had effect west of the Tennessee River, and operated alike in all parts of the State.   *Porterfield v. Clark, 2 Howard, 76.*

SEC. 1201. In directing the selections for orphans, the Creek treaty of 1832 (7 Stat. L., 366) did not intend, and can not admit of the construction, that they might be made on lands selected according to the first part of the second article.   "It is a principle which has always been sacred in the United States that laws by which human action is to be regulated look forward, not backward, and are never to be construed retrospectively, unless the language of the act should render that indispensable."   The last clause in the article can not have been intended to annul or impair a title which was valid under the first clause, and guaranteed from intrusion under the fifth article for five years, unless sooner sold.   *Ladiga v. Roland, 2 Howard, 581.*

SEC. 1202. The decision of a State court upon the merits of a controversy between two parties, one of whom had sold and the other purchased an interest in lands which it was thought could be acquired as Indian reservations under a treaty with the United States, can not be reviewed by the Supreme Court of the United States under the twenty-fifth section (sec. 709, Rev. Stat.) of the judiciary act.   *Maney v. Porter, 4 Howard, 55.*

SEC. 1203. Where bonds were given to the President of the United States and his successors in office, for the use of the orphan children of certain Indians, and the declaration so averred, it was not a good cause of demurrer to allege that they were taken without authority of law. They were valid instruments, though voluntarily given and not prescribed by law.   *Tyler r. Hand, 7 Howard, 572.*

SEC. 1204. In point of law, bonds given to the President of the United States and his successors in office for the use of the orphan children of certain Indians are valid instruments, though voluntarily given and not prescribed by law (5 Pet., 115). It is not the case of a bond given contrary to law or in violation of law, but that of bonds given voluntarily for a consideration expressed in them to a public officer, but not happening to be prescribed by law.   *Ibid.*

SEC. 1205. It was not necessary for the defendants occupying the lands reserved to show that any of the Sac and Fox half-breeds were in existence at the time of the trial of title to land embraced in the reservation made for them by treaty of 1824 (7 Stat. L., 229).
          Marsh r. Brooks, 8 Howard, 223.

SEC. 1206. It is sufficient to show an outstanding title to give in evidence a treaty between the United States and the Sac and Fox Indians in which the land in question, with other lands, was reserved for half-breeds, and an act of Congress passed in 1834 (4 Stat. L., 729) relinquishing the reversionary interest of the United States to these half-breeds.   *Ibid.*

SEC. 1207. If a defendant in an ejectment suit merely sets up the title in an Indian reservee under treaty as an outstanding title, without showing in himself a connection with the title of such reservee, and then a State court decides against him, this court has no jurisdiction to review that decision. In order to give jurisdiction to this court the party must claim the right for himself, and not for a third party in whose title he has no interest.   *Henderson r. Tennessee, 10 Howard, 311.*

SEC. 1208. In Tennessee if a defendant in an ejectment suit claims a right to the possession of land derived under a title which springs from a reservation in a treaty between the United States and an Indian tribe, and a State court decides against the validity of such title, this court has jurisdiction under the twenty-fifth section of the judiciary act (1 Stat. L.,85) to review that decision.   *Ibid.*

SEC. 1209. A law of the legislature of the Territory of Iowa directing that the court should decide suits instituted against "the owners of the half-breed lands in Lee County," without the intervention of a jury to determine matters of fact, was inconsistent with the Constitution of the United States, and in this respect it was void.
          Webster r. Reid, 11 Howard, 436.

SEC. 1210. If no partition of the Sac and Fox half-breed reservation had been made, so that Na Ma Tan Pas could not give an exclusive title to the land, yet, being proved to be an half-breed, he had the power to convey at least his interest in the land, which gave a right of possession to some extent to his grantee.   *Ibid.*

SEC. 1211. Where the legislature of the Territory of Iowa directed that suits might be instituted against the owners of the half-breed lands lying in Lee County, notice thereof being given through the newspapers, and judgments were recovered in suits so instituted, these judgments were nullities and did not authorize the execution on which the lands were sold.   *Ibid.*

SEC. 1212. Apparently the ratification by the Senate of the treaty of 1804 (7 Stat. L., 84) sanctioned, retrospectively, the Sac and Fox claim to the old St. Charles County, Mo., wherein had been established the village of St. Charles twenty years before Louisiana was acquired by the United States, and in like manner the ratification of the treaty of 1824 (7 Stat. L., 229) recognized an existing Indian claim to the Sac and Fox half-breed tract, where the land in dispute lies.   *Marsh v. Brooks, 14 Howard, 513.*

SEC. 1213. The treaty of 1808 (7 Stat. L., 107) had every sanction that a ratification by our Senate could give it, and is a recognition of an Indian title in the Osages to nearly all the territory now embraced in the State of Missouri, and the greater part of Arkansas, and of an Osage right in the land claimed by Riddick up to 1808, and yet the county and town of St. Louis, the seat of the government of Upper Louisiana during the existence of the Spanish colonial government, the post of New Madrid, the county, town, and post of St. Charles were all within that cession, as were also a great mass of Spanish orders of surveys and grants, regarding which this country has been legislating and adjudicating for nearly fifty years without anyone supposing that such concessions were affected by these loose Indian pretensions set up to the country at the time when the concessions were made; pretensions that the Spanish Government notoriously disregarded further than cautious policy required.   *Ibid.*

SEC. 1214. In Louisiana, under Spain, the right of Indians to work their mines on their own account under the Spanish ordinances of May 25, 1783, was at one time questioned, and it was decided that they could do so; and the mines discovered by the Indians were declared to be, in respect to boundaries, on the same footing, without any distinction, as those worked or discovered by Spaniards.   *Chouteau v. Molony, 16 Howard, 203.*

SEC. 1215. Indians, although of age, continued, within the dominions of Spain, to enjoy the rights of minors, to avoid contracts or other sale of their property, particularly real, made without authority of the judiciary or the intervention of their protectors. They were considered as persons under legal disability, and their protectors stood in the light of guardians.   *Ibid.*

SEC. 1216. Mines on public or Indian lands, and whether of the precious or baser metals, formed a part of the royal patrimony of the Spanish Crown, and they were regulated and worked by royal ordinance from the King. The property of the mines was so vested in the King that they were held not to-pass in the land, although not excepted out of the grant, and when included in it the grant was good as to them only during the life of the King who made it, and required confirmation by his successor. *Ibid.*

SEC. 1217. The Spanish law for granting lands (those occupied by Indians as well as public lands) was that the grants be made with formality in the name of the King by the governor-general of the province; that when the order to grant was given a surveyor be appointed to fix the boundaries, and that the order itself should be registered in the land office with the memorials and other papers, whatsoever they might be, which had induced the governor to make the grant. *Ibid.*

SEC. 1218. When the Spanish governors of Louisiana relinquished the interest or title of the Crown in Indian lands the grants were made subject to the rights of Indian occupancy and they did not take effect until that occupancy had ceased, and while it continued it was not in the power of the Spanish governor to authorize anyone to interfere with it. *Ibid.*

SEC. 1219. There is no evidence of fraud practiced in the partition of the Sac and Fox half-breed reservation, which was made at the Sac and Fox treaty of August, 1824 (7 Stat. L., 229), and nothing in the admitted facts to disprove the answer made to complainants' petition. *Coy v. Mason, 17 Howard, 579.*

SEC. 1220. Under section 11 of the act of June, 1812 (2 Stat. L., 755), money due in the District of Columbia to administrators appointed under the laws of the Cherokee Nation should be paid to the attorney in fact of such administrators. *Mackay v. Cox, 18 Howard, 100.*

SEC. 1221. The stipulation in the treaty of 1842 with the New York Indians (7 Stat. L., 586), which required that the appraised value of the improvements on the surrendered reservation should, on delivery of possession, be paid to the President of the United States to be distributed among the owners of the improvements according to the award of the appraisers, shows that the Government was to be present at the surrender and payment for the improvements.
Fellows v. Blacksmith, 19 Howard, 366.

SEC. 1222. The fact that the title set up for the Indians in this case is under a treaty does not avail to give this court jurisdiction under the twenty-fifth section of the judiciary act (1 Stat. L., 85), because neither the Indian himself nor anyone claiming through him is a party. *Verder v. Coleman, 1 Black., 472.*

SEC. 1223. The obligation placed on the President by the Pottawatomie treaty of 1832 (7 Stat. L., 378), to make the selections for the individuals for whose benefit certain lands were reserved, as soon as the lands were surveyed, and to issue the patents, was absolute and imperative and founded upon a valuable and meritorious consideration, the lands reserved constituting a part of the compensation received by the Pottawatomies for the relinquishment of their right of occupancy to the Government.   *Crews v. Burcham, 1 Black, 352.*

SEC. 1224. Fort Leavenworth and its appurtenances were not included in the grant to the Delaware Indians in 1829 (7 Stat. L., 327), which calls for the fort as a boundary.
        United States v. Stone, 2 Wall., 525.

SEC. 1225. The covenant with the Shawnees in the treaty of 1831 (7 Stat. L., 284), that they should not be subjected to the laws of organized States or Territories, nor their lands be included within their boundaries, unless with their own consent signified to the President, must have materially influenced their decision to part with their Ohio possession and join their brethren in Kansas.
        The Kansas Indians, 5 Wallace, 737.

SEC. 1226. Section 107 of the act of 1868 (15 Stat. L., 167) is clear and explicit, and it embraces indisputably the Indian territories, Congress not having thought proper to exclude them, and it is therefore not for the court to make the exception. If the exemption had been intended it would doubtless have been expressed.
        The Cherokee Tobacco, 11 Wallace, 616.

SEC. 1227. When a party, without force or intimidation, and with a full knowledge of all the facts in the case, accepts, on account of an unliquidated and controverted demand, a sum less than what he claims and believes to be due him, and agrees to accept that sum in full satisfaction, he will not be permitted to avoid his act on the ground of duress.
        United States v. Childs, 12 Wallace, 232.   United States v. Old Settlers, 148 United States, 427.

SEC. 1228. A demand by the United States for the proceeds of the Indian trust bonds, unlawfully converted to their own use by persons who had illegally procured and sold them and afterwards become wholly insolvent, is a demand arising upon an implied contract, or one which may be so treated by a waiver of the alleged fraud in the conversion of the bonds.   *Allen v. United States, 17 Wallace, 207;.*

SEC. 1229. A commission called together in pursuance of the Choctaw treaty of 1866 (14 Stat. L., 781) to sell and adjust disputed claims with a view to their ultimate payment and satisfaction is for that purpose a *quasi* court, and there is nothing illegal, immoral, or against public policy in an agreement by an attorney at law to present and prosecute a claim before it, either at a fixed compensation or for a reasonable percentage upon the amount recovered.
        Wright v. Tebbitts, 91 U. S., 252.

SEC. 1230. Where a party under his contracts with the Indian Department was entitled to "all hides of beef cattle slaughtered for

Indians," which the superintendent of Indian affairs should decide were not required for their comfort, and the Commissioner of Indian Affairs directed that the cattle be turned over to the agent who gave them out from time to time to the Indiams by whom they were killed, the order of the Commissioner of Indian Affairs was, in effect, a decision that the hides were required for the comfort of the Indians, and excused the United States from delivery to the contractor.

Lobenstein v. United States, 91 U. S., 324.

SEC. 1231. The statement as made in the contracts of the number of hides not required for the comfort of the Indians to be turned over to the contractor does not create an obligation on the part of the Government to deliver that number, as the condition of the agreement made it impossible for either party to determine how many would be required to be reserved for the Indians, and therefore the number specified could not have been understood as guaranteed.   *Ibid.*

SEC. 1232. Where in contracts with a party the Government agreed that he should receive "all hides of beef cattle slaughtered for the Indians" which the superintendent of Indian affairs decided were not required for the comfort of the Indians, there was no obligation on the part of the United States to slaughter the cattle or any portion of them for the Indians, and they were only bound to deliver the hides of such as they did slaughter in case the superintendent of Indian affairs did not decide that they were not required for the comfort of the Indians.   *Ibid.*

SEC. 1233. The proceeds of Osage lands, ceded in the first article of the treaty of 1865 (14 Stat. L., 687), to be sold by the Government on the most advantageous terms, after deducting enough to repay advances and expenses, were to be placed in the Treasury to the credit of the "civilization fund" for the benefit of the Indian tribes *throughout the country.*   *Leavenworth, etc., R. R. Co. v. United States, 92 U. S., 733.*

SEC. 1234. "A thing which is within the letter of the statute is not within the statute unless it be within the intention of the makers." (1 Bacon's Abridgements, 247.)   *Ibid.*

SEC. 1235. An agreement to pay a contingent compensation for professional services of a legitimate character, in prosecuting a claim against the United States pending in one of the Departments, is not in violation of law or public policy.   *Stanton v. Embery, 93 U. S., 548.*

SEC. 1236. Military officers can no more protect themselves than civilians for wrongs committed in times of peace, under orders emanating from a source which is itself without authority in the premises. Hence a military officer, seizing liquors supposed to be in the Indian country when they are not, is liable to an action as a trespasser.

Bates v. Clark, 95 U. S., 204.

SEC. 1237. If the place where the whisky was seized had been Indian country, and it had turned out that the plaintiffs below had a license, or did not intend to sell or introduce the goods, the fact that the defendants acted on reasonable ground would have exempted them from liability; but the plaintiffs violated no law in having the whisky for sale at the place where seized, and the plea that the defendants had good reason to believe that it was Indian country, and they acted in good faith, while it might · excuse them from punitory damages, is no defense to the action.   *Ibid.*

SEC. 1238. The court having already decided that the Federal questions involved in the case were correctly decided by the State supreme court, the settled rule of the court is that the judgment must be affirmed without determining the other questions not of a Federal character.   *Myrick v. Thompson, 99 United States, 291.*

SEC. 1239. The term "white person" in the Revised Statutes must be given the same meaning it had in the original Indian-intercourse act of 1834 (4 Stat. L., 729). Congress has nowhere manifested an intention of using it in a different sense. While the negro, under the operation of the constitutional amendments, has been endowed with certain civil and political rights which he did not have in 1834, he is no more, in fact, a white person than he was then.
                          United States v. Perriman, 100 U. S., 235; 25—645.

SEC. 1240. If, under claim that they belong to the Government, an officer seizes for the use of an Indian agency a building owned by a private citizen no implied obligation on the part of the United States to pay for the use and occupation of them is thereby raised.
                                  Langford v. United States, 101 U. S., 341.

SEC. 1241. A mixed or half-breed Indian of the tribe of Sac and Fox to whom a patent of land was issued under article seventeenth of the treaty of 1868 (15 Stat. L., 495), by which the tribe ceded all their lands in Kansas to the United States, is not entitled to exemption from taxation on the lands thus held by a title carrying with it absolute ownership with the right of free disposition.
                                  Pennock v. Franklin County, 10 U. S., 44.

SEC. 1242. The Indian trust lands ceded to the Government in trust, to be sold for the benefit of the Indians, by the treaty of 1854 (10 Stat. L., 1048) with the Delawares, and of the same year (10 Stat. L., 1082) with the Kaskaskia, Peorias, Piankeshaws, and Weas, were never public lands of the United States and were never subject to sale at the Lecompton land office. There was never a time that the United States occupied any other position under the cession than that of trustees, with power to sell for the benefit of the Indians. In equity, under the operation of the treaties, the Indians continued, until sales were made, the beneficial owners of all their country ceded in trust.
                                  United States v. Brindle, 110 U. S., 688.

SEC. 1243. It was never any part of the official duty of Brindle, the receiver of public moneys at the Lecompton land office, to sell the

Indian trust lands or receive the payments therefor. His duties in connection with that office were to receive and account for moneys paid for public lands, that is to say, the public moneys of the United States derived from the sale of public lands. The moneys paid for the Indian lands were trust moneys and not public moneys, and they were at all time in equity the moneys of the Indians, subject only to the expenses incurred by the Government for surveying, managing, and selling the lands.   *Ibid.*

SEC. 1244. Brindle's employment was for special service in connection with a special trust assumed by the United States for the benefit of certain Indian tribes, in which express provisions were made for the payment of expenses. So far as is shown the appointment was not made because he was receiver of the land office. The duties to be performed were of a different character and at a different place from those of the land office, and while the exact amount of compensation for this service was not fixed, it was clearly to be inferred that such compensation as the law implies where labor is performed by one at the request of another—that is to say, a reasonable compensation—would be paid.   *Ibid.*

SEC. 1245. When Brindle was appointed special receiver and superintendent, to assist the special commissioner in disposing of the Indian trust lands, he was employed to render a service in no way connected with the office he held—no new duty was imposed on him as receiver of the land office. By express provision of the treaties the expenses incurred by the United States in making the sales were to be paid from the proceeds, and this clearly implied the payment of a reasonable compensation for the service of those employed to carry the trust into effect.   *Ibid.*

SEC. 1246. The members of the Indian tribes within the territorial limits of the United States owed immediate allegiance to their several tribes, and were not part of the people of the United States. They were in a dependent condition, a state of pupilage, resembling that of a ward to his guardian. They and their property were exempt from taxation by treaty or statute of the United States, and could not be taxed by any State. General acts of Congress did not apply to the Indians, unless so expressed as to clearly manifest an intention to include them.   *Elk v. Wilkins, 112 U. S., 94.*

SEC. 1247. The provision in section two of the fourteenth amendment for a proportionate reduction of the basis of the representation of any State in which the right to vote for Presidential electors, Representatives in Congress, or executive or judicial officers or members of the legislature of a State is denied, except for crime, to "any of the male inhabitants of such State, being 21 years of age and a citizen of the United States," can not apply to a denial of the elective franchise to Indians not taxed, who form no part of the people entitled to representation.   *Ibid.*

SEC. 1248. The pension acts exempt Indian claimants of pensions for service in the Army or Navy from the obligation to take the oath to support the Constitution of the United States.   *Ibid.*

SEC. 1249. Any person, whether a citizen or not, unlawfully restrained of his liberty is entitled to the writ of *habeas corpus.*   *Ibid.*

SEC. 1250. It was competent for the Quartermaster's Department of the Army to enter into an agreement binding a contractor to receive from its officers or agents all such military, Indian, or Government supplies as they might deliver to him for transportation; but it had no authority, without reference to the views of the Interior Department and of the officers having special connection with Indian affairs, to control the transportation of Indian supplies of every kind.

Hazlett v. United States, 115 U. S., 291.

SEC. 1251. The contract between the Quartermaster's Department and a contractor, by which said contractor was bound to receive and transport "all military, Indian, and Government supplies turned over to said contractor in good condition by the officers or agents of the Quartermaster's Department," did not obligate the Government to deliver to him, nor did it bind him to receive for transportation, during the period designated, *all* Indian supplies or stores in the hands of its agents or officers of whatever department or branch of the public service.   *Ibid.*

SEC. 1252. As the contractor with the Quartermaster's Department was not bound to receive Indian supplies or stores turned over to him for transportation by the Indian Bureau, the employment by the Commissioner of Indian Affairs of others to effect the transportation of Indian supplies (which were never so far as shown in charge of the Quartermaster's Department for transportation) was not an infringement of his legal rights.   *Ibid.*

SEC. 1253. The fact that in three instances the Indian Department made arrangements with the War Department to transport Indian supplies in the hands of the Quartermaster's Department and that these supplies were delivered by the officers or agents of the Quartermaster's Department to claimant for transportation under the contract of that Department with him, gives no support to the suggestion that the Government recognized claimant's right to transport all Indian supplies for the posts or agencies named in his contract, the Indian Department having reimbursed to the War Department the cost of such transportation.   *Ibid.*

SEC. 1254. The Fort Hall Indian Reservation is subject to the genneral jurisdiction of the Territory of Idaho, as to all matters not interfering with the rights secured to the Indians by treaty.

Utah, etc., Co. v. Fisher, 116 U. S., 28.

SEC. 1255. The principle of settlement adjudged by the Senate in its award, in pursuance of the eleventh article of the Choctaw treaty of 1855 (11 Stat. L., 611), furnishes the nearest approximation to the justice and right of the claim of the Indians that, after this lapse of time, it is practicable for a judicial tribunal to reach.

Choctaw Nation v. United States, 119 U. S., 1.

SEC. 1256. It is notorious as an historical fact, as it abundantly appears from the record in this case, that great pressure had to be brought to bear upon the Indians (Choctaw) to effect their removal, as provided in the treaty of 1830 (7 Stat. L., 333), and the whole treaty evidently and purposely was executed not so much to secure to the Indians the rights for which they had stipulated as to effectuate the policy of the United States in regard to their removal. *Ibid.*

SEC. 1257. When the United States questions the validity of the Senate award under the Choctaw treaty of 1855 (11 Stat. L., 611) by questioning its justice, the burden of proof is upon them to establish by affirmative proof the consideration which ought to constrain the court, as a matter of justice, to altogether disregard it. *Ibid.*

SEC. 1258. It does not give too much effect to the act of March 2, 1861 (12 Stat. L., 238), to treat it as an act of Congress confirming the validity of the award of the Senate under the eleventh and twelfth articles of the Choctaw treaty of 1855 (11 Stat. L., 611), and this view is very much strengthened by the terms of the act of June 23, 1874 (18 Stat. L., 230), from which it appears that at that recent date Congress intended to treat the award as valid and binding, and the report of the Secretary of the Interior as to the balance due to be final.

Ibid.

SEC. 1259. Whatever force might otherwise be supposed to reside in the objections to the validity of the award of the Senate under the Choctaw treaty of 1855 (11 Stat. L., 611) are further answered by a reference to the provisions of the Indian appropriation act of March 2, 1861 (12 Stat. L., 238), making appropriation in part payment of it, and provides for the future adjustment of the claim of the Choctaws under it, and that act would seem to have the effect of confirming the award. *Ibid.*

SEC. 1260. The award of the Senate under the Choctaw treaty of 1855 (11 Stat. L., 611), can not be avoided on the ground of a lack of proper notice to the United States of the intended action of the arbitrator before proceeding to adjudication when it is considered that the Senate of the United States was the arbitrator. Constituting, as it does, a branch of the legislative as well as the treaty-making power of the Government of the United States, it can hardly be contended that the United States had no notice of proceedings taken by the Senate in pursuance of laws or treaties made by the United States. *Ibid.*

SEC. 1261. The award of the Senate under the Choctaw treaty of 1855 (11 Stat. L., 611) can not be avoided on the ground of uncertainty, the award itself having provided the means of reducing the award to a certainty by directing the Secretary of the Interior to cause the account to be stated with the Choctaws, showing what was due them according to the principle of settlement embraced in the award. The stating of the account was merely in execution of the judgment; the principle on which it should proceed was fully, clearly, and finally adjudged. Whatever exception might be taken to the account rendered would not be different from such as in the usual course of equity practice might be taken to the report of a master to whom was referred the statement of the account, the principle of which had been previously settled by a decree of the court fixing and establishing the rights of the parties.   *Ibid.*

SEC. 1262. The language of the question submitted to the Senate by the Choctaw treaty of 1855 (11 Stat. L., 611) is in the alternative "whether the Choctaws are entitled to or *shall be allowed*," and it was sufficient to satisfy the terms of the submission for the Senate to declare, as it did, that the Choctaws should be allowed the proceeds of the sale of the lands which had been ceded by them in the treaty of 1830 (7 Stat. L., 333), and the award can not be avoided on the ground that it did not agree with the submission.   *Ibid.*

SEC. 1263. The language of the act of 1881 (21 Stat. L., 504) in reference to the award made by the Senate under the Choctaw treaty of 1855 (11 Stat. L., 611) does not abrogate it, and does not require as a condition of the exercise of the jurisdiction conferred by the act that the court should entirely disregard it, giving it no effect whatever. There is nothing in the language to prevent the court from giving to that award effect as *prima facie* establishing the validity of the claim so far adjudged in favor of the Choctaw Nation, leaving the representatives of the Government in this litigation the right not only to question the validity of the award as such upon any such ground as might or should invalidate awards ordinarily, either at law or in equity, but also to attack it upon the merits as a finding unsupported by proof, or unjust and unfair in view of all the circumstances, and on that account not to be enforced.   *Ibid.*

SEC. 1264. Under the terms of the act of March 3, 1881 (21 Stat. L., 504), in exercising the jurisdiction thereby conferred the Court of Claims is empowered to review the entire question of differences *de novo*, which may be interpreted to imply that the whole matter was opened from the beginning, with the view of determining what the original treaty rights of the Choctaws were, and how far they have been performed by the United States in its various transactions with them, including the acts done under the authority of the statutes referred to.   *Ibid.*

SEC. 1265. Where, in professed pursuance of treaties, statutes have conferred valuable benefits upon the Choctaw Nation, which that nation have accepted, they partake of the nature of an agreement, the acceptance of the benefits, coupled with the condition, implying an assent on the part of the recipient to the condition, unless that implication is rebutted by other sufficient circumstances.   *Ibid.*

SEC. 1266. Acts of Congress relating to the Choctaws and touching their treaty rights have, in one respect, the force of law, because Congress has full power of legislation over the subject, but, in so far as they may have proceeded upon insufficient or incorrect interpretations of the treaty rights of the Choctaw Nation, or in so far as they may have attempted to modify or disregard those rights, they form the very subjects of complaint on the part of the Choctaw Nation, whose allegation is that the United States by these very statutes, as in other particulars, have broken their treaty obligations.   *Ibid.*

SEC. 1267. The judgment of the Court of Claims in Fremont *v.* United States (2 Court of Claims, 461) did not proceed upon the ground that the claimant was entitled to recover if the case stood on the contract there in question, but upon the ground that certain of the acts of Congress constituted a clear and distinct legislative recognition of the obligation of the United States to pay the fair value of the subsistence furnished for the Indians, as well under the contracts with Fremont, Hensley, and Norris, as under similar contracts with other parties.   *United States v. McDougall's Adm'r., 121 U. S., 89.*

SEC. 1268. The court are unable to find any solid ground upon which to hold the United States legally liable upon the agreement between Wozencraft and McDougall, or for the value of the cattle delivered under it. That Congress, by special acts, made provision for the payment of particular claims of the same class furnishes no ground whatever for the assumption that the Government recognized its legal liability for the amount of such claims, much less for the amount of all other claims of like character.   *Ibid.*

SEC. 1269. The court may properly take judicial notice of the fact that many claims against the United States can not be enforced by suit, but provision for which may be, and upon grounds of equity and justice ought to be, made by special legislation. But the discretion which Congress has in such matters would be very seriously trammeled if the doctrine should be established that it can not appropriate money to pay particular claims except at the risk of thereby recognizing the legal liability of the United States for the amount of other claims of the general class.   *Ibid.*

SEC. 1270. Neither the 5 per cent fund arising under the act of 1811 (2 Stat. L., 641) nor the swamp-land fund arising under the acts of 1850 (9 Stat. L., 519) and 1855 (10 Stat. L., 634) is of such a character that a debt due the United States by the State of Louisiana for overdue coupons on the Indian trust bonds can not be set off against the fund which is in the hands of the United States.

United States v. Louisiana, 127 U. S., 182.

SEC. 1271. The general object of treaties and statutes cited affecting the courts of the Cherokee Nation is to vest in those courts jurisdiction of all controversies between Indians, or where a member of the nation is the only party to the proceedings, and to reserve to the courts of the United States jurisdiction of all actions to which its own citizens are parties on either side.   *In re Mayfield, 141 U. S., 107.*

SEC. 1272. A right of action survives in the Indian Territory against a railroad company inflicting injuries upon a passenger which result in death.   *St. Louis, &c., Ry. Co. v. McBride, 141 U. S., 127.*

SEC. 1273. It was competent for Congress to give the enumerated courts jurisdiction over not only controversies immediately relating to or growing out of the construction of the road, but over all controversies between the nations and tribes, or inhabitants thereof, through whose territory the railroad might be constructed and the company.   *Southern Kansas Ry. Co. v. Briscoe, 144 U. S., 133.*

SEC. 1274. As the Southern Kansas Railway Company acquired all its rights in the matter of construction and operation of its road within the Indian Territory under and by virtue of a law of the United States enacted by Congress in exercise of its power over the Territories, controversies arising by reason of the exercise of its powers therein were necessarily controversies arising under the laws of the United States.

Ibid.

SEC. 1275. The addition of the words "so far as may be necessary to carry out the provisions of this act" to the eighth section of the act of July 4, 1884 (23 Stat. L., 73), was not intended as a limitation of the jurisdiction of the courts of the northern district of Texas and western district of Arkansas to controversies growing out of the construction of the road merely, since the section in terms applies "to all controversies."   *Ibid.*

SEC. 1276. While the plaintiffs in this case were not in 1887 citizens of the United States capable of suing as such in the Federal courts, the courts of Nebraska were open to them, as they are to all persons, irrespective of race or color.   *Felix v. Patrick, 145 U. S., 317.*

SEC. 1277. Twenty-eight years elapsed from the time the scrip was secured from Sophia Felix, and nearly twenty-seven years from the time it went into possession of Patrick, before the bill was filed in this case.   It admits of no doubt that if Sophia Felix and the plaintiffs in this case had been ordinary white citizens, under no legal disabilities, such as those arising from infancy, lunacy, or coverture, this lapse of time would be fatal to a recovery, at least unless it were conclusively shown that knowledge of the fraud was not obtained and could not by reasonable diligence have been discovered within a reasonable time after it was perpetrated. *Ibid.*

SEC. 1278. While upon the facts stated Patrick took these lands as trustee for Sophia Felix, he did not take them under an express trust to hold them for her benefit, in which case lapse of time would be immaterial, but under an implied or constructive trust, a trust created by operation of law, and arising from the illegal practices resorted to in obtaining the power of attorney and deed. Therefore the most important question in this case, and one on which the result must ultimately depend, is laches. *Ibid.*

SEC. 1279. Where the construction of the language of a statute is doubtful, courts will always prefer that which will confirm rather than destroy any *bona fide* transaction or title. The intention and policy of the enactment should be sought for and carried out.

Taylor v. Brown, 147 U. S., 640.

SEC. 1280. While the application of a claimant to the Interior Department, which was paying over to the Indians under treaties, to withhold from them an agreed percentage thereof for services rendered by him to the Indians, may be rightfully regarded as a matter pending in one of the Executive Departments which involves controverted questions of fact or law, within the meaning of the twelfth section of the act of 1887 (24 Stat. L., 505), it can not be regarded as a suit brought against the United States within the contemplation of the ninth section of that act, making provisions for appeals from judgments of the Court of Claims. *In re Sanborn, 148 U. S., 222.*

SEC. 1281. The fact that the Court of Claims was to have "unrestricted latitude in adjusting and determining the said claim, so that the rights, legal and equitable, both of the United States and of the said Indians, may be fully considered and determined," did not mean that either party was "entitled to have or receive, by virtue of the act, anything more than each was entitled to under existing stipulations, or to bring supposed moral obligations into play for the disposal of the case." This language did not involve a confusion of the respective powers of the departments of the Government, nor furnish a basis for an external attack upon the validity of the executive or legislative action. *United States v. Old Settlers, 148 U. S., 427.*

SEC. 1282. The jurisdictional act passed in effectuation of the intention of Congress to obtain a judicial interpretation of the treaties and laws bearing upon the subject, and to be bound by judicial decision in respect of conclusions flowing therefrom and arrived at upon equitable principles, left it open to the courts to readjust the amount, notwithstanding the claim might be theretofore settled. In other words, if the adjustment and settlement were found to have been made upon an erroneous interpretation which led to an obvious mistake, then Congress designed that the mistake should be corrected.   *Ibid.*

SEC. 1283. In view of the terms of the jurisdictional act and conclusion reached with reference to the amount due, it appears that the decision of the Senate in respect of interest is controlling, and that therefore interest must be allowed the Old Settlers upon the balance indicated. Section 1091, Revised Statutes, and the decision of the court in Tellson *v.* United States (100 U. S., 43), holding that interest was not authorized under a private act referring to the Court of Claims a claim founded upon a contract with the United States, which did not expressly authorize interest, do not apply in this case in view of the circumstances.   *Ibid.*

SEC. 1284. The Court of Claims, after delivering its opinion, suspended the entry of the decree which it had indicated its intention to render (that the general liability should be established and the provision made for the individual Old Settlers, or Western Cherokees, to come in and establish their right to share in the fund), and, after argument had upon the question, modified that opinion, and held that the fifth article of the treaty of 1846 (9 Stat. L., 871) applied as to the distribution, and entered a decree accordingly. The court was quite right in holding that the amount due should not be decreed to be received and disbursed by the three petitioners as a commission, and that it was not necessary that the decree should require the beneficiaries to come into that tribunal and prove up against the fund, and the disposition as finally agreed upon is approved as just and appropriate under the circumstances, and a competent exercise of judicial power.   *Ibid.*

SEC. 1285. It is well settled that where the language of a statute is in any manner ambiguous or the meaning doubtful, resort may be had to surrounding circumstances, the history of the times, and the defect or mischief the statute was intended to remedy.

Smith v. Townsend, 148 U. S., 490.

SEC. 1286. Such enactments as sections 2103, 2104, and 2105 of the Revised Statutes, intended to protect the Indians from improvident and unconscionable contracts, by no means create a legal obligation on the part of the United States to see that the Indians perform their part of such contracts.   *In re Sanborn, 148 U. S., 222.*

SEC. 1287. The portion of the Pottawatomie Indians who were permitted to remain east by the supplementary article to the treaty of 1833 (7 Stat. L., 442) are not entitled to the whole of the annuity of $2,000 provided for therein, but only to a just proportion thereof.

Phineas Pam-to-pee v. United States, 148 U. S., 691.

SEC. 1288. The Court of Claims properly held that no power had been given it to convert the perpetual annuities into a sum for present payment, and that matter must be left to be dealt with by Congress.

Ibid.

SEC. 1289. The Court of Claims has the power, under section 1088, Revised Statutes, to grant a new trial at a term subsequent to that at which the original judgment was rendered, on a motion on behalf of the United States, and a mandate from the Supreme Court does not affect that power.   *Belknap v. United States, 150 U. S., 588.*

SEC. 1290. The payment to an Indian agent of the amount appropriated by Congress for the payment of his salary, being less than the amount fixed by the general law as the salary of the office, and his receipt of the sum paid " in full of my pay for services for the period herein expressed," is a full satisfaction of the claim.   *Ibid.*

SEC. 1291. Neither the statutes of Arkansas, which were extended over the Indian Territory by the act of May 2, 1890 (26 Stat. L., 84), nor the decisions of the supreme court of that State, construing those statutes, constitute a rule of decision of the United States court in the Indian Territory when dealing with an instrument made in that Territory before such statutes were so extended to that Territory.
Huntly v. Kingman, 152 U. S., 527.

SEC. 1292. The act of March 1, 1889 (25 Stat. L., 783), establishing a United States court for the Indian Territory, and extending the jurisdiction of the United States courts over the Indian Territory, which was divided and annexed for judicial purposes to the district of Kansas and to the eastern judicial district of Texas, has no application to that portion of the Cherokee Outlet referred to in the ninth section of the act of May 2, 1890 (26 Stat. L., 81), attached to Logan County, Okla., for judicial purposes.   *United States v. Pridgeon, 153 U. S., 48.*

SEC. 1293. The list of half-breeds entitled to participate in the allotment of lands under the treaty of 1830 (10 Stat. L., 332) was not an official record intended as a mode of preserving the recollection of facts, nor was it based upon the personal knowledge of the party making the entry.   It was mere hearsay, and the court did not err in excluding it when offered to prove the ages of a person whose name appears thereon.   *Hegler v. Faulkner, 153 U. S., 109.*

SEC. 1294. Conclusiveness is the characteristic of every tribunal, acting judicially, whilst acting within the sphere of its jurisdiction, where no appellate tribunal is created; but such conclusiveness is restricted to those questions which are directly submitted for decision. In the present case doubtless the identity of the half-breed George Washington and his right to receive the land in question as his share of the lands appropriated by the treaty were conclusively found, but neither the treaty, the act of Congress, nor the instructions of the Department contemplated any special inquiry into the ages of the Indians. The direction to the agent to report as well the age as the sex and tribal relations of the claimants was merely to enable him, when he came to allot the lands, to identify the persons entitled to participate.
Ibid.

SEC. 1295. The President speaks and acts through the heads of the several Departments in relation to subjects that pertain to their regular duties, and the allotment of the half-breed lands by the Indian Department must be considered as made by the President in pursuance of the terms of the act of July 31, 1854 (10 Stat. L., 332), and the treaty of Prairie du Chien (10 Stat. L., 328), and it may be admitted that the decision of the special Indian agent in identifying the Indian half-breeds entitled to participate and in allotting the portion of each would, in the absence of fraud, be conclusive.   *Ibid.*

SEC. 1296. When the allotment to the half-breeds, under the treaty of 1830 (7 Stat. L., 328) and the act of 1854 (10 Stat. L., 332), was completed, and was followed first by a certificate and finally by a patent, the purposes of the inquiry were fulfilled, and the list used to aid the Government functionaries in the task of allotting the lands can not be regarded as a record to be resorted to afterwards in disputes between other parties to prove the age of the Indians.   *Ibid.*

SEC. 1297. While there may be a moral obligation on the part of the Government to reimburse the money of Shawnee orphans embezzled by the Indian superintendent, it is by no means clear that under the acts of 1890 (26 Stat. L., 637) and 1892 (27 Stat. L., 86) the Shawnees were authorized to recover and collect from the Government any other moneys than those which they claimed in their tribal relation or capacity.

United States v. Blackfeather, 155 U. S., 180.

SEC. 1298. The money claimed is not due the Shawnee tribe as such, but to certain individual orphans, who claim to have been defrauded, and it is not clear that the tribe is authorized to recover and collect it; but whether this be so or not, there is nothing in the record to indicate how much of the money was embezzled by the guardians created by the Indian council and how much by the Indian superintendent, so there is in reality no basis for a decree in favor of the tribe, and in this particular there was error in the decree of the Court of Claims. Whether in a suit by the individual orphans they would be held bound by the receipt of the money by the guardians appointed by the council of their tribe, may be a different question.   *Ibid.*

SEC. 1299. While the Shawnee treaty of 1831 (7 Stat. L., 355) bound the Government to pay a 5 per cent annuity until the dissolution of the fund provided for, which dissolution took place September 28, 1852, this dissolution terminated the stipulation for the annuity only *pro tanto*, and if the Government had originally accounted for the whole amount for which the court below held it liable it would have paid 5 per cent upon this amount until the whole fund was paid over; the fund as to the amount being not yet distributed, the obligation to pay the 5 per cent annuity continues until the money is paid over. Upon the whole, the court did not err in allowing interest.   *Ibid.*

Sec. 1300. The provision in the agreement of April 8, 1867, between the Cherokee Nation and the Delaware tribe to sell to the latter for their occupancy a quantity of land equal in the aggregate to 160 acres for each individual Delaware who may "elect to remove to the Indian Territory," the selection of the amounts to be purchased by the Delawares to be made by the said Delawares in any part of the Cherokee Nation east of the ninety-sixth meridian of longitude not already selected and in possession of other parties, contemplates personal selection of separate tracts by individual Delawares.

Cherokee Nation v. Journey Cake, 155 U. S., 196.

Sec. 1301. The members of the Delaware tribe who chose, under the agreement between that tribe and the Cherokee Nation of April 8, 1867, to remove from Kansas not only became members of the Cherokee Nation, but also stand equal with the native Cherokees in all the rights springing out of citizenship in the Cherokee Nation, and whatever rights the Cherokees had the registered Delawares had, and it was an equality not limited to the living Delawares.   *Ibid.*

Sec. 1302. Had Cochrane or his assigns earned under his contract with the Choctaws, and the promise to Mrs. Cochrane been to pay money earned by services fully performed, a question might have arisen as to the power of the Choctaws or of McKee to divert it from the estate in favor of the widow; but as the obligation, if any existed at all, was only a moral one, the parties had a right to discharge it in their own way.   *Gilfillan v. McKee, 159 U. S., 303.*

Sec. 1303. Cochrane's contract with the Choctaws provides for the payment to him of 30 per cent of the amount collected, but it was a contract wholly contingent upon his success, and never was performed by him personally or by his assignees. Nothing was ever earned by them under this contract, and neither Cochrane's executor nor his assignee ever stood in position to sue upon it or to claim anything by virtue of it.   *Ibid; McKee v. Lamon, 159 U. S., 317.*

Sec. 1304. The suit by Lamon, as the successor of Black, Lamon & Co., against McKee, to recover the value of services rendered by Black and Lamon in prosecution of the claim of the Choctaw Nation known as the "net proceeds claim," was neither directly nor indirectly a suit against the Choctaw Nation. The nation had no interest in the fund out of which Lamon claimed his fee should be paid (30 per cent of the net proceeds recovered), and if the nation were made a party defendant in the suit the claimant would be entitled to no relief against it.   *Ibid.*

. Sec. 1305. The agreement on the part of McKee "to adjust the claims of all parties who have rendered service heretofore in the prosecution of said claim, upon the principles of equity and justice, according to the value of the services so rendered," was not needed to indemnify the Choctaws, since no possible action could lie against them after the contract had been abandoned by Black, and it was evidently intended to satisfy any moral obligation for services which had been performed, but not completed, and to throw the burden of adjusting and paying them upon McKee.   *McKee v. Latrobe, 159 U. S., 327.*

SEC. 1306. The act of March 3, 1891 (26 Stat. L., 851), concerning Indian depredations, confers, by section 1, clause 1, no jurisdiction upon the Court of Claims to adjudicate upon such a claim made by a person who was not a citizen of the United States at the time when the injury was suffered, although he subsequently became so; nor by section 1, clause 2, unless the claim was one which, on March 3, 1885, had either been examined and allowed by the Interior Department or was pending therein for examination.   *Johnson v. United States, 160 U. S., 546.*
Marks v. United States, 161 U. S., 297.

SEC. 1307. The act of March 3, 1891 (26 Stat. L., 851), relating to Indian depredation claims, gives either the claimant or the United States the right to reopen a case adjudicated by the Department of the Interior and try the same before the Court of Claims—not a part, but the whole case. If neither party elected to reopen the claimant would be entitled to a judgment for the amount of the allowance without being required to furnish further proof than the action of the Secretary, which action would be sufficient both as to the liability of the Government and the amount of the loss.
Leighton v. United States, 161 U. S., 291.

SEC. 1308. When a plaintiff in an Indian depredation claim which has been allowed by the Secretary of the Interior elects to reopen the claim under the act of March 3, 1891 (26 Stat. L., 851), it is not within his power to reopen the case only partially and, accepting the determination of the Secretary as conclusive upon the question of liability, ask simply an inquiry into the amount of his loss and judgment for a larger sum.   When a case is reopened it stands a new case, to be considered and determined by the court.   *Ibid.*

SEC. 1309. When an Indian tribe is actually engaged in hostilities against the United States for any purpose, it is not an "Indian tribe in amity with the United States" within the meaning of the Indian depredations act of March 3, 1891 (26 Stat. L., 851), giving the Court of Claims jurisdiction of Indian depredation claims.   *Ibid.*

SEC. 1310. If depredations are committed by Indians who are at the time engaged in hostilities against the United States the Court of Claims would not have jurisdiction under the act of March 3, 1891 (26 Stat. L., 851), to render a judgment against the United States, even though the hostilities were carried on for the especial purpose of resisting the opening of a military road, because said act limits the jurisdiction of the Court of Claims to depredations committed by Indian tribes in amity with the United States.   *Ibid.*

SEC. 1311. By the term "in amity with the United States" as used in the act of March 3, 1891 (26 Stat. L., 851), Congress intended that when, as a matter of fact, a tribe of Indians was in the relation of actual peace with the United States, and by some individual or individuals, without the consent or approval of the tribe, a depredation was committed upon the property of citizens of the United States, such depredation might be investigated and the amount of the loss determined and adjudicated by the Court of Claims.

Marks v. United States, 161 U. S., 297.

SEC. 1312. The truth of an allegation that a depredation was committed by an Indian or Indians belonging to a tribe in amity with the United States is not determined by the mere existence of a treaty between the United States and the tribe or the fact that such treaty has never been formally abrogated by a declaration of war on the part of either, but the inquiry is whether, as a matter of fact, the tribe was at the time, as a tribe, in a state of actual peace with the United States.   *Ibid.*

SEC. 1313. A corporation organized under the laws of a State is a citizen of the United States within the meaning of that term as used in the act of March 3, 1891 (26 Stat. L., 851), concerning claims arising from Indian depredations.

United States v. Northwestern Express Co., 164 U. S., 686.

SEC. 1314. When a petition filed in the Court of Claims alleges that a depredation was committed by an Indian or Indians belonging to a tribe in amity with the United States, it becomes the duty of that court to inquire as to the truth of that allegation; and if it appears that the tribe, as a tribe, was engaged in actual hostilities with the United States the judgment of the Court of Claims must be that the allegation of the petition is not sustained, and that the claim is not one within its province to adjudicate.   *Collier v. United States, 173 U. S., 79.*

SEC. 1315. Claims for depredations committed on the property of the Pottowattomie Indians by other Indians were properly allowed by the Secretary of the Interior under the treaty of February 27, 1867 (15 Stat. L., 531), and are valid claims.   *United States v. Navarre, 173 U. S., 77.*

SEC. 1316. It was the manifest purpose of Congress in the act of March 3, 1891, to empower the Court of Claims to receive and consider any document on file in the departments of the Government or in the courts having a bearing upon any material question arising in the consideration of any particular claim for compensation for Indian depredations, the court to allow the documents such weight as they were entitled to have.   *Collier v. United States, 173 U. S., 79.*

SEC. 1317. In a case of an application for dower on the part of the widow in lands held by her husband during coverture the law of the State on limitation applies.   *Pka-o-wah-ash-kum v. Sorin, 8 Fed. Rep., 740.*

SEC. 1318. An Indian agent was commissioned on September 28, 1872; he gave bond, took the oath of office, and was ready for duty October 15.   November 4 he received orders and started for his destination. He arrived at his post and reported for duty January 11, 1873, and on January 20 he took charge of his agency.   *Held*, that he was entitled to his salary from the time he actually went to work for the Government.   *United States v. Roberts et al., 10 Fed. Rep., 540.*

SEC. 1319. An Indian agent, upon assuming his duties, was instructed .to pay interpreters a yearly salary of $500.   Subsequently, without his knowledge, the law was changed and their salaries fixed at $400. *Held*, that he was entitled to credit therefor in his accounts.   *Ibid.*

SEC. 1320. The defendant, as superintendent of Indian affairs, published advertisements in two newspapers inviting proposal for supplies, upon the authority of a general order to that effect, addressed to his predecessor in office by the Commissioner of Indian Affairs, in which it was stated that the order was made by direction of the Secretary of Interior, and attached copies of said order to the bills for publishing such advertisements.   *Held*, that the publication of such advertisements was authorized by the Secretary of Interior within the meaning of section 3828 of the Revised Statutes, and that the payment thereof was a lawful expenditure of public money intrusted to the superintendent and to be allowed in his accounts.

United States v. Odeneal, 10 Fed. Rep., 616.

SEC. 1321. The Commissioner, as to Indian affairs, is the deputy or representative of the Secretary and the lawful channel of communication with Indian superintendents and agents.   The authority professed to come from the head of the Department, and it came through the proper officers.   The money was honestly used for the Government, and defendant should be credited with the amount.   *Ibid.*

SEC. 1322. The Commissioner of Indian Affairs was the proper person for the superintendent to apply to for authority to advertise in the newspapers, and although under section 3828 the authority to do so must "come" from the Secretary, it would, nevertheless, come to the superintendent *through* the Commissioner of Indian Affairs.   It was not necessary for the Secretary to *sign* the order as well as direct the Commissioner to make it.   *Ibid.*

SEC. 1323. Barnhart was appointed agent for the Indians in Washington Territory, and as such gave a bond to account for all money and property that might come into his hands, and was thereupon assigned to duty on the Umatilla Reservation, Oregon, where he acted as agent to the Indians settled thereon, some of whom had previously resided in Washington Territory. *Held*, (1) the condition of the bond did not include or apply to money or property not received by obligor as agent of the Indians in Washington Territory, and (2) that he was not liable on said bond for money received by him while he was acting as agent to the Indians on the Umatilla Reservation.

United States v. Barnhart, 17 Fed. Rep., 579.

Sec. 1324. Officers and agents of the Government are not forbidden to receive extra compensation for services rendered entirely apart from their official functions, but only for services required of them within the scope of employment.   *United States v. Stowe et al., 19 Fed. Rep., 807.*

Sec. 1325. The statutes do not forbid the payment of freight by an Indian agent when supplies are demanded at once by sudden emergency, and an agent paying such charges is entitled to reimbursement.

Ibid.

Sec. 1326. In all cases not provided for by the laws of the United States, the law of the State will apply and govern, and the treaty and local law must be construed together, so that both shall stand as far as they can be reconciled; the law of the treaty prevailing in case of unavoidable conflict.   *Love v. Pamplin, 21 Fed. Rep., 755.*

Sec. 1327. The defendant, Sinnott, employed a person on the Grand Ronde Reservation, as "superintendent of farms and mills," and in reporting the fact to the Commissioner said that he did so at the instance of "some political friends," but there was really no necessity for the employment, and advised that it be disapproved, which was done, but the agent continued the person in such employment, and paid him therefor, and on settlement of his accounts at the Treasury $15,000 was disallowed. *Held*, that the payments being not only without authority, but contrary thereto, were illegal, and the agent and his sureties are liable therefor.   *United States v. Sinnott, 26 Fed. Rep., 84.*

Sec. 1328. The superintendent of Indian affairs in Oregon returned to the Department two vouchers for the payment by him of the salary of the agent of the Grand Ronde Reservation for the second quarter of 1873, each being marked "triplicate," from which the accounting officers assumed that the salary was paid twice, and charged the agent with the amount of such payments in the settlement of his official accounts. *Held*, (1) that on the face of the transaction it was apparent that these two papers were but parts of one voucher taken in triplicate, and that there was but one payment; and (2) that if there had been two payments, the agent, although liable for the excess as an individual, as for money had and received to the use of the United States, was not liable therefor on his bond.   *Ibid.*

Sec. 1329. Lumber made at the sawmill on the Grand Ronde Reservation is in fact the "property" of the Indians located thereon, and not that of the United States within the purview of section 3618 of the

Revised Statutes; and the agent, subject to the instructions of the Commissioner of Indian Affairs, may dispose of any portion of the same and apply the proceeds to the support of the mill or otherwise for the benefit of the Indians, without reference to section 3617 of the Revised Statutes, requiring money received for the use of the United States to be deposited to its credit. *Ibid.*

SEC. 1330. It has always been competent for the State of Indiana to send its officers with process, civil and criminal, into the reservations and lands of the Miamis within its borders, whether held by the tribe or individuals, and, possibly, to exercise police powers over the Indians themselves to some extent. This much it would seem is within the scope of the last clause of the third article of the ordinance of 1787; but quite different, and by no means necessarily implied, would be the right to levy taxes or impose other pecuniary burdens which might work a forfeiture or affect substantially the Indian right of exclusive and free enjoyment.

Wan-pe-man-qua v. Aldrich, 28 Fed. Rep., 489.

SEC. 1331. Without some clause or language to the contrary, in a treaty with Indians with respect to a reservation within the exterior boundaries of a Territory, the lands held by them are a part of the Territory (Idaho), and subject to its jurisdiction, *so that process may run there*, however the Indians may be exempt from that jurisdiction.

Ibid.

SEC. 1332. If the male descendants of Richardville have been voting, they have done it without right, and their acts and their *status* probably can have little or no bearing upon the right of complainant and of those from whom they obtained title. *Ibid.*

SEC. 1333. The Indian who claims exemption from taxation had become, and had been recognized as, a citizen of the State both by the State and the Federal governments, so recognized by the State in the very statute which required the levying of the disputed taxes. *Ibid.*

SEC. 1334. While these Indians, according to the plea, have exercised some rights that belong to the State citizenship, the facts of the case do not show that the United States had, prior to the tax sales in question, surrendered control over them *as Indians*, and as, in fact, a part of the tribe to which they originally belonged. These lands ought now to be subject to taxation, but the way should be opened by Congressional legislation. *Ibid.*

SEC. 1335. In the case of a male Indian child in Alaska, surrendered by its mother to the care of the officers of a Presbyterian mission school there when the child was 5 years old, to remain five years, that the mother could not reclaim him after three years, although the child wished to go back to his mother: *Held*, that the mother should be allowed to visit him at the mission. *In re Can-ah-conqua, 29 Fed. Rep., 687.*

SEC. 1336. Prior to January 6, 1883, the entire Indian Territory was within the jurisdiction of the district court of the western district of Arkansas. On that day an act was passed (22 Stat. L., 400) conferring jurisdiction upon the district court for the district of Kansas.

United States v. Soule, 30 Fed. Rep., 918.

SEC. 1337. A custom prevailing among the uncivilized tribes of Indians in Alaska whereby slaves are bought, sold, and held in servitude against their free will and subjected to ill treatment at the pleasure of the owner, is contrary to the thirteenth amendment to the Constitution of the United States and the civil rights bill of 1866 (14 Stat. L., 27), and a person held in slavery will be released by order of the court upon *habeas corpus.*

In re Sah-quah, 31 Fed. Rep., 327.

SEC. 1338. Under section 2079, Revised Statutes, allowing the actual expenses of persons who are required, under the title relating to Indians, to travel from one place to another, and the act of Congress of March 3, 1875, such persons may be allowed their traveling expenses, including board while actually in transit, but not for board while engaged in inspecting a station. *United States v. Smith, 35 Fed. Rep., 490.*

SEC. 1339. In an action on the bond of a special Indian agent, a Treasury transcript containing a charge " for Government property received at the Western Shoshone Agency and not of property accounted for," but not showing of what the property consisted, nor how the value was ascertained, is insufficient to warrant a judgment for the value of such property, aided by a paper attached thereto describing the property by items, apparently compiled from the original returns and other documents on file, such paper not being admissible. *Ibid.*

SEC. 1340. Under section 886, Revised Statutes, providing for the admission in evidence of copies of books and papers on file in the Treasury Department, a Treasury transcript, certified as therein provided, is competent, in an action on the bond of a special Indian agent, to show what public moneys the defendant received and what disbursements made by him were approved. *Ibid.*

SEC. 1341. The courts of Indian offenses are rot the constitutional courts provided for in section 1, article 3, of the Constitution, which Congress only has the power to "ordain and establish," but mere educational and disciplinary instrumentalities, by which the Government of the United States is endeavoring to improve the condition of the dependent tribes to whom it sustains the relation of guardian.

United States v. Clapox, 35 Fed. Rep., 575.

SEC. 1342. An Indian agent, a part of whose duty it is to receive and disburse public moneys, is "a person accountable for public money" within the meaning of section 886, Revised Statutes, providing that when suit is brought in case of delinquency of a revenue officer or other "person accountable for public money" a transcript from the books and proceedings of the Treasury Department shall be admitted as evidence, and the court trying the case shall be authorized to grant judgment accordingly.   *United States v. Allen, 36 Fed. Rep., 174.*

SEC. 1343. Indians are frequent suitors in the courts of the various States, and while the Supreme Court of the United States reversed the supreme court of Kansas in the case of the Kansas Indians the right of the Indian to sue in the courts of the State was not questioned.   *Felix v. Patrick, 36 Fed. Rep., 457.*

SEC. 1344. Under the Nebraska bill of rights section 13 provides that all courts shall be open, and every person, for any injury done him in his lands, goods, person, or reputation, shall have a remedy, and under section 2126, Revised Statutes, relating to actions between an Indian and a white man about a right of property, an Indian may come into the courts and litigate his title to land, and, where he is not shown to be uneducated or unfamiliar with the laws, the statute of limitations will run against him.   *Ibid.*

SEC. 1345. It is argued because the Indians seek the courts of Kansas for the preservation of rights and redress of wrongs, sometimes voluntarily, and in certain specified cases by direction of the Secretary of Interior, that they submit themselves to all the laws of the State.   *Ibid.*

SEC. 1346. The nations of Indians through whose lands the 120 miles of Southern Kansas Railway runs have many rights that may be affected or destroyed by the tortious acts of the defendant, and Congress did not intend that these Indians should be left without a remedy for an injury to personal property caused by the negligent and tortious acts of the defendant.   *Briscoe v. Railway Co., 40 Fed. Rep., 273.*

SEC. 1347. If the contention of the defendant as to jurisdiction be true, the nation or tribe, or the inhabitants thereof, were left by Congress without any remedy for torts committed by the railroad company; for, as there is no remedy for torts such as was sued for in this case, at the place where the same was committed, there could be no remedy anywhere, as an act for tort not founded upon a breach of contract must be actionable or punishable by the law of the place in which it was done.   *Ibid.*

SEC. 1348. Prior to the act of July 4, 1884, the plaintiff could have no remedy in the Indian country for the injury caused by the tort of the defendant; therefore he had no remedy elsewhere.   *Ibid.*

SEC. 1349. The authority is not given by the act of Congress of July 4, 1884 (23 Stat. L., 73), to the Southern Kansas Railroad Company to lease its road situated in the Indian country. This authority to lease must be expressly given. Congress simply recognized the Southern Kansas Railroad as a Kansas corporation, having an existence under the laws of Kansas, and gave to it certain rights in the Indian country, such as the right to build its road through that country and exercise all the ordinary powers subject to the ownership, construction, and operation of its road. *Ibid.*

SEC. 1350. Every right the defendant has in the Indian country is obtained from the act of Congress (23 Stat. L., 73), and this is sufficient to raise a Federal question. *Ibid.*

SEC. 1351. To give this court jurisdiction, the right to claim it must grow out of the subject-matter. When it appears that some title, right, privilege, or immunity on which the recovery depends will be defeated by one construction of a law of the United States, or sustained by the opposite construction, the case will be one arising under a law of the United States, and one of the Federal courts have jurisdiction, regardless of the citizenship of the parties. *Ibid.*

SEC. 1352. Section 2461, Revised Statutes, which forbids the cutting of timber growing on the lands of the United States which has been reserved or purchased for supplying timber for the Navy, and the cutting and removal from any other land of the United States with intent to export or dispose of the same otherwise than for the use of the Navy, does not apply to Indian reservations in Wisconsin, since its object is to protect timber suitable for the use of the Navy.

United States v. Konkapot, 43 Fed. Rep., 64.

SEC. 1353. An Indian agent who has given bond to faithfully discharge the duties of his office is not responsible for the negligence, error, or breaches of duty of doctors and clerks furnished by the Government, unless by reasonable diligence he could have prevented such negligence, error, or breaches of duty.

United States v. Young, 44 Fed. Rep., 168.

SEC. 1354. When the Government fails to furnish the agent a clerk, he is responsible for the performance of the clerical duties of the agency in the best way practicable for him alone. *Ibid.*

SEC. 1355. The Government is not bound to show that the defendant has converted the property received or the proceeds of the property sold *to his own use.* It is not bound under bond to make out a case of fraud or conversion against him. A failure on the part of the defendant to conform to obligations of bond is sufficient to entitle the Government to recover upon the bond whatever loss it has sustained by reason of failure. *Ibid.*

SEC. 1356. The circuit court of the western district of Arkansas does not have jurisdiction of the case because of the extension of laws of Arkansas over the Indian Territory by the act of May 2, 1890 (26 Stat. L., 81), but it has jurisdiction because there is involved in it a Federal question. *Payne v. Railway Co., 46 Fed. Rep., 546.*

SEC. 1357. The act of Congress approved June 1, 1886 (24 Stat. L., 73), authorized the Kansas and Arkansas Valley Railroad Company to construct and operate a railroad through the Indian Territory and to take and use a certain strip of land for that purpose.   *Ibid.*

SEC. 1358. All contracts or agreements made in violation of any of the conditions prescribed by sections 2103 and 2104, Revised Statutes, are null and void, and it is because of the failure to comply with the provision thereof requiring the approval of certain officers of the Government that this suit is brought.   *United States v. Crawford, 47 Fed. Rep., 561.*

SEC. 1359. In view of the general law as it stood at the time of the adoption by Congress of section 2103, Revised Statutes, the reasonable and just construction of the words "any court of the United States" at the time of their enactment was any circuit or district court where defendant might be found; but since the laws of 1789 and 1875, in regard to the place where suits may be brought, have been repealed by laws of 1887 (24 Stat. L., 552) and 1888 (25 Stat. L., 434), the true and reasonable construction of the words "any court of the United States" seems to be any court of any district of which the party sued is an inhabitant, and that this must be so until Congress, by express legislation, authorizes the service of summons outside the district, and, as this has not been done, the defendant is not in court and can not be brought in unless he becomes an inhabitant of that district or voluntarily appears.   *Ibid.*

SEC. 1360. If the money was paid by officers of the Government, without the direction of the Creek National Council, it would be a payment of money, not in violation of section 2103, Revised Statutes, but of the act of March 3, 1889 (25 Stat. L., 757), and it would be a case where the Government should sue the party who wrongfully received the money for money had and received, but such suit could not be based upon a cause of action arising under section 2103.   *Ibid.*

SEC. 1361. As an incident of the right of the United States to govern Indians by its own laws would be the right to hold lands upon which to locate and maintain them. It was urged that while the United States could have jurisdiction over such lands as far as the Indians are concerned, it would have no right over white men found within an Indian reservation such as the Crow Reservation. The statutes and the ordinance we have been considering say the jurisdiction and control is absolute, not a divided jurisdiction or control, and this seems to be proper.   *United States v. Partello, 48 Fed. Rep., 670.*

SEC. 1362. In actions in the Federal court in the Indian Territory the rule of decision, in the absence of statute, or of proof of the laws, rules, or customs prevailing in the Territory, is the common law, since it is the *lex fori.*   *Pyeatt v. Powell, 51 Fed. Rep., 551.*

SEC. 1363. In the United States, in the absence of statutes, the presumption of the existence of the common laws prevails in all the territory of the original colonies and all newly acquired territory originally settled by Englishmen or their American descendants; but this presumption may not prevail in the Indian Territory, because, before its purchase by the United States, it was part of a territory settled by the subjects and governed by the laws of other nations.

Ibid.

SEC. 1364. Prior to the act of May 2, 1890 (26 Stat. L., 94), extending over the Indian Territory certain statutes of the State of Arkansas, there was no statute in operation in that Territory upon any subject outside those treated in the acts of Congress treating of trade and intercourse with the Indians and punishing offenses against the United States.

Ibid.

SEC. 1365. Statutes of Cherokee Nation, chapter 3, article 19, section 154, as amended by act of December 7, 1889, provide that when in an action of ejectment the district clerk shall give the defendant ten days' notice to show cause why the writ should not issue, and the clerk is authorized to determine upon the showing made whether the writ shall issue. *Held*, that this proceeding is sufficient to constitute due process of law within the meaning of the Federal Constitution.

Mehlin v. Ice, 56 Fed. Rep., 12.

SEC. 1366. The proceedings and judgment of the courts of the Cherokee Nation in cases within their jurisdiction are on the same footing with those of the courts of the Territories of the Union, and entitled to the same faith and credit; and hence, where a party in a Federal court justifies an entry under such writ of ejectment, the sufficiency of the evidence before the clerk to justify its issuance can not be inquired into.

Ibid.

SEC. 1367. It is common knowledge, of which the court should take judicial notice, that the domestic relations of the Indians of this country have never been regulated by the common law of England, and that law is not adapted to the habits, customs, and manners of the Indians.

Davison v. Gibson, 56 Fed. Rep., 443.

SEC. 1368. The court, in making up its opinion of the law of the case, is not limited in its researches to legal literature. It may consult works on collateral sciences, or arts, or history touching the topic on trial, and may appeal to the public archives.

Ibid.

SEC. 1369. In a controversy which involves the right of husband to the personalty of his deceased wife, both of them being citizens of the Creek Nation, where there is no showing as to what was the law or custom of that nation applicable to the matter, it was error to assume that the common law was in force therein and to decide the controversy according to its rules.

Ibid.

SEC. 1370. Where a controversy between citizens of the Creek Nation is an action in the United States court for the Indian Territory, the rule of decision, in the absence of evidence as to what the Creek law is, is the law of the forum, which is to be found in Mansfield's Digest of the Laws of Arkansas, put in force in the Indian Territory by the act of Congress May 2, 1890 (26 Stat. L., 94).   *Ibid.*

SEC. 1371. Where a person responds to the notice issued by the clerk, enters a general appearance, and defends the case on the merits, he thereby waives any exemption from jurisdiction of the courts of the Cherokee Nation to which he, as a white citizen of the United States, may be entitled.   *Mehlin v. Ice, 56 Fed. Rep., 12.*

SEC. 1372. The act of February 18, 1888 (25 Stat. L., 35), conferring upon the circuit and district courts for the western district of Arkansas and the northern district of Texas concurrent jurisdiction of all suits between the Choctaw Coal and Railway Company and the inhabitants of the Indian nations or tribes through which that railway should run, is not repealed by the act of March 1, 1889 (25 Stat. L., 783), establishing a court in the Indian Territory, nor by the act of May 2, 1890 (26 Stat. L., 81), enlarging the jurisdiction of the court.
                    Gowen v. Harley, 56 Fed. Rep., 973.

SEC. 1373. Under the act of February 18, 1888 (25 Stat. L., 35), evidence that plaintiff lived with his wife in his house in the territory of the Choctaw Nation when the cause of the action arose, and for a year thereafter, is sufficient proof of inhabitancy to give the circuit court for the western district of Arkansas jurisdiction of a suit wherein the Choctaw Coal and Railway Company is defendant, whether plaintiff dwelt there rightfully or wrongfully.   *Ibid.*

SEC. 1374. Under the act of May 2, 1890 (26 Stat. L., 94), putting in force in the Indian Territory the statutes of Arkansas, and Mansfield's Digest, Arkansas, sections 1053 and 1061, providing that every poor person not being able to sue may be permitted to bring his action without liability for costs or fees, the privilege of suing in *forma pauperis* under order of court is granted to every poor person in the United States, and not merely to the poor person resident in the Indian Territory.   *Railroad Co. v. Farr, 56 Fed. Rep., 994.*

SEC. 1375. Equitable liens on personalty by contract of the parties being enforceable only in equity, jurisdiction of a case arising in the Choctaw Nation upon suit by nonresidents to enforce such a lien against an administrator is in the United States court for the Indian Territory, and not in the probate court of the Choctaw Nation.
                    Riddle v. Hudgins, 58 Fed. Rep., 490.

SEC. 1376. The defendant is the agent of the Secretary of the Interior. The power of the court to enjoin his agents has not been discussed. Generally the officers of the Department can not be controlled by injunctions or mandamus while acting in a judicial capacity, in which their judgments are to be based upon a consideration of facts; but in this case the action of the land department involved a construction of law, which is not applicable to the same rule.
                    Caldwell v. Robinson, 59 Fed. Rep., 659.

SEC. 1377. An act of the council of the Creek Nation, entitled "An act establishing quarantine regulations against foreign cattle and to prevent smuggling cattle into the Creek Nation," approved October 29, 1891, makes it unlawful for any citizen of the nation "to introduce or invite into the Creek Nation cattle of any kind at any time," except between January 1 and March 31 of each year, and declares that any citizen violating this provision of the act "shall be fined a sum that will be equivalent to $3 per head for each and every head of cattle" unlawfully introduced. The act makes it a lien on the cattle unlawfully introduced.   *Cornells v. Shannon, 63 Fed. Rep., 305.*

SEC. 1378. In a suit by the owners and mortgagees of cattle to declare void a judgment of a court of the Creek Nation imposing a fine on the owners for bringing the cattle into the nation contrary to its law, and making it a lien on the cattle in accordance with such law, it will, on demurrer to the answer, be *held* that the Creek court had the jurisdiction to render the judgment, the answer alleging that such court had jurisdiction of the owners of the cattle.   *Ibid.*

SEC. 1379. The judgments of the courts of the Creek Nation are entitled to the same respect and to the same faith and credit as the judgments of the Territorial courts of the United States, and white men residing in the Indian Territory who appear and submit themselves to the jurisdiction of the courts of the nation are bound by their judgments.   *Ibid.*

SEC. 1380. It is clear that it was never intended there should be within the limits of the towns laid out under the Cherokee act of December 14, 1870, any unappropriated public domain subject to settlement under the general law on that subject. The disposition of the land within these town sites is regulated by laws especially applicable to them. It is not material to inquire whether the railroad company acquired the fee in this ground or only an easement. In either case it acquired a right to the exclusive possession and use of it as against the defendants.   *Bell v. Railroad Co., 63 Fed. Rep., 417.*

SEC. 1381. By act of the national council a certain mile square was segregated from the public domain of the nation and reserved to the nation for a special use, and to be disposed of in a particular manner, and not to be settled upon by the first comer, as is the case with the public domain generally.   *Ibid.*

SEC. 1382. The treaty between the United States and the Cherokee Nation of July 19, 1866 (14 Stat. L., 799), grants certain rights of way and privileges to any corporation authorized by Congress to build a railroad through the nation. By the act of the national council of the Cherokee Nation December 14, 1870, there was reserved to the nation at every railroad station 1 mile square, to include such station, for town sites, to be located by the commissioners, whose duty it shall be also to sell the lots. *Held*, that where such commissioners, in 1871, surveyed and laid off a town pursuant to such act, and set off to a railroad company authorized by Congress to build through the nation, a strip of land 400 feet wide, the company was entitled to the whole of such strip, as against a citizen of the nation or any other person entering thereon after the passage of the act reserving the town site to the use of the nation, and a part of it not actually occupied or needed for present use by the company was not subject to appropriation by a citizen of the nation as part of the public domain thereof.   *Ibid.*

Sec. 1383. The United States court in the Indian Territory has no jurisdiction of an action against the Choctaw Nation or the chief executive officer thereof, when sued in his capacity as such, for an alleged debt or liability of the nation, and when the judgment will operate against the nation. Jurisdiction is not conferred by the act of March 1, 1889 (25 Stat. L., 783), or May 2, 1890 (26 Stat. L., 93).

Thebo v. Choctaw Indians, 66 Fed. Rep., 372.

Sec. 1384. Under the act of March 1, 1889 (25 Stat. L., 783), which created the United States court in the Indian Territory, that court was empowered to grant such relief in equity in cases within its jurisdiction as was consonant with the established rules and practice of courts of chancery, and this authority was confirmed to it by the act of May 2, 1890 (26 Stat. L., 81). That court, therefore, had jurisdiction to enforce express or implied trusts in the absence of the statute of fraudulent conveyances.   *McClellan v. Pyeatt, 66 Fed. Rep., 843.*

Sec. 1385. The supreme court of North Carolina, in Rollins *v.* Cherokees (87 N. C., 229), fully recognized the power and right of the United States to supervise and control the affairs, lands, and contracts of the North Carolina Cherokees. The court refers with approbation to the acts of Congress regulating contracts with the Indians, and expresses the opinion that such laws apply to contracts with the North Carolina Indians.   *United States v. Boyd, 68 Fed. Rep., 577.*

Sec. 1386. By the act of July 27, 1868 (15 Stat. L., 228), Congress authorized and directed the Secretary of Interior and Commissioner of Indian Affairs to take the same supervisory charge of the eastern band of Cherokees as of other tribes; and there is a necessary implication of power that if, in exercise of such supervisory charge, it becomes necessary to resort to a court of equity for remedy and relief, a suit may be properly instituted by such supervisory department in the name of the United States to obtain adequate redress.   *Ibid.*

Sec. 1387. For the purpose of securing the North Carolina Cherokees against the evil consequences of injudicious contracts with more intelligent and designing white men, a State statute was enacted requiring all contracts, equal to $10 or more, with Cherokee Indians to be in writing, signed in the presence of two witnesses who shall subscribe the same (1 Code N. C., sec. 1553). This law of the State imposed upon them a restriction which was not imposed upon other citizens, except as to transactions coming within the statute of frauds and a few other cases. *Ibid.*

SEC. 1388. The act of March 1, 1889 (25 Stat. L., 783) provided for the appointment of certain judicial officers and a court for the Indian Territory and adopted a code of procedure, but did not adopt any substantive laws for the court to enforce, or by which the rights and obligations of the citizens in the Territory subject to the jurisdiction of the court should be regulated and determined.

Manufacturing Co. v. Needles, 69 Fed. Rep., 68.

SEC. 1389. Equity has jurisdiction of a bill brought by the United States as trustee for the Indians to whom lands have been allotted in severalty, pursuant to treaties and acts of Congress providing that the United States will hold the land so allotted in trust for the benefit of the allottees, against persons who have illegally secured leases of such lands and taken possession thereof, such bill seeking to oust such intruders, and to restrain them from inducing the Indians to make further leases, and from interfering with the Indian agent in performance of his duties, since the remedy by action of ejectment, even if such action could be maintained, would be inadequate.

United States v. Real Estate Co., 69 Fed. Rep., 886.

SEC. 1390. A bill in equity by the United States, as trustee for the Indians to whom lands have been allotted in severalty, seeking to oust persons occupying such lands under void leases, and to restrain the making of other such leases, is not multifarious, though exhibited against persons holding under leases from different lessors and having no common interest in the suit, since the United States have one common interest touching the matter of the bill, arising out of the trust relation existing between them and the Indians in regard to the lands. *Ibid.*

SEC. 1391. While it would seem, since Indians are members of a domestic dependent tribe or nation and are regarded as wards of the Government, that the courts of the United States ought to have jurisdiction of civil suits by or against them, it suffices to say that no such jurisdiction has been conferred. Congress has not seen fit to confer upon the Indians, as such, the right to prosecute civil suits in the United States courts or to remove them from the courts of the State into such courts simply on the ground that they were Indians.

Paul v. Chilsoquie, 70 Fed. Rep., 401.

SEC. 1392. The relation of an unnaturalized Indian, segregated from his tribe and residing in a State, in respect of both Federal and State authority and jurisdiction is peculiar, and often gives rise to difficult and perplexing questions. But no such questions are presented by this record; and, inasmuch as there is no provision in the act of March 3, 1887 (24 Stat. L., 505), or the amendatory act of August 13, 1888 (25 Stat. L., 438), or in any act of Congress conferring jurisdiction on the circuit courts of the United States in civil controversies or suit by or against Indians, it follows, necessarily, that the petition for removal must be denied.   *Ibid.*

SEC. 1393. By section 2062 of the Revised Statutes the President is authorized to require of any military officer the performance of the duties of an Indian agent, and thus it appears that Captain Beck, when engaged in performing the duties of agent at the Winnebago Reservation, was an officer of the United States duly charged with the performance of the duties of such office.

United States v. Mullin, 71 Fed. Rep., 682.

SEC. 1394. Indian agents are appointed by the President with the assent of the Senate of the United States, and therefore "officers of the United States" within the meaning of that term as defined by the Supreme Court in United States *v.* Germaine (99 U. S., 508).   *Ibid.*

SEC. 1395. The act of March 1, 1895 (28 Stat. L., 695), creating a court of appeals for the Indian Territory, deprives the circuit court of appeals for the eighth circuit of the power to entertain writs of error and appeals from the United States court in the Indian Territory, and writs of error to said circuit court of appeals allowed by the United States court in the Indian Territory after March 1, 1895, must be dismissed.   *Scott v. Hamner, 72 Fed. Rep., 289.*

SEC. 1396. In Langford *v.* Monteith (102 U. S., 145, 147) it was held that where by treaty the reservation was not excluded from the limits of the Territory civil process in a suit between white men in a court of a Territory may run into the reservation, notwithstanding the Indians themselves are exempt from that jurisdiction.

Truscott v. Land & Cattle Co., 73 Fed. Rep., 60.

SEC. 1397. There is no good reason why the authority of the State may not also include the taxation of all personal property found within its limits, although upon an Indian reservation, provided the Indians are in no way interested in it.   *Ibid.*

SEC. 1398. By section 41 of the Code of Montana it was declared that all legal processes of the State, whether civil or criminal, may be served upon persons and property found within any of the military reservations or on any Indian reservation in all cases where the United States has not exclusive jurisdiction.   *Ibid.*

SEC. 1399. It seems that a suit by the United States to enforce the rights of a tribe of Indians to a fishery is local in its character and properly brought in the district where such fishery is, without regard to the residence of the defendants.   *United States v. Winans, 73 Fed. Rep., 72.*

SEC. 1400. The United States has the right, as guardian and trustee of a tribe of Indians, to bring a suit to protect their rights secured by treaty.   *Ibid.*

SEC. 1401. The failure of an Indian agent, through clerical errors, to include in his accounts property which in fact remains at the agency and is not lost to the Government does not entitle the United States to recover the value thereof in a suit on his bond, and he may show the facts in defense.   The technical failure to account would authorize a recovery of no more than nominal damages.

United States v. Patrick, 73 Fed. Rep., 800.

SEC. 1402. In an action by the United States on the bonds of an Indian agent, defendants pleaded that all the moneys with which the agent had been charged had been properly expended by him, and at the trial offered to prove a specified sum paid to physicians for services to Indians.   *Held,* that the fact that the defendants had not pleaded this claim for a credit did not render proof thereof inadmissible, it appearing that the United States was already correctly informed of the amount and character of the claim, by the reason of its officers having examined and disallowed the same, and that these facts were proved by a transcript from the books of the Treasury Department, in the hands of the United States attorney, who had not moved to make the answer more specific.   *Ibid.*

SEC. 1403. Where, in an action by the United States to recover an alleged shortage due from the Indian agent, the Government introduced a transcript from the books and proceedings of the Treasury Department, which, among the things, contained an opinion by one of the accounting officers disallowing a claim by the agent for one of the items sued for and discussing the vouchers on which the claim was based; *held,* that this was conclusive proof that the claim had been presented to and disallowed by the accounting officers, as required by Revised Statutes, section 951.   *Ibid.*

SEC. 1404. Where the Secretary of the Interior had authority to employ physicians at an Indian agency, and his subordinate, the Indian agent, did employ them, and the Secretary approved their bills and directed the agent to pay them out of funds in his hands; *held,* that the United States and the Secretary were bound by the agent's acts, both because of the ratification thereof and because, by their action, they induced him to expend money which he would not otherwise have disbursed.   *Ibid.*

SEC. 1405. The provision in the Indian appropriation act of March 3, 1875 (18 Stat. L., 420), that the number and kind of employes at each Indian agency shall be prescribed by the Secretary of the Interior, gives him authority to employ physicians to attend Indians; and the fact that during eleven years the Secretary had approved vouchers and directed payment of bills rendered by a particular physician employed at various times by an Indian agent is a sufficient determination by the Secretary that one of the employees of such agency shall be a physician, to be called by the agent from time to time to render medical assistance as the Indians require.   *Ibid.*

SEC. 1406. There can be no recovery, in an action against the bondsmen of an Indian agent, for specific articles or goods not accounted for upon allegations that such agent has failed to account for moneys received by him.   *United States v. McClure, 74 Fed. Rep., 153.*

SEC. 1407. The bondsmen of an Indian agent can not be held liable for a mistake of fact or law, or error of judgment, or misconstruction of authority by such agent in disbursing money in good faith for the benefit of the Government, though the payment has been disallowed in his accounts.   *Ibid.*

SEC. 1408. The mere failure of an Indian agent to file a receipt with his accounts for money actually disbursed for the benefit of the Government is not enough to charge his bondsmen for such money.   *Ibid.*

SEC. 1409. The mere failure of an Indian agent's property return to show the disposition of a large quantity of clothing and provisions is not sufficient, without other evidence to authorize an inference, in an action against his bondsmen, to show that such property has been misapplied.   *Ibid.*

SEC. 1410. The sureties on the bond of a receiver of public moneys at a land office are not liable for moneys received by him as proceeds of the sale of Indian lands made under the act of Congress of September 1, 1888, as such moneys are at all times, in equity, the moneys of the Indians and not public moneys.   *United States v. Rogers et al., 81 Fed., 941.*

SEC. 1411. Under the act of August 15, 1894 (28 Stat. L., 305), giving any person of Indian blood who claims to be entitled to land under any allotment act or grant made by Congress, or to have been unlawfully denied or excluded from any allotment or parcel of land, the right to maintain a suit therefor in the proper circuit court of the United States, and giving such courts jurisdiction to try and determine such suits, their judgments in favor of a claimant, when certified to the Secretary of the Interior, to have the same effect as if the allotment had been allowed him, the jurisdiction of a court over such a suit is not defeated because the title to the land involved remains in the United States, nor is an adverse decision on the claim by the land department conclusive against the legal rights of the claimant.   *Sloan v. United States, 95 Fed. Rep., 193.*

SEC. 1412. There is no ground upon which the United States can maintain a suit in equity against the grantees of an Indian who are in possession of land conveyed to such Indian by patent issued by the land department containing a provision prohibiting its alienation for the purpose of annulling the deed to defendants in the absence of a law forfeiting the grant in case of such alienation.   *United States v. Saunders, 96 Fed. Rep., 268.*

SEC. 1413. A sub-Indian agent has no authority to draw bills of exchange in payment for Indian supplies so as to bind the Government. *Jackson v. United States, 1 C. Cls., 260. Fremont v. United States, Ibid, 461.*

SEC. 1414. War is that state in which a nation prosecutes its rights by force. Troops called into the military service to serve against the Indians are equally entitled with other troops to the various benefits given by Congress. *Alire v. United States, 1 C. Cls., 233.*

SEC. 1415. The obligation of the defendants and the purchases of the Indian agents in California to subsist the Indians in 1851 and 1852 are recognized and ratified by Congress in the appropriation to defray the expenses of subsisting the California Indians (March 3, 1853, 10 Stat. L., 288), and in the acts for the relief of Fremont (10 Stat. L., 804); Hensley (12 Stat. L., 847), and Norris (14 Stat. L., Resolution No. 56). *Fremont v. United States, 2 C. Cls., 461.*

SEC. 1416. Adam Johnson, the Indian agent who made the contract and drew the drafts involved in this suit, was the agent of the United States for a particular purpose, and he derived no authority by virtue of his appointment as such agent to contract debts or pledge the credit of the United States. *Ibid.*

SEC. 1417. Drafts given by a sub-Indian agent for supplies furnished Indians in California were all dishonored by the Government, but Congress subsequently, by a series of enactments, gave a legislative recognition of the obligation of the Government to provide for the wants of these Indians and an implied ratification to the unauthorized acts of their agents. The ratification went only to the extent of paying to the actual parties in interest the actual value of the goods purchased. *Ibid.*

SEC. 1418. An allegation in a petition that an army transportation train "was attacked by a band of hostile Indians" and the claimant's oxen "were captured by the said band of hostile Indians" does not entitle a party to relief under the act of March 3, 1849 (9 Stat. L., 415), which provides that "any person who has sustained damage by the capture by an enemy" shall be paid therefor. The Indian tribes and individuals are subject to the laws of the United States, and it can not be inferred generally that they constitute a public enemy. The words "a hostile band" may imply merely marauders and plunderers, and not a tribe at war with the United States.
Guttman v. United States, 6 C. Cls., 111.

SEC. 1419. Where a contract provides that the Government is "to furnish escort for Mr. Porter's train while en route," and that for delays while "waiting an escort, after application," he shall be paid $10 a day per team, and the contractor, after waiting for an escort a reasonable time, moves off without one, he does so at his own risk and can not recover for oxen killed and captured on the way by Indians.
Porter v. United States, 9 C. Cls., 356.

SEC. 1420. A contract which provides for the sale "*of all the hides of beef cattle slaughtered for Indians*" by the Government at a certain place does not impose an obligation on the Goverment to slaughter any.

Lobenstein v. United States, 11 C. Cls. R., 173.

SEC. 1421. A contract for the sale of "all the hides of beef cattle slaughtered for Indians" at a certain place, "which the superintendent of Indian affairs at that place shall decide are not required for the comfort of the Indians," followed by a decision to turn over all of the cattle on the hoof to the Indians, is in effect a decision that all the hides are required for the comfort of the Indians, and relieves the Government from furnishing any to the contractor.   *Ibid.*

SEC. 1422. When a contract for the sale of hides does not bind the Government to furnish any certain number, but only such as shall not be required for the comfort of the Indians at an Indian agency, an estimate in the contract stating "the number to be about 4,000, more or less," must be construed to be merely a representation of the probable number, and does not bind the Government to furnish any.

Ibid.

SEC. 1423. Where, by the terms of a contract, the claimants are bound and entitled to transport all the goods which may be purchased by the Indian Bureau for the public service, and transported over a certain railroad, under a designated contract with that road, it is not a breach for the Bureau to buy goods deliverable by the vendors at those agencies.   *Piper v. United States, 12 C. Cls., 219.*

SEC. 1424. This court is without jurisdiction to enforce an obligation assumed by the Government for the Indians by treaty. (Sec. 1066, Rev. Stat.)   *Langford v. United States, 12 C. Cls., 338.*

SEC. 1425. The court below holds that where contractors are entitled to transport from the terminus of a railway to certain Indian agencies all the goods of the Indian Bureau which may come over that road under a designated contract with it, it is not a breach for the Bureau to buy goods deliverable at the agencies by the vendors.

Piper v. United States, 13 C. Cls., 525.

SEC. 1426. The act of the Department of the Interior in adjusting and approving a claim for damages suffered by reason of a breach of a certain contract entered into by a superintendent of Indian affairs, and the act of the Treasury in allowing and paying the claim so adjusted, amount to a complete ratification of the contract, and do not leave open the question whether it was approved by the Commissioner of Indian Affairs.   *Neal v. United States, 14 C. Cls., 280.*

SEC. 1427. An appointment by the Secretary of the Interior as commissioner to visit and examine certain Indian agencies is a Federal office in the sense of precluding the commissioner from receiving pay at the same time as a member of the board of health for the District of Columbia.

Cox v. United States, 14 C. Cls., 512.

SEC. 1428. By the act of June 30, 1834 (4 Stat. L., 735), a Department of Indian Affairs was established, with a Commissioner of Indian Affairs as its immediate executive head, and with supervision and appellate powers vested in the Secretary of War. See also act July 9, 1832 (4 Stat. L., 564).

Belt v. United States, 15 C. Cls., 92.

SEC. 1429. The provisions of the act of June 30, 1834 (4 Stat. L., 735), which requires that certain officers "shall be present and certify to the delivery of all goods or money required to be paid or delivered to the Indians" was directory to the officers and not mandatory upon the vendors of the goods.

Ibid.

SEC. 1430. The purchase of supplies to subsist Indians in California in 1851 was a purchase under authority of law within the meaning of the act of June 30, 1834 (4 Stat. L., 729), although the treaty pursuant to which the supplies were purchased had not then been ratified and was subsequently rejected by the Senate.

Ibid.

SEC. 1431. When the Commissioner of Indian Affairs, being informed of the course which a sub-agent intended to pursue, approved it, his approval was a ratification of the agent's acts, rendering them valid.

Ibid.

SEC. 1432. The action of the Commissioner of Indian Affairs must be presumed to be the action of the President.

Ibid.

SEC. 1433. When a statute requires a subordinate officer to obey the instructions of the Secretary of the Interior, and to carry into effect such regulations as the President may prescribe, and his acts receive subsequently the approval of the Commissioner of Indian Affairs, the law is substantially complied with.

Ibid.

SEC. 1434. Under the act of June 30, 1834 (4 Stat. L., 731), the United States is not liable for the theft of cattle from a friendly Indian by a *negro.* Contra, had the theft been committed by a "white person."

Perryman v. United States, 15 C. Cls., 621.

SEC. 1435. The judgment of the court below is affirmed. The Supreme Court now holds that inasmuch as the statutory jurisdiction of the court below is limited to actions on contract, the statute must be construed to refer to actions known at common law as actions *ex contractu,* and that the court therefore had no jurisdiction of this case.

Langford v. United States, 15 C. Cls., 632.

SEC. 1436. In paying these claimants, interpreters, the disbursing officers took a receipt from each one of them on a printed blank, in which it was stated that the sums received by them were "in full of our pay for services for the period herein stated." On the part of the defendants the question is raised whether or not this is not an accord and satisfaction, and a discharge of all obligation to pay the balance.   The court holds that it is not so.

Mitchell v. United States, 18 C. Cls., 281.

SEC. 1437. The act of June 4, 1880 (21 Stat. L., 544), authorized the claimant to bring an action in this court "to recover what may be due to him in justice and equity for the loss inflicted upon him by reason of the seizure of his tobacco factory in the Indian Territory for an alleged violation of the internal-revenue laws, of his property and damages thereto while under seizure, the value of the tobacco, material, etc., and the expenses which he has been subjected to thereby." Judgment for plaintiff.   Boudinot v. United States, 18 C. Cls., 716.

SEC. 1438. A case growing out of Indian depredations which has the approval of the Secretary of the Interior and the Assistant Attorney-General, and which has been submitted by the latter, can not be reopened for the purpose of a reargument without showing fraud, collusion, or manifest mistake on the record.

Wynn, Admr., v. United States, 29 C. Cls., 15.

SEC. 1439. The purpose of the Bowman Act was to authorize the head of an executive department to transmit to this court for judicial examination any claim or matter which the department had power to adjust and settle, and no other.   McClure v. United States, 19 C. Cls., 18.

SEC. 1440. The claimaints cut hay on the Winnebago Reservation in 1868 and immediately file their claims therefor in the Office of Indian Affairs. The papers are transmitted to the Treasury for consideration, and by the Secretary to this court, under the Bowman Act, but not till June 22, 1883. A claim transmitted to this court by the head of an executive department under the Bowman Act (22 Stat. L., 485) is not barred within the meaning of section 3 unless it be barred in such department.   Ibid.

SEC. 1441. Where a statute authorizes a suit in this court by an Indian tribe to be brought by the filing of their petition "verified by the principal chief of said band," verification by the principal chief is a jurisdictional requirement and not a mere matter of pleading.

Eastern Band of Cherokees v. Cherokee Nation West and U. S.,
19 C. Cls., 35.

SEC. 1442. The United States had, many times, in treaties, recognized the principal chief of the Cherokees as the head of the nation; and in the act authorizing this suit Congress saw fit to indicate "the principal chief of the Eastern Band" as the person whose verification should entitle that band to a hearing in this court, and the court has no authority to disregard that legislative indication.   Ibid.

SEC. 1443. The act of March 3, 1883 (22 Stat. L., 585), authorizes the Eastern Band of Cherokees to bring suit in the Court of Claims against the United States to determine the rights of the said band in and to certain moneys held by the United States for the Cherokee Indians.   *Ibid.*

SEC. 1444. Under the Bowman Act (22 Stat. L., 485) the Chickasaw Nation brings suit against the United States for moneys of the nation alleged to have been wrongfully paid out to persons having no right to receive the same. *Held*, that affidavits taken by an officer (United States Indian agent) in the course of an investigation authorized by treaty, are clearly distinguishable from *ex parte* affidavits.

Chickasaw Nation v. United States, 19 C. Cls., 133.

SEC. 1445. When a person is employed to cut and stack hay on an Indian reservation at so much per ton, the place of cutting to be designated by the Government and the hay to be measured when stacked, the contract is for work and service and not for sale and delivery.

McClure v. United States, 19 C. Cls., 173; Davis v. United States, 27 C. Cls., 181.

SEC. 1446. A statute appropriating money to be paid to the Choctaws on account of their claim under a certain treaty, but providing "that in the future adjustment of the claim" the money shall be charged against them, is not a ratification of an award previously made by the Senate.   *Choctaw Nation v. United States, 19 C.Cls., 243.*

SEC. 1447. By the act of March 3, 1881 (1 Supplement to Rev. Stat., 608), Congress authorized the Court of Claims to try all questions of difference arising out of treaties with the Choctaw Nation, and to render judgment thereon.   *Ibid.*

SEC. 1448. When a treaty provides that certain "questions be submitted for adjudication to the Senate" the decision of the Senate is final, unless its finality be set aside by the concurrence of both parties.   *Ibid.*

SEC. 1449. Where the Senate, acting as arbitrator under a treaty, refers a claim to the Secretary of the Interior, with instructions to state an account upon certain principles, and the Secretary states such an account and reports it to Congress, but no action is taken thereon by the Senate, it must be held that the account was for the information of the Senate.   *Ibid.*

SEC. 1450. Where Congress passes an act authorizing this court to take jurisdiction of and try all cases arising out of treaty stipulations with the Choctaws, and providing that the court may "review the entire question of difference de novo, and it shall not be estopped by any action had or award made by the Senate," it must be held that Congress by passing the act and the Choctaw Nation by coming into court and prosecuting their claims thereunder have agreed that the award shall not be final.   *Ibid.*

SEC. 1451. Under the act of March 3, 1883 (22 Stat. L., 585), the claimant brings suit against the United States and the Cherokee Nation to recover a proportional part of two funds held by the United States in trust.   *Eastern Band Cherokees v. United States et al., 20 C. Cls., 449.*

SEC. 1452. The Eastern Band of Cherokees have neither rights nor equities in the funds held by the United States in trust for the Cherokees west of the Mississippi River.   *Ibid.*

SEC. 1453. The effect of the act of 1881 (21 Stat. L., 504) was to remove from the jurisdiction and consideration of this court, as toward the adjudication of the Senate, the technical law of estoppel, and yet to preserve within the jurisdiction the decision of the Senate to be considered by the court as it might determine.
        Choctaw Nation v. United States, 21 C. Cls., 59.

SEC. 1454. When a boundary was fixed by treaty, a claim for an encroachment is a claim founded upon treaty, though the encroachment was sanctioned by statute; of it the court has jurisdiction under the act of 1881 (21 Stat. L., 504).   *Ibid.*

SEC. 1455. As no claims founded on article 19 of the treaty of 1830 with the Choctaws were presented to the commissioners under the act of 1842 (5 Stat. L., 573) they are not barred by that statute.   *Ibid.*

SEC. 1456. The release executed by the Choctaw Nation in consideration of $872,000, pursuant to the act of July 21, 1852 (10 Stat. L., 19), extinguished all demands founded on article 14 of the treaty of 1830, investigated under the act of August 23, 1842 (5 Stat. L., 513), and funded under the act of March 3, 1845 (5 Stat. L., 777). The authority given to this court by the act of 1881 (21 Stat. L., 504), "to review the entire question of difference de novo," does not reopen the final settlement then made, which, however, embraces only claims paid, not claims rejected.   *Ibid.*

SEC. 1457. The emigration subsequent to the year 1843 having been at the instance of the United States and in the absence of any special agreement must be regarded as under the treaty of 1830, and the Choctaws as entitled to the rifles, etc., promised to warriors by article 20 of said treaty.   *Ibid.*

SEC. 1458. Under the peculiar provisions of the act giving this court jurisdiction, as we have held in substance on the demurrer, the sanctity of the adjudication by the Senate has been destroyed by the law of our jurisdiction, and the parties are remitted to their legal rights, as they exist unaffected by the action of the Senate.   *Ibid.*

SEC. 1459. The claimant having voluntarily come into court under the act of March 3, 1881 (21 Stat. L., 504), it becomes the paramount law of the case and destroys the sanctity of the award of the Senate under the treaty of 1855. *Ibid.*

SEC. 1460. The word "liberal" in a treaty or statute can not enlarge the jurisdiction of the court nor authorize it to recognize claims unsupported by legal rights. *Ibid.*

SEC. 1461. There is no express waiver in the Choctaw treaty of 1855 (7 Stat, L., 338) of the proceedings under the act of July, 1852 (10 Stat. L., 19), and the provisions of that treaty proposing a settlement by the arbitration of the Senate does not necessarily destroy the legal effect of any act of the parties, and the only thing which in our inquiry as it may be *de novo* that is affected by direct law is the award of the Senate. *Ibid.*

SEC. 1462. The recognition of the legal effect of what the claimant did under the act of July, 1852 (10 Stat. L., 19), does not violate the justice, fairness, and liberality of the treaty of 1855 (11 Stat. L., 611), unless the parties intended to supersede the legal effect of that act. *Ibid.*

SEC. 1463. At the time the act of 1881 was passed, giving this court jurisdiction to try all questions of difference founded on treaty stipulations, the statute of 1873 was in full force, and the effect of that law was to remit the parties to the rights they had as against each other founded on treaties. *Ibid.*

SEC. 1464. The act of 1842 (5 Stat. L., 513) was not obligatory upon the Choctaws, and did not of itself extinguish claims valid by treaty. The investigations which it authorized were not recognized by them as a nation, and bar only individuals benefited thereby. *Ibid.*

SEC. 1465. The act of March 2, 1861 (12 Stat. L., 238), directing that bonds to the amount of $250,000 be issued to the Choctaws on account of the treaty obligations of the United States vested no right. The refusal of the executive to deliver the bonds, and the act of February 14, 1873 (17 Stat. L., 462), prohibiting the issuing, took away none, but left all treaty obligations unimpaired. *Ibid.*

SEC. 1466. The adjustment and release of claims of the Choctaw Nation under the act of July 21, 1852 (10 Stat. L., 19), extended to interest, it being an incident of the claims released. *Ibid.*

SEC. 1467. Claim of Eastern Band of Cherokees for share of funds of Cherokee Nation. Decision of court below affirmed (117 U. S., 288). *Eastern Band Cherokees v. United States et al., 21 C. Cls., 501.*

SEC. 1468. Indians, not being citizens, are not subject to United States statutes, and where they refer a question to the arbitrament of the Secretary of the Interior by treaty, he can not transmit it to this court for adjudication.   *Chickasaw Nation v. United States, 22 C. Cls., 222.*

SEC. 1469. The Chickasaw treaty, 1852 (10 Stat. L., 974), submits all demands founded on the treaties, 1832 (7 Stat. L., 388) and 1834 (7 Stat. L., 450), to the final decision of the Secretary of the Interior. The authority so conferred is in its nature judicial and can not be delegated.   *Ibid.*

SEC. 1470. The Chickasaw treaty, 1852 (10 Stat. L., 794), authorizes, as preliminary to the Secretary's decision, an investigation which he has the right to depute; and for that purpose he may transmit those claims to this court under section 2 of the Bowman Act (22 Stat. L., 486).   *Ibid.*

SEC. 1471. The jurisdictional restriction of section 1066 of the Revised Statutes, against claims growing out of treaty stipulations, relates to cases of final adjudication defined by sections 1059, 1063, and not to a case transmitted under the Bowman Act, where the decision will be only advisory.   *Ibid.*

SEC. 1472. The only claim or matter excepted from the jurisdiction of this court by the Bowman Act (22 Stat. L., 486) are specifically named in sections 3 and 4, and treaty claims are not among them.
        Ibid.

SEC. 1473. The judgment of the court below is reversed on the ground that while the jurisdictional act did not give the Senate award conclusive effect as *res adjudicata* it did not set it aside or deny its effect as to the validity of the claims allowed under it.   The act opened the award and cast upon the United States the burden of disproving its justice and fairness.   The proceedings under the arbitration were ratified and confirmed by the United States by the acts of March 2, 1861 (12 Stat. L., 238), and of January 23, 1874 (18 Stat. L., 230), and the award of the Senate furnishes the nearest approximation to the justice and right of the case that it is practicable for a court to reach after the lapse of time, and is adopted by the Supreme Court as the basis of its judgment.   *Choctaw Nation v. United States, 29 C. Cls., 476.*

SEC. 1474. Any public officer in an executive department may correct his own errors and open, reconsider, or reverse any case decided by himself.   But this can not be done by his successor in office except under certain circumstances and conditions.
        Rollins & Presbrey v. United States, 23 C. Cls., 106.

SEC. 1475. The act of May 27, 1882 (22 Stat. L., 87), providing that an Indian agent "shall hold his office for the term of four years, and until his successor is duly appointed and qualified," does not extend to one appointed during a recess of the Senate and never confirmed.
        Romero v. United States, 24 C. Cls., 331.

SEC. 1476. An Indian agent commissioned in February, 1876, "to be agent for the Tule River Indians in California" is entitled to the salary of $1,500 appropriated for that agency by the act of June 22, 1874 (18 Stat. L., 146), and subsequent appropriation acts, and is not entitled to the salary of $1,800 prescribed by the Revised Statutes for four agents "for the tribes in California."

Belknap v. United States, 24 C. Cls., 433.

SEC. 1477. The act of March 2, 1889 (25 Stat. L., 1013), provides that the court "may allow a reasonable compensation to the counsel or attorneys of the Citizen Indians of the Wea, Peoria, et al. tribes." Under this the court can not accept the amount claimed in the petition as the sum "actually in controversy."

Citizen Indians of the Weas et al. v. United States, 26 C. Cls., 323.

SEC. 1478. When the Government is sued as trustee of an Indian tribe and the judgment will be satisfied out of a trust fund, interest in the nature of damages can not be recovered. (Sec. 1091, Rev. Stat.)

Ibid.

SEC. 1479. When a treaty reserves a disputed question, and provides that it shall be "submitted to the Senate of the United States for its decision," the decision is as obligatory as the treaty itself.

Western Cherokee Indians v. United States, 27 C. Cls., 1.

SEC. 1480. The statute regulating the recovery of interest against the United States (sec. 1091, Rev. Stat.) does not extend to a case coming into this court under a special act and resting on a treaty which provides for the payment of interest.

Ibid.

SEC. 1481. Sovereignties, corporations, and individuals, or aggregations of individuals, may be parties litigant. The Western Cherokees are not a body corporate; but, as the former owners of communal property, are now severally interested in a common fund. Concerning such litigants equity takes jurisdiction to prevent a multiplicity of suits; one may sue for the benefit of all.

Ibid.

SEC. 1482. The finding and allowance of the Interior Department in such cases become an award, forming the basis of a judgment in which all differences in fact and law are merged; but this court, by its judgment, determines no question applicable to the original controversy.

Hyne v. United States, 27 C. Cls., 113.

SEC. 1483. Under the Indian depredation act, March 3, 1891 (26 Stat. L., 851), the court is required to render judgment for the amount allowed by the Secretary of the Interior in certain cases "unless either the claimant or the United States shall elect to reopen the case."

Ibid.

SEC. 1484. The grass on an Indian reservation, though not the property of the Government, must be treated as such for the purpose of the contract.

Davis v. United States, 27 C. Cls., 181

SEC. 1485. In the Interior Department, in the determination of claims for Indian depredations, it was not necessary that notice be given to the Indians. The jurisdiction of this court now supersedes that of the Secretary of the Interior. *Jaeger v. United States et al., 27 C. Cls., 278.*

SEC. 1486. By the provisions of the statute (26 Stat. L., 851) the United States assume responsibility for the torts of the Indians, charging each tribe with its own depredations, and providing that the Attorney-General shall appear and defend both the Government and the Indians, but allowing the latter to appear by their own attorney if they see fit. The service of the petition on the Attorney-General is the only service of process required, and the Indians are not entitled to other notice. *Ibid.*

SEC. 1487. The Indian depredation act, March 3, 1891 (26 Stat. L., 851), provides "that all claims shall be presented to the court by petition." The filing of the petition is the commencement of the suit.
Ibid.

SEC. 1488. The courts of this country have never been open to Indians, and our civil liberty has never been given to them. *Ibid.*

SEC. 1489. The Indian depredation act, 1891 (26 Stat. L., 851), provides that judgments shall be rendered on claims heretofore allowed by the Secretary of the Interior under prior statutes, unless either the claimant or the United States shall elect to reopen the case, and that "all questions of limitations as to time and manner of presenting claims are hereby waived." If a claim examined by the Secretary prior to the statutes referred to was reexamined subsequently and allowed, it comes within the requirements of the Indian depredation act. *Mitchell, Admr., v. United States et al., 27 C. Cls., 316.*

SEC. 1490. Where the Secretary approved the claim on the merits, but disallowed it on the ground that it was barred, his disallowance is one of the "limitations as to time and manner of presenting claims" expressly waived by the act. *Ibid.*

SEC. 1491. When the defendants have not signified their election whether they will reopen a case, a motion for judgment by the claimant is premature. *Ibid.*

SEC. 1492. A report prepared for the Commissioner of Indian Affairs to sign, but never signed, without date, but supposed to have been drafted in 1890, never transmitted to the Secretary of the Interior, nor approved by him, can not be taken as his examination, approval, and allowance of a claim under the Indian depredation act (26 Stat. L., 851). *Falk v. United States et al., 27 C. Cls., 321.*

SEC. 1493. The court is to determine the aggregate right, leaving the distribution, as the administration of a trust, to the Interior Department. *Pottawatomie Indians v. United States, 27 C. Cls., 403.*

SEC. 1494. The Pottawatomies who remained in Michigan are not entitled to any entire annuity, but only to their *just proportion* in the ratio of those who remained to those who removed.   *Ibid.*

SEC. 1495. In the allowance of fees the court takes no notice of assignees and creditors, even where money was advanced to aid in the prosecution of the claim.   *Beddo v. United States, 28 C. Cls., 69.*

SEC. 1496. Under the Indian depredation act 1891 (26 Stat. L., 851) and the rules of this court, only attorneys who have actually appeared are entitled to an allowance of fees. Associate counsel, assignees, and persons otherwise employed must look to those who employed them.
        Ibid.

SEC. 1497. Prior to 1885 every Indian depredation act provided for indemnity for property destroyed by Indians to any " citizen *or inhabitant*" of the United States, but the act of 1885 (23 Stat. L., 376) provided for the continued examination of claims on behalf of "citizens of the United States," omitting the words "or inhabitants" used in former acts.   *Valk v. United States et al., 28 C. Cls., 241.*

SEC. 1498. Where it is clear that the Secretary of the Interior did not intend to report to Congress any action of his own, but only that of his predecessor prior to the act of March 3, 1885 (23 Stat. L., 376), his report can not be taken as an approval and allowance of a claim within the intent of the act 1891 (26 Stat. L., 851).
        Buchanan v. United States et al., 28 C. Cls., 127.

SEC. 1499. The provision in the act of 1885 (23 Stat. L., 376) which directs the Secretary of the Interior to report certain claims to Congress "at its next regular session" is merely directory.   *Ibid.*

SEC. 1500. Where amity did not exist, and no treaty made a tribe responsible for property taken or destroyed, the court is without jurisdiction of a suit brought under the Indian depredation act, 1891 (26 Stat. L., 851).   *Marks v. United States et al., 28 C. Cls., 147.*

SEC. 1501. No formal declaration of war by Congress, nor proclamation by the President, is necessary to define and characterize an Indian war. It is sufficient that hostilities exist and military operations are carried on.   *Ibid.*

SEC. 1502. The Indian depredation act 1891 (26 Stat. L., 851) provides that this court shall have jurisdiction of claims for property taken or destroyed "by Indians belonging to any band, tribe, or nation in amity with the United States." Treaty relations are not equivalent, within the meaning of the statute, to amity, and do not relieve a claimant from proving a state of amity in cases coming within the first clause of the first section of the statute.   *Ibid.*

SEC. 1503. The act March 3, 1885 (23 Stat. L., 376), provides that the Secretary of the Interior shall report to Congress Indian depredation claims "chargeable against any tribe of Indians by reason of any treaty between such tribes and the United States;" and the Bannock treaty, July 3, 1868 (15 Stat. L., 673), provides that "if bad men among the Indians" shall commit a depredation, the Bannocks "will on proof made to their agent, and notice by him, deliver up the wrongdoer; and in case they willfully refuse so to do, the person injured shall be reimbursed for his loss from the annuities or other moneys due or to become due to them." A claim for property taken or destroyed during the general hostilities of the Bannock war does not come within these provisions.   *Ibid.*

SEC. 1504. The jurisdiction of this court under the Indian depredation act, 1891 (26 Stat. L., 851), is limited to "claims for property of citizens of the United States taken or destroyed by Indians." This must be held to mean citizens at the time the property was taken.   *Valk v. United States et al., 28 C. Cls., 241.*

SEC. 1505. The primary declaration of an alien followed by his subsequent naturalization does not constitute him a citizen within the meaning of the Indian depredation act.   *Ibid.*

SEC. 1506. Where a jurisdictional act adopts the language of a previous statute which had been interpreted for several years in a certain way by an executive department, it must be inferred that Congress intended to use the language as thus interpreted.   *Ibid.*

SEC. 1507. Another defense against the claim is that the Rogue River Indians were not in amity with the United States at the time the property was taken or destroyed; amity being a condition precedent to the right of recovery.   *Ibid.*

SEC. 1508. A treaty is some evidence of amity, to be considered with other facts and circumstances, but is not conclusive.   *Ibid.*

SEC. 1509. Where property intended for delivery to the United States under a contract is captured by the public enemy or by Indians before acceptance and change of possession the loss is the contractor's.
                                          Baker v. United States, 28 C. Cls., 370.

SEC. 1510. Where the authority of the Secretary of the Interior was limited to cases in which he could determine by what tribe a depredation was committed, and that it was chargeable to the tribe by virtue of some treaty, he was without authority to approve and allow other claims.   *Price v. United States, 28 C. Cls., 422.*

SEC. 1511. Where a claim reported by the Secretary of the Interior to Congress was described in a schedule which contained no column for allowances, the court will refer to the action of the Department to determine whether it was approved and allowed within the meaning of the Indian depredation act (26 Stat. L., 851).   *Ibid.*

Sec. 1512. Where the Secretary of the Interior found that the evidence was not sufficient to charge the Kiowa and Comanche Indians with the commission of the injury, his jurisdiction came to an end and he was without authority to approve or allow the claim in pursuance of the act of March 3, 1885 (23 Stat. L., 376).   *Ibid.*

Sec. 1513. Congress having adopted in the statute (26 Stat. L., 851) the language of the act of 1885 (23 Stat. L., 376), it must be inferred that the words "citizens of the United States" were used in the sense that had been given to them by the Interior Department.

Johnson v. United States, 29 C. Cls., 1.

Sec. 1514. The primary declaration to become a citizen under section 2165, Revised Statutes, made before the depredation was committed, did not make the claimant a citizen within the intent of the jurisdictional act.   *Ibid.*

Sec. 1515. Citizenship acquired by being a resident and voter in Nebraska when it was admitted as a State does not relate back to the time when an Indian depredation was committed. Such citizenship was acquired by the act February 9, 1867 (14 Stat. L., 391), and not by the enabling act April 19, 1864 (13 Stat. L., 57).

Hosford v. United States, 29 C. Cls., 42.

Sec. 1516. The Government has a right to press the claim of a citizen as a member of a partnership against a foreign power or an Indian tribe though his partner be alien, and, accordingly, an action may be maintained against such a partner under the Indian depredation act, 1891.   *Ibid.*

Sec. 1517. In the Indian depredation act 1891 (26 Stat. L., 851) citizenship and amity relate to the same time. Hostile Indians were not to be made liable for past depredations by subsequently becoming *in amity*, nor were aliens to acquire new rights by subsequently becoming citizens.   *Valk v. United States, 29 C. Cls., 62.*

Sec. 1518. The omission of the word "inhabitants" used in previous acts relating to Indian depredations was regarded as significant by the Interior Department, and its construction of the act of 1885 was adopted by Congress in the act 1891 (26 Stat. L., 851).   *Ibid.*

Sec. 1519. A treaty provision assuring to aliens "free access to the tribunals of justice" does not prevent this Government from subsequently giving special rights of action to its own citizens against itself to the exclusion of aliens.   *Ibid.*

Sec. 1520. A treaty is evidence of amity, in connection with other facts and circumstances, but not conclusive.   *Ibid.*

Sec. 1521. War supersedes treaties and makes the subjects of contending sovereignties enemies in law.   *Ibid.*

SEC. 1522. The Indian depredation act was framed in accordance with the policy of all governments, not to pay for property destroyed in war.   *Ibid.*

SEC. 1523. Judgment against an Indian tribe is not a necessary condition to judgment against the United States in an action under the Indian depredation act 1891. The court has jurisdiction if the depredation was by Indians in amity with the United States, though the tribe is unidentified.   *Gorham v. United States, 29 C. Cls., 97.*

SEC. 1524. Cases may arise where the mistake, error, or negligence of an officer charged with the defense of the Government is so serious or so palpable that it would be a wrong and injustice to allow a judgment to stand; but where a case has been carefully prepared by a law officer and elaborately argued, the resulting judgment should be set aside only where the fraud, wrong, or injustice complained of is established beyond a reasonable doubt. A different view of the case taken by new counsel for the Government is not sufficient.   *Ibid.*

SEC. 1525. So far as the provisions of section 6 of the act of 1891 (26 Stat. L., 851) are involved, it is manifest that they have no direct bearing upon the action of the court, its jurisdiction and duty, nor upon the liability of the United States as a litigant in court.   *Ibid.*

SEC. 1526. Where a case allowed by the Secretary of the Interior is opened by the claimant on no other ground than the question of damages, and submitted on no other evidence than that which was considered by the Secretary, the court will not lightly disturb the award when computing damages.   *Woolverton v. United States, 29 C. Cls., 107.*

SEC. 1527. Under the Indian depredation act of 1891 the United States are responsible only in two classes of cases: First, where the Indian dependents are responsible but without funds to respond in damages; second, where the depredations were committed by Indians whose tribal relations can not be ascertained.   *Ibid.*

SEC. 1528. An Indian tribe at peace with the United States is not liable for depredations committed by a distinct bānd, previously a part of the tribe, at war with the United States.   *Ibid.*

SEC. 1529. Joseph's band of Nez Percé Indians were in 1877 a distinct Indian organization and their separate existence or autonomy was recognized by the United States. Their nonjoinder as defendants for a depredation known to be committed by them is fatal.
Ibid.

SEC. 1530. Though no statute of limitations may attach to an Indian depredation case, the fact that the Government has again and again notified claimants by statutes to present their claims for the scrutiny and investigation of the Interior Department, and the fact that the claimant has wholly neglected to do so, suggests moral presumptions against the claim.   *Stone v. United States, 29 C. Cls., 111.*

SEC. 1531. When the ownership of the property, the possession of it, the quantity of it, the value of it, and the fact of the depredation depend exclusively upon the testimony of the party in interest and a single witness, a court should proceed with great caution and should not allow such testimony, wholly unsupported, to control a decision, though the witnesses be neither contradicted nor impeached.   *Ibid.*

SEC. 1532. Though a case be not barred by a statute of limitations, the presumption of fact growing out of lapse of time and neglect to file claim must be overcome by satisfactory evidence.   *Ibid.*

SEC. 1533. Where the evidence does not establish a malicious intent on the part of Indians charged with committing a depredation, and does not show such a condition of negligence as would establish a liability at common law for the destruction of property, they are not liable under the Indian depredation act of 1891 (26 Stat. L., 851).
                    Jaeger v. United States, 29 C. Cls., 172.

SEC. 1534. The depredations committed during the Rogue River war were the ravages of war, to be borne by persons upon whom they happened to fall, unless the parties injured were indemnified by treaty.   *Ross v. United States, 29 C. Cls., 176.*

SEC. 1535. The treaty with the Rogue River Indians, September 10, 1853 (10 Stat. L., 1018), reserved $15,000 to pay for the property of the whites destroyed by them. This is the exclusive remedy for persons whose property was destroyed.   *Ibid.*

SEC. 1536. Where a case is not properly an examined and allowed case within the intent of the Indian depredation act (26 Stat. L., 851), the defendants can not be compelled to assume the burden of proof by electing to reopen it.   *Mares v. United States, 29 C. Cls., 197.*

SEC. 1537. A case is not an allowed and preferred case if the Secretary of the Interior had not authority to make an award.
                    Ibid.

SEC. 1538. The act of March 3, 1885 (23 Stat. L., 376), requires the Secretary to designate " the date and clause of the treaty creating the obligation of payment." This does not authorize the Secretary to act where there is no express stipulation in a treaty.
                    Ibid.

SEC. 1539. The treaty with the Jicarilla Apaches (10 Stat. L., 979) contains a general provision requiring the Indians to keep the peace and treat citizens of the United States honestly and humanely. This is not an express stipulation to pay damages for depredations committed by members of the tribe, and does not authorize the Secretary to make awards against the tribe.   *Ibid.*

SEC. 1540. An Indian treaty providing for the payment of depredations committed by members of the tribe can not be construed to include acts of war committed by the tribe. Assuming or imposing such an obligation would be contrary to the general policy of the United States.   *Leighton v. United States, 29 C. Cls., 288.*

SEC. 1541. A treaty obligation "to cease all hostilities against persons and property" is not an obligation to pay depredation claims.   *Ibid.*

SEC. 1542. Under the act of June 30, 1834 (4 Stat. L., 731), the Indian liability arose from the taking or destruction of the property of a citizen or inhabitant by Indians belonging to a tribe in amity with the United States.   *Ibid.*

SEC. 1543. The United States may exact indemnity from an Indian tribe as a condition of peace or for property destroyed in war, but Congress has not conferred jurisdiction on the courts to do so at the suit of a citizen.   *Ibid.*

SEC. 1544. The Indians being within the jurisdiction and control of the United States as "domestic dependent nations," it is their duty to submit to the constituted authorities; but if, instead of submitting, they resort to arms, as a band, tribe, or nation, to maintain or contest their rights, a want of amity *in fact* arises, and by reason of their recognized tribal relations by the political departments and the favorable rules of interpretation to which they are entitled, their rights as belligerents will be respected by the court in construing the remedial act of 1891.   *Ibid.*

SEC. 1545. The action of the Secretary of the Interior under the act May 29, 1872 (17 Stat. L., 190), was advisory to Congress. No right to compensation was created.   *Ibid.*

SEC. 1546. The condition of "amity" imposed by the first jurisdictional clause of the act 1891 extends to the second, i. e., amity is jurisdictional in cases "which have been examined and allowed by the Interior Department" as well as in cases defined in the first clause. (Davis and Nott dissenting for reasons set forth in Love *v.* United States, 29 C. Cls., 332.)   *Ibid.*

SEC. 1547. The act 1891 (26 Stat. L., 851) does not create claims nor impose new liabilities upon Indians; and the liability which the United States assume is only where the Indians are primarily liable.

Ibid.

SEC. 1548. The act 1891 (26 Stat. L., 851) is a recognition of existing claims on the part of citizens and of liabilities on the part of the United States. *Ibid.*

SEC. 1549. The departmental construction of the statutes, viz, that when treaty relations existed amity was not jurisdictional, was erroneous, and there being no ambiguity, it can not be adopted by the judiciary. *Ibid.*

SEC. 1550. Where the political departments continued to recognize a treaty, it must be inferred that the tribe was then recognized as in amity. But such a presumption is not conclusive. *Ibid.*

SEC. 1551. The amity required by the act 1891 is that of the band, tribe, or nation. Amity may exist, though individuals or a party within the tribe raid on citizens of the United States. *Ibid.*

SEC. 1552. Where the political departments of the Government have recognized a band of Indians for the purposes of a treaty, and provided therein for the payment of annuities to the band, irrespective of the nation or tribe of which it was a part, judgment may be rendered against it. *Ibid.*

SEC. 1553. The Indian depredation act 1891 (26 Stat. L., 851) is jurisdictional; it does not create liabilities nor assume them further than this, that where a depredation was committed by Indians, but their tribe can not be identified, or where a tribe is without funds to satisfy a judgment, the United States assume the Indians' liability. But the jurisdiction intended by the act is commensurate with and includes all legal liabilities of Indian defendants for depredations committed on citizens. *Love v. United States, 29 C. Cls., 332.*

SEC. 1554. The only liabilities contemplated by the act 1891 (apart from the above, which are in the nature of guaranties) are those of Indians. The act February 28, 1859 (11 Stat. L., 388), rescinded all liabilities on the part of the United States.

Ibid.

SEC. 1555. The only liabilities which the judiciary can recognize are those which spring from treaty stipulations, from the obligations of international law, from the terms and conditions which may have been imposed as a condition of peace at the termination of an Indian war, or from a statute which prospectively imposed an obligation upon Indian tribes as "domestic dependent relations." *Ibid.*

SEC. 1556. Where war and not amity was the condition of the time, and the taking or destruction of property was the exercise of a belligerent right, the loss, like the losses of other citizens in other wars, must be borne by him upon whom it falls, unless the defendants assumed a liability for war indemnities by treaty or it was imposed as a condition of peace. Conversely, the Indian defendants can not set up their own unlawful acts of violence as a defense. To avoid liability they must show, or it must appear, that the depredation was the taking or destruction of property in the exercise of a belligerent's right to wage war. *Ibid.*

SEC. 1557. "Amity," as used in Indian depredation act, considered at length and construed. *Ibid.*

SEC. 1558. That a depredation was an act of war is a good defense in any depredation case, whether the claim was or was not examined and allowed by the Secretary of the Interior.

Cox v. United States, 29 C. Cls., 349.

SEC. 1559. When an allowed case has been reopened at the election of either party, there is nothing in the act of 1891 which prevents the defendants from setting up any defense which they may set up in other cases. *Ibid.*

SEC. 1560. The only difference between preferred cases reopened and other cases is that the party electing to reopen assumes the burden of proof. *Ibid.*

SEC. 1561. When the defendants elect to reopen a case, they may set up any defense which might have been set up in the Interior Department. *Ibid.*

SEC. 1562. Treaty obligation runs all though the law; it is a tangible, binding obligation upon the Indians, in the creation of which the Indians had a voice, at least. Amity obligation is an intangible, inchoate, *ex parte* obligation, binding only by the edict of law upon a tribe of Indians having no voice in the creation of the law. *Ibid.*

SEC. 1563. Acts of Congress between June 30, 1834, and March 3, 1891, inclusive, relating to Indian depredations, considered and distinguished. *Ibid.*

SEC. 1564. The sworn allegations of the claimant appended to his claim, required by rules prescribed by the Secretary of the Interior, are not evidence within the intent of the act.

Weston v. United States, 29 C. Cls., 420.

SEC. 1565. Ordinarily a claim is pending in a Department as soon as application for payment is made. But in the Indian depredation act, 1891, it is provided that "no case shall be considered as pending unless evidence has been presented therein." *Weston v. United States, 29 C. Cls., 420.*

SEC. 1566. The treaty with the Comanches, 1868 (15 Stat. L., 851), provides, under certain conditions, that a person injured by them shall be reimbursed for his loss.   But the primary object of the provision was the delivery of wrongdoers for punishment, and the words "reimbursed for his loss" are not apt words to describe damages for personal injuries or compensation for carrying away and concealing a child.   *Friend v. United States, 29 C. Cls., 425.*

SEC. 1567. The Indian depredation act, 1891, relates exclusively to claims for property.   Previous statutes examined and their effects stated.   *Ibid.*

SEC. 1568. In February and July, 1859, the Mohave Indians were not in amity with the United States.
                                    Barrow, Porter & Co. v. United States, 30 C. Cls., 54.

SEC. 1569. Where a depredation was committed prior to July, 1865, the demand prosecuted in this court may exceed in amount but not in quantity the claim filed in the Interior Department.   Indian depredation act, 1891, 26 Stat. L., 851. .
                                                              Ibid.

SEC. 1570. Copies of affidavits filed by the claimant in the Interior Department in support of his claim may be treated as admissions of the claimant.   *Ibid.*

SEC. 1571. Where three suits against the United States and three tribes of Indians for distinct causes of action have been audited in one case without objection by the defendants, several judgments against each party defendant must be entered.   *Ibid.*

SEC. 1572. When the Cherokee national council changed the common property of the nation into money, the fund took the place of the lands, and under the constitution was subject to the same limitations and existed for the same beneficiaries.   The national council could not divert the common property from the general welfare and transmit it into a communal fund belonging to a class of citizens, viz, " *Cherokees by blood.*"   *Whitmire, Trustee, v. Cher. Nation et al., 30 C. Cls., 138.*

SEC. 1573. The Cherokee Nation, as a sovereign power, has the right to administer its own affairs in its own way, and to regulate the rights of its citizens by its own laws.   But the legislative authority of the national council is not absolute, being limited and defined by the constitution, and the acts of the council can not control or abrogate the treaty obligations of the nation to the United States.   *Ibid*

SEC. 1574. A decree in equity, so long as the case remains open and within the jurisdiction of the court, may be extended to a subsequently accruing cause of action, the right to which has been determined by the original decision. No new issue, either of law or fact, can be determined upon a motion of this kind.

Journeycake v. Cher. Nation et al., 30 C. Cls., 172.

SEC. 1575. When the original decree fixed the proportional share of the complainants in a certain fund, they can not introduce evidence to show that they were entitled to a larger portion. Such a change is not the correction of an arithmetical mistake or clerical error, but a change of the basis upon which the recovery rests.   *Ibid.*

SEC. 1576. When the complainants do not demand interest before an appeal they can not do so afterwards. Such a demand presents a legal question which should have been presented to the appellate court.   *Ibid.*

SEC. 1577. When the complainants rest content with a decree in their favor, and it having been appealed comes back affirmed, the court can not make a new decision affecting the legal rights of the parties and increasing the amount of the recovery.   *Ibid.*

SEC. 1578. The Secretary of the Interior will cause the "Wallace roll" to be further corrected by adding thereto descendants born since March 3, 1883, and prior to May 3, 1894, and striking therefrom the names of those who have died or ceased to be citizens of the Cherokee Nation, so that when thus amended it shall represent the freedmen entitled to participate in the distribution of the fund now awarded to the complainant.   *Whitmire, Trustee, v. Cher. Nation et al., 30 C. Cls., 180.*

SEC. 1579. The court finds for the purpose of distribution in this suit that the whole number of the citizens of the Cherokee Nation entitled to participate in the fund of $7,240,000 was 28,243, and the number of freedmen, citizens of the nation represented by the trustee, the complainant in this suit, was 3,524, and that their proportionate share or interest in the above fund is $903,365.   *Ibid.*

SEC. 1580. This is not an action to recover damages in the nature of a suit at law, nor is it a proceeding in equity to wind up and dispose of the affairs and assets of a partnership. It is simply a suit in equity, brought by the equitable owners of a specific fund to recover their proportionate share in the same, as contemplated by the jurisdictional act.   *Ibid.*

SEC. 1581. If the funds in question were the property of four joint owners it would be just to award to three of them—the Delawares, Shawnees, and freedmen—the same proportionate amount that has been appropriated to themselves, the native Cherokees. But this may not be the case. Under the decision of this court in the previous cases, affirmed by the Supreme Court, these funds are the common property of all Cherokee citizens.   *Ibid.*

SEC. 1582. A court of equity will not award to a party more than he is legally and equitably entitled to because a second party has appropriated more, and a third party, who may be entitled to participate, is not within the jurisdiction of the court.

Ibid.

SEC. 1583. The court, sitting as a court of equity, must assume, for the purpose of distribution of a fund, that the adopted whites are equally interested in the common property of the nation, and protect their interests to the extent of not awarding their possible share in the fund to parties not strictly entitled to it.

Ibid.

SEC. 1584. A claim for natural increase in the case of the Cherokee freedmen is too uncertain to be adopted as a factor in determining their proportionate number and the consequent amount of their recovery.

Ibid.

SEC. 1585. The Cherokee Nation was directly interested in the census of the Cherokee freedmen made by the United States, generally known as the "Wallace roll," and the nation having had an opportunity to take part in the investigation, and being directly interested in the result, the roll can be used as evidence of the number of the freedmen.

Ibid.

SEC. 1586. Where a new ascertainment of the actual number of the complainants is not a necessity in the case, and will be involved, prolonged, and vexatious, it should be avoided if substantial justice can be done without resorting to it.

Ibid.

SEC. 1587. In a case of joint or communal ownership where the parties recovering must be counted by thousands but are entitled to be paid per capita, the recovery, as against the defendants, must be for a sum in gross; and the amount recovered must constitute a sum for distribution.

Ibid.

SEC. 1588. A "general amnesty of all past offenses" declared by an Indian treaty blots out a depredation, so that in the eye of the law the Indian offenders are as innocent as if the depredation had never been committed.

Garrison v. United States, 30 C. Cls., 272.

SEC. 1589. The term amnesty comprehends every crime and misdemeanor, whether indictable or not, and must be held to include in an Indian treaty an Indian depredation.

Ibid.

SEC. 1590. The liability created by the act of 1834 (4 Stat. L., 731), and the guarantee given by the United States, did not constitute a vested right.

Ibid.

Sec. 1591. A treaty which relieves an Indian nation from penalties that have accrued to the United States does not leave a citizen free to pursue them.   *Ibid.*

Sec. 1592. Under the Indian depredation act, 1891, the court can not render judgment against the United States alone in a case where the claimant has identified the Indians.   *Ibid.*

Sec. 1593. The act of 1891 (26 Stat. L., 851) is a remedial statute, whereby only existing claims against the Indians may be prosecuted to final judgment in this court; and whether or not a judgment can be rendered against the United States, either jointly or alone, depends upon the citizenship of the claimant, the amity of the tribe, band, or nation to which the depredating Indians belonged at the time of the depredation, and whether or not the defendant Indians, known or unknown, are liable for the depredation complained of.   *Ibid.*

Sec. 1594. Under the Indian depredation act a suit may be maintained against the "Sioux Indians" as a tribe, and if there be no more particular identification judgment may be rendered against them.

Graham v. United States, 30 C. Cls., 318.

Sec. 1595. The nation can not be held liable for the acts of the tribes nor the tribe for the acts of the band, if the Indians committing the depredation can be identified as belonging to a particular tribe or band.   *Ibid.*

Sec. 1596. When a claimant has complied with the provisions of section 3 of the act 1891 (26 Stat. L., 851) by averring the Indians who committed the depredation, he has thereby made them parties defendant, and such averment is sufficient notice to the Attorney-General.   *Ibid.*

Sec. 1597. Where judgment was rendered against the tribe when the evidence indicated that a particular band committed the depredation, the judgment will not be disturbed, but an additional finding of fact will be filed sufficient to inform the Interior Department against what band the judgment should be charged.   *Ibid.*

Sec. 1598. A judgment against the Sioux Nation is valid, though technically defective, if it should have been against the "Minneconjou Band of the Sioux Nation."   *Ibid.*

Sec. 1599. When a tribe is brought into court as defendant, the different bands named in a treaty as composing the tribe are in court, and judgment may be rendered against the band which committed the depredation.   *Ibid.*

Sec. 1600. Where two valuations of property, the one by the Commissioner of Indian Affairs and the other by a special agent of the

Department, are before the Secretary of the Interior, and he does not in terms approve either, but directs that the claim shall be reported and the amount of loss be submitted for the determination of Congress, it is not an approval and allowance within the intent of the Indian depredation act (26 Stat. L., 851), and the case is not an allowed claim entitled to priority of consideration. *Hegwer v. United States, 30 C. Cls., 405.*

SEC. 1601. The purpose of the act 1885 (23 Stat. L., 376), in respect to the damages sustained in Indian depredation cases, was that the Secretary should cause such additional investigation to be made as would enable him to determine the value of property taken or destroyed. His judgment and determination, and not that of his subordinates, was what Congress sought by the act. *Ibid.*

SEC. 1602. The provisions in the act 1891 having reference to allowed claims in which the claimant is entitled prima facie to judgment applies only to claims which have been examined and allowed under the act of 1885, and does not extend to claims examined and allowed under the act of May 29, 1872 (17 Stat. L., 190).
Graham v. United States, 30 C. Cls., 405.

SEC. 1603. The act of January 28, 1893 (27 Stat. L., 426), conferring urisdiction on this court to hear and enter judgment "as if it had original jurisdiction of said case," contains no admission of a right. It is a grant of jurisdiction with a waiver of the statute of limitations.
New York Indians v. United States, 30 C. Cls., 413.

SEC. 1604. The Buffalo Creek treaty (7 Stat. L., 550) has expired, leaving no rights or duties behind it, so far as this litigation is involved. Both parties allowed it to lapse. The Indians can not maintain a suit under it for either the lands in Kansas or the lands in Wisconsin. *Ibid.*

SEC. 1605. Legislative action is not necessarily a precedent for judicial. Where Congress awards damages to one Indian tribe and refers the claims of others to this court for investigation and adjudication, it must be deemed that Congress was convinced that the one tribe had been injured, but was not convinced that the others had been. *Ibid.*

SEC. 1606. Where a decree was entered by consent of the defendant's attorneys for a larger amount than the court had decided the complainants were entitled to recover, it will be set aside on the court's own motion. *Journeycake v. Cherokee Nation et al., 31 C. Cls., 140.*

SEC. 1607. Where both parties have classed the "adopted citizens" of the Cherokee Nation as a part of the body of citizens who make up the whole number of the nation, a court of equity will not be justified in awarding a portion of the communal fund, which may be theirs, to the complainants before the court, though the defendants consent thereto. *Ibid.*

SEC. 1608. The treaty with the Cheyenne Indians, July 6, 1825 (7 Stat. L., 255), does not provide for compensation to parties suffering from Indian depredations, but merely that the party guilty shall be given up to the United States and the chiefs exert themselves to recover the stolen property.

Labadi, admr., v. United States et al., 31 C. Cls., 205.

SEC. 1609. There being no undertaking on the part of defendant Indians to pay for property taken or destroyed by members of their tribe, there was no authority in the Secretary of the Interior to allow the claims, and the claimant has no election. *Ibid.*

SEC. 1610. The general traverse puts in issue every material allegation in an Indian depredation case and casts upon the claimant the burden of proof. *King v. United States et al., 31 C. Cls., 304.*

SEC. 1611. A claimant in an Indian depredation case must establish his claim by evidence. If the Attorney-General fails to file a plea, the claimant can not have judgment by default, but must prove his case. *Ibid.*

SEC. 1612. Where a depredation was committed on the 15th of August, 1865, and the claim therefor was never presented to the Interior Department, and the only testimony is the unsupported deposition of the claimant, the case comes within the rule in Stone's case (29 C. Cls. R., 111). *Ibid.*

SEC. 1613. The Kiowa and Comanche Indians were in amity with the United States during the years 1866 to 1874, except during parts of the years 1868, 1869, and 1874, more particularly set forth in the opinion of the court. *Gamel v. United States et al., 31 C. Cls., 321.*

SEC. 1614. In Indian depredation cases the jurisdictional facts, citizenship and amity, are regarded as put in issue by the general traverse; but if either party ask a severance of issues the jurisdictional issues must be first tried and determined. Such a request should be made in due time. *Ibid.*

SEC. 1615. These Indian depredation cases, where a party can bring an action at law twenty-four years after his cause of action arose, without previous notification of any kind, are without a precedent in the history of jurisprudence. *Gossett v. United States et al., 31 C. Cls., 325.*

SEC. 1616. The court reiterates the rule laid down in Stone's case (29 C. Cls., 111). Where a case is first brought to the attention of the defendants by an action in this court after a great number of years, and is supported only by the testimony of the parties in interest, the court will not find the facts, but will dismiss the case as unsupported by sufficient proof. *Ibid.*

SEC. 1617. The fact that a jury may believe or disbelieve testimony is not the sole criterion in the determination of facts. . It is the duty of the court to see that a sufficiently stable foundation is laid upon which to rest a verdict and to set aside verdicts which are against the weight of evidence.   *Ibid.*

SEC. 1618. The purposes of the act 1891 (26 Stat. L., 851) was that a suit should be brought within three years, the cause of action be definitely described, and the depredating Indians named, "as near as may be." When a suit is so brought and its cause of action so defined, the case is subject to all the powers of amendment which a court can exercise in furtherance of justice.   *Duran v. United States et al., 31 C. Cls., 353.*

SEC. 1619. A petition is both process and declaration. A mistake or error in a petition, considered as a declaration, does not nullify it as a process. The provision in the second section of the depredation act, 1891 (26 Stat. L., 851), refers to it as a process; those in the third section as a declaration. A defect in a matter prescribed by the third section may be a matter of amendment and will not go to the jurisdiction.   *Ibid.*

SEC. 1620. In depredation cases the court has power to bring in a new Indian defendant after the statutory period for bringing suits has expired.   *Ibid.*

SEC. 1621. The act is imperative that the court shall render judgment "against the tribe of Indians committing the wrong when such can be identified." This by necessary implication gives the court power to bring in a tribe at any time before judgment, and the exercise of this power is essential to the maintenance of such rights as the United States may have against such a tribe.   *Ibid.*

SEC. 1622. The statutory provisions relating to Indian depredation claims are complex, and with as many different and divers interests and questions in one suit as were probably ever brought together in an action at law. The United States are liable only as guarantors for Indians who are parties to the record or for Indians who are unknown.   *Ibid.*

SEC. 1623. Where suits must be brought within a fixed jurisdictional period, the court will not allow a meritorious cause to fail because of a mistake of parties or attorneys if it can be saved by amendment.
                                              Ibid.

SEC. 1624. The court is inclined to accept the status of Indians for peace or war as defined by the Interior Department. But these Indian wars and hostilities are so frequent, changeable, and ill defined that this can not always be done.   *Valencia v. United States et al., 31 C. Cls., 388.*

SEC. 1625. Where a band of Indians entered into an agreement with the authorized representatives of the United States, ceased to make war, awaited the fulfillment on the part of the United States of an agreement which would make peace permanent, it must be held that they were then in amity.   *Ibid.*

SEC. 1626. Where a judgment has been entered against the Apache Indians and it appears that the depredation was committed by the Mimbres Apaches, a band of the Apache race, the judgment will not be vacated, but will be made definite and certain without disturbing it by filing an additional finding of fact for the information and guidance of the Executive Departments.

Ibid.

SEC. 1627. The purpose of the jurisdictional period prescribed by the act 1891 (26 Stat. L., 851) is like that of the abandoned and captured property act, to bring all claims before the court within a prescribed period. Where the party who instituted the suit is not authorized to bring it, but possesses some legal relation with the proper party concerning the cause of action, the latter may be substituted as claimant.   *Davenport, Admr., v. United States et al., 31 C. Cls., 430.*

SEC. 1628. Where an Indian depredation suit was instituted in due time by the children of the deceased owner, they being the parties really in interest, but not authorized by the law of Texas to maintain an action, the administrator of the estate may be substituted at their consent as party plaintiff after the jurisdictional period has expired.

Ibid.

SEC. 1629. In Indian depredation cases which have been allowed by the Secretary of the Interior, the defendants may file a plea of set-off without electing to reopen the case.

Labadie, Admr., v. United States et al., 31 C. Cls., 436.

SEC. 1630. Where a plea is not filed by the defendants within the sixty days prescribed by the statutes the court may subsequently allow it to be done. The statutory provision is directory to the Attorney-General and not mandatory upon the court.

Ibid.

SEC. 1631. A question involving the right of defendants to set up their counterclaim against one of the partners in an Indian depredation suit brought by the firm will not be considered upon a motion to strike from the files. Such motions go to the regularity of the plea. The question of legal right must be presented by an issue of law or fact.   *Ibid.*

SEC. 1632. The legal right of the defendants to file a plea expires with the time prescribed by the statute for filing it. It then becomes a matter of discretion with the court whether the plea may subsequently be filed.

Ibid.

SEC. 1633. An attack on a military train does not, taken by itself, necessarily imply war, but, taken in connection with prior declarations and subsequent hostile acts of the Indians, it is sufficient to fix the time when hostilities began.   *Levi Carter et al. v. United States, 31 C. Cls.,441.*

SEC. 1634. The war with the Ogalalla Sioux under Red Cloud in 1866 began July 17 and continued during a period not yet determined, extending over many months. *Ibid.*

SEC. 1635. The emigration of the Choctaws between 1834 and 1845 was in pursuance of the policy of the United States; and there being nothing in the treaty of 1830 (7 Stat. L., 340) in the nature of a forfeiture clause, the Choctaws are entitled to recover for the expenses of removal. *Choctaw Nation v. United States, 21 C. Cls., 59.*

SEC. 1636. When an Indian depredation case is reopened by either party the whole case is reopened for trial *de novo*, subject only to the statutory provision concerning the burden of proof.
Leighton v. United States, 29 C. Cl., 288.

SEC. 1637. Where successive attorneys have appeared in a case at different times their fees will be apportioned in proportion to their services. *Beddo v. United States, 28 C. Cl., 69.*

SEC. 1638. When the court has ascertained that a depredation has been committed by Indians belonging to a band, tribe, or nation in amity with the United States, whether recognized as such by treaty or otherwise, the act of 1891 applies, and the court has jurisdiction under it. *Tully v. United States, 32 C. Cl., 1.*

SEC. 1639. When a depredation is alleged to have been committed by a tribe or nation without more particular identification, the defendants may restrict the liability, by showing that the depredation was committed by Indians belonging to a particular band of the tribe.
Ibid.

SEC. 1640. The allowance of the Secretary of the Interior in Indian depredation cases does not have the sanctity of a judicial finding binding upon the rights of the parties, and the only force it has under the act is that upon the consent of the parties it may become the basis of a judgment. But the allowance must have been made in pursuance of law, and have been within the authority of the Secretary.
Crow v. United States et al., 32 C. Cl., 16.

SEC. 1641. There must be an express undertaking in the form of a treaty on the part of the tribe to pay, and no general undertaking to keep the peace is sufficient to authorize an allowance in depredation cases against the Indians under the act of 1885; and where an award was against two tribes for the same depredation, and the Secretary had jurisdiction as to one and not as to the other, the award will be enforced against the former, unless the defendants elect to reopen. *Ibid.*

SEC. 1642. Payment of a claim by the Interior Department under the Indian depredation act need not imply what is technically called a compromise, if the act of the parties be in legal substance a settlement.
Brice v. United States et al., 32 C. Cl., 23.

SEC. 1643. The Secretary of the Interior has no power to adjust and allow a claim for consequential damages growing out of the taking of property, and the court is without jurisdiction under the Indian depredation act to adjudicate a claim for consequential damages growing out of the taking of property.   *Ibid.*

SEC. 1644. A tribe of Indians at war with the United States can not be held responsible for the depredations or crimes of individual members of the tribe.   When amity ceased and war began the purpose of the Indian indemnity statutes was at an end.   The court is without jurisdiction to try a claim growing out of depredations by individuals absent from a tribe which is at war with the United States.

Salois v. United States, et al., 32 C. Cl., 68.

SEC. 1645. It seems impossible to hold that the court has jurisdiction in this case, without necessarily implying that the courts of the State have not; and if they have not, then we decide that the State of Nebraska has not the power to make her ordinary criminal statutes coextensive with the State limits, and enforce them against all persons living or found therein.   Such a power we are not prepared to deny to the State in the absence of some controlling treaty stipulation or valid act of Congress.   *United States v. Yellow Sun, 1 Dill., 271.*

SEC. 1646. In 1866 a State constitution was formed, and in 1867 Nebraska was admitted into the Union "upon an equal footing with the original States in all respects whatever."   There is no exception in the State constitution, or in either of the acts of Congress of the Pawnee Reservation, or the Pawnee Indians, from the territorial or civil jurisdiction of the State.   *Ibid.*

SEC. 1647. Where Indians reside within the limits of a State, the relations which they bear respectively to the State and to the National Government are peculiar, and frequently present perplexing questions. But no such questions now arise, and since there is no provision in the judiciary act, or any other act of Congress, giving to the courts of the United States jurisdiction in civil suits by or against Indians, we need not consider whether such jurisdiction could be constitutionally conferred by Congress as respects Indians not citizens living within State limits, and with respect to cases not arising under the Constitution, laws, or treaties of the United States.

Karrahoo v. Adams, 1 Dill., 344.

SEC. 1648. That Indians are not *foreign* citizens or subjects within the meaning of the Constitution, and that the court has no jurisdiction of the present suit, will further appear by reference to the eleventh section of the judiciary act, which prescribes the jurisdiction of the circuit court of the United States.   This section of the act makes no mention of Indians, does not use the words foreign citizens or subjects.

Ibid.

SEC. 1649. An Indian residing within the United States is not "a foreign citizen or subject" within the meaning of section 2, article 3, of the Constitution, and can not, on the ground that he is "a foreign citizen or subject," maintain a suit in the circuit court of the United States. *Ibid.*

SEC. 1650. Hole-in-the-Day, a chief of the Chippewas, with whom the United States had treaty relations, and an Indian of unmixed blood, and residing at the time of death upon land granted to him by the treaty of May 22, 1855 (10 Stat. L., 1166), was not a citizen of the United States nor of the State of Minnesota, and though said land lay within the territorial limits of Cass County, which was attached to Morrison County, the probate court of the latter county possessed no jurisdiction over his estate. *Note to Karrahoo v. Adams, 1 Dill., 344.*

SEC. 1651. A State court has no jurisdiction over a partition suit in relation to the lands of Shawnee Indians, which have never been conveyed with the approval of the Secretary of the Interior.
Ex parte Forbes and Pucket, 1 Dill., 363.

SEC. 1652. Federal courts can not discharge persons from custody under process for contempt, issued by a State court in the course of a suit pending therein, even though it relates to property of Indians, over which, under special treaties and acts of Congress, such State court has no jurisdiction. *Ibid.*

SEC. 1653. The Wyandotte Council, which is several times referred to in the treaty of 1855 (10 Stat. L., 1159), was an executive and judicial body, and had power, under the laws and usages of the nation, to receive proofs of wills, etc., and this body continued to act, to some extent, after the treaty of 1855. *Gray v. Coffman, 2 Dill., 393.*

SEC. 1654. Relation of the Wyandotte Indians to the civil laws of the Territory of Kansas, in respect to the disposition of property acquired before and after the treaty of 1855, considered. *Ibid.*

SEC. 1655. Passing the question whether it is necessary to valid action by an executor under a will that his appointment should be ratified by some court with probate powers, the only remaining inquiry would be, must Indian wills, after the ratification of the Wyandotte treaty of 1855 (10 Stat. L., 1159) be presented to and allowed by the civil tribunals before acts done thereunder and authorized thereby can be treated as valid. *Ibid.*

SEC. 1656. The laws of the State of Kansas have no application to the mode of alienation of lands granted to the Miami Indians (10 Stat. L., 1093; 11 Stat. L., 430) so long as the title remains in the patentees. The case of the Kansas Indians (5 Wall., 737) applied.
Mungosah v. Steinbrook, 2 Dill., 418.

SEC. 1657. The assignee of the note being within the limits of the Osage Nation, process could not be served on him.

Lemmons v. Choteau, 1 Hemp., 85.

SEC. 1658. In the Osage Nation of Indians there is no mode of coercing the payment of a debt. *Ibid.*

SEC. 1659. J. W. P. Huntington was appointed superintendent of Indian affairs to succeed himself, and at the date of the execution of his second bond there was a balance due the United States of the moneys received by him under his first bond: *Held*, that there could be no presumption that this sum had been illegally appropriated by the officer, but the fact must be proved by the party claiming or alleging it; and that in the absence of such proof the presumption is that this balance was then in the hands of the officer to be applied and accounted for under his second bond. *United States v. Earhart, 4 Sawyer, 245.*

SEC. 1660. The performance of an express contract is not excused by reason of anything accruing after the contract; but in the case of a condition in a bond to do a thing performance is excused when prevented by the law or an overruling necessity.

United States v. Humason, 6 Sawyer, 199.

SEC. 1661. Where an officer is required by his superior, *colore officii*, to give bond, with stipulations or provisions in the condition thereof not required by statute, the bond is void *in toto*. *Ibid.*

SEC. 1662. The defendant having given bond as agent for the Indians in Washington Territory, and having thereupon been assigned to duty on the Umatilla Reservation, Oreg., where he acted as agent for the Indians settled thereon under the treaty of June 9, 1855 (12 Stat. L., 945), the condition of the bond did not include or apply to money or property not received by the obligor as agent of the Indians in Washington Territory; and he was not liable on said bond for money received by him while he was acting as agent for the Indians on the Umatilla Reservation, in Oregon.

United States v. Barnhart, 9 Saw., 159. (Same in Fed. Rep.)

SEC. 1663. The defendant, Sinnott, employed a person on the Grande Ronde Reservation as "superintendent of farms and mills," and in reporting the fact to the Commissioner said that he did so at the instance of "some political friends," but there was really no necessity for the employment, and advised that it be disapproved, which was done; but the agent continued the person in such employment and paid him therefor, and on settlement of his accounts at the Treasury $1,500 thereof was disallowed: *Held*, that the payments not only being made without authority but contrary thereto, were illegal, and the agent and his sureties are liable therefor.

United States v. Sinnott, 1 Saw., 398.

Sec. 1664. The validity and construction of the power of attorney set up by McElrath, and the applicability and construction of the act of Congress July 29, 1846, entitled "An act in relation to the payment of claims," are necessarily involved in the duty required by the Secretary of the Treasury to execute the resolution of March, 1848.

McElrath v. McIntosh, 1 Brunner's Coll. Cases, 559.

Sec. 1665. An indictment for murder in the Indian country was entitled in the caption as follows: "The United States of America, Territory of Dakota, second judicial district, ss.: In the district court in and for the second judicial district and Territory of Dakota, having and exercising the jurisdiction of a United States circuit and district court. United States *v.* Silas Frank Beebe." *Held,* not to show that it was presented to a court not having jurisdiction. A court will take judicial notice of Indian reservations and the leading public proclamations affecting matters relating to its jurisdiction. An indictment charged that "a crime was committed at a place near the Crow Creek Indian Agency, in the Indian country, in a place and district of country under the exclusive jurisdiction of the United States, in the said second judicial district and Territory of Dakota, and within the jurisdiction of this court," sufficiently states the place of the commission of the offense.

Beebe v. United States, 11 N. W. Rep., 505.

Sec. 1666. An offense committed in 1877 in what was then " Indian country" was an offense against the United States, and in 1881 was properly tried in the district court while sitting as and exercising the jurisdiction which pertains to district and circuit courts of the United States.

United States v. Knowlton, 13 Northwestern Reporter, 573.

Sec. 1667. Under the laws of the United States authorizing the condemnation of any boat introducing intoxicating liquor into the Indian country, on a seizure made by the " superintendent of Indian affairs, an Indian agent or subagent, or the commanding officer of a military post," there is no jurisdiction unless the libel shows a seizure by one of the officers; and an amended libel is fatally defective which shows only a seizure by the marshal under a writ based on the original libel.

United States v. The Cora, 46 Northwestern Rep., 503.

Sec. 1668. The district court having on *habeas corpus* remanded a prisoner charged with selling liquor to an Indian, in violation of Revised Statutes United States, section 2139, an appeal lies to the supreme court of the Territory, under Revised Statutes of the United States, section 1869, providing that appeals to that court shall be allowed in all cases under such regulations as may be prescribed by law, and section 1910, providing that in all cases arising under the Constitution and laws of the United States appeals may be had to the supreme court of the Territory, as in other cases.

United States v. Burdick, 46 Northwestern Rep., 571.

SEC. 1669. A trial for homicide in an Indian reservation within a Territory must be had on the Federal side of the Territorial court.

McCall v. United States, 46 Northwestern Rep., 608.

SEC. 1670. Where an Indian belonged to a tribe which is recognized and treated with by the Government, having its chief and tribal laws, kills another of the same tribe, both parties being under the authority and subjection of such tribal laws, the courts of this State, under its general criminal laws, have no jurisdiction of the offense, nor can they have without an affirmative act of the legislature or a self-acting clause in the Constitution.

Nevada, being admitted as a State, on an equal footing in all respects with the other States, the United States courts would have no jurisdiction of the crime, and since our organic act provides that the rights of persons or property now pertaining to the Indians shall not be impaired, so long as they remain unextinguished by treaty between the United States and such Indians, it follows that the authorities of the tribe alone have the right to take cognizance of the crime.

State v. McKenney, 2 Pa. Rep., 171.

SEC. 1671. When both defendant, in a prosecution under an indictment for murder, and the deceased are full-blood Indians, but it does not appear that defendant is a member of any tribe of Indians having its chief or tribal laws, nor that his ancestral tribe had been treated with by the Government, but it does appear that he had lived among the whites several years, the State courts of California have jurisdiction to punish him for the crime.   *People v. Ketchem, 15 Pa. Rep., 353.*

SEC. 1672. A will properly admitted to probate can not be rejected as evidence in a suit between an Indian and white man merely because the will had been proved by the testimony of an Indian witness, it appearing that at the time the will was proved all who were entitled to objections against the will were Indians.

Carroll v. Pathkiller, 3 Porter (Ala.), 279.

SEC. 1673. A grant for lands from certain persons of the Creek tribe of Indians, to whom the chiefs and head men had assigned the same in pursuance of the treaty of the 24th of March, 1832, will not support an action of ejectment, the patent for the same not having issued until after suit commenced.

Fipps v. M' Gehee et al., Porter (Ala.), vol. 5, p. 413.

SEC. 1674. The exception in the statute of limitations that where a debtor is absent from the State at the time the cause of the action accrues suit may be brought "after his return into the State" means after his return within the jurisdiction of the State, where the process of the courts of the State will run. A removal to the Indian nation, where the process of the courts of the State did not run, is not a return within the State, though within its territorial limits.

Smith, Admr., v. The Heirs of Bond (Ala.), vol. 8, p. 386.

SEC. 1675. The decision of the land officers in rejecting the claim of the complainant is that of a legally competent, although special, tribunal, and he can not assail the adjudication on any other ground than a want of power in the officers, or fraud in the defendants, or those under whom they claim, touching the decision.

Cunningham v. Ashley & Beebe, 12 Ark., 296.

SEC. 1676. The courts of this State (Arkansas) will not presume that the common law is in force in the Indian Territory, where no system of laws has been adopted.   *Garner v. Wright, 52 Ark., 385.*

SEC. 1677. When the aid of Arkansas courts is invoked as to a right accruing in the Indian Territory, in the absence of evidence showing the laws in force there, the laws of the State will be applied.   *Ibid.*

SEC. 1678. In an action for an injury to a bystander, caused by blasting rock without warning, the cause of action accrues in this State if the injury occurred here, although the rock was set in motion in the Indian Territory.   *Cameron v. Vandergriff, 53 Ark., 381.*

SEC. 1679. The State is not liable to pay interest upon matured coupons of the Indian war bonds issued under the act of 1851.

Molineux v. State of California, 109 Cal., 378.

SEC. 1680. Scott applied for and obtained a writ of *habeas corpus*, directed to United States marshal, to inquire into the cause of his imprisonment in the United States jail, etc. Upon the return of the writ, and it appearing that the relator was held by the marshal by virtue of a warrant of commitment, issued by a United States commissioner, dated July 8, 1875 (on a charge of giving, bartering, and selling spirituous liquors to an Indian in Yankton, Yankton County, Dak. T., said Indian belonging to the Yankton Indian Reservation and being under the charge of an Indian agent), the United States district attorney suggested to the court that heretofore, to wit, on the 10th of July, 1875, in the district court in and for the second judicial district, upon petition of the same party, and upon similar allegations, and in relation to the same charge and subject-matter, under the same facts and conditions, that court had granted a writ of *habeas corpus* directed to the same officer, upon which the same return as now was made; and that, therefore, in said court, after due hearing and consideration, a final decision or judgment was duly rendered. *Held,* that under the *habeas corpus* act district courts have original concurrent jurisdiction with the supreme court, and their judgments are subject to review as in other cases. After the writ has once been sued out before the supreme or district court, or a judge thereof, and an adjudication had thereof, the principal of *resadjudicator* is applicable, and until that judgment is reversed, the facts and conditions remaining the same, a writ subsequently issued must be abated.

Ex parte Scott, 1 Dakota (Bennett), 140.

SEC. 1681. A trial for homicide committed on an Indian reservation must be had on the Federal side of a Territorial court, and is governed by the United States statutes and the rules of the common law.

McCall v. The United States, 1 Dakota (Bennett), 322.

SEC. 1682. The mere consent of the parties can not confer jurisdiction, unless in a very few special instances. The appellate powers of the supreme court are fixed by law, and can be exercised only in the modes and channels prescribed by the codes. A stipulation of parties as to testimony adduced on the trial below, in the absence of a case made or exceptions settled, will not authorize the appellate court to receive and review *de novo* such uncertified evidence.

Gress v. Evans et al., 1 Dakota (Bennett), 387.

SEC. 1683. The findings of the lower court were that "the land in controversy was entered by what is known as Indian half-breed scrip, in the name of Jane Titus, at the Vermilion land office, in December, 1863, and a patent issued therefor by the United States Government bearing date February 1, 1868, which was filed for record in the office of the register of deeds of Minnehaha County, Dak. T., May 14, 1872. Plaintiff claims under deed, quitclaim in form, executed by Moses S. Titus and Jane Titus, his wife, to Byron M. Smith, dated March 21, 1869, filed for record in Minnehaha County May 14, 1872; and deed from Byron M. Smith and wife to plaintiff, dated April 7, 1870, and filed for record in Minnehaha County, May, 1875. Defendants claim title under two certain deeds, executed by Jane Titus and Moses S. Titus, her husband, in form quitclaim, with special covenants, one dated May 17, 1871, and filed for record May 23, 1871, and the other bearing date August 11, 1871, and filed for record September 18, 1871; and deed from defendant Evans to defendant Burbank, warranty, for the north half of said tract, executed September 2, 1871, and filed for record in Minnehaha County, October 4, 1871. The trial court found for the plaintiff. To this decision is appended the following general exceptions, to wit: "To which finding of facts, conclusions of law, and order of court, the defendants except." Upon appeal it was held that "under the provisions of the code of civil procedure, all distinctions between actions at law and suits in equity and the forms of all such actions and suits have been abolished, and a uniform course of proceeding established."

Ibid.

SEC. 1684. The boundaries of the Territory, its divisions into judicial districts, the limits of such divisions, leading places and geographical features of the land within such limits, leading cities, villages and public places therein, Indian reservations, leading public proclamations affecting matters relative to their jurisdiction, embracing executive decrees, orders, and ordinances of state, are matters of which the courts will take judicial cognizance, and when published in authentic public documents they need not be proved.

United States v. Beebe, 2 Smith (Dakota), 203.

SEC. 1685. The court will take judicial cognizance of the external boundary lines of its jurisdiction, and that a crime committed at a place on an Indian reservation within such boundary lines is within the jurisdiction of the court.   *United States v. Brave Bear, 3 Smith (Dakota), 34.*

SEC. 1686. The revocation of the executive order creating such reservation (an addition to the Sioux Indian Reservation) after the commission of a homicide and before the indictment has been found, does not deprive the court of jurisdiction to indict and try the defendant for such offense.   *Ibid.*

SEC. 1687. In this case the indictment was found in April, 1877, after the proclamation of President Grant of January 11, 1875, and prior to the proclamation of President Hayes of August 9, 1879, which was issued abrogating the proclamation first issued, and restoring the Territory, including the place of the alleged homicide, to the public domain; hence the two proclamations left the *locus in quo* at the time the jury found the bill, in the same condition as if no proclamation had been issued.   *Ibid.*

SEC. 1688. The executive order of January 11, 1875, withdrew the portion of the public domain embraced in the Sioux Reservation from the operation of the criminal laws of the Territory; the trade and intercourse laws were thereby extended over such district of country within the meaning of the acts of Congress extending the crimes act to the Indian country.   *United States v. Knowlton, 3 Smith (Dakota), 59.*

SEC. 1689. The claim of J. to the fund in controversy, as shown by the proceedings in the case, arises thus: He was employed, as he says himself, by Ewing and Adams to assist them in the prosecution of the case of Gerry, who had a claim against the United States for Indian depredations, and for his services in that behalf he was to have a portion of their fee. It is contended that Jackson has a lien upon Adam's share of the fee, and the theory of Jackson seems to be that, notwithstanding the fact that Adams has assigned this interest of his, the lien follows the fund, and the assignee takes it *cum onere*. *Held*, that upon a bill of interpleader where the fund in dispute has been assigned and had been collected by the complainants upon a draft in favor of the assignee, and on his account, it was held that he was entitled to the money against his codefendant, who claimed it upon the ground that he had an attorney's lien upon the fund.

Adams Express Co. v. Adams et al., 1 MacArthur (D. C.), 642.

SEC. 1690. The Iowa territorial district courts were not of inferior jurisdiction. Their jurisdiction in suit to partition the half-breed lands is affirmed. They were invested with the same jurisdiction of a federal character as the circuit and district courts of the United States and also the general common law jurisdiction usually imparted to State courts of record. The territorial district courts, independent of the partition act, had general jurisdiction of the partition proceedings both in law and equity.

Wright v. Marsh, Lee & Delavan. 2 Greene (Iowa), 94. (May, 1849.)

SEC. 1691. The fact that the property was not within the jurisdiction of the court (it being located on the Nez Percé Indian Reservation) constitutes no bar in a court of equity if the person is within the jurisdiction, for a court of equity acts upon the person.

Gamble v. Dunwell et al., 1 Prickett (Idaho), 271.

SEC. 1692. A district court has jurisdiction over Indian reservations in any organized county of this Territory, and its process may run and be served there if there be no treaty to the contrary with the Indians thereof.

Hyde v. Harkness, 1 Prickett (Idaho), 536.

SEC. 1693. Claims on account held against Pottawatomie, Ottawa, and Chippewa tribes in 1847, and which were expected to be paid by the Government of the United States, were assignable in equity so as to enable the assignee, who was the real party in interest, to maintain suits thereon in his own name.   Coquillard's Admr's v. French, 19 Ind., 274.

SEC. 1694. Where an application has been made to and refused by a board of commissioners under the provisions of the act of March 2, 1853 (1 G. & H., 110), for the refunding of taxes illegally assessed and collected, the remedy of the applicant is by appeal to the circuit court and not by mandate.

The State ex rel Godfroy v. The Board of Commissioners of Miami County, 63 Ind., 497.

SEC. 1695. In an action by one Shawnee Indian against another for partition of land which had been patented by the United States to an ancestor, another Shawnee, the record failing to set out the patent or to show under what treaty it was issued, Held, That the court can not presume that it contained restrictions. Also, that the fact that the parties are Shawnees did not deprive the district court nor does it forbid the supreme court from exercising jurisdiction either as to parties or subject-matter.   Swartzel v. Rogers, 3 Kans., 374.

SEC. 1696. John Rubideaux, a Miami Indian chief, bought a piece of land in Miami County, Kans., from Jack Vallie, and in consideration therefor gave a promissory note. After maturity of the note Vallie sued Rubideaux thereon in the district court of Miami County. Held, That said court had jurisdiction to hear and determine the case.

Rubideaux v. Vallie, 12 Kans., 28.

SEC. 1697. Where George set up a claim to certain lands under the Cherokee treaty of July 19, 1866 (14 Stat. L., 799), which he alleges have been awarded and patented to Phillips under article 19 of said treaty upon false testimony, and through bribery and corruption of officials of the United States, the former may come into the courts of the State and litigate the claim, and, upon the proper showing, a patent obtained thus fraudulently by Phillips will inure to George, if George be entitled to recover the lands. *Phillips v. George, 17 Kans., 419.*

SEC. 1698. Plaintiff was injured on defendant's railroad in the Indian Territory while performing his duties as brakeman theron. Objection can not be sustained that the place of injury being the Indian Territory there is no allegation that either plaintiff or defendant had license or legal authority to enter that Territory or engage in the running of trains through it, or that there was any law in force within its limits either giving a cause of action for such wrong, or furnishing a remedy therefor. *Speer v. M., K. and T. Ry. Co., 23 Kans., 571.*

SEC. 1699. Neither the defendants nor the commissioners of Wyandotte County could open or construct a public highway parallel with the track of the railway on the right of way granted by Congress. (See Pierce on Railroads, p. 155; Mills on Eminent Domain, sec. 46.) *U. P. Ry. Co. v. Kindred, 43 Kans., 134.*

SEC. 1700. An action for the conversion of certain corn grown and standing upon land in the Indian Territory, leased in violation of law and the treaty of 1866 with the Cherokees (14 Stat. L., 799), brought by a citizen of Kansas against a person residing in said Territory, but personally served with summons, can not be maintained in Kansas. *Holderman v. Pond, 45 Kans., 411.*

SEC. 1701. Section 2103 of the Revised Statutes of the United States makes void all contracts for leasing land in the Indian country unless executed in the manner therein provided and approved by the Secretary of the Interior. The lease between Pond and Holderman was in violation of this law, and conferred no rights upon Pond to cultivate the land; he was there without authority. *Ibid.*

SEC. 1702. As the plaintiff below had no permit or license to lease the land where the corn was raised, and there being grave doubts as to whether he had any right to recover for the alleged conversion of this property in the Indian Territory, where the tort was committed, and if such right did exist, the jurisdiction was vested in another court, it follows that the court below had no jurisdiction. *Ibid.*

SEC. 1703. The courts of Kansas have been open to Shawnee Indians for the division of lands inherited from allottees, and where partition is so made, and the Secretary of the Interior recognizes the proceedings as legal and approves a deed based thereon, the conveyance is valid. *Ingraham v. Ward, 56 Kans., 550.*

SEC. 1704. There being no provision in any treaty with the Delaware Indians to the contrary, the lands of that tribe within the boundaries of Kansas are included within its limits and jurisdiction. *McCracken v. Todd, 1 Banks & McCahon, 146.*

SEC. 1705. The provisions of the Delaware treaties and of the act of March 3, 1807 (2 Stat. L., 445), prohibit only *settlement* or *survey*, and not the passage to and fro by any person over these lands, nor do they prohibit the government, whether of the territory or of any of its political subdivisions, from establishing its offices, holding its courts, and issuing and executing its processes at any place upon them.   *McCracken v. Todd, 1 Banks & McCahon, 146.*

SEC. 1706. An attorney at law who attends a board of commissioners and obtains the confirmation of the title to a valuable tract of land, may receive a part of the land in payment of his services without incurring the penalty of the law prohibiting attorneys from making bargains with their clients for a share of the property gained in a suit or depending on its result.   *Brent v. Reeves et al., 2 Morgan (La.), 4.*

SEC. 1707. The Spanish law provides that whether the party evicted possessed in good or bad faith, he was not bound to deliver up the premises to the owner until he shall have been paid for the expense incurred on account of them.

So the possessor in bad faith may claim in offset of rents or fruits, which he is condemned to pay, the enhanced value which his improvements added to the property.   *Pearce et al. v. Frantum, 8 Morgan (La.), 649.*

SEC. 1708. When the intention of the parties to a contract is doubtful, under section 1951 of the civil code (Louisiana), the court will inquire into the whole conduct of the parties in relation thereto.   *Wells v. Compton, 3 Robinson (La.), 183.*

SEC. 1709. The statements of witnesses taken down in a suit by a different plaintiff, but to which the defendant was a party, can not as a general rule be received in evidence against the latter. *Aliter*, when the testimony of a witness so taken down is offered to discredit the evidence subsequently given by him, or when the declarations of a deceased surveyor are offered to explain his operations.   *Ibid.*

SEC. 1710. Parish surveyors are regularly appointed officers known to the law, and when dead their declarations taken in other suits may be used, when necessary, as evidence to explain their acts. So plats made by a parish surveyor under orders of court, in a suit to which defendant was a party, are admissible after the decease of the surveyor to prove the declarations of the defendant made at the time of the survey.   *Ibid.*

SEC. 1711. The official acts and certificates of parish surveyors are entitled to full faith and credit in all of the courts of Louisiana.
                                                          Ibid.

SEC. 1712. The *process verbal* of a survey made by a parish surveyor is legal evidence of the acts which it recites, as that notice was given, that the parties attended, etc.   *Ibid.*

Sec. 1713. This may well be understood to have been so expressed in consequence of the previous understanding between the agent and the plaintiff. By the written agreement referred to, a specific portion of the grass, by a description·well understood, is set apart for his benefit. It is equivalent to a declaration of trust in his favor. The plaintiff, however, was to pay a reasonable compensation to Dudley. This was offered by the plaintiff, but Dudley refused to receive it.

Boies v. Black, 13 Maine, 381.

Sec. 1714. General hearsay and public reputation are inadmissible to prove which of two persons claiming by the same name a particular reservation made by the treaty of Saginaw of September 24, 1819, was the person intended. *Campau v. Dewey, 9 Mich. (5 Cooley), 381.*

Sec. 1715. Where a county receives into its treasury taxes illegally assessed an action will lie against it to recover them back.

Foster v. Commissioners of Blue Earth County, 7 Minn. (Gilfillan), 84 (7 Minn. R., 140).

Sec. 1716. There is nothing in the nature of the claims of the parties litigant, or in the source from which they are derived, which confers exclusive jurisdiction on the Federal courts. The twenty-fifth section of the judiciary act of 1789 furnishes a legislative exposition of the second section of the third article of the Constitution directly opposed to proposition that the State court has no jurisdiction.

Land v. Land, 1 S. & M. Chancery (Miss.), 158.

Sec. 1717. The judiciary act provides that the judgments of the highest court of a State in which was drawn in question the construction of any clause of a treaty where the decision is against the title of either party set up under the treaty, such decision may be reexamined, reversed, or reaffirmed by the Supreme Court of the United States.

Ibid.

Sec. 1718. The fact that both parties to a suit in chancery in a State court claim the land in controversy under a treaty to which the United States is a party has in itself nothing to exclude the jurisdiction of the State court. *Ibid.*

Sec. 1719. A party can not trade with Indians in the Indian country under a license which has not been approved by the Commissioner of Indian Affairs.

A license to trade with Indians in the Indian country is a personal privilege to the person therein named, and can not be transferred to other parties.

The organic act creating the Territory of Montana does not repeal the law of the United States which requires persons to obtain a license to trade with the Indians in the Indian country. Goods were legally seized and forfeited under the laws of the United States which were traded for in the Indian country in Choteau County, Mont., by persons without a license therefor from the United States.

United States v. Buffalo Robes, 1 Mon., 487.

SEC. 1720. Where an indictment charged that three persons—an Indian agent, his clerk, and a trader—conspired and agreed together to procure the goods of the United States to be disposed of fraudulently for money, and thereby intended to cheat and defraud the United States, it is held that the indictment is good.

Upon the trial of said persons under said indictment it appeared that said goods had been deposited with said Indian agent for distribution to the Indians. *Held*, that the Government could prove that the Indians had not received the goods. There is no statute of the United States under which an Indian agent can be indicted for embezzlement.

United States v. Upham, 2 Mon., 170.

SEC. 1721. A writ of *habeas corpus* will not lie in favor of an Indian agent to recover the custody of Indian children taken from an agency school by a Catholic priest, it not appearing to have been done against the consent of the parents of such children. Neither by treaty nor statute have the Indians surrendered to the United States the right to compel their children to attend school, nor has the United States assumed to possess or exercise such right. If the Indians fail in their treaty engagements in this respect, neither treaty nor statute provides a penalty, nor does the right of compulsion pass to the United States or its agents. It must be exercised by the parents of such children or the tribe to which they belong. *United States ex rel. Young v. Imoda, 4 Mon., 38.*

SEC. 1722. Section 160, division 4, Compiled Statutes, prohibiting the sale of liquors to Indians, is an act within the police power of the Territorial government, and is not inconsistent with the clause of the Constitution granting to Congress the power to regulate commerce with the Indian tribes, nor with the laws of the United States framed thereunder. *Territory v. Guyott, 9 Mont., 46.*

SEC. 1723. If all persons, without regard to nationality, are in this country allowed to maintain an action to enforce their rights to the enjoyment of all property, personal or real, there is no reason why an Indian who has appropriated water on the public lands of the United States may not maintain an action for the diversion of that water as well as any other person. *Lobdell v. Hall, 3 Nev., 507.*

SEC. 1724. If an Indian could maintain an action for diversion of water, then he certainly would have a fixed interest in the water so diverted and a clear right to repair any temporary damage in his ditch or dam. *Ibid.*

SEC. 1725. The State of Tennessee was admitted into the Union in 1796 "on an equal footing with the original States in all respects whatsoever." In 1833 the legislature extended the civil jurisdiction of several counties to include the territory within the occupancy of the Cherokee Indians. The statute also gave the courts jurisdiction of three crimes committed within the Indian country—murder, rape, and larceny—but allowed to the Indians their usages and customs in all other respects.   *State v. McKenney, 18 Nev., 182.*

SEC. 1726. The act of March 31, 1821, respecting intrusion on Indian lands is not unconstitutional, and the legislature, in prohibiting by said act intrusions upon "lands belonging to or occupied by any nation or tribe of Indians," referred to the tracts of land in different parts of the State which the Indians, in their various cessions, still retained and which were known as reservations.   Where it is admitted in proceedings before a county judge under that act that the persons proceeded against have settled and reside upon land that was a reservation belonging to the Seneca Nation of Indians, and that such persons are of a class to which the prohibition in the act applies, this is sufficiently *prima facie* to give the judge jurisdiction.   If Indians have parted with the title to any of their lands and surrendered the possession to the purchaser or ceased to occupy such lands, the purchasers may enter and they will not be subject to provisions of said act.   But where Indians have always steadily resisted any sale and have denied the binding obligation of any treaty and grant as to the reservation occupied by them, and they still occupy the same under a claim of right, they are entitled to the protection of the act of 1821.

People v. Dibble, 18 Barbour (N. Y.), 412.

SEC. 1727. In June, 1873, certain Indians, members of the Seneca Nation and tribe, were residing upon the Cattaraugus Reservation, in occupation of certain lands thereon inclosed by fences.   Said Indians, each for his own benefit, sold to defendant trees and timber on said land, for which the defendant paid to each Indian full value in money, and afterwards cut and carried away the cordwood, etc.   It was held that under the laws of the State relative to this reservation the acts of the defendant in cutting and removing the timber from the reservation was illegal.   (Chap. 365 of 1847, sec. 20; chap. 294 of 1859; chap. 455 of 1873.)   *Seneca Nation of Indians v. Hammond, 4 Hun. (N. Y.), 417.*

SEC. 1728. Upon an appeal from an order setting aside an execution against property, issued upon a judgment against the plaintiff for costs in favor of the defendant, a railroad company, it appeared that the plaintiff was a Seneca Indian, living and residing with his tribe in this State on the Allegany Reservation, and that the action was in trespass to recover damages for the killing of plaintiff's horse, on the line of the defendant's road, in consequence of the omission of 'the defendant to construct and maintain fences and cattle guards as required by the statutes.   The attorney, appointed by the State for the Seneca Nation of Indians, prosecuted the action in behalf of the plaintiff, and was directed to do so by a resolution of the council, which is the governing body of the Seneca Nation.   Upon the trial of the action the plaintiff was nonsuited.   *Held*, that the provisions contained in chapter 150 of the laws of 1845, which prohibits the issue of an execution to collect a judgment against a Seneca Indian, rendered for costs only, and provides for the payment of such judgment by the State treasurer out of the annuity in his hands belonging to the Seneca Nation, did not apply to this action and prevent the collection of a judgment recovered against an individual Indian out of his individual property, and that the order shall be reversed.

Crouse v. N. Y., Penn. & Ohio R. R. Co., 49 Hun. (N. Y.), 576.

SEC. 1729. An Indian of the Seneca tribe or nation bought a sewing machine under a lease, or by a conditional sale, which provided that, until payment, the title should remain in the vendor. The vendee having failed to make full payment, the vendor demanded the amount due, which was not paid, and therefore demanded the machine, which demand was refused. The vendor then brought an action of replevin to recover the machine. It is forbidden by chapter 92, laws of 1813 (2 R. L., 153, sec. 2), to sue or maintain any action upon a contract against any of the Indians of the Seneca tribe or nation.

Held, that the right of action arose upon the demand and wrongful refusal of the defendant to give up the machine; that, consequently, the action was not on contract, but was one sounding in tort.

Singer Man'f'g Co. v. Hill, 60 Hun. (N. Y.), 347.

SEC. 1730. The act of 1827, chapter 39 (Tennessee), which directed the dismissal of a certain class of suits growing out of the reservations of land to the heads of Indian families under the Cherokee treaties of 1817 and 1819 (7 Stat. L., 156 and 195) upon a certain state of facts being made to appear, is partial, and therefore unconstitutional.

Wally v. Kennedy, 2 Yerger, 554.

SEC. 1731. The act was intended to drive from the courts a few odious persons, who it was supposed had speculated upon the ignorance and necessities of the Indian reservees, and fraudulently obtained their claims for trifling considerations. This part of the act was unconstitutional and void.   *Ibid.*

SEC. 1732. The plaintiff seeks damages for injury to certain real property in the Choctaw Nation of the Indian Territory. Plaintiff's rights grow out of the fact that he had acquired by marriage with an Indian woman membership in the said Choctaw Nation. Plaintiff resides in said nation, and defendant is a Missouri corporation having an office and agent in the county where the suit was brought. *Held*, that the complicated condition of the treaties and statutes of the United States relating to the tribes in the Indian Territory, their rights and manner of enforcing them, offered good reason for the Texas courts to refuse to entertain this action.   *Morris v. M. P. Ry. Co., 78 Texas, 17.*

SEC. 1733. The Missouri Pacific Railway Company, though resident of Missouri, transacts business in Texas and where it has business offices and agents. It is subject to the local jurisdiction of the courts of this State.

An action for injuries done to land situated beyond the limits of this State, and where no part of the injury was committed or performed within the State, is purely local and can not be maintained in any court in this State, but the remedy must be had in the jurisdiction where the land is situated.   *Missouri Pacific Ry. Co. v. Cullers, 81; Texas, 382.*

SEC. 1734. Action for damages for the destruction by fire (by negligence of the defendant) of certain property, including "house, kitchen, and stables" erected upon land not owned by plaintiff. It was not alleged that the *house*, etc., were personal property, or that the plaintiff or the party under whom he sued had the right to move them, nor any other fact showing ownership apart from the land, the land belonging to an Indian tribe in the Indian Territory. *Held*, that the issue of whether the *house*, etc., was part of the realty should have been submitted as a defense. The law presumes that structures belong to the land and are part of the realty.

Ibid.

ARTICLE II.—LAND TITLES AND TREATIES.

CHAPTER I.—TENURE AND TITLES GENERALLY.

SEC. 1735. The nature of the Indian title is not such as to be absolutely repugnant to seizin in fee on the part of the State.

> *Fletcher v. Peck*,[1] *6 Cranch, 142. Johnson v. McIntosh, 8 Wheat., 543.*

SEC. 1736. The Indian title is certainly to be respected by all courts until it be legitimately extinguished.   *Ibid.*

SEC. 1737. The claim of the Government to lands of the Indian tribes extends to the complete ultimate title, charged with their right of possession, and to the exclusive power of acquiring that right.

> *Ibid.   Holden v. Joy, 17 Wall, 211.   Beecher v. Wetherby, 95 U. S., 517.*

---

[1] NOTE.—Fletcher *v.* Peck was the first case brought before the Supreme Court of the United States in which was involved the aboriginal rights of the Indians in the lands occupied and roamed over by them.   The conclusion of a majority of the court was that the Indian right was that of occupancy only, but a right to be respected by the courts until extinguished in a lawful manner; but Mr. Justice Johnson delivered a very strong dissenting opinion on this point in which he very ably contended that the Indian title amounted to a fee because it was a right of use and occupancy limited to the Indians and their heirs forever, and while a fee-simple interest might be held in reversion our law will not admit of the idea of its being limited after a fee simple. Therefore it would appear that the interest of the State of Georgia in the lands of the Indians located in the western part of that State amounted to nothing more than a mere possibility, and that a conveyance of the State, instead of carrying the fee subject to the Indian right of occupancy, could operate legally only as a covenant to convey or to stand seized to a use.   By perusal of the opinion of the court in this case and noting the effect of the decision (especially as more clearly stated in later cases) on the rights of Indians in their lands, in connection with the position taken by Mr. Johnson, it will be readily seen how vastly important was the question before the court and how far-reaching was its opinion.

SEC. 1738. The recognition of the right of the Indians to the soil contained in the memorial from the cabinet of London to that of Versailles, during the controversy between the two nations respecting boundary, which took place in 1775, was made with reference to their character as Indians, and for the purpose of showing that they were fixed to a particular territory, and sustaining the claim of Great Britain to dominion over them.   *Johnson v. McIntosh, 8 Wheat., 543.*

SEC. 1739. It has never been contended that the Indian title amounted to nothing, and their right of possession has never been questioned.
                                                                    Ibid.

SEC. 1740. Admitting the power of Indian tribes to change their laws or usages, so far as to allow an individual to separate a portion of their lands from the common stock and hold it in severalty, still it is a part of their territory, and is held under them by a title dependent on their laws. The grant derives its efficacy from their will, and if they choose to resume it and make a different disposition of the land the courts of the United States can not interpose for the protection of the title.   *Ibid.*

SEC. 1741. The person who purchases lands from the Indians, within their territory, incorporates himself with them, so far as respects the property purchased, holds *their* title under their protection and subject to their laws. If they annul the grant, there is no tribunal which can revise and set aside the proceeding, there being no principle upon which such a case can be distinguished from grants made to a native Indian, authorizing him to hold a particular tract of land in severalty, and such a grant could not separate the Indian from his nation, nor give a title which our courts could distinguish from the title of his tribe, as it still might be conquered from or ceded by his tribe; no legal principle can be perceived which will authorize a court to say that different consequences are attached to a purchase by a stranger because it was made by such.   *Ibid.*

SEC. 1742. The first act to which our attention is called is that by which Georgia ceded her western territory to the United States. That act provides "that all persons who, on the 27th day of October, 1795, were actual settlers within the territory thus ceded shall be confirmed in all grants legally and fully executed prior to that day by the former British Government of west Florida, or by the Government of Spain." On the 3d of March, 1803 (2 Stat. L., 229), Congress passed "An act regulating the grants of land, and provided for the disposal of the lands of the United States south of the State of Tennessee." The first section exacts that any person or persons " who were resident in the Mississippi territory on the 27th day of October, 1795, and who had, prior to that day, obtained, either from the British Government of west Florida or from the Spanish Government, any warrant or order of survey for lands lying within the said territory, to which the

Indian title had been extinguished, and which were on that day actually inhabited and cultivated by such person or persons, or for his or their use, shall be confirmed in their claims to such lands in the same manner as if their titles had been completed." This section places those persons who had obtained a warrant or order of survey on October 27, 1795, on equal ground with those whose titles were completed, provided the Indian title was extinguished, and provided also the land claimed was actually inhabited and cultivated either by the person claiming title or by some other for his use.

Henderson v. Poindexter, 12 Wheat., 535.

SEC. 1743. No Spanish grant made while the country was wrongfully occupied by Spain can be valid, unless it was confirmed by the compact between the United States and the State of Georgia of the 24th of April, 1802, or had been laid before the board of commissioners constituted by the act of Congress of 3d March, 1803, chapter 340, and of March 27, 1804, chapter 414. *Ibid.*

SEC. 1744. The Indians are acknowledged to have an unquestionable, and heretofore an unquestioned, right to the lands they occupy until that right shall be extinguished by a voluntary cession to our Government. They occupy territory to which we assert a title independent of their will, which must take effect, in point of possession, when their right of possession ceases.

Cherokee Nation v. Georgia, 5 Pets., 1.

SEC. 1745. By the compact made with the State of Georgia April 24, 1802, the United States engaged to extinguish, for the use of Georgia, *as early as the same could be peaceably obtained on reasonable terms,* the Indian title to the country of Talassee, and to all the other lands within the State of Georgia; and the United States ceded to Georgia all the claim to the jurisdiction and soil of any lands within the chartered limits of Georgia and east of the line between Alabama and Georgia. This compact could not impair the national character or rights of the Cherokees, who were not parties to it, nor oblige them to part with any portion of their territory without their free and fair consent. *Cherokee Nation v. Georgia (Opinion) Appendix 1, "Peters Cherokee Case," 225.*

SEC. 1746. The Indians are acknowledged to have an unquestionable, and heretofore an unquestioned, right to the lands they occupy until that right shall be extinguished by a voluntary cession to our Government. It may well be doubted whether those tribes which reside within the acknowledged boundaries of the United States can, with strict accuracy, be denominated foreign nations. They may more correctly perhaps be denominated domestic dependent nations. They occupy a territory to which we assert a title independent of their will, which must take effect in point of possession when their right of possession ceases; meanwhile they are in a state of pupilage. Their relations to the United States resemble that of a ward to his guardian. *Ibid.*

SEC. 1747. The territory and sovereignty of the Cherokees have been transmitted to them from their ancestors. They have been in the enjoyment of both from the first settlement of Georgia, with the approbation of the whites, and without any known conflicting claim against them. No better right or title to the territory can exist, either by the law of nature or nations. They have never been conquered.   *Ibid.*

SEC. 1748. The chartered limit of a State gave only a right of pre-emption of the soil after the Indian title had been fairly extinguished, with the consent of the tribe given in a national capacity and nego-tiated under the authority of the United States. The chartered limit and claim were subordinate to the Indian title and sovereignty, and conferred no jurisdiction repugnant thereto.   *Ibid.*

SEC. 1749. As between the Crown and subjects, before the Revolu-tion, and as between the State and its citizens, since our independence, the theory is different so far as that the *seizin* of the Government, under its national boundary or charter limits, can not be drawn in ques-tion. But this fiction of law and this seizin have never been put for-ward (except by Georgia) to any Indian nation, as giving any right or title to their territory, *other than the right of preemption as against other civilized nations.*   *Ibid.*

SEC. 1750. The bill filed on behalf of the Cherokees seeks to restrain a State from forcible exercise of legislative power over a neighbor-ing people asserting their independence, their right to which the State denies. On several of the matters alleged in the bill—for example, on the laws making it criminal to exercise the usual power of self-government in their own country by the Cherokee Nation—this court can not interpose, at least in the form in which those matters are presented. That part of the bill which respects the land occupied by the Indians may be more doubtful. The mere question of right might perhaps be decided by this court, in a proper case, with proper parties; but the court is asked to do more than decide on the title. The bill requires us to control the legislature of Georgia and to restrain the exercise of its physical force. The propriety of such an interpo-sition by the court may well be questioned. It savors too much of the exercise of political power to be within the proper province of the judicial department.   *Ibid.*

SEC. 1751. In 1776 Congress admonished the Indians that "their safety as nations depended on their preserving peace and friendship with the white people of this land;" they declare that they will take all the care in their power that no interruption or disturbance be given to their security and settlement, and that none of the white people should be "suffered by force or fraud to deprive them of any of their land, or to settle them without a fair purchase and their free consent."

Congress in particular guaranteed to the Delawares all their territorial rights in the most ample manner as bounded by former treaties.   *Ibid.*

SEC. 1752. Various acts of the legislature of Georgia furnish conclusive evidence that her former opinion as to the right of the Indians to the lands they occupied concurred with those entertained by the other States and the Government of the United States; that their territory was separate from that of any State within whose chartered limits they might reside by a boundary line established by treaties; that within their boundary they possessed rights with which no State could interfere, and that the whole power regulating intercourse with them was vested in the United States.

Worcester v. Georgia, 6 Pet., 515.

SEC. 1753. All the rights which belong to self-government have been recognized as vested in the Indian nations. Their right of occupancy has never been questioned, but the fee in the soil has been considered in the Government. This may be called the right to the ultimate domain, but the Indians have a present right of possession.

Ibid.

SEC. 1754. The stipulation found generally in Indian treaties by which the Indians acknowledge themselves to be under the protection of the United States and of no other power involved practically no claim to their lands, no dominion over their persons; it merely bound the nation to the Government as a dependent ally, claiming the protection of a powerful friend and neighbor and receiving the advantages of that protection without involving a surrender of their national character. Protection does not imply the destruction of the protected.

Ibid.

SEC. 1755. The royal proclamation of 1763 given at Paris contains the following:

And we do further declare it to be our royal will and pleasure for the present, as aforesaid, to reserve under our sovereignty, protection, and dominion, for the use of said Indians, all the lands and territories lying to the westward of the sources of the rivers which fall into the sea from the west and northwest, as aforesaid; and we do hereby strictly forbid, on pain of our displeasure, all our loving subjects from making any purchases or settlements whatever or taking possession of any of the lands above reserved without our special leave and license for that purpose first obtained, and we do further strictly enjoin and require all persons whatever who have either willfully or inadvertently seated themselves upon any lands within the countries above described, or upon any other lands which, not having been ceded to or purchased by us, are still reserved to the said Indians, as aforesaid.   *Ibid.*

SEC. 1756. At the commencement of the war of the Revolution it was to be expected, on account of Great Britain's policy toward the Indian nation, recognizing their title to the lands they occupied and had not ceded their right of self-government, that as her allies they would add the force of their arms to hers. The early journals of Congress, therefore, exhibit a most anxious desire to conciliate the

Indians.   Far from advancing a claim to their lands or asserting any right of dominion over them, Congress resolved "that the securing and preserving the friendship of the Indians appears to be a subject of the utmost moment to these colonies."   *Ibid.*

SEC. 1757. In Florida, under Spanish law, the fact of the abandonment by the Indians of their lands was an important one to be ascertained.   If voluntary, the dominion of the Crown over it was unimpaired in its plenitude; if by force, the Indians had the right, whenever they had the power or inclination, to return.

United States v. Arredondo, 6 Pets., 691.

SEC. 1758. It was a universal rule that purchases made at Indian treaties, in the presence and with the approbation of the officer under whose direction they were held by authority of the Crown, gave a valid title to the lands.   It prevailed under the laws of the States after the Revolution, and yet continues in those where the right to the ultimate fee is owned by the States or their grantees.   It has been adopted by the United States, and purchases made at treaties held by their authority have been always held good by the ratification of the treaty, without any patent to the purchasers from the United States.   In the colonies it was founded on the settled rule of the law of England that by his prerogative the King was the universal occupant of all the vacant land in his dominions and had the right to grant it at his pleasure by his authorized officers.   *Mitchel v. United States, 9 Pet., 711.*

SEC. 1759. Spain did not consider the Indian right within the Floridas, after their retrocession by Great Britain in 1783, to be that of mere occupancy and perpetual possession, but a right of property in the lands they held under the guarantee of the treaties, which were so highly respected that in the establishment of a military post by the royal order the site thereof was either purchased from the Indians or occupied by their permission.   *Ibid.*

SEC. 1760. The Indian right to lands in the Floridas was not merely of possession; that of alienation was concomitant.   Both were equally secured, protected, and guaranteed by Great Britain and Spain, subject only to ratification and confirmation by the license charter or deed from the governor, representing the King.   *Ibid.*

SEC. 1761. One uniform rule seemed to have prevailed in the British provinces from their first settlement, as appears by their laws, that friendly Indians were protected in the possession of the lands they occupied, and were considered as owning them by a perpetual right of possession in the tribe or nation inhabiting them as their common property, from generation to generation, not as the right of individuals located on particular spots.   *Ibid.*

SEC. 1762. Full statement of the right of the Indians in the Floridas, including the Choctaws and Chickasaws, between the time of treaty of peace of October, 1763, by which they were ceded to Great Britain and their retrocession to Spain in 1783.   *Ibid.*

SEC. 1763. The hunting grounds of the Indians were as much in their actual possession as the cleared field of the whites, and their right to their exclusive enjoyment in their own way aside from their own purposes was as much respected until they abandoned them, made a cession to the Government, or an authorized sale to individuals.   *Ibid.*

SEC. 1764. The principles which had been in force in the colonies as to the tenure of the Indian lands were adopted by the King in the proclamation of October, 1763, and applied to the provinces acquired by the treaty of peace and the Crown lands in the royal provinces as the law which should govern the enjoyment and the transmission of Indian and vacant lands.   *Ibid.*

SEC. 1765. The Indian right of occupancy is considered as sacred as the fee simple of the white man.   *Ibid.*

SEC. 1766. Subject to the Indian right of occupancy, the ultimate fee to the lands within the British colonies was in the Crown and its grantees, which could be granted by the Crown or the colonial legislatures while the lands remained in the possession of the Indians, though possession could not be taken without their consent.   *Ibid.*

SEC. 1767. The colonial charters, a great portion of the individual grants by the proprietary and royal governments, and still greater portion by the States of the Union after the Revolution, were made for the lands within the Indian hunting grounds. The ultimate fee, incumbered with the Indian right of occupancy, was in the Crown previous to the Revolution and in the States of the Union afterwards and subject to grant, but the Indian right of occupancy was protected by the political power and respected by the courts until extinguished, when the patentee took the unincumbered fee.   *Clark v. Smith, 13 Pets., 196.*

SEC. 1768. The native tribes who were found on this continent at the time of its discovery have never been acknowledged or treated as independent nations by the European Governments, nor regarded as the owners of the territories they respectively occupied. On the contrary, the whole continent was divided and parceled out and granted by the Governments of Europe as if it had been vacant and unoccupied land, and the Indians continually held to be and treated as if subject to their dominion and control.   *United States v. Rogers, 4 How., 567.*

SEC. 1769. The land embraced within the section on which a person in whose behalf a reservation had been made in the Choctaw treaty of September 27, 1830 (7 Stat. L., 333), resided was so much excepted from the cession contained in that treaty, and the reservee was entitled to that section embracing his improvements in preference to any other right that could have previously been acquired under the Government. No previous grant of Congress could be paramount.

according to the rights of occupancy which this Government has always conceded to the Indian tribes within her jurisdiction.

Gaines v. Nicholson, 9 How., 356.

SEC. 1770. Land upon which a reservee under the Choctaw treaty of September 27, 1830 (7 Stat. L., 333), resided was so much carved out of the territory ceded, and remained to the Indian occupant, as he had never parted with it.   He holds, strictly speaking, not under the treaty of cession, but under his original title, confirmed by the Government in the act of agreeing to the reservation.   *Ibid.*

SEC. 1771. When the Spanish governors of Louisiana relinquished the interest or title of the Crown in Indian lands, the grants were made subject to the rights of Indian occupancy, and they did not take effect until that occupancy had ceased, and while it continued it was not in the power of the Spanish governor to authorize anyone to interfere with it.   *Chouteau v. Molony, 16 How., 203.*

SEC. 1772. By the laws of Spain the Indians had a right of occupancy, but they could not part with this right except by the consent of the King, which was given either directly under the King's sign manual or by the confirmation of the governors, representing the King.

Ibid.

SEC. 1773. The lands claimed under the Dubuque concession were embraced within territory in the province to which the Indian title had not been extinguished, and Spain did not, in 1796, have the right of occupancy in them.   The Indians had the right to continue it as long as they pleased or to sell any parts of it, the sales being in conformity to the Spanish laws and being afterwards confirmed by the King or his representative, the governor of Louisiana.   *Ibid.*

SEC. 1774. United States *v.* Ritchie (17 How., 525) cited and approved as to status of mission lands.   *United States v. Cervantes, 18 How., 553.*

SEC. 1775. Fort Leavenworth and its appurtenances were not included in the grant to the Delaware Indians in 1829, which calls for the fort as a boundary.   *United States v. Stone, 2 Wall., 525.*

SEC. 1776. All agree that the Indian right of occupancy creates an indefeasible title to the reservation that may extend from generation to generation, and will cease only by the dissolution of the tribe, or their consent to sell to the party possessed of the right of preemption. He is the only party that is authorized to deal with the tribe in respect to their property, and this with the consent of the Government; any other party is an intruder, and may be proceeded against under the twelfth section of the act of June 30, 1834.

The New York Indians, 5 Wall., 761.

SEC. 1777. Until the Indians have sold their lands, and removed from them in pursuance of the treaty stipulations, they are to be regarded as still in their ancient possessions, and are under their original rights entitled to the undisturbed enjoyment of them.   *Ibid.*

SEC. 1778. The exercise by the State of New York of authority over the Indian lands in that State, as in the assessment and levy of taxes on them, is an unwarrantable interference, inconsistent with the original title of the Indians and offensive to their tribal relations.   *Ibid.*

SEC. 1779. The rights of the Indians in their lands do not depend upon the act of 1841, or any other statute of the State of New York, but upon treaties, which are the supreme law of the land; and it is to these treaties that we must look to ascertain the nature of these rights and the extent of them.   *Ibid.*

SEC. 1780. The Indian right of use and occupancy is unlimited and they may exercise it at their discretion. If the lands in a state of nature are not in a condition for profitable use they may be made so, and if desired for the purposes of agriculture they may be cleared of their timber to such an extent as may be reasonable under the circumstances. The timber taken off by the Indians in such clearing may be sold by them. But to justify any cutting of timber, except for use upon the premises as timber or its product, it must be done in good faith for the improvement of the land. The improvement must be the principal thing and the cutting of the timber the incident only. Any cutting beyond this would be waste and unauthorized.

United States v. Cook, 19 Wall., 591.

SEC. 1781. The timber, while standing, is a part of the realty, and can be sold only as the land could be. It can not be rightfully severed, except to improve the land. When rightfully severed it is no longer a part of the land and there is no restriction upon its sale.   *Ibid.*

SEC. 1782. The United States may maintain an action to recover logs sold by Indians from their reservation to a third person where the logs were not cut for improvement of the land.   *Ibid.*

SEC. 1783. Timber growing on Indian reservations can be rightfully severed from the land for the purpose of improving the land, or the better adapting it to convenient occupation, but for no other purpose. Its severance under such circumstances is, in effect, only a legitimate use of the land. In theory, at least, the land is better and more valuable with the timber off than with it on, and it has been *improved* by the removal.   *Ibid.*

SEC. 1784. If the timber should be severed for the purposes of sale alone, in other words, if the cutting of the timber was the principal thing and not the incident, then the cutting would be wrongful, and the timber, when cut, becomes the absolute property of the United States.   *Ibid.*

SEC. 1785. To maintain his title under his purchase it is incumbent on the purchaser of timber from the Indians to show that it was rightfully severed from the land.   *Ibid.*

SEC. 1786. The Indians having only a right of occupancy in the lands, the presumption is against their authority to cut and sell the timber. Every purchaser from them is charged with notice of this presumption. *Ibid.*

SEC. 1787. The right of the Indians to their occupancy is as sacred as that of the United States to the fee, but it is only a right of occupancy, and the possession, when abandoned by the Indians, attaches itself to the fee without further grant. *Ibid.*

SEC. 1788. The Indians have the same right in the lands of their reservations that a tenant for life has in the lands of a remainder-man, and what a tenant for life may do upon the lands of a remainder-man the Indians may do upon their reservations, but no more. The familiar and well-settled principles of law in this country applicable to tenants for life and remainder-men apply to Indians and their use of their reservations. *Ibid.*

SEC. 1789. The doctrine that a tract lawfully appropriated to any purpose becomes thereafter severed from the mass of public lands, and that no subsequent law or proclamation will be construed to embrace it or operate upon it, although no exception be made of it, applies with more force to Indian than to military reservations, inasmuch as the latter are the absolute property of the Government, while in the former other rights are vested. *Railroad Co. v. United States, 92 U. S., 733.*

SEC. 1790. The United States does not recognize in Indian tribes generally any other than a passing title with right of use, until by treaty or otherwise that right is extinguished, and the ultimate title has been always held to be in the United States, with no right in the Indians to transfer it, or even their possession, without the consent of the Government. It is this fixed claim of dominion which lies at the foundation of the act forbidding the white man to make a settlement on the lands occupied by an Indian tribe.
United States v. Joseph, 94 U. S., 614.

SEC. 1791. The right of the Menominee Indians to their lands in Wisconsin was only that of occupancy; and, subject to that right, the State was entitled to every section 16 within the limits of those lands.
Beecher v. Wetherby, 95 U. S., 517.

SEC. 1792. The fee in the lands of the Menominee Indians was in the United States, subject to the right of the Indians to occupy them, and could be transferred by the United States whenever they chose. The grantee, it is true, would take only the naked fee, and could not disturb the occupancy of the Indians. That occupancy could only be interfered with or determined by the United States. *Ibid.*

SEC. 1793. The half-breeds of the Sioux Nation held the tract of land set apart for them as a reservation by the ninth article of the treaty of Prairie du Chien (7 Stat. L., 330) by the same title and in the same manner that other Indian titles are held.

Myrick v. Thompson, 99 U. S., 291.

SEC. 1794. The title to the public domain included within the Territory of Oregon by the donation act of August 14, 1848 (91 Stat. L., 323), was in the United States, subject to possessory Indian title to a portion of the Territory, and there was no law by which any person or company could acquire title from the Government. All persons, therefore, who settled upon the public lands acquired no right thereby as against the United States.   *Missionary Society v. Dallas, 107 U. S., 336.*

SEC. 1795. The title of the Indians was always treated by the governments established by England, and the governments succeeding them, as merely usufructuary, affording protection against individual encroachment, but always subject to the control and disposition of those governments, at least so far as to prevent, without their consent, its acquisition by others. Such superior right rested upon the claim asserted by England of prior discovery of the country, and was respected by other European nations.

The Cherokee Trust Funds Case, 117 U. S., 288.

SEC. 1796. At the time the act of July 2, 1864 (13 Stat. L., 365), was passed, the title of the Indians to the lands in controversy was not extinguished; but that fact did not prevent the grant of Congress from operating to pass a fee of the land to the company. The Indians (Sisseton and Wahpeton) had merely a right of occupancy, a right to use the land subject to the dominion and control of the Government. The grant conveyed the fee subject to this right of occupancy, and the railroad company took the property with this incumbrance.

Buttz v. Railroad Co., 119 U. S., 55.

SEC. 1797. The White Mountain Indian Reservation was a legally constituted Indian reservation. True, when the Territory of Arizona was organized on February 24, 1863, there was no such reservation, and it was created in the first instance by order of the President in 1871. Whatever doubt there might have been, if any, as to the validity of such Executive order, is put at rest by the act of Congress of February 8, 1887 (24 Stat. L., 388), relating to the allotment of lands in severalty to Indians.   *In re Wilson, 140 U. S., 575.*

SEC. 1798. The necessary effect of the legislative recognition in the first clause of section 1 of the act of February 8, 1887 (24 Stat. L., 388), of Executive order reservations, was to confirm the Executive order, and establish beyond challenge the Indian title in the White Mountain Indian Resevation.   *Ibid.*

SEC. 1799. The treaty of 1854 (10 Stat. L., 1109) did not operate to defeat the prior right of occupancy which the Indians had to the particular section 16 in question, but, by including it in the new reservations, made as the condition of the cession of large tracts of land in Wisconsin, continued it in force. The State, therefore, had no such control over that section or right to it as would prevent its being set apart by the United States, with the consent of the Indians, as a part of their permanent reservation.   *United States v. Thomas, 151 U. S., 557.*

SEC. 1800. By authority of their original right of occupancy, which has continuously existed in the Chippewa Indians, as well as by the fact that the section 16 in question is included within the tract set aside as a portion of the permanent reservation in consideration of the cession of lands, the title never vested in the State, except as subordinate to the right of occupation of the Indians.   *Ibid.*

SEC. 1801. By the treaty of 1842 (7 Stat. L., 591) the Chippewa Indians stipulated for the right of occupancy to the lands embracing the sixteenth sections within the Lac Courte d'Orielles Reservation. That right of occupancy gave to them the enjoyment of the land until they were required to surrender it by the President of the United States, which requirement was never made, and whatever right the State of Wisconsin acquired by the enabling act to the sixteenth section was subordinate to this right of occupancy for which the Indians stipulated and which the United States recognized.   *Ibid.*

SEC. 1802. The general rule established by the land department in reference to the school lands in the different States is that the title to them vested in the several States in which the land is situated, subject to any prior right of occupation by the Indians or others, which the Government has stipulated to recognize.   *Ibid.*

SEC. 1803. The term "right and immunities" is often used as descriptive of only policial rights and immunities, and does not necessarily include property rights, but the rights and interest which the native Cherokees had in the reservation and outlet sprang solely from citizenship in the Cherokee Nation, and the grant of equal rights as members of the Cherokee Nation naturally carried with it the grant of all rights springing from citizenship.   *Cherokee Nation v. Journeycake, 155 U. S., 196.*

SEC. 1804. The clear duty rested upon the Government, under the treaty of 1820 (7 Stat. L., 206) with the Chippewa Indians, to see that a tract was reserved for the purposes designated in the treaty, and if a survey was necessary for that purpose it was the duty of the Government to cause such survey to be made. The survey having been made and the Indian reserve having been delineated thereon, the tract so designated having been accepted by both parties to the treaty, the reservation was as effectual as if the particular tract to be used was specifically designated by boundaries in the treaty itself, and the reservation thus created stood precisely in the same category as other Indian reservations, whether established for general or limited uses, and whether made by the direct authority of Congress in a ratification of a treaty or indirectly through the medium of a duly authorized executive officer.	*Spalding v. Chandler, 160 U. S., 194.*

SEC. 1805. The fee of the lands in this country in the original occupation of the Indian tribes was from the time of the formation of this Government vested in the United States, and the Indian title as against the United States was merely a title and right of the perpetual occupancy of the land with the privilege of using it in such mode as they saw fit until such right of occupation had been surrendered to the Government. When Indian reservations are created, either by treaty or Executive order, the Indians hold the land by the same character of title, to wit, the right to possess and occupy the lands for the uses and purposes designated.	*Ibid.*

SEC. 1806. A reservation may be made either by treaty, Executive order, or by act of Congress, and all of these methods are expressly recognized by the homestead and preemption laws.

United States v. Payne, 8 Fed. Rep., 883.

SEC. 1807. The reservation of lands for any specific purpose by the Government is but an expression of a desire of the Government to use them for that purpose. It does not part with its title by reserving them, but simply gives notice to all the world that it desires them for a certain purpose. The same precision and accuracy is not required as in case of conveyance.	*Ibid.*

SEC. 1808. The treaty-making power has a right to convey title to the lands of the United States without an act of Congress, and if a treaty acts directly on the subject of the grant it is equivalent to an act of Congress, and the grantee has a good title.	*Ibid.*

SEC. 1809. No set form of words or phrases need be used to set aside a reservation. It is enough if there are sufficient words to indicate the purpose of the power that acts to show that it intended to act in a given case.	*Ibid.*

SEC. 1810. The fact that the title to land may be in the United States does not necessarily make it that part of the public domain which is subject to settlement by citizens of the United States under the homestead and preemption laws.	*Ibid.*

SEC. 1811. A tract of land lawfully appropriated to any purpose becomes thereafter severed from the mass of public lands, and no subsequent law or proclamation will be construed to embrace it or to operate upon it. Although no exception is made, Congress can not be understood to include it by a law general in its terms. This doctrine applies with more force to Indian than to military reservations.	*Ibid.*

SEC. 1812. As soon as Indians part with their title the land ceases to be Indian country without any further act of Congress, unless by the treaty by which the Indians parted with their title, or by some act of Congress, or some Executive order of the President a different rule was made applicable.   *Ibid.*

SEC. 1813. The language used in the third article of the Seminole treaty of 1866 (14 Stat. L., 755) amounts to the conveyance of the title of the land to the United States; but the fact that the title of the land is in the United States does not necessarily make it that part of the public domain which is subject to entry.   *Ibid.*

SEC. 1814. An Indian reservation can not be established by title or prescription. The fact that a particular tribe or band of Indians have for a long time occupied a particular tract of country does not constitute such tract an Indian reservation. It simply retains the character it had at the beginning, and can only be described as a tract of public land to which the Indian title has not been extinguished.   *43 Gallons Brandy, 14 Fed. Rep., 539.*

SEC. 1815. It was competent for the United States, by the treaty of 1834 (7 Stat. L., 450) with the Chickasaws, to affix conditions to the conveyance of the reservations created by it which should be the valid law of the title, notwithstanding any conflicting State law.
Love v. Pamplin, 21 Fed. Rep., 755.

SEC. 1816. The rights secured to the Indians by any treaty or law of the United States, once vested, became fixed and irrevocable and beyond the reach of State legislation, even when, by extinction of the Indian title on the removal of the tribe beyond the State limits, the legislative authority of the State had become acknowledged and exclusive.   *Ibid.*

SEC. 1817. The Cherokee Nation of Indians holds what is called the "Cherokee Outlet" by substantially the same kind of title it holds its other lands. The title to all their lands was obtained by grant from the United States. This, in fact, puts all the title in the Cherokee Nation.   *United States v. Rogers, 23 Fed. Rep., 658.*

SEC. 1818. Inasmuch as there never was any sale by the Cherokees to the Cheyennes and Arapahoes of the country where this offense was committed, the same was never sold by them and occupied by the Cheyennes and Arapahoes, the country is still in the condition of being set apart and occupied by the Cherokees and does not come under the designation of the *Indian country not set apart* and occupied by the Cherokees.   *Ibid.*

SEC. 1819. The word "occupied" or "occupation" may be so used in law in connection with other expressions, or under the peculiar facts of the case, as to signify actual residence. Under the peculiar facts here, actual residence of the Cherokee Nation here would be an impossibility.   *Ibid.*

SEC. 1820. When Congress, in the act of January 6, 1883 (22 Stat. L. 400), used the word "occupied" it could have meant no more than the possession of the country. To have possession does not mean actual residence.   *Ibid.*

SEC. 1821. The word "occupy," as used in the act of January 6, 1883 (22 Stat. L., 400), means subject to will and control, *possessio pedis*, and it is synonymous with "subjection" to the will and "control." Wherever there is a subjection of land to the will and control of another, with title in him, it is occupied by that other; it is in the actual legal possession of that other.   *Ibid.*

SEC. 1822. The usual legal sense of the word "occupy," as applied to land, is where a person exercises physical control over such land. Hence, when a nation or body of people have the title to land, and the same is subject to its will and control, it is occupied by it, and legally it is in its possession.   *Ibid.*

SEC. 1823. The Cherokee Nation occupies and is in the actual legal possession of all its lands to which it has title and to which it has not relinquished such title.   *Ibid.*

SEC. 1824. The plain meaning of article 16 of the treaty of July 27, 1866 (14 Stat. L., 799), is that when the United States should desire to settle friendly Indians on any part of the Outlet, the Cherokees would sell the same to such Indians, the purchase price to be paid by them or by the United States for them.   *Ibid.*

SEC. 1825. The Cherokee Indians hold what is called the "Cherokee Outlet" by substantially the same kind of title they hold their other lands. The title to all their lands was obtained by grant from the United States. This title is a base, qualified, or determinable fee, without the right of reversion, but only the possibility of reversion, in the United States. This, in effect, puts all the title in the Cherokee Nation.   *In re Wolf, 27 Fed. Rep., 606.*

SEC. 1826. It is a Federal question whether or not, by force of the ordinance of 1787 and of the treaties with the Miami Indians, certain lands in the possession and ownership of a Miami chief and his descendants were exempt from taxation.

Wan-pe-man-qua v. Aldrich, 28 Fed. Rep., 489.

SEC. 1827. The lands patented to Jean Baptiste Richardville, in pursuance of the treaty of October 6, 1818 (7 Stat. L., 189), by force of that and later treaties with the Miamis, and of the ordinance of 1787, were exempt from taxation, and remain exempt while in the possession of his descendants whose tribal relation had not ceased.   *Ibid.*

SEC. 1828. Land owned in fee simple by an Indian, which otherwise would be exempt from taxation, will not be deemed subject to assessment merely because it is free from restriction upon the power of alienation. On the contrary, it would seem that the right of exemption from taxation rests on the fact of the continued tribal organization, which the United States has recognized by treating with the persons concerned as distinct political communities.   *Ibid.*

SEC. 1829. There seems to be no reason, speaking generally, why the unrestricted right to alienate should make Indian lands taxable which otherwise would not be; and, looking at the facts of the case at bar, it would be unreasonable to give that fact controlling significance.
Ibid.

SEC. 1830. While in possession of the chief of the tribe the land was exempt from assessment, and it must be held to have remained so in the possession of his devisees and descendants, members of the tribe, so long as they continued to hold, and were recognized by the United States as holding, tribal relation.   *Ibid.*

SEC. 1831. The land patented to Me-shing-go-me-sia, in trust for the band of Me-to-sin-ia, in conformity with the treaties of 1838 (7 Stat. L., 569) and 1840 (7 Stat. L., 582), were not taxable.   *Ibid.*

SEC. 1832. The Cherokee Outlet was, in a certain sense, "occupied" because the Cherokee Nation had a title and right to possess it; but if Congress had meant by this act (January 6, 1883, 22 Stat. L., 400) to include all land owned by the Cherokees, the words "set apart" would have been ample, and the word "occupied" was superfluous.
United States v. Soule, 30 Fed. Rep., 918.

SEC. 1833. The title to all the land of the Cherokee Nation was obtained by grant from the United States. The title is a base, qualified, or determinable fee, without the right of reversion, but only the possibility of reversion in the United States. This, in effect, puts all the estate in the Cherokee Nation.
Cherokee Nation v. Railroad Co., 33 Fed. Rep., 900.

SEC. 1834. Congress can not grant a right of way over the lands of the Cherokee Nation without its consent, on the ground that the United States has title to the land. If it can do so it must be done because the Government of the United States can exercise, with reference to the lands of the Cherokee Nation, the right of eminent domain.   *Ibid.*

SEC. 1835. By act of Congress April 8, 1864 (13 Stat. L., 40), the President was authorized to set apart not exceeding four tracts of land in California for Indian reservations, and in his discretion to include therein existing reservations. The lands in existing reservations not thus retained were to be sold as therein prescribed. Four reservations were accordingly set apart, among which the previously existing Klamath Reservation was not included, but possession of the latter, which contained about 40 square miles, and on which were about two hundred Indians, was retained by the United States, and steps were taken toward its disposition. *Held*, that the Klamath Reservation was not "Indian country" within the meaning of section 2133, Revised Statutes, prescribing the penalty for unlicensed trading in the Indian country.
United States v. Rising Star Tea, 35 Fed. Rep., 403.

SEC. 1836. Defendant claimed title to a tract of land under a deed alleged to have been executed in behalf of the original locator of Chippewa scrip, which was void, because issued without authority by the Commissioner of Indian Affairs. Plaintiff claimed under a deed subsequently executed by such locator, and alleged that defendant's deed was executed under a forged power of attorney, and was therefore void. In proceedings before the Secretary of Interior, of which plaintiff's grantor had notice, the land was awarded to defendant. *Held*, that defendant was within the provisions of the 17 Stat. L., 340, authorizing the Secretary to give title to lands held under such scrip whenever it shall be shown to his satisfaction that said lands are held by innocent parties, in good faith, and that the locations under such scrip have been made in good faith, and by innocent holders of the same; and that the decision of the Secretary involved no question of law, but simply the question of fact as to the good faith of the claimants, and therefore not subject to review by the court.

Pugsley v. Brown, 35 Fed. Rep., 688.

SEC. 1837. If the Secretary erred only in a matter of fact, it is conceded that his decision is conclusive upon all parties and not subject to review in any other forum.

Ibid.

SEC. 1838. The statute does not define the title which the claimant must have, but refers to him only as an owner and holder in good faith. The Dauphinais patent was void in law for want of authority in the Commissioner of Indian Affairs to issue the scrip on which it was founded.

Ibid.

SEC. 1839. In all cases about the right of property in which an Indian may be a party on one side and a white person on the other, the burden of proof shall rest upon the white person whenever the Indian shall make out a presumption of title in himself from the fact of previous possession or ownership. (Sec. 2126, Rev. Stats.)

Felix v. Patrick, 36 Fed. Rep., 457.

SEC. 1840. On the bill to set aside the even-numbered sections of land granted to the defendant railroad company, the objection that these sections were not the subject of the grant because of the New York Indian Reservation under the treaty of 1838 (7 Stat. L., 550) will not be considered, the Supreme Court, in a former suit against the same company (118 U. S., 682) having held that the odd-numbered sections of the same grant were not affected by that reservation.

United States v. Railroad Co., 37 Fed. Rep., 68.

SEC. 1841. It is a well-known fact that the Missouri, Kansas, and Texas Railroad for many miles runs through the Osage Indian lands, and that by the decision of the Supreme Court of the United States none of these lands passed under this or any other grant to railroads.

Ibid.

SEC. 1842. The act of Congress of August 4, 1886 (24 Stat. L., 219), provides that on the death of an allottee under the treaty of June 28, 1862 (13 Stat. L., 623), with the Kickapoo Indians, leaving heirs, and without having obtained patents, the Secretary of the Interior shall cause patents to issue in fee simple in the name of the original allottee, and that such original allottee shall be regarded as a citizen of the United States and of the State of Kansas; the land to become a part of his estate, to be administered or descend to his heirs, etc. *Held*, that the United States holds the legal title in fee simple in trust for the heirs of the allottee, and the latter are estopped by their warranty deed conveying the land before obtaining a patent from asserting title against the grantee.   *Briggs v. Wash-puk-qua, 37 Fed. Rep., 135.*

SEC. 1843. The right to a patent once vested is treated by the Government, when dealing with the public lands, as equivalent to a patent issued. When in fact the patent does issue, it relates back to the inception of the right of the patentee, so far as it may be necessary to cut off intervening claimants.   *Ibid.*

SEC. 1844. The supreme court of Kansas has decided that a conveyance by an heir of a Pottawatomie Indian allottee, under a treaty similar to the Kickapoo treaty of June 28, 1862 (13 Stat. L., 623), was valid, although made before the patent was issued.   *Ibid.*

SEC. 1845. The title of the Indians to these lands (Chippewa in Michigan) had been fully extinguished. We are not, therefore, embarrassed by the considerations which influenced the court in the case of Railroad Company *v.* United States, 92 U. S., 733, in which it was held that a general grant of lands to a railroad company would not be construed to embrace lands of which an Indian tribe had been granted by treaty the use and possession for an indefinite length of time.
Sherpard v. Insurance Co., 40 Fed. Rep., 341.

SEC. 1846. Where the title of the Indians and their right of occupancy of certain lands had been fully extinguished it was held that they passed under this act (June 3, 1856; 11 Stat. L., 17) notwithstanding that they were held by the United States in trust to sell them for the benefit of the Indians. But even if the lands did not pass under said act, it was held that the defendant, who had taken possession and claimed title under the same act, was estopped from setting up this fact.   *Ibid.*

SEC. 1847. The treaty with the Kickapoo Indians (13 Stat. L., 624) provided that the land allotted to the Indians could not be sold to white men without permission from the President, which permission should be signified by his causing the land to be patented to the Indians "with power of alienation," and that before receiving patent the Indians must appear before the district court, make proof of their intelligence, and take the oath of allegiance. An Indian conveyed his land by warranty deed on the day he made such proof, and after he had obtained his patent conveyed his land to another grantee. *Held*, that the second grantee took the land, since the first deed, being made before patent, was ineffectual to convey the land either indirectly or by estoppel.   *Briggs v. Sample, 43 Fed. Rep., 102.*

SEC. 1848. Prior to the time of the adoption of the Constitution, the States of Massachusetts and New York had each claimed territorial sovereignty over the lands of the Indians in New York; but in 1786 the dispute was settled by a cession from Massachusetts to New York of the "sovereignty and jurisdiction of the lands," and from New York to Massachusetts of the "right of preemption of the soil from the native Indians."   *Benson v. United States, 44 Fed. Rep., 178.*

SEC. 1849. A treaty was entered into between the United States and the Six Nations, November 11, 1794 (7 Stat. L., 44), in which the title to the lands within the Allegany Reservation was acknowledged by the United States to belong to the Seneca Nation of Indians.   *Ibid.*

SEC. 1850. The proviso in the organic act of Oregon Territory (9 Stat. L., 323) confirming title to the land, not exceeding 640 acres, then occupied as missionary stations among Indians, in the religious societies to which said missionary stations respectively belonged, must be construed as a grant of only the specific lands which were at the date of the act so occupied, exclusively, and not in subserviency to another's right.   *Missionary Society v. Gibbon, 44 Fed. Rep., 321.*

SEC. 1851. The Cherokee Nation holds the fee to all the lands to which it has title. Individual citizens of the nation have a right of perpetual occupancy in lands improved and occupied by them under the laws of the Cherokee Nation. By the right of occupancy the individual Indian citizen can hold the lands forever, and fully enjoy all profits arising from them, and their right of occupancy may be transferred by a grant to another citizen of the nation, or it may descend by inheritance. Practically, they get all the productions of the land and are entitled to its increased or peculiar value as though they held it in fee.   *Payne v. Railroad Co., 46 Fed. Rep., 546.*

SEC. 1852. The Cherokee citizen and occupant of land has such a durable and permanent interest in the land as to entitle him to pay for an additional servitude placed upon the same.   *Ibid.*

SEC. 1853. While citizens of the Cherokee Nation do not have a fee to the lands they occupy, they can hold them forever and fully enjoy the profits arising from them, and this right may be granted to their heirs, or may descend by inheritance. Practically, they get all the productions of the land, the same as though they held it in fee.   *Ibid.*

SEC. 1854. The lands in the Bitter Root Valley above the Lo Lo Fork were not public lands such as could pass to the Northern Pacific Railroad by the grant expressed in the act of July 2, 1864, section 3

(13 Stat., L. 365), as of that date; for by the treaty of 1855 (11 Stat. L., 657) with the Flathead Indians it was provided that these lands should be surveyed and examined, and if, in the judgment of the President, they prove to be better adapted to the wants of the Flathead tribe than the general reservation provided therein, then such portions as were necessary should be set apart as a general reservation for the tribe, and that they should not be open to settlement until the decision of the President was made known; and such decision was not made known until 1871, when the President decided not to make the land a reservation.   *Railroad Co. v. Hinchman et al., 53 Fed. Rep., 523.*

SEC. 1855. There is no claim on the part of the Indians residing in the Bitter Root Valley that the same or any part thereof is an Indian reservation, or that the Flathead tribe, to which they belong, has never parted with the title thereto; nor is the tract in controversy claimed by any of said Indians; nor was it so claimed by any of them at the date of the filing of the map of definite location of the plaintiff's road, or at the date of entry thereof by the defendant; nor was the said tract of land embraced in any of the patents mentioned as having been issued to but not accepted by the Indians.   *Ibid.*

SEC. 1856. By the act of June 5, 1872 (17 Stat. L., 226), lands of the Bitter Root Valley were excluded from the general preemption and homestead laws. Certain rights of preemption, without cost, were given to the Indians actually occupying and cultivating any portion thereof.   *Ibid.*

SEC. 1857. The tenure by which the Cherokee Nation holds its lands and its relation to the United States in other respects are widely different from that of the ordinary Indian tribes, by the treaties between the United States and Cherokee Nation of February 14, 1833 (7 Stat. L., 414), and of December 29, 1835 (7 Stat. L., 478).   *Mehlin v. Ice, 56 Fed. Rep., 12.*

SEC. 1858. Plaintiff in ejectment claimed as the grantee of land upon which a half-breed Sioux Indian had located scrip issued to him under the act of July 17, 1854 (10 Stat. L., 304), which scrip was not transferable, but was issued to designated individuals in exchange for the interest acquired by them collectively under a former treaty. *Held,* that the scrip and the location of it did not vest the legal title in the plaintiff's grantor, and it was proper to instruct the jury that they should disregard the location and the deed to plaintiff as evidence of title, and only regard them as evidence explaining his entry, possession, and good faith.   *Carter v. Ruddy, 56 Fed. Rep., 542.*

SEC. 1859. Deeds made to certain Indians of lots of land on the Puyallup Reservation, pursuant to the treaty of December 26, 1854 (10 Stat. L., 1132), with the stipulation that the lands should not be aliened for more than two years, and should be exempt from levy sale or forfeiture, passed the title in fee to the grantees, subject only to conditions subsequent, and left no title or reversionary interest in the United States, but a mere power in the President to reassign or sell for common benefit of the tribe on breach of the conditions.

Ross v. Eells, 56 Fed. Rep., 855.

SEC. 1860. All public lands, including any Indian title thereto, being under the control of the Government, it must follow that any right which Craig may have obtained to the land must have been through the laws of the Government, and any laws which granted him such right must at the same time have operated to extinguish the Indian title thereto. *Caldwell v. Robinson, 59 Fed. Rep., 653.*

SEC. 1861. The lands lying in the Bitter Root Valley, Montana, above the Lo Lo Fork, having been reserved from sale or other disposition until the President should decide whether they should be set aside for the Flathead Indians under the treaty of July 16, 1855 (11 Stat. L., 657), were not public lands and were, therefore, incapable of passing to the Northern Pacific Railroad Company under the act of July 2, 1864 (13 Stat. L., 365), which was a grant in presenti and could never attach to any lands that were not public at that date, though they were afterwards made public by the President's decision.

Railroad Co. v. Maclay, 61 Fed. Rep., 554.

SEC. 1862. The fee of lands in the Cherokee Nation is in the nation. Whatever right a citizen has to occupy any particular portion of the public lands of the nation he must aquire under and in pursuance of the laws of the nation, and not in defiance of them. He can not enter upon land previously dedicated or appropriated to some other person or to some specific use. *Bell v. Railroad Co., 63 Fed. Rep., 417.*

SEC. 1863. A treaty with the Puyallup Indians (10 Stat. L., 1132) allotted the lands in severalty to those who would locate on the same as permanant homes, and authorized the President to prescribe such rules as would insure to the family, in case of the death of its head, possession of such home; to issue a patent to such person or family; cancel it if such family or person rove from place to place. Each patent issued prohibited alienation. The act of February 6, 1887 (24 Stat. L., 388), conferred citizenship on such Indians and provided for leasing the land under the regulations of the Secretary of the Interior, and contemplated that agents shall be in charge of reservations; and the practice of the Department was to maintain such agents. *Held,* that the allotment of such lands in severalty and making the Indians citizens did not revoke the reservation. *Eells v. Ross, 64 Fed. Rep., 417.*

SEC. 1864. The appellees claim contracts with the Indians and a right to occupy the allotted land, and the circuit court held that the Government, by making the Indians proprietors and citizens, lost the power "to coerce such Indians into making or annulling contracts, or of molesting persons upon their premises by their license when not interfering with the operation of the Government or violating any national law." And the court further held that by the issuance of the patent "the Government lost entirely the right to control the use of the land." The patent has clear words of prohibition against alienation, and even if it had omitted them the treaties and law imposed them.   *Ibid.*

SEC. 1865. The right to sell property is not derived from and is not dependent upon citizenship, neither does it detract in the slightest degree from the dignity or value of citizenship that a person is not possessed of an estate, or, if possessed of an estate, that he is deprived for the time being of the right to alienate it. It does not follow, therefore, that the power of these Indians to deal with land which was held in trust for their benefit was sensibly enlarged, or that the restriction against alienation found in the act of February 8, 1887 (24 Stat. L., 388), was removed, because in the sixth section of the same act Congress saw fit to declare Indian allottees to be citizens.

Beck v. Flournoy: &a., Co., 65 Fed. Rep., 30.

SEC. 1866. By the act of February 21, 1863 (12 Stat. L., 659), the Winnebago Indians were removed to a reservation in Nebraska and given allotments of land in severalty thereon "without the right of alienation." Under the act of 1887 (24 Stat. L., 388) other allotments were made to these Indians, such lands to be held in trust for the allottee and his heirs by the United States for twenty-five years, any conveyance of or contract touching such lands being declared null and void. The same act also provided that Indians receiving allotments of land in severalty should thereby become citizens of the United States and entitled to all the rights of such citizens. The Flournoy Live Stock Company, without the sanction of the Commissioner of Indian Affairs, obtained leases from the allottees of large quantities of lands allotted under both acts. *Held*, that the citizenship bestowed on the Indians was in no way inconsistent with the restriction upon their title to the lands, and that the leases obtained by the Flournoy Live Stock Company were utterly void.   *Ibid.*

SEC. 1867. The Flournoy Live Stock Company having obtained an injunction against the Winnebago agent to restrain him from interfering with it in its possession or use of allotted lands leased from the Indians, such injunction was erroneously issued, since the agent had done no more than to give notice, under the direction of his superiors, that the leases were void.   *Ibid.*

SEC. 1868. The clause in the act of February 8, 1887 (24 Stat. L., 388), imposing a limitation upon the power of alienation is not in conflict or inconsistent with the subsequent clause conferring the rights of citizenship. Both provisions may stand well together.   *Ibid.*

SEC. 1869. No reason is known why it was not competent for Congress to declare that allottees should be deemed citizens of the United

States and entitled to the rights, privileges, and immunities of its citizens, while it retained for the time being the title to certain lands in trust for their benefit and withheld from them for a certain period the power to sell, lease, or otherwise dispose of their interest in the said lands.   *Ibid.*

Sec. 1870. By the treaty between the United States and the Choctaw Nation of September 27, 1830 (7 Stat. L., 333), the United States granted to the Indians in fee simple "to inure to them while they shall exist as a nation and live on it" the country now occupied by them; and by the fourth article of this treaty it is provided that the Government and people of the United States are hereby obliged to secure to the said Choctaw Nation of red people the jurisdiction and the government of all the persons and property that may be within their limits, west, so that no Territory or State shall ever have the right to pass laws for the government of the Choctaw Nation of red people and their descendants; and that no part of the land granted them shall ever be embraced in any Territory or State, but the United States shall forever secure said Choctaw Nation from and against all laws, except such as may be from time to time enacted in their own national councils not inconsistent with the Constitution, treaties, and laws of the United States.   *Thebo v. Choctaw Nation, 66 Fed. Rep., 372*

Sec. 1871. In view of the well-known attitude of the United States toward the Indian title, as defined in Johnson *v.* McIntosh (8 Wheat., 574), and taking into consideration the fact that the intercourse act contemplates the residence of the whites within the Indian country as the same is therein defined, the true interpretation of section 11 would seem to be that the lands upon which settlement is therein prohibited are such only as have been confirmed to the Indians by treaty with the United States. The other lands in the Indian country, although they are described in the act as lands to which the Indian title has not been extinguished, were never in fact recognized by the United States as "belonging" to the Indians.   *Robinson v. Caldwell, 67 Fed. Rep., 391.*

Sec. 1872. In Johnson *v.* McIntosh (8 Wheat., 574) the nature of the right of the United States in the Indian country was considered at length, and the conclusion was there reached that the absolute title to all such lands is vested in the United States, subject only to the Indian right of possession, and that the Government possesses the absolute right to extinguish that.   *Ibid.*

Sec. 1873. At the time of the passage of the trade and intercourse act of June 30, 1834 (4 Stat. L., 729), there had been no treaty with the Nez Perces, no lands had, by statute, contract, or treaty, been recognized as belonging to them. In its dealings with the Indians the United States has uniformly denied their title to any of the lands within its domain.   *Ibid.*

SEC. 1874. Even if it should be the fact that the Indians living upon the allotted lands are no longer to be deemed tribal Indians, but have in fact reached the full measure of citizenship, and if it should be held that the allotted lands formed no part of the Indian country, it would be no less true that the United States had agreed that these lands should be set apart for the occupancy and benefit of the Indians, and that Congress, when it authorized the allotment of lands in severalty, had forbidden the alienation of the lands for twenty-five years, except by leasing under the rules and regulations prescribed by the Secretary of the Interior.   *United States v. Flournoy, etc., Co., 69 Fed. Rep., 886.*

SEC. 1875. Whatever may be the relation of the allotted lands to the so-called Indian country, with respect to other provisions of the statutes, such as those regulating the sale of liquors and the like, there can be no question that the title of these lands remains in the United States; that they form part of the lands set apart as a reservation for these Indians by the treaties made with them, and that the duty and consequently the power belongs to the United States to take whatever steps are necessary for the proper performance of the obligations existing upon the part of the United States with regard to these lands.   *Ibid.*

SEC. 1876. The allotments to the Winnebago Indians are not yet perfected. The act of Congress (24 Stat. L., 388) providing therefor expressly restrict all right of alienation and all right of contract between the Indians and the whites for a period of twenty-five years. It can not be known whether all or any of the allottees in severalty will remain on the lands assigned for the period of twenty-five years, and it may be that by abandonment the allottees may fail to perfect an alienable title. Such failure, however, would not deprive the tribe as a whole of their right to the reservation; and it would still be the duty of the United States, under the terms of the treaty, to protect the tribe in the use and occupancy of the reservation.
United States v. Mullin, 71 Fed. Rep., 628.

SEC. 1877. Where chiefs of the Creek Nation obtained, under the treaty of August 9, 1814, a cession of lands which they subsequently occupied, and afterwards, during their lives, sold, without fraud and in good faith on the part of their grantees, assigning as title their certificate of reservation, and such lands passed to the claimant by subsequent intermediate conveyances in fee for a valuable consideration and without fraud. *Held*, that the claimant has no legal cause of action against the United States, and they are not bound to convey to him their interest in the lands.   *Lindsay v. United States, Devereaux's C. Cls., 92.*

SEC. 1878. The effect of the sale in such case by the reservees was to give to the United States a legal right to the land which they had not before the sale,.   *Ibid.*

SEC. 1879. The intention of the treaty of August 9, 1814 (7 Stat. L., 120), with the Creek Indians is not to give to the *reservee* an estate in fee simple in the land, but merely a right of occupancy.   *Ibid.*

SEC. 1880. Under the Creek treaty of 1814 (7 Stat. L., 120), the contingent interest of the United States in reservations of land to any chief or warrior of the Creek Nation does not depend upon the construction of the words "voluntary abandonment."   *Ibid.*

SEC. 1881. The Indian title to that part of the territory which included the Hot Springs, Ark., was extinguished by the Quapaw treaty, August 24, 1818 (7 Stat. L., 176).

Hale et al. v. United States, 10 C. Cls., 289.

SEC. 1882. It has been universally admitted that the act of March 1, 1843 (5 Stat. L., 603), was intended to remove, and did actually remove, the difficulty arising out of the assumed possessory right of the Quapaws.   And the principle is distinctly asserted by this court in Thredgill *v.* Pintard (12 How., 37, 38).   *Ibid.*

SEC. 1883. The plain and palpable intention of the act of 1843 was to *perfect the title*, or to confirm the preemption rights south of the Arkansas River *ab initio;* that is to say, it intended to place the settler in the position he would have occupied if the Indian title had been previously extinguished.   *Ibid.*

SEC. 1884. The Indian title, supposed to have been vested in the Quapaws prior to the treaty of August 24, 1818 (7 Stat. L., 176), has always been put forward as the great obstacle in the way of Percifull's preemption claim to the land in question.   In the case of Thredgill *v.* Pintard (12 How., 24) the Supreme Court seems to have taken it for granted that the Indians had a possessory right to the lands south of the Arkansas River, merely because they assumed to make the cession of a boundless territory by the second article of that treaty.

Ibid.

SEC. 1885. Whatever may be the conclusion of the court sa to the Indian title to the lands south of the Arkansas River prior to the Quapaw treaty of August 24, 1818 (7 Stat. L., 176), there can be no doubt that the obstacle was intended to be wholly removed by the third section of the act of March 1, 1843 (5 Stat. L., 603).   *Ibid.*

SEC. 1886. The treaty made with France, April 30, 1803 (8 Stat. L., 200), conveyed the Louisiana territory to the United States, and the only provision in that treaty bearing on this subject is that which required our Government to respect all treaties which Spain had made with the Indians.   But Spain had made no treaties with the

Indians, and certainly none with the Quapaws.   Spain made grants of land without the least regard to the existence of any Indian title.
Ibid.

SEC. 1887. Though a statutory grant of lands (the Indian title to which has not been extinguished) be absolute in terms, nevertheless it is subject to the outstanding title of the Indians.
Langford v. United States, 12 C. Cls., 338.

SEC. 1888. Though the Washington Territorial act (10 Stat. L., 172) provided that "the title to the land occupied as missionary stations prior to the passage of the act establishing the Territorial government of Oregon be, and is hereby, confirmed and established to the several religious societies to which said missionary stations respectively belong," nevertheless subsequent Indian treaties reserving some of such stations as a part of permanent Indian reservations must be regarded as the paramount law.
Ibid.

SEC. 1889. Estoppel by matter of record does not arise from a judgment by default in an action against an Indian agent for the wrongful occupation of the premises used as an agency, where he did not come in and set up the title either of the United States or of the Indian tribe in whom it really was.   The fact that the agent interposed a demurrer at one stage of the case by order of the Secretary of the Interior does not preclude the Government from setting up the Indian title in a suit against it for use and occupation.
Ibid. ·

SEC. 1890. Where real property is taken by the Government for temporary use an action may lie for the implied rent; but where the taking is in perpetuity, as by a treaty of cession for a permanent Indian reservation, the implied relation of landlord and tenant can not subsist.
Ibid.

SEC. 1891. A judgment in ejectment against an agent of the Government will negative all presumptions of privity of contract in the nature of an implied lease between the owner of the premises and the Government and will defeat an action for the implied rent during the Government's prior occupancy.
Ibid.

SEC. 1892. The court below decides that though the Washington Territorial act (10 Stat. L., 732) confirms "the title to the land" "occupied as missionary stations," the statutory grant nevertheless was subject to the outstanding title of the Indians, and the subsequent treaty with them was paramount law.   Judgment for the defendants affirmed.
Ibid.

SEC. 1893. Certain Chippewa Indians have lands allotted as their individual property and are put in possession.   Before the allotments are approved and patents issue, the Indians, for purposes of improvement and cultivation, cut and sell small quantities of saw logs.   The sale is approved by the Government agent, and the logs are taken possession of by the purchaser. Subsequently agents of the land office, under instructions of the Interior Department, seize and sell the logs, and the proceeds thereof are in the Treasury. Judgment for claimant.   *Thayer v. United States, 20 C. Cls., 137.*

SEC. 1894. Where individual Indians have been put in possession of land as prospective owners, they have a right to cut and sell timber for purposes of cultivation, though the patents conferring a legal title to the land have not issued.   *Ibid.*

SEC. 1895. Where patents have issued the Government is estopped from setting up a claim for waste committed by the patentees on the ceded lands.   *Ibid.*

SEC. 1896. It was decided by the Supreme Court in the case of the United States *v.* Cook (19 Wall., 591) that Indians have a right to cut and sell timber for the purpose of improvement and cultivation of the land. That rule alone would support the claimant's title to the logs, for they were cut for the purpose of cultivation, and with the approval of the Government agent.   *Ibid.*

SEC. 1897. The possession taken in pursuance of the survey and allotment was followed by the approval of the proceedings by the Secretary and the issuing of patents. The title of the Indians being thus completed, related back to its inception in 1878. The Government is thereby estopped from setting up any title or any claim for waste committed in the meantime.   *Ibid.*

SEC. 1898. In 1783 the State of North Carolina granted to the Cherokee Indians a tract of land within its borders, to be "reserved unto the said Cherokee Indians and their nation forever." This grant was held by the supreme court of North Carolina to convey a fee simple estate instead of a mere usufruct conceded by the white race to the aboriginal Indians by right of occupancy. (Eu-che-lah *v.* Welsh, 3 Hawkes, 154.)   *Eastern Band Cherokees v. United States et al., 20 C. Cls., 449.*

SEC. 1899. The treaties of 1866 (14 Stat. L., 799) and 1868 (16 Stat. L., 727) relate principally to the internal government of the nation, authorize the settlement of friendly Indians on their lands by paying for such right and obtaining the consent of the Cherokee council, and cede certain lands to the United States in trust for sale. It is out of sales under these treaties that the land fund now in controversy arises.
                              Ibid.

SEC. 1900. The reservations made by article 19 of the treaty of 1830 with the Choctaws (7 Stat. L., 340) are dedications of certain quantities of land for the benefit of specific classes of persons. A surplus of one can not be applied to a deficiency of another.
                              Choctaw Nation v. United States, 21 C. Cls., 59.

SEC. 1901. The land in New York was disposed of through the States of New York and Massachusetts in negotiations with the Indians. In these transactions the United States were in any way only indirectly interested, and not at all financially interested. The Indian lands in New York did not come into the possession of the United States under the treaty of 1838 (7 Stat. L., 550) or otherwise, and it was never intended that they should do so.   *New York Indians v. United States, 30 C. Cls., 413.*

SEC. 1902. An occupant under an Indian grant, the Indians having afterwards resumed the title and granted it to the Crown, was held to be a tenant at will of the King, whose occupancy no length of time could ripen into a title, by adverse possession.

Jackson ex dem. Sparkman v. Porter, 1 Paine, 457.

SEC. 1903. Where proclamation had been made by the governor of the colony of New York, under orders from the King, that no purchases of lands should be made of the Indians, it was held that a purchaser could not acquire even the Indian title of occupancy.

Ibid.

SEC. 1904. The European nations, by whose subjects the discoveries were made, respected the rights of the natives as occupants, but asserted the ultimate title to be in themselves, and as a necessary consequence thereof claimed and exercised the power of granting the soil while yet in the occupancy of the Indians. Such grants have been universally understood to convey a title to the grantees, subject only to the Indian right of occupancy, and the United States have adopted and acted upon the same principles.   *Ibid.*

SEC. 1905. The title of the Government (English) to the country was placed on the ground of discovery, and which gave to the Government the exclusive right of acquiring the soil from the natives. The Indians were considered as being the rightful occupants of the soil, with a legal as well as just claim to retain possession of it and to use it according to their own discretion; but their rights to complete sovereignty as independent nations were necessarily diminished, and their power to dispose of the soil to whomsoever they pleased was denied.

Ibid.

SEC. 1906. By the Revolution the power of government and right of soil which had been previously in Great Britain passed definitely to these States; and it has never been doubted that either the United States or the several States had a clear title to all the lands within the boundary lines described in the treaty of peace, subject only to the Indian right of occupancy, and that the exclusive power to extinguish that right was vested in the Government, which might constitutionally exercise it.   *Ibid.*

SEC. 1907. The seizin of lands belonging to the Indian tribes is in the sovereign, and the Indians are mere occupants. A purchaser from them can acquire only the Indian title, and they may resume it and make a different disposition of it.   *Ibid.*

SEC. 1908. The Indians, being mere occupants, are deemed incapable of transferring an absolute title to others.   This occupancy is not incompatible with a seizin in fee in the State.   *Ibid.*

SEC. 1909. The land in controversy, being within the limits of Pennsylvania, the Connecticut settlers were in legal estimation trespassers and intruders.   They purchased the land without leave and entered upon it without right.   *Vanhornes, lessee, v. Dorrance, 2 Dallas, 304.*

SEC. 1910. The deed from the Six Nations is invalid under the laws of Pennsylvania, it being provided by the act of February 14, 1729, that purchase from the Indian natives within the State of Pennsylvania "without the order or direction of the proprietary or his commissioners shall be null, void, and of no effect."   *Ibid.*

SEC. 1911. By the charter to William Penn, the right of preemption attached, and was vested in him, to all the lands comprehended within its limits.   The Penn family had exclusively the right of purchasing the lands of the Indians, and indeed the Indians entered into a stipulation of that kind.   *Ibid.*

SEC. 1912. The proclamation by the King of Great Britain, issued some time prior to 1780, directing the governors of the several colonies and provinces in North America to grant tracts of land to British soldiers by way of bounty, prohibited the grant or purchase of lands occupied by Indians.   *Sims's lessee, v. Irvine, 3 Dallas, 425.*

SEC. 1913. Montour's Island, embracing the land in controversy, lay within the country which belonged to the Indians, and could not, therefore, be the subject of a lawful location under a private warrant.   *Ibid.*

SEC. 1914. Without confessing the aboriginal title of the Indian tribes in Montour's Island, it is enough for the lessor of the plaintiff to allege, upon the finding of the special verdict, that before the year 1779 they had abandoned and relinquished all the lands except on the northwest side of the Ohio, and that in pursuance of treaties they have since receded very distantly from that boundary.   *Ibid.*

SEC. 1915. Lands may be acquired by conquest, and a relinquishment in consequence of hostilities is tantamount to conquest.   *Ibid.*

SEC. 1916. The State of Pennsylvania can not urge the treaty at Fort Stanwix, October 22, 1784 (7 Stat. L., 15), as proof that the Indian title had not been previously extinguished.   The State purchased tranquillity from the Indians for the benefit of all who held lands within their hunting grounds, and the deed inured to their use for their prospective proportions and to the State's use only for the residuum.   Besides, the Virginia rights were original charges on the land which she was bound to support and defend.   *Ibid.*

SEC. 1917. The conveyance by deed, in 1740, by John Wells of a tract of land in New Jersey to three Indian chiefs, of whom Jacob Mootes was the survivor, "to them and to their generation, and to endure as long as the waters of the Delaware should run," conveyed only a life estate. *Lessee of Foster v. Joice, 3 Washington, 498.*

SEC. 1918. The defendant set up no other title except a lease made to him in 1806 by certain commissioners appointed under an act of the New Jersey legislature to take care of the land in controversy for the "Cohaxen" Indians, saving the rights of all persons to the same. *Ibid.*

SEC. 1919. The Indian title to the lands in controversy (in Georgia) was extinguished by the treaty of August, 1814. *Bleecker v. Bond, 3 Washington, 529.*

SEC. 1920. In a treaty settling the boundary of the territory of the Indians and extinguishing their title to the rest in the State of Tennessee, the Government had reserved a right to put a garrison on the Indian portion and to use a reserve of three miles square in connection with it, but it happened that the Indian land did not extend above the mouth of the Hiwassee River, and the Government was fortunate enough, through a mistake, to put its garrison above the mouth of the river, on private property, and not below the river, on Indian ground. *The Arlington Case, 3 Hughes, 36.*

SEC. 1921. In the case of Meigs et al. *v.* McClung's lessee, 9 Cranch, 11, the Supreme Court held that the circuit court committed no error in instructing the jury that the Indian title was extinguished in the land in controversy, and that the plaintiff below might sustain his action. *Ibid.*

SEC. 1922. The fee in unsold lands is either in the State or General Government. The Indians have only a right of use, which, however, can not be divested except by purchase or war. *Doe ex dem. Godfrey v. Beardsley, 2 McLean, 412.*

SEC. 1923. The legal title to their lands has never been considered, by any branch of the Federal Government, as vested in the Indians. And hence it has been held that a State might grant the fee in the lands occupied by Indians, subject to their right. The Indian right is that of occupancy, and until this right shall be extinguished by purchase no possession adverse to it can be taken. *Ibid.*

SEC. 1924. Where a grant is made to an individual Indian by treaty or act of Congress, no further evidence of title, such as a patent, is necessary. *Ibid.*

SEC. 1925. An entry of land within the Virginia military district of Ohio, and a survey of the same before the extinguishment of the Indian title, is made void by certain acts of Congress. *Doe ex dem. Chinn v. Darnell, 4 McLean, 440.*

SEC. 1926. The Oneida Indians must be treated as the owners of their land in Wisconsin, their ownership, however, being subject to the rights of sovereignty of the United States.

United States v. Foster, 2 Bissell, 377.

SEC. 1927. A State statute of limitations is not applicable to a sale of lands exempted, by Federal authority, from State taxation.

Swope v. Purdy, 1 Dill., 349.

SEC. 1928. The exemption of the land from State taxation, being an exemption prescribed by Federal authority, no legislation of the State can extend the effect of its laws for taxation over lands exempted by Federal authority.   *Ibid.*

SEC. 1929. It may be doubted whether the Oneida Reservation can be sold by the United States in the present condition of the title, even by act of Congress, without the consent of the Indians themselves, but it is certain that it can not be without an express law, and until the rights of the Indians are purchased, and with their free consent.

United States v. Foster, 2 Bissell, 377.

SEC. 1930. A sale of lands for taxes in Indian reservation not subject to taxation is void.   *Swope v. Purdy, 1 Dill., 349.*

SEC. 1931. The Wyandotte Indians, before their removal from Ohio, had adopted a written constitution and laws, and, among others, laws relating to descent and wills.   These are in the record, and are shown to have been copied from the laws of Ohio and adopted by the Wyandotte tribe, with certain modifications to adapt them to their customs and usages.   *Gray v. Coffman, 2 Dill., 393.*

SEC. 1932. On January 21, 1785, the United States, by treaty of that date, conceded to the Wyandottes and Delawares a large tract of territory, embracing millions of acres, in northern Ohio.   Of these lands, on the 17th of March, 1842, there remained to the Wyandottes, in the county of Crawford, 109,144 acres, which, by treaty of that date (7 Stat. L., 608), were ceded to the United States.

Hicks v. Butrick, 2 Dill., 413.

SEC. 1933. By article 2 of the compact between the Delaware and and Wyandotte Indians, December 14, 1843, the Delawares ceded and quitclaimed to the Wyandottes 36 sections of land in Kansas, in which 36 sections are the lands in controversy.   *Ibid.*

SEC. 1934. The compact of December 14, 1843, between the Delawares and Wyandottes was confirmed by act of Congress approved July 25, 1848 (9 Stat. L., 366), with the proviso that the Wyandotte Nation should take no better right or interest in the lands than was then vested in the Delawares.   This included the lands in controversy.

Ibid.

SEC. 1935. The practical construction of the treaty of 1855 with the Wyandottes (10 Stat. L., 1159), and the coincident judicial construction of it by the supreme court of Kansas (Sumner *v.* Spybuck, 1 Kans., 394), find much support in Wilson *v.* Wall, 6 Wallace, 83. And see 9 Stat. L., 203, as to payment to heads of families.

Ibid.

SEC. 1936. Lands patented to the reservees under the treaty with the Miami Indians, June 5, 1854 (10 Stat. L., 1092), are liable to be taxed by the State authority after the title has passed from the Indian reservee to a citizen.   *Peck v. Miami County, 4 Dill., 370.*

SEC. 1937. At the common law, by a rule which in this country is purely technical, the word "heirs" is necessary in a fee-simple grant. But this rule did not apply to grants to a corporation aggregate, and the Cherokee Nation may be regarded under the law as a corporation aggregate.   *United States v. Reese, 5 Dill., 405.*

SEC. 1938. Were it not for the treaty of 1835 (7 Stat. L., 478) the treaty of 1833 (Id., 414) is broad enough in its terms to convey a fee-simple title.   This treaty is subsequent in date to the act of 1830, which contains the clause that the lands should revert to the United States if the Indians "become extinct or abandon the same."   There is no limitation to the title conveyed by the treaty of 1833.   If the treaty is inconsistent with the law of 1830, it repealed so much of it as was inconsistent.

Ibid.

SEC. 1939. In pursuance with the terms of the treaty of 1835 (7 Stat. L., 478) the President of the United States, on December 31, 1838, executed to the Cherokee Nation a patent for the 7,000,000 acres of land, for the outlet west, as well as for the 800,000 acres of land granted to them by the treaty of 1835.

Ibid.

SEC. 1940. The lands of the Cherokee Nation of Indians can not be held to be "lands of the United States" in the sense of the language used in section 5388 of the Revised Statutes.

Ibid.

SEC. 1941. The Cherokee Indians hold their lands by a title different from the usual Indian title—by occupancy.   They derived it by grant from the United States.   It is a base, qualified, or determinable fee, without the right of reversion, but only the possibility of reversion to the United States.

Ibid.

SEC. 1942. It has been uniformly held by the Supreme Court of the United States that the Indian title was but the right of occupancy, the fee remaining in the United States.   United States *v.* Cook, 9 Wall., 592; Johnson *v.* McIntosh, 8 Wheat., 574; Worcester *v.* Georgia, 6 Pet., 580; Cherokee Nation *v.* Georgia, 5 Pet., 48; Fletcher *v.* Peck, 6 Cranch, 142; 1 Kent Com., 259.   And unless there is a clear and explicit provision in the treaty, showing that the Government intended to make a grant in fee simple, the court will not presume that a new departure has been made or that a different policy from that pursued in the past was intended.   *Goodfellow v. Muckey, 1 McCrary, 238.*

SEC. 1943. In the treaty with the Menomonees of Wisconsin, in 1831 (7 Stat. L., 342), the following language was used: "The following-described tract of land, at present *owned* and *occupied* by the Menomonee Indians, shall be *set apart* and *designated* for their future homes." The Supreme Court in construing this treaty uses the following language: "The land thus recognized as belonging to the Menomonee tribe embraced the section in controversy in this case. * * * But the right that the Indians held was only that of occupancy. The fee was in the United States, subject to that right, and could be transferred by them whenever they chose." (Beecher *v.* Wetherby, 95 U. S., 525.)   *Ibid.*

SEC. 1944. In most treaties the words "set apart" and "reserved" are used in appropriating portions of the public lands for the homes of the Indian tribes.   *Goodfellow r. Joseph Muckey et al., 1 McCrary, 238.*

SEC. 1945. In some instances the Indian's lands have been patented to them in fee simple so long as they should exist as a nation and *remain on the land.* Such were the provisions of the treaties with the Senecas and the Shawnees made in 1861 (7 Stat. L., 349, 352).

Ibid.

SEC. 1946. It has been the policy of the Government in treating with the Indian tribes to reserve from the public domain tracts of land for the use and occupation of the Indian tribes and to limit them to such reservations. The right of the Indians to have and occupy these lands for themselves has been granted in language more or less comprehensive, but always evincing a purpose on the part of the Government to limit the Indian title to the use and occupation of the land.

Ibid.

SEC. 1947. The treaty between the United States and the Pottawatomie tribe of Indians, November 15, 1861 (12 Stat. L., 1192), is not an exception to the general rule that the Indian title is but a right of occupancy and does not amount to a grant *in presenti.*

Ibid.

SEC. 1948. It has been uniformly held by the Supreme Court of the United States that, in the absence of express legislation to the contrary, the Indian title is but a right of occupancy, the fee remaining in the United States.   *Ibid.*

SEC. 1949. If the covenant in a treaty made by the United States with a tribe of Indians that the lands in question "shall be reserved to and for the Great and Little Osage tribes or nations aforesaid, so long as they may choose to occupy the same," is not a reservation by the United States for another purpose than building railroads, it is difficult to comprehend the use of language or what kind of reservation that clause was meant to cover.

United States v. Leavenworth, Lawrence & Galveston R. R. Co., 1 McCrary, 610.

SEC. 1950. Having in view the grant of lands to Kansas for railroad purposes, the treaty of 1865 with the Osages (14 Stat. L., 687), as finally amended and proclaimed, provided as follows: "Said lands shall be surveyed and sold under the direction of the Secretary of the Interior, on the most advantageous terms for cash, as public lands are surveyed and sold under existing laws, *including any act granting lands to the State of Kansas in aid of the construction of a railroad through said lands*, but no preemption claim or homestead settlement shall be recognized."

Ibid.

SEC. 1951. When the act of 1863 (12 Stat. L., 772) was passed, granting certain lands to the State of Kansas to aid in the building of railroads, the lands in controversy were and had for a long time been in the peaceful and undisputed possession of the Osages. And though the treaty of 1825 (7 Stat. L., 240) did not so far vary their tenure as to give them a fee simple title, or, indeed, anything but a usufructuary right, it did guarantee to them the exclusive possession and use of these lands "so long as they may choose to occupy the same."

Ibid.

SEC. 1952. For reasons similar to those stated in the case of the United States *v.* The Leavenworth, Lawrence and Galveston Railroad Company (1 McCrary, 610), the lands reserved for the benefit of the Osage Indians did not pass, under the land grant of Congress, to the State, to aid in the building of railways; approved July 26, 1866.

United States v. M., K. & T. Ry. Co., 1 McCrary, 624.

SEC. 1953. Where a district of country has been, by competent authority, set apart as an Indian reservation, and by treaty stipulation the United States have assumed jurisdiction over it, such district remains an Indian reservation, the Federal jurisdiction over it continues until it is changed by act of Congress or by treaty, or until the Indian title is extinguished; and this notwithstanding it may be embraced within the limits of a State. This jurisdiction extends to and embraces the enforcement of the criminal laws.

United States v. Berry, 2 McCrary, 58.

SEC. 1954. On the 24th of February, 1838, the purchase of the land in question was ordered canceled by the Commissioner of the General Land Office, on the ground that it was not Government land until the ratification of the Quapaw treaty August 24, 1818.

Pintard v. Goodloe et al., 1 Hemp., 502.

SEC. 1955. Rights of preemption can not be acquired to lands whilst the Indian title to occupancy still exists. *Russell v. Beebe et al., 1 Hemp., 704.*

SEC. 1956. The reason given by Estudillo for the nonsignature of the grant, to wit, that he had omitted to settle with the Indians, is not in unison with the practice of making grants subject to the Indian rights. It is further contradicted by the facts in this case that the grant is made to exclude the possessions of the Indians.

Boyreau v. Campbell, 1 McAllister, 119.

SEC. 1957. The grant to Campbell of a certain tract of land in California contained the special condition that the Indians should not be molested. *Ibid.*

SEC. 1958. The Indian tribes have the right of use in the soil, which can only be divested by the United States, with their consent by purchase, or without it by war. *McKay v. Campbell, 2 Sawyer, 118.*

SEC. 1959. The fee of the land covered by the Moapa Reservation, Nevada, is still in the United States, and the land is occupied by the Government as an Indian reservation. *Ex parte v. Sloan, 4 Sawyer, 330.*

SEC. 1960. In the location of Sioux half-breed scrip, the rules and regulations of the United States Land Office requires that in all cases where not located by the party to whom scrip issued in person, the application to locate must be accompanied with a power of attorney from said party authorizing the same. *United States v. Chapman, 5 Sawyer, 528.*

SEC. 1961. While a contest between a purchaser from the State on a State selection, and a claimant under Sioux half-breed scrip location, arising under the provisions of the act of Congress July 23, 1866, is pending and undetermined before the register and receiver of the United States Land Office, no patent can properly issue. *Ibid.*

SEC. 1962. The act of Congress under which the Sioux half-breed scrip was issued does not permit it to be located on land occupied by another; and the land in this case being occupied by the holder of a State title, with valuable improvements thereon, was not subject to location by said scrip. *Ibid.*

SEC. 1963. At the time the State agent applied to select the land in question, January 15, 1868, there being no preemption or other valid claim thereto, the State selection was good as one made on surveyed lands. *Ibid.*

SEC. 1964. The Umatilla Reservation was made by a treaty June 9, 1855 (12 Stat. L., 945), twenty-two days after the admission of Oregon into the Union, and was thereby set apart for the exclusive use of the Indians now occupying it. *United States v. Barnhart, 10 Saw., 491.*

SEC. 1965. In an action brought by the United States to recover damages for cutting and removing timber from the public lands, it was held that the grant to the corporation included lands then occupied by Indians, subject to such occupation, until terminated by Congress. *United States v. Ordway, 12 Saw., 275.*

SEC. 1966. The occupation of Peronto prior to the filing of the maps of either general or definite location of the route of the road could avail him nothing, as the land was not open to preemption, because the Indian title was not then extinguished; and on the filing of the first map the land was specially withdrawn from sale or preemption, irrespective of the Indian title, and on the filing of the second one the right of the corporation at once attached thereto.   *United States v. Ordway, 12 Saw., 275.*

SEC. 1967. Under the act April 8, 1864 (13 Stat. L., 39), four reservations were selected and set apart by the President, viz: The Tule River, by Executive order, October 3, 1873, modified by the order of August 3, 1878; Hoopa Valley, by Executive order, June 23, 1876; Round Valley, by Executive orders, March 30, 1870, April 8, 1873, May 18, 1875, and July 26, 1876; reserves for Mission Indians, by Executive orders, January 31, 1870, December 27, 1875, May 15, 1876, August 25, 1877, and various orders and modifications unnecessary to enumerate.   *United States v. 48 lbs. Rising Star Tea, 13 Saw., 298.   Same in 35 Fed. Rep., 65.*

SEC. 1968. Assuming that the various reserves known as Mission Indian Reserves were made under the provisions of the act April 8, 1864, and constitute one reservation, it would seem that the authority conferred upon the President by that act has been exhausted.   *Ibid.*

SEC. 1969. The Indians known as the "Colus" tribe, in California, were occupying their rancheria about 150 yards from the steamboat landing in the present town of Colusa as late as 1849.
Semple v. United States, 1 Hoffman's Land Cases, 37.

SEC. 1970. John A. Sutter, for Moquelumne Indians, claimant for 4 square leagues in Sacramento County, Cal., granted December 22, 1844, by Manuel Micheltorena to Moquelumne Indians. Claim filed February 28, 1853, and confirmed by the commission November 20, 1855.
1 Hoffman's Land Cases, Appendix, p. 90.

SEC. 1971. Joseph Sadoc Alemany, claimant in behalf of the Christianized Indians formerly connected with the missions of upper California: First, in behalf of the Indians of Santa Clara, under a grant by Manuel Micheltorena, June 10, 1844, for all vacant lands of Santa Clara ungranted before that time; second, in behalf of the Indians for lands known as Las Gallinas, El Nacimiento, and La Estralla, in San Luis Obispo County, under a grant of Manuel Micheltorena, July 16, 1844; third, in behalf of 16 neophytes for small tracts of land in the vicinity of the mission of Santa Ynez, Santa Barbara County; fourth, and in behalf of Indians generally 1 square league in each of the 21 missions. Claim filed February 28, 1853; rejected by the commission December 31, 1855; appeal dismissed for failure of prosecution in the northern district February 23, 1857, and in the southern district December 22, 1857.   *Ibid.*

SEC. 1972. The acts respecting the military and Indian lands had only passed about a year before the first of the two respecting removals. If there were no negative words in the acts respecting the military and Indian lands, it is clear the legislature did not intend by its acts of April, 1784 (chapter 14, section 7), and October, 1784 (chapter 19, section 6), to authorize individuals to appropriate lands within those tracts or portions of country by removal.

Polk's Lessee v. Hill, 1 Brunner's Coll. Cases, 126.

SEC. 1973. At the date of the deed in question, and the first probate and registration thereof, the land lay in the Indian boundary. Watson, to whom the deed was made, resided in North Carolina east of the Cumberland Mountains.

Watson v. Debbins, 1 Brunner's Coll. Cases, 233.

SEC. 1974. The beginning corner of the land called for in the plaintiff's grant was until the year 1806 within the Indian boundary, but that part of the land on which defendant resided was not. Seven years did not elapse between the extinguishment of the Indian title and the commencement of the present action.

McIver's Lessee v. Reagan, 1 Brunner's Coll. Cases, 240.

SEC. 1975. Where, under a grant of land by the United States by a treaty with the Indians (7 Stat. L., 320), the grantee was authorized to convey only with the consent of the President and the grantee executed two conveyances to different persons, the title passed under the one first made effective by the approval of the President.

Lomax v. Pickering, 46 North Eastern Reporter, 238.

SEC. 1976. In ejectment for land originally forming part of an Indian reservation nearly all of which had been allotted to various members of the tribe and their families, *held*, that the want of legal evidence of an allotment to the original grantor, under whom defendant claimed, could not be supplied by general probabilities arising from possession and reputation or by evidence not legally competent, and that defendant showed no title. In an action involving the title to lands originally forming part of an Indian reservation, a table of births, in a book once used as the record of proceedings of the tribe and afterwards of the supervisors of the town, and an entry in a merchant's account book, and in another and otherwise blank book, looking like an attempted copy of some survey or allotment of lands of the tribe to its members and their families, are not admissible as evidence, the same not being authenticated in any way, either as originals or copies of public or official records. *Fowler v. Schafer, 32 N. W. Rep., 292.*

SEC. 1977. In Noonan *v.* Mining Company (121 U. S. 393; 7 Sup. Ct., 911) it was *held* that "where a party was, on the 28th of February, 1877, in possession of a mining claim in the Black Hills of Dakota, within the Indian reservation, with the requisite discovery, with the surface boundaries sufficiently marked, with the notice of location posted, with a disclosed vein of ore, he could, by adopting what had been done, causing a proper record to be made, and performing the amount of labor or making the improvements necessary to hold the claim, date his rights from that date, and such location, labor, and improvements gave him the right of possession.

Scott v. Toomey, 67 N. W. Rep., 840.

SEC. 1978. The exclusive right of preemption to all Indian lands lying within the Territories of the United States is vested in Congress. Title to land is dependent on the law of the nation in the territory of which the land lies. Where lands in California were held by Indians under title by occupying at the time of the treaty of Guadalupe Hidalgo, unless a claim therefor was presented to the commissioners appointed under the act of the United States of March 3, 1851, within the time limited by such act, the land became a part of the public domain, and as such became open to preemption."

Thompson v. Doaksum, sr., 10 Pacific Rep., 199.

SEC. 1979. Under the Creek treaty of 1832, an Indian reservee, when his land had been selected and set apart by location, became entitled to the possession until disposed of by him according to the terms of the treaty or voluntarily relinquished or abandoned; and this right to possession was a legal estate which could be enforced in a court of law. The Indian was authorized to convey his title and interest, with the approval of the President, and after such approval the contract of conveyance became valid, vesting in the grantee all the estate vested in the Indian by the treaty and his location. The action of the President of the United States, in relation to these contracts, is final and conclusive, and precludes any inquiry in a collateral way into the identity or capacity of the Indian parting with his interest, unless in a suit in which one of the parties claims under or through him.

Jones & Parson's Heirs v. Inge & Mardis's Heirs, 5 Porter (Ala.), 327.

SEC. 1980. A *location* or *allotment* of the lands assigned under the sixth article of the treaty of 1832 is necessary to show title in one who claims title previous to the issuance of the patent, and without proof of such allotment or location no action involving the title can be maintained previous to the issuance of the patent. The location or allotment is the mode by which the proper executive officer determines that the choice of land made by the Creek tribe is approved and that the lands are not subject to other claims. When this is done an inchoate legal title is created, capable of transmission by those to whom they are assigned, by the Creek tribe. It is unnecessary to give evidence that the assignment was made by the chiefs and headmen of the tribe or that those who made it were authorized by the tribe. The recognition of these persons by the Government as the chiefs and headmen is conclusive on the courts.　　　　*Johnson v. McGeehee & Thomas, 1 Ala., 186.*

SEC. 1981. Although under the treaty of 1832 a patent is necessary to consummate the title of the reserve or to furnish complete evidence of it, yet the failure to issue the patent does not avoid the title to which the treaty location and continued occupation impart.

Rains v. Ware & Warren, 10 Ala., 623.

SEC. 1982. A purchaser from an Indian reservee acquires no title by his purchase until the contract is approved by the President; when this is done the purchaser is entitled to a patent, and when it issues it vests the fee in the patentee.

Haden v. Ware, 15 Ala., 149.

SEC. 1983. When the Government of the United States has made an appropriation of land to an Indian reservee under the Creek treaty of 1832, a patent subsequently issued by the Government can not defeat the prior right of the Indian or his legal vendee. However, the fact of the previous appropriation can not be proved by the bare recital in another patent subsequently issued, and the plaintiff must prove the location of the Indian reservee, as well as that he succeeded to the rights of such reservee.

Stephens v. Westwood, 20 Ala., 275.

SEC. 1984. A deed from a Creek Indian reservee, under the treaty of March 24, 1832, after it has been approved by the President of the United States, conveys such title to the purchaser as will maintain an action of ejectment.

Long et al. v. McDougald's Admr., 23rd Ala., 413.

SEC. 1985. After the location of an Indian reservee under the treaty of March 24, 1832, no valid entry of the land embraced in the reservation could be made; and consequently, a patent issued on such invalid entry, as against the reservee or those claiming under him, would be void. If the location is proved by the Government records to have been regularly made, it can not be collaterally impeached, even by one holding a patent from the United States.

Stevens v. Westwood, 25 Ala., 716.

SEC. 1986. An assignment, not under seal, of an approved contract for the sale and purchase of an Indian reservation, although it does not convey to the assignee the title conferred by the approved contract, is nevertheless sufficient to authorize the issue of a patent to him; and the validity of a patent, subsequently issued to the assignee, is not affected by the fact that the assignment was not under seal.

Tarver v. Smith, 38 Ala., 135.

SEC. 1987. A purchaser of land from an Indian reservee, under the Indian treaty of 1832, with the approval of the President of the United States, acquired such an interest as was subject to sale under execution in 1852; and its purchase under such sale conferred a title to the land superior to a patent issued to a purchaser from him subsequent to the sale.

Jones' Heirs v. Walker, 47 Ala., 175.

SEC. 1988. The United States holds the fee simple to the lands occupied by Indian tribes, and may, if it seem fit, disregard their right of occupancy, and, before a cession by the Indians, convey either an unencumbered title in fee, to take effect immediately, or a title subject to their right of possession, and to take effect only when they, by voluntary cession, shall have ceded their title.

Gaines et al. v. Hale & Rector, 26 Ark., 168.

SEC. 1989. A deed of conveyance from an Indian to a white person is a nullity on its face, and no one can derive title under it. Such a conveyance is contrary to the policy of Spanish and Mexican as well as American law, and is strictly forbidden. The plan of Iquala, and the Mexican constitutions of 1836 and 1843, and the decrees of 1812 and 1813 did not remove the restrictions on alienation of lands by Indians.

Sunol v. Hepburn, 1 Cal., 255.

SEC. 1990. The lands in controversy were indemnity school lands selected by the State in lieu of a portion of a section sixteen included within an Indian reservation. The selection was subsequently canceled by reason of the relinquishment by the United States of the reservation. Prior to the cancellation the grantors of the plaintiff purchased the lands of the State in good faith, and a patent was issued to them. Ever since the date of their purchase the plaintiff and his grantors have been in the actual possession of the land, cultivating and improving it. Subsequent to the cancellation, and while the plaintiff was so in possession, the defendants, each of whom were qualified to make a homestead entry, applied to enter different portions of the land under the United States homestead laws, and afterwards entered thereon, built houses, and exercised other acts of ownership over the same. The action was brought to quiet title of the plaintiff against the homestead claims of the defendants. *Held*, that the title acquired by the plaintiff, even conceding it to be bad as against the United States, must prevail as against the defendants, because the latter, having forcibly entered upon the land while in the actual possession of the plaintiff, could not acquire any rights under the homestead laws.

Hambleton v. Duhain, 71 Cal., 136.

SEC. 1991. Under section 15 of the act of March 3, 1851, the patent issued in pursuance of the decree confirming the Mexican grant was conclusive only as between the United States and the claimant, and did not terminate the relation between him and the Indians. Under this section the rights of the Indians were preserved without presenting their claims, and the patentee took the legal title in fee, subject to their right of entry.

Byrne v. Alas, 74 Cal., 628.

SEC. 1992. Mission or Pueblo Indians, who by themselves and their ancestors have been in the continuous use, occupation, and possession of lands included within the exterior limits of a Mexican grant from a time prior to the establishment of the Mexican Government, have a right to remain in the occupancy thereof as against the patentee from the United States Government and his grantees, notwithstanding they never presented their claims to the lands to the board of land commissioners appointed by the act of Congress of March 3, 1851, to ascertain and settle private land claims of California.

Byrne v. Alas, 74 Cal., 628 (see 68 Cal., 479, same case).

SEC. 1993. The decisions of this court in the cases of United States *v.* McCall, in Uhlig *v.* Garrison, and in French *v.* Lancaster, wherein it is held that until February 28, 1877, Lawrence County was included within the Sioux Indian Reservation, and that no title could be acquired or transferred to mining grounds and other lands therein situated until that date, is now adhered to.

Golden Terra Mining Co. v. Smith et al., 2 Dakota (Smith), 378.

SEC. 1994. A reservation of land in an Indian treaty of cession simply secures to those in whose favor the reservation is made a continuation of the right of occupancy in the land reserved, while the ultimate title remains in the United States, as before the treaty.

Wheeler v. Me-shing-go-me-sia, 30 Ind., 402.

SEC. 1995. The common-law doctrine that the cutting of standing trees is waste does not apply to the members of a band of Indians in the use of a large tract of wild land in this State granted to them by the United States.   *Ibid.*

SEC. 1996. The act of Congress of June 30, 1834, conferred upon the half-breeds of the Sac and Fox tribes a full-fee simple title as tenants in common to the reserved lands lying in Lee County, Iowa.

Webster v. Reid, 1 Iowa (Morris), 467.

SEC. 1997. By the act of Congress approved June 30, 1834, the qualified interest held by the half-breeds of the Sac and Fox Indians to the half-breed tract in Lee County was converted into an absolute title.   *Wright v. Marsh, Lee and Delavan, 2 Iowa (Greene), 94 (May, 1849).*

SEC. 1998. The act passed for the benefit of settlers on the "half-breed lands" in 1840 can not·be interposed against a title confirmed by the judgment of partition in Spaulding et al. *v.* Antonya et al. Said act became inoperative by its own limitation as soon as the title to said "lands" became settled by due course of law. The judgment of partition is absolute.   *Wright v. Mallard, 3 Iowa (Greene), 86.*

SEC. 1999. The judgment of partition of the half-breed lands in Lee County is final and conclusive of all rights therein adjudicated. Where the land in controversy is shown by the pleadings to be within the venue of the court, proof of its locality is not necessary.

Hypfner v. Walsh et al., 3 Iowa (Greene), 509.

SEC. 2000. The title derived under the decree of partition of the half-breed tract is conclusive as to all those who were parties to it, and can not be controverted by evidence of title to interests or shares acquired prior to it; but the rule is not applicable to conveyances, made prior to such decree, offered in evidence to establish facts essential to a correct ascertainment of the subject-matter of a subsequent conveyance.   *Barney v. Miller, 18 Iowa (Witherow), 460.*

SEC. 2001. On July 22, 1854, Congress passed "An act to dispose of the public lands in the Territory of Kansas to which the Indian title shall have been extinguished." (10 Stat. L., 310.)

State of Kansas v. Stringfellow, 2 Kans., 263.

SEC. 2002. In the case of United States *v.* Brooks (10 How., 445) it was held that the United States, by treating with the Caddoe Indians for the purchase of their lands owned by them in the Red River country while Louisiana was Spanish territory, recognized in said Indians a right to said lands similar to the rights to lands generally recognized in Indian tribes with whom the United States have made treaties; that is, the right to use and the absolute title to such lands as should be *reserved* to the Indians *in severalty.*   *Ibid.*

SEC. 2003. Prior to the treaty of June 3, 1825 (7 Stat. L., 244), with the Kansas Indians, they had the "Indian title," i. e., a life interest in the usufruct of a body of land in Kansas, including that in controversy, the United States holding the ultimate title, charged with this interest of the Indian nation, so long as they should remain a nation.

Brown & Brown v. Belmarde, 3 Kans., 41.

SEC. 2004. The "Indian title" was by the sixth article of that treaty vested in certain individuals; that to the land in question in Lavonture.

Ibid.

SEC. 2005. From the death of Lavonture, in 1847, to the passage of the act of Congress, May 26, 1860, the whole title to the land in question was in the Government, and that act operated as an original grant to certain reservees and the "heirs of deceased reservees" mentioned therein.   *Ibid.*

SEC. 2006. "Heirs of deceased reservees" used in said act of 1860 is *descriptio personœ*, and is to be construed with reference to and determined by the law at the time the estate passed, and whoever under the laws of Kansas would have inherited had Lavonture died May 26, 1860— the date of the approval of the act—are the persons to whose benefit the grant inured, and a charge by the court below to that effect would have been proper in an action of ejectment to recover the land in question.   *Ibid.*

SEC. 2007. There are no words in the treaty of 1825 with the Kansas Indians (7 Stat. L., 244) which upon any known rule of interpretation would create an estate of inheritance. Before the treaty the "United States held the ultimate title charged with the right of undisturbed occupancy and perpetual possession in the Indian nation" so long as it should remain a nation. Had the nation become extinct without a treaty, the lands would have become the property of the United States, disencumbered of the Indian title.   *Ibid.*

SEC. 2008. If the title to the lands in question be in the United States, they are not taxable—this under express treaty stipulation, and without such treaty stipulation.

Blue Jacket v. Comrs. of Johnson Co., 3, Kans., 299.

SEC. 2009. Where a district of country is held in common by an Indian tribe, with or without a patent in fee simple issued pursuant to a treaty, which does or does not give the Government alone the right to purchase from them, such tribe holds the mere right of perpetual possession and enjoyment—though the words of the treaty or patent as between individual Indians or whites and the Government be sufficient to convey title absolutely.   *Ibid.*

SEC. 2010. A contract for the sale of any part of the Delaware trust lands, while they are held in trust, is void; and a note given therefor is without consideration, and, under the Kansas law of 1855 (p. 156, secs. 3, 4), that could be pleaded as a defense to the note in the hands of the assignee.   *Stone v. Young, 4 Kans., 17.*

SEC. 2011. Under the Kickapoo treaty of 1862 (13 Stat. L., 623), which provides that all lands sold under article 5 thereof shall be forfeited to the Government if not fully paid for in accordance with the provisions of said treaty, and which also provides that "none of said land shall be subject to taxation until the patents have been issued therefor," after said land has been sold to the Atchison and Pikes Peak Railroad Company, now known as the Central Branch Union Pacific Railroad Company, and by them sold to an individual who has made valuable improvements thereon, but before said lands have been paid for, *held,* that neither said lands nor the improvements thereon are taxable. .   *Parker v. Winsor, 5 Kans., 362.*

SEC. 2012. If the public lands of the United States, held and occupied by Indian tribes, can not be sold to railroad companies by means of a treaty alone (clause 2, sec. 2, art. 2, U. S. Const.); if it requires an act of Congress to dispose of such lands (clause 2, sec. 1, art 4, U. S. Const.), then of course the land in controversy can not be taxed by the State.   *Ibid.*

SEC. 2013. The title to the same must remain in the United States, and the attempted sale to the railroad company by virtue of the Kickapoo treaty must be a nullity.   *Ibid.*

SEC. 2014. So long as the title to land lying within an Indian reserve remains in the United States, or in the Indians, or in both, the land is not taxable by the State.   *Comsrs. Douglas Co. v. U. P. Ry. Co., 5 Kans., 615.*

SEC. 2015. A mere contingent, conditional, and inchoate equity, obtained by a railway company in such lands, but which does not amount to a title, either legal or equitable, does not so divest the United States of their title to the land as to subject it to taxation.   *Ibid.*

SEC. 2016. Under a conditional purchase of certain Delaware trust lands by the Union Pacific Railway Company, when by the terms of the contract of purchase no patent is to be issued for the land until all the conditions of the purchase are fulfilled, and if any one of the conditions of the purchase is not fulfilled the railway company are to forfeit all their right, title, and interest in and to said land, and the same is to be sold again to other parties, and when it appears from the nature of the contract and the character of the parties that *time* is an essential element of the contract, no title, legal or equitable, passes to the railway company until it fulfills every obligation of its contract.   *Ibid.*

SEC. 2017. The laws and treaties of the United States, and not the laws of the State, must govern in the primary disposal of the soil by the United States.   *Ibid.*

SEC. 2018. If the title had passed so that the land in question belonged to the railway company, it was taxable, but if the title had not so passed, and the lands still belonged to the United States or to the Indians, it was not taxable.   *Ibid.*

SEC. 2019. The maxim in equity that equity will consider that as done which ought to be done, and that it will look upon things agreed to be done as actually performed, never applies where *time* is of the essence of the contract, and where the land is subject to absolute forfeiture on failure of some condition of the sale being performed.

Ibid.

SEC. 2020. The conditions upon which the land was sold had not all been performed when the land was assessed. In 1866 and 1867 the purchase money had not been paid, and, therefore, the patent had not been issued. Hence, in 1866 and 1867 the railroad company had no title to the land, legal or equitable.   *Ibid.*

SEC. 2021. A contract was made for the purchase and sale of certain lots in Leavenworth City, while the title to the lots was still held by the United States in trust for the Delaware Indians. After the vendor and his heir have received all the benefits accruing to them by virtue of said contract, the heir sues the grantee of the vendee to recover of him said lots: *Held*, that the heir is estopped from asserting that said contract is void, and his claim to said lots can not be maintained.

Maduska v. Thomas, 6 Kans., 153.

SEC. 2022. The Indians had a contingent possessory right to every foot of the land reserved to the Shawnees by article 2 of the treaty of 1854 (10 Stat. L., 1053), subject to be converted into an absolute legal right at any time. Such a right, while that condition of things remained, was inconsistent with the right of any other person to obtain any interest in the land, present or prospective, absolute or contingent   *McAlpin v. Henshaw, 6 Kans., 176.*

SEC. 2023. A note given by one citizen of the United States to another for the sale and delivery of possession of a tract of land to which the Indian title has not been extinguished is void.

Vickroy v. Pratt, 7 Kansas (Webb), 238. Same, 7 Kansas (Dassler), 153.

SEC. 2024. In February, 1867, the Missouri River Railroad Company had no such interests in the lands known as the "Delaware Diminished Reserve" as that they could convey the same by deed; and such a deed made at that time, without consideration, and induced by vicious causes, can not be set up as an equitable defense to a suit for the recovery of the lands, as such a deed has no equity and will not be enforced.   *Simpson v. Greeley, 8 Kans. (Dassler), 393.*

SEC. 2025. The chiefs of the Shawnee tribe have no authority, even with the consent and approval of the Secretary of the Interior, to dispose of the "surplus lands" which were set apart for the absentee Indians under the treaty of 1854, and make deeds therefor; and a deed so made confers no title.

Hale v. Wilder, 8 Kansas (Webb), 545. Same, 8 Kansas (Dassler), 365.

SEC. 2026. Each class of beneficiaries under the Shawnee treaty of 1854 received all the land it was entitled to if no mistake had been made. The surplus was more than sufficient to meet the requirements of the absentees, leaving a large residue to be disposed of for the benefit of the Shawnee Nation. The tract in dispute also belongs to the nation, but not as "surplus" lands under the treaty.   *Ibid.*

SEC. 2027. No provision is made for double allotments. The status of the land became fixed by the selections as made and recorded, and the spirit of the treaty is to hold them as allotted lands not taken by the allottees, and thus become the property of the nation, to be disposed of under the direction of the Government.   *Ibid.*

SEC. 2028. The condition of the lands reserved to the Shawnees by the treaty of 1854 is anomalous. That instrument makes no provision for a case of double allotments, such a contingency not having suggested itself to the parties.   *Ibid.*

SEC. 2029. The treaty provides (1) for grants to churches, societies, schools, and a few individuals; (2) for allotments in severalty to those who elect to take them; (3) for a certain portion to be held in common, and (4) the surplus to be set apart in one body of land, in compact form, for use of such absentees as shall return within a given time; and the portion of this tract not so taken within the stipulated time was to be sold for the benefit of the whole tribe. It was after these various selections were made that it became known that there was a small portion that had been double allotted.   *Ibid.*

SEC. 2030. The lands in controversy are a part of the 200,000 acres reserved to the Shawnee Indians by the treaty of 1854 (10 Stat. L., 1053).   *Ibid.*

SEC. 2031. Where, under the treaty of October 14, 1868 (15 Stat. L., 495), the United States became the sole owner of a certain tract of land known as the Sac and Fox Diminished Reservation, proof that a certain smaller tract of land is a part of this reservation is some proof that the Government owned the land at a time when a certain trespass was committed thereon.

State of Kansas v. Herold, 9 Kans. (Dassler), 134.

SEC. 2032. August 31, 1866, the Secretary of the Interior entered into a written agreement with the Missouri River Railroad Company to sell to said company all lands provided to be sold by the Delaware treaty of July 4, 1866 (14 Stat. L., 793).

Bruce v. Luke, 9 Kans. (Dassler), 139.

SEC. 2033. A deed such as was executed by Journeycake to Mrs. Simpson does not estop the grantor, who, at the time of executing the same, had no title to or interest in the land mentioned in the deed, from afterwards acquiring title to or interest in said land as against the grantee, and the after-acquired title or interest will not inure to the benefit of the grantee.   *Ibid.*

SEC. 2034. If the Ottawa Reserve did not, by virtue of the treaty of 1862 (12 Stat. L., 1237), become a part of the State of Kansas, it is not now a part of it. The making of the tribe citizens after five years did not necessarily in terms make the reserve a part of the State, though it must be admitted as one of many stipulations in the treaty abrogating the excluding clause of the treaty of 1831.

McCullagh v. Allen, 10 Kans., 150.

SEC. 2035. If the land in question was a part of the lands belonging to the Cherokee Nation by the treaty of 1835 (7 Stat. L., 478), there can be no doubt that the court below had no jurisdiction, for the fifth article of that treaty expressly stipulates that the lands reserved by that treaty to the Cherokees "shall in no future time, without their consent, be included within the territorial limits or jurisdiction of any State or Territory."   *Ephraim v. Garlick, 10 Kans., 280.*

SEC. 2036. The Secretary of the Interior has declared that the title to certain lands covered by the Osage treaty of 1865 (14 Stat. L., 687) passed to plaintiff on the completion of its road; but the court does not decide that it did or did not.

L., L. & G. R. R. Co. v. Leahy, 12 Kans., 124.

SEC. 2037. Land described as "Cherokee land" is not necessarily land ceded to the Cherokee Nation of Indians by the treaty of 1835 (7 Stat. L., 478).   *Ephraim v. Garlick, 10 Kans., 280.*

SEC. 2038. A description of a tract of land as the SE. ¼ sec. 6, T. 35 S., R. 20 E., does not enable the court to say that the tract so described is within the limits of the lands ceded to the Cherokees by the said treaty of 1835.   *Ibid.*

SEC. 2039. The statute of limitation never runs against the Government (Lindsey *v.* Miller, 6 Peters, 666; Gibson *v.* Chouteau, 13 Wall., 92, 99). Therefore no trespasser can ever obtain any rights upon Government land.   *Wood v. M., K. & T. Ry. Co., 11 Kans., 323.*

SEC. 2040. As against a demurrer, allegations in a petition that the plaintiff is the owner of certain lands under the Osage treaty of 1865 (14 Stat. L., 687) and that the same were not subject to taxation for a given year will be deemed sufficient as statements of fact.

L., L. & G. R. R. Co. v. Leahy, 12 Kans., 124.

SEC. 2041. The lands granted to the State of Kansas under the act of July 25, 1866 (14 Stat. L., 236), to aid in the construction of the Kansas and Neosho Valley Railroad, for which no patents had issued for certain of the lands within this grant in Bourbon County up to April 21, 1871, were subject to taxation for the year 1870.

Gulf R. R. Co. v. Morris, 13 Kans., 302.

SEC. 2042. The portion of the Cherokee neutral lands paid for on the 8th of August and patented on the 2d of November, 1870, were not taxable for the year 1870.   *Ibid.*

SEC. 2043. The only parties who at the time had any rights or interest in the land in question were the Osage Indians, the Government, and Tinker.   No one else could question the validity of the selection, and whether Tinker had any improvements on the land at the time he made his selection or not is a matter into which Rakestraw, holding a subsequently acquired title, can not be permitted to inquire.

Lownsberry v. Rakestraw, 14 Kans., 151.

SEC. 2044. The act of July 28, 1866 (14 Stat. L., 309), entitled "An act for the relief of the trustees and stewards of the Mission Church of the Wyandotte Indians," appears upon its face to be a grant to a church organization among and of Wyandotte Indians, and made by virtue of the governmental protection over these wards of the nation.   *Sarahass v. Armstrong, 16 Kans., 192.*

SEC. 2045. A society of Wyandotte Indians was the beneficiary, and, though the Wyandotte Nation removed from the limits of the State of Kansas, yet while that society was continued in existence among them the parties recognized by the nation as the trustees thereof are the legal custodians of the fund, and may maintain an action in the courts of the State to recover it from one to whom it had been loaned prior to the removal.   *Ibid.*

SEC. 2046. On a construction of the Osage treaty of June 2, 1825 (7 Stat. L., 240), and the subsequent treaty of September 29, 1865 (14 Stat. L., 687), and of the act of March 3, 1863 (12 Stat. L., 772), granting lands to the State of Kansas to aid in the building of railroads, the United States Supreme Court held that lands which, under the said treaty of 1825, had been set apart and reserved for the Osages, and which was in their actual use and occupancy, did not pass under the said railroad grant. Congress did not intend that this grant should reach the Osage lands further than to allow the company to construct its line of road through them.

Note to L., L. & G. Rwy. Co. v. Coffin, 16 Kans., 510.

SEC. 2047. The question in this case—the claim of the plaintiff in error to certain lands in the Osage ceded tract—being one whose ultimate decision belongs to the Supreme Court of the United States, and such question having been decided by that court, must also be decided by this court in the same way, adversely to the claim of the plaintiff in error. *Ibid.*

SEC. 2048. The history of the legal contests with respect to the title and conflicting claims set up to the Osage ceded lands is hardly completed with the mere publication of the final decision in the *Coffin* case. A portion of this history and a discussion of many of the questions involved will be found in the reported cases of Wood *v.* M., K. & T. R. R. (11 Kans., 323); L. L., C. & G. R. R. *v.* Leahy (12 Kans., 124); Lownsberry *v.* Rakestraw (14 Kans., 151).

SEC. 2049. The joint resolution of Congress dated April 10, 1869, in respect to the disposition of the lands ceded by the Osages to the Government by the treaty of 1865 (14 Stat. L., 687), which provided "that the sixteenth and thirty-sixth sections in each township of said lands shall be reserved for State school purposes in accordance with the provisions of the act of admission of the State of Kansas," operated as a grant of said sections to the State for school purposes.

Baker v. Newland, 25 Kans., 25.

SEC. 2050. Such grant was not in violation of the terms of the trust upon which said lands were ceded to the Government, and even if it were, the title of the grantee would not thereby fail, although the Indians might have an equitable claim upon the Government for compensation on account of its breach of trust. *Ibid.*

SEC. 2051. In the Wisconsin case of Beecher *v.* Wetherby (95 U. S., 517), the land was Indian land, set apart for the use of the Indians as these lands in Kansas were set apart for the use of the Osage Indians. In each case the title was in the Government, the right of possession in the Indians. In each case the Government, by compact with the State, by the act of admission, gave the State in one case the sixteenth section and in the other the sixteenth and thirty-sixth sections. This compact having been recognized in Wisconsin and Michigan and elsewhere, as attaching to all the lands in the State in which the Government had not parted with its title, embraces all Indian lands; and when the Indian title is extinguished the lands pass to the State under this compact. *Roberts v. M., K. & T. Ry. Co., 43 Kans., 102.*

SEC. 2052. The criticism that the Osage ceded lands in controversy were not within the meaning of the proviso of the act of March 3, 1863, reserved "to the United States" is unsound.   The treaty reserved them as much to one as to the other contracting party.   In one sense they were reserved to the Indians, but in another and broader sense to the United States for the "use of the Indians."   This proviso construed is exactly the same as the proviso to the act of July 26, 1866, and the subject-matter is the same lands.

Ibid.

SEC. 2053. In construing the act of March 3, 1863 (12 Stat. L., 772), granting lands to the State of Kansas in aid of railroad construction, the United States Supreme Court, in Leavenworth Ry. Co. *v.* United States (92 U. S., 733), said : "All lands heretofore reserved—that is, reserved before the passage of the act 'by competent authority, for any purpose whatsoever,' are excepted by the proviso." This language is broad and comprehensive and unquestionably covers these lands that had been reserved by treaty before the act of 1863 was passed.

Ibid.

SEC. 2054. Under the proviso of the act of Congress (sec. 1, ch. 27, U. S. Rev. Stat., vol. 14) defendants claimed right of way through the land in controversy. The land was Osage ceded land, which was afterwards conveyed to the Government by treaty of 1865 (14 Stat. L., 687).

Ibid.

SEC. 2055. This land being Osage Indian land at the time of the passage of the act of July 26, 1866 (14 Stat. L., 289), was land reserved by the Government from the operation of that grant.

Ibid.

SEC. 2056. The third section of the act of admission of the State of Kansas irrevocably granted to the State for the use of schools the sixteenth and thirty-sixth sections of the public lands, and that grant embraced those sections of Indian lands within the State in which the Indians had a right of possession only.

Ibid.

SEC. 2057. The act of July 26, 1866 (14 Stat. L., 289), gave a right of way over the Osage ceded lands reserved by the United States for the Osage Indians; but such right of way extended only over such lands as had not previously been disposed of by the Government.

Ibid.

SEC. 2058. The right of the United States to dispose of lands to which it holds the fee has ever been recognized by the courts of highest resort in this country, and this rule is true with regard to lands in which the Indians have the right of possession, as well as to the public lands belonging to the Government.

Ibid.

SEC. 2059. The only limitation made by the act of admission of Kansas was that land which had not otherwise been sold or disposed of should be granted to the State for school purposes. The Osage lands were the property of the Government and were subject to grant by the Government.   *Ibid.*

SEC. 2060. The right and power to dispose of the Osage land rested in the Government, and it having that power, then they were not otherwise disposed of and were subject to the grant made to the State. This compact was binding upon the Government and when made and accepted by the State became unalterable except by consent of the State. By this act the Government parted with these lands and they were no longer subject to be disposed of for other purposes.   *Ibid.*

SEC. 2061. The proviso in the organic act of Kansas that the rights of persons or property of Indians should not be impaired, construed to mean with respect to boundary and jurisdiction, and not to fix or determine the grants to the State, or to limit such grants.   *Ibid.*

SEC. 2062. In Railway Co. *v.* Allen, 22 Kans., 485, this court held that where the railway company has only an easement the proprietor of the soil retains the fee of the land and his right for every purpose not incompatible with the rights of the railway company. This rule is recognized everywhere.   *U. P. Ry. Co. v. Kindred, 43 Kans., 134.*

SEC. 2063. Although the abutting land owners have cultivated and inclosed part of the right of way granted by Congress, this possession can not be considered as adverse or hostile. It must be considered as permissive only. If the fee of the land belongs to the United States, then the abutting land owners can acquire no title or claim by possession or limitation.   *Ibid.*

SEC. 2064. If the abutting land owners own the fee of the right of way they may use the land in any way not inconsistent with the permanent rights of the railway company; but such use will not give them adverse possession so as to confer title.   *Ibid.*

SEC. 2065. Section 3, chapter 79, of the laws of 1874 (Kansas), relates to titles procured to Indian lands by a purchaser in good faith for a valuable consideration from the Indian himself, or from his heirs or grantees, and provides that three years' undisturbed actual possession operates as a bar in any action for the recovery of such lands by the holders of any adverse title.   *Forbes v. Higginbotham, 44 Kans., 95.*

SEC. 2066. Under the acts of Congress of August 11, 1876 (Rev. Stat., 1874–1881, p. 237), and May 28, 1880 (Rev. Stat., 1874–1881, p 529), relating to the Osage trust and diminished reserve lands in Kansas, such lands are subject to taxation according to the laws of the State of Kansas, after a sale thereof by the United States to an individual, after the payment of the first installment of the purchase price.   *Logan v. Comsrs. of Clark Co., 51 Kans., 747.*

SEC. 2067. The vendee of one of several coproprietors of a tract of land (the land in dispute being a large tract of land purchased in 1802 of the Choctaw, Biloxi, and Pascagoula Indians by Fulton & Miller), among whom a partition has taken place, can not in case of eviction demand from a vendee of another of the coproprietors a portion of the land sold to him. His remedy is by action of warranty against the vendor. *Compton v. Mathews, 2 Morgan (La.), 82.*

SEC. 2068. A map or plat on which the division lines of several coproprietors of a tract of land (in this case purchased from the Choctaw, Biloxi, and Pascagoula Indians) are traced out and laid down, forms as complete a partition of the joint property as if each line had been actually run and marked by the surveyor. *Ibid.*

SEC. 2069. The right acquired by each of two purchasers of the same tract of land of the same vendor, the title of either of whom requires for its validity as to third persons only a due registry before the other, is a subject of sale or legacy. *Brown v. Frantum, 3 Morgan (La.), 336.*

SEC. 2070. A mandatory under a special power must confine himself strictly within the limits assigned to him, and those dealing with him must at their peril see that he does not exceed his authority; but they need not, in search of his powers and their limitations, look beyond the instrument of mandate. *Ibid.*

SEC. 2071. The certificate of the French officers under the colonial government of Louisiana that the plaintiff's ancestor was in possession of a certain tract of land, under a purchase from the (Biloxi) Indians, etc., is not legal evidence of title, and is inadmissible as evidence in a petitory action. *Billieux's heirs v. Singletary, 9 Morgan (La.), 57.*

SEC. 2072. In an action for slander of title when the defendant reconvenes and sets up title, it becomes essentially a petitory action, and the burden of proof of title rests on the defendant. *Millandon et al. v. McDonough, 9 Morgan (La.), 424.*

SEC. 2073. The last warrantor is the real defendant in a suit against his vendees, not only against the party who cites him, but more particularly against the original actor. *Ibid.*

SEC. 2074. Copies of township maps are not admissible in evidence when better evidence can be procured. *Ibid.*

SEC. 2075. When the expression in a grant or title only conveys a certain front and depth, the grantee or purchaser can not claim by diverging lines to the rear, and thereby obtain more than the superfices contained in a parallelogram. *Ibid.*

SEC. 2076. We are of the opinion that the plat, even if admissible as evidence, is not entitled to any weight as establishing the extent of the claim. Although Patier says he is a sworn surveyor, commissioned by the surveyor-general of the United States, we know of no right that gives him permission to run out claims under the direction of individuals merely, and fix the boundaries of those not recognized by the Government. It is not pretended he acted under any authority from his superior in making what is called a survey; it never was presented to the surveyor-general for his approval, nor does it seem to have had the legal sanction of anyone authorized to act in the premises. Patier does not pretend that it is a regular survey; he says Delille Dupaic had derived his title from the Callapissa Indians and sold it to various persons. He does not seem even to have heard of a grant from the French Government in 1769, or attempted a location in conformity to it. '   *Ibid.*

SEC. 2077. Where the meaning of an instrument is uncertain, the record of another suit, by a different plaintiff, but to which the defendant was a party, will be admissible in evidence to show, by the acts and declarations of the latter, what his understanding of the instrument was. The present plaintiffs not having been parties to the suit can not avail themselves of the statements in the pleadings as judicial admissions absolutely conclusive of the rights of the defendant. They must be considered simply as other declarations.

Wells et al. v. Compton et al., 3 Robinson (La.), 171.

SEC. 2078. Surveyor's plats made under the order of court, in a suit to which the defendant, against whom they are offered, was a party, though the plaintiff was not, are admissible in evidence as circumstances, so far as they show acts of the defendant.   *Ibid.*

SEC. 2079. The vendor of a tract of land is bound to put the purchaser in possession; and when he sells at different times by separate portions, without boundaries, to different persons, the first purchaser must be satisfied before a second can obtain any portion of his.

Ibid.

SEC. 2080. In all surveys, courses and distances must yield to natural and ascertained objects.   *Ibid.*

SEC. 2081. Recognitive acts do not exempt the party offering them from the necessity of producing the primordial title, unless its tenor be therein specially set forth. (C. C. (La.), 2251.)

Brooks v. Norris, 6 Robinson (La.), 175.

SEC. 2082. Recognitive acts are either *ex enta scientia* or *in forma communi.* The former, said to be *in forma speciali et despositiva*, are those in which the primordial title is set forth; they are equivalent to the original title in the event of its loss, and prove its existence against the person making it, dispensing with its production. Recognitive acts *in forma communi* are those in which the tenor of the primordial title is not set forth, serving only to confirm so far as it is true, and to interrupt prescription; they do not prove its existence nor dispense with its production. *Ibid.*

SEC. 2083. By the common law, where the recital of the deed points to higher evidence in the power of the party, the withholding of which creates suspicion of fraud or unfairness, the party will be held to account for the nonproduction of the higher evidence before the recital can avail him. *Brooks v. Norris, 6 Robinson (La.), 182.*

SEC. 2084. An objection to a witness on the ground that a suit was pending against him by the same plaintiff for other tracts of land claimed under the same title, and that he had set up the same defense, goes to his credibility and not to his competency, he being interested in the question, but not in the case. *Ibid.*

SEC. 2085. A stipulation in a contract of sale, to refund to the vendee at a certain rate if the tract purchased proves upon survey to be less than estimated, or if the vendee be evicted from any portion thereof, must be confined to any deficiency ascertained by a survey made "within a reasonable time from the day of the sale." Such stipulations are not contemplated to apply to an eviction occurring at a distant period—ten or eleven years after. For such an eviction the vendee must be compensated for the actual damage sustained, and the measure of such damage is the price paid the United States for the land from which he was so evicted. *Thomas v. Clement, 11 Robinson (La.), 397.*

SEC. 2086. An eviction does not require actual dispossession; it may consist when a party is forced to continue to hold the property under a different title from that transferred to him by his vendor (11 Robinson, 397). Prescription runs against a vendee's action of warranty from date of eviction and not from date of sale. *Ibid.*

SEC. 2087. The plaintiff contends that his claim was confirmed by act of Congress of May 24, 1828, entitled "An act to confirm claims and lands in the district between the Rio Hondo and Sabine rivers, founded on habitation and cultivation" (6 Stat. L., 382). We do not doubt that had it been ascertained at the time of the passage of the act that the claim, No. 14, of Leonard Dyson, as assignee of Edward McLaughlin, did not lie within the Caddo Indians' lands, it would have been confirmed. It is now fully demonstrated that the lands of the Caddo Indians did not cover the claim No. 14 (treaty between the United States and the Caddo Nation, dated July 1, 1835, 7 Stat. L., 470).

We can not, however, give to the act of May 24, 1828, the construction which the plaintiff places on it, for we do not understand the words of the act to say or mean that the claim is confirmed subject to a certain contingency, to wit, that it did not fall within the Caddo Indian Territory. It was not the effect of the confirmation which was suspended, for the act did not confirm the claim, but the action of Congress on the claim itself was suspended and reserved for its subsequent consideration after the ascertainment of a particular fact, thus requiring the further action of Congress to complete the title of the plaintiff. Nor can it be said that the act reserved the land for sale, or precluded the United States from disposing of the same by sale, donation, or otherwise; for the land was not surveyed, located, or described in such a manner as to designate it with sufficient certainty. We are also of the opinion that the title to the land in controversy has passed from Congress and no longer forms a part of the public domain; and also that the apparent title is in the defendant; hence that the pretensions of the litigants must be determed by our State laws and judicature.   *Cannon v. White, 16 Glenn, 89.*

SEC. 2088. It is a recognized principle of jurisprudence in this State (Louisiana) that a perfect grant, imparting a clear devestiture of title from the former sovereign and transfer of that title to the grantee, requires no act of the new sovereign to give it completeness.
                          Nixon v. Houillon, 20 La. (Hawkins), 515.

SEC. 2089. All lands in Louisiana at the time of the cession to the United States which had not passed by a perfect title from the government then having control of the country, vested in the Government of the United States by the act of cession as public domain.
                                                          Ibid.

SEC. 2090. Where a title has been acquired by prescription it may afterwards be lost by subsequent adverse possession of the land, peaceable and undisturbed for more than ten years, by one holding a just title translative of the property.   *Randolph v. Laysard, 36 La. (Davis), 402.*

SEC. 2091. Where the plaintiff in a petitory action claims the land in controversy under a title which he asserts was warranted by the author of the defendant's title opposed to him, and that the defendant is thereby estopped from setting up his title against him, the fact of the warranty must be clearly established and may be disproved by evidence showing a distinct and continued acknowledgment of the title of defendant's author by those from whom or through whom the plaintiff claims.

Such acknowledgment may also be opposed to a claim of title by plaintiff based on presumption.   *Ibid.*

SEC. 2092. The first section of the act of 1693 (Massachusetts) provided for the appointment of persons "to have the inspection and more particular care of the Indians in their respective plantations," and these persons were authorized to determine pleas betwixt party and party and to punish criminal offenses. Such a course of legislative control was continued until Maine was separated from Massachusetts, although contracts called "treaties" were made with them by the colony for the relinquishment of their title to lands. By the act of separation Maine assumed the performance of all the obligations made by Massachusetts to the Indians within her jurisdiction, and in the year 1821 passed an act for the regulation of the Penobscot and Passamaquoddy tribes of Indians.

Moon v. Veazie, 32 Me., 343.

SEC. 2093. The title of the Government is superior to that of the aborigines.

Penobscot tribe v. Veazie, 58 Me., 402.

SEC. 2094. In a deed from the Penobscot Indians to the Commonwealth of Massachusetts, releasing all right, title, and interest to the lands lying on each side of the Penobscot River, was the following clause: "Excepting and reserving to the said tribe all the islands in said river above Oldtown, including said Oldtown Island, within the limits of the said thirty miles," it was held that five islands lying alongside of Oldtown Island were not embraced within the exception.

Ibid.

SEC. 2095. Where the State conveyed land to the grantor of defendant's ancestor more than thirty years ago, and the defendants and those under whom they claim have held the possession and claimed to be owners of the land during all that time, it is not competent for a tribe of Indians who do not appear to have any title in the premises to question the regularity of the sale by the State.

Ibid.

SEC. 2096. The plaintiffs claim that the islands sued for are included in the reservation made in the conveyance of 1796 to Massachusetts. If this were true it would by no means follow that they are entitled to recover. The statute of limitations would still have to be overcome, for the defendants and those under whom they claim have been in the actual possession of the premises under a grant from the State for more than thirty years.

Ibid.

SEC. 2097. The courts have always held that a title derived from the Government is superior to one derived from the aborigines. If it should now be held otherwise, and if it should also be held that the statute of limitations is no bar to a recovery under an Indian title, a door would be opened to endless litigation, and thousands of titles now considered perfectly secure would be instantly destroyed.

Ibid.

SEC. 2098. The reservation referred to in the grant of 1796 by the Penobscot Indians to the State of Massachusetts did not create in the Indians any new title; it did not operate as a grant to them of the islands therein described. Its effect was simply to leave in them the title which they before had, and it is clear that if the plaintiffs prevail it must be upon the ground that the title of the aborigines to the wild lands over which they roamed is superior to that of the Government.

Ibid.

SEC. 2099. The executive and legislative departments of the Government have generally treated with the Indians as though they were the owners of the vast territories over which they had roamed, but when the title to any particular tract has been called in question in the courts of justice no such doctrine has been admitted.

Ibid.

SEC. 2100. It is a well-settled rule of law that in real actions the plaintiff must recover, if he recover at all, upon the strength of his own title, and not upon the weakness of his adversary's. It is clear that the plaintiffs have no title to stand upon.

Ibid.

SEC. 2101. The title to Grass Island did not pass to the Indians by the agreement of 1794 between the Passamaquoddy tribe and the State of Massachusetts.   *Granger v. Avery, 64 Me., 492.*

SEC. 2102. It was determined in Penobscot Tribe *v.* Veazie (58 Me., 402), that the title of the Government was superior to that of the aborigines. The Passamaquoddy tribe had no title originally to the island in controversy; they acquired none by the conveyance from Massachusetts, nor have they since acquired any by adverse possession. The occasional occupation of the island by different Indians for temporary purposes can not constitute a title by disseizin.   *Ibid.*

SEC. 2103. The Prov. St. (13 Will., 3, c. 20) providing that all conveyances of land obtained from the Indians without the license of the general court shall be void applies only to conveyances of land in which aboriginal right of occupancy has never been extinguished; and a purchase from an Indian, without such license, of a lot of land in an old-settled town will be deemed valid, unless it be proved that he held the aboriginal right of occupying the same.

Noah Clark v. William Williams et al., 19 Pickering, 36 Mass., 499.

SEC. 2104. A testator appointed J. P. his executor and S., wife of J. P., executrix, jointly and severally. He then gave a legacy of $200 to be paid by his executor or executrix to a certain charitable society (The Massachusetts Society for the Propagation of the Gospel among the Indians) in one year after his decease, and he said: "To enable my executor or executrix to pay this legacy, I give unto them or either of them, forever, a lot of land," described, "this lot of land being devoted for the payment of this legacy is to be delivered to said society, unless payment is made by my executor or executrix," as aforesaid. The will was proved in 1801, and J. P. alone accepted the trust as executor and paid the legacy according to the will, his wife, S., never having qualified or acted as executrix, and J. P. and S., his wife, jointly occupied the premises until 1827, when J. P. died intestate, leaving several heirs. His widow having had her dower set out to her continued to occupy the whole premises until 1847, when she died, leaving heirs by a former husband. *Held,* that by the devise the fee of the estate vested in J. P. in severalty upon the payment of the legacy.   *Popkin v. Sargent, 64 Mass. (10 Cushing), 327.*

SEC. 2105. Under the third article of the treaty of 1819 with the Chippewa Indians a tract of land was reserved for certain members of the tribe; the section or parcel of each reserve to be afterwards located in such manner as the President of the United States might direct. A certified copy of a map from the General Land Office on which a certain section was designated as the tract of one of said reservees is evidence of the due location of such section according to the conditions of the treaty. The term "reservation" in said treaty is equivalent to an absolute grant, and the title was conferred by the treaty, though not perfect until the location was made, which was necessary to give the grant identity.   *Dewey v. Campau, 4 Mich. (3 Gibbs), 565.*

SEC. 2106. The grant of a sovereignty must have operation according to its intent; it may operate immediately or from time to time, if such appear to be its purpose. The words employed in the proposition relating to school lands in the act of Congress for the admission of Michigan into the Union (Comp. Laws, p. 38) indicate an intent on the part of the United States that the grant should have a continuous operation; and therefore lands reserved for the benefit of Indian tribes by treaties with them prior to the admission of the State will, on the extinguishment of the Indian title, be conclusively presumed as against a trespasser, or one not claiming under the United States, to be embraced within the proposition granting lands to this State contained in the act of admission.

Ballou v. O'Brien, 20 Mich. (2 Clark), 304 (April term, 1870).

SEC. 2107. The Indian reserve at Sault Ste. Marie was not subject to preemption under the preemption law of 1841, even after the surrender by the Chippewa Indians to the United States, August 2, 1855, of the right secured to them therein under the treaty of June 16, 1820, the Government having seen fit to exempt Indian reservations from the provisions of said preemption act even after the Indian title was extinguished. The rights secured to the Chippewa Indians under the treaty of June 16, 1820, in the Indian reserve at Sault Ste. Marie was a *perpetual* one, and when said reserve was set apart and appropriated to their use for a place of encampment the land could not be thereafter used or occupied by anyone else while they occupied and used it, and all of the beneficial attributes and belongings of the fee were theirs as far as any use of the same was concerned.

Spalding v. Chandler, 84 Mich. (Fuller), 140.

SEC. 2108. J. C., a Sioux half-breed, a beneficiary under treaty and act of Congress making the half-breed reservation near Lake Pepin, was, with her husband, in possession of, claiming as their property, a tract within the reservation, and prior to August 20, 1853, they quitclaimed it, with covenant for further assurance to S., and surrendered possession to him, and S. being in possession on August 20, 1853, quitclaimed to A., with covenants to stand seized, and for further assurance. In 1855 S., to correct a supposed misdescription in the first deed, executed to A. another quitclaim deed with covenants of nonclaim to stand seized, and for further assurances whenever he should thereafter acquire from the United States title to the land. In 1857 J. C. entered the land according to the laws and treaties relating to the reservation, and she and her husband conveyed by warranty deed to S. "all their and each of their right, title, interest, estate, property, possession, claim, and demand, of, in, and to" the land. In 1862 S. conveyed to H. all his "right, title, interest, estate, property, possession, claim, or demand whatsoever to said premises." The general deeds were duly recorded in the order as to time in which they were executed. *Held*, that the deed in 1857 from J. C. and husband to S. passed the fee simple; that the deeds from S. to A. were not void as against public policy nor as contrary to acts of Congress; that the covenant for further assurance was binding, and that it was immaterial that S. did not acquire the title direct from the United States; that it is immaterial whether the deeds from S. to A. were recorded, because, as the deed of S. to H. was only of the grantor's "right, title, and interest," H. could take nothing legal or equitable which S. had previously conveyed to A.; that H. took the legal title charged with the trust in favor of A.   *Hope v. Stone, 10 Minn., 141.*

SEC. 2109. The act of Congress of 1854, under which the Sioux half-breed scrip was issued, provides "that no transfer or conveyance of any of said certificates or scrip shall be valid." In the scrip itself he had nothing which he could transfer to another, but his title to the land when perfected under it was as absolute as though acquired in any other way. A simple power of attorney to sell land executed by a Sioux half-breed is good till revoked, and will extend to land subsequently acquired by means of scrip issued under the act of Congress of July 17, 1854, if such lands come within its terms.

Gilbert et al. v. Thompson, 14 Minn., 544.

SEC. 2110. Chapter 83 of the acts of Congress for 1854 (10 Stat. L., 304) authorizes the President to make an exchange with the Sioux half-breeds for their reservation on Lake Pepin by issuing to them certificates or scrip for certain amount of land, and provides that "said certificates or scrip may be located upon any of the lands within said reservation * * * or upon any other unoccupied lands subject to preemption or private sale, or upon any other unsurveyed lands not reserved by Government upon which they have, respectively, made improvements." *Held*, that this provision as to "unoccupied lands" is framed for the *protection* of *occupants*, and that the occupant may waive the same so that a valid location of scrip may be made upon lands of which he is in occupation. *Held further*, that the clause "upon which they have, respectively, made improvements" qualifies the words "other surveyed lands" and not the words "other unoccupied lands."   *Thompson v. Myrick, 20 Minn., 205.*

SEC. 2111. The privilege of the half-breed to select 80 acres of land under the treaty of September 30, 1854, between the United States and the Chippewa Indians of Lake Superior and the Mississippi, was a *personal* right, and therefore the scrip issued as evidence of such right was nonassignable. The transfer of the scrip would not be illegal, but only ineffectual and void, as a transfer of title to the same. The delivery of the lawful possession of said scrip, together with the transfer and delivery of an agreement pertaining to and accompanying the same, and made by the half-breed to whom the scrip was issued, by which he bound himself, for a valuable consideration, to convey, by good and sufficient deed, all such lands as might be selected and entered by him, either in person or by attorney, to such party or parties as should locate the scrip, his or their heirs or assigns, on demand, after the location thereof, *held*, to furnish a valid and sufficient consideration for a promise to pay money.   *Dole v. Wilson, 20 Minn., 356.*

SEC. 2112. The United States Supreme Court has said "it is an universal rule that purchases made at Indian treaties, in the presence of and with the approbation of the officer under whose direction they are held, gave a valid title to the lands. It prevailed under the colonial government and under the laws of the States after the Revolution. It has been adopted by the United States, and purchases made at treaties held by their authority have always been held good by the ratification of the treaty, without any patent to the purchasers from the United States."   *Coleman v. Dee, ex dem. Tish-ho-mah, 12 Miss., 40.*

SEC. 2113. If purchases from Indians are thus deemed complete legal title upon ratification of treaty, reservations to them must stand on as high ground.   *Ibid.*

SEC. 2114. Under article 11 of the Chickasaw treaty of 1834 (7 Stat. L., 450) the residue of the Chickasaw country, after the reservations were located, was the only portion which could be sold as public lands of the United States.   *Wray v. Doe, 18 Miss., 452.*

SEC. 2115. By the proclamation of George III, October 7, 1763, by which, with others, the government of West Florida was created and established over the lands ceded by the treaty of Paris, it was stipulated that the Indian tribes should be protected "in the possession of such parts of our domain and territories as, not having been ceded to or purchased by us, are reserved to them or any of them as their hunting grounds;" and that "no private person do make purchase of any land from any Indians but that the same shall be purchased only for the Government in the name of the sovereign at some public meeting of the Indians." In 1772 the government of West Florida, created under this proclamation, granted a body of land lying between the mouth of the Yazoo and the thirty-first degree of north latitude. It was held that this grant was invalid because the Indian title was not extinguished in the lands thus granted until 1777, and under the proclamation of 1763 the power of the royal governor within the territory reserved was suspended.   *Montgomery v. Ives, 21 Miss., 161.*

SEC. 2116. After the war of 1756, by the treaty concluded in 1763, Spain ceded to Great Britain Florida, Fort St. Augustine, the Bay of Pensacola, and all that she possessed on the continent of North America, to the east or southeast of the Mississippi river. At the same time France also ceded to Great Britain the whole of New France, and all that portion of Louisiana lying upon the east side of the Mississippi River, except the island of New Orleans. Great Britain, by these cessions, became the owner, subject to the Indian right of occupancy, of all the land between the Mississippi River and the Atlantic Ocean.   *Ibid.*

SEC. 2117. The proclamation of George III, October 7, 1763, created four distinct and separate governments within the countries ceded by Spain and France. These were Quebec, East Florida, West Florida, and Grenada. The proclamation also declared "that it is just and reasonable, and essential to our interests and the security of our colonies, that the several nations or tribes of Indians with whom we are connected and who live under our protection should not be molested or disturbed in the possession of such parts of dominions and territories, as not having been ceded to or purchased by us, are reserved to them, or any of them, as their hunting grounds."   *Ibid.*

SEC. 2118. The proclamation of George III further declares a principle which seems to have been adhered to ever since, "that no private person do make purchase of any land from any Indians, but the same shall be purchased only for the Government, in the name of the Sovereign, at some public meeting of the Indians." This principle became incorporated into the intercourse of England with the Indian tribes, and has been adopted and pursued by our own Government in all its transactions with them.   *Ibid.*

SEC. 2119. In the war between the French and Natchez tribe, which terminated about the year 1730 in the extinction of that tribe, the Choctaws were the allies of the French. It is probable, from the fact of the treaty made with them at Mobile in 1777 (7 Stat. L., 21), that they succeeded to and occupied the hunting grounds of the Natchez by virtue of the conquest. They do not appear to have been ceded to anyone (1 Martin's Hist. Louisiana, 280–287; 1 Monethe, 274).   *Ibid.*

SEC. 2120. Be this as it may, when the prohibition on the governor of West Florida to grant lands beyond the limits of his province as then fixed is established, in 1763, it became incumbent on those claiming under his grant to show that the prohibition had been removed.

Ibid.

SEC. 2121. On this part of the proclamation of 1763 the Supreme Court of the United States say:

This reservation is a suspension of the power of the royal governor within the territory reserved. (Fletcher *v.* Peck, 6 Cranch, 142.)

It is because of this suspension, which existed at the date of this grant, that we think it has no intrinsic validity. It is an established principle in our jurisprudence that a grant of land on which the Indian title has not been extinguished is void.

Ibid.

SEC. 2122. The European nations which respectively established colonies in America assumed the ultimate dominion to be in themselves, and claimed exclusive right to grant title to the soil, subject only to the Indian right of occupancy.

Tush-ho-yo-tubby v. Barr, 45 Miss., 189.

SEC. 2123. The natives were admitted to be the rightful owners of the soil, with a legal as well as a just claim to retain possession of it and to use it according to their own discretion, though not to dispose of the soil at their own will, except to the government claiming the right of preemption; and this right was claimed on the ground of prior discovery.

Ibid.

SEC. 2124. This is the view of this subject taken by the Supreme Court of the United States in numerous cases, and this doctrine has always prevailed in this country. The Indians have a kind of nondescript title, which can only be extinguished by purchase.

Ibid.

SEC. 2125. The United States had the power to deal with the lands occupied by the Indian tribes according to its pleasure. It could respect their title and pretensions as it saw fit. But, as the several treaties and acts of Congress show, the Government never regarded the absolute title to the soil as residing in the United States until ceded by the Indians. Nor did they undertake to dispose of them until the acquisition of the Indian title.

Minter v. Shirley, 45 Miss., 376.

SEC. 2126. The various Indian treaties and the acts of Congress show that the Government never regarded the absolute title to the soil as vesting in the United States as proprietors in fee until ceded by the Indians, nor did they undertake to dispose of them by grants to individual purchasers until the acquisition of the Indian title.

Ibid.

SEC. 2127. The statute of 1803, reserving the sixteenth sections for schools, in terms only applied to lands to which the Indian title had been extinguished. The Choctaws and Chickasaws then occupied a large portion of the territory embraced in the limits of Mississippi.

The line which divided Mississippi from the Indian country was at a point at or near the mouth of the Yazoo River. Prior to the extinguishment of the Indian title there was not a vested right either in the State or the inhabitants of a township to the sixteenth section. *Ibid.*.

SEC. 2128. The United States have recognized the Indian nations as so far having the attribute of soverignty as to be capable of making treaties and being bound by them, and as having also such title to the country occupied by them as might be granted by cession to the United States. *Ibid.*

SEC. 2129. By article 19 of the Choctaw treaty of 1830 (7 Stat. L., 333), there were reserved out of the lands ceded by the Choctaws as many quarter sections of land as there were orphans in the Choctaw nation, which lands were to be selected by the Government and sold with the consent of the President, the proceeds to be used for the benefit of the orphans. *Held*, that when the lands were selected as contemplated by the treaty, the title to the whole vested in the United States for the benefit of the orphans as a class, and no particular orphan acquired title to any particular tract thereof. So that the statute of limitations would not run in favor of one in the adverse possession of any of the land, the title being in the United States and not in the orphans. *Bates v. Aven, 60 Miss., 955.*

SEC. 2130. The purchase of and payment for certain land reserved for orphans by the Choctaw treaty of 1830 (7 Stat. L., 333), bought in 1861 from State officers acting under an ordinance passed by the convention which had previously enacted the ordinance of secession, conferred upon the purchaser no right or title against the United States. *Ibid.*

SEC. 2131. If an individual has made a purchase of land from Indians, prohibited by law, for which he might have been punished, and which conveyed no title, so that he might have been removed as an intruder, still if he enters into possession of it and is suffered to remain, he may maintain that possession against persons who have no right to the land. And his quitclaim deed, subsequently made with covenants of warranty against persons claiming under him, will furnish a sufficient consideration for a promise to pay a sum of money if the sale is without fraud and with a knowledge of the circumstances.

It is not sufficient, to avoid a contract of sale, that the price agreed to be paid appears to be excessive. Gross inadequacy of value may be a strong circumstance to show fraud, but if there is no fraud or imposition, the parties have the right to fix the measure of value, and are bound by it. *Bedel v. Loomis, 11 N. H., 9.*

SEC. 2132. Lands purchased for the Brotherton Indians in New Jersey, exempted from taxes by the act authorizing the purchase and afterwards sold by them, are subject to taxation. *State v. Wilson, 2 N. J., 218.*

SEC. 2133. In 1758 the governor and general assembly of the then Colony of New Jersey, at the request of the Indians south of the Raritan, passed a law empowering certain commissioners therein named to purchase a tract of land in the county of Burlington, which was done. The deed was made to those commissioners and their heirs in trust for the use of said Indians and their successors forever; and by a special provision of the act, the Indians were prohibited from leasing or selling any part of their lands, which by the seventh section were thereafter to be exempt from taxation.   *Ibid.*

SEC. 2134. In 1801 the legislature granted the request of the Brothertons that they be allowed to remove to New York, and that their lands be sold for their benefit.   *Ibid.*

SEC. 2135. The lands then sold, under the act of 1801, were sold in fee simple and were therefore subject to taxation.   *Ibid.*

SEC. 2136. It is a matter not clearly settled how the King acquired his right to this country. *Blackstone, 1 Com.*, 108, supposes that he obtained it by treaties, or the right of conquest. *Smith* in his *Hist. of N. J.*, 8, insists that it was acquired by the right of discovery. The right, however derived, was strengthened by the purchase of the Indian title, which was made by the proprietors.   *Arnold v. Mandy, 6 N. J., 1.*

SEC. 2137. In 1758 the government of New Jersey purchased lands for the Indians residing within its borders with a stipulation that the said lands should not be subject to taxation. In 1801 the lands were sold at the request of the Indians, from whom the prosecutors claim to derive title. After the conveyance of the Indian title the lands were taxed in the hands of their grantees. The State courts affirmed the assessments, but on appeal to the Supreme Court of the United States a decision was rendered in 1812 (7 Cranch, 164) denying the right of the State to impose the tax.   *State, Given, prosecutor, v. Wright, 41 N. J., 478.*

SEC. 2138. In 1814, notwithstanding the decision of the United States Supreme Court to the contrary, the lands in question were again taxed, and from that date until the year 1877, taxes upon them have been annually assessed and paid by the prosecutors or their grantors without objection, which raises the conclusive presumption that by some convention with the State the right to exemption was surrendered.   *Ibid.*

SEC. 2139. The case in 7 Cranch, 164, in which the right to tax was denied, was submitted to the court upon a statement of facts, without argument, and a complete history of the case was not before it.   *Ibid.*

SEC. 2140. For the several laws of New Jersey and decisions of its courts relating to Indian lands in that State see   *Ibid.*

SEC. 2141. The inhabitants of the town of Newark trace their titles back to the Indians.   *Stockton v. Newark, 42 N. J. Equity Repts., 531.*

SEC. 2142. The finder of the last Spanish grant to the pueblo of Acoma, dated September 28, 1669, gains no such property in it as authorizes him to estimate its value to the pueblo and to withhold it from the pueblo until the estimated sum is paid.

Victor De La O. v. Acoma, 1 New Mex. (Gildersleeve), 226.

SEC. 2143. When a special verdict stated that A. and others, being some of the proprietors of a patent, in 1763 released part of the patent to certain *Indians* in trust, in which release K., another of the patentees, refused to join, and that in 1764 K. and the other proprietors were seized of the patent and made partition of the whole, including the allotment released to the *Indians*, it was *held* that, the jury having found the fact of seizin, without explaining how the proprietors became reseized, it was to be presumed that they were lawfully reseized, and that any intendment might be made that the fact might require; and that K. having, with a knowledge of the release, united in the partition, and having afterwards made a subdivision of the lot drawn by him with another proprietor, could not question the validity of the partition.   *Jackson v. Richtmyer, 16 Johnson's Reports (N. Y.), 313.*

SEC. 2144. In an action of ejectment brought by the people, the plaintiffs can not recover upon the ground that the Indian title to the lands in question has never been extinguished, where it is not pretended that the State has ever acquired the Indian title by any purchase or treaty, but, on the contrary, it is claimed that the fee of such lands is still in the six nations of Indians.

The People v. Snyder, 51 Barbour (N. Y.), 589.

SEC. 2145. It was not intended by the act "to relieve the Seneca Nation of Indians from certain taxes on the Allegany and Cattaraugus Reservation," passed February 19, 1857, to affect any of the provisions of the general law respecting the property liable to taxation. The tax is not to be assessed or imposed on the reservations, or any part of them, for any purpose so long as the reservations remain the property of the Seneca Nation. But when the Indians enter into a contract with a railroad company by which they give the latter the right to construct its road upon their land, and the road has been constructed thereon, and is used and occupied by the company, it ceases to be the property of the Seneca Nation to the extent specified in the contract. Although the fee of the land does not pass to the company, the possession and use and the right to possess and use pass by such contract, and it is liable to be assessed for taxation as property by the company as a railroad in the town in which it is situated.

The People v. Beardsley, 52 Barbour (N. Y.), 105.

SEC. 2146. Prior to the passage by Congress, in 1875, of the act to authorize the Seneca Nation to lease certain of their lands, leases given by Indians to white persons were, in a strict legal sense, invalid. Said act of Congress confirmed the leases then outstanding and made them valid, and established in the lessees, who had made improvements, a right of renewal for a period not exceeding twelve years, on such conditions as might be agreed upon by them and the councilors of the nation, or, in case of their disagreement, by referees. The plaintiff's lease, being prior in point of time to that given to the defendant, was entitled to priority over it.

As the plaintiff was under said act entitled to a renewal as a matter of right, the conditions only being subject to the action of the councilors of the nation, the defendant could not object to the conditions imposed or as to the mode of their proof, so long as no objections thereto were made by either the plaintiff or the nation.

Baker v. Johns, 38 Hun. (N. Y.), 625.

SEC. 2147. In June, 1872, Casler Redeye, a Seneca Indian of the Allegany Indian Reservation, in Cattaraugus County, leased to plaintiff a piece of land on said reservation for term of thirteen years from November 1, 1872, the land being in one of the villages mentioned in act of Congress of 1875 authorizing the Seneca Nation to lease certain lands and confirming, for the term of not exceeding five years or less, existing leases. On November 13 the plaintiff assigned the lease and possession of the land, including a house and barn, to defendant for $1,100; payment secured by a mortgage on house and barn, etc. Defendant continued in possession, and in April, 1878, default having been made, action for foreclosure of mortgage was begun and judgment entered accordingly in March, 1884. Subsequently defendant moved to modify judgment by striking out the provision that the purchaser at the foreclosure sale be let into possession upon the ground that the lease was void at its execution, and that, even if it were made valid by the act of Congress, it was for five years only from the passage of the act, which term had expired before the action was tried, and the motion was properly denied. The right conferred by the act of Congress upon the Indian nation to the possession of the land at the expiration of five years was subordinate to the right of the owner of the improvements to a renewal of the lease, provided for in said act for twelve years thereafter. Plaintiff's interest as mortgagee of the improvements and of the land gave him the right of renewal under the act, and from the fact that his assignee continued in possession under the lease it would be presumed that the lease had been renewed.

Sheehan v. Mayer, 41 Hun. (N. Y.), 609.

SEC. 2148. Section 6, chapter 150, laws of 1845, in relation to the Seneca Indians, did not preclude the holding of lands, set apart under the provisions thereof, by the descendants of a member of the Seneca Nation, to whom they were originally set apart, although such descendant was a white woman, and her mother was also white. The statute does not impose any restriction upon a half-breed to successorship and occupancy of such land.

The prohibition against the alienation of such land to others than members of the tribe does not apply to the occupancy of one who claims a right to possession as the husband and agent of his half-breed wife or direct descendant of one of the tribe.

A reasonable presumption arises, from the fact of long-continued occupancy by an Indian of the tribe and his ancestors, openly and under the eyes of the whole tribe, that such right of occupancy has been granted by the peacemakers of the tribe.

Seneca Nation v. Lehly, 55 Hun. (N. Y.), 83.

SEC. 2149. A judgment was recovered by the Seneca Nation in an action of ejectment against a person in possession of reservation land under an invalid lease, which judgment was not executed, and after its recovery the defendant continued in possession until his right to a renewal of the lease under the act of Congress of 1875 was recognized, and the lease was renewed accordingly by the Seneca Nation.

Held, that such judgment in the action of ejectment brought by the Seneca Nation against the same defendant did not inure to the benefit of the railroad company claiming a right to the possession of the land under a lease from the Seneca Nation made after the original lease to such defendant.   *Buffalo, etc., R. R. Co., v. Larery, 75 Hun. (N. Y.), 396.*

SEC. 2150. The grant made by the governor in 1717 to the Tuscarora tribe of Indians is absolute and unconditional, and does not require the residence of the Indians upon the land.

The proviso in the act of 1748, chapter 3, section 3, being in derogation of rights actually vested in the plaintiffs, can not be regarded, but if the act of 1748 could rightfully superadd the condition in the proviso, subsequent legislatures had an equal right to modify or abrogate it. And the acts of 1778, chapter 16, and of 1802, make a different appropriation of the land on the happening of either of the events mentioned in the act of 1778 from that made by the act of 1748.

Admitting that the fee simple of the land in the lease, vested by the grant of 1726, mesne conveyances, coupled with the actual removal of the Indians, in William King, the ancestor of the defendants, *yet* he who accepts a lease from another, and those claiming under him, are estopped during the continuance of the lease to deny the title of the lessor.   *Sacarusa v. King's Heirs, 1 Taylor (N. C.), 336.*

SEC. 2151. The right of the Indian tribe to lands is regarded by the European and American governments as a mere possessory right, and the cession of this right by the Cherokee tribe vested the right in North Carolina, and the United States were the agents of North Carolina for that purpose.   *Strother v. Cathey, 1 Murphy (N. C.), 168.*

SEC. 2152. Where a grant has issued irregularly, the party wishing to avoid it must apply to a court of equity. The act of 1783, chapter 2, section 5, providing "that all lands comprehended within the time described in the fifth section of said act shall be, and are hereby, reserved unto the Cherokee Indians and their nation forever," forbids entries or surveys to be made of certain lands set apart for the said Cherokee tribe of Indians.   *Ibid.*

SEC. 2153. The general assembly, in 1849, passed the following resolution:

Resolved, That the Secretary of State be, and he is hereby, authorized and required to issue to Ailsey Medlin, or her heirs and assigns, for the services of the father, etc., or his heirs or assigns, a grant or grants for a quantity of land, not exceeding 640 acres, to be located in one body or in quarter-sections of not less than 160 acres on any of the lands of this State now subject to entry by law; said grant or grants to be issued on the application of the said Ailsey Medlin, her heirs or assigns, as she or they may prefer, in one of four grants. 2. That the said warrant or warrants shall or may be laid so as to include any lands now belonging to the State for which the State is not bound for title: *Provided,* That this act does not extend to any of the swamp lands in this State.

The grant under this resolution issued for land lying in the Cherokee country. *Held,* That the grant was void, having issued for land lying in the Cherokee country, where the lands are prohibited from entry by the general law, and where, indeed, no entry taker's office is established.   *Stanmire v. Powell, 13 Iredell (N. C. L.), 312.*

SEC. 2154. The owner of a tract of land purchased at the Cherokee sales is estopped to deny the right of one who has bought at a sale under an execution against him, though such purchaser at the Cherokee sales has not yet paid the State, and therefore has acquired no legal title. The cases of Jordan *v.* Marsh, 9 Ire., 234; Deaver *v.* Parker, 2 Ire. Eq., 40, and Davis *v.* Evans, 5 Ire., 525, cited and approved.

        Den on Dem. of N. C. to the use of Hunsucker v. Tipton, 13 Iredell (N. C. Law), 481.

SEC. 2155. By an act passed in North Carolina in 1777 it was made lawful for any citizen of the State "to enter any lands not granted before the Fourth of July, 1776, which have accrued or shall accrue to this State by treaty or conquest." An act passed in 1783 reserved to the Cherokee Indians certain lands, and forbade entry or survey, making void all grants issued thereon. By a treaty made in 1791 all Indian titles east of the "Holston treaty line" were extinguished. *Held,* (1) that the legislature had the right to fix and declare the boundaries of this line without affecting the rights of third parties interested; (2) the State can not, without a breach of faith, question such location of boundaries; (3) nor private individuals claiming under it; (4) the State has fixed and declared such boundaries; (5) the Holston line was ascertained and made certain by the Meigs and Freeman survey; (6) a grant of land by the State, depending for its validity upon the location of the boundaries so fixed and declared, is good.

        Brown v. Brown, 15 Davidson (106 N. C.), 451.

SEC. 2156. An action of ejectment was heretofore instituted by the defendants, the heirs of Darling Belk, deceased, to recover from the plaintiff a tract of land which had been reserved unto the Indian chief Yonah, or The Great Bear, in the treaty with the Cherokees of the 27th of February, 1819, and which was alleged to have been conveyed by the said Yonah, first to the said Belk and afterwards to the plaintiff, etc. *Held*, that although proof of the recession of the contract had been offered and received in an action of ejectment between one of the parties and a third party, yet that such proof was not properly admissible on such trial at law, as it did not affect the legal title of said party, but that in this court it was admissible and relevant to show a trust in said party or his heirs, and that therefore the verdict in the ejectment suit was not a bar nor an estoppel to the plaintiff in this court.   *Love v. Belk, 1 Iredell (N. C., Equity Cases), 163.*

SEC. 2157. The late Mr. Grundy, of Tennessee, states that the lands in controversy were within the Indian Territory until the year 1818; that no State tax was imposed on them until 1819, and no tax by the United States at any time. A deed, whether for valuable consideration or not, but good and effectual at law, except for want of registration, and which is lost before registration, will be set up in equity and a decree made for another conveyance by the bargainor or his legal representatives.

Plumer et al. v. Baskerville et al., 1 Iredell (N. C. Equity), 252.

SEC. 2158. A purchaser of the Cherokee lands under the acts of assembly of 1819, 1820, and 1821 (directing the manner of selling the lands acquired by the State under recent treaties with the Cherokee Indians) does not acquire, before the full payment of the purchase money, such a title, either legal or equitable, as can be sold by execution.   *Deaver et al. v. Parker et al., 2 Iredell (N. C. Equity), 40.*

SEC. 2159. A, B, C, and D entered into a copartnership to purchase a tract of land at the Cherokee land sales and to work the same for gold, etc. A and B only gave bonds for the purchase money, with sureties whom they procured. B, C, and D left the country, abandoned the work for several years, and gave no aid to A, either in working on the land or paying the purchase money, but suffered him alone to be pressed for debt. A in good faith, to relieve his sureties, under the act of 1844, surrendered the land to the State, and afterwards, under another act, obtained from commissioners appointed under the act a "preemption right" for the same land, and sold the same for a sum of money. *Held*, that neither the original parties nor their assignees could hold A to an account for this money.

Rhea et al. v. Tathem et al., 1 Jones (N. C. Equity), 290.

SEC. 2160. Where it was alleged that a certificate for a preemption claim, in Cherokee, was obtained from the commissioners appointed under the act of 1850 by false swearing, and the purchaser of such claim, who obtained a grant by virtue of such certificate, answers that he purchased the same for a valuable consideration, without knowledge of the alleged perjury, an injunction obtained to restrain the grantee from taking possession under a recovery in ejectment must be dissolved.   *Evans v. Lovengood et al., 1 Jones (N. C. Equity), 298.*

SEC. 2161. Preemption rights secured to persons residing on Cherokee lands under the act of 1851 which have been passed on by the agent of the State and a certificate granted by such agent for the same may be transferred to a nonresident for a sufficient consideration, and such purchaser will be protected in this court against a fraudulent invasion of his rights.   *Barnett v. Woods, 2 Jones (N. C. Equity), 198.*

SEC. 2162. Allegations that a certificate for a preemption right was obtained from the commissioners of the Cherokee lands by perjury, without specifying the particular perjury, and from a mistake by the commissioners, both in respect of the law and facts, are not sufficient to authorize the interference of this court with the action of the commissioners.   *Burgess v. Lovengood et al., 2 Jones (N. C. Equity), 457.*

SEC. 2163. In locating a preemption right, under the act of 1852, section 7, in respect to Cherokee land, one entitled to locate under the agent's certificate is not bound to respect the advantage or conveniences of one who had an improvement in the vicinity, and who also had a certificate of a preemption right, but obtained subsequently to the other.   *Barnett v. Woods, 5 Jones (N. C. Equity), 428.*

SEC. 2164. The statute of limitations does not affect claims to land until after the Indian title has been extinguished.

Partition of land held in common will bind the owner of an interest, although other persons may have represented his right in the partition proceedings.

Lessee of heirs of Thompson v. Gotham, 9 Ohio (Hammond), 170.

SEC. 2165. It may be conceded that neither the title nor possession of the Indian owner, secured by treaty with the United States Government, can be disturbed by State legislation; and if Mrs. Goodell were plaintiff in the action, seeking to recover possession, it is probable she would be entitled to both land and improvements (though as that question is not before us, we do not decide it).   Kraus *v.* Means, 12 Kans., 26, distinguished.

United States ex rel. v. C., O. & G. R. R. Co., 3 Oklahoma (Dale), 377.

SEC. 2166. The surveillance, protection, and control of the Government, mainly exercised through the Secretary of the Interior, over the rights of the Indian to his land when allotted, which has been uniformerly likened by the courts to that of a guardian over his ward, ceased. He and his rights passed, subject to the provisions mentioned, under the protections of the common law, of the laws of the

United States, and the laws of this Territory, and he became entitled to all the rights and subject to all the duties of a resident, and probably to those also of a citizen of the United States and of the Territory of Oklahoma.   *Ibid.*

SEC. 2167. The Choctaw, Oklahoma and Gulf Railway Company was authorized by the acts of 1888 and 1894 to locate its own line through the section of country wherein "section four" is built, and has located its line by the most feasible and practicable route, and inasmuch as the right of location and construction were dependent only upon the performance of the conditions set forth in the acts, and that these conditions were for the protection of the Indian tribes and nations, or of Indian occupants under the laws, customs, and usages of the Indian tribes or nations, and that the defendant company has fully complied with the conditions; that the defendant company is invested and empowered with the right to locate and construct its line, and to the approval of the Secretary of the Interior therefor, and that the Indian interest having been extinguished, the land became subject to the laws of the Territory of Oklahoma without the intervention of the limitations of the Indian intercourse act, and that the defendant company having complied with the provisions of the laws of this Territory authorizing the laying out and construction of railroads is entitled to locate and construct its line thereunder, and that the approval of the Secretary of the Interior is not necessary under the provisions of this act, and that injunction will not lie to restrain the defendant railroad company from building its line without such approval.   *Ibid.*

SEC. 2168. An improvement on lands purchased by the proprietary from the Indians gives no title, though such improvement be continued after the time of the purchase.

White et al. v. Kyle's, Lessee, 1 Sergeant & Rawle (Penn.), 518.

SEC. 2169. An association of a number of the inhabitants of Connecticut, called the "Susquehanna Company," purchased this district of country of the Six Nations of Indians on the 11th of July, 1754. In August, 1762, two hundred emigrants from Connecticut commenced settlement on these lands, within what is called the Seventeen Townships, under grants from the "Susquehanna Company." These settlements were never abandoned, but were persisted in under the most discouraging and distressing circumstances. The proprietaries of Pennsylvania obtained a deed of the same Indians for the same district of country on the 5th of November, 1768. *Held,* that the seal of the justice is essential to the validity of the certificate of the probate of a deed; and record of a deed without such certificate is not constructive notice of a title conveyed thereby.

The Connecticut settlers under the "Susquehanna Company," within the Seventeen Townships, acquired an equitable interest in the land, upon their making an improvement and permanent settlement thereon, and that as they enlarged their improvements or contributed by personal services or otherwise to the defense of the country, this interest acquired increased strength; and that it was finally matured into a perfect and complete legal title, under the provisions of the act of April 4, 1797, and its supplements.   *Barney v. Sutton, 2 Watts (Penn.), 33.*

SEC. 2170. The title of Connecticut is of no avail, for her charter does not cover the lands in question. The Indian deed is radically defective; fraud is apparent on its face, and particularly the description of the land is written on a razure, and it does not appear to have been executed in that open national manner in which the Indians sell and transfer their lands. If the deed had a legal existence, it would be of no avail, for Pennsylvania had the right of preemption by charter and by treaty stipulation with the Indians; and by the act of assembly of 7th July, 1705 (1 Dall., 5), any person purchasing lands from the Indians without leave from the proprietary the same was void. By the act of assembly of February 14, 1729 (1 Penn. Laws, Dall., 248), every gift, grant, bargain, and sale, etc., with any of the Indian nations was declared void. The lands in controversy being within the chartered limits of Pennsylvania, the Connecticut settlers were in law trespassers, and entered without right.
   Van Horne's Lessee v. Dorrance, 1 Alden (Penn.), 244.

SEC. 2171. This cause depends upon the act of 3d April, 1792, the first section of which· renders the price of all vacant lands, not previously settled or improved, within the limits of the Indian purchase of 1768 and all precedent purchases, to 50s. for every 100 acres; lands of the purchase of 1784 east of the Allegheny and Conewango, to £5; to be granted to purchasers as formerly. The second section offers all the other lands of the State north and west of the Ohio, Allegheny, and Conewango Creek to persons who will cultivate, improve, and settle the same, or cause it to be done, etc. The third section, referring to the above lands, designates the mode of application, by whom to be made, etc. *Held,* that an actual settlement is not constituted by a mere *pedis possessio.* There must be an occupancy accompanied with a *bona fide* intention to reside or live upon the land in person or by agent, etc.

The plaintiff derives no title from his surveys and warrants, because the survey is a mere description of the land.

The warrant (in this case) gives no title; it was a warrant of acceptance, not title; it was not founded on settlement, but improvement, and if it had recited the consideration to be actual settlement, such recital would have been false in fact, and could have produced no legal, valid consequence.   *Balfour's Lessee v. Meade, 1 Alden (Penn.), 427.*

SEC. 2172. By article 1 of the State treaty of 1777 with the Cherokees, the district of country in which the plaintiff's grant was located was ceded to the State of South Carolina. By the second article the

State engaged to permit the Cherokees to inhabit the said district of country "during good behaviour." This was greater than an estate at will.   *Thomas v. Daniel, 2 McCord (S. C.), 354.*

SEC. 2173. No declaration was ever made by the State that the condition requiring good behavior was ever broken. She has on the contrary, by all her acts, evinced the most perfect satisfaction with the conduct of the Indians.   *Ibid.*

SEC. 2174. The land reserved to the Cherokees by the treaty of 1777 with the State was not vacant land within the meaning of the act of the legislature of 1785, and therefore could not be granted.
Ibid.

SEC. 2175. By the act of the legislature March 22, 1786, certain lands in the State of South Carolina were reserved "for the present use and occupation of the Indians." Said act declared "all grants, sales, or conveyances which had before been or should thereafter be obtained within the chartered boundaries of the State to the north and northwest of the said boundary line to be null and void, any law to the contrary notwithstanding.   *Ibid.*

SEC. 2176. The treaty of 1785 with the Cherokees (7 Stat. L., 18) uses the language of "allotting to the Cherokees lands for their hunting grounds." These, with all the treaties, make the Indians acknowledge the protection of the United States, which is very different from the rights of complete sovereignty.   *Glasgow v. Smith, 1 Overton (Tenn.), 111.*

SEC. 2177. Where limits are assigned for the appropriation of particular species of claims, as military or Indian lands, and other kinds of claims are granted, such grants are void.
Polk v. Hill, 2 Overton (Tenn.), 506.

SEC. 2178. The Cherokees, by treaty of January 7, 1806 (7 Stat. L., 101), relinquished to the United States all their title and claim to the tract of country which lies north of Tennessee River and westward of a line directed, etc., excepting two described tracts, "which first reserved tract is to be considered the common property of the Cherokees who now live on the same, including John D. Chisolm." Doublehead's name is not mentioned in the reservation, but it is presumed he was one of the Indians living upon it.   *Drew v. Clarke, 1 Cooke (Tenn.), 285.*

SEC. 2179. The act of Congress prohibiting surveys within Indian reservations, making boundaries, etc., was intended to prevent disturbances with the Indians arising from persons going on their lands and making surveys and marking trees with a view to procuring titles; but if a corner had been marked before the passage of the act, it surely could not have been intended that the owner might not go upon the land to examine for the corner and collect such other proof as would enable him to establish his beginning.   *McIver v. Reagan, 1 Cooke (Tenn.), 297.*

SEC. 2180. Under the third section of the act of Congress prohibiting surveys, marking of boundaries, etc., a license might have been procured from the governor for that purpose. *Ibid.*

SEC. 2181. The North Carolina act of 1777, for the appropriation of vacant lands offered for sale, and which were to be purchased and entered in the public offices, in these words, "lands not heretofore granted by the lords, proprietors, or King of Great Britain, before the 4th of July, 1776, or which have come to this State by treaty or conquest." The latter words are restrictive of the generality of the former and signify that, although the county of Washington extended to the Mississippi and to the southern and northern boundary of the State, it included Indian lands which had not been ceded to the State, and which, therefore, the State did not mean to use.

Cobb v. Conway, 3 Haywood (Tenn.), 18.

SEC. 2182. The Indian claim to the land in controversy was not extinct February 6, 1796. *Gould v. Hoyle, 3 Haywood (Tenn.), 72.*

SEC. 2183. The lands south of French Broad and Holston are in that tract of country which, by the act of 1783 (Tenn.), is reserved for the Cherokee Indians, and are excepted from entry and appropriation by that act. *Ibid.*

SEC. 2184. By the act of 1783, making and stating a reservation to the Cherokees within certain bounds to be theirs forever, the State divested herself of the title until acquired by some future act.

Overton v. Campbell, 5 Haywood (Tenn.), 541.

SEC. 2185. The Cherokees, though living within the limits of Tennessee, and upon lands the dominion of which belongs to this State, and having themselves only the usufruct thereof, are yet an independent nation, subject to laws, both civil and criminal, made by themselves for the regulation of their internal affairs and exterior relations.

Holland v. Pach, 1 Peck (Tenn.), 119.

SEC. 2186. As an independent nation, war is declared, peace made, and treaties entered into with the United States, and sometimes with other nations by the Cherokees under the authority of their own great council. *Ibid.*

SEC. 2187. In an action of ejectment the plaintiffs claimed under a grant from North Carolina in 1800, founded on an entry made in 1783, while the defendant claimed under a reservation in favor of a native Indian by the Cherokee treaty of 1819 (7 Stat. L., 195). *Held*, that the defendant had the better title. *Cornet v. Winton, 2 Yerger (Tenn.), 143.*

SEC. 2188. When the European colonists found the Cherokee Nation of Indians they were residing near to and about the land in controversy, and so continued to reside and enjoy possession up to the treaty of

1819 (7 Stat. L., 195), and to exercise over it as much sovereignty as they did over any other part of the territory of the nation.

Ibid.

SEC. 2189. The possessory right in the Indian nation has long been considered in the nature of a *property* over the soil and subject to any of the Indian natives when the sovereignty of any part of the Indian country was ceded to the United States. From the very nature of the title it must be deemed property.

Ibid.

SEC. 2190. The grant to Stuart by the State having been taken incumbered with the Indian right of possession in the land, which was a r'ght of occupancy and independent of the grant, and this possessory title being the subject of assignment by treaty, to which the Cherokee Nation and the United States should be parties, and the same having been transferred to Brown by this mode, he retains (in "reserve") the title of the Cherokees.

Ibid.

SEC. 2191. That the State recognition of certain rights in the Indians to the soil they occupied and its compact to support those rights by the treaty of 1791 (7 Stat. L., 39) are binding upon the State, has never been questioned.

Ibid.

SEC. 2192. The rights of the Cherokees in their lands are guaranteed to them by the treaties of 1785 (7 Stat. L., 18), 1791 (7 Stat. L., 39), 1794 (7 Stat. L., 43), and 1798 (7 Stat. L., 62).

Ibid.

SEC. 2193. All the lands not ceded to the United States by the treaty of 1794 are guaranteed to the Cherokees by the United States in as apt and strong words as our language is capable of.

Ibid.

SEC. 2194. The Cherokee treaties of 1785, 1791, 1794, and 1798, taken together, not only guarantee the rights of the Indians to the soil undisposed of, but also, to a considerable extent, incorporate the Indians with the Federal Government.

Ibid.

SEC. 2195. The grant by the compact of 1789 between North Carolina and the United States would be equally binding upon both the Governments, as grantors, and consequently upon the State of Tennessee. But the Indian nation was no party to this grant, and its usufructuary title was not thereby affected.

Ibid.

SEC. 2196. North Carolina had no right to take the usufructuary title from the Indians for Stuart's benefit without their consent; their consent they have not given, and therefore no right to prosecute this action to recover possession of the land has ever vested in Stuart.

Ibid.

SEC. 2197. A violation by the United States of the article of the treaty which reserves to certain of the Indians a part of their former possessions, and which reserve was a moving consideration to induce the Indians to part with their title to the lands ceded, *would and ought to* destroy the whole treaty, and leave the Indian title where it was in 1819, before the treaty, in the Cherokee Nation, and not in the grantee, Stuart. *Ibid.*

SEC. 2198. In 1789 the soil and sovereignty of what is now the State of Tennessee was transferred by North Carolina to the United States, and in the same year the treaty-making power and the right to regulate intercourse with the Indians was vested in the United States. *Ibid.*

SEC. 2199. From the passage of the act of 1806 by Congress to 1817 there was no legislation having directly for its object the appropriation of the lands of the Chickasaw Indians.

McLemore v. Wright, 2 Yerger (Tenn.), 326.

SEC. 2200. The treaty of 1816 (7 Stat. L., 150) conferred no powers not previously possessed upon the officers of Tennessee deputed to perfect titles to North Carolina claimants. *Ibid.*

SEC. 2201. The tract in question is within the territory reserved to the Chickasaws prior to the treaty of September 20, 1816 (7 Stat. L., 150). *Ibid.*

SEC. 2202. An entry or grant of land before any power was vested in the officers of the State to permit such entry or make such grant is void; and this was the case with the lands reserved to the Chickasaw Indians prior to the act of 1823 (Tenn.). *Ibid.*

SEC. 2203. North Carolina had the ultimate title, encumbered with the Indian right of occupancy; but that she had the right to exercise legislative power over the nation is negatived by her own acts. Hence the act of 1783 is, in its character, not even conventional in respect to the Cherokees, who were no parties thereto.

Blair v. Pathkiller, 2 Yerger, 407.

SEC. 2204. The North Carolina act of 1783 provides "that the Cherokee Indians shall have and enjoy all that tract of land bounded as follows * * * And that the lands included within the aforesaid bounds shall be and are hereby reserved unto the said Cherokee Indians and their nation forever." The sixth and seventh sections provide that said reserved lands shall not be granted to others or the possession of the Indians obtruded upon. *Ibid.*

SEC. 2205. The act of 1789 transferred the fee from North Carolina to the United States; the act of 1806 transferred the fee to Tennessee, *but expressly reserving the Indian title.* This title, such as it was, the Cherokees transferred to the United States as grantees by the treaty of 1819. *Ibid.*

SEC. 2206. So soon as the Indian title was extinguished, the sovereignty (Tennessee) to which the encumbered fee belonged, or an individual of that sovereignty to whom it had been granted took the land unencumbered, because the Indians had no permanent interest in the soil and nothing passed from them; the right of occupancy was a usufructuary privilege subject to extinction.   *Ibid.*

SEC. 2207. Under the compact of 1806, by which the United States made a cession to the State of Tennessee, the Indian nation was the owner of the possessory right and all the subjects of the nation joint tenants of the whole territory ceded. The reservee, by the treaty, took in severalty, directly from the nation the Indian title as his reasonable portion of the ceded Territory.   *Ibid.*

SEC. 2208. The Cherokees of North Carolina do not pretend to derive title to their lands by virtue of the act of assembly of 1783; they have asserted their right of occupancy by virtue of previous enjoyment of the country, for perhaps, centuries.   · *Ibid.*

SEC. 2209. No fee was taken by the Cherokees by virtue of the act of 1783, and it did not affect the title they already had.   *Ibid.*

SEC. 2210. Previous to 1783 the character of the Cherokee title to the lands ceded by the treaties of 1817 and 1819, and those previously ceded by or conquered from them, was similar to that of all the other tribes of Indians within the limits of the United States, to wit, a right of possession in the Indians, with the ultimate power in the Government to extinguish the same.   *Ibid.*

SEC. 2211. Joint tenancies and tenancies in common were not within the purview of the Cherokee treaties of 1817 and 1819 (7 Stat. L., 156 and 195, respectively).   *McConnell v. Mousepaine, 2 Yerger, 437.*

SEC. 2212. The Duck and Elk River country was surveyed and granted in opposition to the wishes of the Cherokees, and was productive of Indian hostilities for many years.
Singleton v. Whiteside, 5 Yer., 17.

SEC. 2213. The State of Tennessee, under its compact with North Carolina in 1804, recognized and confirmed by the act of Congress 1806, has never possessed or claimed the power to appropriate land to which the Indian title has not been extinguished and entries and grants of such land have invariably been held void.
Gillespie v. Cunningham, 2 Humph. (Tenn.), 19.

SEC. 2214. The land in question lies west of Brown's line (Tennessee), and was still within the Indian reservation as established by the North Carolina act of 1783, although a much larger scope of country was thrown open to entry by this latter act.
Calloway v. Hopkins, 11 Haskell (Tenn.), 349.

SEC. 2215. Where territory is acquired by conquest or cession, in the absence of any order, decree, or law of the new sovereign and in the absence of any treaty stipulations, individual rights of property remain unchanged. The organization of the Indian missions and the character of their grants of land were examined by the court at length and the conclusion arrived at that the Indians were merely tenants at will; that their rights could neither be alienated nor transferred by inheritance, and that after the extinguishment of the missions the lands became a part of the appropriable public domains. All lands sold under laws 15 and 19, title 12, book 4 of the new *recopilacion* were only in composition and the purchasers were merely tenants at will. It is doubtful whether large grants of pasture land were ever authorized in any case by the laws of Spain.

McMullen v. Hodge, 5 Hartly (Texas), 34.

SEC. 2216. The old claims of the Crown, by the treaty of 1763, extended to the Mississippi, and when the dormant title of the Indian tribes was afterwards extinguished by government it enured to the benefit of the citizen who had acquired a title from the Crown, and the land could not be granted anew as waste land. But the Indian title did not impede the grant and location of such lands, although the grantee took the risk of the Indian claim.   *Marshall et al. v. Clark, 4 Call (Va.), 268.*

CHAPTER II.—PURCHASES FROM INDIAN TRIBES.

SEC. 2217. In Pennsylvania the proprietaries had by their charter the exclusive right of preemption to all lands within the province.

Vanhorne v. Dorrance, 2 Dall., 304.

SEC. 2218. In Pennsylvania a grant from the Indians to any other persons than the proprietaries conferred no title.   *Ibid.*

SEC. 2219. The deed from the Six Nations is invalid under the laws of Pennsylvania, it being provided by the act of February 14, 1729, that purchases from the Indian nations within the State of Pennsylvania "without the order or direction of the proprietary or his commissioners, shall be null, void, and of no effect."

Ibid.

SEC. 2220. The land in controversy being within the limits of Pennsylvania, the Connecticut settlers were, in legal estimation, trespassers and intruders. They purchased the land without leave and entered upon it without right.   *Ibid.*

SEC. 2221. The settlers purchased and entered upon the land without the consent of the legislature of Connecticut. Though the legislature subsequently gave approbation, it was posterior to the deed executed by the Six Nations to Penn, at Fort Stanwix, and the principle of relation does not retrospect so as to affect third persons; and the consequence is that the settlers derive no title under the Indian deed.   *Ibid.*

SEC. 2222. The proprietaries, Pennsylvania, while the soil and jurisdiction were vested in them, resisted every attempt of individuals to purchase lands from the Indians, but permitted free access to the land office for the purpose of completing titles within the territory over which they, the proprietaries, had extinguished the Indian claim.

Commonwealth v. Tench Coxe, 4 Dallas, 170.

SEC. 2223. In the year 1792 the State of Pennsylvania completed the present range of her territory by formal grant from the United States of a triangular tract of land bounded by Lake Erie, which tract had been ceded and relinquished by resolutions of Congress June 6 and Sept. 4, 1788, and the Indian title was purchased by commissioners appointed by the State in January, 1789.   *Ibid.*

SEC. 2224. By the charter to William Penn, March 14, he became the proprietor of the soil embraced within the boundaries of Pennsylvania. The charter title, however, was fortified as well since as before the Revolution by successive purchases from the Indians, whose claim may be considered as fairly and finally extinguished throughout the territory of the State by the treaty of Fort Stanwix, October 22, 1784 (7 Stat. L.. 15), and the treaty of Fort McIntosh, January 21, 1785.

Ibid.

SEC. 2225. By the decree of *Trenton* it was settled that Penn had the exclusive right of sovereignty, soil, and preemption as to the lands in question, by a retrospective recognition of the boundaries described in the charter from Charles the Second to William Penn. The laws of Pennsylvania must, therefore, be applied to every transaction respecting those lands, and in the years 1700 and 1729 it had been unlawful to purchase any part of them from the Indians.

Commonwealth v. Franklin, 4 Dallas, 255.

SEC. 2226. Long before the Connecticut claim began to operate, Pennsylvania (in 1729–30) had introduced a similar law to prevent purchases of land from the Indians, to annul all contracts for that purpose, and to extend the English statutes of forcible entries and detainers to the case of entries upon lands not located, or surveyed, by some warrant, or order, from the proprietary.   *Ibid.*

SEC. 2227. Assuming that the Connecticut title began in 1754, as alleged, in a purchase from the Indians, it was by a positive subsisting law (1769) void, and could afford no lawful ground for subsequent contracts.   *Ibid.*

SEC. 2228. Even in the year 1700 (which law was enforced by additional sanctions in 1769, 1 State Laws, 503, Dallas edition) it had been declared "that if any person presume to buy any land of the natives within the limits of the province and territories without leave from the proprietary thereof every such bargain or purchase shall be void and of no effect."

Ibid.

SEC. 2229. A title to lands under grants to private individuals made by Indian tribes or nations northwest of the Ohio River, in 1773 and 1775. can not be recognized in the courts of the United States.

Johnson v. McIntosh, 8 Wheaton, 543.

SEC. 2230. The usual mode adopted by Indians for granting lands to individuals has been to reserve them in a treaty or to grant them under the sanction of the commissioners with whom the treaty was negotiated, and the practice in such cases, to grant to the Crown for the use of the individual, is evidence of a general understanding that validity even of such a grant depended on its receiving the royal sanction.

Ibid.

SEC. 2231. A sound national policy requires that the Indian tribes within our States should exchange their territory upon equitable principles or eventually consent to become amalgamated in our political communities. It would be inconsistent with the political welfare of the States and the social advancement of our citizens that an independent and permanent power should exist within their limits, and this power must give way to the greater power which surrounds it or seek its exercise beyond the sphere of State authority.

Worcester v. Georgia, 6 Pet., 515.

SEC. 2232. Purchases of lands made at Indian treaties, held by the authority of the United States, have always been held good by the ratification of the treaty, without any patent to the purchaser from the United States.

Mitchel v. United States, 9 Pet., 711.

SEC. 2233. Where the Creek and Seminole Indians had granted tracts of land in east Florida to parties, which grants were confirmed by the authorities of Spain before the cession of Florida to the United States, the grants were confirmed under the treaty with Spain.

Ibid.

SEC. 2234. Individuals could not purchase Indian lands without permission or license from the Crown, colonial governors, or according to the rule prescribed by colonial laws; but such purchases were valid with such license or in conformity with the local laws; and by this union of perpetual right of occupancy with the ultimate fee, which passed from the Crown by the license, the title of the purchaser became complete.

Ibid.

SEC. 2235. All titles held under charter or license of the Crown to purchase from the Indians have been held good and such power has never been denied. The right of the Crown to grant being complete, the proclamation of 1763 had the effect of law in relation to such purchases.

Ibid.

SEC. 2236. It was a duty of the governors of the Spanish provinces to examine whether claims against the Indians were well founded, and if so, to contribute by all possible means to their payment, but not to lend their sanction or allow the smallest injury to be done to them. The fact of the supervision of Indian sales of lands by the governors of provinces and commandants of posts in acts of confirmation and putting the purchasers in possession is very clearly established by the reports of the land commissioners of the United States in Louisiana.   *Ibid.*

SEC. 2237. It is a principle established by the King that the Indians were competent judges of the consideration on which they granted their lands; that they might be granted for the payment of debts, and this principle has been fully recognized by the United States.   *Ibid.*

SEC. 2238. The construction of the acts of Virginia of 1778 and 1779 has been that the deed of the Cherokees to Henderson & Co. was void as against the Commonwealth but valid as against the Cherokees, and therefore the title to the lands conveyed passed to the State. This assumption has been maintained from the time the convention sat in 1776, and it received the sanction of the United States at the treaty of Hopewell with the Cherokees in 1785 (7 Stat. L., 18).

Porterfield v. Clark, 2 How., 76.

SEC. 2239. The Cherokee sale to Henderson & Co. stands on the same grounds as if it had been made by the authority of the Crown of Great Britain, so far as the boundary and Indian rights stand affected.

Ibid.

SEC. 2240. A purchase from Indians of land in territory under French authority gave no title unless sanctioned by that authority.

United States v. Rillieux, 14 How., 189.

SEC. 2241. A claim to land in Iowa under an alleged purchase from the Fox Indians by one Dubuque, and a subsequent grant from the Spanish authorities which showed no intention to grant anything more than a mining privilege, did not constitute a complete title protected by the treaty of Paris of April 30, 1803.

Chouteau v. Molony, 16 How., 203.

SEC. 2242. It is unreasonable to suppose that in granting to one Dubuque a mining privilege within a certain territory the Fox Indians intended to sell said territory, which included a large Indian village.

Ibid.

SEC. 2243. If the words of a paper are doubtful as to what the Indians meant to sell, as the copy of the council is written in a language which they could neither read nor fully understand, it will be but right to hold it as an uncertainty, and not permit their bargainee or his alienees to give it a fixed meaning in their own favor.   *Ibid.*

SEC. 2244. Without having a given depth, a tract of land claimed to have been purchased of the Indians could not have been surveyed as to quantities or boundaries, and on that account it would, under the Spanish law as well as our own, have been void for uncertainty.

Ibid.

SEC. 2245. The erection of monuments by Dubuque with the consent of the Fox Indians within certain distances on the river was consistent with the privilege to search for minerals, and in the absence of all words from which it can be inferred that a sale of land was meant, the monuments, as points mentioned on the river, can have no other reference than to the privilege to search for mines.   *Ibid.*

SEC. 2246. Both in Florida and Louisiana it was so well understood that an Indian sale of land before it could take effect at all needed the ratification of the governor, that it was frequently inserted in the act of sale.   *Ibid.*

SEC. 2247. The ground upon which the Supreme Court of the United States placed its judgment in this case is not in conflict with the view taken of the case by the court below, which was the appraisal of the improvements on the Tonawanda reservation, and payment for them were conditions precedent to the surrender of them by the Indians, and that the refusal of the Indians to permit the appraisal did not excuse the performance of these conditions. The performance was not a duty that belonged to the grantees (Ogden & Fellows), but for the Government under the treaty (7 Stat. L., 586).

Fellows v. Blacksmith, 19 How., 366.

SEC. 2248. The stipulation in the treaty of 1842 (7 Stat. L., 586) with the New York Indians, which required that the appraised value of the improvements on the surrendered reservation should on the delivery of possession be paid to the President of the United States to be distributed among the owners of the improvements according to the award of the appraisers, shows that the Government was to be present at the surrender and payment for the improvements.   *Ibid.*

SEC. 2249. Grantees of the lands of the Seneca Indians, who had purchased them under the exclusive right of purchase acquired from Massachusetts, derived no power under the treaty of 1838 (7 Stat. L., 550) or 1842 (7 Stat. L., 586) to dispossess by force the Seneca Indians, or right of entry to sustain an ejectment.   *Ibid.*

SEC. 2250. The treaty of 1842 (7 Stat. L., 586) has made no provision as to the mode or manner in which the removal of the New York Indians or the surrender of their reservations were to take place; it can be carried into execution only by the authority or power of the Government which was a party to it.

Ibid.   New York v. Dibble, 21 How., 366.

SEC. 2251. The New York Indians are to be removed to their new homes provided by the treaties of 1838 (7 Stat. L., 550) and 1842 (7 Stat L., 586) by their guardians, the United States, and can not be expelled by irregular force or violence of the individuals who claim to have purchased their lands, nor even by the intervention of the courts of justice, and until such removal and surrender of possession by intervention of the Government of the United States, they and their possessions are protected by the laws of New York from the intrusion of their white neighbors.   *Ibid.*

SEC. 2252. Where Indians, under arrangements approved by the United States, agree to sell their lands to private citizens, and to give possession of them at the expiration of a term of years named, a taxation of the land before the efflux of the term is premature, even though a sale for the nonpayment of taxes might not take place until after the time when, if they fulfilled their agreements, the Indians would have left the land, and even though such would be subject to the proviso that the right of the Indians to occupy the land should not in any manner be affected thereby.   *The New York Indians 5 Wall., 761.*

SEC. 2253. The cession to the United States by the Cherokees, in the treaty of June 19, 1866 (14 Stat. L., 799), of the "Cherokee neutral lands," owned by them in fee simple, in trust that the United States should sell them and hold the proceeds for the benefit of the said Indians, was a lawful cession and trust, and in accordance with the policy and practice of the Government.   *Holden v. Joy, 17 Wall., 211.*

SEC. 2254. The cession in the Chickasaw treaty of 1832 (7 Stat. L., 381) contemplated the ultimate abandonment of the lands by the Indians. This treaty did not prove satisfactory, and in a second treaty, made in 1834 (7 Stat. L., 450), the United States agreed, when the body of lands were surveyed, to reserve from sale certain limited portions on which the individual reservations should be located. This was done in obedience to a just policy, for it would have been wrong, considering the dependent state of the Indians, to hold them to their original engagement; and it can not be doubted that it was the intention of both parties to the treaty to clothe the reservees with full title, otherwise some words of limitation indicating a different intention would have been used.   *Best v. Polk, 18 Wall., 112.*

SEC. 2255. The acquisition of territory has been the moving cause of all Indian treaties, and will continue to be so until Indian reservations are confined to very narrow limits.
United States v. 43 Gals. Whisky, 93 U. S., 188.

SEC. 2256. The Indian trust lands ceded to the Government in trust to be sold for the benefit of the Indians by the treaty of 1854 (10 Stat. L., 1048) with the Delawares, and of the same year (10 Stat. L., 1082) with the Kaskaskias, Peorias, Piankeshaw, and Weas, were never public lands of the United States, and were never subject to sale at the Lecompton land office. There was never a time that the United States occupied any other position under the cession than that of trustees, with power to sell for the benefit of the Indians. In equity, under the operation of the treaties, the Indians continued until sales were made the beneficial owners of all their country ceded in trust.
United States v. Brindle, 110 U. S., 688.

SEC. 2257. When it is considered that the Choctaw treaty of 1830 (7 Stat. L., 333) was not executed on the part of the United States according to its just intent and spirit, with a' view to securing to the Indians the very advantages which they had a right to expect would accrue to them under it, it would seem as though it were a case where they had lost their lands without receiving the promised equivalent, and in such a case there is a plain equity to enforce compensation by requiring the party in default to account for all the pecuniary benefits it has actually derived from the lands themselves. This is the solid ground on which the justice of the award of the Senate under the treaty of 1855 (11 Stat. L., 611) seems fairly to stand.

Choctaw Nation v. United States, 119 U. S., 1.

SEC. 2258. The obligation on the part of the Sioux Indians in their agreement of 1873, ratified by Congress on June 22, 1874 (18 Stat. L., 167), was only to cede their title. It was not a cession in terms by them, although the officers of the Land Department treated it as an actual cession of title from its date, and the Indians had then retired to the reservation set apart for them by treaty in 1867 (15 Stat. L., 505), thus giving up the occupancy of the other lands. The relinquishment thus made was as effectual as a formal act of cession. Their right of occupancy was in effect abandoned, and full consideration for it being afterwards paid, it could not be resumed.

Buttz v. Railroad Co., 119 U. S., 55.

SEC. 2259. The right to construct railroads and telegraph lines across their lands was secured by treaty, concluded February 19, 1867 (15 Stat. L., 505), with the Sisseton and Wahpeton bands of Sioux. This right was in terms ceded to the United States, but the concession must be construed to authorize any one deriving title from the United States to exercise the same right.

Ibid.

SEC. 2260. By the act of 1876 (19 Stat. L., 176) it was provided that thereafter there should be no appropriation made for the subsistence of the Sioux Indians, unless they should first agree to relinquish all right and claim to so much of their reservation as lay west of the one hundred and third meridian of longitude, which embraced the Black Hills country.

Noonan v. Caledonia Mining Co., 121 U. S., 393.

SEC. 2261. The lands in the Cherokee territory, like the lands held by private owners everywhere within the geographical limits of the United States, are held subject to the authority of the General Government, to take them for such objects as are germane to it, provided only that they are not taken without just compensation being made to the owner.

Cherokee Nation v. Railroad Co., 135 U. S., 641.

SEC. 2262. So far as the question whether the act of Congress prohibiting Indian lands from being conveyed, except by permission of the President, is' satisfied by his approval indorsed upon a deed thirteen years after its execution—and after the death of the grantee and the sale of the land by his administrator is concerned—no reason is known why the analogy of the law of principal and agent is not applicable, viz: That an act in excess of an agent's authority when performed, becomes binding upon the principal if subsequently ratified by him.   *Pickering v. Lomax, 145 U. S., 310.*

SEC. 2263. The Shawnee lands in Ohio ceded to the United States in trust, to be sold at public sale to the highest bidder in the manner of selling public lands, by the treaty of 1831 (7 Stat. L., 355), not having been exposed to public sale, but were sold at private sale, there was a failure on the part of the Government to observe the stipulation of the treaty and a violation of its trust. The obligation being expressed to expose them to public sale, it was incumbent upon the Government to show either that it had done so and failed to find a bidder or for some other reason it had been released from the provisions of the treaty. The privilege of selling the lands "in the manner of selling the public lands" does not nullify the obligation to expose them to public sale, which still remained.   *United States v. Blackfeather, 155 U. S., 180.*

SEC. 2264. The contention that the rights admittedly enjoyed by the Maricopa and Phœnix Railroad are to be treated as if obtained without the consent of the Indians residing on the Gila River Reservation, because it does not appear by the record that such consent, which was a condition attached to the grant, was given, is without force, for the reason that, as the company has taken the rights granted by the statute, the legal presumption of duty performed requires the court to assume that the consent of the Indians was given in accordance with law, and the company can not be permitted to aver its own wrongdoing, trespass, and violation of statute in order to escape its just share of the burden of taxation.   *Maricopa, &c., Railroad v. Arizona, 156 U. S., 347.*

SEC. 2265. It is fairly implied from the language employed in the third article of the Chippewa treaty of 1820 (7 Stat. L., 206) that an encampment location retained, selected, or assigned, as the case might be, reserved for the use specified in the treaty, should not thereafter be appropriated by the Government for other uses than the defenses of any military work. Private rights could not, without authority of Congress, be acquired in the tract during the occupancy of the reservation under the treaty, for the lands lost their character as public lands in being set apart or occupied under the treaty and became exempt from sale and preemption.   *Spalding v. Chandler, 160 U. S., 394.*

SEC. 2266. A treaty between the United States and an Indian tribe having been fulfilled by a conveyance of land, no question can arise as to the character of the conveyance, whether a gift, donation, or grant for value.   *Prentice v. Stearns, 20 Fed. Rep., 819.*

SEC. 2267. An appointment made by an Indian chief of a party to receive title to certain land intended to be conveyed under treaty may be valid. Unless the conveyance describes the land as it really lies, no title can pass to the appointee, whatever may have been the Indian impression as to what its situation was.   *Ibid.*

SEC. 2268. The appointee of an Indian chief to receive title to certain land may afterwards absorb the interest of his cobeneficiaries; but, in a subsequent conveyance by him, he must use language appropriate to his purpose or no title will pass.   *Ibid.*

SEC. 2269. The restrictive clauses of the Chickasaw treaties upon the alienation of Indian lands provided that the reservations to individuals should not be "sold, leased, or disposed of" except in the particular manner pointed out in the treaty, but the terms of the treaty apply only to voluntary conveyance by the Indians, such as were affected by the personal will of the possessor, and not to transmissions of title by operation of law, except where provision is especially made for a peculiar descent on the death of the possessor.   *Love v. Pamplin, 21 Fed. Rep., 755.*

SEC. 2270. It was competent for the United States by treaty, notwithstanding any State law, to prescribe the conditions to the conveyance of Indian lands which should be the law of the title. But on the extinguishment of the original Indian title and the removal of the Indians from the State the laws of the State would come into operation, except so far as modified by the existing treaties and laws of the United States.   *Ibid.*

SEC. 2271. Where the possessor of an Indian reservation of individual lands left his land and rejoined his tribe in the Indian nation, in consequence of which absence from the State the land was attached at the suit of his creditor and sold by the sheriff, the purchaser at the sale took a good title, which must prevail over the claim by his heirs at law under the tribal laws of descent or the ordinary laws of the State.   *Ibid.*

SEC. 2272. Prior to the time of the adoption of the Federal Constitution the States of Massachusetts and New York had each claimed territorial sovereignty over the lands of the Indians in New York, but in 1786 the dispute was settled by a cession from Massachusetts to New York of the "sovereignty and jurisdiction of the lands" and from New York to Massachusetts of the "right of preemption of the soil from the native Indians."   *Benson v. United States, 44 Fed. Rep., 178.*

SEC. 2273. It is contended that the view taken of the pupillary condition of the Cherokees violates the provisions of the constitution and laws of North Carolina forbidding perpetuities. A perpetuity is the attempt to forbid the alienation of lands under any circumstances and to provide for their descent or disposition in a fixed unchangeable way. But the Indians hold these lands to no such purpose. Their realty can be alienated, but the contract is reviewable by the Government for one purpose only—to protect them from fraud or wrong. A condition attached to alienation does not create a perpetuity.

United States v. Boyd, 68 Fed. Rep., 577.

SEC. 2274. The purpose of the Cherokee treaty, 1846 (9 Stat. L., 871), was that the Western Cherokees should surrender their separate sovereignty and sell an undivided two-thirds of their lands in the Indian Territory in consideration of one-third of the price which had been paid to the Eastern Cherokees under the treaty of New Echota for lands east of the Mississippi.

Western Cherokee Indians v. United States, 27 C. Cls., 1.

SEC. 2275. The treaty of 1831 (7 Stat. L., 355) contained a complete bargain by which the Indians surrendered their Ohio lands in consideration of 100,000 acres of land in the West, etc. This part of the consideration having failed, the payment of $66,246.23 under the act of March 3, 1863 (10 Stat L., 236), was in substitution thereof.

Blackfeather v. United States, 28 C. Cls., 447.

SEC. 2276. The United States failed in their duty when they sold any of the lands ceded by the treaty of 1831 (7 Stat. L., 355) otherwise than at public sale to the highest bidder in the manner of selling the public land, and as trustees of these Indians and their guardians are liable to them for any loss which the Shawnees may have sustained.

Ibid.

SEC. 2277. By the treaty of April 3, 1764, the Seneca Nation of Indians ceded to Great Britain a large tract of land in New York, including the tract in controversy. *Ibid.*

SEC. 2278. The purchaser incorporated himself with the Indians, and the purchase is to be considered in the same light as if the grant had been made to an Indian, and might be resumed again and granted over again by the tribe at its pleasure. *Ibid.*

SEC. 2279. The legal effect and operation of an Indian deed was fully considered by the United States Supreme Court in Johnson *v.* McIntosh (8 Wheat., 571), the point of inquiry there being as to the power of the Indians to give and of private individuals to receive a title which could be sustained by the court. *Ibid.*

SEC. 2280. Where one claimed title by an Indian deed, confirmed by an agent of the British Government who could not lawfully have confirmed it, it was held that no other kind of confirmation and no other deed could be set up to help the possession, and that any presumption of the existence of a deed was to be confined to such an one as was originally asserted. *Ibid.*

SEC. 2281. The claim of John Stedman in its broadest extent was no more than the Indian title—occupancy—confirmed by the British agent. *Ibid.*

SEC. 2282. The Indian title to the lands on the west side of the Susquehanna having been extinguished by treaty October 11, 1736, Thomas

Penn, on the 30th of the same month, granted to 52 persons what have been termed licenses.   *Conn. et al. v. Penn et al., 1 Peters (Cir. Ct. Repts.), 497.*

SEC. 2283. The original Dutch purchase of Delaware from the Indians in June, 1620, was concluded by the Indians in person at New York, and recorded there.   *Pea Patch Island Arbitration, 1 Wallace, Jr., Appendix, p. 26.*

SEC. 2284. By the act of March 3, 1793, it was made a penal offense to treat with any Indians for the purchase of land.
Doe ex dem. Chinn v. Darnell, 4 McLean, 440.

SEC. 2285. By treaty of September 24, 1857 (11 Stat. L., 729), the Pawnees ceded, by treaty, their lands in the Territory of Nebraska to the United States, reserving to themselves a certain tract of country therein described.   This treaty provides, among other things, that the Indians shall not alienate their lands except to the United States, that all offenders against the laws of the United States shall be delivered up, etc., but it contains no stipulation as to the jurisdiction over it or over the Indians residing therein when the Territory shall be admitted as a State.   *United States v. Yellow Sun, 1 Dill., 271.*

SEC. 2286. By the seventeenth article of the treaty of July 19, 1866, amended July 31, 1866 (14 Stat. L., 804), the Cherokees ceded in trust to the United States the tract of land in the State of Kansas which was sold to the Cherokees by the United States under the provisions of the second article of the treaty of 1835, and also that strip of land ceded to the nation by the fourth article of said treaty which is included in the State of Kansas; and the Cherokees consented that the said lands may be included in the limits and jurisdiction of said State.   *Langdon v. Joy, 4 Dill., 391.*

SEC. 2287. If Congress had intended to grant these lands, knowing that a treaty for their cession was then under consideration of the Senate, which, by its provisions, appropriated the lands and the proceeds of their sale to other purposes, they surely would have used some language to specifically include these lands, or at least to take them out of the excepting clause.
United States v. M., K. & T. Ry. Co., 1 McCrary, 624.

SEC. 2288. On September 24, 1857, the Pawnees ceded, by treaty of that date, their lands in the Territory of Nebraska to the United States, reserving, however, "out of this cession a tract of country 30 miles long from east to west and 15 miles long from north to south." (11 Stat. L., 729.)   *United States v. Soo-ca-da-cot, 1 Abott, 377.*

SEC. 2289. Upon the approval by the President of a contract made by an Indian reservee under the Creek treaty of 1832 for the sale of his land, the title of the purchaser relates back to the date of the contract, and inures to his intermediate vendee, whether by quitclaim or warranty deed.   *Nolen & Thompson v. The heirs of Gwyn, 16 Ala., 725.*

SEC. 2290. The President's approval of a contract for the sale of an Indian reservation can not be proved by the mere certificate of the Secretary of War, not under the seal of his Department, indorsed on the contract.   *Doe ex dem. Tillman v. Long & Freeman, 29 Ala., 376.*

SEC. 2291. By the Quapaw treaty of August 24, 1818 (7 Stat. L., 176), the lands in question south of the Arkansas River were formally ceded to the Government.   *Gaines et al. v. Hale & Rector, 26 Ark., 168.*

SEC. 2292. August 31, 1866, the Secretary of the Interior entered into a written agreement with the Missouri River Railroad Company to sell to said company all lands provided to be sold by the Delaware treaty of July 4, 1866. (14 Stat. L., 793.)   *Bruce v. Luke, 9 Kans. (Das.), 139.*

SEC. 2293. Under the former government of Louisiana a sale by Indians of land assigned to them did not incapacitate them from acquiring a right to soil in land to which they removed. (5 M., 655.)

Where nullity is only relative the party in interest alone can attach it; it can not be done collaterally. (Ante, 137, and cases noted, 11.)

If a sale by Indians was followed by payment of the price and delivery of the property, no person can take advantage of an informality in the mode of making it but the Indians. The nullity is relative.   *Spencer's heir v. Grimball, 9 Martin (La.), 189; 3 Harrison (La.), 870.*

SEC. 2294. Part of the land in controversy was within the bounds of a tract purchased from the Indians in Maine by Elizabeth Gint, by deed dated anno Domini 1662, and recorded in the old book of eastern records.   *Sewall v. Cargill, 15 Maine, 414.*

SEC. 2295. So early as the year 1633 the general court of Massachusetts ordered "that no person whatsoever shall henceforth buy any land of any Indian without license first had and obtained." In 1650 the French, Dutch, and other foreigners were forbidden to trade with them. In 1657 that Commonwealth declared its right to all the fur trade with them. It had before that time forbidden the sale to them of guns, gunpowder, and other munitions of war. In 1693 an act was passed "for the better rule and government of the Indians in their several places and plantations."   *Moore v. Veazie, 32 Maine, 343.*

SEC. 2296. The United States Supreme Court has said "it is an universal rule that purchases made at Indian treaties, in the presence and with the approbation of the officer under whose direction they are held, gave a valid title to the lands. It prevailed under the colonial government and under the laws of the States after the Revolution. It has been adopted by the United States, and purchases made at treaties held by their authority have always been held good by the ratification of the treaty, without any patent to the purchaser from the United States."   *Coleman v. Doe ex dem. Tish-ho-mah, 12 Miss., 40.*

SEC. 2297. By the proclamation of George III, October 7, 1763, by which, with others, the government of West Florida was created and established out of the lands ceded by the treaty of Paris, it was stipulated that the Indian tribes should be protected "in the possession of such parts of our dominion and territories as, not having been ceded to or purchased by us, are reserved to them or any of them as their hunting grounds," and that "no private person do make purchase of any land from any Indians, but that the same shall be purchased only for the Government in the name of the sovereign, at some public meeting of the Indians." In 1772 the government of West Florida created under this proclamation granted a body of land lying between the mouth of the Yazoo and the thirty-first degree of north latitude. It was held that this grant was invalid, because the Indian title was not extinguished in the land thus granted until 1777, and under the proclamation of 1763 the power of the royal governor within the territory reserved was suspended.   *Montgomery v. Ives, 21 Miss., 161.*

SEC. 2298. The purchase is regulated by treaty, prior to which the Indians are entitled to be protected in their possession. But the fee simple in the soil and the right of preemption belong to the Federal Government. The Indians can sell neither to States nor to individuals. And this principle is now extended to all their commerce, traffic, and intercourse, which are wholly under the control of the Federal Government.   *Tush-ho-yo-tubby v. Barr, 45 Miss., 189.*

SEC. 2299. The Choctaw treaty of January 3, 1786 (7 Stat. L., 21), defined the boundary between the Choctaws and the United States. The treaty of December 17, 1801 (7 Stat. L., 66), established the boundary as previously agreed upon with the British commissioners, and "relinquished and forever quitclaimed to the United States" all their right, title, and pretension to the lands bounded south by the thirty-first parallel of north latitude and north to the point where the boundary line, as defined in the preceding treaty, would strike the Yazoo River.   *Minter v. Shirley, 45 Miss., 376.*

SEC. 2300. The United States in her treaties of acquisition might come under such stipulations and engagements as would defeat a reservation of the sixteenth section in some of the townships, while it would attach in others, or would defeat the reservation in the ceded territory altogether. The Choctaw treaty of 1830 furnishes an example of the former. The Chickasaw treaty of 1832 (7 Stat. L., 388), is a most noted example of the second.   *Ibid.*

SEC. 2301. The cession of the whole reserve by the Choctaw treaty of 1830 (7 Stat. L., 333) was subject to the right to withhold certain parcels, which, when designated by a selection, were excluded from the grant and held by the ancient title of the tribe, quitclaimed and confirmed by the United States.   *Ibid.*

SEC. 2302. In the year 1713 the inhabitants of Newark were incorporated by Queen Anne, it being recited in this charter by the applicants therefor "that their ancestors and predecessors, freeholders of the said town, by license from the proprietor's governor, in the month of July, 1667, had purchased from the Indians all that tract of land now known by the name of Newark," etc.

Newark v. Stockton, 44 N. J. (Equity), 179.

SEC. 2303. The State possesses the power to appropriate to public use the lands of the Indians within its territory upon making compensation therefor, notwithstanding the grant of the right of preemption in such lands to Massachusetts.

Wadsworth v. The Buffalo Hydraulic Association, 15 Barbour (N. Y.), 83.

SEC. 2304. A conveyance by an Oneida Indian in 1791, being previous to the act of the 4th of April, 1801 (see the act relative to the Indians within this State, passed 10th of April, 1813, sess. 36 c. 92, R. N. L., 158), of land of which he was seized in his individual capacity, and distinct from his tribe, as the heir of an Indian to whom it was granted by the State for his services during the Revolutionary war, is valid (S. P. Jackson *v.* Sharpe, 14 Johnson's Rep., 472), although made without special authority from the legislature and without the approbation of the surveyor-general.

Jackson v. Brown, 15 Johnson (N. Y.), 264.

SEC. 2305. Section 12 of the act of Congress of 1802, known as the Indian Intercourse Act, "which invalidates any purchase of lands from Indians unless made by treaty or convention entered into pursuant to the Constitution," applies simply to purchases of Indian lands owned by the United States, for the sale of which its consent is indispensable.   The proviso in said provision making it "lawful for the agent or agents of any State who may be present at a treaty held with the Indians under the authority of the United States, in the presence and with the approbation of the commissioner or commissioners of the United States appointed to hold the same, to propose and adjust with the Indians the compensation to be made for their claims to lands within such State, which shall be extinguished by treaty," was intended to except from the scope of the first part of the section dealings with Indian tribes for the purchase of their right to lands within the State of which the State owned the preemption title. It does not require that the treaty for that purpose shall be one between the United States and the tribes from whom the purchase is made; it is sufficient if the purchase is made at a treaty held "under the authority of the United States," and in the "presence and with the approbation" of its commissioners.   *Seneca Nation v. Christie, 126 N. Y. Appl., 123.*

SEC. 2306. The act of April, 1785, it is true, has been held not to apply to lands within the Indian purchase of 1768, but it tends strongly to mark the sense of the legislature and of the country with respect to surplus land, and, although in the acts of 2d April, 1811, and 13th March, 1817, there has been a partial departure from this policy, yet the interests of those who had previously acquired rights by warrant or improvement were protected.

Blair v. McKee, 6 Sergeant & Rawle (Pa.), 201.

Sec. 2307. The purchase of the Indian title within the supposed charter limits of the colony of Connecticut, on the waters of the Susquehanna, by the Connecticut-Susquenanna Company in 1754, included what was afterwards constituted the town, and later the county, of Westmoreland, under the political jurisdiction of Connecticut, within which were the various townships (of which Wilkesbarre was one). The township of Wilkesbarre was first surveyed by David Meade in 1770. In 1773 a final division was made of the back lots and the town plot; afterwards the borough of Wilkesbarre was laid out.

Bennett et al. v. Norton et al., 171 Pa., 223.

Sec. 2308. By article 1 of tne State treaty of 1777 with the Cherokees, the district of country in which the plaintiff's grant was located was ceded to the State of South Carolina. By the second article the State engaged to permit the Cherokees to inhabit the said district of country "during good behavior." This was greater than an estate at will.

Thomas v. Daniel, 2 McCord (S. C.), 354.

Sec. 2309. From 1777 to 1816 State laws alone were of force in the territory of the Cherokee Nation in South Carolina, and when, in 1816, the State wished to acquire complete sovereignty over this territory, she, under the auspices of the United States Government, entered into negotiations with them which resulted in the treaty of March 22, 1816 (7 Stat. L., 138).

Ibid.

Sec. 2310. By the treaty of March 22, 1816 (7 Stat. L., 138), the Cherokees ceded to the State of South Carolina the same tract of country which was reserved for their use and occupancy by the act of legislature of South Carolina March 22, 1786.

Ibid.

Sec. 2311. A material portion of the consideration for the lands ceded by the Cherokees by their treaties of 1817 and 1819 was the reserves to the individuals who had become cultivators of the soil. Take this part of the consideration away from the reservees and the treaties are violated and annulled.

Blair v. Pathkiller, 2 Yerger, 407.

Sec. 2312. The lands in controversy, entered in 1838, had been ceded to the United States by the Cherokee treaty of 1819.

Crutchfield v. Hammack, 4 Humph. (Tenn.), 203.

Sec. 2313. When the county of Washington was established in 1777, embracing the entire Territory of Tennessee, an entry taker was appointed and numerous entries were made; but previous thereto a

treaty had been made with the Cherokee Indians by which their title
was acquired to all the lands lying east of a certain line, afterwards
known as Brown's line.   *Calloway v. Hopkins, 11 Heiskell (Tenn.), 349.*

CHAPTER III.—TREATIES.

SEC. 2314. In the treaty of October 25, 1805 (7 Stat. L., 93), with
the Cherokees, the reservation of 3 miles square, for a garrison, lies
below and not above the mouth of the Highwassee, where the United
States placed the garrison.   *Meigs et al. v. McClung's Lessee, 9 Cranch, 11.*

SEC. 2315. Construction of the provisions of the treaties with the
Indians made by the State of Georgia relative to boundaries, and of
the acts of the legislature of that State relative to grants of lands
within its territorial limits and which were not within the Indian
boundary line as defined by treaties and as recognized by those acts.
Patterson v. Jenks, 2 Pets., 216.

SEC. 2316. If the State of Georgia have construed their treaty with
the Cherokee Indians by any subsequent acts, manifesting an understanding of it, this court would not hesitate to adopt that construction.
Ibid.

SEC. 2317. The repugnancy of section 107 of the act of 1868 (15
Stat. L., 167) to the tenth article of the Cherokee treaty of 1866
(14 Stat. L., 799) is clear, and they can not stand together. One or the
other must yield. A treaty may supersede a prior act of Congress,
and an act of Congress may supersede a prior treaty. In this case
the act of Congress must prevail as if the treaty was not an element
to be considered, and if a wrong has been done the power of redress
is with Congress, not with the judiciary, and that body, upon being
applied to, it is to be presumed, will promptly give the proper relief.
Foster v. Neilson, 2 Pets., 314. The Cherokee Tobacco, 11 Wall.,
616. Taylor v. Morton, 2 Curtis, 454. The Clinton Bridge,
1 Walworth, 155.

SEC. 2318. The acts of Congress and all treaties duly made and
promulgated are the supreme law of the land, and it is not in the
power of any single State, by any law or ordinance of its own, to
abrogate or impair the binding obligation of the paramount laws and
treaties of the Union.
Cherokee Nation v. Georgia, Appendix 1, "Peters Cherokee Case," 225.

SEC. 2319. Newly asserted title to lands in the possession of the
Indians can derive no aid from the articles, so often repeated in Indian
treaties, extending to them first the protection of Great Britain and
afterwards that of the United States. These articles are associated
with others recognizing their title to self-government. The very fact
of repeated treaties with them recognizes it, and the settled doctrine

of the law of nations is that a weaker power does not surrender its independence—its right to self-government—by associating with a stronger and taking its protection. A weak State, in order to provide for its safety, may place itself under the protection of one more powerful without stripping itself of the right of self-government and ceasing to be a State. *Worcester v. Georgia, 6 Pets., 515.*

SEC. 2320. The language used in treaties with the Indians should never be construed to their prejudice. If words be made use of which are susceptible of a more extended meaning than their plain import, as connected with the tenor of the treaty, they should be considered as used only in the latter sense. How the words of the treaty were understood by this unlettered people, rather than their critical meaning, should form the rule of construction. *Ibid. Jones v. Meehan, 175 U. S., 1.*

SEC. 2321. If the language in a treaty be wholly indefinite, or the natural objects called for are uncertain or contradictory, there is no power, but that which formed the treaty, which can remedy such defects. *Lattimer v. Poteet, 14 Pets., 4.*

SEC. 2322. The stipulations contained in article 5 of the Cherokee treaty of 1835 (7 Stat. L., 478) was not intended or understood to alter in any manner the provisions of section 25 of the act of 1834 (4 Stat. L., 729) extending the criminal laws of the United States over the Indian country. *United States v. Rogers, 4 How., 567.*

SEC. 2323. The treaty of 1808 (7 Stat. L., 107) had every sanction that a ratification by our Senate could give it, and is a recognition of an Indian title in the Osages to nearly all the territory now embraced in the State of Missouri and the greater part of Arkansas, and of an Osage right in the land claimed by Riddick up to 1808, and yet the county and town of St. Louis, the seat of government of Upper Louisiana during the existence of the Spanish colonial government, the post of New Madrid, the county, town, and post of St. Charles, were all within that cession, as were also a great mass of Spanish orders of survey and grants, regarding which this country has been legislating and adjudicating for nearly fifty years, without anyone supposing that such concessions were affected by these loose Indian pretensions set up to the country at the time when the concessions were made— pretensions that the Spanish Government notoriously disregarded, further than a cautious policy required. *Marsh v. Brooks, 14 How., 513.*

SEC. 2324. In respect to the lands in California belonging to the class called Pueblo lands, no opinion is expressed either as to the power of the authorities to grant or the Indians to convey. *United States v. Ritchie, 17 How., 525.*

SEC. 2325. The removal of tribes of Indians under treaties must be made by the United States. They can not be expelled from their homes by the irregular force and violence of individuals who had acquired title to them, or through the intervention of courts of justice.

Fellows v. Blacksmith, 19 How., 366.

SEC. 2326. A treaty with an Indian tribe is the supreme law of the land. Courts can not annul its effect or operation. *Ibid.*

SEC. 2327. The courts can not go behind a treaty, when ratified, to inquire whether or not the tribe was properly represented by its headmen. *Ibid.*

SEC. 2328. The question of the validity of the treaty of 1842 (7 Stat. L., 586) to bind the Tonawanda band of Senecas, is one to be decided by the political power which acted for and with the Indians and not by the courts. So far as the statute of New York prohibiting intrusions on Indian lands is concerned, the Indians are not bound to show that they are owners, but can invoke the aid of the statute against all white intruders so long as they remain in the peaceable possession of their lands. *New York v. Dibble, 21 How., 366.*

SEC. 2329. Rules of interpretation favorable to the Indian tribes are to be adopted in construing our treaties with them, and hence a provision in an Indian treaty which exempts their lands from "levy, sale, and forfeiture" is not, in the absence of expressions so to limit it, to be confined to levy and sale under ordinary judicial proceedings only, but it is to be extended to levy and sale by county officers also for nonpayment of taxes. *The Kansas Indians, 5 Wall., 737.*

SEC. 2330. When the United States acquired and took possession of the Floridas, under the Louisiana treaty, the treaties which had been made with the Indian tribes remained in force over all the ceded territories, as the laws which regulate the relations with all the Indians who were parties to them. They were binding on the United States as fundamental laws of Indian right, acknowledged by royal orders and municipal regulations. By these the Indian right was not merely of possession, but that of alienation. *Wilson v. Wall., 6 Wall., 83.*

SEC. 2331. The register of those who applied to the agent for lands under article 14 of the Choctaw treaty of 1830 (7 Stat. L., 340) contained only the names of heads of families, which would seem to show the Indian construction of the contract or treaty. *Ibid.*

SEC. 2332. The Congress has no constitutional power to settle the rights under treaties except in cases purely political. The construction of them is the peculiar province of the judiciary when a case shall arise between individuals. *Ibid. Jones v. Mechan, 175 U. S., 1.*

SEC. 2333. Treaties with Indian nations within the jurisdiction of the United States, whatever considerations of humanity and good faith may be involved and require their faithful observance, can not be more obligatory than the treaties with foreign nations. They have no higher sanctity, and no greater inviolablity or immunity from legislative invasion can be claimed for them.

The Cherokee Tobacco, 11 Wall., 616.

SEC. 2334. The treaty of December 29, 1835 (7 Stat. L., 478), between the United States and the Cherokee Indians was not made in virtue of the act of May 28, 1830 (4 Stat. L., 411), authorizing an "exchange" of lands west of the Mississippi for the territory claimed or occupied by any tribe of Indians within the limits of any State or Territory, but was made under the treaty-making power vested by the Constitution in the President and Senate.

Holden v. Joy, 17 Wall., 211.

SEC. 2335. The condition in the patent from the United States that if the Indians abandoned the lands they should revert to the United States, if valid, is a condition subsequent, which no one but the *grantor* (?) can set up, and which the parties may waive; and the sale by the Cherokees to the United States did not constitute an abandonment within the condition.

Ibid.

SEC. 2336. On June 2, 1825, the Osage tribes by treaty (7 Stat. L., 240) ceded to the United States all their right to the neutral lands lying west of the Missouri, and the United States acquired the fee-simple title to such lands and could convey the same by treaty to the Cherokee Nation.

Ibid.

SEC. 2337. The lands conveyed to the United States by the Indian treaty of December 29, 1835 (7 Stat. L., 478), were held by the Cherokee under their original title, acquired by immemorial possession; and their title was absolute, subject only to the preemption right of purchase by the United States.

Ibid.

SEC. 2338. The Cherokee treaty of June 19, 1866 (14 Stat. L., 799), is valid, and operated to convey the lands to the United States, and the sale of the neutral lands to Joy, as agreed to by the supplemental treaty of April 27, 1868 (16 Stat. L., 727), and the patent issued therefor to him gave him a valid title.

Ibid.

SEC. 2339. The President and Senate by treaty could lawfully covenant that a patent should issue to convey lands which belong to the United States to an Indian tribe without the consent of Congress. Acts of Congress subsequently validated such treaty.

Ibid.

SEC. 2340. The Indian title to the Hot Springs in Arkansas Territory, with four sections of land including them, was extinguished August 24, 1818, by the treaty with the Quapaws (7 Stat. L., 176).

Rector v. United States, 92 U. S., 698.

SEC. 2341. The Indians could not treat on an equality with the United States if their possessory right were in effect transferred by the United States before it had been acquired from them. They would be constrained to sell, as the United States was obliged to buy, and although it might appear that the sale was voluntary it would, in fact, be compulsory.   *Railroad Co. v. United States, 92 U. S., 733.*

SEC. 2342. It is competent for the United States, in the exercise of the treaty-making power, to stipulate in a treaty with an Indian tribe that, within the territory thereby ceded, the laws of the United States, then or thereafter enacted, prohibiting the introduction and sale of spirituous liquors in the Indian country shall be in full force and effect until otherwise directed by Congress or the President of the United States; and such a stipulation operates *proprio vigore* and is binding upon the courts, although the ceded territory is situated within an organized county of a State.

United States v. 43 Gals. Whiskey, 93 U. S., 188.

SEC. 2343. It has been decided by this court (2 Pets., 314) "that a treaty is to be regarded in courts of justice as equivalent to an act of the legislature whenever it operates of itself without the aid of any legislative provision." No legislation is required to put the seventh article of the Chippewa treaty of 1863 (13 Stat. L., 667) in force; and it must become a rule of action, if the contracting parties had power to incorporate it in the treaty.   *Ibid.*

SEC. 2344. The acquisition of territory has been the moving cause of all Indian treaties, and will continue to be so until Indian reservations are confined to very narrow limits.   *Ibid.*

SEC. 2345. The seventh article of the Chippewa treaty of 1863 (13 Stat. L., 667) is based exclusively on the Federal authority over the *subject-matter*, and there is no disturbance of the principle of State equality.   *Ibid.*

SEC. 2346. The laws of Congress are always to be construed so as to conform to the provisions of a treaty, if it be possible to do so without violence to the language, and this rule operates with special force where a conflict would lead to the abrogation of a stipulation in a treaty making a valuable cession to the United States.   *Ibid.*

SEC. 2347. The treaty of 1828 (7 Stat. L., 311) was made with the chiefs and headmen of the Cherokee Nation of Indians west of the Mississippi, and by that treaty, for the first time, the Cherokees west of the river were recognized as so far a distinct and separate political body from the Cherokees east of the river as to call for separate treaty negotiations with them.   *The Cherokee, &c. Case, 117 U. S., 288.*

SEC. 2348. From the time of the treaty of 1828 (7 Stat. L., 311) until the treaty of 1835 (7 Stat. L., 478) the Cherokees were divided into two branches, so that the United States had separate negotiations with each. The latter treaty was made to put an end to the troubles between the Cherokees composing the branch remaining east and the citizens of the State wherein they resided and secure the reunion of the divided nation.   *Ibid.*

SEC. 2349. The modified Sioux agreement ratified by Congress on June 22, 1872 (18 Stat. L., 167), must be considered as accepted on the part of the United States when it was approved by the Secretary of the Interior on June 19, 1874. Some official recognition was necessary to satisfy those who might be interested as to the good faith of the alleged consent of the Indians, whether the parties acting nominally in their behalf really represented them, and whether their assent was freely given after full knowledge of the import of the legislation by Congress. Proof of these facts was not to rest in the recollection of witnesses, but in the official action of the officers of the Government, or in the legislation of Congress. *Buttz v. Railroad Co., 11 U. S., 55.*

SEC. 2350. Congress did not intend by the thirteenth section of the act of June 30, 1834 (4 Stat. L., 729), to invest the President or the head of a department, or any officer of the Government, with unrestricted authority in the making of treaties with Indians, or in regulating intercourse with them, to purchase merchandise for them, or to make payments of money or goods to them.

United States v. McDougall's Adm.; 121 U. S., 89.

SEC. 2351. Certain sums were appropriated to enable the President to hold treaties with the various Indian tribes in California, and to the extent of such appropriations the President, through persons designated by him, could purchase merchandise required in the making of a treaty, and could make payment of money or goods on account of the Indians, but no officer of the Government was authorized to bind the United States by any contract for subsistence of the Indians not based upon appropriations made by Congress. *Ibid.*

SEC. 2352. As the petitioner was a member of the Cherokee Nation by adoption, if not by nativity, and was the sole party to these proceedings, it is clear that under the treaties and acts of Congress he is amenable only to the courts of the nation, and the fact, if it be so, that the laws of the Cherokee Nation make no provision for the punishment of the crime of adultery, would not extend to the courts of the United States a power to punish this crime that did not otherwise exist. *In re Mayfield, 141 U. S., 107.*

SEC. 2353. Unquestionably a treaty may be modified or abrogated by an act of Congress, but the power to make and unmake is essentially political and not judicial, and the presumption is wholly inadmissible that Congress sought in referring the claim of these Indians to the courts for adjudication to submit the good faith of its own action or the action of the Government to judicial decision by authorizing the stipulations in the Cherokee treaty of 1846 (9 Stat. L., 871) to be overthrown upon an inquiry of the character suggested, and the act of February 25, 1889 (25 Stat. L., 694), giving the courts jurisdiction of this case does not in the least degree justify such inference.

United States v. Old Settlers, 148 U. S., 427.

Sec. 2354. The decision in the United States *v.* Arredondo (6 Pet., 691) is not authority for the proposition that a court is clothed with power to annul a treaty on the ground of fraud or duress in its execution. There is nothing in the jurisdictional act of February 25, 1889 (25 Stat. L., 694), inconsistent with the Cherokee treaty of 1846 (9 Stat. L., 871), and nothing to indicate that Congress attempted by that act to authorize the courts to proceed in disregard thereof. *Ibid.*

Sec. 2355. The acquisition of territory has been the moving cause of all Indian treaties, and will continue to be so until Indian reservations are confined to very narrow limits.

United States v. 43 Gals. Whisky, 93 U. S., 188.

Sec. 2356. A treaty with an Indian tribe has the force and effect of a law of the United States. *United States v. Berry, 4 Fed. Rep., 786.*

Sec. 2357. A treaty, like an ordinary contract or statute, must be construed to give it effect, if possible, and courts always adhere to this rule. In construing a treaty we have a right to take into consideration the situation of the parties to it at the time it was made, the property which is the subject-matter of the treaty, and the intention and purposes of the parties in making the treaty. To get at the intention of the parties we have a right to consider the construction the parties to the treaty, and who were to be affected by it, have given it and what has been their action under it. *United States v. Payne, 8 Fed. Rep., 883.*

Sec. 2358. The construction of a treaty to be taken as the true one is the one which has been adopted and acted upon by all the parties to it, unless the parties to it were mutually led into this construction by fraud or mistake. In a case where the mutual construction was in the face of the language used, and the rights of the third parties had intervened, the language would be taken as governing. *Ibid.*

Sec. 2359. Under the Chickasaw treaty of July 1, 1834 (7 Stat. L., 450), as interpreted by the previous treaty of Pontotoc of March 1, 1832 (7 Stat. L., 381), to which it was a supplement, State legislation that interferes with the national rights of the Chickasaw Indians while in possession of lands under the tribal organizations is extraterritorial, and, so far as conflicting with rights secured by the treaty, unconstitutional, and rights once vested under the treaty are beyond the power of State legislation, even after the removal of the Indians.

Love v. Pamplin, 21 Fed. Rep., 755.

Sec. 2360. The language used in treaties with the Indians should never be construed to their prejudice. If words be made use of which are susceptible of a more extended meaning than their plain import as connected with the tenor of the treaty, they should be considered as used only in the latter sense. *Wan-pe-man-qua v. Aldrich, 28 Fed. Rep., 489.*

Sec. 2361. The doctrine of relation has no application to a case of this kind, where a statute prescribes the time when the bargain shall take effect. *Shepard v. Insurance Co., 40 Fed. Rep., 341.*

SEC. 2362. Where an Indian treaty provided that it should be obligatory as soon as the same should be ratified by the President and Senate, it did not take effect until signed by the President, although it had been previously ratified by the Senate and accepted by the Indians.   *Ibid.*

SEC. 2363. As early as in 1802, by the twelfth section of the act of Congress (2 Stat. L., 139) for regulating trade and intercourse with the Indian tribes, it was declared that no purchase of lands made from any Indian or any Indian tribe or nation within the United States should be "of any validity in law or equity, unless the same be made by treaty or convention entered into in pursuance of the Constitution."

Benson v. United States, 44 Fed. Rep., 178.

SEC. 2364. The treaty between the United States and Makah tribe of Indians (12 Stat. L., 939) gave no rights or privileges to said Indians peculiar from or superior to those of the citizens of this country in general.   *United States v. The James G. Sevan, 50 Feb. Rep., 108.*

SEC. 2365. The only power which can abrogate a treaty, or any provision of a treaty, is the treaty-making power—the United States. The act admitting Wyoming into the Union admits it upon an equal footing with the original States, and makes no reservation whatever regarding the treaty relations then existing between the United States and the Bannock Indians. Neither does it, by express terms, abrogate the treaty or any of its provisions. Hence, if the treaty provisions have been abrogated or repealed by the act admitting Wyoming into the Union (26 Stat. L., 222) it is by implication, because of inconsistent legislation. While repeals by implication are not favored, yet that treaty provisions are repealed by inconsistent Congressional legislation is well settled.   *In re Race Horse, 70 Fed. Rep., 598.*

SEC. 2366. The power to make treaties is, by the Constitution, expressly delegated to the United States and prohibited the States, and that a treaty executed and ratified by the proper formalities is the supreme law of the land, and that, so long as the treaty provision is in force, any State law in conflict with it must give way to its superior authority, because the power to abrogate or place proper limitations upon the treaty provisions is, by the Constitution, expressly delegated to the United States.   *Ibid.*

SEC. 2367. Prior to March 3, 1871, the United States always exercised its power and jurisdiction over the Indian tribes by means of treaties, but on that day a radical change was made in the preexisting policy by the enactment of a law (16 Stat. L., 566) which, while continuing every obligation of any treaty theretofore lawfully made and ratified with any tribe, declared that thereafter "no Indian nation or tribe within the territory of the United States shall be acknowledged or recognized as an independent nation, tribe, or power with whom the United States may contract by treaty."

Truscott v. Hurlbut, &c., Co., 73 Fed. Rep., 60.

SEC. 2368. The enumeration of other rights secured to the Indians by express words negatives any possible presumption of rights by mere implication.   *United States v. Winans, 73 Fed. Rep., 72.*

SEC. 2369. The effect of the admission of Wyoming as a State upon an equal footing with the original States, as well in respect of the exercise of the police power as otherwise, was not to abrogate the provisions of the treaty in reference to the rights of the Indians in the lands within the State.   *In re Race Horse, 70 Fed. Rep., 598.*

SEC. 2370. Parties dealing with Indians must take notice of public treaties and acts of Congress, and do not take land as *bona fide* purchasers relieved of restrictions on alienation merely because no such restriction appears in the patent.   *Laughton v. Nadeau et al., 75 Fed., 790.*

SEC. 2371. It *seems* that the act March 3, 1817 (3 Stat. L., 380), was intended as declaratory of the *meaning* of the treaty of 1814 with the Creeks.   *Lindsay v. United States, Devereaux's (C. Cls. R.), 92.*

SEC. 2372. A treaty is paramount law. It is the duty of Congress to comply with the terms of a treaty, and the Government is not liable because this renders nugatory an assignment from an Indian tribe to its agents.

Kendall v. United States, 1 C. Cls., 261. Same, 7 Wall., 113.
Kansas v. Herold, 9 Kan. (Dassler), 134.

SEC. 2373. By the act of February 27, 1851 (9 Stat. L., 586), Congress directed that all treaties with Indians should be negotiated by such officers and agents of the Indian department as the President should designate for that purpose.   *Norris v. United States, 2 C. Cls. R., 155.*

SEC. 2374. In 1851 the Indians in California entered into certain treaties under the actual pressure of military force, some after defeat in battle, and all under a threat of extermination should they refuse.

Fremont v. United States, 2 C. Cls., 461.

SEC. 2375. Treaties with "Eastern Cherokees" and with "Western Cherokees," or "Old Settlers," considered and construed.

Kendall v. United States, 2 C. Cls., 592.

SEC. 2376. By the Creek treaty of 1866 (14 Stat. L., 785) the United States reserved $100,000 from moneys to be paid the nation, and stipulated that that amount should be divided among the loyal Creeks "in proportion to their several losses;" but they did not thereby assume the losses which loyal individuals suffered by reason of their having faithfully adhered to the Government during the late war.

Connor v. United States, 19 C. Cls., 675.

SEC. 2377. The provision in the Creek treaty of 1866 (14 Stat. L., 785) that "the stipulations of this treaty are to be in full settlement of all claims of said Creek Nation for damages and losses of every kind growing out of the late rebellion" applies to individual and personal, as well as to national, demands.   *Ibid.*

SEC. 2378. The provision in the treaty of 1866 with the Creeks (14 Stat. L., 785) whereby the Government "reaffirms and reassumes all obligations" existing under the previous treaty takes effect from the date of the new treaty, and does not carry back the obligations so as to be operative during the war.   *Ibid.*

SEC. 2379. When the Creek Nation entered into a treaty with the Confederate Government and engaged in war against the United States, the treaty of 1856 (11 Stat. L., 704) was abrogated and the obligation of the Government to individual Creeks at an end.

Ibid.

SEC. 2380. Article 1 of the treaty of 1846, securing the lands west of the Mississippi River to "the whole Cherokee people for their common use and benefit," referred to the three parties into which the Cherokee Nation was then divided, and not to individual Cherokees who remained east of the Mississippi.

Eastern Band Cherokees v. United States et al., 20 C. Cls., 449.

SEC. 2381. An agreement signed by delegates of the Cherokee Nation and of the Western Cherokees, without authority, authorizing the North Carolina Cherokees to participate in the benefits of a treaty which those delegates had just concluded with the United States, can not be enforced unless ratified.

Ibid.

SEC. 2382. Article 10 of the treaty of 1846 (9 Stat. L., 871) was inserted to satisfy the North Carolina Cherokees that certain claims then presented by them should not be abridged by the treaty.

Ibid.

SEC. 2383. That portion of the treaty which was simply directory as to the mode in which the location of the reservation might be made, with reference to the improvement, became, by the requirement of the act of 1842, a condition precedent to the right of reservation, and imposed upon the Indian obligations beyond the requirement of the treaty.   *Choctaw Nation v. United States, 21 C. Cls., 59.*

SEC. 2384. The words "claim" and "rights" as used in the Choctaw treaty of 1855 (11 Stat. L., 611) must necessarily mean to us such claim and such rights as are dependent upon a liberal construction of the Indian's claim, founded upon law, aside from any policy which other Departments of the Government might have the power to exercise toward the claimant. We are not left in the broad field of "natural justice" exercising a jurisdiction of discretion above and beyond the limit of legal right.   *Ibid.*

SEC. 2385. Under the treaty of 1830 (7 Stat. L., 340) the Choctaw Nation is not entitled to the net proceeds of the lands ceded to the United States.   *Ibid.*

SEC. 2386. Under the treaty of 1830 (7 Stat. L., 340) every Choctaw family which complied with the requirements of article 14 had a right to appropriate land and remain east of the Mississippi.

Ibid.

SEC. 2387. The authorities are many that the terms of a treaty can not be changed or affected by the act of one party to the prejudice of the other; and unless the fact that the Indians whose applications were rejected by the board consented to the imposition of new conditions they have a present right to insist through the claimant upon the letter of the treaty.

Ibid.

SEC. 2388. The act of March 2, 1861 (12 Stat. L., 238), directing that bonds to the amount of $250,000 be issued to the Choctaws on account of the treaty obligations of the United States vested no right. The refusal of the Executive to deliver the bonds, and the act of February 14, 1873 (17 Stat. L., 462), prohibiting the issuing, took away none, but left all treaty obligations unimpaired.

Ibid.

SEC. 2389. There was nothing in the treaty in the nature of a forfeiture clause, and if the one party continued to invite or permit emigration, apparently upon the terms of the treaty, and the other continued to emigrate in the belief that the terms of the treaty were still operative to secure the reimbursement of their expenses, there is no reason why the instrument should not be treated like a contract which specifies a time for performance, but contains no forfeiture clause and under which the parties continue to perform by mutual acquiescence after the prescribed period has elapsed.

Ibid.

SEC. 2390. When the Chickasaw treaty of 1852 (10 Stat. L., 974) was approved by the Senate and ratified by the President all the facts were before them.   This is a presumption of law which, in this case, is also established as a fact by the form and phraseology of the treaty and its amendments.   *Chickasaw Nation v. United States, 22 C. Cls., 222.*

SEC. 2391. The rights of the Choctaw Nation are founded upon a treaty, an instrument which is a contract between the parties, and also a law imposed by the Government upon its own citizens and agents. As a contract the Chickasaws are entitled to all its benefits until it is varied by mutual consent or annulled in some manner recognized by law.

Ibid.

SEC. 2392. When a treaty makes the United States the trustee of a fund and charges them with the cost, risk, and responsibility of distribution, the court will decree concerning the unpaid balance that the Government shall continue to act as trustee, and shall pay the balance to the individuals entitled to the fund as ascertained under a provision of the treaty.

Western Cherokee Indians v. United States, 27 C. Cls., 1.

SEC. 2393. The "unrestricted latitude" given by the Western Cherokee act of February, 1889 (25 Stat. L., 694), does not authorize the court to go behind a treaty and declare it to have been procured by duress or fraud.   *Ibid.*

SEC. 2394. The supplemental paragraph attached to the *Supplementary Articles*, September 27, 1833 (7 Stat. L., 442, 445), having been recognized by the Senate and proclaimed by the President as part of the treaty, must be considered as such.

Pottawatomie Indians v. United States, 27 C. Cls., 403.

SEC. 2395. That the commissioners who negotiated a treaty did not sign a supplemental paragraph does not affect its validity if the President and Senate recognized it as a part of the treaty.   *Ibid.*

SEC. 2396. The object of the Pottawatomie treaty of 1833 (7 Stat. L., 431) was to secure the removal of the Pottawatomies west; but it was too late to insist that removal and continued residence form a condition precedent to the right of those who remained in Michigan to participate in the various treaty funds.   *Ibid.*

SEC. 2397. The Delaware-Cherokee agreement of 1867 was something more than a deed of bargain and sale, viz, a treaty. After being executed by the delegates of the nation it was "ratified by the National Committee June 15, 1867."

Journeycake v. Cher. Nation and United States, 28 C. Cls., 281.

SEC. 2398. The treaty with the Klickitat Indians did not take effect until ratified by the Senate March 8, 1859.

Bush v. United States, 29 C. Cls., 144.

SEC. 2399. The Indians and the United States, like all other independent contractors, may agree by the terms of their contract when it shall take effect, and courts will enforce that provision in dealing with the rights and obligations of the parties.   *Ibid.*

SEC. 2400. A treaty which by its terms is to become obligatory "as soon as the same shall be ratified by the President and Senate of the United States," is in the interval only a proposition of the other party and creates no liability.   *Ibid.*

SEC. 2401. Treaties operating upon purely national rights, in the absence of a provision to the contrary, operate from the date of the signature; but a different rule prevails where the treaty operates on individual rights.   *Ibid.*

SEC. 2402. A treaty with an Indian tribe is a part of the law of the land, and where it prescribes a rule by which private rights can be determined a court will apply the rule.

Leighton v. United States, 29 C. Cls., 288.

SEC. 2403. A court can not inquire whether a treaty was properly executed or whether it was procured by undue influence.

Ibid.

SEC. 2404. The act March 3, 1871 (sec. 2079, Rev. Stats.), prohibiting the making of treaties with Indians did not invalidate or impair those theretofore ratified.   *Ibid.*

SEC. 2405. A preamble to a treaty may be consulted when doubt exists; but its function is to state only the general objects of the treaty or the reasons therefor, and not to limit its provisions. "A general amnesty of all past offenses committed by any member of the Creek Nation against the laws of the United States is hereby declared," being clear and comprehensible language, the preamble to the treaty can not be consulted to ascertain its meaning.

Garrison v. United States and the Creek Indians, 30 C. Cls., 272.

SEC. 2406. The acceptance of the treaty of Buffalo Creek, 1838 (7 Stat. L., 550), by certain New York Indian tribes does not appear, but the Senate having passed a resolution stating that it has been "approved by said tribes," and the President having issued a proclamation accepting, ratifying, and confirming the treaty, the court can not go behind this authoritative decision of the treaty-making power.

New York Indians v. United States, 30 C. Cls., 413.

SEC. 2407. The connection which exists by treaty between the Indian tribes and the Federal Government is of a political character; and the enforcement of such stipulations must mainly depend on the Executive power.   *United States v. Bailey, 1 McLean, 234.*

SEC. 2408. Although a treaty is the law of the land, Congress may abrogate it, so far as it is municipal law, provided its subject-matter is within the legislative power of Congress.

United States v. Tobacco Factory, 1 Dill., 264.

SEC. 2409. The treaty-making power of the United States can make a sale or grant of land to an Indian tribe without an act of Congress, and Congress has no right to interfere with rights under treaties, except in cases purely political.   *United States v. Reese, 5 Dill., 405.*

SEC. 2410. The principal object of the Pottawatomie treaty of 1867 (15 Stat. L., 531) was to cause the removal to the Indian Territory of such of the tribe as had not and would not become citizens.

Goodfellow v. Joseph Muckey, 1 McCrary, 238.

SEC. 2411. Treaties of 1825 (7 Stat. L., 240) and 1865 (14 Stat. L., 687) with the Osages construed.

United States v. Leavenworth, Lawrence & Galveston R. R. Co.,
1 McCrary, 610.

SEC. 2412. It will be seen by looking at the date of the act of Congress—July 26, 1866—and the dates of the respective stages of the treaty with the Osages that the treaty had passed the Senate, but with material amendments, June 26, 1866, one month before the approval of this bill by the President; but it had then to .be submitted to the Indians for their action on these amendments. Their approval was given September 21, 1866, two months after the passage of the act of Congress, and the treaty only became valid and operative by the proclamation of the President, January 21, 1867.

United States v. M., K. & T. Ry. Co., 1 McCrary, 624.

SEC. 2413. The treaty-making power has a right to convey title to the lands of the United States without an act of Congress, and if a treaty acts directly on the subject of the grant it is equivalent to an act of Congress, and the grantee has a good title.

United States v. Payne, 2 McCrary, 289. (*Same in 8 Fed. Rep., 883.*)

SEC. 2414. If the treaty of 1868 with the Utes was one of the laws of the United States, which by the terms of the act of June 26, 1876 (19 Stat. L., 61), was to remain in force in the State of Colorado after its admission, it follows that the Ute Reservation remains within the exclusive jurisdiction of the United States by virtue of said treaty.

United States v. Berry, 2 McCrary, 58.

SEC. 2415. Treaties with Indians have the force of law, and when entered into while the reservation is embraced in a Territory are not repealed by implication by the passage of an act authorizing the formation of a State government. *Ibid.*

SEC. 2416. Congress has recognized the obligation of all treaties with the Indian tribes lawfully made and ratified prior to March 3, 1871. (See Revised Statutes, sections 2079, 2080, 2081, 2093, 2094, 2095, 2096, 2097, 2099, 2100, 2101, 2116, 2118.) *Ibid.*

SEC. 2417. According to a well-settled rule of construction, since there is no express repeal of any part of the Ute treaty of 1868 (15 Stat. L., 619), that instrument and the act of 1875 admitting Colorado as a State (18 Stat. L., 474) should be construed together, and as far as possible the provisions of each should be allowed to stand. *Ibid.*

SEC. 2418. The treaty of 1832 between the United States and the Chickasaw Indians, with the supplementary and explanatory articles (7 Stat. L., 381–390), did not invest the reservees with the title to the reserved lands, but clearly prohibited each reservee from selling or leasing his reservation. *Pettit's Admr. v. Pettit's Distributees, 32 Ala., 288.*

SEC. 2419. The President is charged with the duty of maintaining treaty stipulations as the Chief Executive.

Kendall v. United States, 12 Peters, 524.   Echols v. Tate, 53 Ark., 12.

SEC. 2420. If a treaty is made with a tribe of Indians by which they relinquish to the United States their lands, with certain reservations, and the treaty provides that the heads of families in the tribe shall each be entitled to 80 acres of land, to be selected under the direction of the President and to be secured by patents, the officers of the Land

Department can not issue scrip for land selected under the treaty outside of the ceded territory, nor can the President issue patents therefor in the absence of legislation by Congress authorizing it to be done. The treaty with the Chippewas of Lake Superior and the Mississippi, dated September 30, 1854, giving to each head of a family of the mixed bloods of the tribe 80 acres of land, to be selected by the President and patented, does not permit the selection of lands for such mixed bloods on the public domain outside of the territory ceded to the United States by the Indians in the treaty.   *Parker v. Duff, 47 Cal., 554.*

Sec. 2421. By the treaty of 1868, proclaimed by the President February 24, 1869, with the Sioux Indians the district of country known as the Black Hills became an Indian reservation. The agreement passed by Congress, approved February 28, 1877, expressly admits that a reservation was defined by article 2 of said treaty, and modifies the same—abrogates article 16 of the treaty, and relinquishes and cedes the Black Hills country to the United States. By article 8 of said agreement the provisions of the treaty of 1866, except as modified, continued in full force, and, with the provisions of the agreement, apply to any country which may thereafter be occupied by these Indians as a home.   *Uhlig v. Garrison, 2 Dak. (Smith), 71.*

Sec. 2422. The treaty of February 24, 1869, with the Brulé Sioux Indians, as affirmed by the agreement of February 28, 1877, operated of itself without the aid of any legislative enactment, and is equal in vigor and strength to an act of Congress.
United States v. Crow Dog, 3 Dakota (Smith), 106.

Sec. 2423. Chief Justice Marshall, in Foster *v.* Nielson (2 Peters, 314), says: "A treaty is to be regarded in the courts of justice as equivalent to an act of the legislature whenever it operates of itself, without the aid of any legislative provision."   *Ibid.*

Sec. 2424. In 1855 a treaty was made with the Nez Percé tribe of Indians residing within the then Territories of Oregon and Washington, and ratified in 1859, by the provisions of which they were restricted in their rights with the exception of the privileges of hunting, fishing, pasturing, etc. In 1863 a supplemental treaty was made with the Nez Percé tribe of Indians which contained a provision ratifying all the sections of the treaty of 1855 which had not been abrogated or changed. The organic act of Idaho Territory was passed by Congress in 1863, embracing within its limits that portion of Washington Territory upon which was located the Nez Percé Reservation, and that portion of the act respecting the rights of the Indians is much broader and stronger in favor of the authority of the General Government in the premises than were the organic acts of Oregon and Washington Territories.   *Pickett v. United States, 1 Prickett (Idaho), 529.*

SEC. 2425. A condition in an Indian treaty and in a clause in a patent for land granted under a treaty to a person of Indian descent that the land shall never be leased or conveyed by the patentee or any of his heirs, to any one, without the permission of the President of the United States is not void as being a limitation upon a fee.

Pickering v. Lomax et al., 120 Ill., 289.

SEC. 2426. A treaty with the Indians, so far as respects the grants of land to individuals contained in it, is evidence of the grantee's title, and as such proper to be laid before a jury.

Harris v. Doe, ex dem. Barrett et al., 4 Blackf. (Ind.), 370.

SEC. 2427. The treaty of 1824, with the Sac and Fox tribe of Indians, by which certain lands were ceded to the United States, did not include that portion of their lands lying between the rivers Des Moines and Mississippi, which was reserved for the half-breeds belonging to said tribes. By this treaty of 1824 the half-breeds had conferred upon them the right of private property in the lands reserved for their use and not the sovereignty over them. The title of the half-breeds was not disturbed by the second treaty and cession in 1832, as the cession of lands from one nation to another does not affect the right of private property.

Webster v. Reid, 1 (Morris) Iowa, 467.

SEC. 2428. The question whether the President and Senate of the United States have power by treaty to dispose of Indian lands is not an open one. That they have such a power, and the power to pre-scribe the manner in which Indian lands may be sold or conveyed, seems to have been settled by all the departments of the Federal Government.

Wood v. M., K. & T. Ry. Co., 11 Kans., 323.

SEC. 2429. Language in an Indian treaty creating an exemption from taxation should be strictly construed, and should not be extended further than the fair import of the words requires.

Miami Co. v. Brackenridge, 12 Kans., 114.

SEC. 2430. An Indian treaty, like any other instrument, must be construed in the light of its obvious purpose, and general words may often be limited and restricted by such purpose. *Ibid.*

SEC. 2431. An admission in a treaty between the United States and a tribe of Indians as to the limits of the territory occupied by the latter is only binding on the Government and those claiming under it after the date of the treaty; it is not conclusive on those who had previously acquired rights. The latter may go behind the treaty and show that the whole proceeding was, as to them, fraudulent and void.

Brooks v. Norris, 6 Robinson (La.), 186.

SEC. 2432. The treaty of 1725 was after the French and Indian wars of that period, and was between the governors of Nova Scotia, New Hampshire, and Massachusetts Bay on the one hand and "the several tribes, viz, the Penobscot, Norridgewock, St. Johns, Cape Sable, and other tribes inhabiting within New England and Nova Scotia," on the other hand.   *State v. Newell, 84 Me., 465.*

SEC. 2433. In 1749, after another Indian war, commissioners from Governor Phipps made a treaty of peace with "the Indians of the tribes of Penobscot, Norridgewock, St. Francois, and other Indians inhabiting within His Majesty's territory of New England." The conference in 1752 was only a confirmation of the treaty of 1749.   *Ibid.*

SEC. 2434. What is referred to as "the treaty of 1780" appears to be simply a letter of thanks and kindly assurances from Governor Bowdoin to the "different tribes of Indians under Col. John Allen." It makes no mention of hunting and fishing.   *Ibid.*

SEC. 2435. The treaty of 1713 was "the submission and agreement of the Eastern Indians" to and with Governor Dudley at Portsmouth. It purports to be executed by "delegates from all the Indian plantations on the rivers of St. John, Penobscot, Kenybec, Amascogon, Saco, and Merrimack." The conference of 1717 was simply a confirmation of the same treaty.   *Ibid.*

SEC. 2436. In the treaties of 1713, 1725, and 1749 the contracting Indians reserved to themselves "and their natural descendants, respectively, the privilege of fishing, hunting, and fowling, as formerly." These treaties were made by the Crown with actual political communities, with an internal government and an external responsibility, which could wage war and make peace. But whatever may have been the original force and obligation of these treaties, they are now *functus officio.*   *Ibid.*

SEC. 2437. When a treaty has been made by the proper Federal authority and ratified it becomes the law of the land, and no courts have the power to question or in any manner look into the powers or rights recognized by it in the nation or tribe with whom it was made.   *Maiden v. Ingersoll, 6 Mich. (2 Cooley), 373.*

SEC. 2438. The court can not, from a construction of the treaty of Saginaw of September 24, 1819, itself interpret the words "Indians by descent," as used therein, to mean persons of mixed white and Indian blood only, and not full-blooded Indians. Nor can the court say, from the language of said treaty, the policy of the Government as indicated by the Indian treaties, public records and dispatches, and the habits and modes of life of the Chippewa Nation, that a presumption arises that all the reservees in said treaty were persons of mixed white and Indian blood.   *Campau v. Dewey, 9 Mich. (5 Cooley), 381.*

SEC. 2439. Under the practical interpretation put on the Indian treaty of October 18, 1864, by the Government, the selection of lands and the competency of the grantees both became operative together when fixed by the proper official authority, and both were before that ambulatory.   *Raymond v. Shawboose, 34 Mich. (Post), 142.*

SEC. 2440. Where individual rights vest under a treaty, the meaning of the treaty in reference to them is to be ascertained by the same rules of construction which are applied to the interpretation of private contracts.   *Anderson & Orne v. Lewis & Niles, 1 Freeman's Chancery (Miss.), 178.*

SEC. 2441. The instructions from the War Department as to the construction of the Chickasaw treaty, 1834 (7 Stat. L., 450), have no binding force; that Department could add nothing to the terms of the treaty without the consent of the other party thereto, and as the sixth article contained the stipulation that the reservations should be located by the register and receiver, the instructions from the War Department, "that no location under any of the articles of the treaty should be considered as final or as conferring any right whatever until the same should be approved by the President," is not obligatory.

Wray v. Doe, 18 Miss., 452.

SEC. 2442. Under article 4 of the Chickasaw treaty of 1834 (7 Stat. L., 450), which imposes certain conditions on alienation, including the approval of the President, a deed having all the other requisites of the treaty except the approval of the President indorsed on it does not pass the title of the Indian to the vendee so as to entitle him to maintain ejectment for the land; the approval of the President is essential to pass the legal title.   It is the law of the property; it must be conveyed in a prescribed form or no legal title passes.

Harmon v. Partier, 20 Miss., 425.

SEC. 2443. The act of Congress of May 26, 1864, creating the Territory of Montana, excepted therefrom any territory which, by treaty with any Indian tribes, was not, without the consent of said tribe, to be included within the territorial limits or jurisdiction of any State or Territory.   The area of the Crow Indian Reservation, as defined by the treaty of May 7, 1868, was within the boundaries of the Territory of Montana.   *Held*, that said treaty, being subsequent to said organic act of May 26, 1864, and being silent as to the inclusion of the Crow Reservation within the boundaries of said Territory, such reservation became a part of Montana.

Board of Commissioners v. N. P. R. R. Co., 10 Montana, 414.

SEC. 2444. Upon the application of the relators, who claimed to be that portion of the Cayuga Nation of Indians residing in Canada, a writ of *certiorari* was issued requiring the board of commissioners of the land office to return all petitions, papers, and documents pertaining to an application made by the said relators to the said board to receive their share of an annuity which the State of New York had by treaties agreed and promised to pay forever, which application had been rejected by the said board.   *Held*, that section 4 of chapter 234 of 1841 imposed upon the board the duty of hearing and determining the application made by the relators; that the fact that since the war of 1812 no portion of the annuity had been paid to the Canadian branch of the nation, on the ground that they had taken part in that war against the United States, did not authorize the rejection of their claim, if it were otherwise well founded, as it did not appear that the debt due to them had been confiscated either by the State or the United States Government; that the right of the relators to recover a portion of the annuity under the original treaty made with the whole nation could not be affected by the provisions of treaties subsequently made by the State with portions of the nation to which the relators were not parties.   *Cayuga Indians v. Commissioners, 34 Hun (N. Y.), 588.*

SEC. 2445. In the treaties on the part of Ogden and Fellows (January 15, 1838) with the Seneca and also with the Tuscarora nations of Indians, made in the presence of commissioners on the part of the State of Massachusetts and commissioners on the part of the United States, for the purpose, on the part of said Ogden and Fellows, of purchasing from said nations their preemption right to their respective reservations in this State, the United States assumed no obligations and undertook the performance of no duties in respect to the said Ogden and Fellows in their purchase of said reservations. Neither of said treaties contained any stipulations or agreements of anything to be done or performed in respect to said purchase on the part of the United States.   *McKeon v. Tillotson, 1 Keyes (N. Y. App.), 161.*

SEC. 2446. A State or its agent is authorized (section 12, act of 1802) to enter into a treaty or convention with the Indian tribes within its borders for the extinguishment of the Indian title, provided it is entered into in the presence of and with the approval of a commissioner of the United States appointed to attend the same, and such a treaty requires no ratification or proclamation by the Federal authorities.   *Seneca Nation v. Christie, 126 N. Y. App. (Sickels), 123.*

SEC. 2447. When an Indian, under the treaties of 1817 and 1819 (with the Cherokee Indians), after having his reservation allotted to him, voluntarily abandoned it and reunited himself with his tribe west of the Mississippi, it was *held* that his children, after his death, were not entitled to any estate in such reservation. A treaty in its effect is an executory agreement, and where an estate was limited by treaty to one for life, with a remainder to others, on a condition extending to both estates, it was *held* that on breach of such condition both estates were defeated without entry.   *Welch v. Trotter, 8 Jones (N. C. Laws), 197.*

CHAPTER IV.—SETTLEMENT ON INDIAN LANDS.

SEC. 2448. In all acts of the legislature of North Carolina there is a uniform intention manifested to restrict entries from being made on lands included within the Indian boundaries.

Preston v. Browder, 1 Wheat., 115.

SEC. 2449. The acts of assembly of North Carolina passed between the years 1783 and 1789 avoided all entries, surveys, and grants of lands set apart for the Cherokee Indians, and no title can be thereby acquired to such lands.   *Danforth v. Thomas, 1 Wheat., 155.*

SEC. 2450. The boundaries of the Cherokee Reservation have been altered by successive treaties with the Indians, but the mere extinguishment of the Indian title did not subject the land to appropriation unless expressly authorized by the legislature.   *Ibid.*

SEC. 2451. The act of assembly of North Carolina of 1778 was a legislative declaration explaining and amending the act of November, 1777, and no title was acquired by an entry within the Indian boundary contrary to these laws.   *Preston v. Browder, 1 Wheat., 115.*

SEC. 2452. The act of assembly of North Carolina of November, 1777, establishing offices for receiving entries of claims for lands in the several counties of the State, did not authorize entries for lands within the Indian boundary as defined by the treaty of the Long Island of Holston of July 20, 1777.   *Ibid.*

SEC. 2453. The act of North Carolina of 1784, authorizing the removing of warrants which had been located upon lands previously taken up so as to place them upon vacant lands, did not repeal by implication the, previously existing laws which prohibited surveys of land within the Indian boundary.   *Danforth v. Wear, 9 Wheat., 673.*

SEC. 2454. The acts of assembly of North Carolina passed between the years 1783 and 1789 invalidate all entries, surveys, and grants of land within the Indian territory which now forms a part of the territory of the State of Tennessee.   *Ibid.*

SEC. 2455. The State of North Carolina appears to have been sedulous in her efforts to prevent encroachments upon the Indian hunting grounds, and her laws are express and pointed in invalidating entries and grants made within such reservations.   *Ibid.*

SEC. 2456. As to land surveys within the Indian boundary, this court has never hesitated to consider all such surveys and grants as wholly void.   *Ibid.*

SEC. 2457. It is a settled principle that a patent conveying lands lying partly within and partly without the territory retained by the Indians is void as to so much as lie within it.

Patterson v. Jenks, 2 Pets., 216.   Danforth v. Wear, 9 Wheat., 673.

Sec. 2458. Georgia was willing to grant all the lands so far as the Indian boundary, but unwilling to pass that line. The sole object of the act of February, 1807, was to restrain her citizens from passing that boundary by making void all surveys and grants of lands beyond it. *Patterson v. Jenks, 2 Pets., 216.*

Sec. 2459. The act of 1787 for the appointment of commissioners to run the line designating the Indian hunting grounds, although retrospective, manifests, unequivocally, the opinion of the legislature of the State of Georgia that all the surveys and grants which are declared void had been made and issued contrary to positive laws. However this law may be construed, it is obvious that the office was not opened for lands situated within the Indian hunting grounds, and that grants for them were not authorized. *Ibid.*

Sec. 2460. The report of a Committee of Congress on Indian Affairs, consisting of a member from the States of Massachusetts, New York, Pennsylvania, Delaware, and Virginia, had been made in 1787, in which it was stated that encroachments and settlements had been made upon the lands of the Creek and Cherokee nations by people of Georgia and North Carolina, which the Indians, tenacious of their rights, were determined to oppose.

Cherokee Nation v. Georgia, Appendix 1, " Peters Cherokee Case,"
225.

Sec. 2461. Newly asserted title to lands in the possession of the Indians can derive no aid from the articles so often repeated in Indian treaties, extending to them, first, the protection of Great Britain, and afterwards that of the United States. These articles are associated with others recognizing their title to self-government, the very fact of repeated treaties with them recognizes it, and the settled doctrine of the law of nations is that a weaker power does not lose its independence, its right to self-government, by associating with a stronger and taking its protection. A weak State, in order to provide for its safety, may place itself under the protection of one more powerful without stripping itself of the right of self-government and ceasing to be a State. *Worcester v. Georgia, 6 Pets., 515.*

Sec. 2462. To the general pledge of protection contained in Cherokee treaties have been added several specific pledges deemed valuable by the Indians. Some of these restrain the citizens of the United States from encroachments on the Cherokee country and provide for the punishment of the intruders. The faith of the United States is pledged for the protection of the Indians. *Ibid.*

Sec. 2463. "The proclamation issued by the King of Great Britain in 1763, soon after the ratification of the articles of peace, forbids the governors of any of the colonies to grant warrants of survey or pass patents upon any lands whatever, which, not having been ceded to, or purchased by us (the King), as aforesaid, are reserved to said Indians, or any of them." *Ibid.*

SEC. 2464. Grants by North Carolina and Georgia extending partly over the Indian boundary are good so far as they interfere with no prior right of others as to whatever land is not within the Indian Territory.

> *Mitchel v. United States, 15 Pets., 52.   Mitchel v. United States, 9 Pets., 711.   Winn v. Patterson, 9 Pets., 663.*

SEC. 2465. Settlements made by permission of the commanding officer of posts on lands not ceded by the Indians have been held to give a preemption to lands in a proprietary government, and warrants and patents for such lands have been uniformly held good, when knowingly made by the proprietary or his officers, as lands not purchased from the Indians.   *Mitchel v. United States, 9 Pets., 711.*

SEC. 2466. A grant of land in North Carolina lying within the Indian country, founded on entries made in the office of the entry taker in 1795, was void under the North Carolina act of 1773, section 6, reserving this land for the Cherokee Indians.

> *Lattimer v. Poteet, 14 Pets., 4.*

SEC. 2467. The tract of country lying on the west of the Tennessee River was not in 1779 the country of Cherokee Indians, and not within the exemption of the Virginia act of 1779 prohibiting settlement within the Cherokee country.   *Porterfield v. Clark, 2 How., 76.*

SEC. 2468. All lands in the Commonwealth of Virginia not excepted by the land law of 1779 were subject to location on Treasury warrants, although claimed by Indians whose lands were not protected from location by statute.   *Ibid.*

SEC. 2469. A permit given by the lieutenant-governor of Upper Louisiana in 1799 to a person to form an establishment on the Mississippi, followed by actual possession and improvement, entitled the occupant to 640 acres, including his improvements, although the Indian title was not then extinguished.   *Marsh v. Brooks, 14 How., 513.*

SEC. 2470. In the construction of the treaty between the United States and the Sac and Fox Indians (7 Stat. L., 229) the Indians will be assumed to have assented to an occupancy as notorious as their own, although the land occupied was in territory recognized as theirs, especially when the Indians made no complaint.   Under such circumstances the Indian title did not affect the confirmation of the claim by Congress, although the recorder of land titles in his report has added the words "if Indian title extinguished."   *Ibid.*

SEC. 2471. Although the Spanish provincial governor could not give the right of occupancy in lands so as to interfere with the Indian occupancy, they could give the privilege to work mines in lands still in the occupancy of the Indians, because the mines were a part of the royal patrimony of the Crown, and the King had directed that they might be searched out and worked in all his dominions by his subjects, both Spaniards and Indians.   *Chouteau v. Molony, 16 How., 203.*

SEC. 2472. The question of the validity of the treaty of 1842 (7 Stat. L., 586) to bind the Tonawanda band of Senecas is one to be decided by the political power which acted for and with the Indians, and not by the courts. So far as the statute of New York prohibiting intrusions on Indian lands is concerned the Indians are not bound to show that they are owners, but can invoke the aid of the statute against all white intruders so long as they remain in the peaceful possession of their lands.   *New York v. Dibble, 21 How., 366.*

SEC. 2473. The treaty of May 30, 1860 (12 Stat. L., 1129), between the United States and the Delaware Indians, conferred a right to locate grants only on that portion of the Delawares' lands reserved for their "permanent homes" by the treaty of May 6, 1854 (10 Stat. L., 1048), and did not authorize their location on that portion of those lands which by that treaty were to be sold for their uses.
                    United States v. Stone, 2 Wall., 525.

SEC. 2474. A boundary between the lands of an Indian tribe and those of the United States, surveyed by parties, and acquiesced in for more than thirty years, can not be made the subject of dispute by reference to courses and distances called for in the patents under which the parties claimed.   *Ibid.*

SEC. 2475. In only one treaty with the New York Indians is any right stipulated to enter upon the lands reserved to construct roads. That is the treaty of 1794 (7 Stat. L., 44), in which the Seneca Nation cede to the United States the right to make a wagon road from Fort Schlosser to Lake Erie, as far south as Buffalo Creek.   •
                    The New York Indians, 5 Wall., 761.

SEC. 2476. In surrendering the larger part of their immense possessions the Shawnees did not, by treaty of 1854 (10 Stat. L., 1053), part with any right in the lesser part reserved by them so long as the claim of any single member of the tribe, according to the terms of the treaty, was unsatisfied. If one person could acquire a right to any portion of the land thus reserved so could another, and in this way the privilege of free and unrestricted selection would be frittered away. It needed no special provision to secure this freedom of choice, for without it the treaty could not be executed. By virtue of the treaty itself these lands were appropriated to a specific purpose, and whatever interfered with the accomplishment of this purpose was necessarily forbidden.   *Walker v. Henshaw, 16 Wall., 436.*

SEC. 2477. The clause in the Shawnee treaty of 1854 (10 Stat. L., 1053), excluding white persons and citizens from making locations or settlements on the lands reserved to the Indians, was not required by the necessities of the case, as they were excluded without it; and it was doubtless inserted out of superabundant caution and to satisfy the misgivings of the Indians, who, from experience, had good reason to dread the encroachments of this class of people notwithstanding treaty stipulation, and no ground to apprehend interference from other Indians on account of direct control exercised by the Government over the affairs of all Indian tribes.   *Ibid.*

SEC. 2478. The Government at an early day prohibited settlements on Indian lands.   *Holden v. Joy, 17 Wall., 211.*

SEC. 2479. The lands ceded to the United States by the Quapaws in the treaty of 1818 (7 Stat. L., 176) never were subject to preemption claims under the act of 1814 (7 Stat. L., 176) because no settlement or cultivation of the lands prior to that act could have been made consistently with the rightful claims of the Indians.   It was the declared policy of the Government at an early day to prohibit any settlement of lands belonging to the Indians.   A proclamation to this effect was issued by the old Congress, September 22, 1783, and an enactment to the same purport was made by Congress in 1802 (2 Stat. L., 141), which was extended to the Louisiana purchase in 1804 (2 Stat. L., 289).   *Hot Springs Cases, 92 U. S., 698.*

SEC. 2480. When the survey was made in 1820 the act of 1822 was not in existence.   The laws then were, as the Attorney-General held them to be, that unsurveyed lands were not lands the sale of which were authorized by law; and as this doctrine was received and acted upon by the land department of the Government, we should not feel authorized at this late day to reverse it.   *Ibid.*

SEC. 2481. Since 1850 it has been the settled policy of the Government to grant lands in large tracts to the States to aid in works of internal improvement; but such grants have always been recognized as attaching only to so much of the public domain as was subject to sale or other disposal, although the roads of many subsidized companies pass through Indian reservations.   *Railroad Co. v. United States, 92 U. S., 733.*

SEC. 2482. Every tract set apart for special uses is reserved to the Government to enable it to enforce them.   There is no difference in this respect, whether it be appropriated for Indian or other purposes. There is an equal obligation resting on the Government to require that neither class of reservations be diverted from the uses to which it was assigned.   *Ibid.*

SEC. 2483. Only public lands owned absolutely by the United States are subject to survey and division into sections, and to them alone the grant to the State of Kansas to aid in the construction of certain railroads is applicable.   It embraces such lands as could be sold and enjoyed, and not those which the Indians pursuant to treaty were left free to occupy.   *Ibid.*

Sec. 2484. Even if the exception and the proviso were omitted, the language was in the act of March 3, 1863 (12 Stat. L., 772), granting lands in aid of the construction of certain railroads in Kansas can not be construed to include the lands of the Osage Indians.   *Ibid.*

Sec. 2485. The act of March 3, 1863 (12 Stat. L., 772), to aid in the construction of certain railroads in Kansas, embraces no part of the lands reserved to the Great and Little Osages by the treaty of 1825 (7 Stat. L., 240) and the treaty of 1865 (14 Stat. L., 687); neither makes nor recognizes a grant of such lands.   The effect of the treaty is simply to provide that any rights of the companies designated by the State should not be barred or impaired by reason of its general terms.

Ibid.

Sec. 2486. A proviso to an act granting lands to aid in building a railroad, that any and all lands heretofore reserved to the United States, for any purpose whatever, are reserved from the operation of the grant to which it is annexed, applies to lands set apart for the use of an Indian tribe under a treaty.   They are reserved to the United States for that specific use, and, if so reserved at the date of grant, are excluded from its operation, and it is immaterial whether they subsequently become a part of the public lands of the country.   *Ibid.*

Sec. 2487. Where the right of an Indian tribe to the possession and use of certain lands, as long as it may choose to occupy the same, is assured by treaty, a grant of them absolutely or *cum onere* by Congress to aid in building a railroad violates an expressed stipulation, and a grant in general terms of "land" can not be construed as embracing them.   *Ibid.*

Sec. 2488. Neither the act of March 3, 1863 (12 Stat. L., 772), granting lands to the State of Kansas in aid of railroads, nor the Indian treaty, nor a subsequent act relating to the road, grants Osage lands. The lands were otherwise appropriated by the treaty, and hence excepted by the proviso of the act.

Ibid.   Railroad Co. v. United States, 92 U. S., 760.

Sec. 2489. If the defendant is on the lands of the pueblo (of Taos) without the consent of the inhabitants, he may be ejected or punished civilly by a suit for trespass, according to the laws regulating such matters in the Territory.   If he is there with their consent or license, we know of no injury which the United States suffers by his presence, nor any statute which he violates in that regard.

United States v. Joseph, 94 U. S., 614.

Sec. 2490. The people who constitute the pueblo or village of Taos are not an Indian tribe within the meaning of the act of June 30, 1834 (4 Stat. L., 729), which declares that every person who makes a settlement on Indian lands shall be liable to a penalty.   *Ibid.*

Sec. 2491. The 'act of Congress of February 6, 1871 (16 Stat. L., 566), authorizing a sale of the townships occupied by the Stockbridge and Munsee Indians, applies only to those portions which were outside the school sections. *Beecher v. Wetherby, 95 U. S., 517; 24—440.*

SEC. 2492. The whole tract of land embracing what was known as the Red Pipe Stone Quarry was, by the treaty of 1859 (12 Stat. L., 1037), withdrawn from private entry or appropriation until the Government had determined whether any portion less than the whole should be reserved, and its power of selection, if the whole was not retained, could not be restricted by the action of private parties. *U. S. v. Carpenter, 111 U. S., 347.*

SEC. 2493. The treaty is notice that the land will be retained by the Government for the use of the Indians, and this purpose can not be defeated by the action of any officers of the land department. *Ibid.*

SEC. 2494. Where land is reserved for the use of an Indian tribe by treaty it can not be taken up either by settlement or location under the Louisiana agricultural college scrip. *Ibid.*

SEC. 2495. The provisions of section 3 of the act of 1864 (13 Stat. L., 340) limiting the grant to the company to lands to which the United States had then full title, they not having been reserved, sold, granted, or otherwise appropriated, and being free from preemption or other claims of rights, did not exclude from the grant Indian lands not thus reserved, sold, or appropriated which were subject simply to their right of occupancy. *Buttz v. Railroad Co., 119 U. S., 55.*

SEC. 2496. The railroad company could not initiate any preemptive right to the land so long as the Indian title remained unextinguished. The act of Congress (Rev. Stat., sec. 2257) excludes lands in that condition from preemption, but the right of the company, freed from any incumbrance of the Indian title, immediately attached to the alternate sections of the lands. *Ibid.*

SEC. 2497. Where a party was in possession of a mining claim in the Black Hill country on the 28th of February, 1877, the date on which his possession became lawful under the supplementary Sioux agreement (19 Stat. L., 254), with the requisite discovery, with the surface boundaries sufficiently marked, with the notice of location posted, and with a disclosed vein of ore, he could, by adopting what had been done, causing a proper record to be made, and performing the amount of labor or making the improvements necessary to hold the claim, date his rights from that day; and such location, labor, and improvements would give him the right of possession. *Noonan v. Caledonia Mining Co., 121 U. S., 89.*

SEC. 2498. The presence of miners on the Sioux reservation up to the time of the supplementary agreement of February 28, 1877 (19 Stat. L., 254), was illegal, but from that time it was legal, and those then in possession of mining claims which had been taken up and developed in accordance with the rules of miners in mining districts of the country were entitled to protection in their possessory claims as against the intrusion of others. *Ibid.*

SEC. 2499. The railroad authorized by the act of 1884 (23 Stat. L., 73) to be constructed and maintained will have, if constructed and operated, direct relation to commerce with the Indian tribes, as well as with commerce among the States, especially with the States immediately north and south of the Indian Territory; and while it is true that the company authorized to construct and maintain it is a corporation created by the laws of a State, it is none the less a fit instrumentality to accomplish the public objects contemplated by the act, and therefore it was in the power of Congress to adopt it as a means conducive to that end. *Cherokee Nation v. Railroad Co., 135 U. S., 641.*

SEC. 2500. Although the railroad company is authorized to enter upon and use the lands of the Cherokee Nation on the payment into court of a sum double in amount of that awarded by the referees, the title to the land does not pass out of the nation until the just compensation contemplated in the Constitution is ascertained and paid by the company to the nation, and if that just compensation is fixed in an amount greater than has been paid into the court, the railroad company must pay the full sum so fixed before it can acquire the title, and on failure to do so it will become a trespasser and liable for damages as such. *Ibid.*

SEC. 2501. The record shows that the defendant offered to pay into court double the amount of the award made by the referees. The offer to pay is not a compliance with statute. The amount required to be deposited must be actually paid into court before the company can rightfully enter upon the lands sought to be condemned, or proceed with the construction of its road. *Ibid.*

SEC. 2502. The provision of section 3 of the act of 1884 (23 Stat. L., 73), relating to the ascertainment of the compensation justly payable to the Cherokee Nation by the railroad company, is sufficiently reasonable, certain, and adequate to secure the just compensation to which the nation is entitled, and by it the requirements of the Constitution, that the owner of the lands taken for public purposes is entitled to reasonable, certain, and adequate provision for obtaining compensation before his occupancy is disturbed, have been fully met. *Ibid.*

SEC. 2503. The question is no longer an open one as to whether a railroad is a public highway, established primarily for the convenience of the people and to subserve public ends, and, therefore, subject to governmental control and regulation, and it is because it is a public highway and subject to such control that the corporation by which it is constructed and by which it is to be maintained may be permitted under legislative sanction to appropriate private property for the purposes of a right of way, upon making just compensation to the owner, in the mode prescribed by law. *Ibid.*

SEC. 2504. The effect of the treaty of 1868 (15 Stat. L., 619) with the confederated Utes was to exclude all intrusion for mining or other private pursuits upon the territory reserved for the Indians. It prohibited any entry of the kind upon the premises, and no interest could be claimed or enforced in disregard of this provision.

Kendall v. San Juan Mining Co., 144 U. S., 658.

SEC. 2505. The rule in Noonan *v.* Caledonia Mining Co. (121 U. S., 393) was that where a party was in possession of a mining claim on a reservation made by treaty with the Indians, with the requisite discovery, with surface boundaries sufficiently marked, with a notice of location posted, and with a disclosed vein of ore, he could, by adopting what had been done and causing a proper record to be made and performing the amount of labor or making the improvements necessary to hold the claim, date his rights from that day. These conditions do not exist in this case.   *Ibid.*

SEC. 2506. Not until the withdrawal of the land from the Ute Reservation of the treaty of 1868 (15 Stat. L., 619) by a new convention with the Indians, and one which would throw the lands open, could a mining location thereon be initiated, and the location of the lode in question having been made while the treaty was in force, was inoperative to confer any right upon the plaintiffs. Whatever rights to mining lands they subsequently possessed upon the original Indian tract were founded upon a new location made more than two years after the withdrawal of the reservation and after the defendants had located the lode. Had they, immediately after the withdrawal of the reservation, relocated their lode, their position would have been that of original locators, and they would then have been within the rule in Noonan *v.* Caledonia Mining Co. (121 U. S., 393).   *Ibid.*

SEC. 2507. It is a matter of public history, of which the court may take judicial notice, that as the States of Kansas and Texas began to fill up with settlers longing eyes were turned by many upon the lands of the Indian Territory lying between them, occupied only by Indians, and though the Territory was reserved by statute for the occupation of the Indians, there was great difficulty in restraining settlers from entering and occupying it.   *Smith v. Townsend, 148 U. S., 490.*

SEC. 2508. The contention that the rights admittedly enjoyed by the Maricopa and Phoenix Railroad are to be treated as if obtained without the consent of the Indians residing on the Gila River Reservation, because it does not appear by the record that such consent, which was a condition attached to the grant was obtained, is without force, for the reasons that as the company has taken the rights granted by the statute, the legal presumption of duty performed requires the court to assume that the consent was given in accordance with law, and the company can not be permitted to aver its own wrongdoing, trespass, and violation of the statute in order to escape its just share of the burden of taxation.   *Railroad Co. v. Arizona, 156 U. S., 347.*

SEC. 2509. There is no treaty with the Indians occupying the Gila River Reservation in Arizona limiting the power of Congress to grant to the Maricopa and Phoenix Railroad the rights conveyed, and the consent of Congress for the railroad company to enter on the land and use it, as provided in the act (24 Stat. L., 361), was, therefore, a valid exercise of power.   *Ibid.*

SEC. 2510. The fact that Congress reserved the power to alter, amend, or repeal the statute granting the Maricopa and Phoenix Railroad right of way through the Gila River Reservation in no way affected the authority of the Territory over the rights granted, although the duration of that authority may depend upon the exercise by Congress of the rights reserved.   *Ibid.*

SEC. 2511. No trace can be discovered in various legislative enactments relating specifically to the Osage trust lands of any intention upon the part of Congress to disregard the terms of its treaties with the Osage Indians; and consequently the act of December 15, 1880 (21 Stat. L., 311), opening the lands within the abandoned Fort Dodge Military Reservation north of the Atchison, Topeka and Santa Fe Railroad to homestead settlement, should not be construed as impairing the rights of the Indians unless such construction be unavoidable, and it is not unavoidable.   *Frost v. Wenie, 157 U. S., 46.*

SEC. 2512. Looking at the act of December 15, 1880 (21 Stat. L., 311), opening the lands within the abandoned Fort Dodge Military Reservation north of Atchison, Topeka and Santa Fe Railroad to homestead settlement, in connection with prior statutes, particularly the act of May 28, 1880 (21 Stat. L., 143), offering the Osage trust lands to actual settlers only "having the qualifications of preemption on public lands," the lands which that act directed to be opened for entry under the homestead laws were public lands that were within the abandoned military reservation and subject to disposition under general laws relating to "other public lands," and not to lands of an exceptional class that were affected with a trust established for the benefit of Indians by treaty.   *Ibid.*

SEC. 2513. It is fairly implied, from the language employed in the third article of the Chippewa treaty of 1820 (7 Stat. L., 206), that an encampment location retained, or assigned, as the case might be, reserved for the use specified in the treaty, should not thereafter be appropriated by the Government for other uses than the defenses of any military work. Private rights could not, without authority of Congress, be acquired in the tract during the occupancy of the reservation under the treaty, for the lands lost their character as public lands, being set apart or occupied under the treaty, and became exempt from sale and preemption.   *Spalding v. Chandler, 160 U. S., 394.*

SEC. 2514. The land sought to be preempted by the grantor of the plaintiff in error was land which had been an Indian reservation, the Indian title to which had been extinguished while the preemption act of September 4, 1841 (5 Stat. L., 453), was in force, the tenth section of which provided that no "Indian reservation, the Indian title to which has been or may be extinguished by the United States during the operation of this act, shall be liable to entry under and by virtue of the provisions of this act." *Ibid.*

SEC. 2515. Whatever the reason for the omission to make mention of the Indian reserve, the power existed in Congress to invade the sanctity of the reservation and disregard the guarantee contained in the Chippewa treaty of 1820 (7 Stat. L., 206), even against the consent of the Indians, parties to that treaty, and the requirements of the grant to Michigan of the right to locate a canal at the falls of St. Marys River, necessarily demanded the possession of the portion of the reserve through which the canal was to pass, the effect of the act was to extinguish so much of the Indian reservation as was embraced in the grant to the State for canal purposes. *Ibid.*

SEC. 2516. The statute of the Creek Nation prohibiting noncitizen licensed traders from cutting and putting up hay from the common pasturage of the nation implies that citizens of the nation might cut hay without hindrance from such pasturage, as the prohibition is limited to noncitizen traders. *Eddy v. Lafayette, 163 U. S., 456.*

SEC. 2517. When any part of the public lands have been once lawfully reserved, that reservation can not be set aside except by a clear and explicit act of the lawful authority, showing thereby clearly a purpose to open to settlement by the citizen, the land reserved.
United States v. Payne, 8 Fed. Rep., 883.

SEC. 2518. A conspiracy to make settlement on Indian lands and to return to the Indian country, after being removed therefrom, is not an indictable offense within the meaning of the conspiracy clause of chapter 8, Supplement, Revised Statutes, 484, or one that can be prosecuted by criminal proceedings. *Ibid.*

SEC. 2519. The act of May 28, 1880 (21 Stat. L., 143) required that applicants for the settlement of certain lands held in trust for Indians should have the qualifications of preemptors, and that they should be actual settlers and make payment. After final receipts were issued to parties entering upon tracts of such land, and they were bought and paid for by a third party to whom patents were issued, a bill was filed by the Government to set aside the patents on the ground of fraud, and evidence was offered to show that the parties making the entries had never made actual settlement upon the lands, but were generally about a neighboring town or employed in another State. *Held,* that as the Government did not by such evidence clearly and satisfactorily show that it had been defrauded, and that, as the parties entering had the qualifications of preemptors, were actual settlers, and had made payment, and the proceedings in the land office were regular on their face and free from collusion between the purchaser and the parties entering, a decree would be entered dismissing the bill.   *United States v. Edwards, 33 Fed. Rep., 104.*

SEC. 2520. Section 2117, Revised Statutes, provides that "every person who drives or otherwise conveys any stock of horses, mules, or cattle, to range and feed on any land belonging to any Indian or Indian tribe, without the consent of such tribe, is liable to a penalty of one dollar for each animal of such stock." *Held*, that this penalty is recoverable when cattle are driven and permitted to graze on the lands of an Indian tribe a single day without permission.

                                  United States v. Loving, 34 Fed. Rep., 715.

SEC. 2521. One who makes a trail across Indian lands to the nearest accessible point of a permitted trail incurs the penalty prescribed in Revised Statutes, section 2117, for grazing cattle on said lands without permission, although prevented by natural obstructions from entering said lands by the permitted trail.   *Ibid.*

SEC. 2522. The proviso in the organic act of Oregon Territory (9 Stat. L., 323) confirming titles to the land, not exceeding 640 acres, then occupied as missionary stations among Indians, in the religious societies to which said missionary stations respectively belonged, must be construed as a grant of only the specific lands which were at the date of the act so occupied, exclusively, and not in subserviency to another's right.   *Missionary Society v. Gibbon, 44 Fed. Rep., 321.*

SEC. 2523. The right of local self-government has always been claimed and exercised by the Cherokee Nation, and their rights in this regard, so far as they relate to their own country and people, have never been questioned by the United States. Nor is it true that the United States has always denied to the Cherokees jurisdiction over white intruders in their country, such jurisdiction having been expressly conferred by the treaty of July 2, 1791 (7 Stat. L., 40).

                                  Mehlin v. Ice, 56 Fed. Rep., 12.

SEC. 2524. By the treaty of June 9, 1863 (14 Stat. L., 647), it was provided that the entire Nez Perce Reservation, which included Craig's claim, was set apart to the Indians for their exclusive use, and that no white man should "be permitted to reside upon the reservation;" and by the act of March 3, 1873 (17 Stat. L., 627), Craig's rights were expressly construed as a mere right of occupancy. That Congress had the right to thus control the land, even to the cancellation of Craig's right and claim thereto, the cases of Frisbie *v.* Whitney (9 Wall., 187) and the Yosemite Valley case (15 Wall., 77) are invoked.

                                  Caldwell v. Robinson, 59 Fed. Rep., 653.

Sec. 2525. The treaty of June 11, 1855 (12 Stat. L., 957), with the Nez Perces was ratified by Congress. The treaty contained notice to Congress that Craig claimed the title, and not the mere right of occupancy to certain lands, under laws absolutely granting him such right by his compliance with their provisions, and the notice referred to in the treaty as filed in the land office with his proof, would show not only his claim to the land, but also his compliance with the law. Although Congress had such notice of the claim, and recognized Craig's rights to the land as claimed by him by excluding it from the reservation, it has since, by two acts, June 9, 1863 (14 Stat. L., 647), and March 3, 1873 (17 Stat. L., 627), treated the claim of Craig as a mere right of occupancy. *Ibid.*

Sec. 2526. A settler who acquired rights under the provisional government of Oregon, and afterwards complied with the provisions of the donation act (1850), in so far as he was not forestalled by the land officers, but was refused a certificate and patent, acquired a vested right which Congress could not afterwards treat as a mere right of occupancy; and, although the land was subsequently included in an Indian reservation, the Government officials could not disturb the possession of his grantees. *Ibid.*

Sec. 2527. By the provisions of sections 4 and 7 of the Oregon donation act, passed in 1850, all rights to land which accrued under the previous provisional government were recognized, but the grant was finally to pass to the settler only by compliance with the conditions prescribed by the act. *Ibid.*

Sec. 2528. The provision in the intercourse act of 1834 (4 Stat. L., 729), forbidding white persons from settling upon any lands "belonging, secured, or granted by treaty" to any Indian tribe, did not prohibit settlement upon any lands in the Indian country outside of any reservation, and in which the only Indian right was the original Indian right of occupany at the will of the Government. *Ibid.*

Sec. 2529. All public lands, including any Indian title thereto, being under the control of the Government, it must follow that any right which Craig may have obtained to the land must have been through the laws of the Government, and any laws which granted him such right must at the same time have operated to extinguish the Indian title thereto. *Ibid.*

Sec. 2530. Land entered by the complainant under the homestead law, on which he had made valuable improvements, was included by the Government in allotments made to certain Indians on the Colville reservation in fulfillment of a treaty stipulation, and his homestead filing was canceled. *Held,* that the land not being within the boundaries of an Indian reservation, an Indian agent had no authority to dispossess him forcibly, and that complainant's possession should be

protected by injunction pending a determination of the validity of his
claim.   *La Chapelle v. Bubb, 62 Fed. Rep., 545.*

SEC. 2531. At the time of the passage of the trade and intercourse
act of June 30, 1834 (4 Stat. L., 729), there had been no treaty with
the Nez Perces, no land had by statute, contract, or treaty been recognized as belonging to them.   In its dealings with the Indians the
United States has uniformly denied their title to any of the lands
within its domain.   *Robinson v. Caldwell, 67 Fed. Rep., 391.*

SEC. 2532. By article 10 of the treaty of June 11, 1855 (12 Stat. L.,
957), both the contracting parties expressly recognize the right of William Craig and the validity of his entry under the donation act.   The
mention of his notice to the register and receiver serves the double
purpose of identifying his land and acknowledging the character of
his settlement to be that of a donation claimant.   There is, further,
the express stipulation that this land shall never be a part of the
reservation.   *Ibid.*

SEC. 2533. In 1887 the grantees of Craig were informed by the Commissioner of the General Land Office that Craig's proofs were deficient
because unaccompanied by the certificates required by section 12 of
the donation act, and because no certificate had been made by the
surveyor-general or the register and receiver as provided in section 7.
These were not valid reasons.   The affidavits made necessary by section 12 applied only to settlements made subsequent to December 1,
1850, and provisions of section 4, making void all sales and contracts
of sale of lands before patent is issued, were repealed by the act of
1854 (10 Stat. L., 306), and if the provisions of section 7 were not
complied with it was due solely to the nonaction of the officers of the
Government.   *Ibid.*

SEC. 2534. The treaty of the United States with the Nez Perce
Indians of June 11, 1855 (12 Stat. L., 957), relinquished to the United
States the right, title, and interest of the Indians to the country occupied by them, reserving for their own use a specified part.   It also
contained a clause providing that certain land occupied by one Craig,
though within the boundaries of the reserved portion, should not form
part of the reservation.   *Held*, that by this treaty the land so occupied by Craig was fully vested in the United States, and such land
came within the terms of the donation act of September 27, 1850, granting title to settlers upon lands in the Oregon Territory.   *Ibid.*

SEC. 2535. The provisions of the intercourse act of June 30, 1834
(4 Stat. L., 729), did not apply to the Oregon Territory, which did
not become a part of the United States until the treaty of June 15,
1846 (9 Stat. L., 869), and the act of June 5, 1850 (9 Stat. L., 437),
extending the provisions of the intercourse act over the Oregon Territory so far as practicable, did not, through the prohibition in the

intercourse act of settlement upon Indian lands, affect the rights of actual settlers who had taken possession of lands within that Territory before the passage of the act of 1850. *Ibid.*

SEC. 2536. At the date the donation act took effect, 1850, William Craig was a settler who had already resided upon and cultivated his claim for four years, and was in other respects qualified to take as a grantee. He did all that the law demanded of him. That he did not obtain a patent was owing to no fault of his. Even if it should be held that he never became qualified to receive the title, and that he never became the grantee of the soil, he was, nevertheless, entitled to all the relief that was accorded the appellee in the court below in any view of the case, for he had, as was said in Hall *v.* Russell (101 U. S., 510), "a present right to occupy and maintain possession so as to acquire a complete title to the soil," and that right has been lawfully conveyed to the appellee. *Ibid.*

SEC. 2537. A homestead settler whose land has been included by the Government in allotments made to Indians in fulfillment of treaty stipulations, but who has not perfected his right by making proof in the land office of full compliance with the law, is not entitled, in a suit against certain Indians and an army officer who threatens to put them in possession, to a decree declaring him to be the owner of the land and quieting title. But as a bona fide settler and owner of the improvements he is entitled to an injunction protecting him in his possessory rights until the questions of law involved can be determined by a court of competent jurisdiction.
La Chapelle v. Bubb, 69 Fed. Rep., 481.

SEC. 2538. The right of present possession of the allotted tracts on the Winnebago Reservation is in the Indians and not in the United States. The title is held by the Government in trust for the Indians, and it is, to say the least, extremely doubtful whether the United States could maintain an action in ejectment based upon the assertion of a right to immediate possession.
United States v. Flournoy, &c., Co., 69 Fed. Rep., 886.

SEC. 2539. The occupancy of lands and the cultivation thereof by the lessees is wholly inconsistent with the purpose for which the lands were originally set apart as a reservation for the Indians, and with the object of the Government in providing for allotments in severalty.
Ibid.

SEC. 2540. Leases made by members of the Omaha and Winnebago tribes of lands allotted to them in severalty under the acts of February 21, 1863, August 7, 1882, and February 8, 1887 (24 Stat. L., 388), without the authority of the Secretary of the Interior, are wholly void. (65 Fed. Rep., 30, followed.) *Ibid.*

SEC. 2541. Leases made by Indians of lands in severalty under the acts of Congress providing therefor are absolutely void, and neither such leases nor occupancy and planting of crops upon the lands, by the lessees or their subtenants, give to the occupants any right to restrain the officers of the Government from removing them from such lands. (Beck *v.* Real Estate Co., 65 Fed. Rep., 30, followed.)

Pilgrim v. Beck, 69 Fed. Rep., 895.

SEC. 2542. The United States has never yet been released from the treaty stipulations by which it assumed to preserve the lands of the Omaha and Winnebago Indians for their use and benefit.

United States v. Flournoy, &c., Co., 71 Fed. Rep., 576.

SEC. 2543. The fact that Indians, to whom lands have been allotted in severalty, are declared to be citizens of the United States does not render null and void as to them, or as to the remaining portions of their tribes, restrictions upon alienation of their lands contained in the acts of Congress under which allotments in severalty have been made, nor terminate the right and duty of the United States to preserve the reservation lands for the use and benefit of the Indians.   *Ibid.*

SEC. 2544. The act of June 1, 1892 (27 Stat. L., 62), opening a part of the Colville Reservation, annulled from that date the executive order creating the reservation, and restored the lands to the public domain, subject only to the right of the Indians to make selections for allotments in severalty; but the mineral lands contained therein are not subject to such selection, it being the intent of the law to award to each Indian agricultural land for his home.

Collins v. Bubb, 73 Fed. Rep., 735.

SEC. 2545. For the purpose of giving the Indians the full benefit of the right to select from the whole ceded tract of the Colville Reservation, settlements upon and entries of agricultural lands must be postponed, under the act, until six months after the President's proclamation opening the lands to settlement and entry; but prospectors and miners are not required to wait for the proclamation to open the tract to exploration for minerals.   *Ibid.*

SEC. 2546. The lands of the Columbia Reservation in Washington Territory that were erroneously opened to settlement under the agreement of 1884 with Chief Moses never became a part of the public domain which could be lawfully taken up under the homestead law, and neither by estoppel against the Government nor as bona fide purchasers had the settlers acquired any right to hold them.

United States v. La Chappelle et al., 81 Fed. Rep., 152.

SEC. 2547. It was a direct interference with the possessory rights of the Indian tribes on and near these portages, whose titles have not yet been extinguished by the treaty arrangements so generally made with other Indians almost everywhere else in Oregon and the Territory of Washington.   *Johnson v. United States, 2 C. Cls. R., 391.*

SEC. 2548. It has been the declared policy of the Government from an early day to prohibit any settlement of lands belonging to the Indians.   *Hale et al. v. United States, 11 C. Cls., 238.*

SEC. 2549. To give the court jurisdiction under the act of March 2, 1895 (28 Stat. L., 894) the claim must have been wholly disallowed by the Interior Department; the suit must have been commenced within six months after the passage of the act, and it must be the same case in law that was before the Department.

Schewson v. United States, 31 C. Cls., 192.

SEC. 2550. The purpose of the act of March 2, 1895 (28 Stat. L., 894), was to allow damages incidental to removal of settlers from the Crow Creek and Winnebago reservations; without removal there can be no recovery.   *Ibid.*

SEC. 2551. Consequential damages not directly the result of removal from the reservations can not be considered.

Ibid.

SEC. 2562. Where a party did not remove from the reservation within sixty days from April 17, 1885, his delay does not operate as a bar to the suit, but may defeat a right of recovery if it appear that the failure to remove was without good and sufficient reason.

Ibid.

SEC. 2553. Removal is the gravamen of the action given by the statute. If a party removed from the reservation before the President's proclamation, April 17, 1885, there can be no recovery; nor if he purchased the claim of a settler after that day.

Ibid.

SEC. 2554. While the act of March 2, 1895 (28 Stat. L., 899), is a remedial statute and must be liberally construed, the substantial rights of the parties in determining the jurisdiction of the court must be preserved.   *Ibid.*

SEC. 2555. The purpose of the act March 2, 1895 (28 Stat. L., 899), was to compensate the settler for the damages incident to removal, and without removal, either before the expiration of sixty days or within such time as the party was under the circumstances enabled to move, there can be no recovery.   *Ibid.*

SEC. 2556. The authority of the King to regulate and control purchases from the Indians within these colonies was not questioned on the argument and can not be denied. Any purchase made by Stedman in violation of such regulations must be void, and he could acquire no right whatever thereby, not even the Indian right of occupancy, and he must have been an intruder by any entry made under such purchase.

Jackson ex dem. Sparkman v. Porter, 1 Paine, 457.

SEC. 2557. The Army of the United States was opposed to the Indians as to a public enemy from the year 1783 to 1795. At the time of passing the act, April 3, 1792 (Pennsylvania), relative to the settlement of lands, the whole northwestern frontier of the State was in such danger and alarm that the surveyors dared not enter upon the execution of their duties. *Commonwealth v. Tench Coxe, 4 Dallas, 170.*

SEC. 2558. Hostilities between the United States and the Indians were never so entirely discontinued, from the period of the Revolutionary contest until General Wayne's treaty in 1795, as to render it practicable with safety to make actual settlement on the lands in question. *Ibid.*

SEC. 2559. The plaintiff did not forfeit his rights by not making settlement within two years from the date of his warrant. It is notorious that an Indian war existed from the year 1790 until General Wayne's treaty, which was made August 3, 1795, and ratified December 23, 1795. The ratification of the treaty is to be considered as the *terminus a quo*. A man might safely begin a settlement on the western frontier of Pennsylvania. *Morris's lessee v. Neighman, 4 Dallas, 209.*

SEC. 2560. The settler under the act of April 3, 1792 (Pennsylvania), could not excuse himself for not making the settlement and improvements required by that act on the ground of Indian hostilities, the treaty of Greenville having put an end to them in 1795.
Lessee of Brown v. Galloway, 1 Peters (Cir. Ct. Repts.), 291.

SEC. 2561. January 9, 1789, the United States entered into a treaty with the Wyandotte and other nations of Indians (7 Stat. L., 28), in which it was agreed that if any citizen of the United States, or other person not being an Indian, shall settle on their land, such person shall forfeit the protection of the United States, and the Indians were at liberty to punish him or not, as they pleased. And all citizens or inhabitants of the United States were prohibited from hunting or destroying the game, or even entering on the Indians lands without a passport. *United States v. Cisna, 1 McLean, 254.*

SEC. 2562. Rights of "actual settlers" upon the Cherokee neutral lands purchased by the defendant Joy (see Holden *v.* Joy, 17 Wall., 211), under the seventeenth article of the treaty of July 19, 1866 (14 Stat. L., 804), considered and held that an actual settler, whose rights were perfect at the date of the ratification of the treaty, could sell his rights and improvements to another, and that the bill made a case showing in the plaintiff an equitable title in the land in question.
Langdon v. Joy, 4 Dill., 391.

SEC. 2563. In a supplemental article to the treaty of 1866, concluded April 27, 1868 (16 Stat. L., 727), it was provided that Joy should take only the residue of certain lands after securing to "actual settlers" the lands to which they were entitled under the seventeenth article and amendments thereto of the said Cherokee treaty of July 19, 1866, and that the proceeds of the sale of said lands so occupied at the date of said treaty by "actual settlers" should enure to the sole benefit of, and be retained by, the Secretary of the Interior as trustee for the Cherokee Indians.   *Ibid.*

SEC. 2564. The language of the Cherokee treaty of 1866 does not require that the improvements should have been made by the person residing on the land at the date of the signing or ratification of said treaty. But what is required is that they shall be owned by the actual occupant, and that such owner shall in person reside on such improvements at the date of the ratification of the treaty. At this date Vaughan was in possession and the owner of his improvements. His rights were then fixed.   *Ibid.*

SEC. 2565. There was nothing in the treaty that made it necessary that Vaughan should remain in possession and personally make the proof. If he had died his heirs or devisees might personally have made the necessary proof and become entitled to buy. So, also, the actual settler, whose rights were perfect at the ratification of the treaty, might have sold and conveyed his rights to another.   *Ibid.*

SEC. 2566. If Vaughan had not possessed the qualifications of a preemptor, this might possibly have defeated his rights under the treaty; but if he did possess these qualifications at the date of the ratification of the treaty his rights were perfect—he could have bought as soon as the appraisement was made—and there is no public policy, as in the public preemption laws, against the alienation of his rights to others.
                                    Ibid.

SEC. 2567. In the treaty of July 19, 1866, with the Cherokees (14 Stat L., 804), providing for the sale of large tract of land known as the "Cherokee neutral lands," a preference right was given to "actual settlers" to purchase, on certain terms, the land owned and personally occupied by them. *Held,* construing the treaty as amended, that one who is an actual settler, within the meaning of the treaty, at the date of its ratification, and entitled to the benefit of its provisions, may, after that time and before making proof, transfer his right to purchase the land to which he is entitled, and the grantee may make the required proof and purchase the land. *Stroud v. Missouri River, etc., R. R. Co., 4 Dill, 396.*

SEC. 2568. Whether the treaty of July 19, 1866 (14 Stat. L., 804), as finally amended provides for *one* or *two* classes of settlers, discussed, but not decided.   *Ibid.*

SEC. 2569. The case of Stroud *v.* Missouri River, etc., Railroad Co. (4 Dill, 396) followed; and it was held in this case that under the provisions of the treaty of July 19, 1866, with the Cherokees (14 Stat., L., 804), the actual settler whose improvements were wholly upon the west half of the quarter section was entitled to buy only the portion of the quarter section on which the improvements had been made.
                                    Ibid.

Sec. 2570. On a construction of the treaty with the Osage Indians, June 2, 1825 (7 Stat. L., 240), and the subsequent treaty with the same Indians, January 21, 1867 (14 Stat. L., 687), and the act of Congress, March 3, 1863 (12 Stat. L., 772), granting lands to the State of Kansas to aid in the building of railroads: *Held*, that the land which, under the said treaty of 1825, had been set apart and reserved for the said tribe of Indians, and which were in their actual use and occupancy, did not pass under the said railroad grant, and that the United States were entitled to have canceled patents which had issued to the railroad company under the erroneous assumption that the lands were embraced in the railroad grant. · *United States v. L., L. & G. R. R. Co., 1 McCrary, 610.*

Sec. 2571. By joint resolution of April 10, 1869, Congress provided that a *bona fide* settler upon certain lands known as the "Osage ceded lands" in Kansas should have a right to purchase on certain terms. The defendant Snow was such a settler, and, having the right to purchase under said joint resolution, he made the requisite proof and tender of the purchase money to complete such purchase. *Held*, that he was entitled to a patent from Government, and has an equity in the lands and improvements which he is at liberty to sell and convey.

Wallerton v. Snow et al., 5 McCrary, 64.

Sec. 2572. The President having set apart the Pyramid Lake Reservation for the use of Indians, the whites who go upon it to fish do so contrary to law.   *United States v. Sturgeon, 6 Sawyer, 29.*

Sec. 2573. The act of Congress relied on by the plaintiff is in the following words: "If any citizen or other person shall make a settlement on any lands belonging, or secured, or granted by treaty with the United States to any Indian tribe, or shall survey, or attempt to survey, such lands, or designate any of the boundaries by marking trees, or otherwise, such offender shall forfeit a sum not exceeding one thousand dollars and suffer imprisonment not exceeding twelve months."   *McIvers, Lessee, v. Reagan, 1 Brunner's Coll. Cases, 240.*

Sec. 2574. The object of the act was to prevent a disturbance with the Indians arising from persons going on their lands and marking trees and making surveys with a view to procuring titles, but if a corner had been marked before the passage of the act it surely could not have been intended that the owner might not go upon the land to examine for the corner and collect such other proof as would enable him to establish his beginning.   *Ibid.*

Sec. 2575. The provisions of the Delaware treaties and of the act of March 3, 1807 (2 Stat. L., 445), prohibit only settlement or survey, and not the passage to and fro by any person over these lands; nor do they prohibit the Government, whether of the territory or of any of its political subdivisions, from establishing its offices, holding its courts, and issuing and executing its processes at any place upon them.

McCracken v. Todd, 1 Bank & McCahon, 146.

SEC. 2576. Under the treaty of the 20th of October, 1832, between the Chickasaw Nation of Indians and the United States it was not permissible for a reservee, by a lease or sale of his reservation, to introduce into the nation one who was inhibited by the treaty from settling upon the unsold lands.

Lewis v. Love & Lane, 1 Ala., 335.

SEC. 2577. The act of Congress of July 4, 1836, which transferred to the Commissioner of the General Land Office "the executive duties" appertaining to the sale of public lands, conferred upon that officer the authority previously vested in the Secretary of the Treasury to give special directions for the sale of an abandoned reservation under the treaty of Fort Jackson of August 9, 1814. A letter from the Commissioner of the General Land Office to the register and receiver of the local office stating that, in his opinion, since it satisfactorily appeared that the Indian had voluntarily abandoned his reservation under the treaty, "the land is now subject to entry under the preemption law," is a "special direction" to the register and receiver to allow the land to be entered upon under the preemption law.

Saltmarsh v. Crommelin, 39 Ala., 54.

SEC. 2578. The complainant claims the land in controversy by virtue of the location of a Cherokee preemption, and also by virtue of his own claim to a preemption under the act of May 29, 1830 (4 Stat. L., 420), both originating in the favor and founded upon the gratuity of the Federal Government; upon compliance with the terms and conditions of the acts of Congress granting these bounties to the settler he could acquire a vested right, and without such compliance he must be regarded as an intruder, without any color of right at law or in equity, and unless he shows that he has so complied, or has been prevented from so doing by the agents of the Government or the fraudulent acts of the defendants, he can have no claim to relief in equity.

Cunningham v. Ashley et al., 12 Ark., 296.

SEC. 2579. The patents obtained by Ashley and Beebe being founded upon entries under Cherokee scrip which were void are void also so far as they interfere with the preemption right of Cunningham. The decision of the supreme court of Arkansas in this case (12 Ark., 296) is reversed.

Ibid.

SEC. 2580. The certificate of the register of the United States land office that one of the defendants had located with a "Choctaw certificate" the land, for the trespass upon which the suit was brought, was competent evidence to prove that the plaintiff had no title to the close. Such certificate is an instrument of evidence that proves itself.

Floyd v. Ricks, 14 Arkansas, 286.

SEC. 2581. As to surveys within the Indian boundary, this court has never hesitated to regard all such surveys and grants as wholly void. (Danforth v. Wear, 6 Wheat., 675.)   *Gaines et al. v. Hale & Rector, 26 Ark., 168.*

SEC. 2582. *Prima facie* the governor of California, under the Mexican dominion, had the power to make a grant of mission lands to an individual, and a demurrer to a complaint setting forth such a grant on the ground of want of authority in the governor is not sustainable. An officer will not be presumed to have exceeded his authority, especially the officer of a foreign government.   *Den v. Den, 6 Cal., 81.*

SEC. 2583. This action was brought to recover the possession of certain land. The defendants, against whom defaults were taken, are Mission Indians, and by themselves and their ancestors have occupied the land for many years before the commencement of the action. They are very ignorant and helpless, totally unacquainted with judicial proceedings, and, with few exceptions, incapable of speaking the English language. *Held*, that a motion to vacate the defaults was properly granted.   *Byrne v. Alas, 68 Cal., 479.*

SEC. 2584. A mining location made tortiously upon an Indian reservation before the Indian title is extinguished will not avail against a location made after the land is opened for settlement.
          Kendall v. San Juan S. M. Co., 9 Colo., 349.

SEC. 2585. Under the act of Congress of 1854, and the treaty with the Chippewa Indians in pursuance thereto, no authority was given to locate with the "scrip" issued to certain Chippewa half-breeds lands outside the territory thus ceded by the Indians. A patent issued in 1868, under a location with said scrip covering lands in Colorado, was therefore void. The act of 1872 (U. S. Rev. Stat., sec. 2368) authorized the Secretary of the Interior, upon compliance therewith, to issue a patent conveying the Government title to unoffered land outside the territory ceded by the Chippewa Indians, the patentee having in good faith located such lands with Chippewa half-breed scrip and obtained a void patent therefor prior to the adoption of the remedial act.
          Fee v. Brown, 17 Cal., 510.

SEC. 2586. An occupation of Indian lands for grazing purposes only, with the consent of the Indians and in subordination to and recognition of their title, is not forbidden by sections 2117 and 2118 of the Revised Statutes.   *Pike v. Hunter, 4 Mackey (D. C.), 531.*

SEC. 2587. No rights could be acquired to any lands in the Black Hills prior to the 28th of February, 1877, by reason of the existence, until that time, of the Sioux Indian Reservation covering that part of the Territory, following the decisions of this court in Uhlig *v.* Garrison, 2 Dakota, 71; French *v.* Lancaster, id., 276.
          Caledonia Gold Mining Co. v. Noonan, 3 Dakota (Smith), 201.

SEC. 2588. A sale by a sutler (within the county claimed and possessed by the Indians in Florida) on the public lands of the improvements made by him forms a good and sufficient consideration for any contract or price the purchaser may agree to pay for the possession of such improvements.   *Taylor v. Baker, 1 Branch (Fla.), 245.*

SEC. 2589. The treaty between the United States and the Nez Percé tribe of Indians, concluded June 9, 1863, proclaimed April 20, 1867, reserved for the sale, use, and occupation of said tribe the territory or tract of country therein described. Sutlers upon the reservation granted by treaty to the Nez Percé Indians and all others, except such as are permitted by the treaty, who go thereon to occupy or possess any portion of the land embraced therein, are trespassers. No agreement for the use and occupancy of said land between the plaintiff and another white person can be enforced. *Langford v. Monteith, 1 Idaho, 612.*

SEC. 2590. The President of the United States has no power, by virtue of his office and independent of statutory authority, to lease the lead mines in Iowa. There is no law in existence authorizing the President to lease the lead mines.

The act authorizing the President "to lease for a term of five years any lead mine which has been or may hereafter be discovered *in the Indian Territory*," so far from giving the authority contended for, raises a strong inference against it.

Lorimier & Waller v. Lewis et al., 1 Morris, Iowa, 253.

SEC. 2591. A majority of the trustees, under the articles of association, of the New York Company have power to convey the title of said company to lands in the "half-breed tract," and the conveyance may be made by themselves or by their attorney.

The conclusive effect of the judgment of partition of the half-breed lands, as established by Wright *v.* Marsh, Lee & Delavan, is affirmed. *Barney v. Crittenden, 2 Greene (Iowa), 165 (May, 1849).*

SEC. 2592. An occupying claimant of lands situated on the half-breed tract, who acquired his claim or color of title adversely to the decree of partition, and who has, ever since the acquisition of his claim, resisted said decree, believing it to be fraudulent and void, is entitled to compensation for improvements made upon the land. His right to compensation may be assigned, and the assignee is invested with all the rights of his assignor. He is not, in a proper action, entitled to compensation for improvements made after he is found not to be the rightful owner. *Craton v. Wright, 16 Iowa, 133.*

SEC. 2593. A person who, on July 22, 1871, settled upon and occupied a certain piece of land belonging to the United States and situated within the Osage ceded lands had no right to preempt the same, for such lands were not at that time subject to preemption. Such person is a trespasser on Government land and can not maintain an action to quiet his possession against some person who has no interest in the land, but claims that he has. *Wood v. M., K. & T. Ry. Co., 11 Kans., 323.*

SEC. 2594. A settler upon the Osage diminished reserve does not forfeit his right to purchase from the Government the land he has settled upon and occupies by merely agreeing before he has so purchased the same to convey a portion thereof, by way of compromise, to an individual who is contesting his right to so purchase; but if he complies with all the provisions, fulfills all the conditions, and satisfies all the terms of the act of Congress of July 15, 1870 (16 Stat. L., 362), regarding settlers purchasing lands from the Government, he may purchase his land from the Government under said act, whether he could preempt the same under the act of September 4, 1841 (5 Stat. L., 456), or not. *Foster v. Brost, 11 Kans., 350.*

SEC. 2595. Where it appears that Parks was an actual settler on a quarter section of the Sac and Fox lands, and had made improvements thereon; that by treaty with the Sac and Fox Indians these lands were subject to preemption by actual settlers, and that Parks and Bell made a contract whereby, in consideration of $1,500 cash and a note for $500, Parks executed a quitclaim deed of all his right, title, and interest in the land, and delivered the possession of the same, with the improvements, to Bell: *Held*, that in the absence of any fraud or deception there was no failure of consideration of the note, although the improvements were not worth over $700, and the title to the land continued to remain in the Government. *Bell v. Parks, 18 Kans., 152.*

SEC. 2596. Under the act of Congress July 15, 1870 (16 Stat. L., 362), no one but an "actual settler" could purchase any of the Osage diminished reserve land, and he could not purchase more than 160 acres. The Government evidently intended not only that no one but actual settlers should get any portion of said reserve, but also that every quarter section thereof should be occupied by an actual settler. There is no pretense that the plaintiff was ever an actual settler on the land in controversy. Therefore he had no right in himself to purchase said land from the Government, and to procure any other person to purchase it for him would be a fraud on the Government. *Brake v. Ballou, 19 Kans., 397.*

SEC. 2597. The power to correct a mistake or to cancel an unlawful entry of Osage trust and diminished reserve land continues in the executive officers of the United States, and their decisions upon all questions of fact are conclusive upon the parties and binding upon the courts, unless they are vitiated by fraud and imposition. *Freese v. Rusk, 54 Kans., 274.*

SEC. 2598. Questions involved in the inquiry whether a patent for land west of the Tennessee River, granted to G. R. Clark in 1795, upon an entry made, on Treasury warrants, in 1780, and surveyed in 1784, is void or valid; *Held*, that in 1780, when the entry was made, no statute had been enacted reserving the lands west of the Tennessee from appropriation under the Virginia act of 1779, authorizing the appropriation of all the vacant lands within the chartered limits of that State, with certain restrictions; that an inchoate title having been acquired by the entry in 1780, it was not illegal to have it surveyed in 1784, though in the meantime acts had been passed reserving those lands for the officers and soldiers of the Virginia State line and navy; and that the patent issued upon that entry and survey in 1795 was valid and vested the legal title in the patentee, subject only to the right of occupancy conceded to the Choctaws by the treaty of 1786 (7 Stat. L., 21), and the extinguishment of the Choctaw title in 1818 made the title under the patent complete.

Rollins v. Clark, 8 Ky. (Dana), 15.

SEC. 2599. The penalty prescribed by the eleventh section of the intercourse act of 1834 is not recoverable against one settling on land belonging to a pueblo, and particularly to the pueblo of Cochita, that pueblo being a body corporate and having a complete title to its lands, which it can assert and protect in the courts in the same way as other landowners.   *United States v. Lucero, 1 N. M. (Gild.), 422.*

SEC. 2600. The pueblos of New Mexico had an indefeasible title to their lands at the date of the treaty of Guadalupe Hidalgo (9 Stat. L., 992), and that title is guaranteed by the treaty and has been confirmed by Congressional legislation.   *Ibid.*

SEC. 2601. In an action to recover the penalty prescribed in the eleventh section of the Indian intercourse act of 1834 (4 Stat. L., 729) for settlement on Indian lands, it is necessary that there shall be an averment that the settlement was "unlawful" or "wrongful."

Ibid.

SEC. 2602. In an action to recover a penalty under the eleventh section of the Indian intercourse act of 1834 (4 Stat. L., 729) for settling on Indian lands, the declaration must aver that the land settled on belonged to the Indians "by treaty with the United States," or it will be bad on demurrer.

United States v. Lucero, 1 N. M. (Gild.), 422; United States v. Santistevan, 1 N. M. (Gild.), 583; United States v. Varella, 1 N. M. (Gild.), 593.

SEC. 2603. This action was brought to recover for injuries sustained by the plaintiff, by the falling of a bridge, within the boundaries of the town of South Valley, on the ground that it was the duty of the defendant, the commissioner of highways of said town, to keep the same in repair.   The bridge, which, together with the highway leading thereto on either side, was situated on the Allegany Indian Reservation, was constructed by a commissioner appointed by virtue of chapter 473, laws of 1866.   *Held*, that the defendant was not bound to keep the bridge in repair, and that plaintiff was not entitled to recover.

Bishop v. Barton, 2 Hun. (N. Y.), 436.

SEC. 2604. In an action to recover for injuries sustained by a horse of the plaintiff in crossing defendant's tracks, at their intersection with a highway in Cattaraugus Indian Reservation, *held*, that the State had power to construct a highway in such reservation; and that defendant was liable for a neglect to keep its roadway in repair; and that a presumption of negligence arises from the existence of a defect and the fact that an injury was caused thereby.

France v. Erie Railway Co., 2 Hun. (N. Y.), 513.

SEC. 2605. In a proceeding to remove intruders from Indian lands under chapter 204 of the laws of 1821, it is necessary that the persons proceeded against be summoned to appear and answer the complaint in order to give the county judge jurisdiction of the case.

The People v. Soper, 7 Selden (N. Y. App.), 428.

SEC. 2606. The provisions of the act of March 31, 1821, respecting intrusions on Indian lands (chap. 204 of 1821), which authorize the summary removal, by a judge's order, of persons, other than Indians, who settle or reside upon lands belonging to or occupied by any nation or tribe of Indians, are constitutional. A citizen who enters upon their lands before their title has been extinguished and they have removed, or have been removed by the act of the Government, can acquire no such right of property or possession as is within the protection of those provisions of the Constitution which secure the trial by jury and forbid the divesting of property and personal rights otherwise than by proceedings according to the course of the common law. An entry by a person not an Indian upon land included within the bounds of an Indian reservation, which is in the general occupation of a band of Indians, is an intrusion, subjecting the offender to summary removal under chapter 204 of act of 1821, notwithstanding the intruder entered peaceably and with the assent of the individual Indian to whose possession he succeeded, under a title claimed to have been acquired by citizens through a deed of cession recognized by a treaty made between the United States and the Indian nation to which the Indians occupying the reservation belong, and although the lands occupied by the intruder are in a portion of the reservation which is occupied by other citizens, having contiguous possessions forming a white settlement, all claiming ownership under the same title.

People v. Dibble, 16 N. Y. Appls., 203.

SEC. 2607. A person can not lawfully enter on the lands of the Stockbridge Indians and cut and carry away timber growing thereon, even with their consent. When a person, by a written license from the peacemakers of the tribe, entered and cut down trees of which he made shingles, it was held that he was a trespasser, notwithstanding such license, and acquired no property in the timber or shingles.

Chandler v. Edson, 9 Johnson's Reports (N. Y.), 361.

SEC. 2608. The possession of a tract of land by the native Indians does not affect the validity of a patent from the State granting the land to white persons without the consent of the Indians. The legality of such a patent is a political question which can not arise or be discussed in a suit between two of our own citizens. The possession of the native Indians is not such an adverse possession as to render subsequent alienations by the patentees void on the ground of maintenance.

Jackson v. Hudson, 3 Johnson's Reports (N. Y.), 374.

SEC. 2609. Where the consideration of a note is a lease of land within an Indian reservation and the lessor makes title under an Indian, plaintiff can not recover. The lease transferred no title because the lessors possessed no title to transfer; consequently the consideration of the note fails and the plaintiff can not recover.

Chaffee v. Garrett, 6 Ohio (Hammond), 422.

SEC. 2610. Whether a right to an island in the Susquehanna (river) could be acquired by settlement and improvement in the year 1749 *quaere?* A bar to the plaintiff's recovery is that he claims under a violation of law which forbids a settlement on lands not purchased of the Indians. His evidence goes to show that there was an improvement on the island which must have been made prior to the date of the Indian purchase, in which it was included. It has been repeatedly decided that no evidence can be received of a settlement on land not purchased from the Indians. (Sherer *v.* McFarland, 2 Yeates, etc.)

McElear v. Elliot et al., 14 Seargent & Rawle (Penn.), 248.

SEC. 2611. In 1761 the soil belonged to the aborigines, and settlers, before the Indian title was extinguished, had no title to the lands, either under the act of assembly or the proclamation of 1768. By the act it was made penal either to make other settlements on the Indian lands, or not to remove from those already made.

Plumstead et al. v. Rudebaugh, 1 Penn., 555.

SEC. 2612. Action of ejectment for part of the Indian lands in Northumberland County. The plaintiff claims under a warrant, dated May 3, 1785, and survey thereon, 10th of January, 1786. The defendant entered a caveat 20th June, 1785, etc. *Held*, that neither party has right except under the act of 1784. They were trespassers until the act (of 1784) gave right, etc.

Hughs v. Dougherty, 1 Penn., 553.

SEC. 2613. The treaty made between General Wayne and the Indians at Fort Greenville, in August, 1795, was not ratified by the President and Senate of the United States until the 22d day of December, 1795. Up to this period it has been judicially determined that it was unsafe and dangerous to settle lands under the act of 3d of April, 1792 (2 Yeates, 450; 1 Binn., 170). There is no reason why this rule should not be applied to the case of one who had commenced an actual settlement which he was compelled for a while to postpone. An actual settler should be placed at least upon a footing of equality with one who purchases for the profit to be made by a resale.

Patterson v. Ross, 22 Penn., 350.

SEC. 2614. The Cherokee treaty of 1791 (7 Stat. L., 739) abridged the rights of citizens and extended those of the Indians; consequently a great quantity of land sold by North Carolina to her citizens was thrown by this treaty within the Indian boundary. While this was severe it was obligatory, having been made by the United States under the authority of the Constitution.   *Glasgow v. Smith, 1 Overton (Tenn.), 111.*

SEC. 2615. Agreeably to the acts of Congress, individuals could not legally settle on nor occupy land within the Indian limits. The land in question was not purchased until the year 1798, and the line not actually marked until 1799. From either period until the writ issued there was not seven years. The defendants can not avail themselves of a possession previous to that time, for possession before the Indian title was extinguished was illegal.   *Cocke v. Dotson, 1 Overton (Tenn.), 131.*

SEC. 2616. As the defendant was not authorized to make an entry within the Indian hunting ground, the warrant of survey which issued in consequence of it was void and could not authorize the issuing of a grant.   *Dodson v. Cocke, 1 Overton (Tenn.), 249.*

SEC. 2617. The fact that the Indian title to the land in question had not been extinguished at the date of the State constitution, 1796, did not prevent the operation of the occupant and preemption right secured to residents on the land by that instrument.

George v. Gamble, 2 Overton (Tenn.), 549.

SEC. 2618. The bond was given by a citizen of the United States to an Indian, and an Indian countryman, to secure the consideration money for an interest in a tract of land to which the Indian title was not extinguished. The section of the act of Congress, 1806, operates directly on the contract in question, and renders null whatever agreement the complainant and Doublehead may have made with respect to the land.   *Drew v. Clarke, 1 Cooke (Tenn.), 285.*

SEC. 2619. An entry made on lands before the extinguishment of the Indian title gives no title, either legal or equitable.

Cobb v. Conway, 3 Haywood (Tenn.), 18.

SEC. 2620. In an action of ejectment the plaintiffs claimed under a grant from North Carolina in 1800, founded on an entry made in 1783, while the defendant claimed under a reservation in favor of a native Indian by the Cherokee treaty of 1819 (7 Stat. L., 195). *Held*, that the defendant had the better title.   *Cornet v. Winton, 2 Yerger (Tenn.), 143.*

SEC. 2621. The grant to Stuart as between the grantor and grantee (the State of North Carolina and himself) is valid, but it was made to Stuart encumbered with the Indian title to the land granted.

Ibid.

SEC. 2622. The tract in question is within the territory reserved to the Chickasaws prior to the treaty of September 20, 1816 (7 Stat. L., 150.)   *McLemore v. Wright, 2 Yerger (Tenn.), 326.*

SEC. 2623. By the Chickasaw treaty of 1805 (7 Stat. L., 89) the Chickasaw boundary is fixed running up Duck River. The cession act of 1806, which authorizes Tennessee to issue grants upon North Carolina warrants, provides "that nothing therein contained shall be construed so as to affect the Indian title." The treaty of 1805 was the paramount law of the land and fixed the bounds of the first district. The State never authorized her officers to receive these entries, and they are therefore wholly void.

McLemore v. Wright, 2 Yerger (Tenn.), 326.

SEC. 2624. North Carolina, by her legislative acts, had the right to grant lands within the Indian boundary to her citizens, and while such grants were binding between the State and her grantees they did not affect the Indian title. *Blair v. Pathkiller, 2 Yerger (Tenn.), 407.*

SEC. 2625. The attempt to survey lands in the Cherokee country under the act of 1783 was resisted by the Indians to the extent of waging war. *Ibid.*

SEC. 2626. By the fifth section of the act of 1837, chapter 11 (Tennessee), the preference of entry is allowed to any person, except a Cherokee Indian, who was in the actual possession of any vacant and unappropriated land at the time of the passage of the act.

Davis v. Williams, 5 Humph. (Tenn.), 12.

SEC. 2627. War with the Indians made it dangerous to settle in the western part of Pennsylvania during the years 1793, 1794, 1795, and but few settlements were attempted before the spring of 1796.

Balfour's Lessee v. Meade, 1 Washington, 18.

SEC. 2628. The prevalence of an Indian war before the Revolution is no excuse for a neglect by the holder to have a warrant executed beyond the period when the war terminated.

Lessee of Gordon v. Kerr et al., 1 Washington, 322.

SEC. 2629. Lands within the Miami Reservation and patented to a Miami Indian, but sold to a white man and afterwards purchased by a Miami, are not, in the latter's hands, exempt from taxation.

Revoir et al. v. State (Ind.), 36 N. E. Rep., 1109.

SEC. 2630. The territory in which Deadwood is situated was, under he treaty with the Sioux Indians, proclaimed February 24, 1869, and from that date to February 28, 1877, a part of an Indian reservation, and during that time no rights whatever therein could be acquired by any settler. Where prior to the latter date one undertook to lease to another certain lots in Deadwood, then part of an Indian reservation, the contract for such lease was illegal and absolutely void, and the court will not lend their aid to enforce any pretended right resting on such contract. *—Uhlig v. Garrison, 2 N. W. Rep., 253.*

SEC. 2631. A mining location made tortiously upon an Indian reservation before the Indian title is extinguished will not avail against a location made after the land is opened for settlement.

Kendal et al v. San Juan Silver Mining Co., 12 Pacific Reporter, 198.

CHAPTER V.—INDIVIDUAL OWNERSHIP AND RIGHT OF ALIENATION.

SEC. 2632. Where by treaty of 1832 (7 Stat. L., 366), made with the United States, every head of a Creek family should be allowed to select one-half section, a grandmother living with her grandchildren was the head of a Creek family and had a right to make a selection under the first clause of the second article in the treaty, and a sale of her selection under the authority of the President is a nullity.

Ladiga v. Roland, 2 How., 581.

SEC. 2633. The title of the reservees in the supplementary article to the treaty of July 1, 1835 (7 Stat. L., 472), with the Caddo Indians was complete and perfect, as fully so as if derived by patent.

United States v. Brooks, 10 How., 442.

SEC. 2634. A reservee of a specific tract of land in an Indian treaty, the same having been set apart for school purposes under a general law, has the better title, if said reservee resided on the tract.

Gaines v. Nicholson, 9 How., 356.

SEC. 2635. The grantee of a Mexican land grant, who was a civilized Indian, was, under the Mexican laws, competent to take and convey real property.   *United States v. Ritchie, 17 How., 525.*

SEC. 2636. Land reserved to a Creek warrior under act of 1817 (3 Stat. L., 380), passed to carry into effect the treaty with the Creek Indians (7 Stat. L., 120), which had been abandoned by the warrior, became forfeited to the United States, and may be sold.

Minter v. Crommelin, 18 How., 87.

SEC. 2637. The fact of abandonment of lands by Indians the Secretary is authorized to decide. A patent is evidence as to that, and that all incipient steps necessary to its issue have been regularly taken.   *Ibid.*

SEC. 2638. When the United States under a treaty selected the lands reserved to an Indian and made partition (of which the patent is conclusive evidence), his grantees took the interest he would have taken if living.   *Mann v. Wilson, 23 How., 457. Crews v. Burchman, 1 Black, 352.*

SEC. 2639. By the treaty of October 27, 1832 (7 Stat. L., 399), the Pottawatomie Indians ceded to the United States their title to their lands in Indiana and Illinois and Michigan Territory south of Grand River, and reservations were made in favor of individual Pottawatomies, and, to complete their title to reserved lands, the United States agreed that it would issue patents to the respective owners.   *Ibid.*

SEC. 2640. Although the Government alone can purchase lands from an Indian nation, yet when the rights of the nation are extinguished by treaty, an individual of the nation who takes as private owner can sell his reserved interest.   *Ibid.*

Sec. 2641. The reservee took by treaty directly from the nation the Indian title and it was the right of occupancy, and he enjoyed his lands in common with the United States until partition was made.   The treaty (7 Stat. L., 399) itself converted the reserved sections into individual property.   *Ibid.*

Sec. 2642. The recitals in a patent of lands reserved to the Pottawatomie Indians by treaty (7 Stat. L., 399), to be selected by the President for them, that the sections were those selected by the President, and to which the reservees were entitled under the treaty, are conclusive on the point.   *Crews v. Burchman, 1 Black, 352.*

Sec. 2643. A grantee from the head of a Choctaw family would hold such title free from any trust in favor of the children.
                                                        Wilson v. Wall., 6 Wall., 83.

Sec. 2644. The construction given by the representatives of both parties to the treaty and the grants issued under it could not be revoked by a mere legislative act founded on a different construction of a doubtful article of the treaty.   (7 Stat. L., 333).   *Ibid.*

Sec. 2645. Where a patent was issued to a Choctaw head of a family, the full title was conveyed to such head of a family.   *Ibid.*

Sec. 2646. By the treaty (7 Stat. L., 333) with the Choctaw Indians made in 1830 lands were given to each head of family according to the number of his family.   *Ibid.*

Sec. 2647. A joint resolution of Congress removing the restriction on alienation of their lands by the Kansas Indians, passed subsequently to a sale of such lands, can not give validity to the sale.
                                                        Stephen v. Smith, 10 Wall., 321.

Sec. 2648. Under the act of May 26, 1860 (12 Stat. L., 21), which forbade the sale of the lands of the Kansas Indians except by consent of the Secretary of the Interior, an individual Indian could not sell his land without such consent, and a sale by him without such consent was void.   *Ibid.*

Sec. 2649. Congress has the power to impose a restriction on the right of alienation of their lands by Indian reservees as a safeguard against the improvidence of the Indians.
                                                        Wilson v. Wall, 10 Wall., 321.

Sec. 2650. Land claimed or occupied by the Shawnees was not, before it was proclaimed open to preemption and settlement, subject to the location of a Wyandotte float, under article fourteen of the treaty with the Wyandotte Nation ratified October 5, 1842 (11 Stat. L., 581), giving each of several named persons of that nation a section of land not already claimed or occupied.
                                                        Walker v. Henshaw, 16 Wall., 436.

Sec. 2651. After such land was first opened to preemption settlement, one who complied with all the requirements of the preemption law and obtained the usual certificates of purchase is equitably entitled to the land, and the legal title inures to his behalf.   *Ibid.*

SEC. 2652. Chickasaw reservees under the treaty of 1834 (7 Stat. L., 450) are not obliged, in addition to proving that the locations were made by proper officers, to prove also that the conditions on which these officers were authorized to act had been observed by them.

Best v. Polk, 18 Wall., 112.

SEC. 2653. The treaty with the Chickasaw Indians of May 24, 1834 (7 Stat. L., 450), granted the land, but the location had to be fixed before the grant could become operative. A grant raises a presumption that the incipient steps to give it validity have been taken.   *Ibid.*

SEC. 2654. The certificate of the register of the land office is evidence of the location of a reserve of the Chickasaw Indians in an action of ejectment, although not certified by the Commissioner of the General Land Office.   *Ibid.*

SEC. 2655. The location is in itself evidence that the directions of the treaty on the subject were observed; and it will be presumed that the officers empowered to make the location performed their duty.   *Ibid.*

SEC. 2656. The rule that the title to land bounded on a navigable river extends only to high-water mark applies to lands granted to the Sacs and Foxes by the treaty of 1804 (7 Stat. L., 84) bounded on the Mississippi River. The grant to the half-breeds was to them as persons and not as a political body. The political jurisdiction remained in the United States. Had the grant been to them as a political society it would have been a question of boundary between nations or States, and then the line would have been the *medium filium aquia*, as it is now between Iowa and Illinois.   *Barney v. Keokuk, 94 U. S., 324.*

SEC. 2657. If the defendant is on the lands of the Pueblo (of Taos) without the consent of the inhabitants, he may be ejected or punished civilly by a suit for trespass, according to the laws regulating such matters in the Territory. If he is there with their consent or license, we know of no injury which the United States suffers by his presence, nor any statute which he violates in that regard.

United States v. Joseph, 94 U. S., 614.

SEC. 2658. An agreement made by a holder of scrip for land in Minnesota Territory set apart for the Sioux half-breeds, that he would secure the title to the land located under such scrip to be vested in another, is not void under the treaty of July 15, 1830 (7 Stat. L., 328), made at Prairie du Chien, or the act of Congress approved July 17, 1854 (10 Stat. L., 304).   *Myrick v. Thompson, 99 U. S., 291.*

SEC. 2659. An occupant might waive the condition that the scrip should not be located on premises occupied by him.   *Ibid.*

SEC. 2660. When the patents of the Government for lands assigned to members of the confederated Sac and Fox tribes of the Mississippi are once issued, all restrictions upon their alienation, not expressly named, are gone, and without such designation inability to alienate the property would be inconsistent with the perfect title which accompanies the patent.   *Pennock v. Commissioners, 103 U. S., 44.*

SEC. 2661. The circumstances being different in that case, the opinion of the court in the case of the Kansas Indians is not in conflict with the views expressed in this case. The tribal organizations of the Kansas Indians continuing in the State, and the United States treating with them as distinct political communities, the legislature of Kansas could not interfere with their lands or the lands of individual members of the tribes and subject them to taxation.   *Ibid.*

SEC. 2662. The fact that the grantor in this case was an Indian is unimportant. The duty of the officer (a justice of the peace) was precisely the same in respect to him as it was to other men. The officer must, in his case as in others, be satisfied of the identity of the person, as well of the fact of an acknowledgment, and that being done, it was his duty to make the certificate of acknowledgment. There is nothing in Dewey *v.* Campan (4 Mich., 565) to the contrary of this.
                                 Elwood v. Flaningan, 104 U. S., 562.

SEC. 2663. The statutes concerning homesteads, by which the title of the Indian homesteader is made absolutely inalienable for a period, and his right to share in tribal benefits as if he had maintained his tribal relations is preserved, are quite inconsistent with the theory that Indians do or can make themselves independent citizens by living apart from their tribe.   *Elk v. Wilkins, 112 U. S., 94.*

SEC. 2664. A deed from an Indian chief to A, in 1856, of a tract described by metes and bounds, and further as "being the land set off to the Indian Chief Buffalo, at the Indian treaty of September 30, 1854 (10 Stat. L., 1109), and was afterwards disposed of by said Buffalo to said A, and is now recorded with the Government documents," does not convey the equitable interest of the chief in another tract described by different metes and bounds granted to the said chief by a subsequent patent in 1858, in conformity with the said treaty, in such manner that an action at law may be maintained by A or his grantee for recovering possession of the same.   *Prentice v. Stearns, 113 U. S., 435.*

SEC. 2665. The embodiment of the stipulation required in the seventh article of the Ottawa treaty of June 24, 1862 (12 Stat. L., 1238), limiting the power of alienation in the patent to a chief of the Ottawa tribe, the construction of the executive department of the Government that it was applicable to the land granted by the third article, and the acceptance of the patent, seems to imply the acquiescence by the patentee in that construction.   *Libby v. Clark, 118 U. S., 250.*

SEC. 2666. The special allotments to the chiefs and headmen of the Ottawa Indian tribe authorized by the third article of the treaty of

June 24, 1862 (12 Stat. L., 1237), were subject to the limitations on the power of alienation prescribed by the seventh article of the same treaty.   Such limitation on the power of conveyance did not deprive the title of the character of a fee-simple estate.   *Ibid.*

SEC. 2667. The treaty of Prairie du Chien (7 Stat. L., 320) does not provide how or when the permission of the President for the sale of the lands granted to an Indian shall be obtained, and there is certainly nothing that requires that it shall be given before the deed is delivered.   *Pickering v. Lomax, 145 U. S., 310.*

SEC. 2668. The permission of the President for the sale of land granted by the treaty of Prairie du Chien (7 Stat. L., 320) to an Indian was doubtless a condition precedent to a perfect title in the grantee; but the neglect in this case to obtain the approval of the President for thirteen years only shows that for that length of time the title was imperfect, and no action in ejectment would have lain until the condition was performed.   *Ibid.*

SEC. 2669. Had the grantee of land secured to an Indian under the treaty of Prairie du Chien (7 Stat. L., 320), the day after the deed was delivered to him, sent it to Washington and obtained the approval of the President, it would be sticking in the bark to say that the deed was not thereby validated, and a delay of thirteen years is immaterial, provided, of course, that no third parties have in the meantime legally acquired an interest in the land.   *Ibid.*

SEC. 2670. The approval of the President indorsed on a deed of lands granted an Indian by the treaty of Prairie du Chien (7 Stat. L., 320), relates back to the execution of the deed and validates it from that time, and "operates upon the act ratified precisely as though authority to do the act had been previously given, except where the rights of the third parties have intervened between the act and the ratification." The retroactive efficacy of the ratification is subject to this qualification. The intervening rights of third persons can not be defeated by ratification.   *Ibid.*

SEC. 2671. The object of the proviso to article 4 of the treaty of Prairie du Chien (7 Stat. L., 320) was not to prevent the alienation of lands *in toto*, but to protect the Indian against the improvident disposition of his property, and it will be presumed that the President, before fixing his approval, satisfied himself that no fraud or imposition had been practiced upon the Indian when the deed was originally obtained.   *Ibid.*

SEC. 2672. The provision in the treaty of Prairie du Chien (7 Stat. L., 320) continued by its expressed terms to be operative so long as the lands were owned by the grantee or their heirs, and the object of carrying it into the patent was merely intended to warn purchasers of the restrictions imposed by the treaty upon the alienation of the land.

    Ibid.

SEC. 2673. In order to pass the legal title to lands something more is necessary than the signature of the grantor to a blank instrument. There must be an intent to convey, and the delivery of a deed for the purpose of vesting a present title in the grantee and a deed delivered without the consent of the grantor is of no more effect to pass title than if it were a forgery. At best the deed from Sophia Felix, being a quitclaim, conveyed only the interest of the grantor at the date of its delivery, which was nothing. *Felix v. Patrick, 145 U. S., 317.*

SEC. 2674. The power of free alienation is incident to an estate in fee simple, but a condition in a grant preventing alienation to a limited extent or for a certain and reasonable time may be valid and the grantee forfeit his estate by violating it; and while such a result does not ensue in transactions with members of a race of people treated as in a state of pupilage and entitled to special protection, yet the proviso to section 15 of the act of March 3, 1875 (18 Stat. L., 402), may fairly be held to have been adopted in view of general principles.
Taylor v. Brown, 147 U. S., 640.

SEC. 2675. The proviso of section 15 of the act of March 3, 1875 (18 Stat. L., 402), is that the title shall not be subject to alienation in the various ways described and shall be and remain inalienable for a period of five years from the date of the patent. Possibly the language is susceptible of being construed to mean that the land should be inalienable on the day of the issue of the patent and for five years after that date, two periods of time, but the court are of the opinion that the more natural and true construction is that only one period is referred to and that the day the patent issued should not be excluded. *Ibid.*

SEC. 2676. The reservations granted by the seventh clause of article 2 of the Chippewa treaty of 1854 (10 Stat. L., 1109) and provision "first" in section 1 of the act of December 19, 1854 (10 Stat. L., 598), "to provide for the extinguishment of the title of the Chippewa Indians to the lands owned and claimed by them," etc., are limited to the territory ceded by the Indians, both as applied to Indians of pure or mixed blood. *Fee v. Brown, 162 U. S., 602.*

SEC. 2677. The treaty of February 23, 1867 (15 Stat. L., 513), with the Ottawas and other Indians, introduced the limitation of minority upon the inalienability of lands patented to a minor allottee, in that respect changing the provisions of the treaty of July 16, 1862 (12 Stat. L., 1237); and this limitation was applicable to lands then patented to minors under the treaty of 1862, and cut off the right of guardians to dispose of their real estate during their minority, even under direction of the courts of the State in which the land was situated.
Weggan v. Conolly, 163 U. S., 56.

SEC. 2678. A woman of the Pottawatomie tribe whose husband has acquired title to lands by patents from the Government is thereafter

subject to the same laws, and, where the rights of third persons are
concerned, is liable for the consequences of her acts and nonaction, as
any other person.   *Pka-o-wah-ash-kum v. Sorin et al., 8 Fed. Rep., 740.*

SEC. 2679. It can not be maintained that after a perfect title to the
lands exists within this State, by a grant to an Indian, he is exempt, or
the land is exempt, from all the ordinary burdens and incidents which
the law of the State imposes upon owners of land, except probably as
to taxation. He must assert his rights against a trespasser, or a person
in possession under color of title, the same as any other person.   *Ibid.*

SEC. 2680. By the treaty made in 1832 (7 Stat. L., 394) the section of land in controversy was granted to an Indian chief of the Pottawatomie tribe, to whom, two years afterwards, the plaintiff was
married. In the following year, by a deed in which the woman did
not join, the land was deeded away. In 1846 the husband died. The
patent from the Government was not issued until 1846. Thirteen years
after, the widow filed this bill for assignment of dower in the land.
Held, that as against those in possession under the deed of the husband, the bill must be dismissed.   *Ibid.*

SEC. 2681. In Doe *v.* Wilson the reservee died before any patent
was issued, and, long before the patent was issued, the reservee, during his life, had made a conveyance by general warranty deed of lands
granted to him by the treaty (7 Stat. L., 394), and the court decided
that the person holding the grant under the reservee acquired a title by
the issuing of the patent as against his heirs.   *Ibid.*

SEC. 2682. A patent issued to a dead person shall take effect as
though he were living.   *Ibid.*

SEC. 2683. Where a deed of lands purports to have been executed by
the heirs of the deceased Indian, neither the "certificates of identity"
required by the Interior Department nor the formal approval of said
deed by the Secretary are conclusive on the United States courts as to
the identity of grantors.   *Richardville v. Thorp, 28 Fed. Rep., 52.*

SEC. 2684. Where the validity of a deed is in issue before the United
States courts, and the proofs show that the grantors therein falsely
impersonated real heirs, and thereby actually misled the official who
approved the conveyance, the deed will be held void.   *Ibid.*

SEC. 2685. The Secretary of the Interior may prescribe rules and
regulations by which other persons than those who held the real title
can divest the real holder of such title. He can say what evidence
shall be submitted as to the competency of the grantor, the fact that
the money was paid, etc., but beyond that he has not power. He has
no judicial power to judge a forfeiture, to decide questions of inheritance, or to divest the owner of his title without his knowledge or
consent.   *Ibid.*

SEC. 2686. The supreme court of Kansas has decided that a convey-ance by an heir of a Pottawatomie Indian allottee, under a treaty similar to the Kickapoo treaty of June 28, 1862 (13 Stat. L., 623), was valid, although made before the patent was issued.

Briggs v. Wash-puk-qua, 37 Fed. Rep., 136.

SEC. 2687. A deed made in violation of an express statute is not color of title. In such case, the deed from the Indian being void, his execution of the deed and acceptance of the lease do not estop his devisees and their assignees from disputing the title of the grantee.

Smith v. Henry, 41 Fed. Rep., 705.

SEC. 2688. Where an Indian holds land by a patent restricting alienation, attempts to convey such land by a deed, and then accepts a lease of the land from his grantee, his possession is not that of his grantee, so as to set the statute of limitation in motion in favor of the grantee. *Ibid.*

SEC. 2689. The condition of nonalienation imposed upon the fee simple conveyed in the donation act is not repugnant to the nature of the estate and is therefore not void. The old and well-settled rule of the common law does not apply to this legislative grant. The sover-eign power of the legislature is superior to the immemorial rules and usages of the common law. *Ibid.*

SEC. 2690. Under a legislative grant to an Indian, which confers on him the rights of citizenship and gives him title to lands in fee with the right of devising the same, but which expressly withholds from him the right of conveying it, except by lease for a term of two years, a deed of land by such Indian is void, the restraint on alienation not being inconsistent with either the estate granted or the citizenship conferred. *Ibid.*

SEC. 2691. The treaty with the Kickapoo Indians (13 Stat. L., 624) provided that the lands allotted to the Indians could not be sold to white men without permission of the President, which permission should be signified by his causing the land to be patented to the Indians " with power of alienation," and that before receiving patent the Indians must appear before the district court, make proof of their intelligence, and take the oath of allegiance. An Indian conveyed his land by warranty deed on the day he made such proof, and after he had obtained his patent conveyed his land to another grantee. · *Held,* that the second grantee took the land, since the first deed, being made before the patent, was ineffectual to convey the land either directly or by estoppel. *Briggs v. Sample, 43 Fed. Rep., 102.*

SEC. 2692. Deeds made to certain Indians of lots of land on the Puyallup Reservation pursuant to the treaty of December 26, 1854 (10 Stat. L., 1132), with the stipulation that the lands should not be aliened or leased for more than two years, and should be exempt from levy, sale, or forfeiture, pass the title in fee to the grantees, subject only to conditions subsequent, and left no title or reversionary interest in the United States, but a mere power in the President to reassign or sell for the common benefit of the tribe, on breach of the conditions.

Ross v. Eells, 56 Fed. Rep., 855.

Sec. 2693. A deed made by an attorney in fact of an Indian woman, who, though illiterate and unable to converse in English, is possessed of good understanding and capable of acting independently, will not be set aside on the ground that she was imposed upon and induced to give the power without knowledge of its effect, even if voidable for the reason, when it appears that the sale was to the promoters of a town-site company at a price largely in excess of its value at the time; that she made no attempt to repudiate the sale, but accepted and used the money, voluntarily delivered possession of the land, and, although the purchasers were making large expenditures on the property and it was rapidly rising in value, made no claim until it had increased many fold, the mere fact that she still retains the legal title to the land by reason of the issuance to her of a patent by the United States, after the conveyance made by her attorney in fact, will, under the circumstances, give her no right to equitable relief.

Hatch v. Ferguson, 57 Fed. Rep., 959.

Sec. 2694. Where one entitled to select a quantity of land under an Indian treaty makes a deed of such quantity of lands by specific description, adding that "this description is intended to include any land or rights to land secured or intended to be secured" to the grantor by treaty, and thereafter files a survey thereof in the General Land Office, stating that he has selected the described lands, but fails to receive a patent therefor, the deed must be construed to convey only the specific lands, and will not cover other lands selected and patented many years later.   *Pond v. Minnesota Iron Co., 58 Fed. Rep., 448.*

Sec. 2695. A treaty with the Puyallup Indians (10 Stat. L., 1132) allotted the lands in severalty to those who would locate on the same as permanent homes, and authorized the President to prescribe such rules as would insure to the family, in case of the death of its head, possession of such home; to issue a patent to such person or family, and to cancel it if such person or family rove from place to place. Each patent issued prohibited alienation. The act of February 8, 1887 (24 Stat. L., 388), conferred citizenship on such Indians and provided for leasing the lands under regulations of the Secretary of the Interior, and contemplated that agents shall be in charge of reservations, and the practice of the Department was to maintain such agents. *Held,* that the allotment of such lands in severalty and making the Indians citizens did not revoke the reservation.   *Eells v. Ross, 64 Fed. Rep., 417.*

Sec. 2696. The appellees claim contracts with the Indians and a right to occupy the allotted land, and the circuit court held that the

Government, by making the Indian proprietors citizens, lost the power "to coerce such Indians into making or annulling contracts, or of molesting persons upon their premises by their license when not interfering with the operations of the Government or violating any national law;" and the court further held that by issuance of the patent "the Government lost entirely the right to control the use of the land." The patent has clear words of prohibition against alienation, and even if it had omitted them the treaties and law imposed them. *Ibid.*

SEC. 2697. The right to sell property is not derived from and is not dependent upon citizenship; neither does it detract in the slightest degree from the dignity or value of citizenship that a person is not possessed of an estate, or, if possessed of an estate, that he is deprived for the time being of the right to alienate it. It does not follow, therefore, that the power of these Indians to deal with land which was held in trust for their benefit was sensibly enlarged, or that the restriction against alienation found in the act of February 8, 1887 (24 Stat. L., 388), was removed, because in the sixth section of the same act Congress saw fit to declare Indian allottees to be citizens.

Beck v. Flournoy, &c., Co., 65 Fed. Rep., 30.

SEC. 2698. By the act of February 21, 1863 (12 Stat. L., 659), the Winnebago Indians were removed to a reservation in Nebraska and given allotments of land in severalty thereon "without the right of alienation." Under the act of 1887 (24 Stat. L., 388) other allotments were made to these Indians, such lands to be held in trust for the allottee and his heirs by the United States for twenty-five years, any conveyance of or contract touching such lands being declared null and void. The same act also provided that Indians receiving allotments of land in severalty should thereby become citizens of the United States and entitled to all the rights of such citizens. The Flournoy Live Stock Company, without the sanction of the Commissioner of Indian Affairs, obtained leases from the allottees of large quantities of lands allotted under both acts. *Held,* that the citizenship bestowed on the Indians was in no way inconsistent with the restriction upon their title to their lands, and that the leases obtained by the Flournoy Live Stock Company were utterly void. *Ibid.*

SEC. 2699. The Flournoy Company having obtained an injunction against the Winnebago agent to restrain him from interfering with it in its possession or use of allotted lands leased from the Indians, such injunction was erroneously issued, since the agent has done no more than to give notice, under the direction of his superiors, that the leases were void. *Ibid.*

SEC. 2700. The clause in the act of February 8, 1887 (24 Stat. L., 388), imposing a limitation upon the power of alienation is not in conflict or inconsistent with the subsequent clause conferring the rights of citizenship. Both provisions may stand well together. *Ibid.*

SEC. 2701. If the executive branch of the Government deems it necessary, for the proper performance of its treaty stipulations with the Indians, to forbid the occupancy of allotted tracts by white men, it has the right to do so, particularly in view of the fact that, in all the legislation touching the same, Congress has uniformly prohibited the alienation of the lands and has expressly declared that all contracts between the Indians and persons not native members of the tribe shall be wholly null and void.

United States v. Flournoy, &c., Co., 69 Fed. Rep., 886.

SEC. 2702. Leases made by members of the Omaha and Winnebago tribes of lands allotted to them in severalty, under the acts of February 21, 1863, August 7, 1882, and February 8, 1887 (24 Stat. L., 388), without the authority of the Secretary of the Interior, are wholly void. (65 Fed. Rep., 30, followed.)   *Ibid.*

SEC. 2703. The right of present possession of the allotted tracts on the Winnebago Reservation is in the Indians, and not in the United States. The title is held by the Government in trust for the Indians, and it is, to say the least, extremely doubtful whether the United States could maintain an action in ejectment based upon the assertion of a right to immediate possession.   *Ibid.*

SEC. 2704. Leases made by the Indians of lands in severalty, under the acts of Congress providing therefor, are absolutely void; and neither such leases nor occupancy and planting of crops upon the lands by the lessees or their subtenants, give to the occupants any right to restrain the officers of the Government from removing them from such lands. (Beck *v.* Real Estate Co., 65 Fed. Rep., 30, followed.)

Pilgrim v Beck. 69 Fed. Rep., 895.

SEC. 2705. The treaty of October 2, 1863 (13 Stat. L., 667), between the United States and the Chippewa Indians, provided that there should be "set apart from the tract" thereby ceded a reservation of 640 acres near the mouth of Thief River for the chief, Moose Dung. *Held,* that the effect of such provision was to vest in Moose Dung such a title or interest in the 640 acres that, upon selection being made, he could execute a valid lease thereof without the approval of the Secretary of the Interior.   *Meehan v. Jones, 70 Stats., 453.*

SEC. 2706. Where, in a treaty, the lands reserved and granted to individuals can not be conveyed without the permission of the President, that permission may be given in such form as the President may think proper. Such permission having been given by the President, his successor can not revoke or annul it, especially where the rights of third persons are concerned. *Doe ex dem. Godfrey v. Beardsley, 2 McLean, 412.*

SEC. 2707. The United States circuit court will recognize the procedure of a court of probate through which Indian lands have been thus sold, where the court had jurisdiction and the proceedings upon their face appear to have been regular. *Lowry v. Weaver. 4 McLean, 82.*

SEC. 2708. The restriction on alienation by an individual grantee is personal, but such lands are subject to the operation of the State law. The law, thus substituting an agency, conveys the title without the sanction of the President. *Ibid.*

SEC. 2709. Lands reserved to individual Indians under a treaty which vests in them the title, but which restricts them from conveying it except with the consent of the President, descend under the laws of the State, and may be made responsible for the payment of debts. *Ibid.*

SEC. 2710. The deed in question does not come within the provisions of the treaty. The grantee, and perhaps his heirs, may not be able to make a valid conveyance of the land without the approval of the President. That may be considered a condition within the original grant, and is limited to the personal acts of the grantee and his heirs. But the conveyance under consideration is by operation of law. The land is not withdrawn from the sovereign action of the State. Like other lands, it may be taxed by the State and is subject by the local laws to the payment of debts. *Ibid.*

SEC. 2711. The Indians on the Oneida Reservation, Wis., have the right to cut and use the timber thereon, and to sell sufficient to support themselves and families. *United States v. Foster, 2 Bissell, 377.*

SEC. 2712. While there may be some question whether the Indians have the right to commit waste, properly so called, upon the reservation, or to use the timber for the purpose of speculation, there can be no doubt that they would have the right to clear the land for cultivation; and if so, it would seem, to sell the wood thus obtained from the land. *Ibid.*

SEC. 2713. The cases cited by counsel for plaintiff, where land belonging to the Indian tribes has been held to be not taxable under the law of the States, have no application to this case. Here the land was severed from the mass of public lands by the grant, the selection of the President, and the issuing of the patent, and the United States could make no claim that the land belonged to an Indian tribe as such, and the plaintiff has lost to the land thus in possession of the defendants all right to the maintenance of this bill for dower by the delay in the application. *Ash-Kum v. Sorin, 10 Biss., 293.*

SEC. 2714. The fact that complainant was an Indian woman and a member of an Indian tribe did not prevent the Illinois statute, relative to seven years' possession under claim of title, from operating against her and barring her right of dower. *Ibid.*

SEC. 2715. An Indian who gains perfect title to land within a State is not exempt, nor is the land exempt, from any of the ordinary burdens and incidents which the law of the State imposes upon the owners of lands, or upon the lands themselves. *Ibid.*

SEC. 2716. Where the Government agrees to grant certain land and the land is located and surveyed and the boundaries established before the issuing of the patent, the wife of the grantee is thereby clothed with an inchoate right of dower, which becomes consummate on his death, although the patent is not issued until subsequently.

Ibid.

SEC. 2717. The joint resolution of Congress, July 17, 1862 (12 Stat. L., 628), removed the restriction of the right of alienation imposed by the second and third sections of the act of 1860, and therefore the deed made, in 1864 by Butler to plaintiff conveyed the legal title.

Swope v. Purdy, 1 Dill., 349.

SEC. 2718. Although the first section of the act of 1860 (12 Stat. L., 21), concerning the Kaw Reservations in Kansas, if standing alone was sufficient to vest a full fee-simple title in Butler with right of alienation, yet by the second and third sections of that act the right of alienation was taken away and vested in the United States in trust for Butler. The deed of Butler prior to July 17, 1862, therefore, conveyed no title. (Stevens, v. Smith, 1 Kans., 243.)

Ibid.

SEC. 2719. In the case of the Kansas Indians (5 Wall., 737) the United States Supreme Court in speaking of the Shawnees says: "As long as the United States recognize their tribal character they are under the protection of treaties and the laws of Congress, and their property is withdrawn from the operation of State laws." There can be no question of the applicability of this language to the suit in Wyandotte County, Kans. The Secretary of the Interior has never approved the deeds under which petitioners claim, and the deeds are entirely void until approved by that officer. Until they are so approved the lands of the Shawnees are as wholly beyond the jurisdiction of the State courts as if they were situated beyond its geographical limits.

Ex parte Forbes, 1 Dill., 363.

SEC. 2720. The location of the land with the scrip, under the act of Congress, July 17, 1854 (10 Stat. L., 304), passed the fee out of the United States and vested it in the plaintiff as grantee. The scrip and application became the "instruments of title," and conferred upon him the *legal* title as effectually as could have been done by the issuance of a patent.

Larrivierre v. Madegan, 1 Dill., 451.

SEC. 2721. In actions at law the legal title must prevail, and the equities of the parties can not be inquired into. The location with the scrip being equivalent to a patent gives a better title than the preemption entry, and no equitable title can be set up in ejectment in opposition to the legal estate.

Ibid.

SEC. 2722. The issuing of a patent is a ministerial act, and a patent issued without authority is void. The departure of the patent in respect to the name of the grantee from the requirements of the treaty is material, and the patent is therefore a nullity. The effect of this is that the legal title is still in the United States, and of course the plaintiff can not recover in ejectment. *Gray v. Coffman, 2 Dill., 393.*

Sec. 2723. The treaty of 1855 (10 Stat. L., 1159) with the Wyandotte Indians recognizes and provides in several places for the rights of *heirs or legal representatives* of the reservees under the treaty of 1842. These must mean heirs and legal representatives "according to the laws, usages, and customs" of the tribe. See articles 8 and 9 of the treaty of 1855. *Ibid.*

Sec. 2724. The court must give effect to the well-established laws, customs, and usages of the Wyandotte tribe in respect to the disposition of property by descent and will. John Hicks, sr., had a valuable right given by the treaty of 1842 (7 Stat. L., 608)—a right to select and locate 640 acres of land—not land, but a "float" or right to land. He died in 1853, within the limits of what afterwards became the Territory of Kansas. There is no national law of descent and wills; none regulating the rights of members of Indian tribes. *Ibid.*

Sec. 2725. The Wyandotte treaty of 1855 (10 Stat. L., 1159) required the patent to be issued in the *name of the reservee.* The patent of May 3, 1861, was in fact issued, not to John Hicks, the reservee, but to the *heirs of John Hicks.* If it had been issued in the name of John Hicks, though he was then dead, it would, under the act of 1836, have insured to his heirs, devisees, or assigns (5 Stat. L., 31). *Ibid.*

Sec. 2726. By the fourteenth article of the treaty of 1842 with the Wyandottes (7 Stat. L., 608) the United States agree to grant to John Hicks, to his heirs, and to 35 other specified persons of the tribe, 1 section of land each: "The land hereby granted is to be selected by the grantees, surveyed and patented at the expense of the United States, but never to be *conveyed* by them or their heirs without the permission of the President of the United States." *Ibid.*

Sec. 2727. At the date of the death of Francis A. Hicks, August 16, 1855, no statute of descents or will had been passed by the Territorial legislature of Kansas. The council still continued to act, and the will of Hicks was admitted to probate September 25, 1855, the executor gave bond, and was authorized by the council to act as such. January 5, 1863, the will was presented to the regular probate court of Wyandotte County and proved and allowed without any notice being published or otherwise given, so far as appears of record. *Ibid.*

SEC. 2728. The treaty of 1855 with the Wyandottes (10 Stat. L., 1159) requires the patent to issue in the *name of the reservee*, though if he be dead the selection may be made by his "heirs or legal representatives," to be determined by the laws, usages, and customs of the tribe. Whether a patent issued in the name of the heirs of the reservee is void, quære?   *Ibid.*

SEC. 2729. A will of the right to this "float" made and executed according to the laws of the Wyandotte tribe, and proved and allowed by the proper tribunal of the tribe, is valid and will be respected by the civil courts.   *Ibid.*

SEC. 2730. The treaty of March 17, 1842 (7 Stat. L., 608) and of January 31, 1855 (10 Stat. L., 1159), with the Wyandot Indians in respect to the grant to members of the tribe, of a right to select and locate a section of land construed.   *Ibid.*

SEC. 2731. Taking all the provisions of the treaty of 1855 together, it appears that it contemplates that the competent heads of families shall take the lands by patent directly from the United States, and that the Commissioner of Indian Affairs and the land department properly construed the treaty in investing John Hicks as the head of the family with the legal title to the land.   *Hicks v. Butrick, 2 Dill., 413.*

SEC. 2732. In executing the treaty of 1855 with the Wyandottes (10 Stat. L., 1159), the United States construed it as dividing the competent Indians into two classes, to wit: First, individuals or persons without families. Second, heads of families, the members of each separate family being arranged together. The test of competency in the head of the family was, sufficient intelligence and prudence, on the part of the head, to control and manage the affairs and interest of the family.   *Ibid.*

SEC. 2733. By terms of the treaty of January 31, 1855 (10 Stat. L., 1159), between the United States and the Wyandotte tribe of Indians, viewed in the light of the practical construction which it has received and of the patents to lands issued thereunder to the competent heads of families: *Held*, that such patents conveyed to the head of the family the land in fee and not in trust for the wife and other members of his family; approving Summers v. Spybuck, 1 Kans., 394.
                                        Ibid.

SEC. 2734. The laws of the State of Kansas have no application to the mode of alienation of lands granted to the Miami Indians (10 Stat. L., 1093; 11 Stats., 430) so long as the title remains in the patentees. The case of the Kansas Indians (5 Wall., 737) applied.
                              Mungosah v. Steinbrook, 2 Dill., 418.

SEC. 2735. Lands patented to the reservees, under the treaty with the Miami Indians of June 5, 1854 (10 Stat. L., 1092), are liable to be taxed by the State authority after the title has passed out of the Indian reservee to a citizen.   *Peck v. Miami County, 4 Dill., 370.*

SEC. 2736. This being an action in ejectment, the paramount legal title must control, and it is not necessary at this time to decide whether the patentee took the title in trust for the allottee, or in what manner the trust, if any, could be properly executed, or whether notice thereof should be imputed to the purchaser of the legal title.

Goodfellow v. Joseph Muckey et al., 1 McCrary, 238.

SEC. 2737. No reason appears why the United States and the Pottawatomie Indians, having the undoubted right to make provisions in the treaty of 1861, allotting their lands in severalty and for patenting the same as provided therein, had not the same right and power to amend that treaty, and provide for transferring the legal title to the parent or guardian of the allottee.

Ibid.

SEC. 2738. The lands allotted to the Pottawatomies under the treaty of 1861 (12 Stat. L., 1192) were exempt from taxation and sale, and were not alienable by the allottee. That the contracting parties to this treaty did not regard the fee as becoming invested in the allottee by virtue of article two, and the certificate issued in pursuance thereof, is demonstrated by the next article, for it is therein provided how the adult allottees may obtain that title.

Ibid.

SEC. 2739. Grants and reservations claimed under Indian treaties are strictly construed against the grantee or beneficiary.

Ibid.

SEC. 2740. The right of the original grantee, being an Indian, to receive grants of lands in California under the Mexican laws, and to convey the land so granted, considered.

United States v. Briones, 1 Hoffman Land Cases, 110.

SEC. 2741. The Wyandotte treaty of 1855 (10 Stat. L., 1159), is construed to mean that the lands were taken, assigned, and patented to the heads of families "*for*" or *on account of* the other members of the family. The assignment and patent to John Pipe *held* to have vested in him a title in fee simple absolute, according to the intent and meaning of the treaty.

Summer v. Spaybuck, 1 Banks & McCahon, 370.

SEC. 2742. In the provision in article 3 of the Wyandotte treaty of 1855 (10 Stat. L., 1159) for the plat showing "the land assigned to each family and individual," the word "individual" construed to mean a person not a member of a family. The members of families, other than the heads, do not belong to either of the classes reported by the Commissioner of Indian Affairs, nor to those to whom patents are to issue.

Ibid.

SEC. 2743. John Pipe, a Wyandotte Indian, received a patent for land allotted to him as head of a family, consisting of himself, wife, and two minor children. The patent was issued by the General Land Office on report of the commissioners appointed under article 3 of the Wyandotte treaty of January 31, 1855 (10 Stat. L., 1159), purporting to convey it all to him in fee simple absolute. *Held*, that the form of the patent precludes the idea of the land being conveyed by it to him in trust.   *Ibid.*

SEC. 2744. The widow of an Indian is not dowable of lands selected by the husband under the treaty between the United States and Creek tribe of the 24th March, 1832, and by him conveyed, in conformity with that treaty, to a purchaser. If there be a grant to one and his heirs to such uses as he should appoint by deed or will, and for want, or in default of, and in the mean time, and until appointment, to the use of himself, his heirs, and assigns forever; and he make an appointment in fee, his wife has no right of dower. Before such an appointment, he would have a vested fee, and be seized in fee, until appointment. Should he die before such an appointment, his wife would be dowable. But her right would be destroyed by an appointment. When made, the appointee would take the title, as if the original conveyance had been made to himself.

Chumubbee v. Nicks, 3 Por. (Ala.), 362.

SEC. 2745. The reservation of lands to the Cherokee Indians, under the eighth article of the treaty of 1817, inures as a life estate to the reservee only upon compliance with the conditions of continuance thereon as stipulated, and this failing, the fee simple in the land reserved reverts immediately to the United States. The condition of continuance upon the reservation during the lifetime of the reservee is one annexed to the life estate, and upon the breach of it the expectant estate of the reservee's wife and children is at once destroyed. A reservee of lands under this treaty can not make any disposition by lease stipulating a continuance beyond the period of a removal from the land, or the extent of his life, though a lease may be effected of a portion of the land for a time not beyond these periods, if possession is retained.   *Kennedy v. McCartney, 4 Porter (Ala.), 141.*

SEC. 2746. A claim of title under the deed of a Creek Indian to lands selected under treaty of 24th of March, 1832, which deed was made within five years after the treaty, is not held valid, it not being shown that the contract of the Indian had been approved by the President of the United States.   *Herring v. M'Elderry et al., 5 Porter (Ala.), 161.*

SEC. 2747. A contract for the sale of his land by an Indian reservee, located under the treaty of the 24th of March, 1832, and by which the reservee agreed to make title to a contemplated vendee at some future day, requires the certificate of an agent appointed for that purpose and the approval of the President of the United States to render it valid.   *Clarlitko v. Elliott, 5 Porter (Ala.), 403.*

SEC. 2748. The first article of the treaty of 1814 with the Creek Indians, or the act of Congress of 1817 which provides for the location of the lands reserved under that article, and for other purposes, does not invest chiefs, warriors, or other reservees with an estate which he can alienate at pleasure. *James v. Scott, 5 Ala., 579.*

SEC. 2749. Every head of a family of the Creek tribe of Indians who resided on a half section of land, and selected it as his reservation under the treaty of 1832, became thereby entitled to it, and his right could not be divested by the refusal of the locating agent to locate him upon it. He could only be divested of his right within five years by a sale in accordance with the treaty or by abandoning the land; but if he neither sold nor abandoned it within that time his title became perfect and indefeasible. *Rowland & Heifner v. Ladiga's Heirs, 21 Ala., 9.*

SEC. 2750. Under the treaty of 1832 between the United States and the Creek Indians, the title to all the Creek lands was ceded to the United States, and the reservations to the heads of families were of an estate for five years only, to be enlarged into a fee at the expiration of that time on the happening of the contingencies provided for in the treaty. (Overruling *dicta*, to the effect that the reservee took a defeasible fee, in 13 Ala., 793; 15 Ala., 525, and 21 Ala., 9.)
Rose v. Griffin, 33 Ala., 717.

SEC. 2751. Under the fourteenth article of the treaty between the United States and the Choctaw Indians, concluded at Dancing Rabbit Creek September 15, 1830, the reservation to which each "head of a family" was entitled is limited to one section or 640 acres of land; and the other reservations, *to* or *for* each child of the family, were intended to confer a beneficial interest on the children themselves, either to them directly or to their parents in trust for them.
Wilson v. Wall, 34 Ala., 288.

SEC. 2752. A patent being issued to a Choctaw Indian "and his heirs" for all the lands to which he and his several children were entitled as their reservations under the treaty of 1830, a court of equity will hold the legal title subject to the equitable rights secured to the children by the treaty. *Ibid.*

SEC. 2753. A transfer by a Creek Indian of his reservation under the treaty approved by the President of the United States confers on the grantees such title as will support an ejectment, and where the grantees are a partnership, each partner may maintain a separate action for his undivided interest. *Tarver v. Smith, 38 Ala., 135.*

SEC. 2754. The claimant claimed to enter the land in question by virtue of the Cherokee preemption right, as the assignee of the original claimant, under several successive assignments. The application to enter was refused by the district land officers. In the absence of any proof of the genuineness of these assignments, or showing that they were proved before the land officers, the court will presume that their refusal was predicated upon that ground. The land officers could not have allowed such entry with name of the assignee unless they were satisfied of the validity of the assignments.

Cunningham v. Ashley, 12 Ark., 296.

SEC. 2755. Cherokee preemption claims could not be located on the four sections of land including the Hot Springs as their center after the passage of the act of April, 1832.

Gaines et al. v. Hale & Rector, 26 Ark., 168.

SEC. 2756. By the act of Congress (18 Stat. L., 420) under which a patent issued to an Indian on the 15th day of June, 1880, it was declared the land should be inalienable for "five years from the date of the patent." *Held*, in computing the time, that the first day should be included, and that a conveyance made on the 15th of June, 1885, was not within the limitation, and therefore valid. In such cases there is no absolute rule of computation. "From" in its literal and restricted sense means "exclusive," but it may be used in a connection that means "inclusive," and to prevent forfeitures, uphold *bona fide* transactions, and carry out the intention of the parties, courts will always regard it as so used.

Taylor v. Brown, 5 Dakota, 335.

SEC. 2757. Lands acquired by Indians that would abandon their tribal relations, under 18 Stat. L., 420, were declared to be inalienable for five years. Such an Indian, having received a patent which was in the usual form, without any reference to the statutory disability or his being an Indian, executed a conveyance, within the five years, to B. *Held*, that the statute prevailed over the recitals of the patent, that purchasers must take notice thereof, and that the conveyance was void. Under such deed, where the grantee knew his grantor was an Indian, there was no such good faith and color of title as is required for an adverse possession to defeat a subsequent conveyance.

Ibid.

SEC. 2758. Under article 4 of an Indian treaty between the United States and certain Indian tribes, made in 1829, two sections of land in this State were granted to A. R., for himself and children, with the stipulation that such lands should never be leased or conveyed by the grantees or their heirs, to any person whatever, without the permission of the President of the United States, and the patent contained a similar limitation. A partition was had between A. R. and his children, and J. R., one of the children, on August 3, 1858, by his deed conveyed to H. the part set off to him in severalty. Afterwards, on January 21, 1871, the President of the United States indorsed upon this deed his approval. *Held*, that the deed of J. R. to H. was void and passed no title, and that the subsequent permission of the President indorsed thereon did not make it valid.

Pickering v. Lomax, 120 Ill., 289.

SEC. 2759. A treaty with the Indians, so far as respects the grants of land to individuals contained in it, is evidence of the grantee's title, and, as such, proper to be laid before a jury.

Harris v. Doe ex dem. Barnett, 4 Blackf. (Ind.), 370.

SEC. 2760. A special act of Congress respecting a grant of real estate to an individual under an Indian treaty can have no efficacy, if passed subsequently to the grantee's death, in confirming his title; but the act may be evidence for a jury, in explanation of the treaty, relative to the situation of the land.

Ibid.

SEC. 2761. The treaty of 1837 with the Miami Nation of Indians (7 Stat. L., 462), which contained a provision that certain lands should be granted to the persons therein named, did not, of itself, vest the title to said lands in said persons. Before the complainant could claim any tract of land under the treaty, the tract must have been located under the authority of the United States, and a patent to him for the same must have been issued by the President.

Longlois v. Coffin, 1 Indiana, 378.

SEC. 2762. When a treaty says that the title to a certain tract of land is thereafter vested in a certain individual, the treaty operates as a grant of the land. But when it says, as in the present case, that a half section of land at a specified point shall be granted to a certain person, his heirs, and assigns by a patent from the President of the United States, the clause amounts only to a contract that the land shall be afterwards properly located by an agent of the Government, and be conveyed by a patent from the President.

Ibid.

SEC. 2763. The treaty with the Miamis of June 5, 1854 (10 Stat. L., 1093), after providing that Congress may authorize the issuing of patents for the selected lands under restrictions, provides that the lands so patented "shall not be liable to levy, sale, execution, or forfeiture." The patents contain the restriction that said lands shall never be sold or conveyed by the grantee or his heirs without the consent of the Secretary of the Interior, the same as the restrictions in the patents to the Shawnees.

Com'rs of Miami Co. v. Wan-zop-pe-che, 3 Ind., 364.

SEC. 2764. When used with reference to judicial proceedings in civil matters, the words "levy and sale" are equivalent to the word "execution," and each expression means the subjecting of property to the satisfaction of a judgment. Exemption from "taxation" would include exemption from sale for taxes.

Ibid.

SEC. 2765. The sixth article of the Miami treaty of 1818 (7 Stat. L., 189), provided that the several tracts of land granted thereby to individuals should never be conveyed by the grantees or their heirs without the approbation of the President of the United States. Pursuant to the treaty certain tracts were granted to B., an Indian woman, and afterwards the President, upon her petition, gave his approval to her selling a part of the land and to the division of the rest among her children. She did accordingly sell a part of the land, but shortly afterwards died without having made partition of the residue among her children. *Held*, that the children took the land by descent, and could not therefore convey it, and that a deed of conveyance from themselves was not voidable merely, but void.

Harris v. Spencer, 3 Ind., 494.

SEC. 2766. By the Potawatomi treaty of 1832 (7 Stat. L., 399), the United States agreed to grant to one T. a section of land which should be conveyed to him by patent. The land was to be selected under the direction of the President. The agent appointed by the President reported, January 20, 1836, that he had selected the section, a part of which was the land in question, and the President approved the report, but no patent ever issued to T. One H. had, in 1832, located on the land in question, made improvements, and continued to occupy it, and, in 1841, obtained a patent for it under a preemption right. *Held*, that the treaty did not operate as a grant *in præsenti*, but only as a contract for a future conveyance by patent. *Held*, that H.'s title was complete.

Verden v. Coleman, 4 Ind., 457.

SEC. 2767. Where the act or treaty provides for no other mode of conveyance, the courts incline by construction to make the terms of the act or treaty operate as grants where the language, taken altogether in connection with what may be supposed to have been the intention, will admit of it.

Ibid.

SEC. 2768. Money was paid to the county treasurer to redeem tax-sale certificates of lands sold for taxes, which were Indian lands and not subject to assessment and taxation, and at the time of payment the owner of the land denied the legality of the tax on the ground that the lands were not taxable, and paid the money to prevent tax deeds, which were then due, from being made for said lands. *Held*, that such payment was voluntary and could not be recovered back.

Phillips v. Jefferson Co., 5 Ind., 412.

SEC. 2769. Where land is reserved to an Indian under the Potawatomi treaty of 1826 (7 Stat. L., 295–299) and restricted from sale without the consent of the President, it is a question as to whether a court, after the death of such Indian, can order the land to be sold without the consent of the President.

Crews v. Cleghorn, 13 Ind., 438.

SEC. 2770. Land was granted to A., an Indian, under the Potawatomi treaty of 1826 (7 Stat. L., 295) with restriction on alienation without the approval of the President. A., on June 13, 1836, without the approval of the President, executed and delivered to B. a deed for the land in dispute, but the deed was afterwards, on the 14th of December, 1846, approved by the then President of the United States. When the land was conveyed to B. there was no adverse possession, but in 1843 C. went into possession of the land, and at the time of the approval of the deed held it adversely. *Held*, that the deed from A. to B. could not, without the consent of the President, operate as a conveyance, but that his consent to its execution might be given before or after its execution. Also, that the act of the President, in his approval of the deed, related back and gave it validity from the time of its execution.   *Ashley v. Eberts, 22 Ind., 55.*

SEC. 2771. A section of land to be located under the direction of the President was granted to François Dequindre, under the Potawatomi treaty of October 16, 1826 (7 Stat. L., 295); and after the death of the grantee the proper court, upon petition of the guardian of the grantee's heirs at law, ordered the sale of the unlocated section; and the land having been located by the assignee of the purchaser at such guardian's sale, the proper court ordered a conveyance of the specific land to such assignee, which was made but never approved by the President. *Held*, that by the doctrine of relation, the treaty operated instantly in law as a grant, the subsequent location of the land merely ascertaining the specific thing which was granted. Also, that the approval of the President was not necessary to the validity of the guardian's deed.   *Dequindre v. Williams, 31 Ind., 444.*

SEC. 2772. In 1832 A. settled on a tract of land as a preemptioner and made improvements as required by law. In October, 1832, after A. had settled on the land and made improvements, the United States made a treaty with the Potawatomi Indians (7 Stat. L., 394–399) in which she agreed to select and convey some one, but no particular, section to the chief of the tribe, after it had been surveyed. In 1835 the administration determined that the Indian reservations must be located on lands not claimed by preemptioners. In 1836 the location was made for the chief, embracing the land claimed by A., and on which he resided. In 1839 administration set aside the location so far as it embraced the land in question, and in 1843 issued a patent to A. upon his making proof of his claim. *Held*, that A. has a prior equity, and a right to the legal title.   *Sumner v. Coleman, 23 Ind., 91.*

SEC. 2773. The lands reserved by the Miami treaty of 1838 (7 Stat. L., 569) to the band of Meto-sin-ia and referred to in the treaty of 1840 (7 Stat. L., 582), in which the United States agreed to convey by patent said lands to Me-shing-go-me-sia, in trust for his band, are not subject to taxation by the State. Nor are these lands included in the ninth section of the act of June 21, 1852 (1 G. & H., 70).

                                        Me-shing-go-me-sia v. The State, 36 Ind., 310.

SEC. 2774. Title could not pass to the grantees under the Pottawatomie treaty of August 29, 1821 (7 Stat. L., 218), until the tracts of land were located, as it was stipulated in the treaty that "such tracts shall be located after the said cession is surveyed and in conformity with such surveys as near as may be, and in such manner as the President may direct."

The appellants contend that the title vested in the grantees from the date of the treaty, and it may be that when the lands were located the

426 ARTICLE II—LAND TITLES AND TREATIES.

title of the grantees related back to the date of the treaty. But, however this may be, it may be fairly inferred that the land had been located at the time of the execution of the deed by the children of Pierre Moran to Rufus Downing, and, therefore, that the title was then in said children.   *Steeple v. Downing, 60 Ind., 478.*

SEC. 2775. The land in controversy is a part of one of the two sections granted to the children of Pierre Moran, or Peerish, a Pottawatomie chief, by the treaty of August 29, 1821 (7 Stat. L., 218). These lands, by the terms of the treaty, could not be alienated without the consent of the President of the United States. Rufus Downing, the grantee, died soon after the execution of the deed in question.   *Ibid.*

SEC. 2776. The proposition that as Rufus Downing was dead at the time the deed was approved by the President no title passed thereby, there being no grantee *in esse*, can not be maintained. The title to the land vested in the children of Pierre Moran by the terms of the treaty, without any patent from the United States.   *Ibid.*

SEC. 2777. A conveyance by a grantee under the Pottawatomie treaty of 1821 (7 Stat. L., 218) of a specified tract of land afterward conveyed to him by the United States by patent, vested the title in the grantee, though the latter died prior to the issuing of such patent, and prior to the approval of such conveyance by the President, such approval relating back to the execution of the conveyance. A recital in such conveyance that the lands ceded by such treaty had been located under the direction of the President raises the presumption that such location had been made prior to the execution of such conveyance. The production of a conveyance so approved by the heirs of the grantee is presumptive evidence that it had been properly delivered to the grantee, and no new delivery was necessary.   *Ibid.*

SEC. 2778. As it is not averred that the lands taxed were reserved to or held by the Miami Indians as a tribe, or by any subdivision of such Indians as a band, the case does not come within the rule as to the nontaxability of the lands of certain Miami Indians laid down in Me-shing-go-me-sia *v.* The State (36 Ind., 310).
          The State ex rel. Godfroy v. The Board of Com'rs. of Miami Co., 63 Ind., 497.

SEC. 2779. In an action by the State on the relation of one claiming to be an Indian of a certain tribe holding lands reserved to them in the State of Indiana, pursuant to a treaty with the United States, to compel a board of county commissioners, by mandate, to refund certain alleged illegal taxes assessed against such lands and collected from such Indians the complaint failed to allege that such lands were reserved to such Indians as a tribe or band, and not individually.   *Ibid.*

Sec. 2780. By section 10 of the act of December 21, 1872, relative to the assessment of taxes (1 R. S., 1876, p. 72), lands in the State of Indiana reserved to or for any individual under any treaty between an Indian tribe and the United States are taxable from the date of ratification of such treaty.   *Ibid.*

Sec. 2781. The facts of this case are much like those in the case of Lowry *v.* Weaver (4 McLean, 82), wherein it was held that land granted to John W. Burnet, by the Miami treaty of 1818 (7 Stat. L., 189), it being two sections of land on Flint River in Tippecanoe County, was subject to taxation by the State, and subject to the mode prescribed by State laws for the payment of debts.

Taylor, admr., v. Vandegrift, admr., 126 Ind., 325.

Sec. 2782. The question as to whether these lands were subject to taxation by the State does not depend so much upon the question as to whether the owners hold in fee, or a less estate, as it does upon their tribal relations. That the owners of this land constitute a part of the Miami nation, and have kept up their tribal relations, is shown by the special verdict.   *Board of Comsrs. of Allen Co. v. Simons, 129 Ind., 195.*

Sec. 2783. The conclusion that the lands were not taxable is in seeming conflict with the case of the State ex rel. Godfroy *v.* Board, etc. (63 Ind., 497). That was an action by the State, on the relation of Godfroy, to compel the Board of Commissioners of Miami County, by writ of *mandamus*, to refund certain taxes alleged to have been illegally assessed and collected. It was held that mandamus was not the proper remedy. It was also held that the complaint was bad, for the further reason that it did not allege that the land upon which the tax had been assessed was reserved to the Indians as a band and not individually; but the question of the effect of the ordinance of 1787 upon the lands assessed was not decided, and, so far as the court knows, was not considered.   *Ibid.*

Sec. 2784. The lands described in the complaint in this case were not subject to taxation during the period for which they were assessed. What the status of this land is now the court is not called upon to decide.   *Ibid.*

Sec. 2785. The question as to whether the Miami lands in Indiana are exempt from taxation under the treaties and laws of the United States is a Federal question, and it was expressly held in the case of Wau-pe-man-qua *v.* Aldrich (28 Fed. Rep., 489) that they were not subject to taxation, and that the particular tax involved in the suit was void.   *Ibid.*

Sec. 2786. Certain lands which by the Miami treaty of 1818 (7 Stat. L., 189) were granted to the principal chief of the Miami nation in fee simple are not liable to taxation while the owners of the same keep up their tribal relations with the Miami nation. The third article of the ordinance of 1787, relating to the lands and property of the Indians, is in force in Indiana. The language of said clause is broad enough to cover the claims of individual Indians and titles held in fee simple acquired by treaty or otherwise from the United States. The case of the State ex rel. *v.* Board, etc. (63 Ind., 497), distinguished.   *Ibid.*

SEC. 2787. No effort appears to have been made to tax the lands in question prior to 1871. Long acquiescence in the imposition of taxes, unexplained, raises a presumption of a surrender of the privilege of exemption. It not appearing in the special verdict that these lands, prior to that date, had been assessed for taxes, it should be assumed for the purpose of this case that they had not paid taxes up to that time. If, for any reason, they had been legally exempt from taxation between the years 1818 and 1871, the burden of showing that something had occurred between those dates which rendered them liable to taxation rested upon the appellant.   *Ibid.*

SEC. 2788. Under article 3, of the ordinance of 1787 (Rev. Stat., 1881, p. 1430), providing that the lands of the Indians should "never be taken from them without their consent," and under the agreement of the State of Indiana, when admitted into the Union, to protect them in that right, the lands of the Indians reserved or allotted to them by the United States Government are exempt from taxation so long as such lands are held and acquired through such tribal relations; but when any of such lands pass to a white man they are released from such tribal conditions and are subject to taxation, even though they be subsequently reconveyed to Indians.   *Revoir v. The State ex rel. Branyan, 137 Ind., 332.*

SEC. 2789. In an action of right the defendant plead that he held under one Isaac Antaya, a genuine half-breed, who was entitled as such to an interest in the land in controversy, but whose right and claim was not adjudicated in the partition suit in 1841, nor at any other time. *Held*, a demurrer thereto was properly sustained, as the answer set out no facts and circumstances showing when he derived title under Antaya, nor why the interest or claim of the latter was not heard. No reason is shown why the decree should be opened, save the unexplained fact that the interest was not adjudicated.

Kilbourne v. Lockman, 8 Iowa (Clarke), 380.

SEC. 2790. A deed duly acknowledged, dated August 14, 1860, from one of the reservees mentioned in the sixth section of the treaty with the half-breeds of the Kansas tribe, June 3, 1825 (7 Stat. L., 244), to lands reserved thereby to said Indians, it not being the mode of conveyance provided by section 2 of the act of Congress May 26, 1860 (U. S. Stats. of 1860, p. 21), was void and was properly rejected as evidence in an action brought by the grantor therein to recover possession of land therein described.   *Stevens v. Smith, 2 Kans., 243.*

SEC. 2791. At the time of the execution of the deed, the title to the lands in question was, by the treaty and section 1 of the act of May 26, 1860, vested in the then living reservees, and the Secretary of the Interior was, by section 2, authorized to sell the same for the benefit of the reservees, the proceeds of which, under section 3, were to be paid to the reservees or applied for their benefit. The treaty and this act of cession were intended to give the reservees full and complete title, but with restrictions as to mode of conveyance. The removal of these restrictions by joint resolution of Congress July 17, 1862, can not be construed to make a void conveyance valid. *Ibid.*

SEC. 2792. From the lands ceded to the United States by the treaty of 1825 with the Kansas Indians (7 Stat. L., 244) reservations of one mile square were made for each of the half-breeds of the Kansas Nation, including one to Lavonture, the son of Francis Lavonture.

Brown & Brown v. Belmarde, 3 Kans., 41.

SEC. 2793. From the death of Lavonture in 1847 to the passage of the act of Congress May 26, 1860, the whole title to the land in question was in the Government, and that act operated as an original grant to certain reservees and the "heirs of deceased reservees" mentioned therein. *Ibid.*

SEC. 3794. Section 2 of the act of May 26, 1860 (12 Stat. L., 21), provides that in case any of the Kansas Indian reservees or their heirs shall not desire to occupy the lands, the Secretary of the Interior may sell them for their benefit; and the third section directs what shall be done with the proceeds of such sales. July 17, 1862, Congress passed a joint resolution providing: "That sections 2 and 3 'of the above act,' and so much of the first section as authorized the Secretary of the Interior to decide what persons are heirs to deceased reservees, as mentioned therein, be and the same is hereby repealed." *Ibid.*

SEC. 2795. After the treaty of 1825 with the Kansas Indians (7 Stat. L., 244) Lavonture, having but a life estate to the extent of the Indian title in section 9, should he die with or without issue the whole title to that section would vest in the United States. The record shows that he did die in 1847 or 1848. Therefore, from that time to the passage of the act of May 26, 1860, the whole title to the lands in controversy was in the Government. That act operated as an original grant to the persons who shall be ascertained to be meant by the word "heirs" used therein. *Ibid.*

SEC. 2796. Had Lavonture been living at the time of the passage of the act, the title would have vested in him; and if he had died the next day, there can be no question that his heirs would have been determined by the law of the State at the time of his death. The persons who, under the laws of Kansas, would have inherited the real estate of Lavonture had he died on the 26th of May, 1860, are the persons to whose benefit the grant made by the act of Congress of that date inured.   *Ibid.*

Sec. 2797. If the land in controversy was not, under the laws of the United States or treaties with the Wyandottes, subject to sale, that would have been a good reason for setting the sale aside.

White-Crow v. White-Wing, 3 Kans., 276.

Sec. 2798. The test of absolute conveyance as to Indians, taking in severalty, is the intention of the parties evidenced by provisions of patent and treaty, considered in the light of existing circumstances. The Shawnee treaty of May 10, 1854 (10 Stat. L., 1053), provides that "Congress may hereafter provide for issuing to such of the Shawnees as may make separate selections patents for the same, with such guards and restrictions as may seem advisable for their protection therein."

Blue Jacket v. Com. Johnson County, 3 Kans., 299.

Sec. 2799. The Congressional action contemplated by the Shawnee treaty of May 10, 1854 (10 Stat. L., 1053), is found in the act of March 3, 1859 (11 Stat. L., 399), authorizing the Secretary of the Interior to cause patents therefor to issue upon such conditions and limitations and under such guards or restrictions as may be prescribed by the Secretary. The Government assented to the selection of lands, by some, in severalty; when so selected, the title of the tribe of perpetual use and occupation thereto vested in the Indian selecting. Had it been intended that he should not acquire a greater title, further provision would have been unnecessary, but in addition patent might be issued. The object of this provision was not to enable the Government to convey the ultimate title—it could do that without consent; but it was to bind, and the Government was thereby bound to nothing except that *when* it was patented it was to see that the Indian was properly protected.   *Ibid.*

Sec. 2800. By the act of March 3, 1859 (11 Stat. L., 399), Congress provided for issuing patents to the Shawnees holding in severalty, the object of which patenting was to convey the ultimate title, and which in terms conveyed the lands in fee simple, and contained a restriction "that said lands shall never be sold or conveyed by the grantee or his heirs without the consent of the Secretary of the Interior for the time being."   *Ibid.*

Sec. 2801. Where a district of country is held in common by an Indian tribe, with or without a patent, a patent in fee simple issued pursuant to a treaty which does or does not give the Government alone the right to purchase from them, such tribe holds the mere right of perpetual possession and enjoyment—this, though the words of the treaty or patent as between *individual* Indians or whites and the Government be sufficient to convey title absolutely.

Ibid.

SEC. 2802. The restriction on alienation in the patents to the Shawnees does not operate as a condition, because a violation thereof does not affect his title, nor as a limitation on his title, for the whole title of the Government by the patent passed; but it operates as a personal disability, similar to that of a minor, which the Government was competent to impose. *Ibid.*

SEC. 2803. The tribal organization of the Shawnees is still maintained, not, however, to control lands patented in severalty. Such selections are not contiguous, but widely scattered and interspersed by lands of whites, and it was contemplated that the patentees might dispose of some of their lands.

Ibid.

SEC. 2804. There is no express prohibition against taxing the lands of the Shawnees patented to them under the act of March 3, 1859, or the personal property of the Indians residing upon them. It was competent for the Government to have prohibited taxation by the State of these lands, at least while remaining the property of members of the tribe. *Ibid.*

SEC. 2805. The treaties made with Indian tribes under the administration of Commissioner Manypenny may be divided into, *first*, those with no restriction; *second*, those prohibiting alienation without consent of Government; *third*, those exempting lands from levy, sale, execution, or forfeiture; and, *fourth*, those which, in addition, exempt the lands from taxation. In the last class the word "taxation" is added to the terms expressing exemption used in the preceding classes. The treaties of the first three classes had been negotiated prior to the drawing of those of the fourth. The word "taxation," used in the fourth class, was intended to prohibit what had not been provided against in the other classes. Exemption from alienation, therefore, was not intended to include exemption from taxation. *Ibid.*

SEC. 2806. The Secretary of the Interior, having the power, and not having inserted the word "taxation" in the clause of exemptions, it was not the intention that the lands in question should be exempt from taxation. *Ibid.*

SEC. 2807. The words "levy, sale, and forfeiture," used in the treaty with the Miamis (10 Stat. L., 1093) have reference to judicial proceedings alone. The "head rights" of the Miamis are taxable under the State laws. *Comsrs. of Miami Co. v. Wan-zop-pe-che, 3 Kans., 364.*

SEC. 2808. Taxes, like a judgment, are a mere lien upon land to be enforced by a sale, and the title passes and can pass by sale alone; there can be no redemption until after sale. A tax sale is in no sense a forfeiture within the meaning of that word as used in the treaty with the Miamis, and that word can have no application to taxation.

Ibid.

SEC. 2809. In an action by one Shawnee Indian against another for partition of land, which had been patented by the United States to an ancestor, another Shawnee, the record failing to set out the patent or to show under what treaty it was issued. Held, that the court can not presume that it contained restrictions. Also, that the fact that the parties are Shawnees did not deprive the district court, nor does it forbid the supreme court, from exercising jurisdiction either as to parties or subject-matter.   *Swartzel v. Rogers, 3 Kans., 374.*

SEC. 2810. The Kickapoo treaty provides (13 Stat. L., 623) that "none of the lands shall be subject to taxation until the patents have been issued therefor." And hence those who claim that the lands are taxable, notwithstanding the treaty, must claim that this portion of the treaty is a nullity; that it is unconstitutional and void, and that the Government had no power to make it.   *Parker v. Winsor, 5 Kans., 362.*

SEC. 2811. Neither the legal or equitable title to the Kickapoo lands in question has passed. The legal title has not passed because the patent has not been issued, and the equitable title has not passed because the land has not been paid for, and because it is clearly the intention of the parties, as expressed in the treaty, that such title shall not pass until the land is fully paid for. The improvements of a fixed and permanent nature, attached to the soil, are not taxable.   *Ibid.*

SEC. 2812. The Kickapoo Indians had the legal power to hold their lands forever without said lands becoming subject to taxation. The United States had the power, with the consent of the Indians, to purchase this land and hold it forever without becoming subject to taxation. And so long as the Indians or the United States, or both jointly, hold the legal and equitable title to the land, it is exempt from taxation, although there may be a contract between the United States, the Indians, and some individual or corporation, that the United States will at some future time convey the land to such individual or corporation, provided certain things shall be done before that time.   *Ibid.*

SEC. 2813. The State of Kansas can not tax Indian lands, although held by the Indians in severalty, and under patents from the United States, so long as the Indians continue their tribal organizations. (The Kansas Indians, 5 Wallace, 737; overruling the cases of Blue Jacket and Wan-zop-pe-che, 3 Kansas, 299, 364.)   *Ibid.*

SEC. 2814. The legislature and the executive departments of the State of Kansas have recognized the power of the Federal Government, by treaty, to exempt Indian lands from taxation; notably so by the act approved by the governor February 10, 1864.

Ibid.

SEC. 2815. The Blue Jacket case was taken to the Supreme Court of the United States (The Kansas Indians in the case of the Miamis, 5 Wall., 759), and that court went further than the supreme court of

Kansas did, not only holding that the Government, by treaty, had the power to exempt such lands from taxation, but that it had actually done so, holding that the words "levy and sale," as there used, had a broader signification than that given to them by the supreme court of Kansas, holding that these words mean, respectively, a levy of taxes and a sale for taxes, as well as a levy of an execution and a sale on execution, thereby overruling the decision of the supreme court of Kansas in this respect. *Ibid.*

SEC. 2816. In the Blue Jacket case (3 Kans., 368) the court commented upon various treaties exempting lands from taxation, levy, sale, or forfeiture. Elaborate argument was made to prove that the words "levy, sale, and forfeiture," as used in the Miami treaty, do not mean, respectively, a levy of taxes, sale for taxes, or a forfeiture for taxes. But nowhere does it seem to have occurred to the court that the Government had no power to make such a treaty or to exempt such lands from taxation. *Ibid.*

SEC. 2817. The supreme court of Kansas, in the case of Miami County *v.* Wan-zop-pe-che (3 Kans., 364), seems to have recognized the power of the United States to exempt Indian lands from taxation. *Ibid.*

SEC. 2818. Where an individual not a member of the tribe attempted to purchase of a half-breed Sac and Fox Indian lands which were allotted to such Indians under the treaty of October 1, 1859, with the Sac and Fox tribe (15 Stat. L., 467), *held* that a deed made in pursuance of such attempted purchase was a nullity and conveyed no title. Also that provisions of the treaty of 1867 with such tribe (15 Stat. L., 498), recognizing valid sales theretofore made, in no wise affects or refers to or recognizes such void conveyances. *Pennock v. Monroe, 5 Kans., 578.*

SEC. 2819. The condition of the lands reserved to the Shawnees by the treaty of 1854 is anomalous. That instrument makes no provision for a case of double allotments, such a contingency not having suggested itself to parties.

Hale v. Wilder, 8 Kans. (Webb), 545. Same, 8 Kans. (Dassler), 365.

SEC. 2820. Lands that were allotted in severalty to members of the Shawnee tribe, under the second article of the treaty of May 10, 1854 (10 Stat. L., 1053), and afterwards abandoned for other lands, do not become a part of the "surplus lands" which were set apart for the absentee Indians by the President of the United States. *Ibid.*

SEC. 2821. Certain tracts of land in Douglas County, Kans., were not subject to the location of what was known as a "Wyandotte float," secured to certain reservees by the treaty made with the Wyandottes in 1842 (11 Stat. L., 581) and amended by the treaty of 1855 (10 Stat. L., 1159), until July 9, 1858.   And an attempted location of such float on the 8th of May, 1857, was a nullity and conferred no rights.

McAlpin v. Henshaw, 6 Kans., 176.

SEC. 2822. The laws of Kansas formed the law of descent at the death of the Ottawa patentee in 1863, and that law must govern the decision of this case, and not the common law.   *McCullagh v. Allen, 10 Kans., 150.*

SEC. 2823. The Ottawa treaty of 1862 (12 Stat. L., 1237) stipulates that at the expiration of five years the members of the tribe shall become citizens of the United States and their tribal relations dissolved. Meanwhile their lands are to be disposed of by special allotments and sales in various ways.   Some of the stipulations of the treaty are inconsistent with the idea that the reservation is without the limits of the State, while others seem clearly to recognize the laws of Kansas as in force from that time forward.   *Ibid.*

SEC. 2824. As the legal evidence of plaintiff's title was not complete until after the approval of the deed by the Secretary of the Interior, it may be claimed that the plaintiff had only an equitable title up to that time; but it must be admitted that such equitable title was complete, absolute, and perfect, and that land held by such title has everywhere been held to be taxable.   *McMahon v. Welsh, 11 Kans., 280.*

SEC. 2825. Though the land in question was patented to Harley Coon, an incompetent Wyandotte, Mary Nichols, to whom the land descended, must be presumed to be competent and have the unrestricted right of alienation.   The restriction on alienation was not intended to run with the land; and it must have been intended that if land descended from an incompetent to a competent Indian he should have the power to alien it at will.   *Ibid.*

SEC. 2826. Under the treaty of 1855 (10 Stat. L., 1159) the title conveyed by the United States to the competent Wyandottes was a complete, absolute, and unconditional title in fee simple.   This title the Indians could, of course, convey whenever and to whomsoever they chose.   The incompetent Indians unquestionably held the same kind of title to their lands as did the competents, except that the incompetents could not sell or convey their lands for five years without the consent of the President of the United States.   This restriction seems to be purely *personal* to the incompetent Indians and does not affect their title to the land.   It was simply an incapacity to sell, similar to the disability of a minor to sell his lands.   *Ibid.*

SEC. 2827. If the sale and conveyance from Mary Nichols to plaintiff and the Wyandotte treaty of 1867 are valid, the lands were subject to taxation in the year 1870, and the taxes complained of are legal.   If said sale, conveyance, and treaty are void the plaintiff has no title or interest in the land, and for such reason has no right to the remedy of injunction to enjoin the collection of taxes.

Ibid.

SEC. 2828. Under the Wyandotte treaty of January 31, 1855 (10 Stat. L., 1159), a certain piece of land was patented to Harley Coon, an incompetent Wyandotte Indian. In 1857 said patentee died and the land descended to Mary Nichols, his sole heir, who, in 1864, sold the land in question to plaintiff and delivered to him a regular warranty deed therefor. Under the treaty of February 23, 1867 (15 Stat. L., 513), the sale was approved in 1871 by the Secretary of the Interior. In 1870 taxes were levied on said land by the State. *Held* that the plaintiff was not entitled to an injunction to restrain the collection of said taxes.

Ibid.

SEC. 2829. The special clause in the Miami treaty of 1854, which is claimed to create exemption from taxation, declares that "the lands so patented shall not be liable to levy, sale, execution, or forfeiture." These words were construed by this court in 3 Kans., 364, as referring simply to judicial proceedings; but the Supreme Court of the United States, in 5 Wall., 760, held that "such construction would be an exceedingly narrow one, whereas liberal rules of construction are adopted in reference to Indian treaties."

Miami Co. v. Brackenridge, 12 Kans., 114.

SEC. 2830. In the case of the State of New Jersey *v.* Wilson (7 Cranch, 164), it was held that the exemption from taxation was a condition that followed the lands. In that case, which involved the exemption of certain Delaware Indian lands, it was found that there was an express contract by the State that the lands should not thereafter be taxable, a grant of certain nontaxable lands in purchase of other property. This exemption increased the value of the consideration and was itself a part of the consideration. In the case at bar the State is no party to the contract.

Ibid.

SEC. 2831. That the lands of the Miamis, while they remained the property of the reservees, under the treaty of 1854 (10 Stat. L., 1093), were exempt from taxation is settled by the decision of the Supreme Court of the United States in the case of the Miamis (5 Wall., 760), reversing the judgment of the supreme court of Kansas (3 Kans., 364). This exemption did not attach to the land, qualifying the estate, and inuring to the benefit of all subsequent holders of the title, but was simply a personal privilege of the Indian owners.

Ibid.

SEC. 2832. Lands patented to the reservees under the Miami treaty of 1854 (10 Stat. L., 1093) are not exempt from taxation after the title has passed from the Indian owners. Where exemption from taxation is based upon the use to which the lands are put, when the use ceases the exemption also ceases.

Ibid.

SEC. 2833. While it may be doubted whether an Indian owner of land held under treaty stipulation can be compelled to pay for improvements under the "occupying claimant act," yet this immunity, if it exists, is a personal privilege, and the grantee of such owner succeeds only to the title to the land, and has no better right to improvements made by an occupying claimant than any other owner of real estate.   *Krause v. Means, 12 Kans., 335.*

SEC. 2834. Neither the title nor possession of the Indian owner, secured by treaty, can be disturbed by State legislation; and if Mrs. Goodell were plaintiff in the action, seeking to recover possession, it is probable she would be entitled to both land and improvements. But this property protection, guaranteed to the Indian owner, is a personal privilege, and does not run with the land. Mrs. G. has parted with the title, and the protection which the Federal law threw around this land has ceased.   *Ibid.*

SEC. 2835. The land in dispute was assigned to Julia Goodell, a member of the Sac and Fox tribe of the Mississippi, under the treaty of 1859 (15 Stat. L., 467). The deed made by her in 1862 to Fuller, a white man, was, under the treaty, a nullity and conveyed no title. In 1863 Fuller conveyed to Krause, who entered and made valuable improvements. By virtue of the treaty of 1867 (15 Stat. L., 498) the Government conveyed the land in fee simple to Mrs. Goodell, thus abrogating the restraint on alienation imposed by the old treaty. She then conveyed the fee to defendant in error, who brought ejectment and recovered, and who now claims both land and improvements, and denies the right of plaintiff in error to the benefit of the occupying claimant act. That Krause brings his case within the letter and spirit of the law is evident, and he must recover.

Ibid.

SEC. 2836. In accordance with the provisions of the Shawnee treaty of 1854 (10 Stat. L., 1053), and of the act of Congress March 3, 1859 (11 Stat. L., 430), a patent was issued to Thomas Big-Knife, a Shawnee Indian, for the land in controversy containing a restrictive clause on alienation without the consent of the Secretary of the Interior. In 1864 Big-Knife executed and delivered a deed to Scoffins, which was never approved by the Secretary and which was therefore void.

Scoffins v. Grandstaff, 12 Kans., 467.

SEC. 2837. On the 1st of December, 1868, Thomas Big Knife conveyed the land in controversy to McBride, which deed was duly approved by the Secretary of the Interior January 30, 1869, and was a valid conveyance.   *Ibid.*

SEC. 2838. The Wyandotte treaty of 1867 (15 Stat. L., 517) provides for the removal of all restrictions on alienation of lands patented to the incompetents, except in certain specified cases, and in so far as it simply removes the restrictions it is prospective in its operations, and can have no bearing upon prior attempted alienations.

Frederick v. Gray, 12 Kans., 518.

SEC. 2839. It would seem that the parties to the Wyandotte treaty of 1855 intended, after dividing the Indians into competent and incompetent classes, that the restrictions imposed on the latter class should be absolute, and not dependent upon the changes of the future. The competency was determined by the classification, and the restriction followed the classification. It was not during insanity or orphanage that the restriction lasted.   *Ibid.*

SEC. 2840. Each of the provisions of the Wyandotte treaty of 1855 against alienation would, under the "enlarged rules of construction adopted in reference to Indian treaties," have avoided the attempted alienation by sheriff's deed. (The Kansas Indians, 5 Wall., 760; Miami Co. *v.* Wan-zop-pe-che, 3 Kans., 364; Pennock *v.* Monroe, 5 Kans., 578.)   *Ibid.*

SEC. 2841. A sheriff's sale of the lands of an incompetent orphan patentee under the Wyandotte treaty of 1855 (10 Stat. L., 1159) could not, by the approval of the Secretary of the Interior, be made valid so as to divest a purchaser from the heirs of the patentee of the title he had acquired by such purchase.   *Ibid.*

SEC. 2842. By the Wyandotte treaty of January 31, 1855 (10 Stat. L., 1159) the lands belonging to the tribe were allotted in severalty. The patentees were divided into two classes—competents and incompetents. In the latter class were placed the orphans, idiots, and insane. Certain restrictions were, in pursuance of the treaty, incorporated into the patents to the incompetents. *Held*, in the case of an orphan patentee, that the restrictions did not cease to be operative when the orphan became of age, but continued so long as the title remained in the patentee.   *Ibid.*

SEC. 2843. When it was provided by the Osage treaty of 1865 (14 Stat. L., 687) that the Osage "half-breeds, not to exceed 25 in number, who have improvements on the north half of the lands sold to the United States shall have a patent, said half-breeds to be designated by the chief of the tribe," the designation of such chiefs and headmen was conclusive as to the right of the party designated to receive a patent, and in a suit brought by the grantee of such patentee to recover possession of the land no inquiry could be made into the question whether such patentee was a half-breed of the Osage tribe, or whether he had any improvements on the north half of the land sold to the United States.   *Lownsberry v. Rakestraw, 14 Kans., 151.*

SEC. 2844. Where it was provided by the Osage treaty of 1865 (14 Stat. L., 687) that the 25 half-breeds should receive a patent for 80 acres each, "to include as far as practicable their improvements, all of said lands to be selected by the parties, subject to the approval of the Secretary of the Interior," a selection of an 80-acre tract by one of the designated half-breeds, and the approval of that selection by the Secretary, gave to such half-breed a vested interest in the land, and was conclusive against all persons claiming title acquired subsequently to the selection, and the holder of subsequently acquired title could not show as a defense to an action brought by the grantee of such half-breed that such half-breed never had any improvements on the land.   *Ibid.*

SEC. 2845. Where the land selected was incorrectly reported to the Secretary of the Interior, the mistake could be corrected, even after patent issued, and the correct selection submitted to his approval; but where the party making the selection is aware of the mistake, makes no objection thereto or effort to have it corrected, and assents to its submission to the Secretary for approval, such action was virtually a selection of the tract reported to the Secretary.   *Ibid.*

SEC. 2846. Prior to April 10, 1869, Rakestraw's possession and occupancy gave him no rights in the land. He was simply a naked trespasser, whose possession, no matter how long continued, could never ripen into a title. (Wood *v.* The M. K. & T. Ry. Co., 11 Kans., 323.) It is therefore, so far as respects the acquiring by other parties of any title from the United States, under the provisions of the Osage treaty of 1865, as though the land were wholly unoccupied and vacant.
        Ibid.

SEC. 2847. The Osage treaty of 1865 (14 Stat. L., 687) contemplated the possibility that some selections might not cover the party's improvements; hence the mere fact that the selection did not cover the party's improvements would not necessarily defeat the selection.
        Ibid.

SEC. 2848. The only parties who at the time had any rights or interest in the land in question were the Osage Indians, the Government, and Tinker. No one else could question the validity of the selection, and whether Tinker had any improvements on the land at the time he made his selection, or not, is a matter into which Rakestraw, holding a subsequently acquired title, can not be permitted to inquire.
        Ibid.

SEC. 2849. Where a treaty provides that patents are to be issued for the lands in fee simple, which implies a full title free from any restrictions upon alienation, this expression, when used in Indian treaties, carries no such necessary implication.   *Clark v. Libbey, 14 Kans., 435.*

SEC. 2850. Lands patented to the chiefs, councilmen, and headmen of the Ottawas under the first clause of article 3 of the treaty of 1862 (12 Stat. L., 1239), were inalienable to others than Ottawa Indians during the five years succeeding the ratification of that treaty.
        Ibid.

SEC. 2851. A deed made by an Ottawa Indian for land patented to him under the treaty of 1862 (12 Stat. L., 1237), conveying such land to another Ottawa Indian at any time prior to July 4, 1867, without the consent of the Secretary of the Interior, was absolutely void, and could not create even an equitable estate in the lands in favor of the grantee, even though he had paid the purchase money.

Clark v. Akers, 16 Kans., 166.

SEC. 2852. Where an owner of land is legally disabled from selling, conveying, or incumbering it, except with the consent of the Secretary of the Interior, and where the law provides that "any conveyance or incumbrance of said lands done or suffered," except as provided, "shall be null and void," and such owner executes a deed without the consent of the Secretary of the Interior, and subsequently, after all disabilities and restrictions are removed, said owner executes another deed to another grantee for said land, the execution of the second deed, and "willingly putting the same in use as having been made in good faith," is not such a legal fraud upon the first grantee as to prevent the second deed from having full force and effect.   *Ibid.*

SEC. 2853. Early sold the lands in controversy before he became a citizen of the United States, and without the consent of the Secretary of the Interior, and the deeds were therefore void.   *Ibid.*

SEC. 2854. The act of July 28, 1866 (14 Stat. L., 309), "for the relief of the trustees and stewards of the mission church of the Wyandotte Indians," appears upon its face to be a grant to a church organization among and of the Wyandotte Indians, and made by virtue of the governmental protection over these wards of the nation.   *Sarahass v. Armstrong, 16 Kans., 192.*

SEC. 2855. The term "exclusive possession" may imply a repudiation of a cotenant's rights, and therefore indicate an ouster, or it may be used to denote a full and complete and actual possession irrespective of the title under which it is held.   *Squires v. Clark, 17 Kans., 84.*

SEC. 2856. The land in question was originally a part of the Pottawatomie Reservation, and under the provisions of the treaty of 1861 (12 Stat. L., 1192) was allotted to John Riley, a Cherokee by birth, but a Pottawatomie by adoption, and the proper certificate for said land was duly issued to him by the Commissioner of Indian Affairs. Riley had no power to sell or incumber the land, except in a certain manner and under certain terms and conditions. He died and the land descended to his heirs. If the restriction upon the sale of said land was merely personal to Riley, then of course his widow could sell and convey her interest in the land, and in that case the deed that she and her second husband, David Bostick, made to the Lazelles would be considered valid. Contra if the said restriction were not merely personal to Riley.   *Oliver v. Forbes, 17 Kans., 113.*

SEC. 2857. If by a legal fiction, under article 8 of the Pottawatomie treaty of 1867 (15 Stat. L., 531), John Riley, because of his death, was to be considered a citizen of the United States and his estate as that of a citizen, and if by a like legal fiction, under article 6 of the same treaty, his wife and children were to be considered citizens, then the deed executed in 1868 by his widow, Mary Bostick, to the Olivers, must be considered as valid and binding.   *Ibid.*

SEC. 2858. If the patent to Riley was legally issued, then it should have been issued, at the latest, as early as August, 1868, at the time when the treaty of 1867 took effect, which was before Mary Bostick executed the deed to the Olivers; and it is a general rule of law that when a patent is issued, it relates back to the earliest moment when it ought to have been issued.   *Ibid.*

SEC. 2859. If the patent issued in 1870 to Riley for the land in controversy was valid, it was so merely because it was in confirmation of preexisting rights, and not because it created any new rights. And every right existing at the time it was issued, existed at the time and before Mary Bostick and her husband executed the deed to the Olivers. From the time she executed said deed until the patent was issued, nothing transpired to give her any greater rights, powers, or privileges than she previously possessed.   *Ibid.*

SEC. 2860. Where George files his petition alleging he was an occupant of certain lands ceded in trust to the United States by the Cherokee treaty of 1866 (14 Stat. L., 799), and sets forth the fact showing he was entitled to buy the same at its appraised value, and would have obtained a patent therefor except for the false testimony of Phillips, and the corruption and bribery of the commissioners of appraisal, as well as the arbitrary action of the Secretary of the Interior, whereby the lands were awarded and patented to Phillips, the petition is fatally defective if it fails to show that G. paid or offered to pay the United States for the lands, and fails to state what proceedings were taken by G. to contest the right of P. to the lands in controversy prior to the issuance of the patent.   *Phillips v. George, 17 Kans., 419.*

SEC. 2861. Where George set up a claim to certain lands under the Cherokee treaty of July 19, 1866 (14 Stat. L., 799), which he alleges have been awarded and patented to Phillips under article 19 of said treaty upon false testimony, and through bribery and corruption of officials of the United States, the former may come into the courts of the State and litigate the claim, and, upon the proper showing, a patent obtained thus fraudulently by Phillips will inure to George, if he be entitled to recover the lands.   *Ibid.*

SEC. 2862. Under the Cherokee treaty of 1866, no person can obtain title to any of the lands ceded to the United States until a sum of money is paid therefor, except certain Cherokee Indians are entitled to head rights under article 19. If George had complied in every other respect with the provisions of article 17, except paying or offering to pay for the lands, he would not have been entitled to receive a patent.   *Ibid.*

SEC. 2863. Where Hurr, a councilman of the Ottawa tribe, makes a warranty deed to Kalloch for a consideration, under article 3 of the Ottawa treaty of 1862 (12 Stat. L., 1237), which deed is null and void at the time of its execution, and said H., after becoming a citizen of the United States by the terms of the treaty, executes a quitclaim deed to Clark, and thereafter Clark delivers to Hurr, voluntarily and without any consideration, a written agreement to the effect that he will notify certain parties who claim to have title to said lands from H. that he has the same, and that he will offer to protect their title thereto; but if said parties neglect to purchase the title of C. within sixty days, then C. is to be released from any obligation to convey the title to said parties, such agreement is a promise for which there is no consideration and can not be enforced at law. Such agreement under such circumstances is no defense to an action brought by C. against the grantee of K. to recover possession of the land deeded to C by K.   *Clark v. Libbey, 17 Kans., 634.*

SEC. 2864. An allottee under the Ottawa treaty of 1862 (12 Stat. L., 1237), who was only 16 years of age when the treaty of 1867 (15 Stat. L., 513) took effect, was, nevertheless, entitled, under the provisions of article 17 of the latter treaty, to a patent for the land previously allotted to him as soon as he became of age, and when he so became of age, all the restrictions imposed by the former treaty upon his power to alienate his land were removed.

Campbell v. Paramore, 17 Kans., 639.

SEC. 2865. The meaning of the word " tribe," as used in the Ottawa treaty of 1867 (15 Stat. L., 517), evidently means the *members* of the tribe, *and all such members*, and the pronoun "their" evidently means the same thing. Said clause does not provide for issuing patents at the time of making the treaty, or at any particular time; but it provides for issuing patents at some indefinite time in the future—that is, any time in the future. At any time hereafter " patents in fee simple shall be given" "to all who have come of age." And reading the clause in this way, patents should issue to all the allottees of the tribe who are of age, and to all others as they become of age.   *Ibid.*

SEC. 2866. The Ottawa treaty of 1867 (15 Stat. L., 517) evidently intended to remove the restrictions from all of the allottees under the treaty of 1862 who were members of the Ottawa tribe of Indians, and probably did not intend to remove the restrictions from such of the allottees as were not members of said tribe.   *Ibid.*

SEC. 2867. The land in controversy was originally a part of the Osage reserve, but was afterwards, under the provisions of article 14 of the Osage treaty of 1865 (14 Stat. L., 687), allotted to a certain Osage half-breed who subsequently sold it, and the occupying claimant has been in possession ever since. The court below erred in allowing certain purchase money, as the "occupying claimant" act can not have the effect to require the second purchaser under the circumstances to pay said purchase money.   *Lemert v. Barnes, 18 Kans., 9.*

SEC. 2868. Not merely the provision of the patents to issue to the Sac and Fox half-breeds, by article 17 of the treaty of 1867, but the general object and purview of the entire treaty is in conflict with any idea that after said last treaty was proclaimed the lands allotted under article 10 of the treaty of 1859, and patented under article 17 of the new treaty, were to continue to be inalienable. The said lands are, therefore, taxable.   *Comsrs. of Franklin Co., v. Pennock, 18 Kans., 579.*

SEC. 2869. An Indian, under disability to convey his lands without the consent of the Secretary of the Interior, can not of himself make a valid dedication of a portion of said lands to the public for use as a highway; nor can any dedication be presumed by any user of the public highway, or from his acts and conduct in reference thereto.
        The State of Kansas v. O'Laughlin, 19 Kans., 504.

SEC. 2870. The deed dated July 29, 1867, by which Masko, an Ottawa Indian, conveyed the land patented to him under the treaty of 1862 (12 Stat. L., 1237), with restriction on alienation, was valid by virtue of the provisions of the Ottawa treaty of 1867 (15 Stat. L., 513).   *Baldwin v. Squires, 20 Kans., 280.*

SEC. 2871. An Indian owner of land, held under treaty stipulations against alienation, can not be compelled to pay for improvements under the occupying claimant act. The land in controversy was allotted to Susan Maynes, a Pottawatomie woman, under the treaty of 1861 (12 Stat. L., 1191), and was subsequently patented to Anthony F. Navarre under the supposed authority of the treaty of 1867 (15 Stat. L., 531). Navarre conveyed the land by deed, June 25, 1870, to George W. Veale, who subsequently conveyed to others. *Held* that the patent to Navarre was void and that plaintiff was the owner of the land, and the order of the court below granting to the defendants the benefit of the occupying claimant act is reversed.
        Mayne v. Veale, 20 Kans., 374.

SEC. 2872. In a conflict between the law of the State and a treaty of the United States in regard to Indian lands in the State the former must give way. Neither the title nor possession of the Indian owner, secured by treaty, can be disturbed by State legislation, and the occupying-claimant act has no application in this case.
        Ibid.

SEC. 2873. Where a member of the Ottawa tribe of Indians, who, if slfe had lived until after the issuance of patents, would have been entitled to receive one for 80 acres of land under the Ottawa treaty of 1862 (12 Stat. L., 1237), died in the fall of 1862, at the time of her death had an inheritable estate in such lands, which descended under the laws of the State to her heirs.   *Clark v. Lord, 20 Kans., 390.*

SEC. 2874. The restriction upon the alienation of lands reserved and granted to members of the Ottawa tribe contained in article 7 of the treaty of 1862 (12 Stat. L., 1237) do not apply to the heirs of deceased allottees.   *Ibid.*

SEC. 2875. The restriction on alienation is personal, and is not intended to bind the heirs.   While by the terms of the treaty the lands are inalienable in the hands of the original patentee, except as otherwise provided, on the death of such patentee they descend under the laws of the State to the heirs, and in their hands there are no restrictions on the conveyance of the lands so inherited.   *Ibid.*

SEC. 2876. The issuance of a patent is a ministerial act; and a clause inserted therein, not authorized by law, is void

Ibid.

SEC. 2877. The decision of the court below in Maynes *v.* Veale (20 Kans., 374), that the patent issued to Susan Letranch (now Susan Maynes) under the Pottawatomie treaty of 1861 (12 Stat. L., 1191) was valid, and that the patent for the same land issued under the treaty of 1867 (15 Stat. L., 531) to Anthony F. Navarre was void, is reversed on the ground that the treaty of 1867 authorized a patent in fee simple to the head of the family of lands prior thereto allotted to the members of his family, and that such provision was not invalidated by any prior treaties or in derogation of any vested right.

Veale v. Morgan, 23 Kans., 1.

SEC. 2878. The Delawares had stipulated that the L., P. & W. Ry. might have a right of way through their reservation upon compensation being paid.   The United States agreed to extinguish the Indian titles for the right of way of Pacific roads as an additional aid to the enterprises.   The L., P. & W. R. R. was incorporated into the Pacific system, and the United States assumed the obligation to give it the right of way through the Delaware Reservation.   This it could do within the exact terms of the treaty of 1860 (12 Stat. L., 1129) by paying the allottees just compensation therefor.   Whether such allottees have made a demand of the Government for this compensation does not appear; the Government and not the defendant, if anyone, owes the compensation.   *Grinter v. K. P. Ry. Co., 23 Kans., 642.*

SEC. 2879. Special provision had been made in article 3 of the Delaware treaty of 1860 (12 Stat. L., 1129) for a perpetual right of way over the lands allotted to the Delawares for the L., P. & W. Ry. Co. on the payment of a just compensation to the Indians whose lands were to be crossed by the road. This was an agreement between the United States and the Delawares to which the company was not a party, and it could not obtain the benefit of the contract except by permission of Congress. *Ibid.*

SEC. 2880. The company had no authority to exercise the right of eminent domain within the Delaware Reserve, and without the power and obligation of the United States to extinguish for its benefit and use the Indian title, it can hardly be supposed that the company would have assented to the conditions of the act of 1862 (12 Stat. L., 489), or attempted afterwards the construction of its road over and across these Indian lands. *Ibid.*

SEC. 2881. There is nothing in the Delaware treaty of 1860 (12 Stat. L., 1129) to indicate that any other right or title was granted to the allottees than the right of occupancy, with the ultimate fee of the land in the United States. *Ibid.*

SEC. 2882. The plaintiff, a white citizen of Kentucky, went to Kansas in 1853 and married a Delaware Indian woman, but was not himself adopted into the tribe. He lived on the land allotted to his wife under the Delaware treaty of 1860 (12 Stat. L., 1129), and in 1872 brought an action against defendant in the court below for breaking and entering his close. *Held,* that he was not entitled to recover damages notwithstanding the defendant entered and constructed its road over the land so allotted in severalty without paying compensation therefor. *Ibid.*

SEC. 2883. In 1862 Congress had the exclusive right and dominion over the Delaware Reservation in Kansas, and had full power to permit the construction of a railroad over such reservation, either with or without compensation to be paid by the company. *Ibid.*

SEC. 2884. In the case of The Kansas Indians, 5 Wall., 737, the Supreme Court held that "as long as the United States recognizes their national character they are under the protection of treaties and the laws of Congress, and their property is withdrawn from the operation of State laws." This decision was in 1866, and since then it is not pretended that there has been any treaty changing the relations of the Shawnees to the Government, or releasing tribal control of persons or property. *Brown v. Steele, 23 Kans., 672.*

SEC. 2885. It appearing that the tribal organization of the Shawnees was still recognized by the political department of the United States Government, under the decision of the Supreme Court of the United States in the case of The Kansas Indians, 5 Wall., 737, the descent of the lands allotted under the treaty of May 10, 1854 (10 Stat. L., 1053), is governed, not by the Kansas law, but by the Shawnee law. *Ibid.*

Sec. 2886. Where two parties have each a partial possession of and certain improvements upon a single tract of the Kaw Indian trust lands, and claim the right to purchase the tract, and one obtains against the other an *ex parte* restraining order from the probate judge, the district judge may, upon a motion to dissolve this order, modify the same by entering an order restraining each party from interfering with the improvements of the other until the final hearing.

Downing v. Reeves, 24 Kans., 167.

Sec. 2887. Where, after a forfeiture of school lands for the non-payment of the purchase money, the lands are regularly taxed and sold for the nonpayment of taxes, and the purchaser of the tax title pays the balance of the purchase money to the proper authorities and receives a patent from the State, no private individual can question the title thus conveyed. *Baker v. Newland, 25 Kans., 25.*

Sec. 2888. In the case of The Kansas Indians (5 Wall., 737) the United States Supreme Court, while deciding that lands held by the Shawnee Indians in severalty under the treaty of 1854 (10 Stat. L., 1053) were not subject to taxation, failed to hold that all the stipulations of the treaty of 1831 (7 Stat. L., 355) were carried into and became a part of the treaty of 1854. The opinion of the Supreme Court in that case was adverse to the opinion of this court in 3 Kans., 299, and so far is it goes is conclusive. *The State v. O'Laughlin, 29 Kans., 20.*

Sec. 2889. The Supreme Court in the case of The Kansas Indians (5 Wall., 737) did not decide that the lands in question were not within the territorial limits of the State of Kansas, but simply that while owned by the Indians they were not taxable. But in the case at bar the lands are no longer Indian lands. Not only were they set apart in severalty to an Indian and patented, but by such Indian they had been legally conveyed. *Ibid.*

Sec. 2890. Land patented to an individual under the treaty of May 30, 1854, with the confederated Kaskaskias, Peorias, Piankeshaws, and Weas (10 Stat. L., 1082), could not be conveyed without the approval of the Secretary of the Interior. The title held by Pa-kan-giah was simply an Indian title, and the deed executed by him to Baptiste Peoria was null and void for the reason that it was executed without authority and in violation of the terms of the treaty; and he had at the time nothing but a naked allotment to convey.

McGannon v. Straightlege, 32 Kans., 524.

Sec. 2891. The title being an Indian title, or, in other words, the title being vested in the United States and an Indian, no statute of limitations could operate against such title. No statute of limitations began to run against plaintiff's title until his deed was approved by the Secretary of the Interior. *Ibid.*

Sec. 2892. Land allotted to a minor of the Ottawa tribe under the treaty of 1862 (12 Stat. L., 1237) was inalienable by guardian during the minority of allottee. If the contention of plaintiffs in error that the Ottawa Indians, under the terms of the treaty of 1862, became citizens of the United States before the treaty of 1867 (15 Stat. L., 513) took effect were upheld, it would result in nullifying the treaty of 1867, because the President and Senate are not authorized to enter into a treaty with citizens of the United States.

Wiggins v. King, 35 Kans., 410.

SEC. 2893. So much of section 2, chapter 79, laws of 1874 (Kansas), of the "act to protect *bona fide* purchasers of Indian lands," which provides that a person purchasing land from an Indian, allotted under a treaty, can not be evicted by any other person who has obtained the legal title to the same until such subsequent purchaser has repaid the prior purchase money, with interest, is inoperative until the Indian title is extinguished, as violative of a paramount Federal law. If the legislature has the right to impose a lien for $200 or $300 upon this land without the consent of the United States or of the Indian to whom it was allotted, then the legislature would have the power to prescribe under what rules and regulations Indian lands might be sold or conveyed, and would also have the absolute power to deprive the United States and the Indian to whom the land was allotted of all power of alienation.

McGannon v. Straightlege, 37 Kans., 87.

SEC. 2894. The defendant, a white man who had been adopted as a member of the Munsee or Christian Indians, made a deed purporting to convey to plaintiff, a white man who was not a member of any Indian tribe, a tract of land which, under the treaty of 1859 (12 Stat. L., 1109), could not be alienated except to the United States or to some members of the same tribe. Plaintiff paid defendant part of the purchase price and held possession of the land for about sixteen years, when defendant again came into possession. In an action of ejectment against defendant it was held that the deed to him was absolutely void; that plaintiff could not acquire any right in the land in violation of the treaty, nor could he indirectly build up one by adverse possession, estoppel, or any statute of limitations, and that his action must fail.

Sheldon v. Donohue, 40 Kans., 346.

SEC. 2895. Under the act of August 4, 1886 (24 Stat. L., 219), which provides that, on the death of an allottee under the Kickapoo treaty of 1862 (13 Stat. L., 623), leaving heirs, and without having obtained a patent, the Secretary of the Interior shall cause a patent in fee simple to issue in the name of the original allottee, the title passes from the Government to the heirs of the deceased allottee. Under this act of Congress the right to a patent became complete in the allottee. Nothing more remained to be done but the ministerial duty of issuing a patent, and by this act the duty was made imperative.

Briggs v. McClain, 43 Kans., 653.

SEC. 2896. In Stark *v.* Starrs, 6 Wall., 418, Mr. Justice Field says: "The right to a patent once vested is treated by the Government when dealing with the public lands as equivalent to a patent issued. When in fact the patent does issue, it relates back to the inception of the right of the patentee, so far as it may be necessary to cut off intervening claimants."   *Ibid.*

SEC. 2897. The dates of a deed from Je-Mahn and Louisa Je-Mahn, Pottawatomie Indians, had first been written April 30, 1867, and afterwards changed to August 30, 1868. If the deed was executed on the former date it was valid, but if on the latter it was void as to one of the grantors, for prior to that time he died. The court below found that the deed was executed April 30, 1867, and the evidence was sufficient to sustain such finding.   *Forbes v. Higginbotham, 44 Kans., 95.*

SEC. 2898. The grantors were Pottawatomie Indians and the land conveyed by them was Indian land, and the grantees afterwards conveyed the land to the defendant in this case, who was an innocent and *bona fide* purchaser for value, and who afterwards took the actual possession of the property and held the quiet and undisturbed possession thereof for more than three years, and made valuable improvements thereon: *Held,* that under section 3, chap. 79, of the laws of 1874 (Kansas), the defendant had obtained the full, complete, and absolute title to the property.   *Ibid.*

SEC. 2899. Section 2103, United States Revised Statutes, makes void all contracts for leasing land in the Indian country unless executed in the manner therein provided and approved by the Secretary of the Interior. The lease between Pond and Halderman was in violation of this law, and conferred no rights upon Pond to cultivate the land; he was there without authority.   *Halderman v. Pond, 45 Kans., 411.*

SEC. 2900. As the plaintiff below had no permit or license to lease the land where the corn was raised, and there being grave doubts as to whether he had any right to recover for the alleged conversion of this property in the Indian Territory, where the tort was committed, and if such right did exist the jurisdiction was vested in another court, it follows that the court below had no jurisdiction.   *Ibid.*

SEC. 2901. In an action in the nature of ejectment the plaintiff must recover upon the strength of his own title, and not upon the weakness of the title of the defendant who has the actual possession of the land.
                                                 O'Brien v. Bugbee, 46 Kans., 1.

SEC. 2902. In 1860, under the tribal organization of the Shawnees, the descent of real estate was cast in accordance with the customs and decisions of that tribe.   *Ibid.*

SEC. 2903. Where a plaintiff relies upon title to real estate alleged to be cast by descent upon his grantor in accordance with the custom of an Indian tribe, he must establish the custom at the time of the death of the former owner or possession from whom he claims his grantor inherited the property.   *Ibid.*

SEC. 2904. The law or decision of a country, a State, or an Indian tribe may make any person an heir.   An heir at law is simply one who succeeds to the estate of a deceased person under the statute of a country, a State, or the decision of an Indian tribe.   In the absence of any evidence tending to show the law or decision of the Shawnee tribe relating to descent or distribution of lands in 1860, it can not be said what person, if any, succeeded to the estate of Polly Buchanan.   *Ibid.*

SEC. 2905. Where a plaintiff brings his action in the nature of ejectment against a defendant in the actual possession of Indian land properly patented to a member of the Shawnee tribe (now deceased), under the provisions of a treaty between the United States and the Shawnee Indians May 10, 1854 (10 Stat. L., 1053), and the act of Congress March 3, 1859 (11 Stat. L., 399), and such defendant claims color of title and possession under a deed from the chiefs of the tribe, approved by the Secretary of the Interior, the prior possession of such Indian land by the plaintiff is not sufficient for him to recover upon as against such a defendant if such plaintiff fails to show any title or other right of possession on his part.   *Ibid.*

SEC. 2906. The will made by Isaac Johnnycake, a Delaware Indian and member of the Cherokee Nation, was not sufficiently probated or proved to make it effectual to pass title to property situated in Wyandotte County, Kans.   *Meyers v. Smith, 50 Kans., 1.*

SEC. 2907. Where a Kickapoo owner of land in Kansas negligently allows the legal title to go to another and clothes him with apparent power to convey and encumber the same, and such person mortgages it to one who takes the mortgage in good faith and without notice of the fraud, the mortgage will be held valid and in force as against the original grantee.   *Lawrence v. The Guarantee Investment Co., 51 Kans, 222.*

SEC. 2908. Congress having full control over the lands in Kansas known as the "Osage trust and diminished reserve lands," may make them subject to State taxation upon such conditions as are deemed proper, not in conflict with the provisions of the constitution and laws of the State.   *Logan v. Comsrs. of Clark Co., 51 Kans., 747.*

SEC. 2909. All that is required of an applicant to make an entry and purchase of the Osage trust and diminished reserve lands is, that he shall have all the qualifications of a preemptor, that he shall be an actual settler on the land at the date of the entry, and that he shall make full payment therefor.   *Freese v. Scouten, 53 Kans., 347.*

SEC. 2910. A mortgage from an entryman of a tract of Osage trust and diminished reserve lands, after final receipt is given and before the issuance of the patent, takes his mortgage subject to the supervisory power of the Commissioner of the General Land Office of the United States. *Ibid.*

SEC. 2911. Defendant was formerly a member of the Pottawatomie tribe of Indians, and an allotment of 320 acres of land had been made to him in the Indian Territory, March 30, 1888, subject to the approval of the Secretary of the Interior, but it had not been approved at the time of the trial. *Neddo v. Neddo, 56 Kans., 507.*

SEC. 2912. In case of a transfer of land held by a Shawnee Indian in severalty, where the consent of the Secretary of the Interior is required, the approval by him of a deed absolute in form and otherwise sufficient is valid, and will extinguish the Indian title, although the general rules promulgated by that officer for the transfer of such titles have not been strictly pursued. *Ingraham v. Ward, 56 Kans., 550.*

SEC. 2913. Where by treaty and act of Congress, the matter of consent and approval is vested in the Secretary of the Interior, he can modify his own rules with respect to the transfer of such lands and the approval of conveyance, or dispense with them entirely, as the circumstances may warrant, and where he acts and approves the conveyance the transfer is complete. *Ibid.*

SEC. 2914. The deeds to Catharine Swartzel contained no restrictions, and, being absolute in power, the approved deed conveyed to her an absolute title. As to the interest purchased from her coheirs she is to be regarded the same as any other purchaser, and the approved conveyance divested the title of the United States and placed the interest named outside of the restrictions placed upon the sale of Indian lands. *Ibid.*

SEC. 2915. Plaintiff purchased from one Holmes land which had been allotted to a Shawnee Indian. A deed was executed to plaintiff and he took possession. About three years afterwards an action was brought to recover from plaintiff the balance of the purchase money, when he set up as a defense that a prior deed from one of the heirs of the allottee to Holmes had not been approved by the Secretary of the Interior, and he asked for a recission and for damages. There was no fraud or misrepresentation by Holmes in the sale of the land. To cure the alleged defect the vendor asked for the possession of the deed that he might present it to the Secretary and secure the approval thereof, but plaintiff having refused to surrender it, is not entitled to maintain his defense, not to the equitable relief which he sought. If he had allowed the deed to have been approved it would have related back to the execution and validated it from that time. *Ibid.*

SEC. 2916. The courts of Kansas have been open to Shawnee Indians for the division of lands inherited from allottees, and where partition is so made, and the Secretary of the Interior recognizes the proceed-

ings as legal and approves a deed based thereon, the conveyance is
valid.   *Ibid.*

SEC. 2917. Upon the discovery of the American continent the principle was asserted or acknowledged by all European nations that discovery followed by actual possession gave title to the Government by
whose subjects or by whose authority it was made, not only against
other European Governments but against the natives themselves.
While the different nations of Europe respected the rights of the
natives as occupants, they all asserted the ultimate dominion and title
to be in themselves.   *Breaux et al. v. Johns et al., 4 La. (Robinson), 142.*

SEC. 2918. In Martin *v.* Johnson et al. (5 Martin's Reps. 655), it was
in evidence that the Pascagoula and Biloxi tribes of Indians had thus
been removed to bayou Bœuf and located on the *redececion* of the Choctaws with the consent of that tribe.   These regulations were substantially the same as were enforced by England in North America, and
have been enforced by the United States since the Revolution.   In
Louisiana, as in the other States, the nature of the Indian title was not
such as to be repugnant to the right of ultimate domain in the sovereign of the country.   *Ibid.*

SEC. 2919. In the case of Mitchell et al. *v.* The United States (11
Peters, 711) the Indian titles, under which the plaintiffs claimed, rested
upon solemn treaties entered into between Spain and the powerful
tribes of Indians which then occupied the province of Florida.   These
treaties were in derogation of the laws of the Indies, and probably did
vest the absolute title in the Indian tribes.   But no such treaties were
ever made with the tribes which inhabited Louisiana, and that case is
not applicable to the one under consideration.   *Ibid.*

SEC. 2920. We claim the ultimate right to the soil occupied by the
Indians to be in the United States and that, as a consequence of this
ultimate dominion, they have the power to grant the soil while yet in
the possession of the natives.   These grants convey a title to the
grantees, subject only to the Indian right of occupancy.   *Ibid.*

SEC. 2921. The attempt of the defendants to recover from the Indians as warrantors is preposterous.   They, as well as those under whom
they claim, well knew that the title under which they possess was an
absolute nullity, from which no legal effects could result.   *Ibid.*

SEC. 2922. We find that the Chetimacha tribe of Indians had three
villages, two of which have been recognized by the United States as
properly located, and the claim to the other rejected.   The evidence
in the second going to show that the rejected claim was a *redececion*
regularly made under the laws of the Indies is not satisfactory, nor
does it seem to be in accordance with those laws that two such grants
should have been made to the same tribe within 7 or 8 miles of
each other.   But supposing the claim to be valid, the United States

could grant the land it covers, subject to the right of occupancy of the Indians, and as they have ceased to occupy the portion in controversy since 1807 the plaintiffs are entitled to take possession of it under their patent. *Ibid.*

SEC. 2923. Spain, besides claiming as other nations by right of discovery, rested her title to the soil upon the higher sanction of apostolic dispensation. In the exercise of a power then held to be divine, the Pope, Alexander VI, granted to Ferdinand and Isabella all the lands discovered or to be discovered by their subjects on this continent or the islands adjoining it. This grant is found *in extenso* in Salozano, Politica Indiana, book 1, chapter 10, Nos. 23, 24. There can be no doubt from the words used, nor has it ever been doubted by the courts or Government of Spain that it was absolute and vested in the sovereign all the lands discovered or to be discovered, whether or not they were to be appropriated or occupied by the nations at the time of the discovery. We must, therefore, ascertain whether the laws of Spain, after the discovery of America restored the natives to the absolute ownership of the lands allotted to them, there being no doubt those laws were enforced in Louisiana. *Ibid.*

SEC. 2924. Indian tribes in Louisiana to whom lands were allotted by the laws of Spain were never invested by those laws with the absolute ownership. The Indians were not permitted to dispose of those lands without being expressly authorized by the Government. If all died or removed permanently the lands reverted to the Crown, not by forfeiture, but by the implied right of reversion; or, if the population of the Indian villages was greatly reduced in number, the remnants of several villages were united into one, and, in such case, they continued to hold so much of the land originally set apart for them as they stood in need of. *Ibid.*

SEC. 2925. In Martin *v.* Johnson et al. (5 Martin's Rep., 655), and also Reboue *v.* Nero (5 ibid., 490), it was held that the lands assigned to Indian tribes by the Spanish Government were granted in full ownership, and that the Government surveyors were bound to notice their location and could not survey them as vacant. This court is not prepared to give an unqualified assent to those propositions. *Ibid.*

SEC. 2926. A family holding lands belonging to Indians by the right of occupancy, which have been assigned by the Indian agent to the head of said family, receives a base or determinable fee and has the same rights and privileges as if they were tenants in fee simple.

John v. Sabbattis, 69 Maine, 473.

SEC. 2927. The conveyance in question was not approved by the Indian agent, but as it was to a member of the tribe this was not necessary and the deed passed whatever interest in the premises therein described the grantor had to convey. *Ibid.*

SEC. 2928. The lots assigned under chapter 158, laws of 1835 (Maine), according to section 4 of that chapter, could not be sold by the Indians to whom they were assigned to any person in or out of the tribe, with or without the permission of the agent, and the same construction must be given to section 18, chapter 9, Revised Statutes, so far as the sale of lots there ordered to be assigned for agricultural purposes is concerned.   *Ibid.*

SEC 2929. "The permission of the agent" relates to the carrying off of the growth faster than is necessary for cultivation and the leasing of the lots assigned for agricultural purposes, which might be done with the permission of the agent by virtue of section 2, chapter 331, laws of 1838.   *Ibid.*

SEC. 2930. The right to sell, even with the permission of the Indian agent, has never been conferred, expressly or by implication, and the broad prohibition of section 4 that "it shall not be in the power of any Indian to sell his or her lot," is still the law touching lots assigned for agricultural purposes.   *Ibid.*

SEC. 2931. The reservation by the treaty between the United States and Chippewa Indians, made at Saginaw September 24, 1819, of certain designated quantities of land, to be located as the President of the United States might direct, *for the use* of persons therein named, *and their heirs*, was a reservation of an estate in *fee simple*, to each of the individual reservees. The treaty itself operated as a grant of land to each of the several reservees, which became perfect when the land was located under the direction of the President of the United States, and no patent was necessary to perfect the title. A patent issued by the President to a person claiming to be one of the reservees was void, and could in no wise affect the title of the reservees under the treaty.
Stockton v. Williams, 1 Douglas (Mich.), 546.

SEC. 2932. No disposition by an Indian of lands he expected to receive under the treaty of October 18, 1864, which antedates the determination of his competency to take under the terms of the treaty, can be held valid.

The executive department is not so bound by the conduct of Indian agents that it can not repudiate their frauds and decline to follow their false decisions.   *Raymond v. Shawboose, 34 Mich. (post), 142.*

SEC. 2933. Under a patent to a "not-so-competent Indian," in which the power of alienation is suspended except with the consent of the Secretary of the Interior, the patentee has a right to the use, occupancy, and enjoyment of the land, but has no right to alienate it either by direct or indirect means.   *Attorney-General v. Williams, 94 Mich. (Fuller), 180.*

SEC. 2934. The refusal of the agent of the United States to register the application of the Indians claiming under the Choctaw treaty of 1830 (7 Stat. L., 333) does not affect the validity of the claim and application of such Indians. The right of an Indian to the contemplated reservation under the treaty is not made to depend finally and conclusively upon any lawless discretion or caprice which the agent might choose to exercise. Even if the powers of the agent were judicial and conclusive in their character, still his conduct in reference to this claim could in no wise affect its validity, because the sentence or judgment of a judicial tribunal is only conclusive upon the matter actually considered and adjudged. *Land v. Land, 1 S. & M. Chan. (Miss.), 458.*

SEC. 2935. Under the Choctaw treaty 1830, granting reservations of land to each head of family and to each of his children, the treaty intended to secure to the head of family only one section, and to each of the children the amounts stipulated by the treaty; and the bill of a Choctaw Indian setting up title in himself to the portion of land reserved for his children must be dismissed. Whether the language of the treaty vests the technical legal title in the father to the portion reserved for the children, to be held for their use, or whether they take an unincumbered fee independent of the father, is doubtful. It does not appear what construction, in practice, the Government of the United States has placed upon this article in emanating titles under its provisions. *Pickens v. Harper, 1 S. & M. Chan., 539.*

SEC. 2936. Article 14 of the Choctaw treaty of 1830 (7 Stat. L., 333), which provides that each Choctaw head of family who wishes to remain and become a citizen shall have that privilege by signifying his intention to the United States agent within six months from the making of the treaty, and that he shall be entitled to certain reservations of land, and that, if he reside upon the land for five years after the ratification of the treaty a grant in fee simple shall issue, is equivalent to a grant with a condition subsequent. In order to complete the grant it is necessary that the Indian should have resided five years on the land, and parol proof is sufficient to establish residence. It is not necessary that the Indian should have had a residence or improvement on the land at the time of the ratification of the treaty in order to entitle him to a reservation. It seems that it is sufficient if his residence commenced within six months of that time.

Newman v. Doe, 5 Miss., 522.

SEC. 2937. By a provision in the Choctaw treaty of 1830 the Indians had one, two, and three years to remove from the ceded land. This was a length of time which might well justify a claim of citizenship, and without some definite provision they might all have claimed to be citizens; and having signified their intention, every head of a family might have removed with the tribe at the time stipulated without impairing his right to a reservation. The last clause in article 14 provides that "persons who claim under this article shall not lose the privilege of a Choctaw citizen, but if they ever remove, are not to be entitled to any portion of the Choctaw annuity." This means that the treaty had in contemplation and applies to a removal after five years, when they would have a right to do so without further loss of the annuity. If this view be correct it follows that the reservations were made on conditions subsequent, the nonperformance of which put an end to the right, and the court below erred in not receiving the proof of Foster's abandonment.   *Ibid.*

SEC. 2938. The individual Choctaw grants under the treaty of 1830 should be located in a body; but if a different location be recognized by the Government before other rights accrued, it will hold.   *Ibid.*

SEC. 2939. If the title to the soil was in the Indians, the terms used in the treaty of 1830 are sufficient to prevent their right from passing to the United States for such portions as were excepted out of the general cession, and to each head of a family was reserved a certain quantity on his performing certain acts. The reservation secured a right to a portion of that which was before held in common.   *Ibid.*

SEC. 2940. The subsequent provision of the Choctaw treaty of 1830, that a grant in fee simple shall issue, does not destroy the legal effect of the previous part of the article which intended to convey the right. The term "reservation" is a technical one and has been invariably employed to convey title.   *Ibid.*

SEC. 2941. In the case of En-che-lah *v.* Welsh (3 Hawkes R., 155), the words "do agree to allow a reservation of six hundred and forty acres of land to each head of a family formerly residing within the ceded territory" in the Cherokee treaty were held sufficient to convey the title, although it was objected that they only amounted to a promise to convey in future.   *Ibid.*

SEC. 2942. The grant that was to issue at the end of five years was to be an acquittance from the condition or an acknowledgment that it had been performed and that the title had become absolute.   *Ibid.*

SEC. 2943. The court below charged the jury that by signifying his intention to become a citizen within proper time, Foster became entitled to a reservation of 640 acres; and if they believe he had four children at the ratification of the treaty, he was entitled to a further reservation of 640 acres. If by this charge the court intended to convey the idea that the title to the whole 1,280 acres vested in Foster individually and no portion of it in his children, or to him in trust for them, the propriety of the charge may be doubtful.   *Ibid.*

SEC. 2944. Decree of superior court of chancery in Anderson & Orme *v.* Niles & Lewis, involving title to a certain Chickasaw grant under the treaty of May 24, 1834 (7 Stat. L., 450), reported in 1 Freeman's Chancery (Miss.), affirmed.   *Niles et al. v. Anderson et al., 6 Miss., 365.*

SEC. 2945. Under the common law a grantor upon conditions subsequent was compelled to enter or make claim for the breach of conditions, because his failure to do so might be construed as a waiver of the conditions; but his doctrine can not apply as against the United States, against whom no laches are chargeable. But the Choctaw grant was on condition of residence, and if the grantee abandoned the residence he abandoned his right.

Doe ex dem. Harris v. Newman, 11 Miss., 565.

SEC. 2946. The purpose of appointing a locating agent for the reservees under the Choctaw treaty of 1830 must have been to enable the proper department of the Government to ascertain who were entitled to reservations. Assuming that the locating agent acted within the scope of his authority, then his certificate was entitled to credit, and must be regarded as evidence that Foster had brought himself within the provisions of the treaty, so far as to lay a proper foundation for a title afterwards to be consummated. If he afterwards forfeited his right, still the certificate was admissible to show its commencement. *Ibid.*

SEC. 2947. The certificate of the locating agent for the reservees, provided for by the Choctaw treaty of 1830 (7 Stat. L., 333), that Foster was registered for a particular tract of land, etc., is admissible evidence to show that Foster brought himself within the provisions of the treaty so far as to lay a proper foundation for a title afterwards to be consummated. *Ibid.*

SEC. 2948. When a reservee, who holds on condition of residence, abandons the residence, he abandons his rights and thereby avoids it himself, without entry or claim by the grantor. Under the treaty of 1830, if a Choctaw Indian left his home intending to abandon it, he lost his right, whether he afterwards selected another home or not. *Ibid.*

SEC. 2949. The acts of agents in issuing certificates under the Choctaw treaty of 1830 (7 Stat. L., 333) may be impeached for fraud. *Ibid.*

SEC. 2950. An Indian must personally reside for five years on the land he claims as his reservation before he can acquire a title to it under the Choctaw treaty of 1830 (7 Stat. L., 333). The residence of an agent on the land is insufficient. The confirmation of an Indian reservation can not be proved by parol; it is susceptible of higher proof. *Ibid.*

SEC. 2951. Actual registration was not necessary to entitle a Choctaw head of family to a reservation, he becoming entitled thereto by signifying his intention to the agent.

Coleman v. Doe ex dem. Fish-ho-mah, 12 Miss. 40.

SEC. 2952. The attorney-general of this State, in an opinion, says "that all Choctaw heads of families who shall prove by credible evidence, documentary or oral, that they actually and in good faith signified to the proper agent in due time their intention to remain, and who have resided the proper time on the land, are entitled to the reservations secured by the treaty, notwithstanding their names may not have been entered on the list."   *Ibid.*

SEC. 2953. The Choctaw Nation by the treaty of 1830 gave the immediate right of occupancy, the United States gave the ultimate fee, and the reservees thus became clothed with the full title, subject only to be divested in case of failure to comply with the condition of residence of five years.   *Ibid.*

SEC. 2954. A legal title is vested in the Indian who has brought himself within the provisions of the Choctaw treaty of 1830, and no patent from the Government was necessary to complete it. The location of the land claimed by an Indian under that treaty may be proved by parol.   *Ibid.*

SEC. 2955. Where an Indian's right to the section of land secured to him by the Choctaw treaty of 1830 becomes vested by his signifying his intention to remain to the proper agent, the title in the Indian becomes complete, subject to forfeiture by removal within five years; such removal, to constitute a forfeiture, must be *voluntary.*   *Ibid.*

SEC. 2956. An Indian, in whom title to a section of land has vested under the Choctaw treaty of 1830, and who has been dispossessed, may bring his action of ejectment at law and recover the possession.   *Ibid.*

SEC. 2957. It was the duty of the United States not to alienate the lands reserved, while the right of the reservee continued under the Choctaw treaty of 1830, and if they did so, by mistake or otherwise, the grant was void.   *Ibid.*

SEC. 2958. An Indian claiming under article 14 of the Choctaw treaty of 1830 (7 Stat. L., 333), who has brought himself within the provisions of that article, is clothed with a legal title, which will prevail against a patent, subsequently issued by the Government, to the reservation of such Indian.   *Hit-tuk-Ho-mi v. Watts, 15 Miss., 363.*

SEC. 2959. The court below erred in instructing (1) that a patent is the highest evidence of title, and that it is evidence that all the prerequisites have been complied with and can not be questioned; (2) that before any title can be gained by a second patentee the first patent must be set aside *by a court of equity;* (3) that priority of date of patent is the best evidence of title, although the opposite party made the first entry.   *Ibid.*

SEC. 2960. In Stoddard *v.* Chambers (2 How., S. C., 317) the court say: "On these facts the important question arises, whether the defendant's title is not void. The question is as well examinable at law as in equity. * * * The patent of the defendant having been for land reserved from such appropriation is *void.*"   *Ibid.*

SEC. 2961. A patent may be impeached for illegality or fraud, and declared void in a court of law, as well as in chancery. A patent which issues from the General Government for land which has been previously appropriated by the Government and reserved from entry is void. *Ibid.*

SEC. 2962. If a Choctaw Indian has been prevented by *force* from complying with the condition of the treaty of 1830 requiring five years continued residence, it will be regarded as if they had complied.

Wade v. Amc'n Colonization Society, 15 Miss., 665.

SEC. 2963. Where by a written contract Jacoway set over to Young one-fourth part of the interest of two Indians in land reserved to them under the Choctaw treaty of 1830 (7 Stat. L., 333) it was held, in an action by J. against Y., on a note given in consideration therefor, that writing was unambiguous, and that J. could not show by parol that he thereby intended to sell Y. his interest in the land without warranty, and that such was also Y.'s understanding; nor could he show by parol the nature of his interest in the land.

Young v. Jacoway, 17 Miss., 212.

SEC. 2964. In an action of ejectment by an Indian claiming under article 6 of the Chickasaw treaty, 1834, the Indian having shown the reservation and the location on the land in controversy, it was held not to be necessary for him to show that a list, including himself, was furnished by the seven chiefs and filed with the agent; nor to produce the agent's certificate of its believed accuracy furnished to the register and receiver prior to the location; the location in itself was evidence that all the prerequisites were complied with. *Wray v. Doe, 18 Miss., 452.*

SEC. 2965. By statute of Mississippi (How. and Hatch., 605) copies of records appertaining to land offices, duly authenicated, are made evidence; in an action of ejectment, therefore, by an Indian claiming under article 6 of the Chickasaw treaty, 1834 (7 Stat. L., 450), the certificate of the register of the land office, showing the date of the location of the Indian on the land in dispute, is competent evidence.

Ibid.

SEC. 2966. Under the Chickasaw treaty, 1834 (7 Stat. L., 450) the term "reservation" is equivalent to an absolute grant, and it needs only the *location* of the land to give the reservation identity, to make the title in the reservee absolute and complete; and where, after such location, the Government issues a patent to the same land to a third party, the patent will be *void*, even at law. *Ibid.*

SEC. 2967. In an action of ejectment by an Indian claiming under the Chickasaw treaty, 1834, it is not competent for the defendant to show what certificate was appended to the roll of the reservees, when it appeared that the name of the Indian plaintiff was in the list; the Indians had done all in their power to secure their reservations by being enrolled, and if the agent afterwards neglected his duty by failing to annex a proper certificate to the roll, the Indian is not to be prejudiced thereby. *Ibid.*

SEC. 2968. Under article 11 of the Chickasaw treaty of 1834 the *residue* of the Chickasaw country, after the reservations were located, was the only portion which could be sold as public lands of the United States.   *Ibid.*

SEC. 2969. The instructions from the War Department as to the construction of the Chickasaw treaty of 1834 (7 Stat. L., 450), have no binding force; that Department could add nothing to the terms of the treaty without the consent of the other party thereto, and as the sixth article contained the stipulation that the reservations should be located by the register and receiver, the instructions from the War Department "that no location under any of the articles of the treaty should be considered as final, or as conferring any right whatever until the same should be approved by the President," is not obligatory.   *Ibid.*

SEC. 2970. The Chickasaw treaty of 1834 (7 Stat. L., 450), provided that none of the allotted tracts should be sold without the certificate of *at least* two of seven named persons, of whom five signed the treaty for the Indians, that the grantor was competent, etc.; which fact should also be certified by the agent.   One of the seven persons, the certificate of two of whom was required to make a sale valid, sold his reservation without having procured his certificate.   *Held*, that the spirit of the treaty did not embrace those who were by the treaty itself appointed to judge of the capability of others, and that the sale by him, without such certificate, would be valid.
Pointer v. Trotter, 18 Miss., 538.

SEC. 2971. It has been insisted that the Indian acquired an absolute title by the treaty, according to the decisions in Newman *v.* Harris (5 Miss.) and Niles *v.* Anderson, and that no limit to the power of alienation could be imposed, but it does not appear that the power to impose these restrictions has ever been questioned.
Harman v. Partier, 20 Miss., 425.

SEC. 2972. In the case of Pointer *v.* Trotter (18 Miss., 537) it was decided that a conveyance by one of the persons appointed by the treaty of 1834 to certify to the capability of others, to wit, Henry Love, was not within the spirit and meaning of this provision.   But at the same time it was held that the certificates constituted prerequisites to a good title.   By reference to that case it will be seen upon what ground the exception was placed.   *Ibid.*

SEC. 2973. It would not have been in the power of the Indians or of the Government by treaty stipulation, without the express assent of the State, to vest the Indian with the absolute property in the land, and at the same time say it shall not be subject to execution for debts lawfully contracted.   That would be trenching too far on State sovereignty.
Saffarans v. Terry, 20 Miss., 690.

SEC. 2974. Although article 4 of the Chickasaw treaty of 1834 imposes certain conditions and restrictions on alienation it was held that a sale under execution upon an attachment for debt was valid, and passed the title to the purchaser without compliance with either of the stipulations of the treaty, and that the purchaser's title, thus acquired, would be better than that of a vendee, by subsequent deed of the Indian, in which all the treaty stipulations were complied with.   *Ibid.*

SEC. 2975. The act of Congress (7 Stat. L., 21) provides for the survey and sale of the lands in West Florida to which the Indian title had been extinguished, but withholds from the operation of the law all such lands as the Indians had not ceded. The treaty of cession between Georgia and the United States itself provides that the latter Government shall extinguish the Indian title to all the lands in Georgia.

Montgomery v. Ives, 21 Miss., 161.

SEC. 2976. In 1834 Niles made contracts with various Chickasaw Indians for fifty sections of land to which the Indians were entitled under the treaty of 1834 (7 Stat. L., 450); but afterwards, in 1835, Niles entered into an agreement with plaintiff by which he was to furnish to them an interest in the contracts which he had made with the Indians, so as to procure title to the fifty sections, for which plaintiffs were to pay $50,000, and Niles was to attend to the location and survey for the company. *Held*, that plaintiffs designed by this contract to take in effect in place of Niles in the purchase of the land.

Stebbins v. Niles, 25 Miss., 267.

SEC. 2977. The titles to seven of the sections of land which fell to the defendant, by the division under the compromise, were afterwards found to be imperfect, in that the deeds made by the Indians to Niles were not approved by the President according to the stipulations of the Chickasaw treaty.   *Ibid.*

SEC. 2978. The treaty in this case is the source of the Indians' title; the location is intended to identify the land granted; the two together, the treaty and the location, constitute the title. The treaty being the source of title, must be treated as the substantial part of the transaction, to which the title itself will have relation when completed by a location of the land.   *McAfee v. Lynch et al., 26 Miss., 257.*

SEC. 2979. The defendants claimed title to the land in controversy as assignees of a Choctaw Indian, to whom a half section of land, to be located on any unoccupied land in the district in which he lived, was granted by the treaty of 1830 (7 Stat. L., 333). Defendants had become the owner of this land in 1832, and one of them, some time during the year 1833, applied to the locating agent for the purpose of locating the land for the said Indian, but the agent refused to locate the land, on the ground that he had not opened an office in that district.   *Ibid.*

SEC. 2980. The certificate is evidence of itself that all the prerequisites were complied with, and a violation of duty on the part of the officers who made the location is not to be presumed. The diagram and plat offered in evidence was only admissible on the ground that it was "a record appertaining to the land office," and it was not susceptible of parol explanation in its material parts.

Hardin v. Ho-yo-po-nubby's lessee, 27 Miss., 567.

SEC. 2981. The certificate shows that the location of the land in behalf of plaintiff's lessor by the agent was in June, 1838, before the register and receiver were furnished with a list, as required by the treaty of 1834, which was not done until November, 1838. This list is provided for in the first clause of the sixth article of the treaty, which does not require the list to be filed before the location can be made. All that is required to be filed with these officers is the agent's certificate of the believed accuracy of the list. *Ibid.*

SEC. 2982. As to the validity of the certificate of the register of the land office at Pontotoc, showing the location of the land under the sixth article of the treaty of 1834 with the Chickasaws, which was offered in evidence by the plaintiff's lessor in the circuit court, see the case of Wray *v.* Doe (18 Miss., 452), in which this court decided such to be competent testimony, and which decision is here affirmed. *Ibid.*

SEC. 2983. Some time previous to the year 1830, Smith, a white man, married a woman of the Choctaw Nation, and the parties, after marriage, continued to reside on certain land granted by article 19 of the Choctaw treaty of 1834 (7 Stat. L., 450) which provides that each head of family who had cultivated 30 acres of land during the year 1830 should have three quarter sections to include improvements. Smith located the land in the name of himself and wife, and in 1835 he sold it to Hall, from whom Fish derives his title. *Held,* that the treaty has reference to the heads of families living under the dominion of the Choctaw Nation, but it does not say that a white man may not according to the usages and customs of that nation, be the head of a family. *Turner v. Fish, 28 Miss., 306.*

SEC. 2984. The Government having recognized the location of the land by Smith, and the sale by him to Hall, in the absence of any showing to the contrary, the validity of the action of the Government whose duty it was to carry out the stipulations of the treaty will be presumed. *Ibid.*

SEC. 2985. A patent for a tract of land reserved to a Choctaw Indian under the treaty of 1830, issued by the United States to the vendee of the Indian, and reciting a sale by the reservee to the patentee and its approval by the Government, is evidence of a good title to the land in the patentee against all persons except the Indian or his heirs, or a party claiming title under him by a purchase duly approved, according to the terms of the treaty. *Johnston v. Horne, 32 Miss., 151.*

SEC. 2986. A deed by a reservee under the supplemental Choctaw treaty of 1830 (7 Stat. L., 340) to land in the adverse possession of a third person, though valid as between the grantee and grantor, is absolutely void as to him in possession; and it therefore constitutes no obstacle to a subsequent complete conveyance of the grantor's title as it existed before the execution of the deed to the adverse holder.

Betsey v. Torrance, 34 Miss., 132.

SEC. 2987. A patent for land issued by the Government is evidence of the existence and due performance of all the conditions upon which its issuance depended. And hence a patent issued to a Chickasaw Indian, under the provisions of the treaty of 1834, is evidence that the patentee was entitled to a reservation under the eighth article of the treaty, and that the land had been regularly surveyed and located for his benefit. *Harris v. McKissack, 34 Miss., 464.*

SEC. 2988. It will not be presumed, in the absence of all proof on the subject, that a minor, to whom land was reserved under the Chickasaw treaty of 1834 (7 Stat. L., 450), had arrived at full age in 1854, so as to avoid a sale then made by the President of the land so reserved.

Ibid.

SEC. 2989. The rights of that class of persons to which the patentee belonged depended exclusively on the stipulations of the treaty of 1834 (7 Stat. L., 450) with the Chickasaws. The title, at least the beneficial ownership of the lands, reserved by the eighth article of the treaty, never attached in the United States. They were reserved and appropriated by the treaty itself. *Ibid.*

SEC. 2990. Although the Chickasaw treaty of 1834 contemplated the speedy sale of the lands reserved and located under the eighth article, if the parties designated should deem it advisable, and that the power of the President over the subject of such sale terminated with the minority of the persons entitled to the reservations, the objection urged thereto is untenable. *Ibid.*

SEC. 2991. The appellee can not claim to stand in the attitude of a *bona fide* purchaser without notice. He knew that the land in question was a reservation under the eighth article of the treaty of 1834, and was presumed to know the authority under which the register and receiver claimed to act. As the sale was illegal and void, the appellee did not acquire even an equity in virtue of the sale. *Ibid.*

SEC. 2992. The President, by the terms of the Chickasaw treaty of 1834 (7 Stat. L., 450), was vested with authority, upon the recommendation of a majority of the chiefs, designated under the fourth article of the treaty, to order a sale of the lands reserved under the eighth article, and also to designate the time and place, mode and manner of sale; and his directions on this subject constitute the law, to which not only the subordinate officers must conform in making a sale, but they are also binding on the President; and hence where the land of a reservee was sold in larger quantities and at a lower price than was authorized by the President's instructions, the sale is absolutely void, notwithstanding his subsequent approval of it. *Ibid.*

SEC. 2993. An objection to the introduction in evidence of a deed made by a Chickasaw Indian "that it was not made and certified to according to the requirements of the treaty of 1834," is bad; the objection should have pointed out specifically in what respect the deed and certificate were not in accordance with the treaty.

New Orleans, J. and G. N. R. R. Co. v. Moye, 39 Miss., 374.

SEC. 2994. The interest of a Chickasaw Indian in land situated in Mississippi is subject to the bar created by adverse possession for the time prescribed in the statute of limitations. *Ibid.*

SEC. 2995. Where the declaration in an action of ejectment by a reservee under the Chickasaw treaty of 1834 (7 Stat. L., 450) does not show that the defendant was in possession of the land, the character of that possession and the length of time for which enjoyed, the question of the bar of the statute of limitations on account of the adverse possession can not be raised by a demurrer to the declaration.

Tush-ho-yo-tubby v. Barr, 41 Miss., 52.

SEC. 2996. Under the act of Congress April 20, 1832, for the relief of Jefferson College (6 Stat. L., 484) requiring that the lands granted should be located in bodies of not less than two sections and that each location should be of one body of contiguous lands and on unappropriated land, such location, where it afterwards appears that part of the land was an Indian reservation and another part was a preemption claim, together covering nearly one-half, is void only as to so much as was embraced in the reservation and preemption and good for the rest, although the contiguity of the remaining parts was destroyed. *Shelton v. Keirn, 45 Miss., 106.*

SEC. 2997. A decision by the Commissioner of the General Land Office, or of any other officer, in respect to conflicting claims to land, does not affect the power of the courts to decide on the facts and law of a case involving them, and has no binding force on the courts. The power given to a register to decide between conflicting claims clearly relates to the claim to make the *entry*, on which the grant of the patent is to be founded, and this decision is to be made at the time of the application to make such entry. *Ibid.*

SEC. 2998. A continued residence of the plaintiff in ejectment for land, since the year 1838, in the Indian Territory, west of the State of Arkansas, is not such absence without the limits of the United States as will prevent the bar of the statute of limitations from attaching to the action. *Tush-ho-yo-tubby v. Barr, 45 Miss., 189.*

SEC. 2999. It would be error to instruct a jury in an action of ejectment that "presumptions of law from lapse of time, coupled with possession, in favor of the existence of a deed or other muniment of title, or right of possession, are weaker and less conclusive against a plaintiff in ejectment than the statute of limitations." *Ibid.*

SEC. 3000. In the execution of Indian treaties the Government had uniformly permitted "reservees" to make locations on any sections, including the sixteenth. Such was the opinion given by the Attorney-General to the Commissioner of the General Land Office in 1838.

Minter v. Shirley, 45 Miss., 376.

SEC. 3001. The cession of the whole reserve by the Choctaw treaty of 1830 (7 Stat. L., 333), was subject to the right to withhold certain parcels which, when designated by a selection, were excluded from the grant and held by the ancient title of the tribe, quitclaimed and confirmed by the United States. *Ibid.*

SEC. 3002. The reservation by article 2 of the Choctaw treaty, 1830, to Robert Jones of the right to locate a section upon any unoccupied and unimproved land, gave him the right to locate upon a sixteenth section, which was unoccupied and unimproved; and his assignee, receiving a patent from the United States to a sixteenth section, located by virtue of his claim, acquired a good title. *Ibid.*

SEC. 3003. The act of Congress, August 23, 1842, provides that the patent for lands should be issued to the Indian, if living, who took under the treaty of 1830 (7 Stat. L., 733). *Ibid.*

SEC. 3004. The covenant of the United States was that the reservee might place his "float" upon any lands within the ceded territory not "improved and not occupied." This would give him the right to locate it upon sixteenth sections. *Ibid.*

SEC. 3005. If the sixteenth section should include an "improvement," which by the treaty was reserved to a particular Indian, it is clear that the reservee would have a good title; for the very parcel of land described and designated is excepted out of the cession to the United States. (Gaines v. Nicholson, 9 How., 356.) The court, however, forebore to express an opinion as to whether the same result would ensue if a reservee had located his "float" on a sixteenth section. *Ibid.*

SEC. 3006. Whether Istonche had a title to the land under the Choctaw treaty of 1830 was directly involved and decided in the chancery suit (1 S. & M. Chancery, 158). The plaintiffs in error, privies in estate with Silas Land, are estopped from affirming or claiming that the land had not been appropriated to her, and are also estopped from setting up a title which is founded on a denial of that fact. *Land v. Keirn, 52 Miss., 341.*

SEC. 3007. The application to register satisfies the requirements of the Choctaw treaty of 1830, although the agent may fail to do his duty. In order to work a forfeiture by removal from the land within five years the removal must be voluntary and not forcible. *Ibid.*

SEC. 3008. A reservation under the Choctaw treaty of 1830 separates the land reserved from the public lands, and operates as a grant of the reserve, which takes effect upon the particular parcel, when specified and located, as completely as if the treaty had assigned the particular parcel. The grant being complete in itself, a patent is unnecessary, and a patent which attempts to convey land previously reserved or appropriated is void.   *Ibid.*

SEC. 3009. The bond gives no other designation of the land than the vague and indefinite description that it is for the conveyance of five sections of land claimed by Davis of certain Indians, claiming under the fourteenth article of the Dancing Rabbit Creek treaty.   It is therefore void.   *Wilkinson v. Davis's Admr., 1 Freeman's Chancery (Miss.), 53.*

SEC. 3010. When a party representing himself as the assignee of certain Choctaw Indians who were entitled to certain lands under the Choctaw treaty of 1830 (7 Stat. L., 333) sold said land and it afterwards appeared that he was not the assignee of said Indians, but had contracted to become their assignee upon certain conditions, which he had not complied with, it was held to be a fraud, and the contract for the sale of said land was rescinded.   *Ibid.*

SEC. 3011. Every contract for the conveyance of land must define its identity and fix its locality, or there must be such description of the land that parol evidence will readily point to its locality and boundaries.   There is no proof that Davis was the assignee of a single Indian title, except some negative parol proof which is inadmissible.   *Ibid.*

SEC. 3012. The certificate of the agent as to competency and adequacy of consideration were mere preliminaries to a sale, and were not obligatory upon anyone, as the President still had the power to approve or disapprove the same.
        Anderson & Orne v. Lewis & Niles, 1 Freeman's Chancery (Miss.), 178.

SEC. 3013. By article 6, Chickasaw treaty, 1834 (7 Stat. L., 455), it is provided that a section of land within the territory, which was the principal subject of the treaty, should be reserved to each male and female of the tribe, not being the heads of families, who were of the age of 21 years and upwards.   This treaty vests a right in the persons thus described to one section of land, and that right may be conveyed to a third party even before the land is located, if the conveyance is made according to the forms prescribed in the treaty.   *Ibid.*

SEC. 3014. It is now well-settled doctrine that even a mere possibility, clothed with an interest in real estate, may be made a subject of a contract, which a court of equity will enforce.   *Ibid.*

SEC. 3015. The certificates required by the Chickasaw treaty to pass the title of an Indian to his land are conditions subsequent.   Where an estate is granted upon a condition subsequent, and that condition becomes impossible by inevitable accident or the performance of it is prevented by the grantor, in both cases the estate granted becomes absolute and unconditional. *Ibid.*

SEC. 3016. Where an Indian claiming a section of land under the Chickasaw treaty of 1834 sold the same for a fair consideration, and the purchaser was prevented from perfecting his title according to the form prescribed in the treaty, by the fraud of a third party, who obtained a deed to the same land with full knowledge of the previous sale, it was held that this was a sufficient excuse for the failure of the first purchaser to perfect his title, and that a court of equity would perfect the same. *Ibid.*

SEC. 3017. The Chickasaw treaty of 1834 requires that where an Indian sells his reservation, certain officers, appointed for that purpose under the treaty, shall certify that said Indian is competent to contract, and that a fair consideration has been paid him, whereupon the President shall approve the sale. Such a conveyance is *prima facie* evidence of good title, but the same may be contested in a court of equity and vitiated for fraud. *Ibid.*

SEC. 3018. The acts of officers who certify to the competency of an Indian to contract, etc., are purely ministerial, and partake no more of the character of a judicial sentence than the certificate of a clerk or justice of the peace of the acknowledgment of a deed. *Ibid.*

SEC. 3019. By the language of article 6 of the Chickasaw treaty of 1834 (7 Stat L., 450) a title in fee passed to such persons as were over 21 years of age. The term "reservation" was equivalent to an absolute grant. The same term used in the Choctaw treaty was held to pass title, although it was then provided that a grant should issue. Although the title was conferred by treaty, it was not perfect until location was made; location was necessary to give identity. *Ibid.*

SEC. 3020. The question as to whether the Indian, from whom the defendants claim title, could convey any water right to them or not, referred to but not discussed. *Labdell v. Simpson, 2 Nev., 274.*

SEC. 3021. Any person getting possession of any dam or ditch, for the diversion of water from an Indian, although there be no deed of conveyance, has the same right to maintain and enjoy such dam and ditch as the Indian had. *Labdell v. Hall, 3 Nev., 507.*

SEC. 3022. An Indian who has appropriated water on the public lands of the United States may maintain an action for the diversion of that water, as well as any other person. *Ibid.*

SEC. 3023. When a patent for a lot of land was granted in 1791 to an Oneida Indian as a bounty for his services as a soldier during the Revolutionary war, " to hold unto him and his heirs and assigns forever," and the patentee died leaving two sons, his heirs, who sold and conveyed the land to A, it was held that the sale and conveyance were void.   Indians residing in the State of New York can not, according to the constitution and laws of the State, alienate their lands without the consent of the legislature or the approbation of the surveyor-general.   *Jackson v. Wood, 7 Johnson's Reports (N..Y.), 290.*

SEC. 3024. Under the third article of the treaty of 1819, between the United States and the Cherokee Indians, the particular Indians, residing within the limits of North Carolina, to whom reservations in fee simple were made, had a right to alienate the tracts reserved as they thought proper, prior to and independent of any act of the State legislature.   The condition annexed to this article does not require a perpetual residence on tracts reserved, but only a notification of an intent to reside, which is a condition precedent, and when complied with, the estate becomes absolute.
Den. ex dem. Belk. et al. v. Love, 4 Hawks. (N. C.), 65.

SEC. 3025. The Cherokees, by treaty of January 7, 1806 (7 Stat. L., 101), relinquished to the United States all their title and claim to the tract of country which lies north of Tennessee River, and westward of a line directed, etc., excepting two described tracts, etc., "which first reserved tract is to be considered the common property of the Cherokees who now live on the same, including John D. Chisolm," etc.   Doublehead's name is not mentioned in the reservation, but it is presumed he was one of the Indians living upon it.
Drew v. Clarke, 1 Cooke (Tenn.), 285.

SEC. 3026. The reservation of 640 acres to the head of every Indian family made by the Cherokee treaties of 1817 (7 Stat. L., 156) and 1819 (7 Stat. L., 195), upon certain conditions therein specified, are valid and binding on the State of Tennessee and all persons claiming under the State.   The head of a family, in selecting his tract, was not limited to the place where he resided at the date of the treaty.
Blair v. Pathkiller, 2 Yerg. (Tenn.), 407.

SEC. 3027. To the reserves taken by the treaties of 1817 and 1819, Tennessee never has had the right of possession, and could not, therefore, communicate it to the purchaser from her.   *Ibid.*

SEC. 3028. Pathkiller was given a reservation of 640 acres under the Cherokee treaties of 1817 and 1819 (7 Stat. L., 156 and 195, respectively) with a life estate therein to himself and a reversion in fee simple to his children.   *Ibid.*

SEC. 3029. Article 8 of the treaty of 1817; and articles 2 and 3 of the treaty of 1819, relative to allotments in severalty to Cherokees, construed.   Pathkiller removed to the land in controversy in April or May following the treaty of February 27, 1819, having previously resided at a place several miles distant.   He had no right to claim the land in controversy as a reserve for want of residence thereon at date of treaty, and the judgment below should be reversed.   *Ibid.*

SEC. 3030. Under the compact of 1806, by which the United States made a cession to the State of Tennessee, the Indian nation was the owner of the possessory right and all the subjects of the nation joint tenants of the whole territory ceded. The reservees, by the treaty, took in severalty directly from the nation the Indian title as his reasonable portion of the ceded territory. *Ibid.*

SEC. 3031. A material portion of the consideration for the lands ceded by the Cherokees by their treaties of 1817 and 1819 was the reserves to the individuals who had become cultivators of the soil. Take this part of the consideration away from the reservees and the treaties are violated and annulled. *Ibid.*

SEC. 3032. By article 3 of the treaty of 1817, the time for registering the name for life reservations was made coextensive with the time for taking the census, which was during the month of June, 1818. History of the time shows that the census was not taken at the time appointed, and as the removal of the Cherokees to Arkansas continued, in proportion to the numbers removed the right of cession accrued to the United States of lands lying east of the Mississippi.

Grubbs v. McClatchy, 2 Yerg., 431.

SEC. 3033. By article 8 of the Cherokee treaty of 1817 the registry of the name of the head of a family residing on the east side of the Mississippi River entitled him to a reservation of 640 acres, which reservation with his name was to be filed in the office of the Cherokee agent, the office to have been kept open for that purpose as stipulated in article 3 of the treaty. *Ibid.*

SEC. 3034. A registry for a reservation of land by the head of an Indian family under the Cherokee treaties of 1817 and 1819 is valid if made before January 1, 1820, and parol testimony is not admissible to show that the Indian making the registry had enrolled himself as a Kansas emigrant, nor is the right affected by a removal from the land, unless made with the intention of abandonment. *Ibid.*

SEC. 3035. The reservation given to the heads of families by the Cherokee treaties of 1817 and 1819 extended only to such persons as answered the description at the date of the treaty of 1819. Luna Riley, not being then the head of a family, was, by the terms of the treaty, excluded, and the registration of his name for a reservation unauthorized. *Riley v. Elliston, 2 Yerg., 431.*

SEC. 3036. Joint tenancies, and tenancies in common, were not within the purview of the Cherokee treaties of 1817 and 1819 (7 Stat. L., 156 and 195). *McConnell v. Mousepaine, 2 Yerg. (Tenn.), 437.*

SEC. 3037. The treaty of 1817 was prospective in its operation, contemplating a cession on the part of the Cherokees of all their claim to territory east of the Mississippi, and much was to be done to execute the treaty. It was supposed by the Cherokees to operate harshly upon them, and to put an end to its future effects the treaty of 1819 was made (7 Stat. L., 195). The treaty of 1819 spoke in the present, and its object was to operate upon the state of things as they then were. Instead of allowing to each head of an Indian family resid- ing on the east side of the Mississippi 640 acres, it allowed to each head of a family upon the territory then ceded to the United States that quantity.   *Ibid.*

SEC. 3038. A registry for a reservation by the head of a family under the treaties of 1817 and 1819 with the Cherokees is valid if made before January 1, 1820, and a subsequent removal by force, or threats of force, will not affect the rights thus acquired.   *Ibid.*

SEC. 3039. The treaty vested a right in Mousepaine to the 640 acres. It was an inchoate right, subject to be retained or forfeited by him for whose benefit it was made. He had an election (the United States had none) to divest or alter the title created by the treaty.   *Ibid.*

SEC. 3040. Although the Cherokee treaty of 1819 vested the right in Mousepaine to 640 acres of land, if he failed to register as a reservee before January 1, 1820, he forfeited. But if he registered, then, by force of the treaty, he became a citizen of the United States. If he failed to do this, he forfeited his right to become a citizen and his title to the land with it.   *Ibid.*

SEC. 3041. A voluntary removal from the land reserved at any time after the treaty was made and the title vested was a forfeiture. This was a prominent condition of the grant, and such being the condition attached to Mousepaine's title, no act on the part of the agents of the United States or by the legislature of Tennessee could divest this vested right.   *Ibid.*

SEC. 3042. Mousepaine's tract was located with reference to the improvements. This alone gave it locality, without which it would have been void.   *Ibid.*

SEC. 3043. The question of abandonment of a tract granted to an individual under the Cherokee treaty of 1817 (7 Stat. L., 156) is a question of fact for a jury.   *Grubb v. McClatchy, 3 Yer., 442.*

SEC. 3044. Under the Cherokee treaty of 1819 (7 Stat. L., 195) actual occupation of the land claimed before, at, or after the making of the treaty, and within the time therein limited, is necessary to communicate title to the claimant.   *West v. Donoho, 3 Yer., 445.*

SEC. 3045. The act of marrying an Indian woman would not of itself give a white man a right to a reservation under the Cherokee treaties of 1817 and 1819; but the forming of such a connection, taking up a residence among the Indians, and identifying himself with them, would constitute him the head of a family, which, coupled with residence and enrolling his name for a reservation, would give him such right.

Taten v. Martin, 3 Yer., 452.

SEC. 3046. The fact that a person's name was registered with the Cherokee agent for a reservation under the Cherokee treaties of 1817 and 1819 within the time prescribed in those treaties is conclusive evidence that such person was the head of an Indian family and resided within the ceded territory. *Jones v. Evans, 5 Yer., 323.*

SEC. 3047. A removal of the reservee by force will not work a forfeiture of his title, and he may recover the possession by ejectment against the defendant not concerned in such expulsion. *Ibid.*

SEC. 3048. The sale of the reservee's life estate, or a part of it, will not work forfeiture, provided he remain resident in even the least part of the 640-acre tract reserved to him. The reservee could not sell more than his life estate, and the treaty does not restrict the free exercise of the right of selling that. *McIntosh v. Cleveland, 7 Yer., 46.*

SEC. 3049. Possession of the land intended to be held as a reservation on the 1st of January, 1820, was indispensable to acquire title thereto under the Cherokee treaties of 1817 and 1819, but whether the reservee was possessed of any particular spot before that time or not would be immaterial. *Ibid. Neddy v. The State, 8 Yer., 247.*

SEC. 3050. Where the reservee had two improvements and might elect to take either, his election, when made, would be conclusive on himself and his heirs, and the specification of the place where he registered his name, together with other acts of his, might be taken by the jury as evidence of his intention as to the locality of his reservation. *McConnell v. McGee, 7 Yer., 63.*

SEC. 3051. No right to any particular tract of land could vest in a Cherokee reservee before January 1, 1820. The registration of his name would entitle him to take a reservation, but it would be a floating claim, capable of being located or not, up to the day upon which he must be found upon the spot he might wish to appropriate. If a right were vested before the 1st of January, 1820, to the place of which a party may have been in possession, although by the treaty his removal would forfeit his title, yet that forfeiture would have no effect, for he might return to it at pleasure before the 1st of January, 1820, and be vested with just as good right as he had forfeited. *Neddy v. The State's Lessee, 8 Yer. (Tenn.), 248.*

SEC. 3052. Under the Cherokee treaty of 1817 the only fact which works a forfeiture of the title of the Indian reservee is removal from the land, and it must be voluntary. *Evans v. Jones, 8 Yer., 461.*

SEC. 3053. Although it has been held (3 Yerg., 452; 2 Yerg., 432, 450) that a white man, a citizen of the United States, by marrying an Indian woman, taking up his residence among the Cherokee Indians and identifying himself with them, is constituted the "head of a family," yet the children born of such Indian wife alone are entitled to the remainder reserved under the eighth article of the Cherokee treaty of 1817 (7 Stat. L., 156).   The children of a marriage of such white man with a white woman, either before or after the marriage with the Indian woman, are neither within the letter nor policy of the treaty.   *Taten v. Byrd, 1 Swan (Tenn.), 108.*

SEC. 3054. After defendant's father, a person of Indian descent, had long been in the exclusive occupancy of a certain tract of land as his farm and home, and it had been allotted to him and he had cultivated and improved it and otherwise treated it in every respect as his private property, an act of Congress passed for his exclusive benefit authorized the payment to him of a certain sum of money belonging to the Stockbridge tribe, and granted said tract to him "in fee simple and to his heirs and assigns forever," in lieu of all his rights in the lands and annuities of the Stockbridge tribe, etc.; and neither the father nor the son appears ever to have submitted to any of the laws, customs, or regulations of any tribe, but adopted and always retained the manners, habits, and industries of civilized life.   *Held*, that both father and son are within the provisions of subdivision 4, section 1, article 3 of the State (Wisconsin) constitution, providing that "civilized persons of Indian descent, not members of any tribe," having the prescribed qualifications as to sex, age, and residence shall be qualified electors in this State; and that said tract of land now owned by defendant is held by "purchase" within the meaning of the laws of this State, and subject to taxation.

Helgurs v. Quimey, 3 Wis., 347.   Same, 8 N. W. Rep., 17.

SEC. 3055. A patent of land situated in this State (Wisconsin) issued by the United States to one of the tribes of Winnebago Indians, in pursuance of a treaty made with them, declared that the land was "not to be leased or sold by the grantee to any person or persons whatever without the permission of the President of the United States."   *Held*, that the restriction was valid and a conveyance made by the grantee in contravention thereof was void.   Such restriction was, however, personal to the grantee, and did not bind his heirs.

Subdivision 7, section 4, chapter 18, Revised Statutes, exempts from taxation "the property of all Indians who are not citizens, except lands held by them by purchase."   *Held*, that the lands reserved by the treaty (August 1, 1829; 7 Stat. L., 323) to one of the members of the tribe, and subsequently patented by the United States to him (he not being a citizen) were not held "by purchase" within the meaning of the provision, and were exempt from taxation.

Farrington v. Wilson, 29 Wis., 383.

SEC. 3056. An allotment of a portion of the Brothertown reservation to a member of that tribe under the act of Congress of March 3, 1839, vested in the allottee the whole beneficial interest in the land allotted, and such allotment never having been vacated or set aside, a patent for the same land subsequently issued to certain persons in

trust for the Brothertown Indians, under the act of April 20, 1878, is void.
Fowler et al. v. Scott, 64 Wis., 509.

SEC. 3057. The treaty between the United States and the Ottawa, Chippewa, and Pottawatomie Indians, providing in article 4 (7 Stat. L., 371) that the two sections of land required thereby to be granted to one "Alexander Robinson, for himself and children," should "never be leased or conveyed by the grantees, or their heirs, without the permission of the President of the United States." The patent to Robinson, in 1843, contained the same condition. Partition was had between Robinson and his children in 1847, and the part set off to one of the children (Joseph) was conveyed by him and his wife in 1858. The approval of the President was subsequently indorsed on this deed in 1871. *Held,* in ejectment by one claiming under the said Joseph through mesne conveyances, to recover the land so conveyed, that there was no compliance with the conditions upon which the sale might be made, and that the deed from Joseph was void.
Pickering v. Lomax et al., 11 North Eastern Reporter, 175.

SEC. 3058. Under the treaty between the United States and the confederated tribes of Kaskaskias, Peorias, Piankashaws, and Weas, of May 30, 1854 (10 Stat. L., 1082), an Indian was allotted a certain piece of land, and before the patent was issued he executed a deed therefor to the defendant's grantor. Such deed has never been approved by the Secretary of the Interior. The defendant and his grantor have been in the quiet and peaceable possession ever since, and for more than fifteen years prior to the commencement of this action. After the patent was issued to said Indian, and after his death, and on June 22, 1882, his sole surviving heir executed a deed of conveyance for the land to the plaintiff, and on October 10, 1882, such deed was approved by the Secretary of the Interior, and on April 25, 1883, the plaintiff commenced this action against the defendant to recover the land. *Held,* that neither this action nor the plaintiff's title to the land is barred by any statute of limitations.
McGannon v. Straightlege, 4 Pacific Reporter, 1042.

SEC. 3059. Under the treaties of 1862 and 1867, land allotted to an Ottawa Indian can not be alienated by a guardian's sale and deed while he is a minor.
Wiggin et al. v. King, 11 Pacific Reporter, 140.

SEC. 3060. The provision of article 2 of the treaty of 1805 with the Flathead Indians, that there might be placed on their reservation "other friendly bands of Indians of the Territory of Washington," who might agree to be consolidated with the Flathead Nation, does not authorize the adoption into the tribe of a quarter-breed Chippewa who is married to a Flathead woman.
Stiff v. McLaughlin, 48 Pacific Reporter, 232.

SEC. 3061. W., who had been a member of the Kickapoo tribe of Indians became a citizen of the United States, and thereafter executed a deed of conveyance, with the general covenants of warranty, for certain Indian lands in which he had an interest, but not the legal title, to one L., not an Indian, and to whom a conveyance of such lands was at the time not authorized by law. Subsequently, the legal title to said lands becoming vested in W. with full power of conveyance, he executed another deed for the same to N., who took with notice of the prior deed. *Held*, that W. and his second grantee were estopped from setting up a title adverse to that attempted to be conveyed by deed to L.   *Letson v. Roach et al., 47 Pacific Reporter, 321.*

SEC. 3062. Under article 3 of the treaty of the United States with the Kickapoo Indians, June 28, 1862 (13 Stat. L., 623) the lands allotted to a member of the said tribe of Indians became alienable and said Indian ceased to be a member of said tribe and became a citizen of the United States, when his application was acted upon by the President and a patent issued therefor and not at the time he appeared before the district court, made the required proof, and took the oath of allegiance as provided for in said article.
Baldwin v. Letson et al., 49 Pacific Rep., 619.

SEC. 3063. Montour's Island was within the original charter boundaries of Virginia; so that as far as royal jurisdiction and Indian surrender are involved, the sovereignty and property of that State was complete.   *Sims's Lessee v. Irwin, 3 Dallas, 425.*

CHAPTER VI.—EXTINGUISHMENT OF THE INDIAN TITLE.

SEC. 3064. When the Indians abandoned their hunting grounds, made a cession of them to the Government, or an authorized sale to an individual, their right became extinct, and the lands could be granted disencumbered of the right of occupancy, or enjoyed in full dominion by the purchasers from the Indians. Such was the tenure of the Indian lands by the laws of Massachusetts, Connecticut, Rhode Island, New Hampshire, New York, Pennsylvania, Maryland, Virginia, North Carolina, South Carolina, Georgia, and Congress.
Mitchel v. United States, 9 Pet., 711.

SEC. 3065. The Cherokee town of Tellico, near the Tennessee River, in what is now Monroe County, Tenn., continued to be an Indian town until the treaty of 1819 (7 Stat. L., 195), when the Cherokees extinguished their title to the country there.
Porterfield v. Clark, 2 How., 76.

SEC. 3066. A forcible removal of an Indian tribe from their ancient home to a new country provided for them by treaty must be made, if made at all, under the direction of the United States.
Fellows v. Blacksmith, 19 How., 366.

SEC. 3067. The cession in the Chickasaw treaty of 1832 (7 Stat. L., 381) contemplated the ultimate abandonment of the lands by the Indians.   This treaty did not prove satisfactory and in a second treaty made in 1834 (7 Stat. L., 450) the United States agreed, when the body of the lands were surveyed, to reserve from sale certain limited portions on which the individual reservations should be located.   This was done in obedience to a just policy, for it would have been wrong, considering the dependent state of the Indians, to hold them to their original engagement, and it can not be doubted that it was the intention of both parties to the treaty to clothe the reservees with the full title, otherwise some words of limitation indicating a different intention would have been used.   *Best v. Polk, 18 Wall., 112.*

SEC. 3068. The Indian title to the Hot Springs in Arkansas Territory, with four sections of land including them, was extinguished August 24, 1818, by the treaty with the Quapaws.   (7 Stat. L., 176.)
Rector v. United States, 92 U. S., 698.

SEC. 3069. The act of Congress of March 3, 1863 (12 Stat. L., 793) authorizing treaties for the removal of the several tribes of Indians from the State of Kansas, and for the extinction of their title, and a subsequent act for the relocation of a part of the road of the Leavenworth, Lawrence and Galveston Railroad Company (17 Stat. L., 5) neither recognize nor confer a right to the lands within the Osage country.   *Railroad Co. v. United States, 92 U. S., 733.*

SEC. 3070. The policy of the removal of Indian tribes, a favorite one with the Government and always encouraged by it, looked to the extinguishment of the Indian title for the general good and not for the special benefit of any particular interest.   *Ibid.*

SEC. 3071. The propriety or justice of the action of the United States toward the Indians with respect to their lands is a question of governmental policy, and is not a matter open to discussion in a controversy between third parties, neither of whom derives title from the Indians.   *Beecher v. Wetherby, 95 U. S., 517.*

SEC. 3072. The obligation on the part of the Sioux Indians in their agreement of 1873, ratified by Congress on June 22, 1874 (18 Stat. L., 167), was only to cede their title.   It was not a cession in terms by them, although the officers of the Land Department treated it as an actual cession of title from its date, and the Indians had then retired to the reservation set apart for them by the treaty in 1867 (15 Stat. L., 505), thus giving up the occupancy of the other lands.   The relinquishment thus made was as effectual as a formal act of cession.   Their right of occupancy was in effect abandoned, and full consideration for it being afterwards paid, it could not be resumed.
Buttz v. Railroad Co., 119 U. S., 55.

SEC. 3073. Considering the Sioux agreement, ratified in 1874 (18 Stat. L., 167), in connection with the actual retirement of the Indians from the land, the agreement may properly be treated as establishing the extinguishment of the Indian title from its date, or so far as the United States is concerned.   *Ibid.*

SEC. 3074. That the policy pursued by Wozencraft and his colleagues was the only one that would give peace to the inhabitants of California; that the Indians were induced by the promises of subsistence held out to them to abandon their lands to the whites and settle upon reservations selected for them, and that the United States thereby acquired title to the lands so abandoned, are considerations to be addressed to Congress in support of a special appropriation to pay the claim of McDougall's administrator, but they do not establish, or tend to establish, a claim against the United States enforcible by suit.   *United States v. McDougall's Admr., 121 U. S., 89.*

SEC. 3075. By virtue of the treaty of 1842 (7 Stat. L., 591), in the absence of any proof that the Chippewa Indians have surrendered their right of occupancy, the right still remains with them, and the title and right which the State may claim ultimately to the sixteenth section of every township for the use of the schools is subordinate to this right of occupancy of the Indians, which has never been released to any of their lands except as it may be inferred from the provisions of the treaty of 1854 (10 Stat. L., 1109).   *United States v. Thomas, 151 U. S., 577.*

SEC. 3076. The general authority conferred upon the President by the act of March 1, 1847 (9 Stat. L., 146) to set apart such portion of lands within the land district then created as were necessary for public uses, can not be considered as empowering him to interfere with reservations existing by force of treaty. The land was appropriated in a sense which exempted it from a reservation made in such general terms, at least so long as the Indian right of user remains unextinguished.   *Spalding v. Chandler, 160 U. S., 394.*

SEC. 3077. Where the title of the Indians and their right of occupancy of certain lands had been fully extinguished it was held that they passed under this act (June 3, 1856; 11 Stat. L., 17) notwithstanding that they were held by the United States in trust to sell them for the benefit of the Indians. But even if the lands did not pass under said act it was held that the defendant, who had taken possession and claimed title under the same act, was estopped from setting up this fact.   *Shepard v. Insurance Co., 40 Fed. Rep., 341.*

SEC. 3078. The title of the Indians to these lands (Chippewa in Michigan) had been fully extinguished. We are not therefore embarrassed by the considerations which influenced the court in the case of Railroad Company *v.* United States (92 U. S., 733), in which it was held that a general grant of lands to a railroad company would not be construed to embrace lands of which an Indian tribe had been granted by treaty the use and possession for an indefinite length of time.   *Ibid.*

SEC. 3079. The lands in Bitter Root Valley above the Lo Lo Fork were not public lands such as could pass to the Northern Pacific Railroad by the grant expressed in the act of July 2, 1864, section 3, as of that date, for by the treaty of 1855 (12 Stat. L., 975) with the Flathead Indians it was provided that these lands should be surveyed and examined, and if, in the judgment of the President, they proved to be better adapted to the wants of the Flathead tribe than the general reservation therein provided, then such portions as were necessary should be set apart as a general reservation for the tribe, and that they should not be open to settlement until the decision of the President was made known; and such decision was not made known until 1871, when the President decided not to make the lands a reservation.

Railroad v. Henchman et al., 53 Fed. Rep., 523.

SEC. 3080. There is no claim on the part of the Indians residing in the Bitter Root Valley that the same or any part thereof is an Indian reservation, or that the Flathead tribe, to which they belong, has never parted with the Indian title thereto; nor is the trust in controversy claimed by any of said Indians; nor was it so claimed by any of them at the date of the filing of the map of definite location of the plaintiff's road, or at the date of entry thereof by defendant; nor was the said tract of land embraced in any of the patents mentioned as having been issued to but not accepted by the Indians.   *Ibid.*

SEC. 3081. All public lands, including any Indian title thereto, being under the control of the Government, it must follow that any right which Craig may have obtained to the land must have been through the laws of the Government, and any laws which granted him such right must, at the same time, have operated to extinguish the Indian title thereto.   *Caldwell v. Robinson, 59 Fed. Rep., 653.*

SEC. 3082. The theory that lands conveyed by the Government patents after being so conveyed and appropriated by individual citizens still remain subservient to use and occupancy by the Indians for travel over the same, otherwise than by lawfully established public highways and for camping grounds, finds no support in the provisions of the treaty (Yakima, 12 Stat. L., 951) nor in the rules for the construction and interpretation of statutes which must be applied in the interpretation of the treaty and of the public land laws of the United States.   *United States v. Winans, 73 Fed. Rep., 72.*

SEC. 3083. It was an invasion of the rights of the Yakima indians under their treaty (12 Stat. L., 951) to exclude them from fishing in the Columbia River at a place to which, at and prior to the making of the treaty, the Indians were accustomed to fish, though the lands bordering on the river at such place had been patented to private citizens, but that the right of the Indians to erect temporary buildings on any particular lands ceased when such land was so patented and vested in private citizens.   *Ibid.*

SEC. 3084. The Government of the United States is the primary source of title to the public lands, the Indians having only a right of occupancy, which may at any time be extinguished by Congress.

United States v. Four Bottles Sour Mash Whiskey, 90 Fed. Rep., 720.

SEC. 3085. The provisions of the act of July 1, 1898 (30 Stat. L., 593), authorizing the entry of mineral lands in the Colville Indian Reservation, in the State of Washington, under the laws of the United States relating to the entry of mineral lands, necessarily gave prospectors and miners the right to explore the reservation for minerals, and authorized citizens who make discovery of valuable minerals therein to locate claims and work them as required to obtain title under the mineral land laws. The effect of such a valid location is to segregate the claim from the reservation, and extinguish the Indian title thereto, which is merely possessory, so that the land embraced in such location ceases to be Indian country, within the meaning of of sections 2139 and 2140, Revised Statutes, and the act of January 30, 1897 (29 Stat. L., 506), prohibiting introduction of liquor into the Indian country.   *Ibid.*

SEC. 3086. The Indians on these portages (in Oregon) had claimed and enjoyed the right of carriage of goods over them; and when it will be seen through the proofs that no special treaty has even to this day extinguished the Indian title just there, while we have treaties with these tribes shingling over nearly the whole State of Oregon and Washington Territory, any such action for damages as this of the Younger Johnson may be better understood.

Johnson v. United States, 26 Cls. R., 391.

SEC. 3087. By the treaty at the rapids of Maumee, September 29, 1817 (7 Stat. L., 160), a large tract of land was ceded to the United States, within which the land in controversy was situated. It seems, then, that any entry made within this territory prior to said cession was contrary to law.   *Doe. ex dem. Chinn. v Darrell, 4 McLean, 440.*

SEC. 3088. Without a law the President is not authorized to sell the public lands, so that this treaty, though so far as the Indians were concerned was the supreme law of the land, yet as regards the proceeds of the tract in question, an act of Congress is required.

Turner v. Amc'n Baptist Missionary Union, 5 McLean, 344.

SEC. 3089. There was no valid subsisting treaty by which the Indian title to the lands in controversy was extinguished when the act of July 26, 1866, granting lands to Kansas for railroad purposes became a law.   *United States v. M., K. and T. Ry. Co., 1 McCrary, 624.*

SEC. 3090. This case differs from that of the same plaintiff against the Leavenworth, Lawrence and Galveston Railroad Company in this, that the act of Congress, which is the foundation of the defendant's claim to the lands in controversy, was passed July 26, 1866. The significance of this difference in the dates of the grants is found in the assertion of the defendants that the lands in question had then been ceded to the United States.

Ibid.

SEC. 3091. The first article of the treaty of 1814 with the Creek Indians confers upon the chiefs and warriors provided for a qualified inheritable estate, which is determined by the sale of the reservee, the cesser of occupation, and his removal from the State; and immediately upon such abandonment of possession, the reservation becomes a part of the public domain, without any positive assertion of right on the part of the United States. But the reservation thus abandoned is not subject to entry under the preemption laws of Congress.

Crommelin v. Minter et al., 9 Ala., 594.

SEC. 3092. The failure of an Indian reservee, or his or her heirs, under the provisions of the treaty of the 24th of March, 1832, with the Creek tribe of Indians, to take possession of the land allotted to them, or in any manner to signify a desire to remain in the State after the five years expired, determined the estate to which they would otherwise have been entitled, and the land reverts to the United States without an entry or other act on the part of its agent.

Wells & Wells v. Thompson, 13 Ala., 793.

SEC. 3093. If an Indian reservee under the Creek treaty of 1832 fails to sell and convey his reservation in five years, in the mode prescribed by the treaty, and at the end of that period manifests no desire to remain in the State, his reservation will revert to and vest in the United States without an entry or other act on the part of its agents.

Corprew v. Arthur et al., 15 Ala., 525.

SEC. 3094. Where an Indian reservee, the head of a family, made application to the locating agent to be located on her reservation, which application was improperly refused, and she continued to reside on the land until interrupted in her possession by intruders, and then went to a relative's to reside, this is not an abandonment of the land, notwithstanding she is afterwards removed from the country by the force of the Government.

Rowland & Heifner v. Ladiga's heirs, 21 Ala., 9.

SEC. 3095. The policy of the Government has been to protect the lands occupied by the Indians from settlement, and not to convey the title until the possessory rights of the Indians have been extinguished; therefore, it is not to be presumed that the United States intended that the act of April 12, 1814 (3 Stat. L., 121) should extend to lands south of the Arkansas River, the title to which was not ceded to the Federal Government until August, 1818.

Gaines et al. v. Hale & Rector, 26 Ark., 168.

SEC. 3096. Under Mexican law the approbation and consent of the Government was necessary to make a conveyance of land by an Indian to a white person valid; and such consent being wanting, *held*, that a conveyance was void upon its face and transferred no title, and that the party claiming under it was chargeable with knowledge of its invalidity.   *Sunol v. Hepburn, 1 Cal., 255.*

SEC. 3097. A grant of land by the Mexican Government to a tribe of Indians, if of any validity, is for the benefit of the Indian community at large, and the individual members composing the tribe can not make any valid conveyance of all or any portion of the same.
                                             Hicks v. Coleman, 25 Cal., 122.

SEC. 3098. Lands in California in the occupancy of Indian tribes at the date of the treaty of Guadalupe Hidalgo became a part of the public domain, and subject to preemption, if no claim therefor was presented by the occupants to the land commissioners appointed under the act of Congress of March 3, 1851, within two years after the date of the act.   *Thompson v. Doaksum, 68 Cal., 593.*

SEC. 3099. There is no provision in the act of July 2, 1864 (13 Stat. L., 365), by which the lands were to revert to the grantor in case of a failure to perform the conditions. The title to the land would be unaffected by such failure until Congress should see fit to enforce a forfeiture. The words used are terms of present grant, but at the time this act was passed that portion of the grant lying west of the Red River, embracing the land in this contention, was Indian territory, in the possession of the Wahpeton and Sisseton bands of Indians; hence the act provided that the United States should extinguish, as rapidly as consistent with public policy and the welfare of the Indians, this title to all lands falling under the operation of the act.
                            Northern Pacific Ry. Co. v. Peronto, 3 Dakota (Smith), 227.

SEC. 3100. By the removal of the Indian reservation (by Executive order) on February 28, 1877, the Black Hills country was open to legal settlement.   *Hawke v. Deffebach, 4 Dakota (Smith), 37.*

SEC. 3101. The United States, acting in aid of the Wyandottes in the transfer of the ferry to plaintiff in error and conveying only "the rights of the Wyandottes in said ferry," did not thereby convey to plaintiff in error any interest or easement in their own land.
                                           Walker v. Armstrong, 2 Kans, 198.

SEC. 3102. Congress, by the second section of the act of July 1, 1862 (12 Stat. L., 489), granted the right of way for the railroad through the Delaware diminished reserve, and agreed to extinguish as rapidly as possible the Indian title required for such right of way. This grant was for 400 feet—200 feet in width on each side of the railroad. (Grinter *v.* Railway Co., 23 Kans., 642.)
                                       U. P. Ry. Co. v. Kindred, 43 Kans., 134.

Sec. 3103. In the treaty between the United States and the Caddo Indians of the 1st of July, 1835, that tribe was not treated with as the owners, but merely as the occupants of the territory from which it was the object of the Government to induce them to remove.

Brooks v. Norris, 6 Robinson (La.), 175.

Sec. 3104. The so-called treaty of 1794 was simply a grant by the Commonwealth to the Passamaquoddy tribe of Indians of certain lands and the privilege of fishing in the Schoodiac River in consideration of their releasing all claims to other lands in the Commonwealth. The defendant gains no right to hunt under that grant.

State v. Newell, 84 Me., 465.

Sec. 3105. By a treaty made in 1807 between the United States and the Chippewa, Ottawa, Pottawatomie, and Wyandotte tribes of Indians, certain lands near Detroit, among others, were reserved to these tribes. The treaty did not show on its face what tribe was in the occupancy of these lands. By another treaty with the Pottawatomies in 1827, these lands, therein stated to have been before "reserved to the use of said tribe," were ceded to the United States. *Held,* that this treaty having recognized the right to this reserve to have been in the Pottawatomies, the courts are bound so to regard it, and must consider the treaty of 1827 as extinguishing the reserve.

Maiden v. Ingersoll, 6 Mich. (2 Cooley), 373.

Sec. 3106. Congress, by the act passed to carry the cession made by Georgia into effect, directs that those persons who had obtained, either from the British Government of West Florida, or the Spanish Government, any warrant or order of survey for lands in said territory, to which the Indian title had been extinguished, should be confirmed therein. The inference is that, in the opinion of Congress, no grant would have been made of land to which the Indian title was not extinguished at the time, or if made, that it would not be valid.

Montgomery v. Ives, 21 Miss., 161.

Sec. 3107. On this part of the proclamation of 1763 the Supreme Court of the United States say: "This reservation is a suspension of the powers of the royal governor within the territory reserved." Fletcher *v.* Peck, 6 Cranch, 142. It is because of this suspension, which existed at the date of this grant, that we think it has no intrinsic validity. It is an established principle in our jurisprudence that a grant of land on which the Indian title has not been extinguished is void. *Ibid.*

Sec. 3108. The Indian title to the country in which the land in controversy lies was not extinguished until May, 1777, when the Choctaws relinquished their title to it by treaty at Mobile with the British superintendent of Indian affairs. This is the relinquishment referred to in the act of the legislature of Georgia, creating the county of Bourbon in 1785, and it was confirmed by the treaty between these Indians and the United States, January 3, 1786 (7 Stat. L., 21). See 5 Hall. Law Journal, 363–390.   *Ibid.*

SEC. 3109. The proclamation of George III further declares a principle which seems to have been adhered to ever since, "that no private person do make purchase of any land from any Indians, but the same shall be purchased only for the Government, in the name of the Sovereign, at some public meeting of the Indians." This principle became incorporated into the intercourse of England with the Indian tribes and has been adopted and pursued by our own Government in all its transactions with them.   *Ibid.*

SEC. 3110. The statute of 1803, reserving the sixteenth sections for schools, in terms only applied to lands to which the Indian title had been extinguished. The Choctaws and Chickasaws then occupied a large portion of the territory embraced in the limits of Mississippi. The line which divided Mississippi from the Indian country was at a point at or near the mouth of the Yazoo River. Prior to the extinction of the Indian title there was not a vested right, either in the State or the inhabitants of a township, to the sixteenth sections.
Minter v. Shirley, 45 Miss., 376.

SEC. 3111. Features of cession and boundary are found in the Chickasaw treaty of September 20, 1816 (7 Stat. L., 150), the Choctaw treaties of October 24, 1816 (7 Stat. L., 152), and October 18, 1820 (7 Stat. L., 210). Finally, the treaty of 1830 (7 Stat. L., 333–340) extinguished their title to all their lands east of the Mississippi River, except certain reservations therein made.   *Ibid.*

SEC. 3112. The several acts of Congress respecting the survey and sale of public lands distinctly keep in view the fact "that the Indian title must first have been extinguished and acquired by the United States before individual right to any part of the soil can be derived and vest." An example is furnished by the Chickasaw treaty of 1834 "of a paramount obligation resting on the Government" which interposes "a legal obstacle to the reservation in controversy for the use of schools."   *Ibid.*

SEC. 3113. Prior to 1758 the remnant of the Delaware tribe had claims to a large portion of lands in New Jersey, which the Government and proprietors, under the conveyance from Charles II to the Duke of York, desired to extinguish. To effect that object a convention was held in February, 1758, between the Indians and the commissioners appointed by New Jersey, at which the Government purchased the tract of land in litigation, on which the Indians might reside, in consideration of which they released their claim to all other lands in New Jersey south of the Raritan.   *State, Given, pros., v. Wright, 41 N. J., 478.*

SEC. 3114. When the defendant in ejectment sets up an outstanding title, it must be a present, subsisting, and operative title, otherwise the presumption is that such title in a stranger has been extinguished. An outstanding title in certain Indians of the Mohawk tribe was held to be extinguished, as the title had never been claimed or asserted, and the tribe or nation had become extinct.

Jackson v. Hudson, 3 Johnson's Reports (N. Y.), 374.

SEC. 3115. This court will take judicial notice of the fact that the tract of land known as the "Pulteney estate" was ceded by the State of New York to the State of Massachusetts by the treaty and deed of cession executed December 16, 1786, and that under the proper authority, State and national, the Indian title to said lands has been extinguished. As to whether the fact that the Indian right of occupancy of lands within this State had not been extinguished with the sanction of the State government or abandoned by the Indians can be set up by one without title as against the owner in fee subject to such rights, *quære.*

Howard et al. v. Moot, 64 N. Y. App. (Sickels), 262.

SEC. 3116. On the declaration of independence the colonies became sovereign States, and, as such, succeeded to the title of the Crown to all the ungranted lands within their respective boundaries, with the exclusive right to extinguish by purchase the Indian titles, and to regulate dealings in regard thereto with the Indian tribes, which power they retained after the adoption of the Federal Constitution. The provisions of the Constitution of the United States, prohibiting any State from entering into "any treaty, alliance, or confederation" (sec. 10, art. 1), and conferring upon the President the treaty-making power (sec. 2, subd. 2, art. 2), do not apply to negotiations or dealings between a State and Indian tribes therein for the extinguishment of the Indian title to land in the State. Such a dealing is not a treaty in the constitutional sense, nor is it inconsistent with the exercise by the United States of its general jurisdiction for the protection of the Indians in their right of occupancy of their land.

The Seneca Nation v. Christie, 126 N. Y. App. 122.

SEC. 3117. In July, 1791, a treaty was made by William Blount on behalf of the United States with the Cherokee Indians, and it is stipulated in said treaty that "the chiefs and warriors of the Cherokee Nation for themselves and the whole Cherokee Nation, their heirs and decendants, for a consideration therein expressed, relinquish, release, recede, etc., all the land to the right of the line therein described."

Strother v. Cathey, 1 Murphy (N. C.), 168.

SEC. 3118. To resist the intrusions of Maryland, encouragement was offered by Sir William Keith to a number of Germans, and by them accepted, for forming settlements on the tract; and in 1736, the Indian title being extinguished, Thomas Penn empowered Samuel

Blunston to grant licenses for 12,000 acres to satisfy the rights of those who had settled within the tract of land commonly called "Springetsbury Manor," under the invitation of Sir William.

Penn's Less. v. Klyne, 1 Alden·(Penn.), 443.

SEC. 3119. The fact that the Indian title to the land in question had not been extinguished at the date of the State constitution, 1796, did not prevent the operation of the occupant and preemption right secured to residents on the land by that instrument.

George v. Gamble, 2 Overton (Tenn.), 549.

SEC. 3120. The bond was given by a citizen of the United States to an Indian countryman to secure the consideration money for an interest in a tract of land to which the Indian title was not extinguished. The section of the act of Congress of 1806 operates directly on the contract in question and renders null whatever agreement the complainant and Doublehead may have made with respect to the land.

Drew v. Clarke, 1 Cooke (Tenn.), 285.

SEC. 3121. From the words of the treaty of 1806 (7 Stat. L., 101) with the Cherokees, as well as the spirit of it, it would seem that as to the excepted tract the Indian title is not extinguished, because it is appropriated by the Indians themselves to a particular part of their nation. It is certainly true that in the reservation there are no words of inheritance by which to transmit the interest of the heirs of those for whom it was reserved; but to whom it is to belong after their death, whether to the whole nation or to any particular part of it, is unimportant.

Ibid.

SEC. 3122. By the Cherokee treaty of 1791 (7 Stat. L., 39) the Indian claim was extinguished to a certain portion of the tract reserved to them by the Tennessee act of 1783, and the treaty of 1789 (7 Stat. L., 62) extinguished the claim to the remainder of said tract.

Gould v. Hoyle, 3 Haywood (Tenn.), 72.

SEC. 3123. In 1807 (ch. 42), Tennessee made an appropriation for the extinguishment of the Cherokee title within her limits, but it was impossible to accomplish this until 1817 and 1819, when the title was extinguished by the United States as the agent of Tennessee.

Blair v. Pathkiller, 2 Yerg., 407.

SEC. 3124. The right of the reservee, once vested, was subject to be forfeited by one act, and one alone. That act is specified in the proviso to the eighth article of the treaty of 1817, in the following words: "*Provided*, That if any of the heads of families for whom reservations shall be made should remove therefrom, then, in that case, the right to revert to the United States." The stipulated act for which a forfeiture was to take place being a removal from the land reserved, the removal, if involuntary, coupled with or succeeded by any possible state of mind, can not work a forfeiture. No length of absence from the land; no manifestation of purpose not to return can forfeit his right, for by force of the treaty nothing can work a forfeiture but removal from the land. But if others get into possession under another title, and hold adversely for seven years, before suit, the Indian right is gone.   *McIntosh v. Cleveland, 7 Yerg., 46.*

SEC. 3125. If the reservee was deprived of the possession of his land by force, fear, or fraud, and afterwards determined to expatriate himself and not return to the land, it would not be a forfeiture or defeat recovery. Fear, operating to induce a removal which will not work a forfeiture, must be a fear superinduced by some act of others, with a design to affect thereby the reservee's removal. For if the reservee should commit a crime and remain away through fear of punishment, such removal would work a forfeiture.   *Ibid.*

SEC. 3126. The act of 1809, chapter 100 (Tennessee), declared that deeds of lands to which the Indian title was not extinguished at the time of execution should be good to pass the title when the Indian title shall be extinguished.   *Gordon v. Overton, 8 Yerg., 119.*

SEC. 3127. A line run by commissioners of the United States and the Indians, in compliance with treaty provisions, and acquiesced in by them, is conclusive in a question between individuals as to whether certain land is within or without the territory to which the Indian titles had not been extinguished.   *Gillespie v. Cunningham, 2 Humph. (Tenn.), 19.*

SEC. 3128. The State of Tennessee, under its compact with North Carolina in 1804, recognized and confirmed by the act of Congress in 1806, has never possessed or claimed the power to appropriate land to which the Indian title has not been extinguished, and entries and grants of such land have invariably been held void.   *Ibid.*

SEC. 3129. The Indian title to Jollys Island was extinguished by the Cherokee treaty of 1819 (7 Stat. L., 195).

Calloway v. Hopkins, 11 Haskell (Tenn.), 349.

SEC. 3130. If the Indian title to the lands granted (by act of Congress of August 8, 1846, to aid in the improvement of the Fox and Wisconsin rivers, etc.) was not extinguished, the power to extinguish that title was vested in the Government of the United States, and it becomes its duty to remove any incumbrance thereon.

Veeder et al. v. Guppy, 3 Smith (Wisc), 502.

SEC. 3131. In 1829 the land was not the subject of preemption, because the Indian title had not been extinguished. By Vanmatre's death the defendant's rights were extinguished so far as a preemption was concerned. Bracken and Parkinson were in reality the two first settlers, and were entitled to divide the quarter section between them, and this was the result of the decision of the Department and they are now bound by it. After examination of pleadings and evidence court *held* that this is not such a case either of fraud or mistake as to authorize this court in disturbing the patent of defendant.

Bracken v. Parkinson et al., 1 Pinney (Wisc), 685.

SEC. 3132. When a judgment by default in an action of ejectment has been entered against Indians who are ignorant and unacquainted with modes of judicial proceedings, it may be reopened and affidavits of merits, though made by counsel, received as sufficient.

Byrne v. Alas et al., 9 Pacific Reporter, 851.

SEC. 3133. In a lease of lands occupied and held by the Indians on the Uintah Reservation according to the provisions of the law of Congress passed February 28, 1891 (Sup. Rev. Stats., 2d ed., pp. 897, 898), the words "bought and paid for" were not intended by Congress to be a limitation to lands which had been actually paid for in cash, or to lands which had been patented and the title thereto actually parted with by the United States. It was doubtless the intention of Congress that the statute and those words should apply to all lands which had been purchased by the Indians either by the payment of money, or exchange, or by the surrender of the possession of other property.

The surrender of the rights of the Uintah Indians to other lands constituted a valuable and moving consideration for the land which they acquired for their places of abode in the future, and which, by the terms of the lease, passed to the plaintiff, for a term of years, for grazing purposes.   *Strawberry Valley Cattle Co. v. Chipman, 45 Pa. Rep., 348.*

CHAPTER VII.—BOUNDARIES OF THE INDIAN COUNTRY.

SEC. 3134. The boundaries of the Cherokee reservation have been altered by successive treaties with the Indians, but the mere extinguishment of the Indian title did not subject the land to appropriation, unless expressly authorized by the legislature.

Danforth v. Thomas, 1 Wheat., 155.

SEC. 3135. It was within the powers of the Intendent of Cuba and the Floridas, under the royal order of September 3, 1817, to decree officially, whether from the nature of the Indian right of occupancy, it had in law and by the actual condition of the land in fact, reverted to and become annexed to the royal domain by the abandonment of the occupancy, on report from the attorney-general as to the law on the subject and from the surveyor-general as to the fact of the abandonment.   *United States v. Arredondo, 6 Pet., 691.*

SEC. 3136. When it is considered that at the treaty of Holston (7 Stat. L., 43) the Cherokee Indians refused to make the ridge which divides the waters running into Little River from those running into the Tennessee River the boundary, and would agree to no other than a straight line; and that neither party seems to have considered the place of crossing at the mouth of the Holston, a liberal construction should be given to the clause in the treaty affecting the question.

Lattimer v. Poteet, 14 Pet., 4.

SEC. 3137. It is a sound principle of national law, and applies to the treaty-making power of this Government, whether exercised with a foreign nation or an Indian tribe, that all questions of disputed boundaries may be settled by the parties to the treaty.   And to the exercise of these high functions by the Government, within its constitutional powers, neither the rights of a State nor those of an individual can be interposed.   *Ibid.*

SEC. 3138. By the treaty of Long Island, made in July, 1777, between the Cherokees and Virginia the eastern line of the Indians in that State was removed west commencing 6 miles above the island and running with the Holston River to the mouth of Clouds Creek, the second creek below Rogersville, in Hawkins County, Tenn., and a few miles below that place; thence to a high point of Cumberland Mountain, a few miles below the Gap.   This was the only line between Virginia and the Indians in 1779 (when the land law was passed) except the boundaries established by the grant of March, 1776, to Richard Henderson and company.   *Porterfield v. Clark, 2 How., 76.*

SEC. 3139. The Cherokee town of Tellico near the Tennessee River, in what is now Monroe County, Tenn., continued to be an Indian town until the treaty of 1819 (7 Stat. L., 195), when the Cherokees extinguished their title to the country there.   *Ibid.*

SEC. 3140. The Cherokee sale to Henderson & Company stand on the same grounds as if it had been made by the authority of the Crown of Great Britain so far as the boundary and Indian rights stand affected.   *Ibid.*

SEC. 3141. The lands west of the line on the ridge from the Cherokee corner north to the Ohio River below the Chickasaws in 1779, when the Virginia land law was passed.   This is confirmed in a remarkable degree by the treaty of Hopewell with the Chickasaws (7 Stat. L., 25), and the intercourse had with them respecting that line.   *Ibid.*

SEC. 3142. During the British colonial government of Virginia, by different treaties prior to 1777, the eastern limits of the Cherokees commenced 6 miles above the Long Island in Holston River (now in the county of Sullivan, Tenn.), from thence to Cumberland Gap, thence to the head of the Kentucky River, and down the same to the Ohio.   *Ibid.*

SEC. 3143. The Chickasaw line established by the treaty of Hopewell (7 Stat. L., 25), from the Cherokee corner to the Ohio River, was conclusive as the true line of that people, anterior to any date known to Virginia as a Commonwealth.   *Ibid.*

SEC. 3144. The tract of country lying on the west of the Tennessee River was not, in 1779, the country of the Cherokee Indians, and not within the exemption of the Virginia act of 1779, prohibiting settlement within the Cherokee country.   *Ibid.*

SEC. 3145. Spain had no treaty with any of the Indian tribes in Louisiana, fixing limits to their claims, so far as we are informed; but the Indians were kept quiet, and at peace with Spanish subjects by kind treatment and due precautions, which did not allow obtrusion on lands claimed by them without written permits from the governor; but that such permits were usual, can not be doubted.

Marsh v. Brooks, 14 How., 513.

SEC. 3146. A boundary between the lands of an Indian tribe and those of the United States, surveyed by the parties, and acquiesced in for more than thirty years, can not be made the subject of dispute by reference to courses and distances called for in the patents under which the parties claimed.

United States v. Stone, 2 Wall., 525.

SEC. 3147. It was not until the act of 1864 (13 Stat. L., 40) that the survey of Indian lands was placed under the direction and control of the General Land Office.

McKee v. United States, 1 C. Cls., 341.

SEC. 3148. Where a boundary was fixed by treaty, a claim for an encroachment is a claim founded upon treaty, though the encroachment was sanctioned by statute; of it the court has jurisdiction under the act of 1881 (21 Stat. L., 504)

Choctaw Nation v. United States, 21 C. Cls., 59.

SEC. 3149. The western boundary of Arkansas having been fixed by the treaty of 1855, the Choctaws were not bound by an erroneous survey, nor by the act of March 3, 1875 (18 Stat. L., 476), which adopts the survey and makes the encroachment a part of the public domain.

Ibid.

SEC. 3150. The boundary of the lands of the claimant was fixed by the treaty of 1855, as well as other treaties; such boundary became as to it a claim founded on treaty stipulation, and it had a right to have such lands as were designated as forming a part of the territory ceded to it by treaty protected from the use and appropriation of the United States.

Ibid.

SEC. 3151. The registration act of 1881, chapter 122, section 15, applies to countries bordering on the Missouri River, etc. The act of 1873, chapter 16, section 26, bounds Buffalo County by the Missouri River. Counties are the creatures of statute, and, as the law creating Buffalo County extends it to and bounds it on one of its sides by the Missouri River, the position taken by the appellants that it is not so bounded because that portion of Buffalo County bordering on the Missouri River is Indian reservation, is clearly untenable. The fact that a portion of the county is Indian reservation can not and does not, in our opinion, change the boundary thereof.

Farren v. Comrs. of Buffalo Co., 5 Dakota (Tripp) 45.

SEC. 3152. The settlers on the section of country known as the neutral territory, between the Arroyo Hondo and the Sabine, within the limits of the present State of Louisiana, acquired no title to the lands occupied by them under any custom or usage of the Spanish Government independent of the act of Congress by which their titles were confirmed.   *Brooks v. Norris, 6 Robinson (La.), 187.*

SEC. 3153. Certain Indians, in a grant of land, made a reservation of a tract bounded north on a line some miles in length, "running a due west course" from a given point. In a controversy arising more than a hundred years after between parties owning land on different sides of the Indian line, it was held that evidence of general tradition and reputation and of the understanding and occupation of the owners of lands bounding on the line, and of deeds made by them, and acts of the legislature referring to the line, would warrant the jury in inferring that a line, varying some degrees from a due west course, was located, laid out, assented to, and adopted by the parties; and that if the jury did so find, the line so established must be taken as the true Indian line.   *Kellogg v. Smith, 61 Mass., 376.*

SEC. 3154. Whether that portion of the lands ceded to Great Britain by France and Spain in 1763, lying between the mouth of Yazoo River and the thirty-first degree of north latitude, ever constituted a part of the government of West Florida, created in that year by royal proclamation, so that they would pass by a grant from the British governor of that colony, dated in 1772, discussed by Mr. Justice Clayton, and its decision left to depend upon the fact whether the limits of the province of West Florida, as defined by the proclamation of 1763, were afterwards extended north from the thirty-first degree of north latitude to the mouth of Yazoo River, by commissions to governors of that province, issued in 1764 and 1770.   *Montgomery v. Ives, 21 Miss., 161.*

SEC. 3155. Action of ejectment by defendant in error to recover possession of a lot of land in the town of Catskill, in the county of Greene. Defendant in error gave in evidence certain Indian deeds, etc. Plaintiff in error set up that the premises in question were comprehended in an older patent, called the Catskill patent, etc. *Held*, that according to the true construction of the Catskill patent, its boundaries are to be ascertained by lines 4 miles distant, in every direction from the five plains mentioned in the patent, so as to make the exterior lines of the patent correspond as far as possible with the sinuosities of the plains, and so that a line 4 miles long extended from any part of the exterior sides of the plains will touch some part of the exterior boundary of the patent.

Van Gorden v. Jackson, 5 Johnson's Reports (N. Y.), 440.

SEC. 3156. Pursuant to act of Congress of 1878 (chap. 139), authorizing a resurvey of the reservation, a survey was made and duly approved. By this the south line in question was run as a straight line; plaintiff claimed under this survey. *Held*, that the survey so made did not, by changing the location of the line, have the effect to enlarge the reservation. *Seneca Nation v. Hugaboom, 132 N. Y. App. (Sickels), 493.*

SEC. 3157. A survey made of Cherokee lands, at the instance of an individual, independently of the action of the commissioners intrusted with the survey and sale of these lands, was *held* not to be sufficient to control or contradict the calls of a grant as to course and distance.

Addington v. Jones, 7 Jones (N. C. Law), 582.

SEC. 3158. This survey does not fall within the provision of the fifteenth section of the act of 8th of April, 1785, by which it is declared that "every survey made by any deputy surveyor out of his proper district shall be void and of no effect," because it has been settled that that provision was confined to the lands contained within the purchase lately made by the Commonwealth, of the Indians at Fort McIntosh, of all the residue of waste lands within the charter bounds of Pennsylvania.

Creek et al. v. Moon, 7 Sergeant & Rawle (Pa.), 334.

SEC. 3159. By mistake of the commissioners on behalf of the United States appointed to run the lines of the country reserved to the Cherokees under the treaty of July 2, 1791 (7 Stat. L., 39), Smith, one of the defendants, lives on the Indian side of the line. The Cherokee boundary was not actually run and marked until the year 1797, agreeably to article 2 of the treaty of 1794 (7 Stat. L., 43).

Glasgow v. Smith, 1 Overton (Tenn.), 111.

SEC. 3160. By the Chickasaw treaty of 1805 (7 Stat. L., 89) the Chickasaw boundary is fixed running up Duck River. The cession act of 1806 which authorizes Tennessee to issue grants upon North Carolina warrants provides "that nothing therein contained shall be construed so as to affect the Indian title." The treaty of 1805 was the paramount law and fixed the bounds of the first district. The State never authorized her officers to receive these entries, and they are therefore wholly void. *McLemore v. Wright, 2 Yerg. (Tenn.), 326.*

SEC. 3161. A line run by commissioners of the United States and the Indians in compliance with treaty provisions, and acquiesced in by them, is conclusive in a question between individuals as to whether certain land is within or without the territory to which the Indian title had not been extinguished. *Gillespie v. Cunningham, 2 Humph. (Tenn.), 19.*

SEC. 3162. By article 5 of the Cherokee treaty of 1819 (7 Stat. L., 195) it is provided that the boundary lines necessary to designate the land ceded by that treaty shall be run by commissioners appointed by the United States and by the Cherokees, and that all white intruders on the lands reserved for the Indians shall be removed.

Ibid.

SEC. 3163. Where a survey and patent called for "on Trammel's Trace, including a place known as the old Choctaw village," and the survey was properly made and the lines distinctly marked, but the surveyor, in making up the field notes, called for east instead of south, by mistake, which would have excluded all the land actually surveyed,

and the mistake was not discovered until after the issue of the patent. *Held*, that the mistake did not affect the right of the patentee to the land surveyed.
Urquart v. Burleson, 6 Hartly (Texas), 502.

SEC. 3164. An Indian reservation may be included within the boundaries of a town.
Schriber v. The Town of Langlade, 66 Conover (Wisc.), 616.

SEC. 3165. In a treaty made with the Seneca Nation in 1802, the southern boundary of their reservation was described as beginning at a certain point and running "thence west 482 chains 31 links to a post." A survey of the reservation was made in 1798, by which the southern boundary of the reservation was run between the points named in the treaty, but not in a straight line. The lines of this survey were plainly marked on the ground at the date of the treaty, and some of its lines were referred to in the treaty. The line as so surveyed was treated as the boundary line from the earliest time within the memory of witnesses. *Held*, that the true boundary line was the one so surveyed, and not a direct east and west line between the termini. (9 N. Y. Supp., 699, affirmed.)
Seneca Nation v. Hugaboom, 30 N. E. Rep., 983.

CHAPTER VIII.—SOME PARTICULAR TITLES.

SEC. 3166. In directing selections for orphans, the Creek treaty of 1832 (7 Stat. L., 366), did not intend that they might be made on lands selected according to the first part of the second article. "It is a principle which has always been sacred in the United States, that laws by which human action is to be regulated look forward, not backward, and are never to be construed retrospectively, unless the language of the act should render that indispensable." The last clause in this article can not have been intended to annul or impair a title which was valid under the first clause, and guaranteed from intrusion under the fifth article for five years, unless sooner sold.
Ladiga v. Roland, 2 How., 581.

SEC. 3167. The clause in the Choctaw treaty of September 27, 1830 (7 Stat. L., 333), reserving to Wall among others a section of the land ceded, has been properly given a liberal construction by the officers of the Government, and which was inculcated by the eighteenth article of the treaty itself, by which the reservee is allowed a section, although not a resident at the time, and without having made any improvements upon the particular tract. In cases of residence and improvements the location must be such as shall include them.
Gains v. Nicholson, 9 How., 356.

SEC. 3168. The reservation in the Caddo treaty of 1835 (7 Stat. L., 470), to the Grappes, "their heirs and assigns forever," creates as absolute a fee as any subsequent act upon the part of the United States could make, and nothing further was contemplated by the treaty to perfect the title.   *United States v. Brooks, 10 How., 442.*

SEC. 3169. The Spanish law for granting lands (occupied by the Indians as well as public lands) was, that the grants were to be made with formality, in the name of the King, by the governor-general of the province; that when the order to grant was given that a surveyor be appointed to fix the boundaries, and that the order itself should be registered in the land office, with the memorials and other papers, whatsoever they might be which had induced the governor to make the grant.   *Chouteau v. Molony, 16 How., 203.*

SEC. 3170. Under the laws of the Mexican Congress of 1833 and 1834 the authorities empowered to grant the public lands have dealt with the mission establishments in Upper and Lower California the same as with any other portion of the public domain; the clergy, who previously had the charge and control of them, being confined simply to the ecclesiastical and spiritual direction and government of the missions.   *United States v. Ritchie, 17 How., 525.*

SEC. 3171. The large tracts of land appurtenant to the mission establishments were never vested in the church or any other corporation, or individual, by any legal title. The missionaries and Indians had an usufruct or occupancy of the land at the will of the sovereign.
                              United States v. Cervantes, 18 How., 553.

SEC. 3172. It was the practice and usage of the Mexican Government in California to set apart, for the use of the Indians, small lots of land appurtenant to the houses in which they lived around the mission, and where a person claims a lot under such distribution among the Indians of a mission and shows that the grantee and his assigns have lived upon it for a long time, the title ought to be confirmed.
                              United States v. Wilson, 1 Black, 267.

SEC. 3173. The agreement between the Government and Potawatomies at the treaty of 1832 (7 Stat. L., 378) respecting the survey, selection, and patent of the individual tracts reserved, was one which if entered into by an individual a court of chancery would have enforced by compelling the selection of lands and the conveyance in favor of the reservee, or, in case he had parted with his interest, in favor of his grantees, and the obligation is not the less imperative and binding because entered into by the Government. The equitable right therefore to the lands in the grantee of a Potawatomie reservee, when selected, was perfect.   *Crews v. Burcham, 1 Black, 352.*

SEC. 3174. It could never have been intended by the Government to make a distinction in favor of the Shawnee Indians in Kansas who held their lands in common and against those who held in severalty. If the Indians thus holding had less rights than their more favored brethren, who enjoy their possession in common and in compact form, good faith would require that it should have so stated in the treaty.

The Kansas Indians, 5 Wall., 737.

Sec. 3175. A provision in an Indian treaty whereby it is agreed that on the performance of certain conditions a varying quantity of lands should be patented to heads of Indian families did not operate as a grant, and a patent was necessary to the person who alone could perform the conditions. *Wilson v. Wall, 6 Wall., 83.*

Sec. 3176. It had been the uniform construction of the War Department of the words used in article 14 of the Choctaw treaty of 1830 (7 Stat. L., 333), as giving to the head of a Choctaw family title to all the lands selected for such family under said article, and patents were issued accordingly and no doubt was entertained of the correctness of such interpretation of that article. *Ibid.*

Sec. 3177. From an early period in the Government it has been the practice of the President to order, from time to time, as the exigencies of the public service required, parcels of land belonging to the United States to be reserved from sale and set apart for public uses, and the authority of the President in this regard is recognized in numerous acts of Congress. This recognition is to be found in the preemption acts of May 29, 1830 (4 Stat. L., 421), and September 4, 1841 (5 Stat. L. 456), and also in the act of March 3, 1853 (10 Stat. L., 246).

Grisar v. McDowell, 6 Wall., 381.

Sec. 3178. The Cherokee treaty of December 29, 1835 (7 Stat. L., 478), made a sale in fee simple to the Cherokee Indians of lands west of the Mississippi, known as the "Cherokee neutral lands," and the fact and validity of the sale have been recognized by Congress through appropriations made in execution of the treaty making it.

Holden v. Joy, 17 Wall., 211.

Sec. 3179. The Indian tribes are capable of taking as owners in fee simple lands by purchase where the United States in form, and for a valuable and adequate consideration, so sell them to them, and such sale is properly made by a treaty. *Ibid.*

Sec. 3180. For all practical purposes the Osages owned their land, as the actual right of possession, the only thing they deemed of value, was secured to them by treaty until they should elect to surrender it to the United States. In the free exercise of their choice they might hold it forever, and whatever changed this condition or interfered with it violated the guaranties under which they had lived.

Leavenworth, etc., Railroad Co., 92 U. S., 733.

Sec. 3181. Had the grant to the Sac and Fox half-breeds been to them as a political society the boundary would have been as between States or nations and the line would have been the *medium filum aquæ,* as it is between Iowa and Illinois, but the grant was to them as individuals—as tenants in common—and is to be construed as any other grant or sale to individuals.   *Barney v. Keokuk, 94 U. S., 324.*

SEC. 3182. The grant of what was known as the half-breed Sac and Fox Reservation to the half-breeds was to them as persons and not as a political body. The political jurisdiction remained in the United States.   *Ibid.*

SEC. 3183. The peculiar origin of the title to the "Half-breed Sac and Fox Reservation" in the peninsula lying between the rivers Mississippi and Des Moines did not take it out of the general rule in Iowa that the title of riparian proprietors on the banks of the Mississippi extends only to ordinary high-water mark.   *Ibid.*

SEC. 3184. If the Pueblo Indians differ from the other inhabitants of New Mexico in holding lands in common, and in a certain patriarchal form of domestic life, they only resemble in this regard the Shakers and other communistic societies in this country, and can not for that reason be classed with the Indians to whom the intercourse act applies.   *United States v. Joseph, 94 U. S., 614.*

SEC. 3185. The Pueblo Indians hold their lands by a right superior to that of the United States. Their title dates back to grants made by the Government of Spain before the Mexican revolution, a title which was fully recognized by the Mexican Government, and protected by it in the treaty of Guadalupe Hidalgo.   *Ibid.*

SEC. 3186. By the compact between the United States and the State of Wisconsin on the admission of that State, the sixteenth section in every township in the State which had not been sold or otherwise disposed of were withdrawn from any other disposition and set apart from the public domain, so that no subsequent laws authorizing the sale of it could be construed to embrace them, although they were not especially accepted, and they could not be diverted from their appropriation to the State.   *Beecher v. Wetherby, 95 U. S., 517.*

SEC. 3187. The logs in question were cut in the winter of 1872 and 1873; and they were therefore timber on the land when the patent of 1870 was issued by the State of Wisconsin to the defendant, and also when the patent of 1872 was issued by the United States to the plaintiff, and as such constituted a portion of the realty. Although when severed from the soil the timber became personalty, the title to it remained unaffected, and the owner of the land could equally as before claim its possession and pursue it wherever it was carried.   *Ibid.*

SEC. 3188. It was an unalterable condition of the admission of the State of Wisconsin, obligatory upon the United States, that section 16 in every township of the public lands in the State which had not been sold or otherwise disposed of should be granted to the State for the use of the school.   *Ibid.*

SEC. 3189. Title to two sections of land selected under treaty for a chief of the Pottawatomie Indians and aliened by him before patent, which was issued after his death, was vested in his grantee.

Elwood v. Flannigan, 104 U. S., 562.

SEC. 3190. The act of 1862 (12 Stat. L., 543) in express terms granted to the State of Iowa for the use of its grantee "the alternate sections designated by odd numbers lying within five miles of said river, between the Raccoon Fork of the Des Moines River and the northern boundary of the State." At this time there was no Indian title in the way of the grant, and if the reservation was good as against the railroad companies in 1856, the title of the Des Moines Valley Company, the grantee of the State, was perfected.

Railroad Co. v. Railroad Co., 109 U. S., 329.

SEC. 3191. To leave the question of the construction of the act of 1846 (9 Stat. L., 77), granting lands to the State of Iowa for the improvement of the Des Moines River, that is, the effect of the grant, "entirely open," as the intention of the Secretary of the Interior expressed in his letter of October 29, 1851, to the Commissioner of the General Land Office, all the lands within the limit, surveyed or unsurveyed and encumbered by an Indian title or unencumbered, were reserved from sale until the "action of the judiciary." This reservation was in force when the act of 1856 (11 Stat. L., 9) was passed, and it is *the* reservation which the court has held prevented the grant under that act from attaching to the lands within the limits of the river grant as claimed by the State.

Ibid.

SEC. 3192. In 1774 the tribes of Indians known as the Homnas and Bayou Goula tribes had possession of lands on the left bank of the Mississippi River, about 22 leagues above New Orleans, by a right which appears to have been that of occupancy subject to the will of the governor of the province. This interest they sold on that date to two parties, named Mauric Conway and Alexander Latil, who paid $150 for it, the conveyance being made before a notary public by one Calajero, who is described as the chief of the tribes by appointment of the governor.

Slidell v. Grandjean, 111 U. S., 412.

SEC. 3193. The claim of the Cherokees of North Carolina to a share of the commuted fund of $214,000 and of the funds arising from the sales of Cherokee lands west of the Mississippi rests on no solid foundation. The lands from the sales of which the proceeds of the latter funds were derived belonged to the Cherokee Nation as a body politic, and not to its individual members. They were held, it is true, for the common benefit of all the Cherokees, but that does not mean that each member had such an interest as a tenant in common that he could claim a *pro rata* proportion of the proceeds of sales made of any part of them.

Cherokee, etc., Case, 117 U. S., 288.

SEC. 3194. An individual member of the Cherokee Nation had a right to use parcels of the lands held by the nation for the benefit of all its members, subject to such rules as its governing authority might prescribe; but that right neither prevented nor qualified the legal power of that authority to cede the lands and the title of the nation to the United States. The Cherokee treaties of cession must therefore be held not only to convey the common property of the nation, but to divest the interest therein of each of its members.   *Ibid.*

SEC. 3195. The embodiment of the stipulation required in the seventh article of the Ottawa treaty of June 24, 1862 (12 Stat. L., 1238), limiting the power of alienation in the patent to a chief of the Ottawa tribe, shows the construction of the executive department of the Government, that it was applicable to the land granted by the third article, and the acceptance of the patent seems to imply the acquiescence by the patentee in that construction.   *Libby v. Clark, 118 U. S., 250.*

SEC. 3196. Neither the treaty of 1835 (7 Stat. L., 473), whereby the United States covenanted and agreed that the land ceded to the Cherokee Nation should at no future time without their consent be included within the territorial limits or jurisdiction of any State or Territory, and that the Government would secure to that nation " the right by their national council to make and carry into effect all such laws as they may deem necessary for the government of the persons and property within their own country, belonging to their people, or such persons as have connected themselves with them;" nor the treaties of 1846 (9 Stat. L., 871), and 1866 (14 Stat. L., 799), guaranteeing to the Cherokees the title and possession of their lands and jurisdiction over their country, nor any previous treaties evinced any intention upon the part of the Government to discharge them from their condition of pupilage or dependency and constitute them a separate, independent, sovereign people, with no superior within its limits.
Cherokee Nation v. Railroad Co., 135 U. S., 641.

SEC. 3197. The record shows that the defendant offered to pay into court double the amount of the award made by the referees. The offer to pay is not a compliance with the statute. The amount required to be deposited must be actually paid into court before the company can rightfully enter upon the lands sought to be condemned or proceed with the construction of its road.   *Ibid.*

SEC. 3198. The fact that the Cherokee Nation hold their lands in fee simple under patents from the United States is of no consequence in the present discussion; for the United States may exercise the right of eminent domain, even within the limits of the several States, for purposes necessary to the execution of the powers granted to the General Government by the Constitution. It would be very strange if the National Government in the execution of its rightful authority could exercise the power of eminent domain in the several States, and could not exercise the same power in a territory occupied by an Indian nation or tribe, the members of which were wards of the United States and directly subject to its political control.   *Ibid.*

Sec. 3199. The lands in the Cherokee territory, like the lands held by private owners everywhere within the geographical limits of the United States, are held subject to the authority of the General Government to take them for such objects as are germane to the execution of the powers granted to it; provided only that they are not taken without just compensation being made to the owner.   *Ibid.*

Sec. 3200. In an official communication from the Commissioner of the General Land Office to the Secretary of the Interior under date of January 29, 1886, embodied in a report made on February 11, 1886, by the Judiciary Committee of the House of Representatives (H. R. Report No. —, Forty-ninth Congress, first session), upon a proposed bill extending the laws of the United States over certain "unorganized territory south of Kansas," it was stated that "it appears that the Cherokees claimed the Public Land Strip, now so called as the Outlet above mentioned, and the official maps down to 1869 or later designated said strip as a part of the Indian Territory."
Cook v. United States, 138 U. S., 157.

Sec. 3201. The treaties of 1853 (10 Stat. L., 1013), 1865 (14 Stat. L., 717), and 1867 (15 Stat. L., 581), show that as late as 1867 the Public Land Strip (No Mans Land) in the mode of its use had some connection with Indians west of the Mississippi and especially with some of those now occupying permanent reservations in the Indian Territory. That strip has not been occupied by Indians since 1867, but it was not open to settlement and could have been used for any of the purposes that the Government had in view for Indians.   *Ibid.*

Sec. 3202. In order to pass the legal title to lands something more is necessary than the signature of the grantor to a blank instrument. There must be an intent to convey, and the delivery of a deed for the purpose of vesting a present title in the grantee and a deed delivered without the consent of the grantor is of no more effect to pass title than if it were a forgery. At best, the deed from Sophia Felix, being a quitclaim, conveyed only the interest of the grantor at the date of its delivery, which was nothing.   *Felix v. Patrick, 145 U. S., 317.*

Sec. 3203. As the power of attorney and quitclaim deed from Sophia Felix, whose Sioux half-breed scrip was used in locating the land in dispute, were received by the defendant in blank, he is clearly chargeable with notice that they were intended as a device to evade the law against the assignment of the scrip.   *Ibid.*

Sec. 3204. Although half-breed scrip issued under the Sioux treaty of 1830 (7 Stat. L., 328) and the act of July 17, 1854 (10 Stat. L., 304), could not be transferred or conveyed, the moment the scrip was located in the name and for the benefit of the person to whom it was issued and the title in the land vested in him it became subject to his disposition, precisely as any other land would be.   *Ibid.*

SEC. 3205. Whenever a person obtains the legal title to land by artifice or concealment or making use of facilities intended for the benefit of another, a court of equity will impress upon the lands so held by him a trust in favor of the party who is justly entitled to them and will order the trust to be executed by decreeing their conveyance to the party in whose favor the trust was created. It is of no consequence in this connection that Sophia Felix was ignorant of the defendant's acts or the trust thereby created, since she was at liberty, upon discovering it, to affirm the trust and enforce its execution.
                                                                            Ibid.

SEC. 3206. As Patrick had no right to locate the Sioux half-breed scrip issued to Sophia Felix for his own benefit, he must be deemed to have located for Sophia Felix and as her representative. This is in accordance with the rule established in 1810 in Massie *v.* Wall, 6 Cranch, 148, "that if an agent locate land for himself which he ought to locate for his principal, he is in equity a trustee for his principal."   *Ibid.*

SEC. 3207. No additional right was acquired by Patrick under the acts of July 25, 1868, and February 2, 1869, confirming the title to the lands to the parties holding by deed from the patentees. Such acts might estop the Government itself from taking proceedings to cancel the patent already issued, or to oust Patrick, but to hold them operative as affecting the rights of the third parties would be virtually recognizing judicial power in the legislature. In no possible view of legislative authority can it be assumed that an act of Congress can declare that lands to which one party is entitled by law shall belong to another.   *Ibid.*

SEC. 3208. The power of attorney and quitclaim deed under which Patrick claims to be the grantee of the patentee (Sophia Felix), being in blank when they passed from the possession of Sophia Felix, were inoperative to convey her title to any particular land, and Patrick was not "holding by deed from the patentee within the meaning of the acts of July 25, 1868 (15 Stat. L., 186), and February 2, 1869 (15 Stat. L., 269). Nor can it be claimed that Sophia Felix ever authorized the blanks to be filled, and neither the person to whom she delivered them nor Patrick himself could be considered her agent for filling them out. Such agency, if it exists must be exercised before the deed is delivered.
                                                                            Ibid.

SEC. 3209. No ground can be discovered for the revival of the controversy by the Western Cherokees (Old Settlers) as to their ownership of or rights in the lands west of the Mississippi, and any such claim in respect thereof as is put forward in their petition in this case can not be successfully maintained from any point of view. If any matter ever can be put at rest that has been, and the treaty of 1846 (9 Stat. L., 871) has presented for nearly fifty years an insuperable bar to any such contention. *United States v. Old Settlers, 148 U. S., 427.*

SEC. 3210. The Cherokee treaty of 1835 (7 Stat. L., 478) by which the conveyance of land by the treaties of 1828 (7 Stat. L., 311) and 1833 (7 Stat. L., 414) is declared to have been to the Cherokee Nation of Indians, and 800,000 acres additional was agreed to be conveyed for a consideration that there might be no question as to there being a sufficient quantity of land for the accommodation of the whole nation on their removal west, was wholly inconsistent with the attitude subsequently assumed by the Old Settlers. *Ibid.*

SEC. 3211. In the provision contained in the Chippewa treaty of 1854 (10 Stat. L., 1109), for the Lac Courte d'Oreilles and other reservations in the State of Wisconsin, nothing was said of the sixteenth section of any townships, and it is clear that it was not contemplated that any section should be left out of any one of them. The land reserved was to be, as near as possible, in a compact form, except so far as the meandered lakes were concerned. When the townships composing these reservations were surveyed, the sixteenth section was already disposed of in the sense of the enabling act of 1846 (9 Stat. L., 56), and it had been included within the limits of the reservations.

United States v. Thomas, 151 U. S., 577.

SEC. 3212. The President speaks and acts through the heads of the several departments in relation to subjects that pertain to their regular duties, and the allotment of the half-breed lands by the Indian Department must be considered as made by the President in pursuance of the terms of the act of July 3, 1854 (10 Stat. L., 332) and the treaty of Prairie du Chien (7 Stat. L., 328), and it may be admitted that the decision of the special Indian agent in identifying the Indian half-breeds entitled to participate and in allotting the portion of each would, in the absence of fraud, be conclusive.

Hegler v. Faulkner, 153 U. S., 109.

SEC. 3213. As a further consideration for the payment of the sum for the purchase of homes, the Delawares were guaranteed not merely the continued occupancy thereof, but also in case of a subsequent allotment in severalty of the entire body of lands among the members of the Cherokee Nation, they should receive any aggregate amount equal to that which they had purchased and such disposition as would secure to them the homes upon which they had settled, together with their improvements, so that if, when the allotment was made, there was for any reason not land enough to secure to each member of the Cherokee Nation 160 acres, the Delawares were to have at least that amount, and the deficiency would have to be borne by the native Cherokees *pro rata*.   *Cherokee Nation v. Journeycake, 155 U. S., 196.*

SEC. 3214. The laws of the Cherokee Nation provided for the appropriation by the several Cherokees of lands for personal occupation, and the purchase by the Delawares was with the view of securing to the individual Delawares the like homes, but the lands thus purchased and paid for still remained a part of the Cherokee Reservation.   *Ibid.*

SEC. 3215. Given, the two propositions that the lands are the common property of the Cherokee Nation, and that the registered Delawares have become incorporated into the Cherokee Nation and are members and citizens thereof, it follows necessarily that they are equally with the native Cherokees the owners of and entitled to share in the profits and proceeds of these lands.   *Ibid.*

SEC. 3216. By the patent issued to the Cherokees in December, 1838, for the lands granted by various treaties, whatever of title was conveyed was conveyed to the Cherokees as a nation, and no title was vested in severalty in the Cherokees, or any of them.   *Ibid.*

SEC. 3217. The necessary effect of the act of January 17, 1887 (24 Stat. L., 361), granting the Maricopa and Phœnix Railroad Company a right of way through the Gila River Reservation, was, to the extent of the grant and for the purposes thereof, to withdraw the land from the prior act of February 28, 1859 (11 Stat. L., 401), establishing the reservation, and the immediate consequence of such withdrawal, so far as it affected the property and rights withdrawn, was to reestablish the full sway and dominion of the territorial authority.

Railroad Co. v. Arizona, 156 U. S., 347.

SEC. 3218. It is fairly implied from the language employed in the third article of the Chippewa treaty of 1820 (7 Stat. L., 206) that an encampment location retained, selected, or assigned, as the case might be, reserved for the use specified in the treaty, should not thereafter be appropriated by the Government for other uses than the defenses of any military work. Private rights could not, without authority of Congress, be acquired in the tract during the occupancy of the reservation under the treaty, for the lands lost their character as public lands in being set apart or occupied under the treaty and became exempt from sale and preemption.   *Spalding v. Chandler, 160 U. S., 394.*

SEC. 3219. The act of June 8, 1872 (17 Stat. L., 340), "to perfect certain land titles," etc., was intended to permit a purchaser of Chippewa half-breed scrip certificates, who through them had acquired an invalid title to public land, to perfect that title by compliance with the terms of that statute.   *Fee v. Brown, 162 U. S., 602.*

SEC. 3220. Chippewa half-breed scrip certificates were intended to be located only by half-breeds to whom they were issued, and patents were to be issued only to the persons named in those certificates; and, consequently, the right to alienate the lands was not given until after the issue of the patents. *Ibid.*

SEC. 3221. The reservations granted by provision "First" in section 1 of the act of December 19, 1854 (10 Stat. L., 598), "to provide for the extinguishment of the title of the Chippewa Indians to lands owned and claimed by them," etc., are limited to the territory ceded by the Indians, both as applies to Indians of pure blood and to Indians of mixed blood. *Ibid.*

SEC. 3222. As to Indian reservations made subsequently to the grant to the railroad company contained in the act of July 27, 1866 (14 Stat. L., 292), there was no restriction upon the right of the Government to dispose of public lands in any way it saw fit prior to the filing of the map of definite location; and if it assumed to dispose of lands within the grant after the rights of the railroad company had attached, such action would be void, but it would be no answer to the obligation of the company to complete its road within the stipulated time. *A. and P. R. R. v. Mingus, 165 U. S., 413.*

SEC. 3223. Lands in the Indian Territory belonging to the Indians did not pass under the grant to the Atlantic and Pacific Railroad Company by the act of July 27, 1866 (14 Stat. L., 292), and the United States were not required by the statutes to extinguish the Indian title for the benefit of the railroad company, nor could they be reasonably expected to do so. *Ibid.*

SEC. 3224. The circumstances under which the Indian tribes in the Indian Territory hold their lands preclude the idea that it could be expected that the United States should be called upon to extinguish for the benefit of a railroad company which had chosen to locate its route through the Territory a title guaranteed to the Indians by solemn treaties and which had been possessed by them for upward of forty years with the powers of an almost independent government. *Ibid.*

SEC. 3225. It is open to serious doubt whether that large tract of land known distinctly as the Indian Territory is a Territory of the United States within the meaning of the act of July 27, 1866 (14 Stat. L., 292), granting land to the Atlantic and Pacific Railroad. While, for certain purposes, such, for instance, as the enforcement of the criminal and internal-revenue laws, it has been recognized as such, and within the jurisdiction of the United States, a reference to some of the treaties under which it is held by the Indians indicates that it stands in an entirely different relation to the United States from other Territories and that for most purposes it is to be considered as an independent country. *Ibid.*

SEC. 3226. The provision in the treaty of June 15, 1838 (7 Stat. L., 550), with the New York Indians that the United States will set apart as a permanent home for them the tract therein described in what afterwards became the State of Kansas was intended to invest a present legal title thereto in the Indians, which title has not been forfeited and has not been reinvested in the United States; and the Indians are not estopped from claiming the benefit of such reservation.

N. Y. Inds. v. U. S., 170 U. S., 1.

SEC. 3227. It appears by the record of the proceedings of the Senate that several amendments were made to the treaty of 1838 (7 Stat. L., 550) with the New York Indians, including a new article; that the ratification was made subject to a proviso, the text of which is stated in the opinion of the court, and that in the official publication of the treaty and in the President's proclamation announcing it all the amendments except said proviso were published as part of the treaty, and it was certified that "the treaty, as so amended, is, word for word, as follows," omitting the proviso. *Held*, that it is difficult to see how the proviso can be regarded as part of the treaty, or as limiting at all the terms of the grant.   *Ibid.*

SEC. 3228. The effect of the treaty of October 2, 1863 (13 Stat. L., 667), between the United States and the Red Lake and Pembina bands of Chippewa Indians, by which those bands ceded to the United States all their right, title, and interest in a large tract of country, and by which "there shall be set apart from the tract hereby ceded a reservation of 640 acres near the mouth of the Thief River for the Chief Moose Dung," was to grant him an alienable title in fee in the quantity of land at the designated place subject only to its selection in due form and to the definition of its boundaries by survey and patent.

Jones v. Meehan, 175 U. S., 1.

SEC. 3229. The right of inheritance, at the time of the death of the grantee in 1872, in land granted in fee by the United States by an Indian treaty to a member of an Indian tribe whose tribal organization was still recognized by the Government of the United States is controlled by the laws, usages, and customs of the tribe and not by the law of the State in which the land lies, nor by any action of the Secretary of the Interior.   *Ibid.*

SEC. 3230. When the United States, in a treaty with an Indian tribe, and as part of the consideration for the cession by the tribe of a tract of country to the United States, make a reservation to a chief or other member of the tribe of a specified number of sections of land, whether already identified, or to be surveyed and located in the future, the treaty itself converts the reserved sections into individual property. The reservation, unless accompanied by words limiting its effect, is equivalent to a present grant of a complete title in fee simple; and that title is alienable by the grantee at his pleasure, unless the United States, by a provision of the treaty, or of an act of Con-

gress, have expressly or impliedly prohibited or restricted its alienation.   *Ibid.*

SEC. 3231. A good title to parts of the lands of an Indian tribe may
be granted to individuals by a treaty between the United States and
the tribe without any act of Congress or any patent from the executive authority of the United States. The question in every case is
whether the terms of the treaty are such as to manifest the intention
of the parties to make a present grant to the persons named.   *Ibid.*

SEC. 3232. It is not an offense within the meaning of section 2116,
Revised Statutes, to negotiate, without authority from the United
States Government, a lease of lands for grazing purposes from an
Indian tribe to a corporation.   *United States v. Hunter, 21 Fed. Rep., 615.*

SEC. 3233. By implication, an Indian tribe may *consent* to the use
of their lands for grazing purposes, or, at least, that if it does not
consent no penalty attaches; and, if the tribe may so consent, it may
express such consent in writing, and for any brief and reasonable
time.   *Ibid.*

SEC. 3234. The Secretary of the Interior may prescribe rules and
regulations by which other persons than those who held the real title
can divest the real holder of such title. He can say what evidence
shall be submitted as to the competency of the grantor, the fact that
the money was paid, etc., but beyond that he has no power. He has
no judicial power to adjudge a forfeiture, to decide questions of
inheritance, or to divest the owner of his title without his knowledge
or consent.   *Richardville v. Thorp, 28 Fed. Rep., 52.*

SEC. 3235. Some half-breed scrip for Government land, a blank
power of attorney for its location and conveyance, and a blank quitclaim deed were obtained from the owner by fraud and came into the
hands of the defendant, who used the scrip to obtain a patent to land
of which he was in possession. The patent was taken in the name of
the owner of the scrip, which was not transferable, and the blank instruments were filled out, conveying the land to the defendant. At that
time the land was only of nominal value, but it afterwards became
very valuable. *Held*, that the acts of defendant being in violation of
the original owner's rights, there was no express relation of trust, and
that the owner and her heirs having contributed nothing to increase
the value of the land, and having delayed to bring the action to declare
the defendant trustee and to cancel the conveyances until after the
period of limitation, were precluded by their laches.
                                       Felix v. Patrick, 36 Fed. Rep. 457.

SEC. 3236. The defendants held the lands allotted to them in severalty, and they had no right to cut or remove timber from the
unallotted lands for the purpose of erecting upon their allotted land
any buildings or tenements whatever, and that the reservation or

unallotted land was held in trust for the other Indians entitled to
allotment, or in trust for the common benefit of the tribe, and could
not be despoiled for the purpose of improving allotted land.

United States v. Konkapot, 43 Fed. Rep., 64.

SEC. 3237. While citizens of the Cherokee Nation do not have a
fee to the lands they occupy, they can hold them forever, and fully
enjoy the profits arising from them, and their right may be granted
to their heirs, or may descend by inheritance.

Payne v. Railroad Co., 46 Fed. Rep., 546.

SEC. 3238. The Cherokee citizen and occupant of land has such a
durable and permanent interest in his land as to entitle him to pay for
an additional servitude placed upon the same.   *Ibid.*

SEC. 3239. The Cherokee Nation holds the fee to all the lands to
which it has title.   Individual citizens of the nation have a right of
perpetual occupancy in lands improved and occupied by them under
the laws of the Cherokee Nation.   By this right of occupancy the
individual Indian citizen can hold the lands forever, and fully enjoy
all profits arising from them, and their right of occupancy may be
transferred by a grant to another citizen of the nation, or it may descend
by inheritance.   Practically they get all the productions of the land,
and are entitled to its increased or peculiar value as though they held
it in fee.   *Ibid.*

SEC. 3240. By the act of June 5, 1872 (17 Stat. L., 226), the lands
of the Bitter Root Valley were excluded from the general preemption
and homestead laws.   Certain rights of preemption without cost,
were given to the Indians actually occupying and cultivating any portion thereof.   *Railroad Co. v. Hirchman, 53 Fed. Rep., 523.*

SEC. 3241. The tenure by which the Cherokee Nation holds its lands,
and its relation to the United States in other respects, are widely different from that of the ordinary Indian tribes.   By the treaties between
the United States and the Cherokee Nation of February 14, 1833
(7 Stat. L., 414), and of December 29, 1835 (7 Stat. L., 478), the
United States granted to the Cherokee Nation, in fee simple, the land
now occupied by them.   -   *Mehlin v. Ice, 56 Fed. Rep., 12.*

SEC. 3242. Plaintiff in ejectment claimed as the grantee of land upon
which a half-breed Sioux Indian had located scrip issued to him under
the act of July 17, 1854 (10 Stat. L., 304), which scrip was not transferable, but was issued to designated individuals in exchange for the
interest acquired by them collectively under a former treaty.   *Held,*
that the scrip and the location of it did not vest the legal title in the
plaintiff's grantor, and it was proper to instruct the jury that they
should disregard the location and the deed to plaintiff as evidence of
title, and only regard them as evidence explaining his entry, possession, and good faith.   *Carter v. Ruddy, 56 Fed. Rep., 542.*

SEC. 3243. Deeds made to certain Indians of lots of land on the Puyallup Reservation pursuant to the treaty of December 26, 1854 (10 Stat. L., 1132), with the stipulation that the lands should not be aliened or leased for more than two years, and should be exempt from levy, sale, or forfeiture, passed the title in fee to the grantees, subject only to conditions subsequent, and left no title or reversionary interest in the United States, but a mere power in the President to reassign or sell for the common benefit of the tribe on breach of the conditions.   *Ross v. Eells, 56 Fed. Rep., 855.*

SEC. 3244. The fee of lands in the Cherokee Nation is in the nation. Whatever right a citizen has to occupy any particular portion of the public lands of the nation he must acquire it under and in pursuance of the laws of the nation, and not in defiance of them. He can not enter upon land previously dedicated or appropriated to some other person or to some specific use.   *Bell v. Railroad Co., 63 Fed. Rep., 417.*

SEC. 3245. A treaty with the Puyallup Indians allotted the lands in severalty to those who would locate on the same as permanent homes, and authorized the President to prescribe such rules as would insure to the family, in case of the death of its head, possession of such home; to issue a patent to such person or family, and to cancel it if such person or family rove from place to place. Each patent issued prohibited alienation. The act of February 8, 1887 (24 Stat. L., 388), conferred citizenship on such Indians and provided for leasing the lands under regulations of the Secretary of the Interior, and contemplated that agents shall be in charge of reservations; and the practice of the Department was to maintain such agents. *Held*, that the allotment of such lands in severalty and making the Indians citizens did not revoke the reservation.   *Eells v. Ross, 64 Fed. Rep., 417.*

SEC. 3246. No reason is known why it was not competent for Congress to declare that allottees should be deemed citizens of the United States and entitled to the rights, privileges, and immunities of citizens, while it retains for the time being the title to certain lands in trust for their benefit, and withheld from them for a certain period the power to sell, lease, or otherwise dispose of their interest in said lands.   *Beck v. Flournoy, &c., Co., 63 Fed. Rep., 30.*

SEC. 3247. By the treaty between the United States and the Choctaw Nation of September 27, 1830 (7 Stat. L., 333), the United States granted to the Choctaw Nation in fee simple "to enure to them while they shall exist as a nation and live on it," the country now occupied by them; and by the fourth article of this treaty it is provided that the Government and people of the United States are hereby obliged to secure to the said Choctaw Nation of red people the jurisdiction and government of all the persons and property that may be within their limits west, so that no Territory or State shall ever have a right to pass laws for the government of the Choctaw Nation of red people and their descendants; and that no part of the land granted them shall ever be embraced in any Territory or State; but the United States shall forever secure said Choctaw Nation from and against all laws, except such as may from time to time be enacted in their own national councils not inconsistent with the Constitution, treaties, and laws of the United States.   *Thebo v. Choctaw Tribe, 66 Fed. Rep., 372.*

SEC. 3248. It is contended that the view taken of the pupillary condition of the Cherokees violates the provisions of the constitution and laws of North Carolina forbidding perpetuities. A perpetuity is the attempt to forbid the alienation of lands under any circumstances, and to provide for their descent or disposition in a fixed, unchangeable way. But the Indians hold these lands to no such purpose. Their realty can be alienated, but the contract is reviewable by the Government for one purpose only—to protect them from fraud or wrong. A condition attached to alienation does not create a perpetuity.

        United States v. Boyd, 68 Fed. Rep., 577.

SEC. 3249. The action of the Secretary of the Interior, the Attorney-General, and district attorney in procuring, by procedure in this court, execution of the new deed under which the Eastern Band of Cherokees now hold their lands in fee simple as a corporation neither expressly nor by implication relieved the United States of any obligation or duty imposed or waived any power conferred by the Constitution, treaties, or acts of Congress.   *Ibid.*

SEC. 3250. Even if it should be the fact that the Indians living upon the allotted lands are no longer to be deemed tribal Indians, but have in fact reached the full measure of citizenship, and if it should be held that the allotted lands form no part of the Indian country, it would be no less true that the United States had agreed that these lands should be set apart for the occupancy and benefit of the Indians, and that Congress, when it authorized the allotment of lands in severalty, had forbidden the alienation of the lands for twenty-five years except by leasing under the rules and regulations prescribed by the Secretary of the Interior.   *United States v. Flournoy, &c., Co., 69 Fed. Rep., 886.*

SEC. 3251. Whatever may be the relation of the allotted lands to the so-called Indian country, with respect to other provisions of the statutes, such as those regulating sale of liquors and the like, there can be no question that title to these lands remains in the United States; that they form part of the lands set apart as a reservation for these Indians by the treaties made with them, and that the duty, and consequently the power, belongs to the United States to take whatever steps that are necessary for the proper performance of the obligations existing upon the part of the United States with regard to the lands.   *Ibid.*

SEC. 3252. The tract of country within which the elk were killed by Race Horse constituted unoccupied lands of the United States within the meaning of the treaty of July 3, 1868 (15 Stat. L., 673), with the Bannock Indians, notwithstanding the presence of a few settlers thereon and the fact that it was within the boundaries of the State of Wyoming.   *In re Race Horse, 70 Fed. Rep., 598.*

SEC. 3253. The allotments to the Winnebago Indians are not yet perfected.   The acts of Congress providing therefor expressly restrict all right of alienation and all right of contract between the Indians and the whites for a period of twenty-five years.   It can not be known whether all or any of the allottees in severalty will remain on the lands assigned for the period of twenty-five years, and it may be that, by abandonment, the allottees may fail to perfect an alienable title. Such failure, however, would not deprive the tribe, as a whole, of their right to the reservation, and it would still be the duty of the United States, under the terms of the treaty, to protect the tribe in the use and occupancy of the reservation.   *United States v. Mullin, 71 Fed. Rep., 682.*

SEC. 3254. The theory that lands conveyed by Government patents, after being so conveyed and appropriated by individual citizens, still remain subservient to use and occupation by the Indians for travel over the same otherwise than by lawfully established public highways and for camping grounds, finds no support in the provisions of the treaty nor in the rules for the construction and interpretation of statutes, which must be applied in the interpretation of the treaty and of the public-land laws of the United States.
                                   United States v. Winans, 73 Fed. Rep., 72.

SEC. 3255. The location of a tract of public land by an alleged beneficiary under the seventh clause of the second article of the treaty of September 30, 1854 (10 Stat. L., 1109), between the United States and the Chippewa Indians of Lake Superior, segregates the tract from the public domain and appropriates it to private use.   While such a location remains in force, Porterfield warrants issued under the act of April 11, 1860 (12 Stat. L., 836), can not be lawfully located on the same land, because that land has been otherwise appropriated by the prior location whether right or wrong.   *Hartman v. Warren et al., 76 Fed. Rep., 157.*

SEC. 3256. Where, in a treaty made subsequently to a road grant, Indian lands are ceded to the United States with a reservation of a right to a residence on part of them "until otherwise directed by the President," such reserved right is not a new right founded on the treaty, but the restricted right is a continuous one, and is prior and superior to the road grant.
                    California and Oregon Land Co. v. Worden, 85 Fed. Rep., 94.
                    California and Oregon Land Co. v. Rankin, 87 Fed. Rep., 532.

SEC. 3257. Under the act of August 7, 1882 (22 Stat. L., 341), providing for the allotment of lands to the Indians of the Omaha tribe, no distinction can be made as to whether they were of full or mixed blood, or on account of the length of their residence on the reservation; and it is immaterial that an applicant for an allotment was not residing with the tribe in 1865, at the time of the treaty under which previous allotments were made. Neither is the right of an Indian who was a member of the tribe when the act was passed, and residing on the reservation, to an allotment affected by the fact that allotments had been made to his ancestors under previous acts or treaties.

Sloan v. United States, 95 Fed. Rep., 193.

SEC. 3258. Act of August 7, 1882 (22 Stat. L., 341), relating to the lands of the Omaha tribe of Indians in Nebraska, and providing for allotments therefrom in severalty, superseded all prior acts and treaties on the subject, and all subsequent allotments are governed solely by its provisions, both as to the right to allotment and the quantity of land.   *Ibid.*

SEC. 3259. The provision of the general act of July 4, 1884 (23 Stat. L., 96), giving Indians the right to avail themselves of the homestead laws, and providing that patents for homesteads taken by Indians shall be of the legal effect and declare that the United States will hold the land in trust for twenty-five years, during which time it shall be exempt from taxation, is prospective only in its operation, and does not affect land to which an Indian had perfected his right of homestead under the act of 1875, prior to its passage.

United States v. Saunders, 96 Fed. Rep., 268.

SEC. 3260. Act of January 18, 1881 (21 Stat. L., 315), relating to homesteads acquired by Indians, is a special act, which by its terms applies only to the Winnebagoes of Wisconsin; and a clause in a patent issued to an Indian of a different tribe for a homestead acquired under the act of March 3, 1875, embodying the provision of section 5 of the act of 1881, which prohibits the alienation of the land for twenty years is void, but the insertion of such void limitation in a paragraph separate from the granting clause does not affect the validity of the patent to convey the land to the patentee, and he takes the title in fee simple without any restrictions upon his power of alienation.   *Ibid.*

SEC. 3261. If the "whole Cherokee people" mentioned in the treaty of 1846 included the North Carolina Cherokees, the very language repels the idea of any partition between them. To enjoy the benefit of the common lands they must go and enjoy the same with their brethren according to the customs, laws, and usages of the nation. There is not a word in either of the treaties that implies a partition of lands or division of the funds of the Cherokee Nation.

Eastern Band Cherokees v. United States et al., 20 C. Cls., 449.

SEC. 3262. The agreement of April 8, 1867, between the Delawares and Cherokees, whereby the former became a part of the Cherokee

Nation, expressly excluded the Cherokees from any right of property in the lands conveyed to the Delawares, and, by implication, the Delawares from any right of property in the lands retained by the Cherokees, the result being that there were two communities in the Cherokee country, each in the matter of property independent of each other, but both subject to the laws and constitution of the Cherokee Nation.

Journeycake v. Cherokee Nation and U. S., 28 C. Cls., 281.

SEC. 3263. All Indian lands were originally communal, the fee being vested in the community as such with a mere right of occupancy in members of the community. But in the Cherokee country the control has passed from the communal owners and become lodged in the State, and the unoccupied lands or "public domain" analogous to the public lands of the United States is held absolutely by the Government as a trust for governmental purposes and the general welfare.

Ibid.

SEC. 3264. The legislation of the Cherokees recognizes again and again the communal character of the seizin or occupancy of the land. It is not "lawful for any citizen of the Cherokee Nation to sell any farm or other improvement in said nation to any person other than to a 'bona fide' citizen thereof;" nor "to rent any farm or other improvement to any other person than a citizen of the Indian Territory." *Ibid.*

SEC. 3265. The constitution and laws of the Cherokee Nation, since that people came within the confines of civilization, have followed, in a limited extent, the traditions and usages of the race, and have embodied in them in varying degrees the fundamental principles and characteristics of communial property. *Ibid.*

SEC. 3266. The claim of the Delawares springs out of an agreement dated April 8, 1867, whereby they were admitted into and became a part of the Cherokee Nation. The principal objects of this agreement were (1) for the purchase by the Delawares of homes within the Cherokee country; (2) for their joint ownership and equal participation in the national fund held in trust by the United States for the benefit of the Cherokees; (3) for the adoption of the Delawares and their children after them as "members of the Cherokee Nation with the same rights and immunities as native Cherokees." *Ibid.*

SEC. 3267. Under the agreement of 1867, the Cherokees as grantors conveyed no right or interest other than in the lands sold, and the Delawares as grantees acquired no right or interest in lands other than those for which they paid. As to the communal element of the estate conveyed, considered in the abstract, it is manifest that while the lands granted remained communal they were not owned in common by the Cherokees. *Ibid.*

SEC. 3268. While there may still be in the Cherokee Nation property which is communal but not common, that is, property which is held for a portion of the people and not for national purposes, when the national council changed the common property of the nation into money, the fund took the place of the lands, and under the constitution was subject to the same limitations and existed for the same beneficiaries. The national council could not divert the common property from the general welfare and transmute it into a communal fund belonging to a class of citizens.   *Whitmire v. Cherokee Nation, 30 C. Cls., 138.*

SEC. 3269. Payment *per capita*, or the right to payment *per capita*, must be regarded as the badge or recognition of an individual communal interest. Funds payable *per capita* are trusts for the benefit of designated individuals or communities. Over them the Cherokee government has no control, and in them the Cherokee freedmen have no estate or interest.   *Ibid.*

SEC. 3270. The Delawares entered into an express agreement with the Cherokees, and paid for the homesteads which they acquired. The rights of the freedmen depend exclusively upon the constitution of the Cherokee Nation and the treaty of 1866 (14 Stat. L., 799) with the Cherokees.   *Ibid.*

SEC. 3271. The land is not "mineral land" within the meaning of the treaty, because a coal deposit underlies it.
        Stroud v. Missouri River, etc., R. R. Co., 4 Dill., 396.

SEC. 3272. The Cherokee Indians hold their lands by a title different from the usual Indian title—by occupancy. They derived it by grant from the United States. It is a base, qualified, or determinable fee, without the right of reversion, but only a possibility of reversion in the United States.   *United States v. Reese, 5 Dill., 405.*

SEC. 3273. The lands of the Cherokee tribe of Indians can not be held to be "lands of the United States" in the sense of the language used in section 5388 of the Revised Statutes.   *Ibid.*

SEC. 3274. In pursuance of the terms of the treaty of July 29, 1835 (7 Stat. L., 478), the President of the United States on December 31, 1838, executed to the Cherokee Nation a patent for the 7,000,000 acres of land, and for the outlet west, as well as for the 800,000 acres of land granted to them by the treaty of 1835.   *Ibid.*

SEC. 3275. Were it not for the treaty of 1835 (7 Stat. L., 478) the treaty of 1833 is broad enough in its terms to convey a fee simple title. This treaty is subsequent in date to the act of 1830, which contains the clause that the land should revert to the United States if the Indians "become extinct or abandon the same." There is no limitation to the title conveyed by the treaty of 1833. If such treaty is inconsistent with the law of 1830 it repealed so much of it as was inconsistent.   *Ibid.*

SEC. 3276. At the common law, by a rule which in this country is purely technical, the word "*heirs*" is necessary in a fee simple grant.

But this rule did not apply to grants to a corporation aggregate, and the Cherokee Nation may be regarded under the law as a corporation aggregate.   *Ibid.*

SEC. 3277. A Cherokee preemption can not be located upon the same tract of land upon which a preemption has been proved and allowed and a patent certificate issued.   *Hale v. Gaines et al., 19 Ark., 94.*

SEC. 3278. Where the members of the Mohegan tribe of Indians owned as joint tenants a certain farm, and some of them owned in severalty certain adjoining lands which they conveyed, it was held that the latter could not by their conveyance create a way of necessity in favor of the grantees over the farm. The tribe held the farm under certain laws of the State which forbade their selling it. *Held,* that there could not be a prescriptive right of way over it, since a prescription presumes a grant and could not exist where there was no power to grant.   *Woodworth v. Raymond, 51 Conn., 70.*

SEC. 3279. Lands included in the grant by act of Congress of July 2, 1864, to the Northern Pacific Railway Company are not within the operation of the act of March 3, 1875, granting the right of way to railroads, etc.   *Wash. and I. R. Co. v. Northern Pacific R. Co., 2 Idaho, 514. Hamilton v. Spokane and P. Ry. Co., 2 Idaho, 906.*

SEC. 3280. The electors' oath enacted at the first session of the legislature of the State of Idaho, and approved February 25, 1891, *Held,* not to be an *ex post facto* law, not in the nature of a bill of attainder, and to be clearly within the constitutional power of the legislature.
                                                          Shepherd v. Grimmett, 2 Idaho, 1126.

SEC. 3281. The United States has, by grant, confirmed to the inhabitants of the village of Cahokia the use of the "commons" adjacent to the village. The parishioners not living in the village, worshiping at the church in the village, do not, of right, participate in the use of the "commons." Parties deriving title from original Indian inhabitants of the village of Cahokia do not enjoy rights of common which might have pertained to their grantors if the grantees have abandoned the village.   *Hebert v. Lavalle, 27 Ill., 447.*

SEC. 3282. A certificate of the Commissioner of the General Land Office, made under the act of Congress of July 17, 1854, showing the location of half-breed Dakota or Sioux scrip on certain of the public lands, and that the location thereof was made by the party authorized to do so, is competent evidence in an action to show title in the location, and it is not essential that a copy of the scrip should be attached to and form a part of such certificate.   *Wilcox v. Jackson, 109 Ill., 261.*

SEC. 3283. One tenant in common may be liable to his cotenant for waste; but certainly the owner in fee of an undivided interest in land can not maintain an action of trespass against one whom he has himself licensed to do the act complained of.
                                          Wheeler v. Me-shing-go-me-sia, 30 Ind., 402.

SEC. 3284. Under the treaty the legal title to the land was vested in the appellee in trust for himself and the other members of the band. Both Me-shing-go-me-sia and Wa-co-co-nah were tenants in common with the other members of the band of the land in question.   *Ibid.*

SEC. 3285. By the Miami treaty, November 28, 1840 (7 Stat. L., 582), the United States agreed to convey by patent to Me-shing-go-me-sia, son of Ma-to-sin-ia, the tract of land reserved by the second article of the treaty of 1838.(7 Stat. L., 569) to the band of Ma-to-sin-ia, to be held in trust by Me-shing-go-me-sia for his band; and the proceeds thereof, when the same shall be alienated, to be equally distributed to said band, under the direction of the President.   *Ibid.*

SEC. 3286. The real estate of a member of the Ma-to-sin-ia band of Indians who died in 1880, having received a title to his land under the act of Congress of 1872 (17 Stat. L., 213), did not descend to his heirs free from the demands of creditors. Said land, on proper petition, might be sold to pay the claim of a creditor of the decedent, whose claim did not belong to the class the payment of which said act of Congress provided should never be enforced against the land to which the act referred.   *Taylor, Admr., v. Vandegrift, Admr., 126 Ind., 325.*

SEC. 3287. The grant of land by act of Congress of June 30, 1834 (4 Stat. L., 740), to the half-breeds was to them as persons, and not as a body politic. They take as individuals, tenants in common, and the grant is to be construed as made to individuals, and does not convey the land between high water and low water mark on navigable rivers.   *Haight v. The City of Keokuk, 4 Iowa (Clarke), 199.*

SEC. 3288. In an action of right the defendant will not be allowed to impeach a decree of partition upon the ground of fraud against his grantor, or third parties, when they have not complained of such fraud, and he was not a party to the decree. As Francois Herbert, the half-breed, under whom the defendant claims by purchase since the decree of partition, has not, in any manner, questioned its fairness, the defendant can not be permitted to question it for her.
          Wright v. Keithler, 7 Iowa (Clarke), 92.

SEC. 3289. The provision of the first supplementary article of the treaty of 1835 (7 Stat. L., 470–472) between the United States and the Caddo Indians, relative to a reservation in favor of the heirs of Francois Grappe, is a mere confirmation of such grant as may have been made by that tribe in 1801, and not a substantial grant of so much land from the Government. The recital by the Indians that they had made such a grant is not conclusive upon the Government.
          Brooks v. Norris, 6 Robinson (La.), 184.

SEC. 3290. The Penobscot Indians own all the islands in the Penobscot River above Oldtown Falls, some of which they occupy. Said tribe of Indians always have been and now are under the jurisdiction and guardianship of the State.   *Moor v. Veazie, 32 Maine, 343.*

SEC. 3291. The statute of 1701, entitled "An act to prevent and make void clandestine and illegal purchases of lands from the Indians," rendered void, as the foundation of title, all deeds made by Indians without the license or approbation of the legislature, after the year 1633.   *Brown et al. v. Inhabitants of Wenham, 51 Mass. (10 Metcalf), 495.*

SEC. 3292. The deed from the Indians in 1686 purports upon its face to be only a release or confirmation of titles already held by the town of Lyn or by the proprietors of the lands; and all conveyances from Indians of their aboriginal title, without the license or approbation of the general court, were of no validity whatever.

Lyn v. Nahant, 113 Browne (Mass.), 449.

SEC. 3293. Subsequently to the treaty of Saginaw of September 24, 1819, an act of Congress was passed for the issue of a patent for the land reserved to a person claiming to be assignee of the reservee, on proof being taken of the assignment. Proofs were taken and patent issued. *Held,* that as the title was beyond the control of Federal legislation the act and proceedings under it could not be given in evidence in this suit for the purpose of showing that the assignor of the patentee bore the name of the reservee named in the treaty.

Campau v. Dewey, 9 Mich. (5 Cooley), 381.

SEC. 3294. One of the adverse claimants under the treaty of Saginaw of September 24, 1819, was an Indian child of the full blood, 6 years of age at the date of the treaty. Evidence that for seven years after the treaty the witness heard no claim made by the band to which this child belonged, that any reserves were made for Indians of full blood, is not competent for the purpose of showing that she was not the reservee intended, since neither the neglect of others to make the claim, nor of herself at that age could affect her rights.   *Ibid.*

SEC. 3295. The Indian names "Che-gaw-*ge*-quay" and "Che-gaw-*go*-quay" may be regarded as of the same sound.

Where under an Indian treaty the selections of land were in writing oral testimony of such fact is incompetent in the absence of a legal excuse for the nonproduction of the writing or of a certified copy.

In an action of ejectment involving the identity of the patentee, a witness who can not identify the land in dispute with that he was on when he had a conversation with the occupant as to who selected the latter parcel, can not testify to such conversation in the absence of evidence of the identity of the two parcels.

Brown v. Quinland, 75 Mich., 289.

SEC. 3296. The purchase of and payment for certain land reserved for orphans by the Choctaw treaty of 1830, bought in 1861 from State officers acting under an ordinance passed by the convention which had previously enacted the ordinance of secession, conferred upon the purchaser no right or title against the United States.

Bates v. Aven, 60 Miss., 955.

Sec. 3297. By article 19 of the Choctaw treaty, 1830, there were reserved out of the lands ceded by the Chotaws as many quarter sections of land as there were orphans in the Choctaw Nation, which lands were to be selected by the Government and sold with the consent of the President, the proceeds to be used for the benefit of the orphans. *Held*, that when the lands were selected as contemplated by the treaty, the title to the whole vested in the United States for the benefit of the orphans as a class, and no particular orphan acquired title to any particular tract thereof. So that the statute of limitations would not run in favor of one in the adverse possession of any of this land, the title being in the United States and not in the orphans.   *Ibid.*

Sec. 3298. The right of the head of a Choctaw family to a reservation under the treaty of 1830 *vested* whenever such Choctaw signified his intention to the agent of the United States of becoming a citizen of the State; and that right became *complete* whenever a residence on the land for five years subsequent to the ratification of the treaty was accomplished.   *Land v. Land, 1 H. M. Chancery (Miss.), 158.*

Sec. 3299. The court will take judicial knowledge of the history and status of the Pueblo Indians and of the title by which they hold their lands.   *United States v. Lucero, 1 N. M. (Gild.), 422.*

Sec. 3300. The thirty-seventh article of the constitution of this State, making void purchases of lands of the *Indians* within this State, applies to purchases of such lands only as they possess in their national capacity or as communities, and not to lands acquired by an Indian as an individual and distinct from his tribe; and the prohibition of the constitution is not extended by the statute of the 18th March, 1788. Therefore when an Indian being seized of land which had been granted to him by patent for his military services during the Revolutionary war conveyed the same on the 22d December, 1791, it was held that the conveyance was valid, being anterior to the act of the 4th April, 1801 (sess. 36, chap. 147), which was more extensive in its operation than the act of 1783.

Jackson v. Sharp, 14 Johnson's Reports (N. Y.), 473.

Sec. 3301. In 10 Massachusetts Reports, 155, it was held that where the legislature by a resolve declared that a monument mentioned in the resolve was, and should be, considered as the one intended in an Indian deed under which a title was derived to certain properties, it was held the Commonwealth was thereby estopped.   *Doe v. Roe, 4 Hawks (N. C.), 119.*

Sec. 3302. The right to a reservation of land granted by the treaty with the Cherokee Indians in 1817 to each head of an Indian family choosing to remain in this State does not attach to the land ceded by the treaty of 1785.   *Den. ex. Dem. Sutton v. Moore et al., 3 Iredell (N. C. Law), 66.*

Sec. 3303. Under the acts for the sale of the Cherokee Indian lands the purchaser has a right, upon the certificate of his purchase from the commissioner, to institute an action of ejectment, in the name of the State, against any person in possession. The person so in possession can not set up as a defense to this action that he had received a deed ·from the purchaser, which had never been registered, but which was alleged to be lost or destroyed by an agent of the purchaser.

The State ex rel. Lindsay v. England, 7 Iredell (N. C. Law), 153.

SEC. 3304. The case depends upon a proper construction of the act of 1852, chapter 169, entitled "An act to bring into market the lands pledged for the completion of the Western Turnpike Road." Section 1 of said act provides for the opening of an entry taker's office and the election of an entry taker in the county of Cherokee, and the second section authorizes the entry of the unsold lands in that county at certain rates, and the third section declares "that it shall be lawful for all enterers of vacant land in said county of Cherokee to file bonds, with approved security, with an entry taker, payable to the State in four equal annual installments, which shall, when paid, be in full of such purchase money, for the tracts so entered; and upon proof of such payment as herein provided the secretary of state shall issue the grant or grants according to the entry and survey thereon." *Held*, that under said act of 1852, chapter 169, it is the duty of the entry taker to demand and receive bonds for the purchase money for the land before he takes the entry.   *State ex rel. Jarrett v. Krugzey, 3 Jones (N. C. Law), 489.*

SEC. 3305. The acts of assembly of 1783, 1819, 1836, and other acts relating to the sales, etc., of Cherokee lands, prior to that of 1852, confer special authority and jurisdiction; to give effect therefore to a grant issued by virtue of these acts, the cases to which they are restricted must be shown.   *Horshaw v. Taylor, 3 Jones (N. C. Law), 513 and 515.*

SEC. 3306. The title to the unsold Cherokee lands in county of Haywood was, by the act of 1835, vested in the justices of that county, and when their commissioner, whose duties and powers were limited by the resolution of the court appointing him to three months, executed a deed for a portion of said lands at the end of three years, it was *held* to be inoperative and void.   *Cooper v. Gibson, 6 Jones (N. C. Law), 512.*

SEC. 3307. The act of 1824, by which the long terms for years, created by the Tuscarora Indians, are, for certain purposes, made real estate, has no effect upon the reversions expectant on those terms.

Burnett v. Thompson, 6 Jones (N. C. Law) 210. Same, 7 Jones (N. C. Law), 407.

SEC. 3308. When an Indian under the treaties of 1817 and 1819 (with the Cherokee Nation), after having his reservation allotted to him, voluntarily abandoned it and reunited himself with his tribe, west of the Mississippi, it was held that his children, after his death, were not entitled to any estate in such reservation. A treaty in its effect is an executory agreement, and where an estate was limited by treaty to one for life, with a remainder to others, on a condition extending to both estates, it was held that on breach of such condition, both estates were defeated without entry.   *Welch v. Trotter, 8 Jones (N. C. Law), 197.*

SEC. 3309. There is nothing in the constitution or laws of North Carolina which forbids Cherokee Indian residents from taking and holding land by grant.   *Calvord v. Monroe, 2 Phillips (63 N. C.), 288.*

SEC. 3310. Where enterers of Cherokee lands, as to the acquisition of which a mode of procedure different from that applicable to other public lands was in force prior to November 1, 1883 (see secs. 2465, 2466, and 2467 of the Code), laid their entries in 1855 and 1860, and failed to comply with the requirements of law and to pay the purchase money and take out grants until February, 1890. *Held,* that their long delay was an abandonment of the equity which their entry gave them to acquire title to the lands so entered, and having obtained grants they held the legal title to the lands in trust for a grantee of the same land issued in October, 1890, under an entry made in December, 1889, and this would be so even if the later grantee had made his entry with notice of the previous entries of 1855 and 1860.
        Kimsey et al. v. Munday et al., 1 Gray (112 N. C.), 816.

SEC. 3311. The Cherokee Nation holds the lands in the Cherokee Outlet by the same title as they hold the lands ceded and granted to them for a permanent home, but their estate in the lands in the Cherokee Outlet is a base, qualified, or determinable fee, with the qualification annexed to the use.   *Jordan v. Goldman, 1 Okl. (Green), 406.*

SEC. 3312. The lands in the Cherokee Outlet were ceded and granted to the Cherokee Nation as an outlet, and for the purposes of an outlet only, and not for residence and cultivation, and, in such case the law annexes the qualification, or condition, that the estate shall continue in the Cherokee Nation only so long as the lands are used as an outlet, and no longer, and when the Cherokee Nation ceases to use the land as an outlet such cesser of the use determines their estate, and the lands revert to United States.   *Ibid.*

SEC. 3313. The qualification annexed to a base, qualified, or determinable fee may be either one of two kinds. It may be a qualification which is attached to the use of the land itself, so that the estate is held to be granted for that use and purpose only, and expires on the cessation of the use. Or it may be one which is concerned with the happening of a more strictly collateral event, leaving the use free for any purpose, but limiting its existence only by the event contemplated. The estate of the Cherokee Nation in the Cherokee Outlet is of the first class.   *Ibid.*

SEC. 3314. If the Cherokee Nation has ceased to use the lands of the "Cherokee Outlet" as an outlet, such cesser has terminated their estate and the lands have reverted to the United States. But whether there has been such a cesser of use is a political rather than a judicial question, and should be settled by Congress and the Chief Executive of the nation. *Ibid.*

SEC. 3315. The Cherokee Nation has no right to use the lands of the Cherokee Outlet for the purpose of operating a stone quarry therein and selling and shipping the rock, and could give the complainants, by license, no greater right than the nation itself has, and the operating of the stone quarry by the complainants is wrongful and a court of equity will not protect them by injunction in such wrongful act.

Ibid.

SEC. 3316. The lands in the Cherokee Outlet having been ceded and granted as an outlet, they can not be lawfully used for any other purpose, either by the Cherokee Nation or persons claiming by license or lease under the Cherokee Nation; and the subjection of the lands to any other use is wrongful and a breach of the qualification or condition annexed to the estate and works a termination of the estate, and the lands revert to the United States. *Ibid.*

SEC. 3317. By the purchase of all lands west of the Cherokee Outlet from Mexico by the United States and the voluntary sale and conveyance by the Cherokee Nation for cash of more than 2,000,000 acres at the east end thereof, the Cherokee "outlet west" has ceased to be an outlet to the west or any outlet in any sense to any place. Its character has been changed and the object for which it has been granted has been defeated and totally destroyed by the voluntary acts of the Cherokee Nation, which constituted an abandonment of any title theretofore vested, and there is now no tract or parcel of land that answers to the description of "outlet to the west," as used in the patent to the Cherokee Nation. *Guthrie v. Hall, 1 Okl. (Green), 454.*

SEC. 3318. Nothing appears in the treaties showing that one of these claims destroyed the other. They are different in kind and dependent upon different articles of the treaties, between which there is no connection. The third article of the treaty of 1819, which gives the reservation to the wife, has no connection with the second and seventh articles of the same treaty and the eighth article of the treaty of 1817, which gives a reservation to the husband. *Morgan v. Fowler, 2 Yerg., 450.*

SEC. 3319. The original title to the vast body of wild lands lying in the new States and Territories, subject to such rights as are recognized in the Indian tribes, is in the United States. In respect to these lands it has pursued a wise and liberal policy. It has caused them to be surveyed as the advancing tide of settlement required, has disposed of them at small cost to individuals, and has frequently granted large tracts to aid in various public improvements. This has been and is well understood to be the purpose for which the Government holds these lands, and the phrase "public lands" has a well-known signification, limited to these only. *Spaulding et al. v. Martin et al., 11 Smith (Wisc.), 273.*

SEC. 3320. Where commissioners appointed under the act of Congress of February 21, 1823, to ascertain and decide on the rights of persons claiming lands at Green Bay, Prairie du Chien, etc., have determined the rights of claimants, and their report is confirmed by the act of April 17, 1828, the courts of Wisconsin will not enter upon an examination of the testimony to ascertain what facts are established by it. The court can not go behind the decision and report of the commissioners and the confirmation of that report by Congress, or inquire into the sufficiency and nature of the evidence introduced before them.   *Challefaux v. Ducharme, 8 Smith (Wisc.), 288.*

SEC. 3321. By the act of Congress of August 3, 1843, allotting certain lands to the Stockbridge Indians as soon as the report of the commissioners therein provided for showing the allotment had been transmitted to the President of the United States, and before the issue of any patent by the President, the title to the several lots became vested in the allottees, respectively, as grantees under the act in fee simple; and the act of August 6, 1846, repealing the act of 1843, could not divest the title thus acquired, and even if it did such title was restored and confirmed by the subsequent treaties with the said Indians (in 1848 and 1856) to all the allottees who had accepted the lands allotted to them and to their assigns.   *Ruggles v. Marsilliott, 19 Conover (Wisc.), 159.*

SEC. 3322. Proof of possession by an Indian and of common reputation of his ownership of a part of the reservation of his tribe not shown to have been allotted to him in severalty, and of continuous possession for more than forty years under conveyances from him and his grantees, witnessed by and acknowledged before members of the same tribe, is not sufficient to establish an equitable title in him or his grantees as against such tribe.   *Fowler v. Schafer, 69 Conover (Wisc.), 23.*

SEC. 3323. Act of Congress, 1872 (17 Stat. L., 213), authorized partition among the survivors of the Me-shin-go-me-sia band of Indians of the tract of land ceded to Me-shin-go-me-sia by treaty of 1840, and provided that patent issue to each person in fee simple, and that the title so conveyed should descend as other lands in Indiana, but provided that the land should not be subject to any debt contracted prior to the partition, nor subject to levy, sale, forfeiture, or mortgage prior to January 1, 1881, nor be sold by the owner prior to that date. *Held,* that the land of one of the tribe who died in 1880, leaving debts not within the prohibited class, descended, subject to be applied in payment of such debts, as provided by section 2332, revised statutes of Indiana, as in case of other lands.

Taylor v. Vandergrift, 25 N. E. Rep., 548.

SEC. 3324. Under the provisions of the first clause of section 6 of the act of Congress entitled "An act to provide for the allotment of lands in severalty to Indians," etc., approved February 8, 1887 (24 Stat. L., 388), in order to establish an Indian right to citizenship and hence to vote at an election in this State, *held*, that it must be proven that such Indian was born within the territorial limits of the United States and that an allotment of land in fact has been made to such Indian by the Government of the United States in pursuance of said act, or of like authority of law or treaty of the United States.

State ex rel. Fair v. Frazier, 44 N. W. Rep., 471.

SEC. 3325. The descent of lands patented to a Shawnee Indian under the treaty of May 10, 1854, is to be determined by the laws and rules established by the tribe. Laws giving title to lands by inheritance are purely arbitrary, and the lawmaking power may cast the descent on whomsoever it will, or provide that, at the death of the owner. the whole estate shall go to the tribe, State, or other sovereignty.

Hannon v. Taylor et al., 45 Pacific Reporter, 51.

SEC. 3326. Where a Shawnee Indian, owning lands patented to him under the treaty of 1854, died in 1862, unmarried and without issue, leaving as his nearest relatives a half-brother, *held*, that a deed executed in 1862 by·the surviving half-brother, accompanied by certificates of the two chiefs showing that he was the only surviving heir of the patentee, and upon such certificates, approved by the Secretary of the Interior, under which the defendants received and held possession of the land for more than twenty-five years, passed a full title under the Shawnee law in force at that time, as disclosed by the evidence in this case; and that a deed executed by the daughter and heirs of the widow of the deceased half-brother in 1887, though approved by the Secretary of the Interior, conveyed no title.   *Ibid.*

SEC. 3327. We are of opinion that the grant of a right of way to defendant in error by the act of February 18, 1888, as amended February 13, 1889, was a "present absolute grant," subject to certain conditions subsequent in that part of said territory remaining under Indian occupancy, and, so far as they were applicable in that part, thrown open to settlement.   *Churchill v. Choctaw Ry. Co., 46 Pacific Rep., 505.*

CHAPTER IX.—RIGHTS OF DISCOVERERS.

SEC. 3328. The royal proclamation of 1763, reserving under the dominion and protection of the Crown for the use of the Indians "all the land and territories lying to the westward of the sources of the rivers which fall into the sea from the west and northwest," and forbidding all British subjects from making any purchases or settlements whatever, or taking possession of the reserved lands, was within the constitutional power of the Crown and binding so far as it affected the lands reserved.   *Johnson v. McIntosh, 8 Wheat., 543.*

SEC. 3329. In her discussion with France and Great Britain and with the United States respecting boundary, Spain did not rest her title in

America solely on the grant of the Pope, but she placed it on the right given by discovery. Portugal sustained her claim to the Brazils by the same title, and France founded her title to vast territories she claimed in America on discovery.   *Ibid.*

SEC. 3330. While the different nations of Europe respected the right of the natives as occupants, they asserted the ultimate dominion to be in themselves, and claimed and exercised as a consequence of this ultimate dominion a power to grant the soil while yet in the possession of the natives. These grants have been understood by all to convey a title to the grantees, subject only to the Indian right of occupancy.   *Ibid.*

SEC. 3331. The claim of the Dutch was always contested by the English; not because they questioned the title given by discovery, but because they insisted on being themselves the rightful claimants under that title.   *Ibid.*

SEC. 3332. All the nations of Europe who have acquired territory on this continent have asserted in themselves, and have recognized in others, the exclusive right of the discoverer to appropriate the lands occupied by the Indians, and the United States adopted this principle.   *Ibid.*

SEC. 3333. The validity of the power of the United States (which resided in the Crown or its grantees while we were colonies) has never been questioned in our courts, and it has been exercised uniformly over territory in the possession of the Indians. The existence of this power must negative the existence of any right which may conflict with and control it.   *Ibid.*

SEC. 3334. The principle "that discovery of parts of the continent of America gave title to the Government by whose subjects or by whose authority it was made, against all other European Governments, which title might be consummated by possession," acknowledged by all Europeans, because it was the interest of all to acknowledge it; gave to the nation making the discovery, as its inevitable consequence, the sole right of acquiring the soil and of making settlements on it.
Worcester v. Georgia, 6 Pet., 515.

SEC. 3335. The preemption rights of the discoverer were based on an exclusive principle which shut out the right of competition among those who had agreed to it, no one of which could annul the previous rights of those who had not agreed to it; it regulated the right given by discovery among the European discoverers, but could not affect the rights of those already in possession, either as aboriginal occupants or as occupants by virtue of a discovery made before the memory of man; it gave the exclusive right to purchase, but did not found that right on the denial of the right of the possessor of the soil.   *Ibid.*

SEC. 3336. The charters granted by the King soon after Great Britain determined to plant colonies in America purported generally to convey the soil, from the Atlantic to the South Sea, which was occupied by numerous and warlike nations, equally willing and able to defend their possessions.   The extravagant and absurd idea that the feeble settlements made on the seacoast or the companies under whom they were made acquired legitimate power by them to govern the people or to occupy the lands from sea to sea did not enter the mind of any man; they were all understood to convey the title, which, according to the common law of European sovereigns respecting America, they might rightfully convey, and no more.   This was the exclusive right of purchasing such lands as the natives were willing to sell.   *Ibid.*

Sec. 3337.   The relation between the Europeans and the natives was determined in each case by the particular Government which asserted and could maintain the preemptive privilege in the particular place. The United States succeeded to all the claims of Great Britain, both territorial and political, but no attempt, so far as it is known, has been made to enlarge upon them; so far as they existed merely in theory or were in their nature only exclusive of the claims of other European nations they still retain their original character and remain dormant; so far as they have been practically exerted they exist in fact, are understood by both parties, are asserted by the one and admitted by the other.   *Ibid.*

Sec. 3338.   In the management of their internal concerns the Indians are dependent on no power.   They punish offenses under their own laws, and in doing so they are responsible to no earthly tribunal. They make war and form treaties of peace.   The exercise of these and other powers gives to them a distinct character as a people and constitutes them in some respects a State, although they may not be admitted to possess the right of soil.   *Ibid.*

Sec. 3339.   The actual state of things at the time the various royal charters were granted by Great Britain and all history since explain them, the King at the treaty of peace could cede only what belonged to his Crown.   *Ibid.*

ARTICLE III.

CHAPTER I.—STATUS OF TRIBES.

Sec. 3340. The Indian tribes within the Louisiana purchase are in fact independent, yet any attempt of others to intrude into that country would be considered as an aggression which would justify war; and our late acquisitions from Spain are of the same character.

Johnson v. McIntosh, 8 Wheat., 543.

Sec. 3341. The Indian nations may, perhaps, be more correctly denominated domestic, dependent nations. Their relation to the United States resembles that of a ward to his guardian.

Cherokee Nation v. Georgia, 5 Pet., 1.

Sec. 3342. An Indian nation within the United States is not a foreign State in the sense of the United States Constitution and can not maintain an action as such in the United States courts. *Ibid.*

Sec. 3343. The Indians and their country are considered by foreign nations, as well as ourselves, as being so completely under the sovereignty and dominion of the United States that any attempt to acquire their lands or to form a political connection with them would be considered by all as an invasion of our territory and an act of hostility.

Ibid.

Sec. 3344. The Indians within the acknowledged boundaries of the United States are in a state of pupilage. Their relations to the Government resemble those of a ward to his guardian, and they look to it for protection, rely upon its kindness and its power, appeal to it for relief of their wants, and address the President as their Great Father.

Ibid.

Sec. 3345. The condition of the Indians in relation to the United States is, perhaps, unlike that of any other peoples in existence. In general, nations not owing a common allegiance are foreign to each other, and the term foreign nations is with strict propriety applicable by either to the other; but the relation of the Indians to the United

521

States is marked by peculiar and cardinal distinctions which exist nowhere else. *Ibid.*

SEC. 3346. The Cherokees are a State; they have been uniformly treated as a State since the settlement of our country; the numerous treaties made with them by the United States recognize them as being a people capable of maintaining the relations of peace and war. *Ibid.*

SEC. 3347. The Cherokee Nation has been recognized as being responsible in their political character for any violation of their engagements, or for any aggressions committed on citizens of the United States by any individual of their community. *Ibid.*

SEC. 3348. Even though the Cherokee Nation be not a foreign State in the sense of the Constitution, John Ross, or the principal chief of the Cherokee Nation, and duly authorized by them to represent them and their rights, is entitled to sue out from the circuit court of the United States process of injunction against the officers of Georgia, acting in execution of the statute of Georgia.

Opinion of Chancellor Kent as counsel in Cherokee Nation v. Georgia, "Peters Cherokee Case," 225.

SEC. 3349. The Indian nations are to be considered not only as States, but as foreign States, because they do not constitute any ingredient or essential part of our body politic. *Ibid.*

SEC. 3350. The chartered limits of the individual States have never been construed by the United States, in any period of its history, to confer jurisdiction over territories contained within those limits, and claimed, defined, and occupied, not by wandering savages, as in New South Wales, but by tribes of Indians acting regularly in a national capacity. *Ibid.*

SEC. 3351. The territory and sovereignty of the Cherokees have been transmitted to them from their ancestors. They have been in the enjoyment of both from the settlement of Georgia with the approbation of the whites and without any known conflicting claim against them. No better right or title to territory can exist either by law of nature or nations. They have never been conquered. *Ibid.*

SEC. 3352. The Cherokee Nation of Indians are an independent people, placed under the protection of the United States, and entitled to the privileges of self-government within their own territory, and to the exclusive use, enjoyment, and government of their laws, except so far as those rights have not been expressly surrendered or modified by treaty. *Ibid.*

SEC. 3353. It is difficult to conceive of any political transaction which could carry with it more explicit and conclusive evidence of the recognition on the part of the United States of the competence of the Cherokee Nation to treat and act as a sovereign and independent nation than the treaty made with the Cherokees at Holston July 2, 1791 (7 Stat. L., 39). *Ibid.*

SEC. 3354. By Indians *not members of any State*, were intended all those tribes which remained upon their own territory and in the exercise of their original independence, notwithstanding their lands were included within the chartered limits of the Colonies, and in some instances nearly surrounded by white settlements. It is well known that the Colonies claimed under their charters to an indefinite extent, and covered *all the Indian territories within the United States;* and the clause in question in the Articles of Confederation must have had reference to Indians *within the chartered limits of the States* who were not at the time members of the State nor subject to its municipal jurisdiction. Under any other construction the clause would have been inoperative, repugnant, and void. *Ibid.*

SEC. 3355. January 21, 1785, Congress made a treaty with the Wyandot, Delaware, Chippewa, and Ottawa nations of Indians and gave them peace. They had previously declared, in 1783, that *they waived the right of conquest* over the northern and western nations of Indians. These Indian nations "acknowledged themselves and all their tribes to be under the protection of the United States and of no other foreign sovereign whatever." *Ibid.*

SEC. 3356. Under the Articles of Confederation Congress continued to treat with the Indians *within the chartered limits of the States* as distinct, independent nations, and as possessing the sole and exclusive right to protect them and maintain political relations with them. In 1781 they sanctioned a negotiation for a treaty of peace with the Cherokee and Chickasaw Indians as being the means "to put a stop to the ravages of *those nations.*" *Ibid.*

SEC. 3357. From the first formation of the Union, and prior to the adoption of the Articles of Confederation, Congress treated with the Indians, spread over every part of the country covered by the colonial charters, as separate and independent nations, and appointed commissioners for the three Indian departments to treat with them in the name and on the behalf of the United Colonies. The Cherokees were mentioned as included in the southern department. *Ibid.*

SEC. 3358. The Cherokee Nation, whom the act of the legislature of Georgia (December 19, 1829) in a manner destroyed, had existed from time immemorial as a separate tribe in the exercise of the power of self-government and with the attributes of a nation competent to make treaties and to maintain the customary relations of war and peace. The Cherokees had been constantly recognized in their national character by the British and colonial authorities prior to our Revolution. The same character was conceded to them by the Government of the United States ever since we became an independent nation. *Ibid.*

SEC. 3359. Congress has passed acts to regulate trade and intercourse with the Indians which treat them as nations, respect their rights, and manifest a firm purpose to afford the protection which treaties stipulate. All these acts, and especially that of 1802 (2 Stat. L., 139), manifestly consider the several Indian nations as distinct political communities having territorial boundaries, within which their authority is exclusive, and having a right to all the lands within those boundaries, which is not only acknowledged but is guaranteed by the United States.   *Worcester v. Georgia, 6 Pet., 515.*

SEC. 3360. All the rights which belong to self-government have been recognized as vested in the Indian nations. Their right of occupancy has never been questioned, but the fee in the soil has been considered in the Government. This may be called the right to the ultimate dominion, but the Indians have a present right of possession.
Ibid.

SEC. 3361. In the management of their internal concerns the Indians are dependent on no power. They punish offenses under their own law, and in doing so they are responsible to no earthly tribunal. They make war and form treaties of peace. The exercise of these and other powers gives to them a distinct character as a people and constitutes them in some respects a State, although they may not be admitted to possess the right of soil.   *Ibid.*

SEC. 3362. The exercise of the power of the General Government over the Indians within the limits of a State must, in its nature, be limited by circumstances. If a tribe of Indians shall become so degraded or reduced in numbers as to lose the power of self-government, the protection of the local law of necessity must be extended over them.   *Ibid.*

SEC. 3363. The Cherokee Nation is a distinct community, occupying its own territory, with boundaries accurately described, in which the laws of Georgia can have no force, and which the citizens of Georgia have no right to enter but with the assent of the Cherokees themselves or in conformity with the treaties and the acts of Congress. The whole intercourse between the United States and this nation is by our Constitution and laws vested in the Government of the United States.   *Ibid.*

SEC. 3364. The stipulation found generally in Indian treaties by which the Indians acknowledge themselves to be under the protection of the United States and of no other power involve practically no claim to their lands—no dominion over their persons. It merely bound the nation to the Government as a dependent ally claiming the protection of a powerful friend and neighbor, and receiving the advantages of that protection without involving a surrender of their national character. Protection does not imply the destruction of the protected.
Ibid.

SEC. 3365. Our history furnishes no example since the first settlement of our country of any attempt on the part of the Crown to interfere with the internal affairs of the Indians further than to exclude the agents of foreign powers, who, as traders or otherwise, might seduce them into foreign alliances. The King never intruded into the interior of their affairs or interfered with their self-government so far as respected themselves only. *Ibid.*

SEC. 3366. The words "treaty" and "nation" are words of our own language, selected in our diplomatic and legislative proceedings by ourselves, having each a definite and well-understood meaning. We have applied them to the Indian as we have applied them to the other nations of the earth; they are applied to all in the same sense. *Ibid.*

SEC. 3367. The relations between the Indians and the Government of Spain were considered as matters of deepest political concern, in no wise connected with its fiscal operations; the commerce with the Indians was intrusted exclusively to the governors of the Spanish provinces. It was a part of his oath as prescribed by the laws of the Indies "that you shall take care of the welfare, increase, and protection of the Indians." *Mitchel v. United States, 9 Pet., 711.*

SEC. 3368. The treaty with the Cherokees allows the Indian council to make laws for their own people or such persons as have connected themselves with them; but it also provides that such laws shall not be inconsistent with acts of Congress. *United States v. Rogers, 4 How., 567.*

SEC. 3369. The native tribes who were found on this continent at the time of its discovery have never been acknowledged or treated as independent nations by the European Governments nor regarded as the owners of the territories they respectively occupied. On the contrary, the whole continent was divided and parceled out and granted by the Governments of Europe as if it had been vacant and unoccupied land, and the Indians were continually held to be and treated as if subject to their dominion and control. *Ibid.*

SEC. 3370. It is the duty of the courts to expound and execute the law as they find it. It is too firmly and clearly established to admit of dispute that the Indian tribes residing within the territorial limits of the United States are subject to their authority, and where the country occupied by them is not within the limits of one of the States, Congress may by law punish any offense committed there, no matter whether the offender be a white man or an Indian.
United States v. Rogers, 4 How., 572. The Cherokee Tobacco, 11 Wall., 616.

SEC. 3371. Indians within the Spanish domains, whether Christianized or not, were considered in a state of tutelage, and a part of the official oath of the Spanish governors was that they would look to the welfare, augmentation, and preservation of the Indians.
Chouteau v. Malony, 16 How., 203.
(The report of this case contains, at page 237, many valuable references to Spanish laws.)

SEC. 3372. Under the act of June 24, 1812, authorizing administrators appointed in a Territory to sue in the District of Columbia, money could be paid to administrators of a deceased Cherokee Indian appointed under the laws of the Cherokee Nation, and receipted for by them in that District. *United States v. Cox, 18 How., 100.*

SEC. 3373. The Cherokees are within our jurisdiction, and bear relation to our Government similar, in some respects, to that of a domestic Territory. *Ibid.*

SEC. 3374. The principal difference between the relation to the Federal Government of the Cherokee Nation and that of a Territory in its second grade of government consists in the fact that the Cherokees enact their own laws, under the restriction stated in the treaty of 1835, article 5, appoint their own officers, and pay their own expenses. This, however, is no reason why the laws and proceedings of the Cherokee Territory, so far as relates to rights claimed under them, should not be placed on the same footing as other Territories in the Union. It is a domestic Territory—a Territory originated under our constitution and laws. *Mackey v. Coxe, 18 How., 100.*

SEC. 3375. The treaty of 1838 (7 Stat. L., 550) with the New York Indians did not separate them from the care and protection of the Government on its ratification, but contemplated further duties toward them, and for which means were supplied.
Fellows v. Blacksmith, 19 How., 366.

SEC. 3376. Whether any particular class of Indians are still to be regarded as a tribe or have ceased to hold the tribal relation is primarily a question for the political departments of the Government, and if they have decided it the court will follow their lead.
United States v. Holliday, 3 Wall., 407.

SEC. 3377. The facts show distinctly "that the Secretary of the Interior and the Commissioner of Indian Affairs deem that it is necessary in order to carry into effect the provisions of said treaty that the tribal organization should be preserved." In reference to all matters of this kind it is the rule of the court to follow the action of the executive and other political departments of the Government whose more especial duty it is to determine such affairs. If by them those Indians are recognized as a tribe, the court must do the same; if they are a tribe, then, by the Constitution, they are placed for certain purposes within the control of the laws of Congress. This control extends to the subject of regulating the liquor traffic with them, and this power, residing in Congress, that body is necessarily supreme in its exercise. *Ibid.*

SEC. 3378. The situation of the Miamies in Kansas is the same as that of the Shawnee and Wea tribes. It is sufficient to state that they are a nation of people, recognized as such by the General Government in the making of treaties with them, and the relations always maintained toward them, and can not therefore be taxed by the authorities of Kansas. *The Kansas Indians, 5 Wall., 737.*

SEC. 3379. The situation of the Weas and their property in the State of Kansas is the same as that of the Shawnees, and the fact that they have applied to the courts of the State some times voluntarily, and, in certain specified cases, by the Secretary of the Interior, does not necessarily imply that they have submitted themselves to all the laws of the State, and until the tribe is disbanded the Indians can not look to Kansas for protection, nor can the general laws of the State taxing real estate within its limits reach their property. *Ibid.*

SEC. 3380. Numerous treaties made with the Indian tribes recognize them as a people capable of maintaining the relations of peace and war, of being responsible in their political character for any violations of their engagements, or for any aggression committed on citizens of the United States by any individual of their community, and laws have been enacted by Congress in the spirit of those treaties.
Holden v. Joy, 17 Wall., 211.

SEC. 3381. Indian tribes are States in a certain sense, although not foreign States, nor States of the United States, within the meaning of the Constitution of the United States.
Ibid. Warner v. Joy, 17 Wall., 253.

SEC. 3382. The cession in the Chickasaw treaty of 1832 (7 Stat. L., 381) contemplated the ultimate abandonment of the lands by the Indians. This treaty did not prove satisfactory, and in a second treaty made in 1834 (7 Stat. L., 450) the United States agreed, when the body of the lands were surveyed, to reserve from sale certain limited portions on which the individual reservations should be located. This was done in obedience to a just policy, for it would have been wrong, considering the dependent state of the Indians, to hold them to their original engagement, and it can not be doubted that it was the intention of both parties to the treaty to clothe the reservees with the full title, otherwise some words of limitation indicating a different intention would have been used. *Best v. Polk, 18 Wall., 112.*

SEC. 3383. The power of Congress to regulate commerce with the Indian tribes is in no wise affected by the magnitude of the traffic or the extent of the intercourse. As long as these Indians remain a distinct people with an existing tribal organization, recognized by the political departments of the Government, Congress has the power to say with whom and on what conditions they shall deal and what articles shall be contraband. *United States v. 43 Gallons of Whiskey, 93 U. S., 188.*

SEC. 3384. The court being informed who they are by the description of them in the petition as "Pueblo Indians of the pueblo of Taos," is not bound by the use of the additional word "tribe" to disregard that knowledge and assume that they are tribal Indians within the meaning of the statute regulating the intercourse of the white with this latter class of Indians.   *United States v. Joseph, 94 U. S., 614.*

SEC. 3385. The degree of civilization which the Pueblo Indians had attained centuries before their willing submission to all the laws of the Mexican Government, the full recognition by that Government of all their civil rights, including that of voting and holding office, and their absorption into the general mass of the population, all forbid the idea that they should be classed with the Indians for whom the intercourse acts were made, or that in the intent of the act of 1851 (9 Stat. L., 452), its provisions were applicable to them.   *Ibid.*

SEC. 3386. The tribes for whom the act of 1834 (4 Stat. L., 729), was made were those semi-independent tribes whom our Government has always recognized as exempt from our laws, whether within the limits of an organized State or Territory and in regard to their own rules and traditions; in whom we have recognized the capacity to make treaties and with whom the governments, State and national, deal, with few exceptions only, in their national or tribal character and not as individuals.   *Ibid.*

SEC. 3387. If the Pueblo Indians differ from the other inhabitants of New Mexico in holding lands in common, and in a certain patriarchal form of domestic life, they only resemble in this regard the Shakers and other communistic societies in this country, and can not for that reason be classed with the Indians to whom the intercourse act applies.   *Ibid.*

SEC. 3388. The status of the Pueblo Indians is not, in the face of all the facts stated, to be determined solely by the circumstance that some officer of the Government has appointed an agent for them, even if the court could take judicial knowledge of the existence of that fact.   *Ibid.*

SEC. 3389. The circumstances being different in that case the opinion of the court in the case of the Kansas Indians is not in conflict with the views expressed in this case. The tribal organizations of the Kansas Indians continuing within the State, and the United States treating with them as distinct political communities, the legislature of Kansas could not interfere with their lands or the lands of individual members of the tribes and subject them to taxation.   *Pennock v. Commissioners, 103 U. S., 44.*

SEC. 3390. The pledge contained in the eighth article of the Sioux agreement embodied in the act of 1877 (19 Stat. L., 256) to secure to the Indians an orderly government by appropriate legislation thereafter to be framed and enacted, necessarily implies, having regard to all the circumstances attending the transaction, that among the arts of civilized life, which it was the very purpose of all these arrangements to introduce and naturalize among them, was the highest and best of all, that of self-government, the regulation by themselves of their own domestic affairs, the maintenance of order and peace among their own members by the administration of their own laws and customs.   *Ex parte Crow Dog, 109 U. S., 556.*

SEC. 3391. The Sioux Indians notwithstanding the pledge contained in their agreement that the United States would secure them in self-government, were to be subject to the laws of the United States, not in the sense of citizens but as they had always been, as wards subject to a guardian; not as individuals, constituted members of the political community of the United States with a voice in the selection of representatives and the framing of the laws, but as a dependent community, who were in a state of pupilage, advancing from the condition of a savage tribe to that of a people who, through the discipline of labor and by education, it was hoped might become a self-supporting and a self-governing society.   *Ibid.*

SEC. 3392. The laws of the United States to which the Sioux were declared by the agreement of 1877 (19 Stat. L., 256) to be subject were the laws then existing and which applied to them as Indians, and, of course, they included the statute excepting from the operation of the general laws of the United States crimes committed within the Indian country by one Indian upon the person or property of another Indian. Declaring them subject to the laws made them so, if it effected any change in their situation, only in respect to laws in force and existing, and did not effect any change in the laws themselves.   The phrase can not have a more extensive meaning than the acknowledgment of their allegiance as Indians to the laws of the United States, made or to be made in the exercise of legislative authority over them as such.   *Ibid.*

SEC. 3393. The expressions contained in the Sioux agreement of 1877 (19 Stat. L., 256), promising that the United States would secure the Indians in an orderly government and declaring them subject to laws of the United States, must be taken in connection with the entire scheme of the agreement, including those parts not finally adopted, as throwing light on the remainder; and looking at the purpose so clearly disclosed in the rejected clause of the removal of the whole body of the Sioux Nation to the Indian Territory proper, it is manifest that the provisions had reference to their establishment as a people upon a definite reservation as a permanent home.   *Ibid.*

SEC. 3394. The Indian tribes, being within the territorial limits of the United States, were not, strictly speaking, foreign States, but they were alien nations—distinct political communities—with whom the United States might, and habitually did, deal as they thought fit, either through treaties made by the President and Senate, or through acts of Congress in the ordinary forms of legislation.
                                    Elk v. Wilkins, 112 U. S., 94.

SEC. 3395. The remarks by Chief Justice Taney in his opinion in case of Scott *v.* Sanford (19 How., 393) cited in this case for the plaintiff, did not affirm or imply that either the Indian tribes, or individual members of those tribes, had the right, beyond other foreigners, to become citizens of their own will without being naturalized by the United States.   *Ibid.*

SEC. 3396. Indians born within the territorial limits of the United States, members of and owing immediate allegiance to one of the Indian tribes (an alien though dependent power), although in a geographical sense born in the United States, are no more "born in the United States and subject to the jurisdiction thereof" within the meaning of the first section of the fourteenth amendment to the Constitution than the children of subjects of any foreign government born within the domain of that government, or of children born within the United States of ambassadors or other ministers of foreign nations.   *Ibid.*

SEC. 3397. The national legislation has tended more and more toward the education and civilization of the Indians and fitting them to be citizens, but the question whether any Indian tribes, or any members thereof, have become so far advanced in civilization that they should be let out of the state of pupilage and admitted to the privileges and responsibilities of citizenship is a question to be decided by the nation whose wards they are and whose citizens they seek to become and not by each Indian for himself.   *Ibid.*

SEC. 3398. The provision of the act of March 3, 1871 (16 Stat. L., 566) that "hereafter no Indian nation or tribe within the territory of the United States shall be acknowledged or recognized as an independent nation, tribe, or power with whom the United States may contract by treaty," is coupled with a provision that the obligations of any treaty already lawfully made is not to be thereby invalidated or impaired; and its utmost possible effect is to require the Indian tribes to be dealt with for the future through the legislative and not through the treaty-making power.   *Ibid.*

SEC. 3399. The Cherokees of North Carolina are not entitled to a share of the commuted fund of $214,000, and of the fund created by the sales of Cherokee lands west of the Mississippi; such Indians must be readmitted to citizenship in the Cherokee Nation in compliance with its constitution and laws if they wish to enjoy the benefits of its common property.   *Cherokee Trust Funds, 117 U. S., 288.*

SEC. 3400. The acts of our Government recognize the Cherokee Nation as a State, and the courts are bound by those acts.

Cherokee Nation v. Georgia, 5 Pets., 1. Cherokee Trust Funds, 117 U. S., 288.

SEC. 3401. The Cherokees of North Carolina dissolved their connection with their nation when they refused to accompany the main body of it on its removal west; and they have since had no separate political organization. *Cherokee Trust Funds, 117 U. S., 288.*

SEC. 3402. The treaty of 1828 (7 Stat. L., 311) was made with the chiefs and headmen of the Cherokee Nation of Indians west of the Mississippi, and by that, for the first time, the Cherokees west of the river were recognized as so far a distinct and separate political body from the Cherokees east of the river as to call for separate treaty negotiations with them. *Ibid.*

SEC. 3403. The number of Cherokees that were permitted to remain under the twelfth article of the treaty of 1835 (7 Stat. L., 478) was between eleven and twelve hundred. They were without organization or a collective name and they ceased to be a part of the Cherokee Nation, and henceforth they became citizens of and were subject to the laws of the State in which they resided. The name of the " Eastern Cherokees " accompanied those who emigrated, to distinguish them from those who had preceded them, and who were called "Old Settlers." *Ibid.*

SEC. 3404. Whatever union the Cherokees in North Carolina have had among themselves has been merely a social or business one. It was formed in 1868 at the suggestion of an officer of the Indian Office for the purpose of enabling them to transact business with the Government with greater convenience. Although its articles are drawn in the form of a constitution for a separate civil government, they have never been recognized as a separate nation by the United States; no treaty has been made with them; they can pass no laws; they are citizens of the State, and bound by its laws. *Ibid.*

SEC. 3405. The band of Cherokees in North Carolina, organized as it is now, is not the successor of any organization recognized by any treaty or law of the United States. *Ibid.*

SEC. 3406. In several opinions of the courts the Indians have been variously spoken of as "wards of the nation," as "pupils," as local dependent communities, and in this spirit the United States have conducted its relations to them from its organization, but after an experience of an hundred years of the treaty-making system of the Government, Congress has determined upon a new departure—to govern them by acts of Congress.
United States v. Kagama, 118 U. S., 375.

SEC. 3407. The recognized relation between the United States and the Choctaw Nation is that between a superior and an inferior, whereby the latter is placed under the care and control of the former, and which, while it authorizes the adoption on the part of the United States of such policy as their own public interests may dictate, recognizes, on the other hand, such an interpretation of their acts and promises as justice and reason demand in all cases where power is exerted by the strong over those to whom they owe care and protection. The parties are not on an equal footing, and inequality is to be made good by the superior justice which looks only to the substance of the right without regard to technical rules framed under a system of municipal jurisprudence, formulating the rights and obligations of private persons equally subject to the same laws. *Choctaw Nation v. United States, 119 U. S., 1.*

SEC. 3408. The Choctaw Nation is capable, as an Indian tribe, under the terms of the Constitution, of entering into treaty relations with the Government, although, from the nature of the case, they are subject to the power and authority of the laws of the United States when Congress shall choose to exert its legislative power.   *Ibid.*

SEC. 3409. While the proceedings instituted by the Cherokee Nation could not be regarded as technically a suit in equity, of which the court might take cognizance under the general statutes defining its jurisdiction, no reason is perceived why, in view of the broad terms of the act of July 4, 1884 (23 Stat. L., 73), granting the Southern Kansas Railway Company a right of way through the lands of the nation and of the peculiar relations which the nation sustains to the Government and people of the United States—relations which forbid, if to be avoided, the application of strict rules of interpretation—the bill should not have been treated simply as an original petition of appeal by the plaintiff for a trial of the case between it and the railway company upon the issue as to damages.

Cherokee Nation v. S. Kan. Ry. Co., 135 U. S., 641.

SEC. 3410. The proposition that the Cherokee Nation is sovereign, in the sense that the United States or the several States are sovereign, and that the nation alone can exercise the power of eminent domain within its limits finds no support in the numerous treaties with the Cherokee Indians, in the decisions of the courts, or in the acts of Congress defining the relations of that people with the United States.

Ibid.

SEC. 3411. From the beginning of the Government to the present time the Cherokee Indians have been treated as "wards of the nation," "in a state of pupilage," "dependent political communities," holding such relations to the General Government that they and their country, as declared in Cherokee Nation *v.* Georgia, are considered by foreign nations, as well as ourselves, as being so completely under the sovereignty and dominion of the United States that any attempt to acquire their lands or to form a political connection with them would be considered by all as an act of hostility.   *Ibid.*

SEC. 3412. It is true that the treaties and laws of the United States contemplated the Indian Territory as completely separated from the States and the Cherokee Nation as a distinct community, and that, as stated by Mr. Justice McLean in Worcester *v.* Georgia "in the executive and judicial branches of our Government we have admitted, by the most solemn sanction, the existence of the Indians as a separate and distinct people and as being vested with rights which constitute them a State or separate community," but that falls far short of saying that they are a sovereign State, with no superior within the limits of its territory.   *Ibid.*

SEC. 3413. Neither the treaty of 1835 (7 Stat. L., 473), whereby the United States covenanted and agreed that the lands ceded to the Cherokee Nation should at no future time, without their consent, be included within the territorial limits or jurisdiction of any State or Territory, and that the Government would secure to that nation "the right by their national council to make and carry into effect all such laws as they may deem necessary for the government of the persons and property within their own country, belonging to their people, or such persons as have connected themselves with them," nor the treaties of 1846 (9 Stat. L., 871) and 1866 (14 Stat. L., 799), guaranteeing to the Cherokees the title and possession of their lands and jurisdiction over their country, nor any previous treaties, evinced any intention upon the part of the Government to discharge them from their condition of pupilage or dependency and constitute them a separate, independent, sovereign people, with no superior within its limits.   *Ibid.*

SEC. 3414. Whatever may have been the injustice visited upon this unfortunate race of people (the Indians) by their white neighbors this court has repeatedly held them to be the wards of the nation, entitled to a special protection in its courts, and as persons "in a state of pupilage." Congress, too, has recognized their dependent condition and their hopeless inability to withstand the wiles or cope with the power of the superior race by imposing restrictions upon their right to alienate lands assigned to them in severalty, either by making their scrip nonassignable, as in this case, or by requiring the assent of the President to their execution of deeds, as in the case of Pickering *v.* Lomax (*ante*, 310). The court in this case fully coincides with what was said by Mr. Justice Davis in the case of the *Kansas Indians*, that "the conduct of Indians is not to be measured by the same standard which we apply to the conduct of other people."

Felix v. Patrick, 145 U. S., 317.

SEC. 3415. The very analogy of the Indians to persons under guardianship suggests a limitation to their pupilage, since the utmost term of disability of an infant is but 21 years, and it is very rare that the relations of guardian and ward under any circumstances, even those of lunacy, are maintained for a longer period than this.   *Ibid.*

SEC. 3416. The "Old Settlers" or Western Cherokees are not a governmental body politic nor have they a separate existence nor any capacity to act collectively. The money decreed in this judgment belongs to them as individual members of an Indian community, recognized as such by the treaty of 1846 (9 Stat. L., 871) and treated as distinct and separate from the Cherokee Nation so far as necessary to enable the Government to accord to them their treaty rights. They are described in the treaty of 1846 as "all those Cherokees west of the Mississippi who emigrated prior to 1835;" and they may be held to include those now living who so emigrated, together with the descendants of those who have died, the succession to be determined by the Cherokee law. The petition does not set forth their names nor the extent of the right and interests claimed, respectively; but the evidence is quite inadequate to justify the recognition of the immediate petitioners as appointed by all the beneficiaries as their agents to receive and disburse the amount awarded.

United States v. Old Settlers, 148 U. S., 427.

SEC. 3417. The Indians of the country are considered as wards of the nation, and whenever the United States set apart any land of their own as an Indian reservation, whether within a State or Territory, they have full authority to pass such laws and authorize such measures as may be necessary to give to these people full protection in their persons and property, and to punish all offenses committed against them or by them within such reservation.

United States v. Thomas, 151 U. S., 577.

SEC. 3418. By treaties and statutes of the United States the right of the Cherokee Nation to exist as an autonomous body, subject always to the paramount authority of the United States, has been recognized. (5th art. treaty, 1835, 7 Stat. L., 478; 13th art. treaty, 1866, 14 Stat. L., 799; secs. 30 and 31, act May 2, 1890, 26 Stat. L., 81.) And from this fact there has consequently been conceded to exist in that nation power to make laws defining offenses and providing for the trial and punishment of those who violate them when the offenses are committed by one member of the tribe against another one of its members within the territory of the nation.   *Talton v. Mayes, 163 U. S., 376.*

SEC. 3419. The Indians are not a portion of the political community called the "people of the United States," and, although not foreign nations or persons, they have always been regarded and treated as distinct and independent political communities.

United States v. Osborn, 2 Fed. Rep., 58.

SEC. 3420. The Indian tribes, or the members thereof, are not subject to the jurisdiction of the United States, and therefore such Indians are not made citizens by the fourteenth amendment.   *Ibid.*

SEC. 3421. The Indian tribes in the United States, or the members thereof, are not born "subject to the jurisdiction of the United States."   *Ibid.*

Sec. 3422. The several Indian tribes or nations belong to the Republic, though they are neither a State nor Territory.

Ex parte Morgan, 20 Fed. Rep., 298.

Sec. 3423. The Indian tribes have always been considered by every department of the Government—legislative, executive, and judicial—as distinct, independent political communities, differing in so many essential particulars from States and Territories in the American Union as not to come under the designation of either.   *Ibid.*

Sec. 3424. While the Indian tribes and nations and their lands are within the general sovereignty of the United States, yet the Government has always recognized a *quasi* national existence on the part of each Indian tribe, and has uniformly dealt with these tribes by treaty.

United States v. Hunter, 21 Fed. Rep., 615.

Sec. 3425. The alien and dependent condition of the members of the Indian tribes could not be put off at their own will without the action or assent of the United States. They were never deemed citizens of the United States, except under explicit provision of treaty or statute to that effect, either declaring a certain tribe or such members of it as chose to remain behind on the removal of the tribe westward to be citizens, or authorizing individuals of particular tribes to become citizens on application for naturalization and satisfactory proof of fitness for civilized life.   *Wau-pe-man-qua v. Aldrich, 28 Fed. Rep., 489.*

Sec. 3426. The Alaska Indians are dependent allies under the protection of the laws, and subject to such restraints in their tribal relations as may be deemed necessary for their welfare, promotion, and protection, and they must recognize the binding force of their obligations.   *In re Can-ah-conqua, 29 Fed. Rep., 687.*

Sec. 3427. No treaty having ever been made with the Alaska Indians or tribal independence recognized, they are not to be regarded as within the operation of the custom and policy of the Government arising out of the ordinance of 1787, relating to the Northwest territory, whereby the Indian tribes of the United States have been treated as free and independent within their respective territories, governed by their tribal laws and customs in all matters pertaining to their internal affairs.   *In re Sah-quah, 31 Fed. Rep., 327.*

Sec. 3428. The act of March 3, 1873 (17 Stat. L., 530), extending to Alaska two sections of the act of June 30, 1834 (4 Stat. L., 729), known as the "Indian intercourse laws," and relating principally to the interdiction of the liquor traffic among the Indians, is to be construed to make said territory "Indian country" only to the extent of the prohibited commerce, and did not put the Alaska Indians on a general footing with Indians in other parts of the United States.   *Ibid.*

Sec. 3429. The Cherokee Nation, while it owns the soil of its country, is under the political control of the United States and is depend-

ent on it for its political rights.   This, as the history of the country
has so often demonstrated, is necessary for the protection of its
people.   *Cherokee Nation v. So. Kan. R. Co., 33 Fed. Rep., 900.*

SEC. 3430. The Cherokee Nation is not sovereign, for its depend-
ence on the United States forbids the idea of sovereignty in it as
against the United States.   If not sovereign it can not, as against the
United States, have the right of eminent domain as an inherent right.
It can not have it because it has not been granted to it by the Government, as the Government can not grant away the sovereign powers
of the people.   *Ibid.*

SEC. 3431. The tribal organization of the Cherokees is recognized
by the political departments of the National Government as existing,
although their primitive habits and customs are largely broken into
by the progress they have made toward civilization.   Yet, while the
intercourse laws enacted by the National Government are applicable
to them, though they may have a local government of their own, it
can not with any reason be said that, as against the Government of the
United States, they are a sovereign people or have the power which is
inherent in sovereignty.   That they are not sovereign is apparent
from the treaties made with them by the United States, from the laws
of Congress enacted for their government, and from the opinions as to
their *status* delivered at different times in the history of the country
by the Supreme Court of the United States.   *Ibid.*

SEC. 3432. The Indian tribes are wards of the nation.   They are
communities dependent on the United States; dependent largely for
their daily food; dependent for their political rights.   They owe no
allegiance to the States and receive from them no protection.
                               United States v. Clapax, 35 Fed. Rep., 575.

SEC. 3433. The Government of the United States has always regarded
the Indian tribes as distinct communities, in a state of semiindependence and pupilage, between which and it certain international relations
were to be maintained; and both the legislative and judicial departments of the National Government have always emphatically asserted
that the Indian tribes possess such a national character as to be within
the treaty-making power of the Constitution and outside the sphere of
State jurisdiction over their persons or their lands so far as the national
authority has intervened.   *Benson v. United States, 44 Fed. Rep., 178.*

SEC. 3434. Even if section 5391 of the Revised Statutes could be
considered as applicable to the law of Montana, it does not apply to an
offense committed by one Indian against another on the Flathead Reservation, because Indians living in the tribal relation are not subject,
in their internal social relations, either to the laws of the State or of
the United States.   *United States v. Barnaby, 51 Fed. Rep., 20.*

SEC. 3435. Indian tribes were and always have been regarded as having a semiindependent position when they preserve their tribal relations—not as States, not as nations, not as possessed of the full attributes of sovereignty, but as a separate people, with the power of regulating their internal social relations, and thus far not brought under the laws of the Union or of the State within whose limits they resided. *Ibid.*

SEC. 3436. The social and political condition of the Cherokee Nation is imperfectly understood by many. By intermarriage with the whites they have to a considerable extent come to be of mixed blood. Generations ago they abandoned the chase and the warpath and adopted the pursuits of civilized man. As far back as 1827 they adopted a written constitution, modeled after the constitutions of the States then surrounding their country. *Mehlin v. Ice, 56 Fed. Rep., 12.*

SEC. 3437. The right of local self-government has always been claimed and exercised by the Cherokee Nation, and their rights in this regard, so far as they relate to their own country and people, have never been questioned by the United States. Nor is it true that the United States has always denied to the Cherokees jurisdiction over white intruders in their country, such jurisdiction having been expressly conferred by the treaty of July 2, 1791 (7 Stat. L., 40). *Ibid.*

SEC. 3438. The nature and character of the Cherokee Nation as a political body, and the faith and credit due to the proceedings of its courts, have been the subject of consideration by the Supreme Court. The probate court of the Cherokee Nation issued letters of administration to Mackey and two others on the estate of Samuel Mackey, of the Cherokee Nation. In the case of Mackey *v.* Coxe (18 How., 100) it became necessary to consider the validity of these letters and the faith and credit due them, and the court reviewed at length the status, condition, and government of the Cherokees. *Ibid.*

SEC. 3439. The Creek Nation has long been recognized by the United States as a " separate dependent nation," as a State in a certain sense, though not a foreign State or a State of the Union, as a distinct community with boundaries accurately described, and as a domestic territory. The right of local self-government has been accorded the Creeks from the earliest times. The laws and customs of the nation adopted for the government and protection of the members thereof have never been interfered with by the United States.

Davidson v. Gibson, 56 Fed. Rep., 443.

SEC. 3440. Rights acquired under the laws and customs of the Creek Nation have been respected and enforced. In Mackey *v.* Coxe (18 How., 100), the Supreme Court said there was no "reason why the laws and proceedings of the Cherokee Territory, so far as relates to rights claimed under them, should not be placed upon the same footing as other Territories in the Union." The Creek Nation stands on the same footing. *Ibid.*

SEC. 3441. The two cases—United States *v.* Cook (19 Wall., 591) and Leavenworth, Lawrence and Galveston R. Co. *v.* United States (92 U. S., 733)—cited by defendant's counsel, are concerning lands within Indian reservations, and can not be considered controlling in this case. This right of general occupancy to the public domain is quite different from that given the Indians when a special reservation is by law or treaty assigned to them; this the Government treats as something tangible, and of it they are never deprived until they relinquish their title. *Caldwell v. Robinson, 59 Fed. Rep., 653.*

SEC. 3442. The Choctaw Nation is identical in all respects, so far as relates to its independence and form of government, with the Cherokee Nation. *Thebo v. Choctaw Indians, 66 Fed. Rep., 372.*

SEC. 3443. The political departments of the United States Government, by treaties, by acts of Congress, and by Executive action, have always recognized the Choctaw Nation "as a State and as a distinct political society, separate from others, and capable of managing its own affairs and of governing itself," and the courts are bound by those acts of the political departments of the Government. *Ibid.*

SEC. 3444. It has been the policy of the United States to place and maintain the Choctaw Nation and the other civilized tribes in the Indian Territory, so far as relates to suits against them, on the plane of independent States. A State, without its consent, can not be sued. *Ibid.*

SEC. 3445. The civilized nations in the Indian Territory are probably better guarded against suits than the States themselves, for the States may consent to be sued, but the United States has never given its permission that these Indian nations might be sued generally, even with their consent. *Ibid.*

SEC. 3446. The right of independent self-government guaranteed to the Choctaw Nation by the treaty of September 27, 1830 (7 Stat. L., 333), has been fully exercised, and the rights of the nation in this regard have never been questioned by the United States. The nation has long had a written constitution and laws modeled after those of the States of the Union and differing from them in no essential respect. *Ibid.*

SEC. 3447. While the Choctaw Nation has many of the attributes of the political unit which constitutes the civil and self-governing community called a "State" or "nation," it is not a sovereign State, but it is a domestic and dependent State subject to the jurisdiction and authority of the United States. Being a domestic and dependent State the United States may authorize a suit to be brought against it, but for obvious reasons this power has been sparingly exercised. *Ibid.*

Sec. 3448. The Eastern Band of Cherokee Indians is not a part of the Cherokee Nation with which this Government treats, and they have no recognized separate political existence, but at the same time their distinct unity is recognized and the fostering care of the Government is over them as such unit. This being so the United States have the right in their own courts to bring such suits as may be necessary to protect them. *United States v. Boyd, 68 Fed. Rep., 577.*

Sec. 3449. Congress has repeatedly recognized the distinctive character of the Eastern Band of Cherokees. It has legislated for their benefit, and has always treated this band as a distinct unit. They are not dealt with as individuals who gradually are absorbed into the community, but as a band isolated from—cared for apart from—other inhabitants. *Ibid.*

Sec. 3450. The policy of State legislation seems to have recognized the quasi tribal organization of the North Carolina Cherokees and regarded them as a peculiar class of citizens, worthy of and needing the kindly supervision and care of the State and National governments. *Ibid.*

Sec. 3451. The forefathers of the North Carolina Cherokees availed themselves of a provision in the treaty of New Echota (7 Stat. L., 478) and remained in the State of North Carolina; and the civil laws of the State were extended over them from the period of the removal of the Cherokee Nation to their territory west of the Mississippi River. The North Carolina Cherokees, by reason of their birth and residence, became citizens under the general provisions of the State constitution and not by any special law conferring upon them the rights of citizenship. *Ibid.*

Sec. 3452. The political departments of the Government have certainly recognized and treated the Eastern Band of Cherokees as a quasi tribal organization for social and business purposes, and have made liberal appropriations of money, appointed Indian agents to reside among them, and employed efficient means to enlighten their minds and guard them against the injurious consequences of their own ignorance and the frauds of unscrupulous white men. *Ibid.*

Sec. 3453. By numerous acts of Congress, the legislative department of the Government has recognized the Eastern Band of Cherokee Indians as being under the supervisory care of the United States. (A number of the acts are cited in the report of the case.) *Ibid.*

Sec. 3454. The act of July 27, 1868 (15 Stat. L., 228), in express terms placed the Eastern Cherokees in the same situation toward the Government as other tribes of Indians. The court is strongly inclined to the opinion that the act of Congress restored them to their former tribal relations as wards of the Government, subject to its control, and entitled to its care and protection. *Ibid.*

SEC. 3455. The fathers of the Eastern Band of Cherokees were members of the tribe of Cherokee Indians recognized by the Government as a nation. By the treaty of New Echota (7 Stat. L., 478) individuals and families who were averse to removal with the nation were suffered to remain in the States in which they were living if they were qualified to take care of themselves and their property, and were desirous of becoming citizens of the United States. Those who exercised this privilege terminated their connection with the Cherokee Nation, but this did not make them citizens.   *Ibid.*

SEC. 3456. The Indians belonging to the Eastern Band of Cherokees in the State of North Carolina never became citizens of the United States, and the Federal courts have jurisdiction to entertain a suit brought by the United States, as guardian of such Indians, for the protection of their interests.   *Ibid.*

SEC. 3457. In the absence of direct Congressional action on the subject, it is for the executive branch of the Government, acting through its appropriate channels, to determine when a given tribe of Indians or any portion thereof has sufficiently advanced in the ways of civilized life, etc., as to warrant the termination of Federal control over them, leaving them to the protection only of the general laws of the country.   *United States v. Flournoy, &c., Co., 69 Fed. Rep., 886.*

SEC. 3458. By the express terms of the treaties made with the Omahas and Winnebagos, the United States assumed the duty of preserving the reservations for use, occupancy and benefit of the Indians, and this duty is still incumbent upon it.   *Ibid.*

SEC. 3459. Indian tribes residing within the territorial limits of the United States are not foreign nations or States. In the case of Cherokee Nation *v.* Georgia (5 Pet., 1), it was held that an Indian tribe or nation within the United States was not a foreign State, in the sense of the Constitution, and that it could not maintain an action in the courts of the United States on the ground that it was a foreign State. The doctrine of that case has never been departed from, but often affirmed.   *Paul v. Chilsoque, 70 Fed. Rep., 401.*

SEC. 3460. Lapse of time and allotment of portions of their reservations in severalty do not terminate the tribal relations of Indians, nor remove them from the supervision and control of the Interior Department of the Government.   *United States v. Flournoy, &c., Co., 71 Fed. Rep., 576.*

SEC. 3461. The Cherokees east of the Mississippi do not form a nation. Their organization by the Indian Office under the name of the Eastern Band was for the purpose of facilitating business with the Government and is at most a social organization.   *Eastern Band of Cherokees v. United States et al., 20 C. Cls., 449.*

SEC. 3462. The Cherokee Nation, as litigants, have a right to stand upon their treaties in relation to the funds in suit, and neither an act of Congress nor the proceedings of the political departments of the Government can take away their vested rights guaranteed by treaty.

Ibid.

SEC. 3463. The relations of the Cherokee Nation to the United States are fixed by contracts, set out in treaties and laws, to which, as a nation, it has given its assent. The United States, by the terms of those contracts, have become trustee of its funds, which they have agreed to administer according to the provisions of those contracts.

Ibid.

SEC. 3464. No treaty was ever made with the Eastern Band of Cherokees nor with the people composing its membership. All the connection the band has with the United States is such as has been created by the laws of Congress, which may be altered by the same power that enacted them; and Congress may make no laws in relation to the band which are in conflict with the laws and constitution of the State of North Carolina, to which these Indians are subject.   *Ibid.*

SEC. 3465. The "whole Cherokee people" referred to in the treaty of 1846 (9 Stat. L., 871) were the three parties into which the Cherokee Nation was then divided by dissensions, and not by locality—*first*, the "Eastern Cherokees," meaning those who removed west after the the treaty of 1835–36, and who constituted the governing party, or, as their delegates signed themselves, the "government party;" *second*, the "treaty party," and *third*, "Old Settlers," all mentioned in that treaty.   *Ibid.*

SEC. 3466. History of the several bands of Cherokees and their rights under various treaties stated at length.   *Ibid.*

SEC. 3467. The relation of trustee and *cestui que trust* does not, as a matter of law, exist between the parties in this case.

Choctaw Nation v. United States, 21 C. Cls., 59.

SEC. 3468. The law of guardian and ward does not prevail in suits between the United States and the Indian tribes, but doubts are to be resolved in favor of the Indians, and words of doubtful construction are to be taken most strongly against the United States.   *Ibid.*

SEC. 3469. Indians not being citizens are subject to United States statutes, and where they refer a question to the arbitrament of the Secretary of the Interior by treaty, he can not transmit it to this court for adjudication.   *Chickasaw Nation v. United States, 22 C. Cls., 222.*

SEC. 3470. Sovereignties, corporations, and individuals, or aggregations of individuals may be parties litigant. The Western Cherokees are not a body corporate, but as the former owners of communal property, are now severally interested in a common fund. Concerning such litigants equity takes jurisdiction to prevent a multiplicity of suits; one may sue for the benefit of all.

Western Cherokee Indians v. United States, 27 C. Cls., 1.

Sec. 3471. Whenever Indians have asserted a legal capacity, it has been in pursuance of some statute especially conferring upon them the civil rights of suitors. *Jaeger v. United States et al., 27 C. Cls., 278.*

Sec. 3472. By the Delaware-Cherokee agreement, 1867, two independent bodies politic united and became one, the lesser, according to its terms, being merged in the greater. The compact regulated and guaranteed the individual and political rights of those who surrendered their independent political existence and became members of the Cherokee nationality. It received them as members of the Cherokee Nation with the same rights and immunities as native Cherokees.
Journeycake v. Cher. Nation and U. S., 28 C. Cls., 281.

Sec. 3473. The Delawares were Indians; they became legally members of the Cherokee Nation by adoption, and, by the terms of the agreement of 1867, they must be "taken and deemed to be citizens" identical in all constitutional rights with "native-born Cherokees."
Ibid.

Sec. 3474. Since the agreement of 1867 was entered into more than a quarter of a century has passed and it must be assumed that nearly half of the citizens of the Cherokee Nation have been born during this period. As against those who are of Delaware parentage no possible discrimination can be made, either under the Constitution or under the agreement. *Ibid.*

Sec. 3475. It does not appear that the Yuma Indians ever entered into treaty relations with the United States or that they have been recognized as having a tribal character capable of making treaties or that they are more than a race. *Jaeger v. United States, 29 C. Cls., 172.*

Sec. 3476. The Supreme Court decided in the case of United States *v.* Joseph (94 U. S., 614) that the act of June 30, 1834 (sec. 2118, Rev Stat.), does not apply to the Pueblo Indians of New Mexico; that they should not "be classed with the Indian tribes for whom the intercourse acts were made," and that "the tribes for whom the act of 1834 was made were those semiindependent tribes whom our Government has always recognized as exempt from our laws." *Ibid.*

Sec. 3477. "The Pueblo Indians," the court says in United States *v.* Joseph (94 U. S., 614), "if indeed they can be called Indians, have nothing in common with this class." Their holding lands in common the court likens to "the Shakers and other communistic societies in this country." *Ibid.*

Sec. 3478. The status of the Pueblo Indians is not to be determined solely by the circumstance that some officer of the Government has appointed for them an agent. *Ibid.*

Sec. 3479. The Sioux Nation is composed of different tribes or bands which have always been recognized as belonging to the Sioux family or race; and the treaty, February 16, 1869 (15 Stat. L., 635), " with

the representatives of the Sioux Nation," recognizes the different bands in their dual capacity as a nation and as separate bands composing the nation.
Graham v. United States, 30 C. Cls., 318.

SEC. 3480. When the national or tribal relations of Indian bands has been established by the political departments the courts are bound by it.
. *Ibid.*

SEC. 3481. The United States by treaty July 1, 1852 (10 Stat. L., 979), recognized the Apache Indians "situate and living within the United States" as a nation. Three other treaties made subsequently were with a lesser number of Indians, but the United States have never recognized the separate bands of the Apaches by treaty.
Tully v. United States, 32 C. Cls., 1.

SEC. 3482. The policy of the United States has been to accept the subdivisions of the Indians as by them adopted and to treat them accordingly, and if a subdivision has been recognized by the proper officers of the Government the court will accept that as a sufficient recognition upon which to rest a judgment.
Ibid.

SEC. 3483. The relations which Indians residing within State limits sustain to the State and the United States, and their respective laws, discussed.
United States v. Sa-coo-da-cot, 1 Abb., 377.

SEC. 3484. Under the treaty-making power certain political relations have been established between the United States and the Indian tribes.
United States v. Cisna, 1 McLean, 254.

SEC. 3485. The fact that the woman was a Pottawatomie Indian did not exempt her from the operation of the general rules applicable in such cases, and no special disability attaches to her social and political status.
Ash-Kum v. Sorin, 10 Bissell, 393.

SEC. 3486. The treaty of January 31, 1855 (10 Stat. L., 1159), dissolves the tribal relations of the Wyandot Indians, and declares them to be citizens of the United States to all intents and purposes and subject to the laws of the United States and of the Territory of Kansas. But this treaty excepted, in this particular, such Indians as applied to be exempt from its operation, among whom was the plaintiff. Since then Kansas has been admitted into the Union as a State.
Karrahoo v. Adams, 1 Dill., 344.

SEC. 3487. Indian tribes residing in the United States are not foreign States. In the case of the Cherokee Nation *v.* The State of Georgia (5 Pet., 1, 19), the Supreme Court of the United States held " that an Indian tribe or nation within the United States is not a foreign State or nation within the sense of the Constitution, and can not maintain an action in the courts of the United States on such grounds." If, as thus held, the tribe is not a foreign State it necessarily results that the persons composing it are not foreign citizens or subjects.
Ibid.

Sec. 3488. Since the Indians are within the jurisdiction and subject to the laws of the United States or the States within which they reside, or both, it is difficult to see on what ground or with what propriety they can be regarded as *foreign* citizens or subjects.   (Mackey *v.* Coxe, 18 How., 100, 104; Worcester *v.* Georgia, 6 Pet., 515.)   *Ibid.*

Sec. 3489. Where Indians reside within the limits of a State, the relations which they bear respectively to the State and to the National Government are peculiar, and frequently present perplexing questions. But no such questions now arise, and, since there is no provision in the judiciary act, or any other act of Congress giving to the courts of the United States jurisdiction in civil suits by or against Indians, we need not consider whether such jurisdiction could be constitutionally conferred by Congress as respects Indians not citizens living within State limits, and with respect to cases not arising under the Constitution, laws, or treaties of the United States.   *Ibid.*

Sec. 3490. Senator Carpenter, of the Senate Judiciary Committee, which was instructed to inquire into the effect of this amendment (fourteenth) upon Indian tribes and treaties, reported to the Senate, December 14, 1870, that the committee was of opinion "that the Indian tribes within the limits of the United States and the individual members of such tribes, while they adhere to and form a part of the tribes to which they belong, are not, within the meaning of the fourteenth amendment, *subject to the jurisdiction* of the United States by virtue of that amendment; and if so, it follows that the treaties heretofore made between the United States and the Indian tribes are not annulled by that amendment."   *Ibid.*

Sec. 3491. Under the laws as they now are, these Indians, if members of a tribe, are not citizens or members of the body politic.   The tribes are permitted by the United States to exist as distinct nations or as distinct political societies—separated from others, capable of managing their own affairs, and governing themselves.

Ex parte Reynolds, 5 Dill., 394.

Sec. 3492. The Cherokee Nation is a State, a distinct political society, separated from others, and capable of managing its own affairs and governing itself.   (Cherokee Nation *v.* Georgia, 5 Pet., 1.)   *Ibid.*

Sec. 3493. The numerous treaties made with the Cherokees recognize them as a people capable of maintaining the relations of peace and war, of being responsible in their political character for any violation of their engagements or for any aggressions committed on the citizens of the United States by any individual of that community. The acts of the Government plainly recognize the Cherokee Nation as a State, and the courts are bound by these acts.   *Ibid.*

Sec. 3494. In Worcester *v.* Georgia (6 Pet., 515), Chief Justice Marshall again reviewed the relations existing between the Government and the Indian tribes. In speaking of the relation of the Cherokee Nation to the United States, he says: "This relation was that of a nation claiming and receiving the protection of one more powerful; not that of individuals abandoning their national character and submitting as subjects to the laws of the master." *Ibid.*

Sec. 3495. The principle to be deduced from the decisions of the Supreme Court in The Kansas Indians (5 Wall., 737), Dred Scott *v.* Sandford (19 How., 403), and Worcester *v.* Georgia, in which the political status of the Indian is so fully discussed, is, that in cases where the United States has not, by its legislative or other acts, incorporated these people into the political body known as the people of the United States, who, according to our republican institutions, form the sovereignty, and who hold the power and conduct the government, they are not citizens. These nations or tribes may not be absolutely independent powers—they may be domestic dependent nations; but as long as the Government of the United States, through its legislative department, continues to treat them as beyond the jurisdiction of the United States, so long they must be held to be quasi foreign nations, whose citizens are not regarded as American citizens and not subject to the full responsibility of such citizens. If the Government has never recognized them as subject to its jurisdiction, and they have never been treated as citizens, they occupy the same position before the law as though they were citizens of a foreign power. *Ibid.*

Sec. 3496. It is provided by the thirty-eighth article of the Choctaw treaty of 1866 (14 Stat. L., 769) that every person who, having married a Choctaw or Chickasaw, resides in the said Choctaw or Chickasaw Nation, or who has been adopted by the legislative authorities, is to be deemed a member of said nation, and shall be subject to the laws of the Choctaw or Chickasaw nations, according to his domicile, and to prosecution and trial before their tribunals according to their laws, in all respects as though he were a native Choctaw or Chickasaw. This article of the treaty permits a citizen of the United States, by joining himself in marriage to a Choctaw or Chickasaw Indian and by residence in their country, to place himself beyond the jurisdiction of the laws of the United States. *Ibid.*

Sec. 3497. If Indian tribes are to be regarded and treated as separate dependent nations, there can be no serious difficulty as to the question whether an Indian can withdraw from his tribe, sever his relation therewith, and terminate his allegiance thereto. If they are not to be treated as separate dependent nations, then no allegiance is owing from an individual Indian to his tribe, and he could, therefore, withdraw therefrom at any time. *United States v. Crook, 5 Dill., 453.*

Sec. 3498. The Osage Nation is not so far independent as a nation as to be exempt from the constitutional power of Congress to pass

H. Doc. 538——35

laws punishing its members for crimes and offenses committed against the United States. *United States v. Cha-to-kah-na-pe-sha, 1 Hemp., 27.*

SEC. 3499. A white person, by adoption by a tribe of Indians, may become entitled to certain privileges in the tribe and also make himself amenable to their laws and usages. *United States v. Ragsdale, 1 Hemp., 497.*

SEC. 3500. The United States have never acknowledged or treated the native tribes of Indians as independent nations, nor regarded them as the owners of the territory they respectively occupied. On the contrary, they have always treated them as independent nations or tribes, subject to their dominion and control, and have exercised legislative power over them by the punishment of crimes committed within their limits whether the offender be a white man or an Indian. *Ibid.*

SEC. 3501. The Indian tribes within the territory of the United States are independent political communities, and a child or member thereof, though born within the limits of the United States, is not a citizen thereof because not born subject to its jurisdiction.
McKay v. Campbell, 2 Sawyer, 118.

SEC. 3502. Indian tribes within the limits of the United States have always been held to be distinct and independent political communities, retaining the right of self-government, though subject to the protecting power of the United States. (Worcester *v.* Georgia, 6 Pet., 574.)
Ibid.

SEC. 3503. The recognition or dissolution of the tribal relation is a matter in which the courts usually follow the action of the political departments of the Government.
United States v. Holliday, 3 Wall., 415; United States v. Earl, 9 Saw., 79.

SEC. 3504. In the absence of proof that a savage tribe of Indians have laws or customs having the force of laws relating to descent of property, the presumption arises that the property of a deceased person would belong to the first occupant. After the extension of the laws of the State over the tribe, property in the *possession* of the Indians is *prima facie* liable to the payment of their debts.
Brashear v. Williams, 10 Ala., 630.

SEC. 3505. The Indians upon our western frontier since their removal from their former homes east of the Mississippi, have been, to some extent, under the parental guardianship and protection of the Government of the United States, have been receiving annuities under treaty stipulations, and being of an inferior race and easily imposed upon, Congress deemed it expedient to pass the clause in section 3 of the act of March 3, 1847 (9 Stat. L., 203), to guard them against imposition.
Clark v. Crosland, 17 Ark., 43.

SEC. 3506. The act of April 22, 1850, for the protection and punishment of Indians, was intended to be applied to Indians in tribes, or when living in separate communities or companies, and not to a case where an Indian has been living among white men.

The People v. Juan Antonio, 27 Cal., 404.

SEC. 3507. But few of the particulars enumerated as constituting a State exist in a tribe of North American Indians.

Roche v. Washington, 19 Ind., 53.

SEC. 3508. The Indians are not educated above the condition of nomadic pastoral tribes, if up to it. Neither were these tribes conceded to be States or nations in the political or international sense of the terms. *Ibid.*

SEC. 3509. Admitting that the Miami tribe of Indians constitutes an international political State, and that it is a civilized one, still the State of Indiana is not bound by international comity to give effect, in her courts, to all the laws and customs of such State; but only to such as are not repugnant to her own laws and policy. *Ibid.*

SEC. 3510. The Miami tribe of Indians is not a nation, or independent people, between which and ourselves the principles and regulations of international law can apply or be enforced. *Ibid.*

SEC. 3511. The General Government never recognized the Shawnee tribe as a distinct nationality, except in connection with the country they occupied, and as occupying exclusively a particular district of country. *Blue Jacket v. Comsr's of Johnson Co., 3 Kans., 299.*

SEC. 3512. In pursuance of the treaty of July 19, 1866 (14 Stat. L., 799), an agreement was entered into between the Shawnees and the Cherokee Nation by which the Shawnees, upon certain terms and conditions, were incorporated into the Cherokee Nation, on equal terms in every respect and with all the privileges and immunities of native citizens of the Cherokee Nation. The Shawnees were to abandon their tribal organization and the agent of the Cherokees was to act for the Shawnees. *Ingraham v. Ward, 56 Kans., 550.*

SEC. 3513. In the Spanish colonies land was not assigned to the Indians by actual survey. They were permitted to occupy a specified spot, and the law gave them a right to 1 league around it. (*Post*, 655; 7 N. S., 315; 4 A. R., 141.)

Rebaus v. Nero, 2 Martin (La. Sup. Ct. Reps.), 576.

SEC. 3514. In Rebaus *v.* Nero and Martin *v.* Johnson it has already been decided that tribes of Indians to whom lands were allotted by the Spanish officers of Louisiana, in pursuance of the laws of the Indies, acquired a legal title to the soil. That they were in every respect as completely owners of it as those who held under a complete grant, although being considered under a state of pupilage, the authority of the public officers who were constituted their guardians was necessary to a valid alienation of their property.

Spencer's Heirs v. Grienball, 9 Martin (La. Sup. Ct. Reps.), 190, and 3 Harrison (La.), 870.

SEC. 3515. Nor did the American Government, the successor of Spain, ever recognize the Caddo tribe as the owners of any lands within the limits of Louisiana. The Commissioner was instructed to procure from them a cession of their right of occupation of the district in which they resided. (See House Doc. No. 1035, second session Twenty-seventh Congress.) *Brooks v. Norris, 6 Robinson (La.), 183.*

SEC. 3516. The Penobscot tribe of Indians always have been and now are under the jurisdiction and control of this State. This tribe can not, therefore, be one of those referred to in the Constitution of the United States. *Moore v. Veazie, 32 Me., 343.*

SEC. 3517. The wandering and improvident habits of the remnants of the Indian tribes in the State of Maine led the legislature at an early day to make them the wards of the State, and especially to take the control and regulate the tenure of their lands. Numerous acts looking to this end were passed in different years, which are now gathered together in chapter 9 of the revised statutes. *John v. Sabattis, 69 Me., 473.*

SEC. 3518. In the treaties of 1713, 1725, and 1749, the contracting Indians reserved to themselves "and their natural descendants, respectively, the privilege of fishing, hunting, and fowling, as formerly." These treaties were made by the Crown with actual political communities with an internal government and an external responsibility, which could wage war and make peace. But whatever may have been the original force and obligation of these treaties, they are now *functus officio.* *State v. Newell, 84 Me., 465.*

SEC. 3519. Whatever the status of the Indian tribes in the West may be, all the Indians of whatever tribe remaining in Massachusetts and Maine have always been regarded by those States and by the United States as bound by the laws of the State in which they live. Their position is like that of those Cherokees who remained in North Carolina. *Ibid.*

SEC. 3520. It is not found that the Federal Government ever by treaty or statute recognized these Indians as being a political community or an Indian tribe, within the meaning of the Federal Constitution. *Ibid.*

SEC. 3521. The statutes of 1870, chapter 293, section 6, providing that any justice of the superior court, upon the application of the selectmen of the town of Mashpee, after hearing all parties interested, may appoint commissioners to make partition of "any or all of the common lands of said town or of the people heretofore known as the Mashpee tribe of Indians," and that he may direct that the same or any part thereof be sold and the proceeds paid over to the treasurer of the town, is constitutional; and if, upon a petition presented by the selectmen, a sale of a portion of the common lands has been ordered by the court, the selectmen may, while the first petition is still pending, file a second petition for the sale of the lands not included in the order. *Coombs et al., Petitioners, 127 Mass., 278.*

SEC. 3522. By the statutes of 1869, chapter 463, all Indians within the Commonwealth (Massachusetts) were declared to be citizens, entitled to the rights and subject to the duties of other citizens of the Commonwealth. Previously to that statute they were the wards of the Commonwealth, and the title to the lands occupied by the several tribes was in the Commonwealth, and its use and improvement were regulated from time to time by the legislature (Danzell *v.* Webquish, 108 Mass., 133; Stat., 1862, c. 184). In thus enfranchising the Indians and conferring on them the rights of citizens, it was not the intention of the legislature to give at once to the several tribes or to the individual Indians composing those tribes the absolute and unqualified control of common lands occupied by them. Not only does the statute provide for the division or sale of common lands, but also for the collection of all funds and the sale of property held in trust for any tribe and the division of the same among them. The guardianship of the State was thus to be exercised over all Indians included within the terms of the act after they were declared to be citizens, and provision was made for the final distribution among them of property thus held in common. *Ibid.*

SEC. 3523. The United States have recognized the Indian nations as so far having the attributes of sovereignty as to be capable of making treaties and being bound by them, and as having also such title to the country occupied by them as may be granted by cession to the United States. *Minter v. Shirley, 45 Miss., 376.*

SEC. 3524. In 1870 the Senate Judiciary Committee, of which Mr. Carpenter was chairman, was instructed by resolution "to inquire into and report to the Senate the effect of the fourteenth amendment to the Constitution upon the Indian tribes of the country," etc. The report is No. 268, Forty-first Congress, third session, and shows that the said amendment has no effect whatever on the *status* of the Indian tribes and does not annul the treaties previously made with them.
State v. McKenney, 18 Nev., 182.

SEC. 3525. The Pueblo Indians of New Mexico are not Indian tribes within the meaning of the intercourse act of 1834 (4 Stat. L., 729), and no action lies under that act for a penalty for settling on the lands secured to them by patent from the United States, their rights and remedies as to such lands being the same as those of other persons owning lands. *United States v. Santislevan, 1 N. Mex. (Geld.), 583.*

SEC. 3526. The provisions of the Constitution and bill of rights respecting a *trial by jury* are not applicable to cases of a disturbance of the friendly relations between the State and the Indian nations or tribes within the State. *The People v. Dibble, 18 N. Y. (Barbour), 412.*

Sec. 3527. The Brothertown Indians are subject to the civil and criminal jurisdiction of this State (New York). The Brothertown Indians are not a distinct nation or tribe. They are not, in this respect, like some of the Indian tribes within this State, whose situation is peculiar, and who, as to offenses committed by the individuals within their tribes against each other, have claimed and exercised a criminal jurisdiction.

The Case of George Peters, a Brothertown Indian, 2 Johnson's Cases (N. Y.), 344.

Sec. 3528. The Brothertown, Oneida, and Stockbridge Indians can sue and be defended only by their attorney commissioned for that purpose pursuant to the act. (Session 36, ch. 92, sec. 27.)

Jackson v. Reynolds, 14 Johnson's Reports (N. Y.), 335.

Sec. 3529. As to the grants or cessions made by the Indians to the United States, it is a sufficient answer to say that the Indians have never been recognized as the absolute owners of the soil, or as a source of title to lands in this State. Their right to the *use* of the lands occupied by them has been admitted. But these very *Six Nations* of *Indians* had before ceded all their rights to Great Britain, and so, in truth, they had nothing to grant to the United States. There can be no source of title to land acknowledged but what is derived from the State.

The People v. Godfrey, 17 Johnson's Reports (N. Y.), 228.

Sec. 3530. The St. Regis Indians, though authorized by an act of the legislature at their annual meeting to make such rules, orders, and regulations respecting their lands as they shall judge necessary, etc., can not maintain an action of assumpsit for use and occupation against a white man who had occupied their land under a parol agreement as a tenant from year to year, at an annual rent, pursuant to the rules made by the plaintiffs at their annual meetings as to the improvement of their lands.

The St. Regis Indians v. Drum, 19 Johnson's Reports (N. Y.), 126.

Sec. 3531. The acts of a band of Indians forming part of the Seneca Nation in resisting the entry upon their reservation by the arbitrators appointed under the treaty to appraise and determine the value of their improvements, did not excuse the grantees under the treaty from a compliance with the conditions precedent before entering upon the lands, because, first, the "bands" were not as individuals parties to the treaty, and second, in this case it was not shown that the appraisement and award might not have been made without an actual entry upon the reservation.

Blacksmith v. Fellows et al., 7 Selden (N. Y. App.), 401.

Sec. 3532. The act (1841) authorizing the sale of the lands for the collection of unpaid taxes, but providing that such sale should not affect the Indian right of occupancy, is valid as against the objection that it conflicts with the treaties (January 5, 1838, between the United States and the several tribes of New York Indians, including the

Senecas; and May 20, 1842, between United States and Seneca Nation) by which the United States guarantee the Indian tribes against being disturbed in the free use and enjoyment of their lands, or the acts of Congress regulating intercourse with the Indian tribes. It operates only as against the preemption rights of white purchasers. The act, however (ch. 254 of 1840), authorizing the taxation and sale of Indian lands, without any reservation of the rights of Indian occupants is unconstitutional and void. The lands of Indian tribes were not subject to assessment for taxes under the general provisions of the Revised Statutes. The policy of our laws, until changed by the statute of 1840, regarded the Indians within our borders as distinct communities, not embraced within the administrative arrangement of towns and counties, though resident within their bounds.

Fellows v. Denniston, 23 Smith (N. Y. App.), 420.

SEC. 3533. Certain persons styling themselves "That portion of the Cayuga Nation of Indians residing in Canada," presented a claim to the board of audit for a share of annuities agreed to be paid by the State to said nation by treaties of 1789 and 1795. *Held*, that the claim was properly denied; that the claimants have no personal or associate character authorizing them to present the claim; that the treaty contract was between the State and the Cayuga Nation of Indians, and if violated only the contracting parties, not a citizen of the State or a member of the nation, or any portion of such members, unless recognized by the State as such, could demand satisfaction; that so long as the State recognizes the tribal organization as existing and deals with it as a nation the courts and officers of the State must so regard it; also that if any claim existed it was not a private one, and so was not within the jurisdiction of the board.

Cayuga Nation v. State, 99 N. Y. (Sickles), 235.

SEC. 3534. It was claimed on behalf of the plaintiff that the Indians, being wards of the nation, could not be bound by practical location founded on acquiescence. *Held*, untenable; that as plaintiffs right to sue was given by and dependent upon the said act of 1845, which provides that actions "may be brought and maintained * * * in the same manner * * * as if brought by citizens of the State," in adopting a remedy, it was taken subject to the conditions.

Seneca Nation v. Hugaboom, 132 N. Y. App. (Sickles), 493.

SEC. 3535. The rights of the aborigines in that State are best understood by referring to the acts of North Carolina when possessing jurisdiction over the country, now the State of Tennessee, the Constitution of the United States, and the laws made in pursuance thereof.

Glasgow v. Smith, 1 Overton (Tenn.), 111.

SEC. 3536. The rights of the aborigines as a sovereign people are not recognized, neither in the charter of Charles II nor the constitution of North Carolina. The first does not seem to recognize them at all, and the second in very different language from that which is usual when mentioning a people sovereign in fact. *Ibid.*

SEC. 3537. The Cherokees, though living within the limits of Tennessee, and upon lands the dominion of which belongs to this State, and having themselves only the usufruct thereof, are yet an independent nation, subject to laws, both civil and criminal, made by themselves for the regulation of their internal affairs and exterior relations.
Holland v. Pack, 1 Peck (Tenn.), 119.

SEC. 3538. The theory of legislating for the Cherokees, which is supposed to have been assumed by North Carolina, was visionary. The treaty under consideration admits the Indians not to be citizens, and the eighth article provides the mode of their naturalization.
Blair v. Pathkiller, 2 Yerg., 407.

SEC. 3539. For history, government, and status of Cherokees in North Carolina and Tennessee see *The State v. Foreman, 8 Yerg., 256.*

SEC. 3540. The Cherokee Nation did not cease to exist east of the Mississippi and within the limits of Tennessee upon the ratification of the treaty of 1835 (7 Stat. L., 478) for their removal west of the river, but remained a nation, subject to the laws of the United States, during the two years allowed for removal; and it was therefore a good defense to an action of trespass for destroying liquors within the limits of the nation that the liquor had been brought into the nation contrary to the laws of the United States, and that the defendant had destroyed it under the order of the military commander assigned to command the public forces in that nation. *Morrow v. Blevins, 4 Humph., 223.*

SEC. 3541. The Indians did not lose their character of tribe or nation and become a mass of unorganized individuals *eo instanti* upon the ratification of the Cherokee treaty of 1835 (7 Stat. L., 478). Their organization during the two years following the treaty was just the same as before, and the intercourse laws of the United States were unaffected and unimpaired by the condition of things after the treaty.
Ibid.

SEC. 3542. Chief Justice Marshall, in delivering his opinion in the Supreme Court of the United States, on the final decision of the controversy between the Cherokee Nation and the State of Georgia, places them with reference to the General Government in the same relation as that of ward to his guardian, and after reciting the fact that those Indians occupied a territory to which the Government of the United States asserted a title, decided that "whilst they so resided within the limits of that Government they were in a state of *pupilage,*" and that they looked to the Government for protection and relied upon its kindness and power. The Indian tribes on our frontier stand necessarily in the same relation to this Government, and although there may be occasional resistance they are still subject to be controlled by the Government. *Doss v. Crodock, 1 Dallam's Digest (Texas), 595.*

SEC. 3543. No territorial limits were ever assigned by the Mexican Government to the various tribes of Indians in Texas, and if we look to the treaty of 1832 between Mexico and the United States we will find that the former Republic then designated them as "Indian tribes" and not "Indian nations." In conformity with the views of the parent government, the congress of Coahuila and Texas, in the nineteenth article of the colonization law of 1825, have enacted "That Indians of all the wandering tribes within the limits of the State who may wish to establish themselves in any of the settlements, after declaring themselves in favor of the institutions and religion of the Government, shall be admitted as settlers." By our Constitution and laws the Indians have been reduced to a level with free negroes and mulattoes. The Indian tribes of Texas can not be regarded as independent of other nations since they are under the control of this Government and their territorial limits may be extended or reduced at the will of Congress. All States of the Union where Indians were residing have held them in strict obedience to the laws so far as public policy required. *Ibid.*

SEC. 3544. An Indian sustaining tribal relations is as capable of entering into binding contracts as any other alien, except in the particular instance prohibited by section 3, act of Congress March 3, 1847 (9 Stat. L., 203), which concludes in these words, "and all executory contracts made and entered into by any Indian for the payment of money or goods shall be deemed and held to be null and void and of no binding effect whatsoever." *Gho v. Julles, 1 Allen (Wash.), 325.*

SEC. 3545. The relations of the Government to the Indian tribes is of a political character, and their rights growing out of their occupancy of the soil can not be brought in question in a suit between individuals both of whom claim title through the same grant of Congress.
Challefaux et al. v. Ducharre et al., 8 Smith (Wisc.), 288.

SEC. 3546. The tribal records of the Brotherhood Indians, purporting to have been made by the "town clerk," and shown to have been for many years in the office of the town clerk of Brotherhood, are held to be *ancient instruments*, and, as such, admissible in evidence to show an allotment of lands within their reservation to members of the tribe in severalty, made at a "town meeting" in 1835. The commissioners elected to make partition of lands among the Brotherhood Indians in 1839 allotted one tract to "Hannah Paul" and another to "the wife of Solomon Paul," whose name, in fact, was "Hannah Paul." *Held*, that under the circumstances of this case it will not be presumed that there was but one person of that name or that the allotments were not made to different persons. *Fowler et al. v. Scott, 64 Conover (Wisc.), 510.*

SEC. 3547. *Quære*, whether the act of Congress of March 3, 1839 (5 Stat. L., 349), put an end to the existence of the tribe of Brothertown Indians as such, and whether, if so, the act of April 20, 1878

(20 Stat. L., 513), did not restore the tribal functions sufficiently to enable the members of the tribe as such to take as beneficiaries of the trust thereby created. *Ibid.*

SEC. 3548. The United States Government recognizes the authority of the Indian tribes to make contract and treaties, and asserts no authority over them except with their consent.

United States ex rel. Young v. Imoda, 1 Pacific Reporter, 721.

SEC. 3549. In Boyer *v.* Dively (58 Mo., 529) the court say: "The Constitution of the United States and the statutes passed in pursuance thereof undoubtedly recognized the Indian tribes as a peculiar people, having relations to the Government totally different from citizens of the States. Although located within the State lines, yet so long as their tribal customs are adhered to and the Federal Government manages their affairs by agents, they are not regarded as subject to the State laws so far, at least, as marriage, inheritance, etc., are concerned." * * *

State v. McKenney, 2 Pacific Reporter, 178.

SEC. 3550. *Quære,* whether the tribal character of the Brothertown Indians has entirely ceased. The tribal records of the Brothertown Indians are held to be admissible in evidence to show the allotments of land made under the acts of Congress.

Fowler et al. v. Scott, 25 Northwestern Reporter, 716.

SEC. 3551. An Indian tribe within the State (Minnesota), recognized as such by the United States Government, is to be considered as a separate community or people, capable of managing its own affairs, including the domestic relations, and those persons belonging to the tribe who are recognized by the custom and laws of the tribe as married persons must be so treated by the courts, and the children of such marriages can not be regarded as illegitimate.

Earl et al. v. Godley et al., 44 N. W. Reporter, 254.

SEC. 3552. Indians while preserving their tribal relations and residing on a reservation set apart for them by the United States are the wards of the General Government, and as such the subject of Federal authority, and the power to legislate for them is exclusively in Congress; and for acts committed within the limits of the reservation, they are not subject to the criminal laws of the State.

State v. Campbell et al., 55 N. W. Rep., 553.

SEC. 3553. The Omahas are a tribe of Indians having their residences chiefly in Thurston County, Nebr. They were formerly in possession of a reservation, but by virtue of certain treaties and acts of Congress a portion of their land was sold for their benefit, and a large portion of the remainder was allotted in severalty to members of the tribe. There remained unallotted a considerable body of land, subject to lease for grazing purposes, under certain supervision by the Indian Bureau, for the benefit of the tribe. While the members of the tribe have adopted the habits of civilized life, a council composed of 12 members is retained, and exercises a certain control over property still enjoyed by members of the tribe in common. It is to this communal property that this suit relates. Plaintiff is a member of the Omaha tribe and charges acts of a conspiracy on the part of certain parties to injure her rights in a lease of certain grazing lands, etc. *Held*, that in order to justify the admission in evidence, for the purpose of establishing the conspiracy of such acts of individuals, it is not necessary to first prove by other evidence the existence of the company.   *Farley v. Peebles, 70 N. W. Rep., 232*

CHAPTER II.—OF INDIVIDUALS.

SEC. 3554. Indians within the Spanish dominions, whether Christianized or not, were in a state of tutelage, and a part of the official oath of the Spanish governors was that they would look to the welfare, augmentation, and preservation of the Indians.
Chouteau v. Molony, 16 How., 203.

SEC. 3555. Indians, although of age, continued, within the dominions of Spain, to enjoy the rights of minors, to avoid contracts or other sales of their property—particularly real—made without authority of the judiciary or the intervention of their protectors. They were considered as persons under legal disability, and their protectors stood in the light of guardians.   *Ibid.*

(In the report of this case full references are made to Spanish law.)

SEC. 3556. The solemn declarations of the Mexican Government in the adoption of the "Plan of Iguala," on February 24, 1821, the treaty of Cardova, August 24, 1821, the delaration of independence, September 28, 1821, and the subsequent decrees of the first Mexican Congress had the effect, necessarily, to invest the Indians with the privileges of citizenship as effectually as had the Declaration of Independence of the United States of 1776 to invest all persons with these privileges residing in the country at the time and who adhered to the interests of the colonies.   *United States v. Ritchie, 17 How., 525.*

SEC. 3557. As a race it is impossible to deny that under the constitution and laws of Mexico, after the adoption of the "Plan of Iguala," in 1821, no distinction was made as to the rights of citizenship and the privileges belonging to it between the Indian and the European or Spanish blood.   *Ibid.*

SEC. 3558. Notwithstanding the citizenship of the Indians in Mexico under the "Plan of Iguala" and other solemn acts of the political authorities of the Mexican Republic, and their improvement under the influence of the missionary establishments, from their degraded condition and ignorance generally, the privileges extended to them in the administration of the Government must have been very limited, and they still, doubtless, required its fostering care and protection. · *Ibid.*

Sec. 3559. Where an Indian to whom liquor was sold had a piece of land on which he lived, and voted in county and town, as he was authorized to do by the laws of the State, still if he lived with his tribe and received his annuities he was a member of his tribe and under the charge of an Indian agent.

United States v. Holliday, 3 Wall., 407.

Sec. 3560. By conferring rights and privileges on the Indians the State of Kansas can not affect their situation, which can only be changed by treaty stipulation or a voluntary abandonment of their tribal organization.   *The Kansas Indians, 5 Wall., 737.*

Sec. 3561. American half-breed Indians, male and female, were included in the Oregon donation act of September 27, 1850.   (9 Stat. L., 496.)   *Silver v. Ladd, 7 Wall., 219.*

Sec. 3562. The cession in the Chickasaw treaty of 1832 (7 Stat. L., 381) contemplated the ultimate abandonment of the lands by the Indians.   This treaty did not prove satisfactory, and in a second treaty made in 1834 (7 Stat. L., 450) the United States agreed, when the body of the lands were surveyed, to reserve from sale certain limited portions on which the individual reservations should be located.   This was done in obedience to a just policy, for it would have been wrong, considering the dependent state of the Indians, to hold them to their original engagement, and it can not be doubted that it was the intention of both parties to the treaty to clothe the reservees with the full title, otherwise some words of limitation indicating a different intention would have been used.   *Best v. Polk, 18 Wall., 112.*

Sec. 3563. The status of the Pueblo Indians is not, in the face of all the facts stated, to be determined solely by the circumstance that some officer of the Government has appointed for them an agent, even if the court could take judicial notice of the existence of that fact.

United States v. Joseph, 94 U. S., 614.

Sec. 3564. The degree of civilization which the Pueblo Indians had attained centuries before their willing submission to all the laws of the Mexican Government, the full recognition by that Government of all their civil rights, including that of voting and holding office and their absorption into the general mass of the population, all forbid the idea that they should be classed with the Indians for whom the intercourse acts were made, or that in the intent of the act of 1851 its provisions were applicable to them.   *Ibid.*

Sec. 3565. The rule that the title to land bounded on a navigable river extends only to high-water mark applies to lands granted the Sacs and Foxes by the treaty of 1804 (7 Stat. L., 84), bounded on the Mississippi River.   The grant to the half-breeds was to them as persons and not as a political body. The political jurisdiction remains in the United States. Had the grant been to them as a political society it would have been a question of boundary between nations or States, and then the line would have been the *medium filium aqua*, as it is now between Iowa and Illinois.   *Barney v. Keokuk, 94 U. S., 324.*

SEC. 3566. The court being informed who they are by the description of them in the petition as " Pueblo Indians of the pueblo of Taos," is not bound by the use of the additional word "tribe" to disregard that knowledge and assume that they are tribal Indians within the meaning of the statute regulating the intercourse of the white man with this latter class of Indians.   *United States v. Joseph, 94 U. S., 614.*

SEC. 3567. Abiding by the rule which ought always to govern the court, to decide nothing beyond what is necessary to the judgment the court are to render, the question of whether the Pueblo Indians are citizens of the United States is left until it shall be made in some case where the rights of citizenship are necessarily involved.   *Ibid.*

SEC. 3568. The people who constitute the pueblo or village of Taos are not an Indian tribe within the meaning of the act of June 30, 1834 (4 Stat. L., 729), which declares that every person who makes a settlement on Indian lands shall be liable to a penalty.   *Ibid.*

SEC. 3569. A mixed or half-blood Indian of the tribe of Sacs and Foxes, to whom a patent for land was issued under article 17 of the treaty of 1868 (15 Stat. L., 495), by which the tribe ceded all their lands in Kansas to the United States, is not entitled to exemption from taxation on the lands thus held by a title carrying with it absolute ownership, with the right of free disposition.

Pennock v. Franklin County, 103 U. S., 44.

SEC. 3570. By accepting the provisions of article 10 of the Sac and Fox treaty of 1859 (15 Stat. L., 467) and the benefits arising out of that article and article 17 of the treaty of 1867 (15 Stat. L., 495) a half-breed Indian woman of the confederated Sac and Fox tribes of the Mississippi, who was married to a white man, had renounced all claim to share in the proceeds of lands in the reservation sold by the United States under said treaty of 1859 and her subsequent relation to her tribe as a member of it if she chose to keep it up, can not affect the jurisdiction of the State over her property for governmental purposes. She might have followed her tribe—she can now do it—but as the tribe has left the State of Kansas while she remains, and has taken a title carrying with it absolute ownership, with a right of free disposition at her will, she and her property have come under the control of the State and are subject to its laws, entitled to its protection, and bound to bear a portion of its burdens.   *Ibid.*

SEC. 3571. The Sioux Indians, notwithstanding the pledge contained in their agreement that the United States would secure them in self-government, were to be subject to the laws of the United States, not in the sense of citizens, but as they had always been, as wards subject to a guardian; not as individuals, constituted members of the political community of the United States, with a voice in the selection of representatives and the framing of the laws, but as a dependent community who were in a state of pupilage, advancing from the condition of a savage tribe to that of a people who, through the discipline of labor and by education, it was hoped might become a self-supporting and a self-governing society.   *Ex parte Crow Dog, 109 U. S., 556.*

SEC. 3572. It was no part of the design of the Sioux agreement of 1877 (19 Stat. L., 256) to treat the individuals of the Sioux Nation as separately responsible and amenable in all their personal and domestic relations with each other to the general laws of the United States, outside of those which were enacted expressly with reference to them as members of an Indian tribe, but to urge them as a people, as far as it could be successfully done, into the practice of agriculture, and to teach their children the arts and industry of civilized life.   *Ibid.*

SEC. 3573. A petition alleging that the plaintiff is an Indian, and was born within the United States, and has severed his tribal relations to the tribe of Indians and fully and completely surrendered himself to the jurisdiction of the United States, and is a *bona fide* resident of Omaha, in the State of Nebraska, does not show that he is a citizen of the United States under the fourteenth amendment to the Constitution.   *Elk v. Wilkins, 112 U. S., 94.*

SEC. 3574. An Indian born a member of one of the Indian tribes within the United States, which still exists, who has voluntarily separated himself from his tribe and taken up his residence among the white citizens of a State, but who has *not* been naturalized, or taxed, or recognized as a citizen by the United States or by the State, is not a citizen of the United States within the meaning of the fourteenth amendment of the Constitution.   *Ibid.*

SEC. 3575. The remarks by Chief Justice Taney in his opinion in Scott *v.* Sanford (19 How., 393), cited in this case for the plaintiff, did not affirm or imply that either the Indian tribes or individual members of those tribes had the right, beyond other foreigners, to become citizens of their own will without being naturalized by the United States.   *Ibid.*

SEC. 3576. The national legislation has tended more and more toward the education and civilization of the Indians and fitting them to be citizens; but the question whether any Indian tribes, or any members thereof, have become so far advanced in civilization that they should be let out of the state of pupilage and admitted to the privileges and responsibilities of citizenship, is a question to be decided by the nation whose wards they are and whose citizens they seek to become, and not by each Indian for himself.   *Ibid.*

Sec. 3577. Indians born within the territorial limits of the United States, members of and owing immediate allegiance to one of the Indian tribes (an alien, though dependent power), although in a geographical sense born in the United States, are no more "born in the United States and subject to the jurisdiction thereof," within the meaning of the first section of the fourteenth amendment, than the children of subjects of any foreign government born within the domain of that government, or of children born within the United States of ambassabors or other public ministers of foreign nations. *Ibid.*

Sec. 3578. The members of the Indian tribes within the territorial limits of the United States owed immediate allegiance to their several tribes, and were not part of the people of the United States. They were in a dependent condition, a state of pupilage, resembling that of a ward to his guardian. They and their property are exempt from taxation by treaty or statute of the United States, could not be taxed by any State. General acts of Congress did not apply to the Indians unless so expressed as to clearly manifest an intention to include them. *Ibid.*

Sec. 3579. The alien and dependent condition of the members of the Indian tribes can not be put off at their own will without the action or assent of the United States. They were never deemed citizens of the United States except under explicit provisions of treaty or statute to that effect, either declaring a certain tribe, or such members of it as chose to remain behind on the removal of the tribe westward, to be citizens or authorizing individuals of particular tribes to become citizens on application to a court of the United States for naturalization and satisfactory proof of fitness for civilized life. *Ibid.*

Sec. 3580. Slavery having been abolished, and the persons formerly held as slaves made citizens, the clause in the second section of the fourteenth amendment fixing the apportionment of representatives has abrogated so much of the corresponding clause of the original Constitution as counted only three-fifths of such persons; but Indians not taxed are still excluded from the count, for the reason that they are not citizens, and their absolute exclusion from the basis of representation, in which all other persons are now included, is wholly inconsistent with their being considered citizens. *Ibid.*

Sec. 3581. The Indians, then, not being citizens by birth, can only become citizens in the second way mentioned in the fourteenth amendment—by being "naturalized in the United States" by or under some treaty or statute—and the action of the political departments of the Government, not only after the proposal of the amendment by the Congress to the States in June, 1866, but since the proclamation in July, 1868, of its ratification by the requisite number of States, accords with this construction. *Ibid.*

Sec. 3582. Since the ratification of the fourteenth amendment Congress has passed several acts for naturalizing Indians of certain tribes, which would have been superfluous if they were, or might become, without any action of the Government, citizens of the United States.

Ibid.

SEC. 3583. The Cherokees of North Carolina are not entitled to a share of the commuted fund of $214,000 and of the fund created by sales of Cherokee lands west of the Mississippi. Such Indians must be readmitted to citizenship in the Cherokee Nation in compliance with its constitution and laws if they wish to enjoy the benefits of its common property.   *Cherokee Trust Funds, 117 U. S., 288.*

SEC. 3584. The Cherokees in North Carolina can not live out of the territory of the Cherokee Nation west of the Mississippi, evade the obligations and burdens of citizenship, and at the same time enjoy the benefits of the funds and common property of the nation. Those funds and that property were dedicated by the constitution of the Cherokees, and were intended by the treaties with the United States for the benefit of the united nation, and not in any respect for those who had separated from it and become aliens to their nation.   *Ibid.*

SEC. 3585. The band of Cherokees in North Carolina, organized as it now is, is not the successor of any organization recognized by any treaty or law of the United States.   *Ibid.*

SEC. 3586. The number of Cherokees that were permitted to remain under the twelfth article of the treaty of 1835 (7 Stat. L., 478) was between 1,100 and 1,200. They were without organization or a collective name and they ceased to be a part of the Cherokee Nation, and henceforth they became citizens of and were subject to the laws of the State in which they reside. The name of the *Eastern Cherokees* accompanied those who emigrated to distinguish them from those who had preceded them and who were called "Old Settlers."   *Ibid.*

SEC. 3587. The Cherokees of North Carolina dissolved their connection with their nation when they refused to accompany the main body of it on its removal west, and they have since had no separate political organization.   *Ibid.*

SEC. 3588. In several opinions of the courts the Indians have been variously spoken of as "wards of the nation," as "pupils," as "local dependent communities," and in this spirit the United States has conducted its relations to them from its organization; but, after an experience of a hundred years of the treaty-making system of the Government, Congress has determined upon a new departure—to govern them by acts of Congress.   *United States v. Kagama, 118 U. S. 375.*

SEC. 3589. From the beginning of the Government to the present time the Cherokee Indians have been treated as "wards of the nation," "in a state of pupilage," "dependent political community," holding such relations to the General Government that they and their country, as declared in Cherokee Nation *v.* Georgia, "are considered by foreign nations, as well as ourselves, as being so completely under the sovereignty and dominion of the United States that any attempt to acquire their lands, or to form a political connection with them, would be considered by all as an invasion of our territory and an act of hostility."   *Cherokee Nation v. S. Kan. Ry. Co., 135 U. S., 641.*

SEC. 3590. As the petitioner was a member of the Cherokee Nation by adoption, if not by nativity, and was the sole party to these proceedings, it is clear that under the treaties and acts of Congress he is amenable only to the courts of the nation, and the fact, if it be so, that the laws of the Cherokee Nation make no provision for the punishment for the crime of adultery, would not extend to the courts of the United States a power to punish this crime that did not otherwise exist.   *In re Mayfield, 141 U. S., 107.*

SEC. 3591. Whatever may have been the injustice visited upon this unfortunate race of people (the Indians) by their white neighbors, this court has repeatedly held them to be the wards of the nation, entitled to a special protection in its courts and as persons "in a state of pupilage." Congress, too, has recognized their dependent condition and their hopeless inability to withstand the wiles or cope with the power of the superior race by imposing restrictions upon their right to alienate lands assigned to them in severalty, either by making their scrip nonassignable, as in this case, or by requiring the assent of the President to their execution of deeds, as in the case of Pickering *v.* Lomax (*ante*, 310). The court in this case fully coincides with what was said by Mr. Justice Davis in the case of the *Kansas Indians*, that "the conduct of Indians is not to be measured by the same standard which we apply to the conduct of others."   *Felix v. Patrick, 145 U. S., 317.*

SEC. 3592. The very analogy of the Indians to persons under guardianship suggests a limitation to their pupilage, since the utmost term of disability of an infant is but twenty-one years, and it is very rare that the relations of guardian and ward under any circumstances, even those of lunacy, are maintained for a longer period than this.   *Ibid.*

SEC. 3593. While the plaintiffs in this case were not, in 1887, citizens of the United States, capable of suing as such in the Federal courts, the courts of Nebraska were open to them, as they are to all persons irrespective of race or color.   *Ibid.*

SEC. 3594. Twenty-eight years elapsed from the time the scrip was secured from Sophia Felix, and nearly twenty-seven years from the time it went into the possession of Patrick, before the bill was filed in this case. It admits of no doubt that if Sophia Felix and the plaintiffs in this case had been ordinary white citizens, under no legal disabilities, such as those arising from infancy, lunacy, or coverture, this lapse of time would be fatal to a recovery, at least unless it was conclusively shown that knowledge of the fraud was not obtained, and could not by reasonable diligence have been discovered, within a reasonable time after it was perpetrated. *Ibid.*

Sec. 3595. The power of free alienation is incident to an estate in fee simple, but a condition in a grant preventing alienation to a limited extent or for a certain and reasonable time may be valid, and the grantee forfeit his estate by violation of it, and while such a result does not ensue in transactions with members of a race of people treated as in a state of pupilage and entitled to special protection, yet the proviso to section 15 of the act of March 3, 1875 (18 Stat. L., 402), may fairly be held to have been adopted in view of general principles.

Taylor v. Brown, 147 U. S., 640.

Sec. 3596. The "Old Settlers" or "Western Cherokees" are not a governmental body politic, nor have they a corporate existence, nor any capacity to act collectively. The money decreed in this judgment belongs to them as individual members of an Indian community, recognized as such by the treaty of 1846 (9 Stat. L., 871), and treated as distinct and separate from the Cherokee Nation, so far as necessary to enable the Government to accord to them their treaty rights. They are described in the treaty of 1846 as "all those Cherokees west of the Mississippi who emigrated prior to 1835," and they may be held to include those now living who so emigrated, together with the descendants of those who have died, the succession to be determined by the Cherokee law. The petition does not set forth their names, nor the extent of the right and interests claimed, respectively; but the evidence is quite inadequate to justify the recognition of the immediate petitioners as appointed by all the beneficiaries as their agents to receive and disburse the amount awarded. *United States v. Old Settlers, 148 U. S., 427.*

Sec. 3597. The fact that Gentry (the alleged murdered man) said he lived in southern Kansas, without any evidence showing how he came to live there, under what circumstances, or how long he lived there, does not constitute any evidence of his being a white man, or that, being an Indian, he had severed his tribal relations and became a citizen of the United States. *Smith v. United States, 151 U. S., 50.*

Sec. 3598. It was held in Elk *v.* Wilkins (112 U. S., 94), that an Indian born a member of one of the Indian tribes within the United States, which still exists and is recognized as a tribe by the Government of the United States who has voluntarily severed himself from his tribe and taken up his residence among the white citizens of a State, but who has not been naturalized, taxed, or recognized as a citizen, either by the United States or the State, is not a citizen of the United States within the fourteenth amendment to the Constitution. Much more is that the case where it appears that the Indian was but temporarily a resident of a State, and that he had done nothing to indicate his intention to sever his tribal relations. *Ibid.*

SEC. 3599. Conclusiveness is the characteristic of every tribunal, acting judicially, whilst acting within the sphere of its jurisdiction, where no appellate tribunal is created, but such conclusiveness is restricted to those questions which are directly submitted for decision. In the present case doubtless the identity of the half-breed, George Washington, and his right to receive the land in question as his share of the lands appropriated by the treaty was conclusively found, but neither the treaty, the act of Congress, nor the instructions of the Department, contemplated any special inquiry into the ages of the Indians, the direction to the agent to report, as well the age as the sex and tribal relations of the claimants was merely to enable him, when he came to allot the lands, to identify the persons entitled to participate. *Hegler v. Faulkner, 153 U. S., 109.*

SEC. 3600. The last clause in the agreement between the Cherokee Nation and the Delaware tribe, containing the express declaration that the children of the registered Delawares should in all respects be regarded as native-born Cherokees, was not inserted with a view to giving additional rights to such children, but to prevent any question as to their inheritance of all the rights which their fathers received under the agreement. *Cherokee Nation v. Journeycake, 155 U. S., 180.*

SEC. 3601. The members of the Delaware tribe who chose under the agreement between that tribe and the Cherokee Nation of April 8, 1867, to remove from Kansas not only became members of the Cherokee Nation, but also stand equal with the native Cherokees in all the rights springing out of citizenship in the Cherokee Nation, and whatever rights the Cherokees had the registered Delawares also had, and it was an equality not limited to the living Delawares. *Ibid.*

SEC. 3602. The laws of the Cherokee Nation provided for the appropriation by the several Cherokees of lands for personal occupation, and the purchase by the Delawares was with the view of securing to the individual Delawares the like homes; but the lands thus purchased and paid for still remained a part of the Cherokee Reservation. *Ibid.*

SEC. 3603. The terms "rights and immunities" are often used as descriptive of only political rights and immunities, and do not necessarily include property rights, but the rights and interests which the native Cherokees had in the reservation and outlet sprang solely from citizenship in the Cherokee Nation, and the grant of equal rights as members of the Cherokee Nation naturally carried with it the grant of all rights springing from citizenship. *Ibid.*

SEC. 3604. As a further consideration for the payment of the sums for the purchase of homes the Delawares were guaranteed not merely the continued occupancy thereof, but also that in case of a subsequent allotment in severalty of the entire body of lands among the members of the Cherokee Nation they should receive an aggregate amount equal to that which they had purchased, and such disposition as would secure to them the homes upon which they had settled, together with their improvements; so that if, when the allotment was made, there was for any reason not land enough to secure to each member of the Cherokee Nation 160 acres, the Delawares were to have at least that amount, and the deficiency would have to be borne by the native Cherokees *pro rata*.   *Ibid.*

SEC. 3605. For the reasons stated in the opinion in the case of Cherokee Nation *v.* Journeycake (*ante*, 196), it may be held that the stipulations in the agreement of June 7, 1869, between the Cherokee Nation and the Shawnee tribe, secured to the Shawnees equal rights with the native Cherokees in that which was the common property of the Cherokee Nation, to wit, the reservation and the outlet, as well as all profits and proceeds thereof.   *Cherokee Nation v. Blackfeather, 155 U. S., 218.*

SEC. 3606. The first clause of section 2146, Revised Statutes, is taken from the twenty-fifth section of the act of June 30, 1834 (4 Stat. L., 729, 733), and it was held in United States *v.* Rogers (4 How., 567) that an adoption into an Indian tribe did not bring the party thus adopted within the scope of such exception, the court saying: "Whatever obligations the prisoner may have taken upon himself by becoming a Cherokee by adoption, his responsibility to the laws of the United States remained unchanged and undiminished. He was still a white man of the white race, and therefore not within the exception in the act of Congress." The term "Indian" in the section is one descriptive of race, and therefore the defendant described as a white man and not an Indian, is shown to be outside the first two clauses of the section.   *Westmoreland v. United States, 155 U. S., 545.*

SEC. 3607. Duncan was the illegitimate child of a Choctaw Indian by a colored woman, who was not his wife, but a slave in the Cherokee Nation. As his mother was a negro slave, under the rule *partus sequiter ventrem*, he must be treated as a negro by birth, and not as a Choctaw Indian, and there is an additional reason for this in the fact that he was an illegitimate child, and took the *status* of the mother.
                        Alberty v. United States, 162 U. S., 499.

SEC. 3608. Duncan came to the Cherokee Nation when he was about 17 years of age and married a freed woman, and a citizen of that nation. "It would seem, however, from such information as we have been able to obtain of the Cherokee laws, that such a marriage would not confer upon him the rights and privileges of Cherokee citizenship beyond that of residing and holding personal property in the nation; that the courts of the nation do not claim jurisdiction over such persons, either in criminal or civil suits, and they are not permitted to vote at any elections."   *Ibid.*

SEC. 3609. Under the treaty of 1867 (15 Stat. L., 513) the Ottawas of Blanchard's Fork and Roche de Bœuf, who had not prior to July

16, 1869, become citizens of the United States by applying to the courts as provided in said treaty, remained members of the tribe that they might remove to the Indian Territory and continue their tribal relations. *Wiggan v. Conolly, 163 U. S., 56.*

SEC. 3610. The Ottawa tribe of Indians, including the bands of Blauchard's Fork and Roche de Bœuf, proposed to continue its organization and relations to the United States and the Government accepted the proposition. The State of Kansas has never objected, even if it had any right to object, and it does not lie in the power of an individual to assert any supposed political rights of the State or challenge the action of the nation and the Indians in this behalf. The treaty of 1867 (15 Stat. L., 513), was valid and determined the status of the Indians politically and in respect to their property. *Ibid.*

SEC. 3611. The negotiations in February, 1867, with the Ottawa Indians of Blauchard's Fork and Roche de Bœuf were while the tribal organization and relations to the United States continued, and they amounted substantially to a proposition by the tribe to change the treaty of 1862 (12 Stat. L., 1237) and continue the tribal organization and relations with the United States; this was a valid act on the part of the tribe, and though the proposition was not accepted by the United States until after July 16, 1867, yet when accepted the acceptance related back to the date of the proposition. *Ibid.*

SEC. 3612. In the Cherokee Nation the fact that a marriage license was issued to a white man carries with it a presumption that all statutory prerequisites thereto had been complied with. This is the general rule in respect to official action, and one who claims that any such prerequisite did not exist must affirmatively show the fact. *Nofire v. United States, 164 U. S., 657.*

SEC. 3613. A white man who enters the office of the district clerk in the Cherokee Nation for the purpose of taking out a marriage license, and finds there a person in charge of it and transacting its business in a regular way, is not bound to ascertain his authority to act; but to him he is an officer *de facto*, to whose acts the same validity and the same presumptions attach as to those of an officer *de jure*. *Ibid.*

SEC. 3614. The evidence shows that deceased, a white man, sought in his lifetime to become a citizen of the Cherokee Nation by intermarriage, took all the steps he supposed necessary therefor, considered himself a citizen, and that the Cherokee Nation in his lifetime recognized him as a citizen and still asserts his citizenship. *Held*, that under those circumstances it must be adjudged that he was a citizen by adoption, and consequently that the jurisdiction over the offense charged is, by the laws of the United States and treaties with the Cherokee Nation, vested in the courts of that nation. *Ibid.*

SEC. 3615. A right of citizenship in an Indian nation, conferred by an act of its legislature, can be withdrawn by a subsequent act, and this rule applies to citizenship created by marriage with such citizens.

Roff v. Burney, 168 U. S., 218.

SEC. 3616. While the Indians and the territory which may have been specially set apart for their use are subject to the jurisdiction of the United States, and Congress may pass such laws as it sees fit prescribing the rules governing the intercourse of the Indians with one another and with citizens of the United States, and also the courts in which all controversies to which an Indian may be a party shall be submitted, the mere fact that a citizen of the United States has become a member of an Indian tribe by adoption may not necessarily cancel his citizenship.   *Ibid.*

SEC. 3617. A right of citizenship in an Indian nation conferred by an act of its legislature can be withdrawn by a subsequent act; and this rule applies to citizenship created by marriage with such a citizen. Whether any rights of property could be taken away by such subsequent act is not considered or decided.   *Ibid.*

SEC. 3618. The statute of Georgia could not make the Cherokees citizens, for it belongs exclusively to the Congress of the United States to prescribe the rule of naturalization; and no alien can be made a citizen but in the mode directed by the act of Congress.

Opinion of Chancellor Kent as counsel in Cherokee Nation v. Georgia, "Peters Cherokee Case," p. 225.

SEC. 3619. By Indians, *not members of any State*, were intended all those tribes which remained upon their own territory and in the exercise of their original independence, notwithstanding their lands were included within the chartered limits of the colonies, and in some instances nearly surrounded by white settlements. It is well known that the colonies claimed under their charters to an indefinite extent, and covered *all the Indian territories within the United States;* and the clause in question in the Articles of Confederation must have had reference to Indians *within the chartered limits of the States* who were not at the time members of the State nor subject to its municipal jurisdiction. Under any other construction the clause would have been inoperative, repugnant, and void.   *Ibid.*

SEC. 3620. An Indian occupying land in severalty, and voting at elections in the State of Michigan, can not be sold liquor without violation of the law.   *United States v. Osborn, 2 Fed. Rep., 58.*

SEC. 3621. The disposition of spirituous liquors to an Indian, under the charge of an agent, who has abandoned his nomadic habits and tribal relations and adopted the habits of civilized life, is a violation of section 2139, Revised Statutes.   *Ibid.*

SEC. 3622. The Indian tribes, or the members thereof, are not subject to the jurisdiction of the United States, and therefore such Indians are not made citizens by the fourteenth amendment.   *Ibid.*

SEC. 3623. The Indian tribes in the United States, or the members thereof, are not born "subject to the jurisdiction of the United States.   *Ibid.*

SEC. 3624. The offspring of a white man and a half-breed Indian woman was entitled to vote in Ohio.   *In re Camille, 6 Fed. Rep., 256.*

SEC. 3625. A person of half white and half Indian blood is not a "white person" within the meaning of this phrase as used in the naturalization laws, and therefore he is not entitled to be admitted to citizenship thereunder.   *Ibid.*

SEC. 3626. Indians on a reservation within a State are not citizens or members of the body politic, but are considered as dependent tribes, governed by their own usages and chiefs.
                Note to "43 Gallons Cognac Brandy," 11 Fed. Rep., 51.

SEC. 3627. When a tribe of Indians is placed under the charge of an Indian agent by treaty or otherwise each member of such tribe is under the charge of the agent, within the purview of section 2139 of the Revised Statutes, and no member thereof can dissolve his tribal relation or escape from such charge by absenting himself from the reservation of his tribe otherwise, without the consent of the United States.   *United States v. Earl, 17 Fed. Rep., 75.*

SEC. 3628. The recognition of the dissolution of tribal relations is a matter in which the courts usually follow the action of the political departments of the Government.   *Ibid.*

SEC. 3629. It may be admitted that an Indian who had separated from his tribe before the Government took cognizance of it as such, by treaty or otherwise, and did not return thereto or claim or enjoy any right or privilege as a member of such tribe, is not under the charge of an agent within the meaning of section 2139 of the Revised Statutes.   *Ibid.*

SEC. 3630. An Indian boy in Oregon who left his tribe and lived with a white family until his tribe had entered into treaty relations with the United States and gone upon a reservation in pursuance of such treaty, and until he was 23 years of age, and then went to live upon such reservation as a member of his tribe, could not thereafter by simply absenting himself from the reservation dissolve his tribal relation or cease to be under the charge of the agent of such reservation.   *Ibid.*

SEC. 3631. If the male descendants of Richardville have been voting, they have done it without right; and their acts and their status probably can have little or no bearing upon the rights of complainant and of those from whom she obtained title.

Wau-pe-man-qua v. Aldrich, 28 Fed. Rep., 489.

SEC. 3632. The alien and dependent condition of the members of the Indian tribes could not be put off at their own will without the action or assent of the United States. They were never deemed citizens of the United States, except under explicit provisions of treaty or statute to that effect, either declaring a certain tribe, or such members of it as chose to remain behind on the removal of the tribe westward, to be citizens, or authorizing individuals of particular tribes to become citizens on application for naturalization and satisfactory proof of fitness for civilized life.   *Ibid.*

SEC. 3633. The Indian who claimed exemption from taxation had become and had been recognized as a citizen of the State both by the State and Federal governments—so recognized by the State in the very statute which required the levying of the disputed taxes.   *Ibid.*

SEC. 3634. While these Indians, according to the plea, have exercised some rights that belong to State citizenship, the facts of the case do not show that the United States had prior to the tax sales in question surrendered control over them *as Indians* and as, in fact, a part of the tribe to which they originally belonged. These lands ought now to be subject to taxation, but the way should be opened by Congressional legislation.   *Ibid.*

SEC. 3635. A custom prevailing among the uncivilized tribes of Indians in Alaska, whereby slaves are bought, sold, and held in servitude against their free will and subjected to ill treatment at the pleasure of the owner, is contrary to the thirteenth amendment to the Constitution of the United States and the civil-rights bill of 1866 (14 Stat. L., 27), and a person held in slavery will be released by order of the court upon *habeas corpus.*   *In re Sah-quah, 31 Fed. Rep., 327.*

SEC. 3636. The recognized relation between the parties to this controversy, therefore, is that between a superior and an inferior, whereby the latter is placed under the care of the former, and which, while it authorizes the adoption on the part of the United States of some such policy as their own public interests may dictate, recognizes on the other hand such an interpretation of the acts and promises as justice and reason demand in all cases where power is exerted by the strong over those to whom they owe care and protection.

Cherokee Nation v. So. Kan. Ry. Co., 33 Fed. Rep., 900.

SEC. 3637. The defendant's case must be tried as that of any other man, and he must be given the same consideration regardless of his race, color, or condition of life. The same law governs in this case as in any other case of the same character and circumstances.

United States v. Les Claya, 35 Fed. Rep., 493

SEC. 3638. An Indian reservation is in the nature of a school, and the Indians are gathered there under the charge of an agent for the purpose of acquiring the habits, ideas, and aspirations which distinguish the civilized from the uncivilized man.

United States v. Clapox, 35 Fed. Rep., 575.

SEC. 3639. It is well known that many of these Indians, especially the half-breeds are well educated, intelligent, and as fully competent to look after their business affairs as any person; and the fact that they were Indians and maintained tribal relations and were in a certain sense the wards of the Government did not debar them from a hearing in the courts of Nebraska.

Felix v. Patrick, 36 Fed. Rep., 457.

SEC. 3640. In ex parte Reynolds (5 Dill., 403) it was pointed out that the common-law rule respecting the offspring of a connection between a freeman and a slave was reversed with regard to the offspring of free persons, as their offspring follows the condition of the father.

United States v. Ward, 42 Fed. Rep., 320.

SEC. 3641. The statutes of the United States nowhere define an "Indian." As a matter of fact, the defendant is no more an Indian than he is a negro and no more a negro than he is an Indian. In United States *v.* Sanders (1 Hemp., 486) the court held that the quantum of Indian blood in the veins did not determine the condition of the offspring of a union between a white person and an Indian, but further held that the condition of the mother did determine the question, and the court referred to the common law as authority for the position that the condition of the mother fixed the status of the offspring.

Ibid.

SEC. 3642. By the act of March 1, 1889 (25 Stat. L., 757), Congress intended to change the rule as prescribed by section 2103, Revised Statutes, and by said act it provided when a contract with an Indian or with an Indian tribe for the payment of money to an agent or attorney was a valid contract and when money might be legally paid by an officer of the Government to an agent or attorney of an individual Indian or Indian tribe without violating the law. But the said act of 1889 was only intended to apply to the particular case embraced in the act. Congress in said act used appropriate language to change the law as prescribed by the Revised Statutes, as far as the case embraced in the act was concerned.

United States v. Crawford, 47 Fed. Rep., 561.

SEC. 3643. The principle applicable to the case of an Indian who, by absenting himself from his home for pleasure or profit, temporarily places himself beyond the physical power of his superintendent or agent, should be applied to this case. Neither the Indians themselves, the officers of the Army who induce them to enlist, or officers of the Interior Department who consent to it, have any power to change the laws, and no act of either, affecting for the time being the actual situation of an Indian, can change his status from that of a ward of the nation. *United States v. Hurshman, 53 Fed. Rep., 542.*

SEC. 3644. When an Indian enlists in the military service, the officers of Indian affairs are only partially relieved of their charge concerning him, and but temporarily deprived of power to control his person. While he is in the Army said officers continue to be charged with the duty of caring for his family and property and interests as a member of his tribe, and upon his discharge from the Army their right to control him will be fully restored. *Ibid.*

SEC. 3645. An Indian of the Nez Percé tribe, a soldier in the United States Army, is within the meaning of section 2139, Revised Statutes, prohibiting the sale of liquor to Indians, an " Indian under the charge of an agent." *Ibid.*

SEC. 3646. The grantees of certain lots on the Puyallup Reservation under the treaty of December 26, 1854 (10 Stat. L., 1132), were, by the act of February 8, 1887 (24 Stat. L., 388), made citizens of the United States, with all the rights, privileges, and immunities of other citizens, and subsequently the Territory was admitted as a State. This deprived the Government of the power to coerce such Indians into making or annulling contracts, or to molest persons who were on the granted premises by the license of the grantees, and transferred to the State government the power to preserve peace and good order, regulate the making of private contracts, and the use and descent of private property, and, therefore, no power remained in the United States to interfere with a person who was building a railroad across the granted lands with the consent and approval of the grantees, and an injunction *pendente lite* would be granted to restrain an army officer attempting such interference. *Ross v. Eells, 56 Fed. Rep., 855.*

NOTE.—This was reversed on error to the circuit court of appeals. (See Eells v. Ross, 64 ibid., 417.)

SEC. 3647. An Indian woman who marries a citizen of the United States, voluntarily takes up her residence apart from the tribe and adopts the habits of civilized life, becomes a citizen of the United States and of the State in which she resides, and may maintain a suit in the Federal courts against a citizen of another State.
Hatch v. Ferguson, 57 Fed. Rep., 957.

SEC. 3648. The act of 1887 (24 Stat. L., 388), which confers citizenship, clearly does not emancipate the Indians from all control or abolish the reservations. *Eells v. Ross, 64 Fed. Rep., 417.*

SEC. 3649. Section 3 of the act of 1887 (24 Stat. L., 388) provides for leasing lands under the regulations of the Secretary of the Interior, and the proviso of the section contemplates agents in charge of the reservations. Besides, the practice of the Department is and has been to maintain them, and this practice is respectable evidence of a correct interpretation of the statute by officers who may have suggested the policy and written the provisions of the law.   *Ibid.*

SEC. 3650. No reason is known why it was not competent for Congress to declare that allottees should be deemed citizens of the United States and entitled to the rights, privileges, and immunities of citizens, while it retained for the time being the title to certain lands in trust for their benefit, and withheld from them for a certain period the power to sell, lease, or otherwise dispose of their interest in said lands.   *Beck v. Flournoy, &c., Co., 65 Fed. Rep., 30.*

SEC. 3651. The Indians belonging to the Eastern Band of Cherokees in the State of North Carolina never became citizens of the United States, and the Federal courts have jurisdiction to entertain a suit brought by the United States, as guardian of such Indians, for the protection of their interests.   *United States v. Boyd, 68 Fed. Rep., 577.*

SEC. 3652. It must not be understood that the Eastern Band of Cherokees, although not citizens of the United States, and still under pupilage, are independent of the State of North Carolina. They live within the territory of that State and hold lands under its sovereignty and by its tenure. They are not a nation nor a tribe. They can enjoy privileges that the State may grant and are subject to its criminal laws. None of the laws applicable to Indian reservations apply to them. All that is decided is that the Government of the United States has not ceased its guardian care over them nor released them from pupilage. The Federal courts can still, in the name of the United States, adjudicate their rights.   *Ibid.*

SEC. 3653. It is true that the North Carolina Cherokees are citizens of the State of North Carolina, and have not been recognized as a separate nation or tribe, with treaty-making power; but it seems to the court that the mere fact that they are citizens of the State does not necessarily deprive them of the legitimate guardianship and care of the United States where there is no State or national legislation indicating such a purpose.   *Ibid.*

SEC. 3654. "An act in favor of Chief Junaluska" was passed by the legislature of North Carolina on January 2, 1847, conferring upon him all the rights of citizenship, and directing the Secretary of State to grant to him in fee simple a valuable tract of land in Cherokee County without the power of alienation by deed, and it was held in this court, in Smythe v. Henry (41 Fed. Rep., 417), that such restriction upon the power of alienation was not inconsistent with the rights of citizenship.   *Ibid.*

SEC. 3655. The alien and dependent condition of the members of the Indian tribes could not be put off at their own will without the action or assent of the United States. They were never deemed citizens of the United States except under explicit provisions of treaty or statute to that effect, either declaring a certain tribe, or such members of it as chose to remain behind on the removal of the tribe westward, to be citizens on application to an United States court for naturalization and satisfactory proof of fitness for civilized life.   *Ibid.*

SEC. 3656. It is urged with great force that the State of North Carolina recognizes the Cherokee Indians in that State as citizens; that they vote, pay taxes, and perform all the duties of citizens. But a citizen of the United States takes this privilege as a gift of the General Government. It can be acquired only under its laws and in the mode prescribed by it.   *Ibid.*

SEC. 3657. There is nothing in the record going to show that the members of the Eastern Band of Cherokees were ever naturalized. The clause in the treaty relating to those members of the band who desired to remain behind is in these words:

ART. 12. * * * Such heads of Cherokee families as are desirous to reside within the States of North Carolina, Tennessee, and Alabama, subject to the laws of the same, and who are qualified or calculated to become useful citizens shall be entitled to a prescriptive right to certain lands.

This does not confer on them citizenship. It only authorizes them to become citizens under certain circumstances. If the words of the treaty do not make them citizens of the United States and only gives them the right to become citizens upon showing the desire to that end, then there was but one way for them to attain citizenship, and that is pointed out in the statutes relating to naturalization.   *Ibid.*

SEC. 3658. A number of Indians had been taken at a dance house and a fight had occurred there to which the prisoner and the deceased were parties; at the breaking up of the dance the prisoner and another, who was also charged with the murder, were walking together toward their homes, when the deceased came up, and another fight ensued between the prisoner and his companion on one side and the deceased upon the other, in the course of which the killing occurred. *Held,*

I. That these facts constituted no evidence of a combination between the persons charged to commit the homicide.

II. That it was error to instruct the jury that if there were previous malice on the part of the prisoner toward the deceased, then, even in case the prisoner fought in self-defense, he was guilty of murder; and as the court to which the prisoner appealed could not tell how much the latter may have been prejudiced by the charge, even where the verdict was for manslaughter only, a new trial should be granted.

State v. Ta cha na tah, 3 Phillips (64 N. C.), 614.

SEC. 3659. The citizenship bestowed upon Indians to whom lands had been allotted in severalty was in no way inconsistent with the restriction imposed upon their titles, and under these restrictions the leases by the Winnebagos are wholly void.

United States v. Flournoy, &c., Co., 69 Fed. Rep., 886.

SEC. 3660. The defendant is not a citizen of the United States nor of the State of Indiana. She could only become such either by being naturalized in a court of competent jurisdiction in accordance with the laws of the United States, or by having the right of citizenship conferred upon her by an act of Congress, or by the treaty-making power. *Paul v. Chilsoquie, 70 Fed. Rep., 401.*

SEC. 3661. A member of an Indian tribe residing within the limits of the United States, who has not been naturalized, is not a citizen of the United States nor of the State of his residence, nor is he a citizen or subject of a foreign State within the meaning of the statutes conferring jurisdiction on the Federal courts, and such unnaturalized Indian can not remove into a Federal court a civil suit brought against him in a State court, unless it appears upon the face of the complaint or declaration that a Federal question is necessarily involved. *Ibid.*

SEC. 3662. Indians born within the territorial limits of the United States, members of and owing immediate allegiance to one of the Indian tribes (an alien, though dependent, power), although, in a geographical sense, born in the United States, are no more "born in the United States and subject to the jurisdiction thereof," within the meaning of the first section of the fourteenth amendment, than the children of subjects of any foreign government born within the domain of that government, or the children born within the United States of ambassadors or other public ministers of foreign nations. *Ibid.*

SEC. 3663. It not unfrequently happens that in cases of the acquisition of territory by conquest or purchase, the Government binds itself to confer citizenship upon the inhabitants of the acquired territory, and also to recognize and protect the title held by them; and it has never been held that the acquisition of the status of citizenship deprives the individual of his right to insist that the treaty obligation providing for the recognition and protection to the title to property should be observed and fulfilled. *United States v. Mullin, 71 Fed. Rep., 682.*

SEC. 3664. The fact that Indians to whom lands have been allotted in severalty are declared to be citizens of the United States, does not render null and void as to them, or as to the remaining portions of their tribes, restrictions upon alienation of their lands contained in the acts of Congress under which allotments in severalty have been made, nor terminate the right and duty of the United States to preserve the reservation lands for the use and benefit of the Indians. *United States v. Flournoy, &c., Co., 71 Fed. Rep., 576.*

SEC. 3665. The treaty with the Pottawatomie Indians of 1861 (12 Stat. L., 1191), by article 2 restrained an allottee of lands from alienating the same without the President's consent, under regulations established by the Secretary of the Interior. By article 3 members of the tribe being adult males and heads of families, with the consent of the President and on becoming naturalized before the United States court, could receive patents for their lands, with full power to sell the same. Under the treaty of 1867, when an allottee died, a patent was issued to deceased and his heirs, and the land was administered under the Kansas laws. *Held*, that an Indian boy, 11 years old, whose patent was obtained by false representations that he was dead, could not alienate his land, nor could a guardian appointed by the probate court do so. *Laughton v. Nadeau et al., 75 Fed. Rep., 789.*

SEC. 3666. Half-breeds who never received recognition from their white parents, but are left to be nurtured during childhood by Indian relatives, and live as savages, and are subjects of governmental care, have the status of Indians. *United States v. Hadley, 99 Fed. Rep., 437.*

SEC. 3667. Children born in lawful wedlock within the United States, the father being a white man and a citizen of the United States and the mother an Indian woman, who has adopted the habits of civilized life and lives apart from her tribe, are by virtue of the fourteenth amendment and section 1992, Revised Statutes, citizens of the United States, and their status is not changed by residence upon an Indian reservation and receiving allotments of Indian land. Half-breeds, who are citizens by birth, can not be brought to trial in the Federal courts under a statute which limits the jurisdiction to offenses committed by Indians. *Ibid.*

SEC. 3668. One born of a white father and an Indian mother, and who is a recognized member of a tribe of Indians to which his mother belongs, is an Indian and not subject to taxation under the laws of the State in which he resides on the reservation of his tribe.
United States v. Higgins, 103 Fed. Rep., 348.

SEC. 3669. The claimant, Hall, is a man of color, of Indian and African descent, and claims to have been freeborn. His mother was of Indian extraction, residing at the time of his birth in the city of Alexandria as a free woman. Hall was, therefore, always a free man or entitled to his freedom. *Hall v. United States, 11 C. Cls. R., 197.*

SEC. 3670. The appellant's mother resided in Virginia, where he was born. She was an Indian, and her status as a free woman is clearly established by the decisions of the courts of that State. "All Indians and their descendants in the natural line, brought into Virginia since the year 1705, and their descendants in the female line, are free." (Hodgins *v.* Wright, 1 Hen. & Mumf., 134.)
Ibid.

SEC. 3671. If a female ancestor of a person asserting a right to freedom, whose geneology is traced back to such ancestor through females only, be proved to have been an Indian, it seems incumbent on those who claim such person as a slave to show that such ancestor, or some female from whom she descended, was brought into Virginia between the years 1679 and 1691, and under circumstances which, according to the laws then in force, created a right to hold her in slavery.

Ibid.

SEC. 3672. The North Carolina Cherokees were not made parties to the Cherokee treaty of 1846 (9 Stat. L., 871) and were not regarded by the treaty-making power as forming a part of the Cherokee Nation.

Eastern Band of Cherokees v. United States et. al., 20 C. Cls., 449.

SEC. 3673. The Cherokees who remained east of the Mississippi after the removal of the nation thereby severed their connection with the Cherokee Nation.   *Ibid.*

SEC. 3674. All citizens of the Cherokee Nation, adopted as well as those of Cherokee blood, must be regarded in the administration of their constitutional rights, civil, political, and personal, as Cherokees. The national council is prohibited by the Constitution from making discriminations between different classes of citizens, and is without power to perceive differences which exist only in race or blood. So much of the acts of May 18, 1883, and November 25, 1890, as restricts the payment of funds derived from the public domain to "citizens of the Cherokee Nation by blood, is unconstitutional and void; and complainants in this suit are entitled to participate in those funds as if no such restriction had been exacted."   *Journeycake v. Cher. Nation, 28 C. Cls., 281.*

SEC. 3675. By virtue of the provisions of the Cherokee constitution, 1866, the freedmen became citizens equally with the Cherokees, and equally interested in the common property and equally entitled to share in its proceeds when distributed per capita.

Whitmire, Trustee v. Cherokee Nation et al., 30 C. Cls., 138.

SEC. 3676. By virtue of the provisions of the Cherokee constitution of 1866 the freedmen became citizens equally with the Cherokees, and equally interested in the common property and equally entitled to share in its proceeds when distributed *per capita.*   *Ibid.*

SEC. 3677. The Secretary of the Interior will cause the "Wallace Roll" to be further corrected by adding thereto descendants born since March 3, 1883, and prior to May 3, 1894, and striking therefrom the names of those who have died or ceased to be citizens of the Cherokee Nation, so that when thus amended it shall represent the freedmen entitled to participate in the distribution of the fund now awarded to the complainant.   *Ibid.*

SEC. 3678. The court, sitting as a court of equity, must assume for the purpose of distribution of a fund that the adopted whites are equally interested in the common property of the nation and protect their interests to the extent of not awarding their possible share in the fund to parties not strictly entitled to it.   *Ibid.*

SEC. 3679. Indians living in a State and doing business as merchants, are responsible, by the laws of the State, for the payment of their debts. This presupposes that they are not under the laws of the United States.   *Lowry v. Weaver, 4 McLean, 82.*

SEC. 3680. Hole-in-the-day, a chief of the Chippewas with whom the United States had treaty relations, and an Indian of unmixed blood, and residing at the time of death upon land granted to him by the treaty of May 22, 1855 (10 Stat. L., 1166), was not a citizen of the United States, nor of the State of Minnesota, and though said land lay within the territorial limits of Cass County, which was attached to Morrison County, the probate court of the latter county possessed no jurisdiction over his estate.

Note to Karrahoo v. Adams, 1 Dill., 344.

SEC. 3681. An Indian residing in the United States is not a "foreign citizen or subject" within the meaning of section 2, article 3, of the Constitution, and can not, on the ground that he is a "foreign citizen or subject," maintain a suit in the circuit court of the United States.   *Ibid.*

SEC. 3682. That Indians are not foreign citizens or subjects within the meaning of the Constitution and that the court has no jurisdiction of the present suit will further appear by reference to the eleventh section of the judiciary act, which prescribes the jurisdiction of the circuit courts of the United States. This section makes no mention of Indians and does not use the words " foreign citizens or subjects."

Ibid.

SEC. 3683. An Indian may abandon his tribe and, for the purpose of jurisdiction, become a member of the body politic known as citizens of the United States.   *Ex parte Kenyon, 5 Dill., 385.*

SEC. 3684. Before a citizen—that is, one of the sovereign people, a constituent member of the sovereignty—can expatriate himself under the thirty-eighth article of the Choctaw treaty of 1866 and place himself beyond the jurisdiction of the courts of the United States there must be a concurrence of certain things, to wit, marriage to a Choctaw or Chickasaw and residence in one or the other of those tribes.   *Ex parte Reynolds, 5 Dill., 394.*

SEC. 3685. The status of the offspring of a union between a citizen of the United States and one who is not a citizen, e. g., an Indian living with his people in a tribal relation, is that of the father. The rule of the common law and of the Roman civil law, as well as the law of nations, prevails in determining the status of the child in such cases.   *Ibid.*

SEC. 3686. Indians who maintain their tribal relations are the subjects of independent governments, and, as such, not within the jurisdiction of the United States within the meaning of the Constitution and laws of the United States, because the Indian nations have always been regarded as distinct political communities, between which and our Government certain international relations were to be maintained. These relations are established by treaties to the same extent as with foreign powers. They are treated as sovereign communities, but in consideration of protection, owing a qualified subjection to the United States. *Ibid.*

SEC. 3687. When the members of a tribe of Indians scatter themselves among the citizens of the United States, and live among the people of the United States, they are merged in the mass of our people, owing complete allegiance to the Government of the United States, and, equally with the citizens thereof, subject to the jurisdiction of the courts thereof. *Ibid.*

SEC. 3688. In United States *v.* Sanders (1 Hemp., 483) the court held that the quantum of Indian blood in the veins did not determine the condition of the offspring of a union between a white person and an Indian; but further held that the condition of the mother did determine the question. The court is sustained in this position by the common law if applied to the offspring of a connection between a freeman and a slave, but this rule is reversed with regard to the offspring of free persons, which offspring follow the condition of the father. *Ibid.*

SEC. 3689. It can make but little difference whether we accord to the Indian tribes a national character or not, the individual Indian possesses the clear right to withdraw from his tribe and forever live away from it, as though it had no further existence. *United States v. Crook, 5 Dill., 453.*

SEC. 3690. The right of expatriation is a natural, inherent, and inalienable right, and extends to the Indian as well as to the white race. *Ibid.*

SEC. 3691. The *habeas corpus* act describes applicants for the writ as *persons* or *parties* who may be entitled thereto. It nowhere describes them as *citizens*, nor is citizenship in any way or place made a qualification for suing out the writ. And an Indian is a *person*. *Ibid.*

SEC. 3692. An Indian is a *person* within the meaning of the *habeas corpus* act and is entitled to sue out a writ of *habeas corpus* in the Federal courts when it is shown that he is deprived of liberty under color of authority of the United States, or is in custody of an officer in violation of the Constitution or a law of the United States, or in violation of a treaty made in pursuance thereof. *Ibid.*

SEC. 3693. Colored persons who were never held as slaves in the Indian country, but who may have been slaves elsewhere, are like other citizens of the United States, and have no more rights in the Indian country than other citizens of the United States. *United States v. Payne, 2 McCrary, 289. Same, 8 Fed. Rep., 883.*

SEC. 3694. The child must partake of the condition of the mother; and if the mother is an Indian, the child will be so considered, for the purposes of the intercourse act of 1834, whether the father is a white man or an Indian.   *United States v. Sanders, 1 Hemp., 483.*

SEC. 3695. The declarations of a father as to the maternity of his child are competent evidence, but the circumstances under which they were made and the weight to be given them must be left to the jury.
                                                                    Ibid.

SEC. 3696. The child of a white woman, by an Indian father, would be deemed of the white race; the condition of the mother, and not the quantum of Indian blood in the veins, determining the condition of the offspring.   *Ibid.*

SEC. 3697. A white man who is incorporated with an Indian tribe at mature age by adoption does not thereby become an Indian, so as to cease to be amenable to the laws of the United States.
                              United States v. Ragsdale, 1 Hemp., 497.

SEC. 3698. The fourteenth article of the Constitution of the United States, commonly called the fourteenth amendment, is only declaratory of the common-law rule on the subject on citizenship by birth, and therefore does not include Indians or others not born subject to the jurisdiction of the United States.   *McKay v. Campbell, 2 Sawyer, 118.*

SEC. 3699. The son of a Chinook Indian woman by a British subject is either to be deemed to follow the condition of the mother and be considered a Chinook Indian, or that of his father and be considered a British subject; but in either case he was not born a citizen of the United States.   *Ibid.*

SEC. 3700. A half-breed Indian being denied the right to vote in Oregon, it is held that whether such refusal was wrongful or not, under the State law, the plaintiff not being a citizen of the United States, it is not within the purview of article fifteen of the Constitution of the United States, or the act of Congress entitled "An act to enforce the right of citizens of the United States to vote in the several States of the Union, and for other purposes" (16 Stat. L., 740), and therefore can not maintain an action on account of such refusal to recover the penalty given by section 2 of said act of Congress.
                                                                    Ibid.

SEC. 3701. Article 15 of the Constitution simply provides that the right of citizens of the United States to vote shall not be denied or abridged * * * on account of race, color, or previous condition of servitude. But as to who are "citizens of the United States," this article is silent—it being understood that that matter had been regulated or defined by article 14, section 1, which enacts: "All persons born or naturalized in the United States, and subject to the jurisdiction thereof, are citizens of the United States and of the State wherein they reside."   *Ibid.*

SEC. 3702. To be a citizen of the United States by reason of his birth, a person must not only be born within its territorial limits, but he must also be born subject to its jurisdiction—that is, in its power and obedience. *Ibid.*

SEC. 3703. Under article 15 of the Constitution, an Indian, whether of the whole or half blood who is a citizen of the United States is entitled to vote, or rather he can not be excluded from this privilege on the ground of being an Indian, as that would be to exclude him on account of race. *Ibid.*

SEC. 3704. According to the case of the United States *v.* Sanders (1 Hemp., 483), the plaintiff follows the condition of his mother, and is an alien. It was held in that case that the issue of an Indian woman and a white man is an Indian, and *vice versa;* that the rule of the civil law—*partus sequitur ventrem*—prevailed. But the contrary is the rule of the common law in the analogous case of a marriage between a freeman and a slave. *Ibid.*

SEC. 3705. The plaintiff ought to be deemed to follow the condition of his father. Congress seems to have taken this view of the matter in the passage of the act of September 27, 1850 (9 Stat. L., 496), section 4 of which grants land to each white settler on the public lands who is a citizen of the United States, or who has or will declare his intention to become such, "American half-breed Indians included," thereby excluding half-breeds, the children of alien fathers, as not Americans, but aliens. *Ibid.*

SEC. 3706. As the law now stands, the plaintiff can not be admitted to citizenship, because he is neither a "white alien" nor a person of "African nativity or descent;" but that is a matter within the exclusive jurisdiction of Congress. *Ibid.*

SEC. 3707. All Indians born and resident in Oregon are *prima facie* members of some Oregon tribe, and are therefore under the charge of the superintendent of Indian affairs in Oregon, appointed in pursuance of the act of June 5, 1850 (9 Stat. L., 437), within the meaning of section 20 of the act of June 30, 1834 (4 Stat. L., 729), as amended by section 1 of the act March 16, 1864 (15 Stat. L., 29).

United States v. Wirt, 3 Sawyer, 161.

SEC. 3708. An Indian born in Minnesota is *prima facie* not a member of an Oregon tribe, though he might become such by adoption.

Ibid.

SEC. 3709. When a tribe of Indians is placed under the charge of an Indian agent, by treaty or otherwise, each member of such tribe is under the charge of such agent within the purview of section 3129 of the Revised Statutes, and no member thereof can dissolve his tribal relation or escape from such charge by absenting himself from such reservation, or otherwise without the consent of the United States.

United States v. Earl, 9 Saw., 79.

SEC. 3710. An Indian who had separated from his tribe before the Government took cognizance of it as such, by treaty or otherwise, and did not return thereto or claim or enjoy at the hands of the Government any right or privilege as a member of such tribe, is not under the charge of an agent within the meaning of section 2139 of the Revised Statutes. *Ibid.*

SEC. 3711. An Indian boy in Oregon who left the locality of his tribe and lived with a white family until his tribe had entered into treaty relations with the United States, and moved on a reservation in pursuance of such treaty, and until he was 25 years of age, and who then went to live upon such reservation as a member of his tribe, could not thereafter by simply absenting himself from the reservation dissolve his tribal relation, or cease to be under the charge of the agent of such reservation. *Ibid.*

SEC. 3712. In the absence of any law authorizing severance of the tribal relation by an individual, mere absence from the reservation, however prolonged, is not proof of consent or acquiescence by the United States, because it may occur without the approval of the Government, and it may take place with the consent of the agent for some lawful purpose, and with intent to return. *Ibid.*

SEC. 3713. Who are citizens of the United States in Alaska under article 3 of the treaty of 1867 may be a difficult question to determine. Under that treaty the inhabitants of Alaska at that date who did not return to Russia within three years thereafter became citizens of the United States excepting members of the uncivilized tribes.

Kie v. United States, 11 Saw., 579.

SEC. 3714. A marriage between two Indians belonging to the Choctaw tribe, entered into according to the laws and customs of that tribe at a place where such laws and customs were in force, is recognized as a valid marriage by the laws of Alabama, the laws of Alabama having been extended over the territory where the parties so married resided. The laws and customs of the Choctaws were not abrogated, so far as members of the tribe were affected, by the extension of the jurisdiction of the State over the country occupied by them. When, by the law of an Indian tribe, the husband has the capacity to dissolve the marriage at pleasure, and his abandonment of his wife, he remaining within the jurisdiction of his tribe, is evidence that he has done so, the effect of this dissolution of the marriage is the same as if directed by a lawful decree. *Wall v. Williamson, 8 Ala., 48.*

SEC. 3715. Marriage among the Indian tribes must generally be considered as taking place in a state of nature, and if according to the usages and customs of the particular tribe, the parties are authorized to dissolve it at pleasure, the right of dissolution will be considered a term of the contract. The act of 1832 extending the jurisdiction of this State over the Indian territory does not take from a marriage between members of the Choctaw tribe its dissoluble quality at the pleasure of the parties, nor can the asking a reservation under the treaty of Dancing Rabbit Creek, the acceptance of a patent from the United States for the land embraced by it, and the continued cohabitation in the State for more than five years after the ratification of the treaty and the departure of the mass of their tribe to the west have that effect. The concurrence of all these facts will not take from a reservee his citizenship as a Choctaw, the treaty securing the right of resuming his status in the tribe at pleasure.   *Ibid.*

SEC. 3716. A grandmother of the Creek tribe of Indians, with whom her grandchildren resided, was held to be the head of a family within the meaning of the second article of the treaty with the Creek Indians of March 24, 1832.   *Rowland and Heifner v. Ladiga's Heirs, 21 Ala., 9.*

SEC. 3717. The testimony of a witness that he was intimately acquainted with a party, and believed that he was a native of the Chickasaw tribe of Indians, without stating upon what facts the belief rests, or that it is common reputation, is not sufficient to establish the fact against the positive denial of the answer.

                                    Dyer v. Bean, 15 Arkansas, 519.

SEC. 3718. "The various regulations in the act of 1801 all show the sense of the legislature, that an Indian in his individual capacity is, in a great degree, *inops consilii*, and unfit to make contracts, unless with the consent and under the protection of a civil magistrate. The same provisions prevail in the Spanish colonies.

                                    Sunol v. Hepburn, 1 Col., 255.

SEC. 3719. The fourteenth section of the statute of this State "concerning crimes and punishments," which provides that "no Indian, or person having one-half or more of Indian blood, or Mongolian, or Chinese, shall be permitted to give evidence in favor of or against any white person" (Stat. L., 1863, p. 69), so far as it discriminates against persons on the score of race or color, born within the United States and not subject to any foreign power, excluding Indians not taxed, has, by the force and effect of the "civil rights bill" (14 Stat. L., p. 27), become null and void.

        The People of the State of California v. George Washington, 36 Cal., 658.

SEC. 3720. Section 397 of the Penal Code forbids the sale or giving of liquors to Indians of full blood without reference to the question whether they have or have not adopted the habits of civilization, or separated themselves from tribal relations, or have become citizens of the United States; and construed as applying to all Indians is not in conflict with any provision of the Constitution of the United States or of this State, and does not deprive any citizen of his privileges and immunities as such.   *People v. Bray, 105 Cal., 344.*

SEC. 3721. After the ratification of the Sioux Indian treaty by Congress on the 28th of February, 1877, the governor appointed the officers for said counties, among others the appellant as register of deeds and *ex officio* county clerk of Lawrence County, and issued commissions to his appointees running until January 1, 1879, and until their successors should be elected and qualified. *Held*, that county officers appointed by the governor on the organization of a new county hold until the next general election ensuing after such organization, in which their successors must be elected.

The Territory ex rel. McKinnis v. Hand, 1 Dakota (Bennett), 437.

SEC. 3722. When the land in dispute lies and the contract of lease is to be performed in the said Indian country or reservation, the relation of landlord and tenant can not legally exist.

Uhlig v. Garrison, 2 Dakota (Smith), 71.

SEC. 3723. A party in possession of a mining claim on the 28th day of February, 1877 (located on the Sioux Indian reservation in the Black Hills), with the requisite discovery, with the surface boundaries sufficiently marked, with the notice of location posted, and with a disclosed vein of ore, could, by manifesting his adoption of these facts, and subsequently causing a proper record to be made and performing the amount of labor, or making the improvements necessary to hold the claim, date his right from that day; and such location and subsequent labor and improvements would give him the right to possession from that date. *Caledonia Gold Mining Co. v. Noonan et al., 3 Dakota (Smith), 202.*

SEC. 3724. Several freeborn negroes and mulattoes were offered as witnesses to support the prosecution (in an indictment for assault and battery). The counsel for defense objected and contended that they were not competent witnesses, being disqualified by the act of assembly of Maryland (1717, ch. 13) by which it was enacted "That no negro or mulatto slave, free negro, or mulatto born of a white woman, during his time of servitude by law, or any Indian slave, or free Indian, native of this or the neighboring provinces, be admitted and received as good and valid evidence in law in any matter or thing whatsoever depending before any court of record wherein any Christian white person is concerned." *Held*, that freeborn negroes, not subject to any term of servitude by law, are competent witnesses in all cases. Color alone is no objection to a witness. *United States v. Mullany, 1 Cranch, (D. C.), 517.*

SEC. 3725. A statute prohibiting the intermarriage of a white person with an Indian, enacted after such a marriage, will have no bearing upon the validity of the marriage.

Every child born in wedlock is presumed to be legitimate. And when a person's mother was an Indian proof that he was a colored man will not be sufficient to overcome such presumption, as the color will be referred to that derived from his mother.

The Illinois Land and Loan Co. v. Bonner, 75 Ill., 315.

SEC. 3726. An Indian is not a competent witness under the statute of the State; but the Supreme Court can not presume that a witness, admitted as competent in the circuit court, was an Indian, merely because he was the principal chief of an Indian nation.

Harris v. Doe, ex dem. Barnett et al., 4 Blackf, Ind., 370.

SEC. 3727. An Indian, consistently with the provisions of section 1, page 232, 1 Rev. Stat., 1852 (Indiana), may be a *bona fide* resident of the *United States*, although not a citizen, and may therefore transfer property by will. *Scott v. Sanford, 19 How., 361. Parent v. Walmsly, 20 Ind., 82.*

SEC. 3728. The generous intentions of the legislature are to be carried out by such a construction as will secure the contemplated relief to the Indian, holding it rigidly to all who assume to deal with him in derogation of the statute.

Wendover v. Tucker, 4 Ind., 381. Doe ex dem. Lafontaine v. Avaline, 8 Ind., 6.

SEC. 3729. Section 4 of the Indian act of February 3, 1841, provides "that in all cases the provisions of this act shall extend to all persons of Indian descent who are recognized as members of any tribe residing in the State of Indiana, down to those having one-eighth Indian blood. *Doe ex dem. Lafontaine v. Avaline, 8 Ind., 6.*

SEC. 3730. A person recognized as an Indian by the community, by the Indians themselves, by the State and Federal authorities, stamped as such by birth, education, and language, and having three-eighths Indian blood, is held to be an Indian within the meaning of the statutes of this State relative to Indians. *Ibid.*

SEC. 3731. An Indian may, like the subjects of any other foreign government, be naturalized by the authority of Congress and become a citizen of the State and of the United States; and if an individual should leave his tribe and take up his abode among the white population, he would be entitled to all the rights and privileges which would belong to an emigrant from any other foreign people.

Scott v. Sanford, 19 How., 361. Parent v. Walmsly, 20 Ind., 86.

SEC. 3732. The plaintiff's father was a mixed blood—three-fourths white and one-fourth Indian—and his mother was a white woman. He was, therefore, a "white male citizen" and a legal voter within the meaning of section 2, article 2 of the constitution of Indiana, provided he was 21 years of age. *Smith v. Jeffries, 25 Ind., 376.*

SEC. 3733. An Indian is not incompetent as a witness because he does not know the nature of an oath exactly, or the penalties for perjury, but thinks he will be hanged if he tells a lie.

Smith v. Brown, 8 Kans. (Webb), 608. Same, 8 Kans. (Dassler), 409.

SEC. 3734. Early, Jones, and King were Ottawa Indians. Early obtained all the land now in controversy by virtue of the provisions of the treaty with the Ottawa Indians of June 24, 1862 (12 Stat. L., 1237).

By that treaty the Ottawa Indians were to become citizens of the United States July 16, 1867. By the treaty of February 23, 1867 (15 Stat. L., 517), the time for them to become citizens was extended to July 16, 1869.   *Clark v. Akers, 16 Kans., 166.*

SEC. 3735. The Pottawatomie treaty of 1867 (15 Stat. L., 531) provides that "Where allottees under the treaty of 1861 shall have died or shall hereafter decease, such allottees shall be regarded, for the purposes of a careful and just settlement of their estates, as citizens of the United States and of the State of Kansas." * * * And where any member of the tribe shall become a citizen under the provisions of the said treaty, the families of said parties shall also be considered as citizens.   *Oliver v. Forbes, 17 Kans., 113.*

SEC. 3736. If by a legal fiction under article 8 of the Pottawatomie treaty of 1867 (15 Stat. L., 531) John Riley, because of his death was to be considered a citizen of the United States and his estate as that of a citizen, and if, by a like legal fiction under article 6 of the same treaty, his wife and children were to be considered citizens, then the deed executed in 1868 by his widow, Mary Bostick, to the Olivers must be considered as valid and binding.   *Ibid.*

SEC. 3737. The plaintiff is not a member of the Delaware tribe nor entitled to the rights of an allottee. He is an intruder on the lands of the tribe and has no right to plead the treaty of 1860 (12 Stat. L., 1129) in his behalf, nor is he authorized to claim any of its guaranties.
                    Grinter v. K. P. Ry. Co., 23 Kans., 642.

SEC. 3738. The rule is that a person visibly a negro is *prima facie* a slave, but that one apparently a white person or an Indian is *prima facie* free. For, as to Indians, though it was declared by a Virginia statute of 1679 that Indian captives, and, by a statute of 1682, that Indians sold as slaves by their neighboring tribes should be deemed as slaves. These enactments were constructively repealed by an act of the Virginia legislature of 1691, for encouraging a *free* trade among the Indians.   *Gentry v. Polly McMinnis, 3 Ky. (Dana), 385.*

SEC. 3739. Under the French Government in Louisiana some Indians were held in slavery, and the freedom of such was not acquired by the establishment of the Spanish Government.
            *Seville v. Chretien, 2 Martin (La. Sup. Ct., comprising Vols. IV and
            V U. S. of term reports), p. 474, and 1 Harrison (La.), 367.*

SEC. 3740. This is an action in which the plaintiffs, who aver that they are descended from Indians, now claim their freedom. The issue joined is *liberi vel non.* The cause was submitted to a jury on special facts, who have found that the petitioners are descended from an Indian woman of the Chickasaw tribe, and that the defendant has shown no title to hold them as slaves. *Held,* the duty of the court is very simple. If the defendant hold the plaintiffs in slavery without any title he does so illegally and they must be set free.

Ulzire et al. v. Palyfavre, 7 Martin (La., comprising vols. 10 and 11, U. S. term reports), p. 256, and 2 Harrison (La.), 727.

SEC. 3741. The officers of the French Government could only certify such records or documents as were deposited in their departments and such documents should be produced. If they certify of their personal knowledge they should be sworn.

Billieux's Heirs v. Singletary, 9 Morgan (La.), 57.

SEC. 3742. That the defendant was an Indian of the Penobscot tribe furnishes no defense to an action upon a promissory note made by him. The slightest imposition, however, in obtaining the note would prevent a recovery upon it. *Murch v. Tomer, 21 Maine (8 Shepley), 535.*

SEC. 3743. There was in Abigail Jones but one-sixteenth part of Indian blood and she must be considered a white woman. She was married to a mulatto, who can not be regarded as a white man.

Bailey v. Fiske, 34 Maine, 77.

SEC. 3744. Within the import of the Massachusetts act of 1786, prohibiting the marriage of a white person with any Indian, negro, or mulatto, a person having but one-sixteenth (or perhaps one-eighth) of the colored blood is to be considered a white person. The marriage of such person with a mulatto was null, and the children of such marriage, being illegitimate, could not take their father's land by inheritance. *Ibid.*

SEC. 3745. The Indians resident in the State of Maine are not "Indian tribes" within the treaty-making powers of the Federal Government; nor are they in political life or territory the successors of any of the various "eastern tribes of Indians" with whom treaties were made by the Crown or the Colonies in colonial times, and hence they can not effectually claim any exemptions or privileges under such treaties. *State v. Newell, 84 Me., 465.*

SEC. 3746. A child of Indian parents, who was not born upon the lands belonging to the Herring Pond tribe of Indians and never resided thereon, whose father is not known to have been a member of the tribe or to have ever resided on their lands, and whose mother, although a proprietor of those lands and born thereon, resides with her husband and children elsewhere, is not entitled to the division of those lands under the statute of 1869, chapter 463, section 3.

Danzell et al. v. Webquish et al., 108 Mass., 133.

SEC. 3747. All persons in whom white blood so far preponderates that they have less than one-fourth of African blood are within the meaning of that clause of the constitution of Michigan which limits the elective franchise to "white male citizens," and no other person of African descent can be so regarded.

The People v. Dean, 14 Mich. (1 Jennison), 406.

SEC. 3748. By a provision in the Choctaw treaty of 1830 (7 Stat. L., 333) the Indians had one, two, and three years to remove from the ceded land. This was a length of time which might well justify a claim of citizenship, and without some definite provision they might all have claimed to be citizens; and having signified their intention, every head of a family might have removed with the tribe at the time stipulated without impairing his right to a reservation. *Newman v. Doe, 5 Miss., 522.*

SEC. 3749. A transcript of the registry of names kept by the United States Indian agent of the applications of Choctaw Indians to become citizens under the treaty of 1830 (7 Stat. L., 333) is admissible in evidence without first showing that the names were those of heads of families. The presumption must be that the agent complied with the requirements of the treaty, so far as the powers of his office extended. Application to become a citizen under article 14 of the treaty of 1830, by letter to the Indian agent, designating particularly the lands claimed under the treaty, is sufficient notice of intention to claim the benefit of the treaty, and become a citizen; and such letter, together with the certificate of application and location by the agent, are admissible in evidence to prove the identity of the land claimed. Where the original application and certificate of location are in the custody of the department for Indian affairs, and beyond the control of the claimant, copies certified by the proper officer are admissible in evidence in an action of ejectment. *Ibid.*

SEC. 3750. Where an Indian relinquished to the State his rights to citizenship, but the United States subsequently treated with him as an Indian, and allowed him a reservation of land as such, it was held that such relinquishment of citizenship did not affect his title to land acquired under the treaty, and could not be inquired into in an action in ejectment; it being a matter between the Indian and the Federal Government. *Ibid.*

SEC. 3751. By the act of 1829 (Mississippi) all the privileges, immunities, and franchises of white persons were extended to Indians. *Doe, ex dem. Harris v. Newman, 11 Miss., 565.*

SEC. 3752. Since the act of 1829 (Mississippi) the Indians are competent witnesses in any case in which white persons would be. *Ibid.*

SEC. 3753. Where a white man married a woman who was a member of an "Indian nation," whether he became the head of the family or not must depend upon the law and custom regulating the marital rights of the parties in such a case; and "head of family" mentioned in the treaty is presumed to mean one who is so in the Choctaw sense of the term or according to the usages and customs of that nation. *Held,* that these usages and customs, as far as the courts of the State are concerned, must be regarded as facts that must be averred and proven. The court can only take judicial notice of the law or the acts of certain officers of the Government, but can not take judicial notice of local customs. *Turner v. Fisher, 28 Miss., 306.*

SEC. 3754. Among the savage tribes of North American Indians marriage is merely a natural contract, and neither law, custom, nor religion has affixed any conditions, limitations, or forms other than those which nature herself has prescribed. Permanency is not to be regarded as an essential element of such marriage; otherwise, all such connections as have taken place among the various tribes, either between pure Indians or Indian half-breeds, or between the white and Indian races, must be regarded as illicit and the offspring illegitimate, for the husband may dissolve the contract at his pleasure. A mere casual commerce between the sexes does not constitute a marriage by the law of nations, but where there is cohabitation by consent for an indefinite period for the procreation and bringing up of children, that, in state of nature, would be marriage. It is well settled as a general proposition that a marriage valid according to the law as custom of the place where it is contracted is valid everywhere.

Johnson v. Johnson's Admr., 30 Mo., 72.

SEC. 3755. The Constitution of the United States and the statutes passed in pursuance thereof recognize the Indians as a peculiar people, having relations to the Government totally different from citizens of the States; and although located within State lines, yet, so long as their tribal customs are adhered to and the Federal Government manages their affairs by agent they are not regarded as subject to the laws, at least so far as marriages and inheritances are concerned. The Constitution of the United States especially authorizes Congress to regulate commerce with the Indian tribes as with foreign nations. The customs and laws of the Indians then prevailed among the remnants of tribes located in this State in 1829 and 1830, and would continue unless positively changed by the legislature of the State, and no such legislation has ever been attempted. A marriage therefore among them according to their customs would, for the purpose of inheritance, at least be valid. *Boyer v. Dively, Admr., 58 Mo., 510.*

SEC. 3756. The principles announced in Johnson *v.* Johnson's Admr., 30 Mo., 72, and Boyer *v.* Dively, Admr., 58 Mo., 510, in regard to marriages of white persons with Indians, approved.

La Riviere v. La Riviere et al., 77 Mo., 512.

SEC. 3757. It is not necessary to the validity of a marriage, according to the custom of the Ponca Indians, that it be actually contracted on the territory set off to or occupied by them.

La Riviere v. La Riviere, 97 Mo., 80.

SEC. 3758. Under the provisions of the first clause of section 6 of the act of Congress entitled "An act to provide for the allotment of lands in severalty to Indians," etc., approved February 8, 1887, in order to establish an Indian's right to citizenship, and hence to vote at an election in this State, it must be proven that such Indian was born within the territorial limits of the United States, and that an allotment of land in fact has been made to such Indian by the Government of the United States in pursuance of said act or of like authority of law or treaty of the United States.   *State ex rel. Fair v. Frazier, 28 Nebraska, 438.*

Sec. 3759. In 1798 the legislature enacted that every negro, Indian, mulatto, or mestee within this State who, at the time of passing the act, was a slave for his or her life should continue to be such unless manumitted and set free in the manner prescribed by law.
State v. Emmons, 2 N. J., 5.

Sec. 3760. The act of Congress of February 8, 1887, entitled "An act to provide for the allotment of lands in severalty to Indians on the various reservations and to extend the protection of the laws of the United States and the Territories over the Indians, and for other purposes," is not in conflict with the United States Constitution, article 1, section 8, which provides that Congress shall have power to establish an uniform rule of naturalization."

By the provisions of said act all Indians born within the territorial limits of the United States to whom allotments of land in severalty have been made under the provisions of said law or other law or treaty, and all Indians born as aforesaid who have voluntarily taken up their residence in the United States separate and apart from any tribe of Indians therein, and adopted the habits of civilized life are made citizens of the United States, and such Indians residing in the State are citizens thereof. The *actual issuance* or *receipt* by an Indian of a patent for lands allotted to him under the act is not necessary to constitute him a citizen of the United States. When he has accepted the land allotted, taken possession thereof, and otherwise complied with the law he becomes entitled to his patent and his citizenship attaches.   *State ex rel. Crawford v. Norris, 37 Nebr., 299.*

Sec. 3761. In the "act for regulating of slavery" passed March 11, 1713–14 (Allinson, 18), Indians are coupled with negroes. In the act of May 10, 1768 (Allinson, 307), regulating the trial of slaves for murder and other crimes, and in the act of November 16, 1769, no discrimination is made between negroes and Indians.
State v. Van Waggoner, 6 N. J., 374.

Sec. 3762. The question as to the slavery of Indians has on several occasions come before the courts of Virginia. (See Jenkins v. Tom, 1 Wash., 123; Coleman v. Dick, ib., 233; Pallas v. Hill, 2 Hen. and Munf., 149.) The slavery of Indians was, in that State, founded upon an act of assembly in 1679, which declared Indian prisoners taken in war to be slaves. This act was repealed in 1691, since which time Indian slavery has not been recognized in Virginia.   *Ibid.*

SEC. 3763. The Pueblo Indians of New Mexico were, at the date of the treaty of Guadalupe Hidalgo, citizens of the Mexican Republic and by virtue of the provisions of that treaty became citizens of the United States, none of them having elected to retain the character of Mexican citizens. Their property rights are therefore guaranteed by the treaty equal with those of other Mexican citizens of the Territory.

United States v. Lucero, 1 N. Mex. (Gildersleeve), 422. United States v. Santistevan, 1 N. Mex. (Gildersleeve), 583.

SEC. 3764. The Pueblo Indians of New Mexico are not within the provisions of the intercourse act of 1834 (4 Stat. L., 729), not being tribal Indians, and are not subject to the jurisdiction of the Indian Department of the United States Government.

United States v. Lucero, 1 N. Mex. (Gild.), 422.

SEC. 3765. The Indian tribes within this State are subject to the jurisdiction and laws of this State. These Indians are not aliens but citizens, owing allegiance to the Government and entitled to its protection. They may acquire property by purchase or descent, and alien or transmit the same as natural-born citizens; subject, however, to such regulations as the legislature may prescribe for their security against imposition and fraud. A deed, therefore, executed in 1797, in the usual form, by the only son of an Indian to whom lands had been granted by the State for his services as a soldier in the Revolutionary war, claiming and holding the same as heir to his father, is valid, there being at the time of the conveyance no law of the State disabling individual Indians seized of real estate from alienating their lands or regulating the manner of their conveyance.

Jackson v. Goodell, 20 Johns, 188.

SEC. 3766. A native Indian of the Seneca Nation in the actual and separate occupation of lands upon the Tonawanda Reservation had, under the treaty of May 20, 1842, between the United States and the Seneca Nation (7 Stat. L., 586), a right of occupancy until the amount which he was entitled to receive "as an individual Indian," for his improvements should be determined and awarded in the manner provided in the fourth article of the treaty. This determination was a condition precedent to the extinction of the Indian title. He may maintain an action of trespass for the lands so occupied by him separately, and not in common with the rest of the nation.

Blacksmith v. Fellows, 7 Selden (N. Y. App.), 401.

SEC. 3767. The act, section 36, chapter 92, relative to the Indians within this State (2 R. L., 153) does not merely protect Indians of the Oneida Nation from suits on contracts while residing on the lands reserved to that nation, but extends to suits against such Indians wherever their residence may be; and an Indian sued upon a contract may plead this act in bar, and is not restricted to pleading it in abatement.

Dana v. Dana, 14 Johnson's Reports (N. Y.), 181.

Sec. 3768. The court refused to grant an attachment for costs on a judgment against an Oneida Indian who was the lessor of the plaintiff in an action of ejectment; but they granted a rule to show cause on the attorney who brought the suit, not being the agent or attorney appointed by the State to manage the affairs of the *Indians*, why an attachment should not issue against him.

Jackson v. King et al., 18 Johnson's Reports (N. Y.), 506.

Sec. 3769. A patent for land to J. S., an Oneida Indian, and his heirs and assigns forever, is to him and his *Indian* heirs, whatever their civil condition and character may be, whether aliens or citizens. The Indians in this State are not citizens, but are distinct tribes or nations living under the protection of the Government.

No white person can lawfully purchase any right or title to land from any Indian or Indians without the authority and consent of the legislature. *Goodell v. Jackson, 20 Johnson's Reports (N. Y.), 693.*

Sec. 3770. Cherokee Indians in possession of lands within the limits of North Carolina, reserved under the treaties of 1817 and 1819 made by the United States and the Cherokee Nation, are to be considered as purchasers of the land. The exercise of power by the commissioners of the United States is legitimate; and, moreover, the stipulations in these treaties having been recognized by several acts of the legislature of North Carolina passed since, she must be considered as assenting to them. A grant of the land to the Indian in possession is not necessary, for it is not claimed under those laws which point out the manner of acquiring title to vacant lands in this State, and title may be complete in some cases without the grant.

Doe ex dem. of Eu-che-lah v. Welsh, 3 Hawks (N. C.) 155 and 174.

Sec. 3771. The certificate of the "chief of the Cherokee Nation," under its great seal, that a judge before whom the probate of a deed is taken is such judge, etc., is sufficient to entitle the deed to probate and registration in this State. The word "governor" in the statute must be taken to mean the chief executive officer of a State or Territory having its great seal. *Whitsett v. Forehand, 79 N. C. Rep., 230.*

Sec. 3772. When the plaintiff, by *mandamus*, attempted to compel the admission of his children into a public school established for the Croatan Indians there was evidence that the plaintiff's father was a white man and his wife, the mother of the children, was a Croatan Indian, and that the plaintiff was a slave before 1865. The plaintiff asked the court to charge, in effect, that if the jury believed the evidence their answer should be that the plaintiff's children were not negroes. The court refused, but charged that if the plaintiff was a slave there was a presumption that he was negro. *Held*, no error.

McMillan v. School Committee, 107 N. C., 609.

Sec. 3773. The legislature is not prohibited by the Constitution from providing separate schools for the Croatan Indians, and the act of

1885, chapter 51, and the act of 1889, amendatory thereof, providing such schools, are valid.   The legislature has power outside of the constitutional grant to classify pupils according to race.

Ibid.

SEC. 3774. A person, the offspring of a white man and a half-breed Indian woman, is a lawful voter.

Jeffries v. Ankeny et al., 11 Ohio (Stanton), 372.

SEC. 3775. Youth of negro, Indian, and white blood, but of "more than one-half white blood," are entitled to the benefit of the common school fund.   (Polly Gray v. The State, 4 Ohio, 353; Williamson v. The School Directors, Wright, 578; Jefferies v. Ankeny, 11 Ohio, 372; Thacker v. Hawk and others, ibid, 376, are affirmed.)

Lane v. Baker et al., 12 Ohio (Stanton), 237.

SEC. 3776. The surveillance, protection, and control of the Government, mainly exercised through the Secretary of the Interior, over the rights of the Indian to his land when allotted, which has been uniformly likened by the courts to that of a guardian over his ward, ceased.   He and his rights passed, subject to the provision mentioned, under the protection of the common law, of the laws of the United States, and the laws of this Territory, and he became entitled to all the rights and subject to all the duties of a resident and probably to those also of a citizen of the United States and the Territory of Oklahoma.

United States ex rel. v. C. O. and G. R. R. Co., 3 Okla. (Dale), 482.

SEC. 3777. Exemptions in act of 1740, in favor of "free Indians in amity with the Government," apply to what "free Indians."

State v. Belmont, 4 Strob. (S. C.), 445.

SEC. 3778. The exceptions in the act of 1740 in favor of "free Indians in amity with this Government" apply to "free Indians" and their descendants domiciled in the State of South Carolina, although disconnected with any tribe, and not merely to Indians preserving a national character and in amity with the State.   *Ibid.*

SEC. 3779. The South Carolina act of 1740 also provides that in all suits for the freedom of a negro "it shall be always presumed that every negro, mulatto, and mestizo is a slave unless the contrary can be made to appear (the Indian in amity with this Government excepted).

Vinyard v. Passalaigue, 2 Strobhard (S. C.), 536.

SEC. 3780. The State policy in making slaves of the Indians was temporary, arising out of the necessity of frequent wars with the savage tribes.   It was to deter their inroads by the intimidations of slavery, so hateful to Indian instincts.   *State v. Belmont, 4 Strobhard (S. C.), 445.*

SEC. 3781. Indians are not entitled to the elective franchise in South Carolina under any conditions.   *State v. Managers, 1 Bailey, 215.*

SEC. 3782. An Indian is not entitled to the elective franchise in South Carolina; nor can merit, services, or other circumstances alter the conditions of his birth under the existing provisions of the constitution.   *Ibid.*

SEC. 3783. The provision in the act of 1740 (South Carolina) that the offspring of slaves, whether negroes, mulattoes, mestizos, or Indians, shall follow the condition of the mother, relates only to the question of *slavery or freedom;* and whenever the words *negro, mulatto,* etc., are used in the act for the purpose of designating *a class,* they are to be interpreted by the common acceptation of the terms, and not by the rule *partus sequitur ventrem.*

                                                State v. Scott, 1 Bailey (S. C.), 270.

SEC. 3784. The term, "mestizo," used in the act of 1740, is confined to admixtures of the Indian and negro races.

                                        Miller v. Dawson & Brown, 1 Dudley (S. C.), 174.

SEC. 3785. Considering the act of 1740 as applicable to free Indians separated from their tribes, the construction must either be, that if the Indian himself was in friendly relations with the whites, or that he belonged to a tribe of Indians in amity with the State, in either case they were to be treated as free Indians in amity, and not liable to be tried under the said act of 1740. If the Indian belonged to an extinct tribe, the amity required to give him a status in society, would, from necessity, be personal; but if his tribe still existed it would be necessary to show, actually or by presumption, that such tribe was in a relation of amity with the State.   *Ibid.*

SEC. 3786. The early history of South Carolina shows that there were several tribes of Indians within the State, maintaining sometimes pacific and sometimes hostile relations to the State; and that many members of these tribes, either upon their tribes becoming extinct or from some other cause, resided among the whites and have been considered as standing in a different order or caste from free negroes.

                                                                              Ibid.

SEC. 3787. The act of 1740 and the early history of the State point to the fact that Indians in South Carolina were regarded as slaves under some circumstances; presumably, such as were taken in war were treated as the property of the captors. Section 14 of the act of 1740 was intended to regulate the trial of free Indians not in amity with the State. It must have applied alone to such as were within the limits of the State; whether residing with the tribe or not does not seem to be distinguished by the act.   *Ibid.*

SEC. 3788. The words "free Indians in amity with this Government" employed in the fourteenth section of the act of 1740 (South Carolina) are applicable to one who has no connection with any tribe and is domiciled in the State.   *Ibid.*

SEC. 3789. Words "free Indians in amity with this Government" employed in the fourteenth section, act of 1740, applicable to one connected with no tribe and domiciled in South Carolina.   *Ibid.*

SEC. 3790. By the constitution of the republic of Texas, section 10, it is provided: "All persons, Africans, the descendants of Africans, and Indians excepted, who were residing in Texas on the day of the Declaration of Independence shall be considered citizens of the republic and entitled to all the privileges of such. All citizens now living in Texas who shall not have received their portion of land in like manner as colonists shall be entitled to their land in the following proportion and manner: Every head of a family shall be entitled to 1 league and labor of land," etc.   *Russell v. Randolph, 11 Hartly (Texas), 464.*

SEC. 3791. On the question of the condition of slavery the doctrine is too well settled to require a reference to authority that the offspring follows the condition of the mother. If the mother was a slave, so also would be the child, with this qualification, that the mother was in lawful slavery. If the mother was of the pure white race, unmixed with African blood, her being *de facto* held in slavery would not be lawful and could not entail her own illegal slavery upon her child. So if she was of Indian and not of African blood she could not be held in slavery *de jure*. Lawful slavery is confined to the African race.   *Gaines v. Ann., 17 Hartly (Texas), 214.*

SEC. 3792. An Indian, and certainly a civilized one, is entitled to own personal effects and to be protected in their enjoyment until deprived of them by due course of law. Article 2103 of the Revised Statutes of the United States does not inhibit an Indian from assigning his claim for the value of property illegally destroyed. Such assignment was legal and the assignee would have the right to recover.   *Missouri Pacific Ry. Co. v. Cullers, 81 Texas, 383.*

SEC. 3793. A citizen of a State sued upon a claim in part assigned him by an Indian and a citizen of the Indian Territory. Objection was made to that part so assigned. *Held*, the objection did not raise the issue as to the right of the Indian to sue, but to the right of the Indian to assign his claim to the plaintiff who could sue. An Indian of a civilized tribe is *a person*, and entitled to protection in the courts of this State of his rights of person and property.   *Ibid.*

SEC. 3794. A white man recognized as a member of the Cherokee Nation by being treated with as a commissioner of the nation in the treaty of 1819, and married to an Indian woman, although he exercised the privileges of a citizen of the State, is the head of an Indian family within the meaning of the treaties of 1817 and 1819, and as such is entitled to a grant under those treaties, although a reservation in fee was given to his wife by the treaty of 1819.   *Morgan v. Fowler, 2 Yerg., 450.*

SEC. 3795. The Cherokee treaties of 1817 and 1819 (7 Stat. L., 156 and 195) secured to the reservees the rights of citizenship. In 1827 they held the same relation to the body politic and were entitled to the same measure of constitutional protection as the citizens of Tennessee.   *Wally v. Kennedy, 2 Yerger, 554.*

SEC. 3796. Ross was one of the fee-simple reservees provided for by the treaty of 1819, but this is not the description of person contemplated by the act of 1833. He did not have the rights of citizenship extended to him by any law of the State, so as to confer on him the full benefit of those laws by which alone he can be made subject to their penalty.   *The State v. Ross, 7 Yerg., 74.*

SEC. 3797. Reputation or hearsay is admissible evidence of descent from Indian ancestors and may be used as a part of the chain of proof to establish freedom.   *Vaughan v. Phebe, 1 Martin & Yerger (Tenn.), 389.*

SEC. 3798. Although an Indian taken into Virginia between 1679 and 1691 might be a slave, yet all American Indians and their descendants are *prima facie* free, and where the fact of their nativity and descent in a maternal line is satisfactorily established the burden of proof thereafter lies upon the party claiming to hold them as slaves.   *Ibid.*

SEC. 3799. Since the year 1705 no American Indian could be held as a slave, but foreign Indians coming within the description of the act of 1705, chapter 49, might be made slaves. If in an action for freedom the jury find that the plaintiff is descended from an Indian who was brought into this State generally, without saying from whence, it is sufficient for the plaintiff.   *Coleman v. Dick, 1 Washington (Va.), 300.*

SEC. 3800. Act 1723, chapter 4, section 22, "When any female mulatto or Indian, by law obliged to serve till the age of thirty or thirty-one years, shall, during the time of her servitude, have any child born of her body, every such child shall serve the master or mistress of such mulatto or Indian until it shall attain the same age the mother of such child was obliged by law to serve unto."
                    Howell v. Netherland, 1 Jefferson (Va.), 91.

SEC. 3801. In questions of freedom (of Indian slaves) evidence that there had been a belief in the neighborhood some fifty or sixty years before that the female ancestor of the plaintiff was entitled to her freedom is not admissible. A full review given of all laws in Virginia concerning Indian slavery.   *Gregory v. Baugh, 4 Randolph (Va.), 611.*

SEC. 3802. *Quære*, whether in the case of a person claiming freedom on the ground of descent from a female Indian ancestor, hearsay would be admissible, not only to prove the plaintiff's pedigree, but also to prove that the female ancestor, from whom he derives his descent, was an Indian. The court (four judges sitting) being divided on the point.   *Gregory v. Baugh, 2 Leigh (Va.), 665.*

SEC. 3803. Where white persons or native American Indians or their descendants in the maternal line are claimed as slaves, the *onus probandi* lies on the claimant, but it is otherwise with respect to native Africans and their descendants who have been and are now held as slaves. It seems that no native American Indian could be made a slave under the laws of Virginia since the year 1691.

Hudgins v. Wrights, 1 Henning & Mumford (Va.), 133.

SEC. 3804. The manuscript act of 1691 and not the printed revisal of 1705 fixes the period at which the right of making slaves of Indians was restricted. *Pallas et al. v. Hill, 2 Henning & Mumford (Va.), 149.*

SEC. 3805. In tracing a pedigree in a suit for freedom, what a witness swore to on the executing of a writ of inquiry between the mother of the plaintiff and another person may be given in evidence to prove the said mother to have been descended from a female Indian ancestor. The record of the verdict and judgment upon a writ of inquiry in a suit by the mother of the plaintiff against a third person, in which record the ground of the judgment does not appear, may be given in evidence to prove that the mother had recovered her freedom; not that she was entitled to it "by reason of being descended in the maternal line from an Indian ancestor imported into this State since the year 1705," but questions upon what ground the judgment in that suit was rendered and whether the descendant was born after her mother acquired her right to freedom or not ought to be left open.

Pegram v. Isabell, 2 Henning & Mumford (Va.), 193.

SEC. 3806. A native American Indian, brought into Virginia since the year 1691, could not lawfully be held in slavery here, notwithstanding such Indian was a slave in the country from which he or she was brought. *Butt v. Rachel, 4 Mumford (Va.), 209.*

SEC. 3807. In an action to cancel a deed, where the evidence shows that the plaintiff is an ignorant Indian, with a very limited knowledge of the English language and with no knowledge of legal transactions or the force or effect of legal instruments, the burden of proof is shifted from defendant to show that the import of the deed was understood by plaintiff at the time he signed it. In such a case, when the certificate of the officer taking the acknowledgment fails to show that he made known the contents of the deed to the grantor before acknowledgment, the certificate can not be accepted as proof of the grantor's knowledge of the contents of the deed. *Jackson v. Tatebo, 3 Wash., 457.*

SEC. 3808. Where a white man procures an Indian woman to live with him on the payment of a few dollars to her relatives, no marriage ceremony being celebrated, the issue of such a union is illegitimate and incapable of inheriting the father's estate.

Kelly v. Kitsap County, 5 Wash. (Kreider), 521.

SEC. 3809. The fact that the law forbidding a white person to marry an Indian was repealed within a short time after the celebration of such forbidden marriage, and that cohabitation was continued subsequent to such repeal, would not constitute a marriage.

In re Wilber's Estate, 8 Wash. (Kreider), 35.

SEC. 3810. The marriage of a white man to a Swinomish Indian woman, although contracted on the reservation of that tribe and persuant to its custom, was void if celebrated while the territorial law of 1866 forbidding marriages between Indians and white persons was in force, as, under the organic act of this Territory and the treaty with said tribe, such reservation was left within and a part of the Territory for all legislative and judicial purposes not affecting the personal rights and the lands and other property of the Indians.

Ibid.

SEC. 3811. An information filed in the superior court of a county containing within its limits a part or the whole of an Indian reservation against a person described as an Indian need not, in order to confer jurisdiction, aver either that such person *does not* sustain tribal relations, or that the offense *was not* committed within the limits of such reservation. *State v. Williams, 13 Wash. (Kreider), 336.*

SEC. 3812. An Indian who retains his tribal relations may be prosecuted in the courts of this State for offenses committed at a place not within the limits of an Indian reservation. *Ibid.*

SEC. 3813. An Indian who has severed his tribal relation may be prosecuted in the courts of this State whether the offense was committed within or without the limits of a reservation. *Ibid.*

SEC. 3814. The passage of the act of 1875 regulating the descent of property did not operate to prevent the act passed on the same day relating to adoption (November 12, 1875) from becoming a law, but the two must be construed together as one act.

In re Wilbur's Estate, 14 Wash. (Kreider), 242.

SEC. 3815. The marriage of a white man and an Indian woman in the year 1868 according to the customs in vogue among the Swinomish tribe of Indians, followed by cohabitation as man and wife, was not a legal marriage, even if there were no miscegenation acts in force at the time thereof. *Ibid.*

SEC. 3816. After defendant's father, a person of Indian descent, had long been in the exclusive occupancy of a certain tract of land as his farm and house, and it had been allotted to him, and he had cultivated and improved it and otherwise treated it in every respect as his private property, an act of Congress, passed for his exclusive benefit, authorized the payment of a certain sum of money belonging to his tribe (Stockbridge) and granted said tract to him "in fee simple and to his heirs and assigns forever" in lieu of all his rights in the lands and annuities of the Stockbridge tribe, etc.; and neither the father nor the son appears ever to have submitted to any of the laws, customs, or regulations of any tribe, but adopted and always retained the manners, habits, and industries of civilized life. *Held,* that both father and son are within the provisions of subdivision 4, section 1, article 3 of the State (Wisconsin) constitution providing that "civilized persons of Indian descent, not members of any tribe," having the prescribed qualifications as to sex, age, and residence, shall be qualified electors in this State; and that said tract of land now owned by the defendant is held "by purchase," within the meaning of the laws of this State, and is subject to taxation.

Helgurs v. Quimey, 8 Norw. Rep., 17. Same, 3 Wis., 347.

SEC. 3817. The fact that the alleged wards (the person who claimed to be the guardian of the infant heirs having applied to the probate court for license to sell the lands, etc.,) were members of an Indian tribe, recognized as a distinct nation of people, does not invalidate such appointment of a guardian, the probate courts of a country having power to appoint guardians for persons resident therein who have a different nationality, as well as guardians for the property situated therein of persons who are residents and citizens of a foreign country.

Farrington v. Wilson, 29 Wisc., 385.

SEC. 3818. The Territory has no right to tax the property of a post trader at a military post situated upon an Indian reservation, and the tax, if paid, can be recovered back. It is immaterial that such trader furnished the lists and valuations on which the taxes were levied. The right to impose a tax, and as preliminary to it to take a list and valuation of property intended to be taxed, depends not upon the consent of the party taxed, but upon the power of the government which assumes to exercise the right and upon the functions of the officers through whom it assumes to exercise it. The Territory is totally excluded from the exercise of political power over the Indian country, either to regulate the intercourse of its subjects with it or to extend its municipal authority into it. *Moore v. Commissioners, 11 Wyoming, 8.*

SEC. 3819. Cohabitation of an Indian chief, who has a wife living, and another woman, followed by a voluntary separation of the parties to the alleged second marriage, and the forming of new relations with others by both parties, can not, contrary to the recognized laws of all Christian nations, be upheld as a valid marriage according to Indian customs; and a child born as the fruit of the cohabitation with the second woman can not be considered legitimate and entitled to inherit from her father as such. In this case not only does the evidence fail to establish a valid marriage and the legitimacy of the child from whom complainant has taken an assignment of the claim set up in the bill, but the claim is itself barred by the lapse of time, and the bill must be dismissed. *Compo v. Jackson Iron Co., 16 Northwestern Reporter, 295.*

SEC. 3820. An Indian may testify as a witness under laws of Dakota, 1862, page 99, section 308, making competent "every human being who understands the nature of an oath, and 13 Stat. L., 351, 533, and 12 Stat. L., 588, providing that in the Federal courts no witness shall be excluded on account of color, and that in other respects the competency of a witness shall be determined by the law of the State in which the court is held.   *Brugier v. United States, 46 Northwestern Rep., 502.*

SEC. 3821. When a certain territory was situated in the limits of the county of Benson in this State (North Dakota), and also within the limits of the Devils Lake Indian Reservation, and where said territory had, under an act of Congress, been allotted to certain Indians and persons of Indian descent in severalty, and the preliminary patent therefor issued to such persons, and where said persons were living upon their respective allotments and farming the same it was the duty of the county commissioners of Benson County to establish a voting precinct within or for said territory. Such Indians and persons of Indian descent so residing upon lands allotted to them in severalty, and for which the preliminary patents had been issued, are citizens of the United States, and qualified electors of this State.

Denover et al v. County Comrs., 72 N. W. Rep., 1014.

SEC. 3822. Where an Indian tribe is located upon a reservation by the Government of the United States under a treaty which does not provide that the reservation shall not be included within Territorial or State jurisdiction, and the reservation is afterwards included in an organized county and Territory, and the tribe surrenders its interest in its reservation and the several members of it take allotments, they become residents of the Territory and county and are "persons" in contemplation of law, and their personal property is subject to assessment and taxation by the proper authorities of the county in which they reside.   *Keokuk v. Ulam, 38 Pacific Reporter, 1081.*

SEC. 3823. An Indian who has severed his tribal relations may be prosecuted in the courts of the State, whether the crime was committed within or without the reservation. An Indian who retains his tribal relations may be prosecuted in the courts of a State for a crime committed at a place without the limits of a reservation. An information filed in the superior court of a county containing within its limits an Indian reservation, against a person described in the information as an Indian, need not aver that such person does not sustain tribal relations or that the offense was not committed within such reservation.   *State v. Williams, 43 Pa. Rep., 15.*

SEC. 3824. Compiled Laws, 1877, chapter 3, section 3 (Arizona), declaring marriages between white persons and Indians illegal and void, renders void a marriage between a white man and an Indian woman contracted on an Indian reservation within the Territory in accordance with the law of the tribe of which the woman was a member, though followed by cohabitation on the reservation; hence, a child of the union has no right of heirship from the father. Revised statutes (Arizona), paragraph 1470, providing that the issue also of marriages deemed null in law shall nevertheless be legitimate, does not render legitimate the children of a pretended marriage between a white man and an Indian woman celebrated on a reservation within the Territory in accordance with the laws of the tribe of which the woman was a member, but not in accordance with the requirements of the laws of the Territory, there being in such case no marriage in fact.

In re Walker's Estate, 46 Pa. Rep., 67.

SEC. 3825. One not an Indian acquires no tribal relations by marriage with an Indian woman and residence on an Indian reservation.

Stiff v. McLaughlin, 48 Pacific Rep., 232.

SEC. 3826. Under article 3 of the treaty of the United States with the Kickapoo Indians, June 28, 1862 (13 Stat. L., 623), the lands allotted to a member of the said tribe of Indians became alienable, and said Indian ceased to be a member of the tribe and became a citizen of the United States when his application was acted upon by the President and a patent issued therefor, and not at the time he appeared before the district court, made the required proof, and took the oath of allegiance as provided for in said article. *Baldwin v. Letson, 49 Pacific Rep., 619.*

INDEX.

O